PEARSON CUSTOM BUSINESS RESOURCES

Compiled by

DePaul University
ACC 303
Managerial Accounting

PEARSON

Senior Vice President, Editorial: Patrick F. Boles
Sponsoring Editor: David J. Maltby
Development Editor: Megan Tully
Editorial Assistant: Hannah Coker
Operations Manager: Eric M. Kenney
Production Manager: Jennifer Berry
Art Director: Renée Sartell
Cover Designer: Renée Sartell

This special edition published in cooperation with Pearson Learning Solutions.

Printed in the United States of America.

Please visit our website at *www.pearsonlearningsolutions.com*.

Attention bookstores: For permission to return any unsold stock, contact us at *pe-uscustomreturns@pearson.com*.

Pearson Learning Solutions, 501 Boylston Street, Suite 900, Boston, MA 02116
A Pearson Education Company
www.pearsoned.com

ISBN 10: 1-256-62705-4
ISBN 13: 978-1-256-62705-0

PEARSON

Contents

2 An Introduction to Cost Terms and Purposes

2

An Introduction to Cost Terms and Purposes

What does the word cost mean to you?

Is it the price you pay for something of value? A cash outflow? Something that affects profitability? There are many different types of costs, and at different times organizations put more or less emphasis on them. When times are good companies often focus on selling as much as they can, with costs taking a backseat. But when times get tough, the emphasis usually shifts to costs and cutting them, as General Motors tried to do. Unfortunately, when times became really bad GM was unable to cut costs fast enough leading to Chapter 11 bankruptcy.

GM Collapses Under the Weight of its Fixed Costs[1]

After nearly 80 years as the world's largest automaker, General Motors (GM) was forced to file for bankruptcy protection in 2009. Declining sales and the rise of Japanese competitors, such as Toyota and Honda, affected GM's viability given its high fixed costs—costs that did not decrease as the number of cars that GM made and sold declined.

A decade of belt-tightening brought GM's variable costs—costs such as material costs that vary with the number of cars that GM makes—in line with those of the Japanese. Unfortunately for GM, a large percentage of its operating costs were fixed because union contracts made it difficult for the company to close its factories or reduce pensions and health benefits owed to retired workers.

To cover its high fixed costs, GM needed to sell a lot of cars. Starting in 2001, it began offering sales incentives and rebates, which for a few years were somewhat successful. GM also expanded aggressively into China and Europe.

But in 2005, growth efforts slowed, and GM lost $10.4 billion. As a result, GM embarked on a reorganization plan that closed more than a dozen plants, eliminated tens of thousands of jobs, slashed retirement plan benefits for its 40,000-plus salaried employees, and froze its pension program.

Despite these cuts, GM could not reduce its costs fast enough to keep up with the steadily declining market for new cars and trucks. In the United States, as gas prices rose above $4 a gallon, GM's product

[1] *Sources:* Loomis, Carol. 2006. The tragedy of General Motors. *Fortune*, February 6; *New York Times*. 2009. Times topics: Automotive industry crisis. December 6. http://topics.nytimes.com/top/reference/timestopics/subjects/c/credit_crisis/auto_industry/index.html; Taylor, III, Alex. 2005. GM hits the skids. *Fortune*, April 4; Vlasic, Bill and Nick Bunkley. 2008. G.M. says U.S. cash is its best hope. *New York Times*, November 8.

mix was too heavily weighted toward gas-guzzling trucks, pickup trucks, and sport utility vehicles, all of which were experiencing sharp decreases in sales.

In late 2008, as the economic crisis worsened, GM announced plans to cut $15 billion in costs and raise $5 billion through the sale of assets, like its Hummer brand of off-road vehicles. "We're cutting to the bone," said Fritz Henderson, GM's president. "But given the situation, we think that's appropriate."

It was appropriate, but it wasn't enough. By November 2008, GM had lost more than $18 billion for the year, and the government loaned the company $20 billion to continue operations. Ultimately, its restructuring efforts fell short, and the weight of GM's fixed costs drove the company into bankruptcy. In court papers, the company claimed $82.3 billion in assets and $172.8 billion in debt.

When it emerges from bankruptcy, GM will be a much smaller company with only four brands of cars (down from eight), more than 20,000 fewer hourly union workers, and as many as 20 additional shuttered factories.

As the story of General Motors illustrates, managers must understand costs in order to interpret and act on accounting information. Organizations as varied as as the United Way, the Mayo Clinic, and Sony generate reports containing a variety of cost concepts and terms that managers need to run their businesses. Managers must understand these concepts and terms to effectively use the information provided. This chapter discusses cost concepts and terms that are the basis of accounting information used for internal and external reporting.

Costs and Cost Terminology

Accountants define **cost** as a resource sacrificed or forgone to achieve a specific objective. A cost (such as direct materials or advertising) is usually measured as the monetary amount that must be paid to acquire goods or services. An **actual cost** is the cost incurred (a historical or past cost), as distinguished from a **budgeted cost**, which is a predicted or forecasted cost (a future cost).

When you think of cost, you invariably think of it in the context of finding the cost of a particular thing. We call this thing a **cost object**, which is anything for which a measurement of costs is desired. Suppose that you were a manager at BMW's Spartanburg, South Carolina, plant. BMW makes several different types of cars and sport activity vehicles (SAVs) at this plant. What cost objects can you think of? Now look at Exhibit 2-1.

You will see that BMW managers not only want to know the cost of various products, such as the BMW X5, but they also want to know the costs of things such as projects,

Learning Objective 1

Define and illustrate a cost object

. . . examples of cost objects are products, services, activities, processes, and customers

Exhibit 2-1

Examples of Cost
Objects at BMW

Cost Object	Illustration
Product	A BMW X5 sports activity vehicle
Service	Telephone hotline providing information and assistance to BMW dealers
Project	R&D project on enhancing the DVD system in BMW cars
Customer	Herb Chambers Motors, the BMW dealer that purchases a broad range of BMW vehicles
Activity	Setting up machines for production or maintaining production equipment
Department	Environmental, health, and safety department

services, and departments. Managers use their knowledge of these costs to guide decisions about, for example, product innovation, quality, and customer service.

Now think about whether a manager at BMW might want to know the *budgeted cost* of a cost object, or the *actual cost*. Managers almost always need to know both types of costs when making decisions. For example, comparing budgeted costs to actual costs helps managers evaluate how well they did and learn about how they can do better in the future.

How does a cost system determine the costs of various cost objects? Typically in two basic stages: accumulation, followed by assignment. **Cost accumulation** is the collection of cost data in some organized way by means of an accounting system. For example, at its Spartanburg plant, BMW collects (accumulates) costs in various categories such as different types of materials, different classifications of labor, and costs incurred for supervision. Managers and management accountants then *assign* these accumulated costs to designated cost objects, such as the different models of cars that BMW manufactures at the plant. BMW managers use this cost information in two main ways:

1. when *making* decisions, for instance, on how to price different models of cars or how much to invest in R&D and marketing and

2. for *implementing* decisions, by influencing and motivating employees to act and learn, for example, by rewarding employees for reducing costs.

Now that we know why it is useful to assign costs, we turn our attention to some concepts that will help us do it. Again, think of the different types of costs that we just discussed—materials, labor, and supervision. You are probably thinking that some costs, such as costs of materials, are easier to assign to a cost object than others, such as costs of supervision. As you will see, this is indeed the case.

Decision Point ▶

What is a cost object?

Direct Costs and Indirect Costs

We now describe how costs are classified as direct and indirect costs and the methods used to assign these costs to cost objects.

Learning Objective 2

Distinguish between direct costs

. . . costs that are traced to the cost object

and indirect costs

. . . costs that are allocated to the cost object

- **Direct costs of a cost object** are related to the particular cost object and can be traced to it in an economically feasible (cost-effective) way. For example, the cost of steel or tires is a direct cost of BMW X5s. The cost of the steel or tires can be easily traced to or identified with the BMW X5. The workers on the BMW X5 line request materials from the warehouse and the material requisition document identifies the cost of the materials supplied to the X5. In a similar vein, individual workers record the time spent working on the X5 on time sheets. The cost of this labor can easily be traced to the X5 and is another example of a direct cost. The term **cost tracing** is used to describe the assignment of direct costs to a particular cost object.

- **Indirect costs of a cost object** are related to the particular cost object but cannot be traced to it in an economically feasible (cost-effective) way. For example, the salaries of plant administrators (including the plant manager) who oversee production of the many different types of cars produced at the Spartanburg plant are an indirect cost of the X5s. Plant administration costs are related to the cost object (X5s) because plant administration is necessary for managing the production of X5s. Plant administration costs are indirect costs because plant administrators also oversee the production of other

TYPE OF COST	COST ASSIGNMENT	COST OBJECT
Direct Costs Example: Cost of steel and tires for the BMW X5	**Cost Tracing** based on material requisition document	
Indirect Costs Example: Lease cost for Spartanburg plant where BMW makes the X5 and other models of cars	**Cost Allocation** no requisition document	Example: BMW X5

Exhibit 2-2

Cost Assignment to a Cost Object

products, such as the Z4 Roadster. Unlike the cost of steel or tires, there is no requisition of plant administration services and it is virtually impossible to trace plant administration costs to the X5 line. The term **cost allocation** is used to describe the assignment of indirect costs to a particular cost object. **Cost assignment** is a general term that encompasses both (1) tracing direct costs to a cost object and (2) allocating indirect costs to a cost object. Exhibit 2-2 depicts direct costs and indirect costs and both forms of cost assignment—cost tracing and cost allocation—using the example of the BMW X5.

Challenges in Cost Allocation

Consider the cost to lease the Spartanburg plant. This cost is an indirect cost of the X5—there is no separate lease agreement for the area of the plant where the X5 is made. But BMW *allocates* to the X5 a part of the lease cost of the building—for example, on the basis of an estimate of the percentage of the building's floor space occupied for the production of the X5 relative to the total floor space used to produce all models of cars.

Managers want to assign costs accurately to cost objects. Inaccurate product costs will mislead managers about the profitability of different products and could cause managers to unknowingly promote unprofitable products while deemphasizing profitable products. Generally, managers are more confident about the accuracy of direct costs of cost objects, such as the cost of steel and tires of the X5.

Identifying indirect costs of cost objects, on the other hand, can be more challenging. Consider the lease. An intuitive method is to allocate lease costs on the basis of the total floor space occupied by each car model. This approach measures the building resources used by each car model reasonably and accurately. The more floor space that a car model occupies, the greater the lease costs assigned to it. Accurately allocating other indirect costs, such as plant administration to the X5, however, is more difficult. For example, should these costs be allocated on the basis of the number of workers working on each car model or the number of cars produced of each model? How to measure the share of plant administration used by each car model is not clear-cut.

Factors Affecting Direct/Indirect Cost Classifications

Several factors affect the classification of a cost as direct or indirect:

- **The materiality of the cost in question.** The smaller the amount of a cost—that is, the more immaterial the cost is—the less likely that it is economically feasible to trace that cost to a particular cost object. Consider a mail-order catalog company such as Lands' End. It would be economically feasible to trace the courier charge for delivering a package to an individual customer as a direct cost. In contrast, the cost of the invoice paper included in the package would be classified as an indirect cost. Why? Although the cost of the paper can be traced to each customer, it is not cost-effective to do so. The benefits of knowing that, say, exactly 0.5¢ worth of paper is included in each package do not exceed the data processing and administrative costs of tracing the cost to each package. The time of the sales administrator, who earns a salary of $45,000 a year, is better spent organizing customer information to assist in focused marketing efforts than on tracking the cost of paper.

■ **Available information-gathering technology.** Improvements in information-gathering technology make it possible to consider more and more costs as direct costs. Bar codes, for example, allow manufacturing plants to treat certain low-cost materials such as clips and screws, which were previously classified as indirect costs, as direct costs of products. At Dell, component parts such as the computer chip and the CD-ROM drive display a bar code that can be scanned at every point in the production process. Bar codes can be read into a manufacturing cost file by waving a "wand" in the same quick and efficient way supermarket checkout clerks enter the cost of each item purchased by a customer.

■ **Design of operations.** Classifying a cost as direct is easier if a company's facility (or some part of it) is used exclusively for a specific cost object, such as a specific product or a particular customer. For example, the cost of the General Chemicals facility dedicated to manufacturing soda ash is a direct cost of soda ash.

Decision Point ▶

How do managers decide whether a cost is a direct or indirect cost?

Be aware that a specific cost may be both a direct cost of one cost object and an indirect cost of another cost object. *That is, the direct/indirect classification depends on the choice of the cost object.* For example, the salary of an assembly department supervisor at BMW is a direct cost if the cost object is the assembly department, but it is an indirect cost if the cost object is a product such as the BMW X5 SAV, because the assembly department assembles many different models. A useful rule to remember is that the broader the definition of the cost object—the assembly department rather than the X5 SAV—the higher the proportion of total costs that are direct costs and the more confidence a manager has in the accuracy of the resulting cost amounts.

Cost-Behavior Patterns: Variable Costs and Fixed Costs

Learning Objective 3

Explain variable costs and fixed costs

. . . the two basic ways in which costs behave

Costing systems record the cost of resources acquired, such as materials, labor, and equipment, and track how those resources are used to produce and sell products or services. Recording the costs of resources acquired and used allows managers to see how costs behave. Consider two basic types of cost-behavior patterns found in many accounting systems. A **variable cost** changes *in total* in proportion to changes in the related level of total activity or volume. A **fixed cost** remains unchanged *in total* for a given time period, despite wide changes in the related level of total activity or volume. Costs are defined as variable or fixed with respect to *a specific activity* and for *a given time period*. Surveys of practice repeatedly show that identifying a cost as variable or fixed provides valuable information for making many management decisions and is an important input when evaluating performance. To illustrate these two basic types of costs, again consider costs at the Spartanburg, South Carolina, plant of BMW.

1. **Variable Costs:** If BMW buys a steering wheel at $60 for each of its BMW X5 vehicles, then the total cost of steering wheels is $60 times the number of vehicles produced, as the following table illustrates.

Number of X5s Produced (1)	Variable Cost per Steering Wheel (2)	Total Variable Cost of Steering Wheels (3) = (1) × (2)
1	$60	$ 60
1,000	60	60,000
3,000	60	180,000

The steering wheel cost is an example of a variable cost because *total cost* changes in proportion to changes in the number of vehicles produced. The cost per unit of a variable cost is constant. It is precisely because the variable cost per steering wheel in column 2 is the same for each steering wheel that the total variable cost of steering wheels in column 3 changes proportionately with the number of X5s produced in column 1. When considering how variable costs behave, always focus on *total* costs.

Exhibit 2-3

Graphs of Variable and Fixed Costs

PANEL A: Variable Cost of Steering Wheels at $60 per BMW X5 Assembled

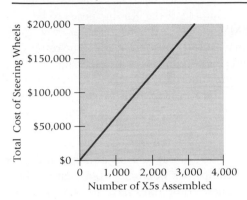

PANEL B: Supervision Costs for the BMW X5 assembly line (in millions)

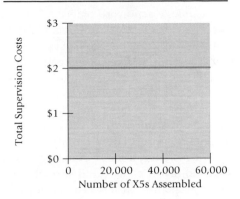

Exhibit 2-3, Panel A, graphically illustrates the total variable cost of steering wheels. The cost is represented by a straight line that climbs from left to right. The phrases "strictly variable" and "proportionately variable" are sometimes used to describe the variable cost in Panel A.

Consider an example of a variable cost with respect to a different activity—the $20 hourly wage paid to each worker to set up machines at the Spartanburg plant. Setup labor cost is a variable cost with respect to setup hours because setup cost changes in total in proportion to the number of setup hours used.

2. **Fixed Costs:** Suppose BMW incurs a total cost of $2,000,000 per year for supervisors who work exclusively on the X5 line. These costs are unchanged in total over a designated range of the number of vehicles produced during a given time span (see Exhibit 2-3, Panel B). Fixed costs become smaller and smaller on a per unit basis as the number of vehicles assembled increases, as the following table shows.

Annual Total Fixed Supervision Costs for BMW X5 Assembly Line (1)	Number of X5s Produced (2)	Fixed Supervision Cost per X5 (3) = (1) ÷ (2)
$2,000,000	10,000	$200
$2,000,000	25,000	80
$2,000,000	50,000	40

It is precisely because *total* line supervision costs are fixed at $2,000,000 that fixed supervision cost per X5 decreases as the number of X5s produced increases; the same fixed cost is spread over a larger number of X5s. Do not be misled by the change in fixed cost per unit. Just as in the case of variable costs, when considering fixed costs, always focus on *total costs*. Costs are fixed when total costs remain unchanged despite significant changes in the level of total activity or volume.

Why are some costs variable and other costs fixed? Recall that a cost is usually measured as the amount of money that must be paid to acquire goods and services. Total cost of steering wheels is a variable cost because BMW buys the steering wheels only when they are needed. As more X5s are produced, proportionately more steering wheels are acquired and proportionately more costs are incurred.

Contrast the description of variable costs with the $2,000,000 of fixed costs per year incurred by BMW for supervision of the X5 assembly line. This level of supervision is acquired and put in place well before BMW uses it to produce X5s and before BMW even knows how many X5s it will produce. Suppose that BMW puts in place supervisors capable of supervising the production of 60,000 X5s each year. If the demand is for only 55,000 X5s, there will be idle capacity. Supervisors on the X5 line could have supervised the production of 60,000 X5s but will supervise only 55,000 X5s because of the lower demand. However, BMW must pay for the unused line supervision capacity because the cost of supervision cannot be reduced in the short run. If demand is even lower—say only 50,000 X5s—line supervision costs will still be the same $2,000,000, and idle capacity will increase.

Unlike variable costs, fixed costs of resources (such as for line supervision) cannot be quickly and easily changed to match the resources needed or used. Over time, however, managers can take actions to reduce fixed costs. For example, if the X5 line needs to be run for fewer hours because of low demand for X5s, BMW may lay off supervisors or move them to another production line. Unlike variable costs that go away automatically if the resources are not used, reducing fixed costs requires active intervention on the part of managers.

Do not assume that individual cost items are inherently variable or fixed. Consider labor costs. Labor costs can be purely variable with respect to units produced when workers are paid on a piece-unit (piece-rate) basis. For example, some garment workers are paid on a per-shirt-sewed basis. In contrast, labor costs at a plant in the coming year are sometimes appropriately classified as fixed.

For instance, a labor union agreement might set annual salaries and conditions, contain a no-layoff clause, and severely restrict a company's flexibility to assign workers to any other plant that has demand for labor. Japanese companies have for a long time had a policy of lifetime employment for their workers. Although such a policy entails higher fixed labor costs, the benefits are increased loyalty and dedication to the company and higher productivity. As the General Motors example in the chapter opener (p. 26) illustrated, such a policy increases the risk of losses during economic downturns as revenues decrease, while fixed costs remain unchanged. The recent global economic crisis has made companies very wary of locking-in fixed costs. The Concepts in Action box on page 33 describes how a car-sharing service offers companies the opportunity to convert the fixed costs of owning corporate cars into variable costs by renting cars on an as-needed basis.

A particular cost item could be variable with respect to one level of activity and fixed with respect to another. Consider annual registration and license costs for a fleet of planes owned by an airline company. Registration and license costs would be a variable cost with respect to the number of planes owned. But registration and license costs for a particular plane are fixed with respect to the miles flown by that plane during a year.

To focus on key concepts, we have classified the behavior of costs as variable or fixed. Some costs have both fixed and variable elements and are called *mixed* or *semivariable* costs. For example, a company's telephone costs may have a fixed monthly payment and a charge per phone-minute used. We discuss mixed costs and techniques to separate out their fixed and variable components in Chapter 10.

> **Decision Point** ▶
>
> How do managers decide whether a cost is a variable or a fixed cost?

Cost Drivers

A **cost driver** is a variable, such as the level of activity or volume that causally affects costs over a given time span. An *activity* is an event, task, or unit of work with a specified purpose—for example, designing products, setting up machines, or testing products. The level of activity or volume is a cost driver if there is a cause-and-effect relationship between a change in the level of activity or volume and a change in the level of total costs. For example, if product-design costs change with the number of parts in a product, the number of parts is a cost driver of product-design costs. Similarly, miles driven is often a cost driver of distribution costs.

The cost driver of a variable cost is the level of activity or volume whose change causes proportionate changes in the variable cost. For example, the number of vehicles assembled is the cost driver of the total cost of steering wheels. If setup workers are paid an hourly wage, the number of setup hours is the cost driver of total (variable) setup costs.

Costs that are fixed in the short run have no cost driver in the short run but may have a cost driver in the long run. Consider the costs of testing, say, 0.1% of the color printers produced at a Hewlett-Packard plant. These costs consist of equipment and staff costs of the testing department that are difficult to change and, hence, are fixed in the short run with respect to changes in the volume of production. In this case, volume of production is not a cost driver of testing costs in the short run. In the long run, however, Hewlett-Packard will increase or decrease the testing department's equipment and staff to the levels needed to support future production volumes. In the long run, volume of production is a cost driver of testing costs. Costing systems that identify the cost of each activity such as testing, design, or set up are called *activity-based costing systems*.

Concepts in Action

How Zipcar Helps Reduce Twitter's Transportation Costs

Soaring gas prices, high insurance costs, and hefty parking fees have forced many businesses to reexamine whether owning corporate cars is economical. In some cities, Zipcar has emerged as an attractive alternative. Zipcar provides an "on demand" option for urban individuals and businesses to rent a car by the week, the day, or even the hour. Zipcar members make a reservation by phone or Internet, go to the parking lot where the car is located (usually by walking or public transportation), use an electronic card or iPhone application that unlocks the car door via a wireless sensor, and then simply climb in and drive away. Rental fees begin around $7 per hour and $66 per day, and include gas, insurance, and some mileage (usually around 180 miles per day). Currently, business customers account for 15% of Zipcar's revenues, but that number is expected to double in the coming years.

Let's think about what Zipcar means for companies. Many small businesses own a company car or two for getting to meetings, making deliveries, and running errands. Similarly, many large companies own a fleet of cars to shuttle visiting executives and clients back and forth from appointments, business lunches, and the airport. Traditionally, owning these cars has involved very high fixed costs, including buying the asset (car), costs of the maintenance department, and insurance for multiple drivers. Unfortunately, businesses had no other options.

Now, however, companies like Twitter can use Zipcar for on-demand mobility while reducing their transportation and overhead costs. Based in downtown San Francisco, Twitter managers use Zipcar's fleet of Mini Coopers and Toyota Priuses to meet venture capitalists and partners in Silicon Valley. "We would get in a Zipcar to drive down to San Jose to pitch investors or go across the city," says Jack Dorsey, the micro blogging service's co-founder. "Taxis are hard to find and unreliable here." Twitter also uses Zipcar when traveling far away from its headquarters, like when visiting advertisers in New York and technology vendors in Boston, forgoing the traditional black sedans and long taxi rides from the airport.

From a business perspective, Zipcar allows companies to convert the fixed costs of owning a company car to variable costs. If business slows, or a car isn't required to visit a client, Zipcar customers are not saddled with the fixed costs of car ownership. Of course, if companies use Zipcar too frequently, they can end up paying more overall than they would have paid if they purchased and maintained the car themselves.

Along with cutting corporate spending, car sharing services like Zipcar reduce congestion on the road and promote environmental sustainability. Users report reducing their vehicle miles traveled by 44%, and surveys show CO_2 emissions are being cut by up to 50% per user. Beyond that, each shared car takes up to 20 cars off the road as members sell their cars or decide not to buy new ones—challenging the whole principle of owning a car. "The future of transportation will be a blend of things like Zipcar, public transportation, and private car ownership," says Bill Ford, Ford's executive chairman. But the automaker isn't worried. "Not only do I not fear that, but I think it's a great opportunity for us to participate in the changing nature of car ownership."

Sources: Keegan, Paul. 2009. Zipcar – the best new idea in business. *Fortune*, August 27. http://money.cnn.com/2009/08/26/news/companies/zipcar_car_rentals.fortune/; Olsen, Elizabeth. 2009. Car sharing reinvents the company wheels. *New York Times*, May 7. http://www.nytimes.com/2009/05/07/business/businessspecial/07CAR.html; Zipcar, Inc. Zipcar for business case studies. http://www.zipcar.com/business/is-it/case-studies (accessed October 8, 2009)

Relevant Range

Relevant range is the band of normal activity level or volume in which there is a specific relationship between the level of activity or volume and the cost in question. For example, a fixed cost is fixed only in relation to a given wide range of total activity or volume (at which the company is expected to operate) and only for a given time span (usually a particular budget period). Suppose that BMW contracts with Thomas Transport Company (TTC) to transport X5s to BMW dealers. TTC rents two trucks, and each truck has annual fixed rental costs of $40,000. The maximum annual usage of each truck is 120,000 miles. In the current year (2011), the predicted combined total hauling of the two trucks is 170,000 miles.

Exhibit 2-4 shows how annual fixed costs behave at different levels of miles of hauling. Up to 120,000 miles, TTC can operate with one truck; from 120,001 to 240,000 miles, it operates with two trucks; from 240,001 to 360,000 miles, it operates with three trucks. This

Exhibit 2-4

Fixed-Cost Behavior at
Thomas Transport
Company

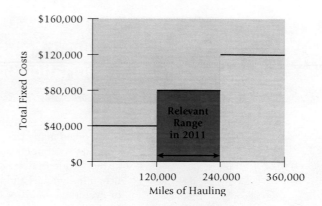

pattern will continue as TTC adds trucks to its fleet to provide more miles of hauling. Given the predicted 170,000-mile usage for 2011, the range from 120,001 to 240,000 miles hauled is the range in which TTC expects to operate, resulting in fixed rental costs of $80,000. Within this relevant range, changes in miles hauled will not affect the annual fixed costs.

Fixed costs may change from one year to the next. For example, if the total rental fee of the two trucks is increased by $2,000 for 2012, the total level of fixed costs will increase to $82,000 (all else remaining the same). If that increase occurs, total rental costs will be fixed at this new level of $82,000 for 2012 for miles hauled in the 120,001 to 240,000 range.

The basic assumption of the relevant range also applies to variable costs. That is, outside the relevant range, variable costs, such as direct materials, may not change proportionately with changes in production volume. For example, above a certain volume, direct material costs may increase at a lower rate because of price discounts on purchases greater than a certain quantity.

Relationships of Types of Costs

We have introduced two major classifications of costs: direct/indirect and variable/fixed. Costs may simultaneously be as follows:

- Direct and variable
- Direct and fixed
- Indirect and variable
- Indirect and fixed

Exhibit 2-5 shows examples of costs in each of these four cost classifications for the BMW X5.

Exhibit 2-5

Examples of Costs in
Combinations of the
Direct/Indirect and
Variable/Fixed Cost
Classifications for a Car
Manufacturer

| | Assignment of Costs to Cost Object | |
	Direct Costs	**Indirect Costs**
Variable Costs	• Cost object: BMW X5s produced Example: Tires used in assembly of automobile	• Cost object: BMW X5s produced Example: Power costs at Spartanburg plant. Power usage is metered only to the plant, where multiple products are assembled.
Fixed Costs	• Cost object: BMW X5s produced Example: Salary of supervisor on BMW X5 assembly line	• Cost object: BMW X5s produced Example: Annual lease costs at Spartanburg plant. Lease is for whole plant, where multiple products are produced.

Cost-Behavior Pattern

Total Costs and Unit Costs

The preceding section concentrated on the behavior patterns of total costs in relation to activity or volume levels. We now consider unit costs.

Unit Costs

Generally, the decision maker should think in terms of total costs rather than unit costs. In many decision contexts, however, calculating a unit cost is essential. Consider the booking agent who has to make the decision to book Paul McCartney to play at Shea Stadium. She estimates the cost of the event to be $4,000,000. This knowledge is helpful for the decision, but it is not enough.

Before a decision can be reached, the booking agent also must predict the number of people who will attend. Without knowledge of both total cost and number of attendees, she cannot make an informed decision on a possible admission price to recover the cost of the event or even on whether to have the event at all. So she computes the unit cost of the event by dividing the total cost ($4,000,000) by the expected number of people who will attend. If 50,000 people attend, the unit cost is $80 ($4,000,000 ÷ 50,000) per person; if 20,000 attend, the unit cost increases to $200 ($4,000,000 ÷ 20,000).

Unless the total cost is "unitized" (that is, averaged with respect to the level of activity or volume), the $4,000,000 cost is difficult to interpret. The unit cost combines the total cost and the number of people in a handy, communicative way.

Accounting systems typically report both total-cost amounts and average-cost-per-unit amounts. A **unit cost**, also called an **average cost**, is calculated by dividing total cost by the related number of units. The units might be expressed in various ways. Examples are automobiles assembled, packages delivered, or hours worked. Suppose that, in 2011, its first year of operations, $40,000,000 of manufacturing costs are incurred to produce 500,000 speaker systems at the Memphis plant of Tennessee Products. Then the unit cost is $80:

$$\frac{\text{Total manufacturing costs}}{\text{Number of units manufactured}} = \frac{\$40,000,000}{500,000 \text{ units}} = \$80 \text{ per unit}$$

If 480,000 units are sold and 20,000 units remain in ending inventory, the unit-cost concept helps in the determination of total costs in the income statement and balance sheet and, hence, the financial results reported by Tennessee Products to shareholders, banks, and the government.

Cost of goods sold in the income statement, 480,000 units × $80 per unit	$38,400,000
Ending inventory in the balance sheet, 20,000 units × $80 per unit	1,600,000
Total manufacturing costs of 500,000 units	$40,000,000

Unit costs are found in all areas of the value chain—for example, unit cost of product design, of sales visits, and of customer-service calls. By summing unit costs throughout the value chain, managers calculate the unit cost of the different products or services they deliver and determine the profitability of each product or service. Managers use this information, for example, to decide the products in which they should invest more resources, such as R&D and marketing, and the prices they should charge.

Use Unit Costs Cautiously

Although unit costs are regularly used in financial reports and for making product mix and pricing decisions, *managers should think in terms of total costs rather than unit costs for many decisions.* Consider the manager of the Memphis plant of Tennessee Products. Assume the $40,000,000 in costs in 2011 consist of $10,000,000 of fixed costs and $30,000,000 of variable costs (at $60 variable cost per speaker system produced). Suppose the total fixed cost and the variable cost per speaker system in 2012 are expected to be unchanged from 2011. The budgeted costs for 2012 at different production levels, calculated on the basis of total variable costs, total fixed costs, and total costs, are as follows:

Units Produced (1)	Variable Cost per Unit (2)	Total Variable Costs (3) = (1) × (2)	Total Fixed Costs (4)	Total Costs (5) = (3) + (4)	Unit Cost (6) = (5) ÷ (1)
100,000	$60	$ 6,000,000	$10,000,000	$16,000,000	$160.00
200,000	$60	$12,000,000	$10,000,000	$22,000,000	$110.00
500,000	$60	$30,000,000	$10,000,000	$40,000,000	$ 80.00
800,000	$60	$48,000,000	$10,000,000	$58,000,000	$ 72.50
1,000,000	$60	$60,000,000	$10,000,000	$70,000,000	$ 70.00

A plant manager who uses the 2011 unit cost of $80 per unit will underestimate actual total costs if 2012 output is below the 2011 level of 500,000 units. If actual volume is 200,000 units due to, say, the presence of a new competitor, actual costs would be $22,000,000. The unit cost of $80 times 200,000 units equals $16,000,000, which underestimates the actual total costs by $6,000,000 ($22,000,000 − $16,000,000). *The unit cost of $80 applies only when 500,000 units are produced.*

An overreliance on unit cost in this situation could lead to insufficient cash being available to pay costs if volume declines to 200,000 units. As the table indicates, for making this decision, managers should think in terms of total variable costs, total fixed costs, and total costs rather than unit cost. As a general rule, first calculate total costs, then compute a unit cost, if it is needed for a particular decision.

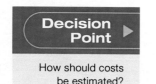

Decision Point ▶

How should costs be estimated?

Business Sectors, Types of Inventory, Inventoriable Costs, and Period Costs

In this section, we describe the different sectors of the economy, the different types of inventory that companies hold, and some commonly used classifications of manufacturing costs.

Learning Objective 5

Distinguish inventoriable costs

. . . assets when incurred, then cost of goods sold

from period costs

. . . expenses of the period when incurred

Manufacturing-, Merchandising-, and Service-Sector Companies

We define three sectors of the economy and provide examples of companies in each sector.

1. **Manufacturing-sector companies** purchase materials and components and convert them into various finished goods. Examples are automotive companies such as Jaguar, cellular phone producers such as Nokia, food-processing companies such as Heinz, and computer companies such as Toshiba.

2. **Merchandising-sector companies** purchase and then sell tangible products without changing their basic form. This sector includes companies engaged in retailing (for example, bookstores such as Barnes and Noble or department stores such as Target), distribution (for example, a supplier of hospital products, such as Owens and Minor), or wholesaling (for example, a supplier of electronic components, such as Arrow Electronics).

3. **Service-sector companies** provide services (intangible products)—for example, legal advice or audits—to their customers. Examples are law firms such as Wachtell, Lipton, Rosen & Katz, accounting firms such as Ernst and Young, banks such as Barclays, mutual fund companies such as Fidelity, insurance companies such as Aetna, transportation companies such as Singapore Airlines, advertising agencies such as Saatchi & Saatchi, television stations such as Turner Broadcasting, Internet service providers such as Comcast, travel agencies such as American Express, and brokerage firms such as Merrill Lynch.

Types of Inventory

Manufacturing-sector companies purchase materials and components and convert them into various finished goods. These companies typically have one or more of the following three types of inventory:

1. **Direct materials inventory.** Direct materials in stock and awaiting use in the manufacturing process (for example, computer chips and components needed to manufacture cellular phones).

2. **Work-in-process inventory.** Goods partially worked on but not yet completed (for example, cellular phones at various stages of completion in the manufacturing process). This is also called **work in progress.**

3. **Finished goods inventory.** Goods (for example, cellular phones) completed but not yet sold.

Merchandising-sector companies purchase tangible products and then sell them without changing their basic form. They hold only one type of inventory, which is products in their original purchased form, called *merchandise inventory*. Service-sector companies provide only services or intangible products and so do not hold inventories of tangible products.

Commonly Used Classifications of Manufacturing Costs

Three terms commonly used when describing manufacturing costs are direct material costs, direct manufacturing labor costs, and indirect manufacturing costs. These terms build on the direct versus indirect cost distinction we had described earlier, in the context of manufacturing costs.

1. **Direct material costs** are the acquisition costs of all materials that eventually become part of the cost object (work in process and then finished goods) and can be traced to the cost object in an economically feasible way. Acquisition costs of direct materials include freight-in (inward delivery) charges, sales taxes, and custom duties. Examples of direct material costs are the steel and tires used to make the BMW X5, and the computer chips used to make cellular phones.

2. **Direct manufacturing labor costs** include the compensation of all manufacturing labor that can be traced to the cost object (work in process and then finished goods) in an economically feasible way. Examples include wages and fringe benefits paid to machine operators and assembly-line workers who convert direct materials purchased to finished goods.

3. **Indirect manufacturing costs** are all manufacturing costs that are related to the cost object (work in process and then finished goods) but cannot be traced to that cost object in an economically feasible way. Examples include supplies, indirect materials such as lubricants, indirect manufacturing labor such as plant maintenance and cleaning labor, plant rent, plant insurance, property taxes on the plant, plant depreciation, and the compensation of plant managers. This cost category is also referred to as **manufacturing overhead costs** or **factory overhead costs.** We use *indirect manufacturing costs* and *manufacturing overhead costs* interchangeably in this book.

We now describe the distinction between inventoriable costs and period costs.

Inventoriable Costs

Inventoriable costs are all costs of a product that are considered as assets in the balance sheet when they are incurred and that become cost of goods sold only when the product is sold. For manufacturing-sector companies, all manufacturing costs are inventoriable costs. Consider Cellular Products, a manufacturer of cellular phones. Costs of direct materials, such as computer chips, issued to production (from direct material inventory), direct manufacturing labor costs, and manufacturing overhead costs create new assets, starting as work in process and becoming finished goods (the cellular phones). Hence, manufacturing costs are included in work-in-process inventory and in finished goods inventory (they are "inventoried") to accumulate the costs of creating these assets.

When the cellular phones are sold, the cost of manufacturing them is matched against **revenues**, which are inflows of assets (usually cash or accounts receivable) received for products or services provided to customers. The cost of goods sold includes all manufacturing costs (direct materials, direct manufacturing labor, and manufacturing overhead costs) incurred to produce them. The cellular phones may be sold during a different accounting period than the period in which they were manufactured. Thus, inventorying manufacturing costs in the balance sheet during the accounting period when goods are manufactured and expensing the manufacturing costs in a later income statement when the goods are sold matches revenues and expenses.

For merchandising-sector companies such as Wal-Mart, inventoriable costs are the costs of purchasing the goods that are resold in their same form. These costs comprise the costs of the goods themselves plus any incoming freight, insurance, and handling costs for those goods. Service-sector companies provide only services or intangible products. The absence of inventories of tangible products for sale means there are no inventoriable costs.

Period Costs

Period costs are all costs in the income statement other than cost of goods sold. Period costs, such as marketing, distribution and customer service costs, are treated as expenses of the accounting period in which they are incurred because they are expected to benefit revenues in that period and are not expected to benefit revenues in future periods. Some costs such as R&D costs are treated as period costs because, although these costs may benefit revenues in a future period if the R&D efforts are successful, it is highly uncertain if and when these benefits will occur. Expensing period costs as they are incurred best matches expenses to revenues.

For manufacturing-sector companies, period costs in the income statement are all nonmanufacturing costs (for example, design costs and costs of shipping products to customers). For merchandising-sector companies, period costs in the income statement are all costs not related to the cost of goods purchased for resale. Examples of these period costs are labor costs of sales floor personnel and advertising costs. Because there are no inventoriable costs for service-sector companies, all costs in the income statement are period costs.

Exhibit 2-5 showed examples of inventoriable costs in direct/indirect and variable/fixed cost classifications for a car manufacturer. Exhibit 2-6 shows examples of period costs in direct/indirect and variable/fixed cost classifications at a bank.

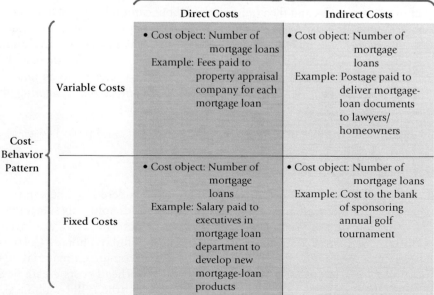

Exhibit 2-6		Assignment of Costs to Cost Object	
Examples of Period Costs in Combinations of the Direct/Indirect and Variable/Fixed Cost Classifications at a Bank		Direct Costs	Indirect Costs
	Variable Costs	• Cost object: Number of mortgage loans Example: Fees paid to property appraisal company for each mortgage loan	• Cost object: Number of mortgage loans Example: Postage paid to deliver mortgage-loan documents to lawyers/homeowners
Cost-Behavior Pattern	**Fixed Costs**	• Cost object: Number of mortgage loans Example: Salary paid to executives in mortgage loan department to develop new mortgage-loan products	• Cost object: Number of mortgage loans Example: Cost to the bank of sponsoring annual golf tournament

Illustrating the Flow of Inventoriable Costs and Period Costs

We illustrate the flow of inventoriable costs and period costs through the income statement of a manufacturing company, for which the distinction between inventoriable costs and period costs is most detailed.

Manufacturing-Sector Example

Follow the flow of costs for Cellular Products in Exhibit 2-7 and Exhibit 2-8. Exhibit 2-7 visually highlights the differences in the flow of inventoriable and period costs for a manufacturing-sector company. Note how, as described in the previous section, inventoriable costs go through the balance sheet accounts of work-in-process inventory and finished goods inventory before entering cost of goods sold in the income statement. Period costs are expensed directly in the income statement. Exhibit 2-8 takes the visual presentation in Exhibit 2-7 and shows how inventoriable costs and period expenses would appear in the income statement and schedule of cost of goods manufactured of a manufacturing company.

We start by tracking the flow of direct materials shown on the left of Exhibit 2-7 and in Panel B of Exhibit 2-8.

Step 1:   Cost of direct materials used in 2011. Note how the arrows in Exhibit 2-7 for beginning inventory, $11,000 (all numbers in thousands), and direct material purchases, $73,000, "fill up" the direct material inventory box and how direct material used, $76,000 "empties out" direct material inventory leaving an ending inventory of direct materials of $8,000 that becomes the beginning inventory for the next year.

The cost of direct materials used is calculated in Exhibit 2-8, Panel B (light blue shaded area) as follows:

Beginning inventory of direct materials, January 1, 2011	$11,000
+ Purchases of direct materials in 2011	73,000
− Ending inventory of direct materials, December 31, 2011	8,000
= Direct materials used in 2011	$76,000

Exhibit 2-7 Flow of Revenue and Costs for a Manufacturing-Sector Company, Cellular Products (in thousands)

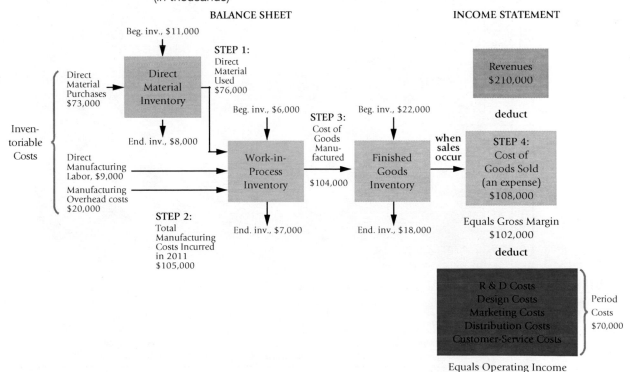

Exhibit 2-8   Income Statement and Schedule of Cost of Goods Manufactured of a
Manufacturing-Sector Company, Cellular Products

	A	B	C	D
1	**PANEL A: INCOME STATEMENT**			
2	**Cellular Products**			
3	**Income Statement**			
4	**For the Year Ended December 31, 2011 (in thousands)**			
5	Revenues		$210,000	
6	Cost of goods sold:			
7	Beginning finished goods inventory, January 1, 2009	$ 22,000		
8	Cost of goods manufactured (see Panel B)	104,000		
9	Cost of goods available for sale	126,000		
10	Ending finished goods inventory, December 31, 2009	18,000		
11	Cost of goods sold		108,000	
12	Gross margin (or gross profit)		102,000	
13	Operating costs:			
14	R&D, design, mktg., dist., and cust.-service cost	70,000		
15	Total operating costs		70,000	
16	Operating income		$ 32,000	
17				
18	**PANEL B: COST OF GOODS MANUFACTURED**			
19	**Cellular Products**			
20	**Schedule of Cost of Goods Manufactured[a]**			
21	**For the Year Ended December 31, 2009 (in thousands)**			
22	Direct materials:			
23	Beginning inventory, January 1, 2009	$11,000		
24	Purchases of direct materials	73,000		
25	Cost of direct materials available for use	84,000		
26	Ending inventory, December 31, 2009	8,000		
27	Direct materials used		$ 76,000	
28	Direct manufacturing labor		9,000	
29	Manufacturing overhead costs:			
30	Indirect manufacturing labor	$ 7,000		
31	Supplies	2,000		
32	Heat, light, and power	5,000		
33	Depreciation—plant building	2,000		
34	Depreciation—plant equipment	3,000		
35	Miscellaneous	1,000		
36	Total manufacturing overhead costs		20,000	
37	Manufacturing costs incurred during 2009		105,000	
38	Beginning work-in-process inventory, January 1, 2009		6,000	
39	Total manufacturing costs to account for		111,000	
40	Ending work-in-process inventory, December 31, 2009		7,000	
41	Cost of goods manufactured (to income statement)		$104,000	
42	[a]Note that this schedule can become a schedule of cost of goods manufactured and sold simply by including the beginning and ending finished goods inventory figures in the supporting schedule rather than in the body of the income statement.			

STEP 4 (rows 6–11)

STEP 1 (rows 22–27)

STEP 2 (rows 28–37)

STEP 3 (rows 37–41)

Step 2: Total manufacturing costs incurred in 2011. Total manufacturing costs refers to all direct manufacturing costs and manufacturing overhead costs incurred during 2011 for all goods worked on during the year. Cellular Products classifies its manufacturing costs into the three categories described earlier.

(i) Direct materials used in 2011 (shaded light blue in Exhibit 2-8, Panel B)	$ 76,000
(ii) Direct manufacturing labor in 2011 (shaded blue in Exhibit 2-8, Panel B)	9,000
(iii) Manufacturing overhead costs in 2011 (shaded dark blue in Exhibit 2-8, Panel B)	20,000
Total manufacturing costs incurred in 2011	$105,000

Note how in Exhibit 2-7, these costs increase work-in-process inventory.

Step 3: Cost of goods manufactured in 2011. Cost of goods manufactured refers to the cost of goods brought to completion, whether they were started before or during the current accounting period.

Note how the work-in-process inventory box in Exhibit 2-7 has a very similar structure to the direct material inventory box described in Step 1. Beginning work-in-process inventory of $6,000 and total manufacturing costs incurred in 2011 of $105,000 "fill-up" the work-in-process inventory box. Some of the manufacturing costs incurred during 2011 are held back as the cost of the ending work-in-process inventory. The ending work-in-process inventory of $7,000 becomes the beginning inventory for the next year, and the cost of goods manufactured during 2011 of $104,000 "empties out" the work-in-process inventory while "filling up" the finished goods inventory box.

The cost of goods manufactured in 2011 (shaded green) is calculated in Exhibit 2-8, Panel B as follows:

Beginning work-in-process inventory, January 1, 2011	$ 6,000
+ Total manufacturing costs incurred in 2011	105,000
= Total manufacturing costs to account for	111,000
− Ending work-in-process inventory, December 31, 2011	7,000
= Cost of goods manufactured in 2011	$104,000

Step 4: Cost of goods sold in 2011. The cost of goods sold is the cost of finished goods inventory sold to customers during the current accounting period. Looking at the finished goods inventory box in Exhibit 2-7, we see that the beginning inventory of finished goods of $22,000 and cost of goods manufactured in 2011 of $104,000 "fill up" the finished goods inventory box. The ending inventory of finished goods of $18,000 becomes the beginning inventory for the next year, and the cost of goods sold during 2011 of $108,000 "empties out" the finished goods inventory.

This cost of goods sold is an expense that is matched against revenues. The cost of goods sold for Cellular Products (shaded brown) is computed in Exhibit 2-8, Panel A, as follows:

Beginning inventory of finished goods, January 1, 2011	$ 22,000
+ Cost of goods manufactured in 2011	104,000
− Ending inventory of finished goods, December 31, 2011	18,000
= Cost of goods sold in 2011	$108,000

Exhibit 2-9 shows related general ledger T-accounts for Cellular Products' manufacturing cost flow. Note how the cost of goods manufactured ($104,000) is the cost of all goods completed during the accounting period. These costs are all inventoriable costs. Goods completed during the period are transferred to finished goods inventory. These costs become cost of goods sold in the accounting period when the goods are sold. Also note that the direct materials, direct manufacturing labor, and manufacturing overhead costs of the units in work-in-process inventory ($7,000) and finished goods inventory ($18,000) as of December 31, 2011, will appear as an asset in the balance sheet. These costs will become expenses next year when these units are sold.

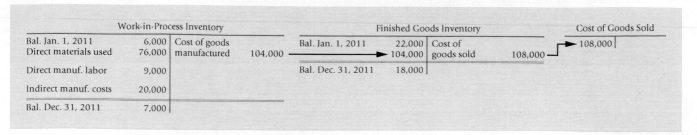

Exhibit 2-9 General Ledger T-Accounts for Cellular Products' Manufacturing Cost Flow (in thousands)

We are now in a position to prepare Cellular Products' income statement for 2011. The income statement of Cellular Products is shown on the right-hand side of Exhibit 2-7 and in Exhibit 2-8, Panel A. Revenues of Cellular Products are (in thousands) $210,000. Inventoriable costs expensed during 2011 equal cost of goods sold of $108,000.

$$\text{Gross margin} = \text{Revenues} - \text{Cost of goods sold} = \$210{,}000 - \$108{,}000 = \$102{,}000.$$

The $70,000 of operating costs comprising R&D, design, marketing, distribution, and customer-service costs are period costs of Cellular Products. These period costs include, for example, salaries of salespersons, depreciation on computers and other equipment used in marketing, and the cost of leasing warehouse space for distribution. **Operating income** equals total revenues from operations minus cost of goods sold and operating (period) costs (excluding interest expense and income taxes) or equivalently, gross margin minus period costs. The operating income of Cellular Products is $32,000 (gross margin, $102,000 – period costs, $70,000). Those of you familiar with financial accounting will note that period costs are typically called selling, general, and administrative expenses in the income statement

Newcomers to cost accounting frequently assume that indirect costs such as rent, telephone, and depreciation are always costs of the period in which they are incurred and are not associated with inventories. When these costs are incurred in marketing or in corporate headquarters, they are period costs. However, when these costs are incurred in manufacturing, they are manufacturing overhead costs and are inventoriable.

Recap of Inventoriable Costs and Period Costs

Exhibit 2-7 highlights the differences between inventoriable costs and period costs for a manufacturing company. The manufacturing costs of finished goods include direct materials, other direct manufacturing costs such as direct manufacturing labor, and manufacturing overhead costs such as supervision, production control, and machine maintenance. All these costs are inventoriable: They are assigned to work-in-process inventory until the goods are completed and then to finished goods inventory until the goods are sold. All nonmanufacturing costs, such as R&D, design, and distribution costs, are period costs.

Inventoriable costs and period costs flow through the income statement at a merchandising company similar to the way costs flow at a manufacturing company. At a merchandising company, however, the flow of costs is much simpler to understand and track. Exhibit 2-10 shows the inventoriable costs and period costs for a retailer or wholesaler who buys goods for resale. The only inventoriable cost is the cost of merchandise. (This corresponds to the cost of finished goods manufactured for a manufacturing company.) Purchased goods are held as merchandise inventory, the cost of which is shown as an asset in the balance sheet. As the goods are sold, their costs are shown in the income statement as cost of goods sold. A retailer or wholesaler also has a variety of marketing, distribution, and customer-service costs, which are period costs. In the income statement, period costs are deducted from revenues without ever having been included as part of inventory.

Decision Point ▶

What are the differences in the accounting for inventoriable versus period costs?

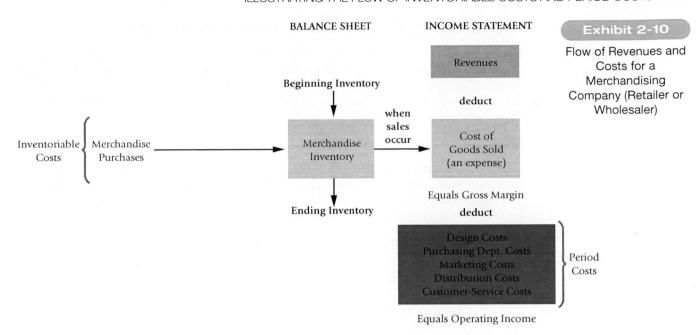

Exhibit 2-10

Flow of Revenues and Costs for a Merchandising Company (Retailer or Wholesaler)

Prime Costs and Conversion Costs

Two terms used to describe cost classifications in manufacturing costing systems are prime costs and conversion costs. **Prime costs** are all direct manufacturing costs. For Cellular Products,

$$\text{Prime costs} = \text{Direct material costs} + \text{Direct manufacturing labor costs} =$$
$$\$76{,}000 + \$9{,}000 = \$85{,}000$$

As we have already discussed, the greater the proportion of prime costs in a company's cost structure, the more confident managers can be about the accuracy of the costs of products. As information-gathering technology improves, companies can add more and more direct-cost categories. For example, power costs might be metered in specific areas of a plant and identified as a direct cost of specific products. Furthermore, if a production line were dedicated to the manufacture of a specific product, the depreciation on the production equipment would be a direct manufacturing cost and would be included in prime costs. Computer software companies often have a "purchased technology" direct manufacturing cost item. This item, which represents payments to suppliers who develop software algorithms for a product, is also included in prime costs. **Conversion costs** are all manufacturing costs other than direct material costs. Conversion costs represent all manufacturing costs incurred to convert direct materials into finished goods. For Cellular Products,

$$\text{Conversion costs} = \frac{\text{Direct manufacturing}}{\text{labor costs}} + \frac{\text{Manufacturing}}{\text{overhead costs}} = \$9{,}000 + \$20{,}000 = \$29{,}000$$

Note that direct manufacturing labor costs are a part of both prime costs and conversion costs.

Some manufacturing operations, such as computer-integrated manufacturing (CIM) plants, have very few workers. The workers' roles are to monitor the manufacturing process and to maintain the equipment that produces multiple products. Costing systems in CIM plants do not have a direct manufacturing labor cost category because direct manufacturing labor cost is relatively small and because it is difficult to trace this cost to products. In CIM plants, the only prime cost is direct material costs, and conversion costs consist only of manufacturing overhead costs.

Measuring Costs Requires Judgment

Measuring costs requires judgment. That's because there are alternative ways in which costs can be defined and classified. Different companies or sometimes even different sub-units within the same company may define and classify costs differently. Be careful to define and understand the ways costs are measured in a company or situation. We first illustrate this point with respect to labor cost measurement.

Measuring Labor Costs

Consider labor costs for software programming at companies such as Apple where programmers work on different software applications for products like the iMac, the iPod, and the iPhone. Although labor cost classifications vary among companies, many companies use multiple labor cost categories:

- Direct programming labor costs that can be traced to individual products
- Overhead (examples of prominent labor components of overhead follow):
  - Indirect labor compensation for
    Office staff
    Office security
    Rework labor (time spent by direct laborers correcting software errors)
    Overtime premium paid to software programmers (explained next)
    Idle time (explained next)
  - Managers', department heads', and supervisors' salaries
  - Payroll fringe costs, for example, health care premiums and pension costs (explained later)

Note how *indirect labor costs* are commonly divided into many subclassifications, for example, office staff and idle time, to retain information on different categories of indirect labor. Note also that managers' salaries usually are not classified as indirect labor costs. Instead, the compensation of supervisors, department heads, and all others who are regarded as management is placed in a separate classification of labor-related overhead.

Overtime Premium and Idle Time

The purpose of classifying costs in detail is to associate an individual cost with a specific cause or reason for why it was incurred. Two classes of indirect labor—overtime premium and idle time—need special mention. **Overtime premium** is the wage rate paid to workers (for both direct labor and indirect labor) in *excess* of their straight-time wage rates. Overtime premium is usually considered to be a part of indirect costs or overhead. Consider the example of George Flexner, a junior software programmer who writes software for multiple products. He is paid $20 per hour for straight-time and $30 per hour (time and a half) for overtime. His overtime premium is $10 per overtime hour. If he works 44 hours, including 4 overtime hours, in one week, his gross compensation would be classified as follows:

Direct programming labor: 44 hours × $20 per hour	$880
Overtime premium: 4 hours × $10 per hour	40
Total compensation for 44 hours	$920

In this example, why is the overtime premium of direct programming labor usually considered an overhead cost rather than a direct cost? After all, it can be traced to specific products that George worked on while working overtime. Overtime premium is generally not considered a direct cost because the particular job that George worked on during the overtime hours is a matter of chance. For example, assume that George worked on two products for 5 hours each on a specific workday of 10 hours, including 2 overtime hours. Should the product George worked on during hours 9 and 10 be assigned the overtime premium? Or should the premium be prorated over both products? Prorating the overtime premium does not "penalize"—add to the cost of—a particular product solely because it happened to be worked on during the overtime hours. *Instead, the overtime premium is considered to be attributable to the heavy overall volume of work. Its cost is regarded as part of overhead, which is borne by both products.*

Sometimes overtime is not random. For example, a launch deadline for a particular product may clearly be the sole source of overtime. In such instances, the overtime premium is regarded as a direct cost of that product.

Another subclassification of indirect labor is the idle time of both direct and indirect labor. **Idle time** is wages paid for unproductive time caused by lack of orders, machine or computer breakdowns, work delays, poor scheduling, and the like. For example, if George had no work for 3 hours during that week while waiting to receive code from another colleague, George's earnings would be classified as follows:

Direct programming labor: 41 hours × $20/hour	$820
Idle time (overhead): 3 hours × $20/hour	60
Overtime premium (overhead): 4 hours × $10/hour	40
Total earnings for 44 hours	$920

Clearly, the idle time is not related to a particular product, nor, as we have already discussed, is the overtime premium. Both overtime premium and idle time are considered overhead costs.

Benefits of Defining Accounting Terms

Managers, accountants, suppliers, and others will avoid many problems if they thoroughly understand and agree on the classifications and meanings of the cost terms introduced in this chapter and later in this book.

Consider the classification of programming labor *payroll fringe costs* (for example, employer payments for employee benefits such as Social Security, life insurance, health insurance, and pensions). Consider, for example, a software programmer, who is paid a wage of $20 an hour with fringe benefits totaling, say, $5 per hour. Some companies classify the $20 as a direct programming labor cost of the product for which the software is being written and the $5 as overhead cost. Other companies classify the entire $25 as direct programming labor cost. The latter approach is preferable because the stated wage and the fringe benefit costs together are a fundamental part of acquiring direct software programming labor services.

Caution: In every situation, pinpoint clearly what direct labor includes and what direct labor excludes. Achieving clarity may prevent disputes regarding cost reimbursement contracts, income tax payments, and labor union matters. Consider that some countries such as Costa Rica and Mauritius offer substantial income tax savings to foreign companies that generate employment within their borders. In some cases, to qualify for the tax benefits, the direct labor costs must at least equal a specified percentage of the total costs.

When direct labor costs are not precisely defined, disputes have arisen as to whether payroll fringe costs should be included as part of direct labor costs when calculating the direct labor percentage for qualifying for such tax benefits. Companies have sought to classify payroll fringe costs as part of direct labor costs to make direct labor costs a higher percentage of total costs. Tax authorities have argued that payroll fringe costs are part of overhead. In addition to fringe benefits, other debated items are compensation for training time, idle time, vacations, sick leave, and overtime premium. To prevent disputes, contracts and laws should be as specific as possible regarding definitions and measurements.

Different Meanings of Product Costs

Many cost terms found in practice have ambiguous meanings. Consider the term *product cost*. A **product cost** is the sum of the costs assigned to a product for a specific purpose. Different purposes can result in different measures of product cost, as the brackets on the value chain in Exhibit 2-11 illustrate:

- **Pricing and product-mix decisions.** For the purposes of making decisions about pricing and which products provide the most profits, the manager is interested in the overall (total) profitability of different products and, consequently, assigns costs incurred in all business functions of the value chain to the different products.

- **Contracting with government agencies.** Government contracts often reimburse contractors on the basis of the "cost of a product" plus a prespecified margin of profit. Because of the cost-plus profit margin nature of the contract, government agencies provide detailed guidelines on the cost items they will allow and disallow

Learning Objective 6

Explain why product costs are computed in different ways for different purposes

. . . examples are pricing and product-mix decisions, government contracts, and financial statements

Exhibit 2-11

Different Product Costs
for Different Purposes

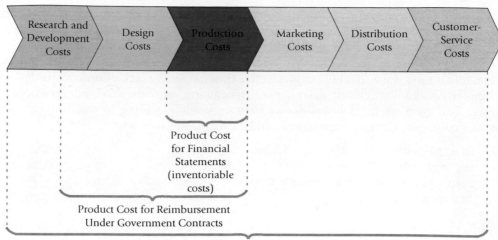

when calculating the cost of a product. For example, some government agencies explicitly exclude marketing, distribution, and customer-service costs from the product costs that qualify for reimbursement, and they may only partially reimburse R&D costs. These agencies want to reimburse contractors for only those costs most closely related to delivering products under the contract. The second bracket in Exhibit 2-11 shows how the product-cost calculations for a specific contract may allow for all design and production costs but only part of R&D costs.

■ **Preparing financial statements for external reporting under generally accepted accounting principles (GAAP).** Under GAAP, only manufacturing costs can be assigned to inventories in the financial statements. For purposes of calculating inventory costs, product costs include only inventoriable (manufacturing) costs.

**Decision
Point** ▶

Why do managers
assign different
costs to the same
cost object?

As Exhibit 2-11 illustrates, product-cost measures range from a narrow set of costs for financial statements—a set that includes only inventoriable costs—to a broader set of costs for reimbursement under a government contract to a still broader set of costs for pricing and product-mix decisions.

This section focused on how different purposes result in the inclusion of different cost items of the value chain of business functions when product costs are calculated. The same caution about the need to be clear and precise about cost concepts and their measurement applies to each cost classification introduced in this chapter. Exhibit 2-12 summarizes the key cost classifications.

Using the five-step process described in Chapter 1, think about how these different classifications of costs are helpful to managers when making decisions and evaluating performance.

1. *Identify the problem and uncertainties.* Consider a decision about how much to price a product. This decision often depends on how much it costs to make the product.

2. *Obtain information.* Managers identify direct and indirect costs of a product in each business function. Managers also gather other information about customers, competitors, and prices of substitute products.

Exhibit 2-12

Alternative
Classifications of Costs

1. Business function
   a. Research and development
   b. Design of products and processes
   c. Production
   d. Marketing
   e. Distribution
   f. Customer service
2. Assignment to a cost object
   a. Direct cost
   b. Indirect cost

3. Behavior pattern in relation to
   the level of activity or volume
   a. Variable cost
   b. Fixed cost
4. Aggregate or average
   a. Total cost
   b. Unit cost
5. Assets or expenses
   a. Inventoriable cost
   b Period cost

3. *Make predictions about the future.* Managers estimate what it will cost to make the product in the future. This requires predictions about the quantity of product that managers expect to sell and an understanding of fixed and variable costs.

4. *Make decisions by choosing among alternatives.* Managers choose a price to charge based on a thorough understanding of costs and other information.

5. *Implement the decision, evaluate performance, and learn.* Managers control costs and learn by comparing actual total and unit costs against predicted amounts.

The next section describes how the basic concepts introduced in this chapter lead to a framework for understanding cost accounting and cost management that can then be applied to the study of many topics, such as strategy evaluation, quality, and investment decisions.

A Framework for Cost Accounting and Cost Management

Three features of cost accounting and cost management across a wide range of applications are as follows:

1. Calculating the cost of products, services, and other cost objects
2. Obtaining information for planning and control and performance evaluation
3. Analyzing the relevant information for making decisions

We develop these ideas in Chapters 3 through 12. The ideas also form the foundation for the study of various topics later in the book.

> **Learning Objective 7**
>
> Describe a framework for cost accounting and cost management
>
> . . . three features that help managers make decisions

Calculating the Cost of Products, Services, and Other Cost Objects

We have already seen the different purposes and measures of product costs. Whatever the purpose, the costing system traces direct costs and allocates indirect costs to prod-ucts. Chapters 4 and 7 describe systems, such as activity-based costing systems, used to calculate total costs and unit costs of products and services. The chapters also discuss how managers use this information to formulate strategy and make pricing, product-mix, and cost-management decisions.

Obtaining Information for Planning and Control and Performance Evaluation

Budgeting is the most commonly used tool for planning and control. A budget forces managers to look ahead, to translate strategy into plans, to coordinate and communicate within the organization, and to provide a benchmark for evaluating performance. Budgeting often plays a major role in affecting behavior and decisions because managers strive to meet budget targets. Chapter 6 describes budgeting systems.

At the end of a reporting period, managers compare actual results to planned performance. The manager's tasks are to understand why differences (called variances) between actual and planned performances arise and to use the information provided by these variances as feedback to promote learning and future improvement. Managers also use variances as well as nonfinancial measures, such as defect rates and customer satisfaction ratings, to control and evaluate the performance of various departments, divisions, and managers. Chapters 7 and 8 discuss variance analysis. Chapter 9 describes planning, control, and inventory-costing issues relating to capacity. Chapters 6, 7, 8, and 9 focus on the management accountant's role in implementing strategy.

Analyzing the Relevant Information for Making Decisions

When making decisions about strategy design and strategy implementation, managers must understand which revenues and costs to consider and which ones to ignore. Management accountants help managers identify what information is relevant and what information is irrelevant. Consider a decision about whether to buy a product from an outside vendor or to make it in-house. The costing system indicates that it costs $25 per unit to make the product in-house. A vendor offers the product for $22 per unit. At first glance, it seems it will cost less for the company to buy the product rather than make it. Suppose, however, that of the $25 to make the product in-house, $5 consists of plant lease costs that the company has already paid under the lease contract. Furthermore, if the product is bought, the plant will remain idle. That is, there is no opportunity to profit by putting the plant to some alternative use. Under these conditions, it will cost less to make the product than to buy it. That's because making the product costs only an *additional* $20 per unit ($25 − $5), compared with an *additional* $22 per unit if it is bought. The $5 per unit of lease cost is irrelevant to the decision because it is a *past* (or *sunk*) cost that has already been incurred regardless of whether the product is made or bought. Analyzing relevant information is a key aspect of making decisions.

When making strategic decisions about which products and how much to produce, managers must know how revenues and costs vary with changes in output levels. For this purpose, managers need to distinguish fixed costs from variable costs. Chapter 3 analyzes how operating income changes with changes in units sold and how managers use this information to make decisions such as how much to spend on advertising. Chapter 10 describes methods to estimate the fixed and variable components of costs. Chapter 11 applies the concept of relevance to decision making in many different situations and describes methods managers use to maximize income given the resource constraints they face. Chapter 12 describes how management accountants help managers determine prices and manage costs across the value chain and over a product's life cycle.

Decision Point ▶

What are the three key features of cost accounting and cost management?

Later chapters in the book discuss topics such as strategy evaluation, customer profitability, quality, just-in-time systems, investment decisions, transfer pricing, and performance evaluation. Each of these topics invariably has product costing, planning and control, and decision-making perspectives. A command of the first 12 chapters will help you master these topics. For example, Chapter 13 on strategy describes the balanced scorecard, a set of financial and nonfinancial measures used to implement strategy that builds on the planning and control functions. The section on strategic analysis of operating income builds on ideas of product costing and variance analysis. The section on downsizing and managing capacity builds on ideas of relevant revenues and relevant costs.

Problem for Self-Study

Foxwood Company is a metal- and woodcutting manufacturer, selling products to the home construction market. Consider the following data for 2011:

Sandpaper	$ 2,000
Materials-handling costs	70,000
Lubricants and coolants	5,000
Miscellaneous indirect manufacturing labor	40,000
Direct manufacturing labor	300,000
Direct materials inventory Jan. 1, 2011	40,000
Direct materials inventory Dec. 31, 2011	50,000
Finished goods inventory Jan. 1, 2011	100,000
Finished goods inventory Dec. 31, 2011	150,000
Work-in-process inventory Jan. 1, 2011	10,000
Work-in-process inventory Dec. 31, 2011	14,000
Plant-leasing costs	54,000
Depreciation—plant equipment	36,000
Property taxes on plant equipment	4,000
Fire insurance on plant equipment	3,000
Direct materials purchased	460,000
Revenues	1,360,000
Marketing promotions	60,000
Marketing salaries	100,000
Distribution costs	70,000
Customer-service costs	100,000

1. Prepare an income statement with a separate supporting schedule of cost of goods **Required** manufactured. For all manufacturing items, classify costs as direct costs or indirect costs and indicate by V or F whether each is basically a variable cost or a fixed cost (when the cost object is a product unit). If in doubt, decide on the basis of whether the total cost will change substantially over a wide range of units produced.
2. Suppose that both the direct material costs and the plant-leasing costs are for the production of 900,000 units. What is the direct material cost of each unit produced? What is the plant-leasing cost per unit? Assume that the plant-leasing cost is a fixed cost.
3. Suppose Foxwood Company manufactures 1,000,000 units next year. Repeat the computation in requirement 2 for direct materials and plant-leasing costs. Assume the implied cost-behavior patterns persist.
4. As a management consultant, explain concisely to the company president why the unit cost for direct materials did not change in requirements 2 and 3 but the unit cost for plant-leasing costs did change.

Solution

1.

Foxwood Company
Income Statement
For the Year Ended December 31, 2011

Revenues		$1,360,000
Cost of goods sold		
Beginning finished goods inventory January 1, 2011	$ 100,000	
Cost of goods manufactured (see the following schedule)	960,000	
Cost of goods available for sale	1,060,000	
Deduct ending finished goods inventory		
December 31, 2011	150,000	910,000
Gross margin (or gross profit)		450,000
Operating costs		
Marketing promotions	60,000	
Marketing salaries	100,000	
Distribution costs	70,000	
Customer-service costs	100,000	330,000
Operating income		$ 120,000

Foxwood Company
Schedule of Cost of Goods Manufactured
For the Year Ended December 31, 2011

Direct materials		
Beginning inventory, January 1, 2011		$ 40,000
Purchases of direct materials		460,000
Cost of direct materials available for use		500,000
Ending inventory, December 31, 2011		50,000
Direct materials used		450,000 (V)
Direct manufacturing labor		300,000 (V)
Indirect manufacturing costs		
Sandpaper	$ 2,000 (V)	
Materials-handling costs	70,000 (V)	
Lubricants and coolants	5,000 (V)	
Miscellaneous indirect manufacturing labor	40,000 (V)	
Plant-leasing costs	54,000 (F)	
Depreciation—plant equipment	36,000 (F)	
Property taxes on plant equipment	4,000 (F)	
Fire insurance on plant equipment	3,000 (F)	214,000
Manufacturing costs incurred during 2011		964,000
Beginning work-in-process inventory, January 1, 2011		10,000
Total manufacturing costs to account for		974,000
Ending work-in-process inventory, December 31, 2011		14,000
Cost of goods manufactured (to income statement)		$ 960,000

2. Direct material unit cost   = Direct materials used ÷ Units produced
                               = $450,000 ÷ 900,000 units = $0.50 per unit
   Plant-leasing unit cost   = Plant-leasing costs ÷ Units produced
                               = $54,000 ÷ 900,000 units = $0.06 per unit

3. The direct material costs are variable, so they would increase in total from $450,000 to $500,000 (1,000,000 units × $0.50 per unit). However, their unit cost would be unaffected: $500,000 ÷ 1,000,000 units = $0.50 per unit.

   In contrast, the plant-leasing costs of $54,000 are fixed, so they would not increase in total. However, the plant-leasing cost per unit would decline from $0.060 to $0.054: $54,000 ÷ 1,000,000 units = $0.054 per unit.

4. The explanation would begin with the answer to requirement 3. As a consultant, you should stress that the unitizing (averaging) of costs that have different behavior patterns can be misleading. A common error is to assume that a total unit cost, which is often a sum of variable unit cost and fixed unit cost, is an indicator that total costs change in proportion to changes in production levels. The next chapter demonstrates the necessity for distinguishing between cost-behavior patterns. You must be wary, especially about average fixed cost per unit. Too often, unit fixed cost is erroneously regarded as being indistinguishable from unit variable cost.

Decision Points

The following question-and-answer format summarizes the chapter's learning objectives. Each decision presents a key question related to a learning objective. The guidelines are the answer to that question.

Decision	Guidelines
1. What is a cost object?	A cost object is anything for which a separate measurement of cost is needed. Examples include a product, a service, a project, a customer, a brand category, an activity, and a department.
2. How do managers decide whether a cost is a direct or an indirect cost?	A direct cost is any cost that is related to a particular cost object and can be traced to that cost object in an economically feasible way. Indirect costs are related to the particular cost object but cannot be traced to it in an economically feasible way. The same cost can be direct for one cost object and indirect for another cost object. This book uses *cost tracing* to describe the assignment of direct costs to a cost object and *cost allocation* to describe the assignment of indirect costs to a cost object.
3. How do managers decide whether a cost is a variable or a fixed cost?	A variable cost changes *in total* in proportion to changes in the related level of total activity or volume. A fixed cost remains unchanged *in total* for a given time period despite wide changes in the related level of total activity or volume.
4. How should costs be estimated?	In general, focus on total costs, not unit costs. When making total cost estimates, think of variable costs as an amount per unit and fixed costs as a total amount. The unit cost of a cost object should be interpreted cautiously when it includes a fixed-cost component.
5. What are the differences in the accounting for inventoriable versus period costs?	Inventoriable costs are all costs of a product that are regarded as an asset in the accounting period when they are incurred and become cost of goods sold in the accounting period when the product is sold. Period costs are expensed in the accounting period in which they are incurred and are all of the costs in an income statement other than cost of goods sold.

6. Why do managers assign different costs to the same cost objects?

Managers can assign different costs to the same cost object depending on the purpose. For example, for the external reporting purpose in a manufacturing company, the inventoriable cost of a product includes only manufacturing costs. In contrast, costs from all business functions of the value chain often are assigned to a product for pricing and product-mix decisions.

7. What are the three key features of cost accounting and cost management?

Three features of cost accounting and cost management are (1) calculating the cost of products, services, and other cost objects; (2) obtaining information for planning and control and performance evaluation; and (3) analyzing relevant information for making decisions.

Terms to Learn

This chapter contains more basic terms than any other in this book. Do not proceed before you check your understanding of the following terms. Both the chapter and the Glossary at the end of the book contain definitions.

actual cost (**p. 27**)
average cost (**p. 35**)
budgeted cost (**p. 27**)
conversion costs (**p. 43**)
cost (**p. 27**)
cost accumulation (**p. 28**)
cost allocation (**p. 29**)
cost assignment (**p. 29**)
cost driver (**p. 32**)
cost object (**p. 27**)
cost of goods manufactured (**p. 41**)
cost tracing (**p. 28**)
direct costs of a cost object (**p. 28**)

direct manufacturing labor costs (**p. 37**)
direct material costs (**p. 37**)
direct materials inventory (**p. 37**)
factory overhead costs (**p. 37**)
finished goods inventory (**p. 37**)
fixed cost (**p. 30**)
idle time (**p. 45**)
indirect costs of a cost object (**p. 28**)
indirect manufacturing costs (**p. 37**)
inventoriable costs (**p. 37**)
manufacturing overhead costs (**p. 37**)
manufacturing-sector companies (**p. 36**)

merchandising-sector companies (**p. 36**)
operating income (**p. 42**)
overtime premium (**p. 44**)
period costs (**p. 38**)
prime costs (**p. 43**)
product cost (**p. 45**)
relevant range (**p. 33**)
revenues (**p. 38**)
service-sector companies (**p. 36**)
unit cost (**p. 35**)
variable cost (**p. 30**)
work-in-process inventory (**p. 37**)
work in progress (**p. 37**)

Assignment Material

Questions

2-1 Define cost object and give three examples.

2-2 Define direct costs and indirect costs.

2-3 Why do managers consider direct costs to be more accurate than indirect costs?

2-4 Name three factors that will affect the classification of a cost as direct or indirect.

2-5 Define variable cost and fixed cost. Give an example of each.

2-6 What is a cost driver? Give one example.

2-7 What is the relevant range? What role does the relevant-range concept play in explaining how costs behave?

2-8 Explain why unit costs must often be interpreted with caution.

2-9 Describe how manufacturing-, merchandising-, and service-sector companies differ from each other.

2-10 What are three different types of inventory that manufacturing companies hold?

2-11 Distinguish between inventoriable costs and period costs.

2-12 Define the following: direct material costs, direct manufacturing-labor costs, manufacturing overhead costs, prime costs, and conversion costs.

2-13 Describe the overtime-premium and idle-time categories of indirect labor.

2-14 Define product cost. Describe three different purposes for computing product costs.

2-15 What are three common features of cost accounting and cost management?

MyAccountingLab

Exercises

2-16   Computing and interpreting manufacturing unit costs. Minnesota Office Products (MOP) produces three different paper products at its Vaasa lumber plant: Supreme, Deluxe, and Regular. Each product has its own dedicated production line at the plant. It currently uses the following three-part classification for its manufacturing costs: direct materials, direct manufacturing labor, and manufacturing overhead costs. Total manufacturing overhead costs of the plant in July 2011 are $150 million ($15 million of which are fixed). This total amount is allocated to each product line on the basis of the direct manufacturing labor costs of each line. Summary data (in millions) for July 2011 are as follows:

	Supreme	Deluxe	Regular
Direct material costs	$ 89	$ 57	$ 60
Direct manufacturing labor costs	$ 16	$ 26	$ 8
Manufacturing overhead costs	$ 48	$ 78	$ 24
Units produced	125	150	140

Required

1. Compute the manufacturing cost per unit for each product produced in July 2011.
2. Suppose that in August 2011, production was 150 million units of Supreme, 190 million units of Deluxe, and 220 million units of Regular. Why might the July 2011 information on manufacturing cost per unit be misleading when predicting total manufacturing costs in August 2011?

2-17   Direct, indirect, fixed, and variable costs. Best Breads manufactures two types of bread, which are sold as wholesale products to various specialty retail bakeries. Each loaf of bread requires a three-step process. The first step is mixing. The mixing department combines all of the necessary ingredients to create the dough and processes it through high speed mixers. The dough is then left to rise before baking. The second step is baking, which is an entirely automated process. The baking department molds the dough into its final shape and bakes each loaf of bread in a high temperature oven. The final step is finishing, which is an entirely manual process. The finishing department coats each loaf of bread with a special glaze, allows the bread to cool, and then carefully packages each loaf in a specialty carton for sale in retail bakeries.

Required

1. Costs involved in the process are listed next. For each cost, indicate whether it is a direct variable, direct fixed, indirect variable, or indirect fixed cost, assuming "units of production of each kind of bread" is the cost object.

Costs:
Yeast	Mixing department manager
Flour	Materials handlers in each department
Packaging materials	Custodian in factory
Depreciation on ovens	Night guard in factory
Depreciation on mixing machines	Machinist (running the mixing machine)
Rent on factory building	Machine maintenance personnel in each department
Fire insurance on factory building	Maintenance supplies for factory
Factory utilities	Cleaning supplies for factory
Finishing department hourly laborers	

2. If the cost object were the "mixing department" rather than units of production of each kind of bread, which preceding costs would now be direct instead of indirect costs?

2-18   Classification of costs, service sector. Consumer Focus is a marketing research firm that organizes focus groups for consumer-product companies. Each focus group has eight individuals who are paid $50 per session to provide comments on new products. These focus groups meet in hotels and are led by a trained, independent, marketing specialist hired by Consumer Focus. Each specialist is paid a fixed retainer to conduct a minimum number of sessions and a per session fee of $2,000. A Consumer Focus staff member attends each session to ensure that all the logistical aspects run smoothly.

Classify each cost item (**A–H**) as follows:

Required

a. Direct or indirect (D or I) costs with respect to each individual focus group.
b. Variable or fixed (V or F) costs with respect to how the total costs of Consumer Focus change as the number of focus groups conducted changes. (If in doubt, select on the basis of whether the total costs will change substantially if there is a large change in the number of groups conducted.)

You will have two answers (D or I; V or F) for each of the following items:

Cost Item	D or I	V or F
A. Payment to individuals in each focus group to provide comments on new products		
B. Annual subscription of Consumer Focus to *Consumer Reports* magazine		
C. Phone calls made by Consumer Focus staff member to confirm individuals will attend a focus group session (Records of individual calls are not kept.)		
D. Retainer paid to focus group leader to conduct 20 focus groups per year on new medical products		
E. Meals provided to participants in each focus group		
F. Lease payment by Consumer Focus for corporate office		
G. Cost of tapes used to record comments made by individuals in a focus group session (These tapes are sent to the company whose products are being tested.)		
H. Gasoline costs of Consumer Focus staff for company-owned vehicles (Staff members submit monthly bills with no mileage breakdowns.)		

2-19 **Classification of costs, merchandising sector.** Home Entertainment Center (HEC) operates a large store in San Francisco. The store has both a video section and a music (compact disks and tapes) section. HEC reports revenues for the video section separately from the music section.

Classify each cost item (**A–H**) as follows:

Required

a. Direct or indirect (D or I) costs with respect to the total number of videos sold.
b. Variable or fixed (V or F) costs with respect to how the total costs of the video section change as the total number of videos sold changes. (If in doubt, select on the basis of whether the total costs will change substantially if there is a large change in the total number of videos sold.)

You will have two answers (D or I; V or F) for each of the following items:

Cost Item	D or I	V or F
A. Annual retainer paid to a video distributor		
B. Electricity costs of the HEC store (single bill covers entire store)		
C. Costs of videos purchased for sale to customers		
D. Subscription to *Video Trends* magazine		
E. Leasing of computer software used for financial budgeting at the HEC store		
F. Cost of popcorn provided free to all customers of the HEC store		
G. Earthquake insurance policy for the HEC store		
H. Freight-in costs of videos purchased by HEC		

2-20 **Classification of costs, manufacturing sector.** The Fremont, California, plant of New United Motor Manufacturing, Inc. (NUMMI), a joint venture of General Motors and Toyota, assembles two types of cars (Corollas and Geo Prisms). Separate assembly lines are used for each type of car.

Classify each cost item (**A–H**) as follows:

Required

a. Direct or indirect (D or I) costs with respect to the total number of cars of each type assembled (Corolla or Geo Prism).
b. Variable or fixed (V or F) costs with respect to how the total costs of the plant change as the total number of cars of each type assembled changes. (If in doubt, select on the basis of whether the total costs will change substantially if there is a large change in the total number of cars of each type assembled.)

You will have two answers (D or I; V or F) for each of the following items:

Cost Item	D or I	V or F
A. Cost of tires used on Geo Prisms		
B. Salary of public relations manager for NUMMI plant		
C. Annual awards dinner for Corolla suppliers		
D. Salary of engineer who monitors design changes on Geo Prism		
E. Freight costs of Corolla engines shipped from Toyota City, Japan, to Fremont, California		
F. Electricity costs for NUMMI plant (single bill covers entire plant)		
G. Wages paid to temporary assembly-line workers hired in periods of high production (paid on hourly basis)		
H. Annual fire-insurance policy cost for NUMMI plant		

2-21 Variable costs, fixed costs, total costs. Bridget Ashton is getting ready to open a small restaurant. She is on a tight budget and must choose between the following long-distance phone plans:

Plan A: Pay 10 cents per minute of long-distance calling.

Plan B: Pay a fixed monthly fee of $15 for up to 240 long-distance minutes, and 8 cents per minute thereafter (if she uses fewer than 240 minutes in any month, she still pays $15 for the month).

Plan C: Pay a fixed monthly fee of $22 for up to 510 long-distance minutes and 5 cents per minute thereafter (if she uses fewer than 510 minutes, she still pays $22 for the month).

Required

1. Draw a graph of the total monthly costs of the three plans for different levels of monthly long-distance calling.
2. Which plan should Ashton choose if she expects to make 100 minutes of long-distance calls? 240 minutes? 540 minutes?

2-22 Variable costs and fixed costs. Consolidated Minerals (CM) owns the rights to extract minerals from beach sands on Fraser Island. CM has costs in three areas:

a. Payment to a mining subcontractor who charges $80 per ton of beach sand mined and returned to the beach (after being processed on the mainland to extract three minerals: ilmenite, rutile, and zircon).
b. Payment of a government mining and environmental tax of $50 per ton of beach sand mined.
c. Payment to a barge operator. This operator charges $150,000 per month to transport each batch of beach sand—up to 100 tons per batch per day—to the mainland and then return to Fraser Island (that is, 0 to 100 tons per day = $150,000 per month; 101 to 200 tons per day = $300,000 per month, and so on).

    Each barge operates 25 days per month. The $150,000 monthly charge must be paid even if fewer than 100 tons are transported on any day and even if CM requires fewer than 25 days of barge transportation in that month.

CM is currently mining 180 tons of beach sands per day for 25 days per month.

Required

1. What is the variable cost per ton of beach sand mined? What is the fixed cost to CM per month?
2. Plot a graph of the variable costs and another graph of the fixed costs of CM. Your graphs should be similar to Exhibit 2-3, Panel A (p. 31), and Exhibit 2-4 (p. 34). Is the concept of relevant range applicable to your graphs? Explain.
3. What is the unit cost per ton of beach sand mined (a) if 180 tons are mined each day and (b) if 220 tons are mined each day? Explain the difference in the unit-cost figures.

2-23 Variable costs, fixed costs, relevant range. Sweetum Candies manufactures jaw-breaker candies in a fully automated process. The machine that produces candies was purchased recently and can make 4,100 per month. The machine costs $9,000 and is depreciated using straight line depreciation over 10 years assuming zero residual value. Rent for the factory space and warehouse, and other fixed manufacturing overhead costs total $1,200 per month.

Sweetum currently makes and sells 3,800 jaw-breakers per month. Sweetum buys just enough materials each month to make the jaw-breakers it needs to sell. Materials cost 30 cents per jawbreaker.

Next year Sweetum expects demand to increase by 100%. At this volume of materials purchased, it will get a 10% discount on price. Rent and other fixed manufacturing overhead costs will remain the same.

Required

1. What is Sweetum's current annual relevant range of output?
2. What is Sweetum's current annual fixed manufacturing cost within the relevant range? What is the annual variable manufacturing cost?
3. What will Sweetum's relevant range of output be next year? How if at all, will total annual fixed and variable manufacturing costs change next year? Assume that if it needs to Sweetum could buy an identical machine at the same cost as the one it already has.

2-24 Cost drivers and value chain. Helner Cell Phones (HCP) is developing a new touch screen smartphone to compete in the cellular phone industry. The phones will be sold at wholesale prices to cell phone companies, which will in turn sell them in retail stores to the final customer. HCP has undertaken the following activities in its value chain to bring its product to market:

> Identify customer needs (What do smartphone users want?)
> Perform market research on competing brands
> Design a prototype of the HCP smartphone
> Market the new design to cell phone companies
> Manufacture the HCP smartphone
> Process orders from cell phone companies
> Package the HCP smartphones
> Deliver the HCP smartphones to the cell phone companies
> Provide online assistance to cell phone users for use of the HCP smartphone
> Make design changes to the smartphone based on customer feedback

During the process of product development, production, marketing, distribution, and customer service, HCP has kept track of the following cost drivers:

> Number of smartphones shipped by HCP
> Number of design changes
> Number of deliveries made to cell phone companies
> Engineering hours spent on initial product design
> Hours spent researching competing market brands
> Customer-service hours
> Number of smartphone orders processed
> Number of cell phone companies purchasing the HCP smartphone
> Machine hours required to run the production equipment
> Number of surveys returned and processed from competing smartphone users

1. Identify each value chain activity listed at the beginning of the exercise with one of the following value-chain categories:

   Required

   a. Design of products and processes
   b. Production
   c. Marketing
   d. Distribution
   e. Customer Service

2. Use the list of preceding cost drivers to find one or more reasonable cost drivers for each of the activities in HCP's value chain.

2-25 Cost drivers and functions. The list of representative cost drivers in the right column of this table are randomized with respect to the list of functions in the left column. That is, they do not match.

Function	Representative Cost Driver
1. Accounting	A. Number of invoices sent
2. Human resources	B. Number of purchase orders
3. Data processing	C. Number of research scientists
4. Research and development	D. Hours of computer processing unit (CPU)
5. Purchasing	E. Number of employees
6. Distribution	F. Number of transactions processed
7. Billing	G. Number of deliveries made

1. Match each function with its representative cost driver.

   Required

2. Give a second example of a cost driver for each function.

2-26 Total costs and unit costs. A student association has hired a band and a caterer for a graduation party. The band will charge a fixed fee of $1,000 for an evening of music, and the caterer will charge a fixed fee of $600 for the party setup and an additional $9 per person who attends. Snacks and soft drinks will be provided by the caterer for the duration of the party. Students attending the party will pay $5 each at the door.

1. Draw a graph depicting the fixed cost, the variable cost, and the total cost to the student association for different attendance levels.

   Required

2. Suppose 100 people attend the party. What is the total cost to the student association? What is the cost per person?

3. Suppose 500 people attend the party. What is the total cost to the student association and the cost per attendee?

4. Draw a graph depicting the cost per attendee for different attendance levels. As president of the student association, you want to request a grant to cover some of the party costs. Will you use the per attendee cost numbers to make your case? Why or why not?

2-27 Total and unit cost, decision making. Gayle's Glassworks makes glass flanges for scientific use. Materials cost $1 per flange, and the glass blowers are paid a wage rate of $28 per hour. A glass blower blows 10 flanges per hour. Fixed manufacturing costs for flanges are $28,000 per period. Period (nonmanufacturing) costs associated with flanges are $10,000 per period, and are fixed.

Required

1. Graph the fixed, variable, and total manufacturing cost for flanges, using units (number of flanges) on the *x*-axis.

2. Assume Gayle's Glassworks manufactures and sells 5,000 flanges this period. Its competitor, Flora's Flasks, sells flanges for $10 each. Can Gayle sell below Flora's price and still make a profit on the flanges?

3. How would your answer to requirement 2 differ if Gayle's Glassworks made and sold 10,000 flanges this period? Why? What does this indicate about the use of unit cost in decision making?

2-28 Inventoriable costs versus period costs. Each of the following cost items pertains to one of these companies: General Electric (a manufacturing-sector company), Safeway (a merchandising-sector company), and Google (a service-sector company):

a. Perrier mineral water purchased by Safeway for sale to its customers

b. Electricity used to provide lighting for assembly-line workers at a General Electric refrigerator-assembly plant

c. Depreciation on Google's computer equipment used to update directories of Web sites

d. Electricity used to provide lighting for Safeway's store aisles

e. Depreciation on General Electric's computer equipment used for quality testing of refrigerator components during the assembly process

f. Salaries of Safeway's marketing personnel planning local-newspaper advertising campaigns

g. Perrier mineral water purchased by Google for consumption by its software engineers

h. Salaries of Google's marketing personnel selling banner advertising

Required

1. Distinguish between manufacturing-, merchandising-, and service-sector companies.

2. Distinguish between inventoriable costs and period costs.

3. Classify each of the cost items (**a–h**) as an inventoriable cost or a period cost. Explain your answers.

MyAccountingLab

Problems

2-29 Computing cost of goods purchased and cost of goods sold. The following data are for Marvin Department Store. The account balances (in thousands) are for 2011.

Marketing, distribution, and customer-service costs	$ 37,000
Merchandise inventory, January 1, 2011	27,000
Utilities	17,000
General and administrative costs	43,000
Merchandise inventory, December 31, 2011	34,000
Purchases	155,000
Miscellaneous costs	4,000
Transportation-in	7,000
Purchase returns and allowances	4,000
Purchase discounts	6,000
Revenues	280,000

Required

1. Compute (**a**) the cost of goods purchased and (**b**) the cost of goods sold.

2. Prepare the income statement for 2011.

2-30 Cost of goods purchased, cost of goods sold, and income statement. The following data are for Montgomery Retail Outlet Stores. The account balances (in thousands) are for 2011.

Marketing and advertising costs	$ 24,000
Merchandise inventory, January 1, 2011	45,000
Shipping of merchandise to customers	2,000

Building depreciation	$ 4,200
Purchases	260,000
General and administrative costs	32,000
Merchandise inventory, December 31, 2011	52,000
Merchandise freight-in	10,000
Purchase returns and allowances	11,000
Purchase discounts	9,000
Revenues	320,000

Required

1. Compute **(a)** the cost of goods purchased and **(b)** the cost of goods sold.
2. Prepare the income statement for 2011.

2-31 Flow of Inventoriable Costs. Renka's Heaters selected data for October 2011 are presented here (in millions):

Direct materials inventory 10/1/2011	$ 105
Direct materials purchased	365
Direct materials used	385
Total manufacturing overhead costs	450
Variable manufacturing overhead costs	265
Total manufacturing costs incurred during October 2011	1,610
Work-in-process inventory 10/1/2011	230
Cost of goods manufactured	1,660
Finished goods inventory 10/1/2011	130
Cost of goods sold	1,770

Required

Calculate the following costs:

1. Direct materials inventory 10/31/2011
2. Fixed manufacturing overhead costs for October 2011
3. Direct manufacturing labor costs for October 2011
4. Work-in-process inventory 10/31/2011
5. Cost of finished goods available for sale in October 2011
6. Finished goods inventory 10/31/2011

2-32 Cost of finished goods manufactured, income statement, manufacturing company. Consider the following account balances (in thousands) for the Canseco Company:

	Home	Insert	Page Layout	Formulas	Data	Review	View		
	A							B	C
1	**Canseco Company**							**Beginning of**	**End of**
2								**2011**	**2011**
3	Direct materials inventory							$22,000	$26,000
4	Work-in-process inventory							21,000	20,000
5	Finished goods inventory							18,000	23,000
6	Purchases of direct materials								75,000
7	Direct manufacturing labor								25,000
8	Indirect manufacturing labor								15,000
9	Plant insurance								9,000
10	Depreciation—plant, building, and equipment								11,000
11	Repairs and maintenance—plant								4,000
12	Marketing, distribution, and customer-service costs								93,000
13	General and administrative costs								29,000

Required

1. Prepare a schedule for the cost of goods manufactured for 2011.
2. Revenues for 2011 were $300 million. Prepare the income statement for 2011.

2-33 Cost of goods manufactured, income statement, manufacturing company. Consider the following account balances (in thousands) for the Piedmont Corporation:

Piedmont Corporation	Beginning of 2011	End of 2011
Direct materials inventory	65,000	34,000
Work-in-process inventory	83,000	72,000
Finished goods inventory	123,000	102,000
Purchases of direct materials		128,000
Direct manufacturing labor		106,000
Indirect manufacturing labor		48,000
Indirect materials		14,000
Plant insurance		2,000
Depreciation—plant, building, and equipment		21,000
Plant utilities		12,000
Repairs and maintenance—plant		8,000
Equipment leasing costs		32,000
Marketing, distribution, and customer-service costs		62,000
General and administrative costs		34,000

Required

1. Prepare a schedule for the cost of goods manufactured for 2011.
2. Revenues for 2011 were $600 million. Prepare the income statement for 2011.

2-34 Income statement and schedule of cost of goods manufactured. The Howell Corporation has the following account balances (in millions):

For Specific Date		For Year 2011	
Direct materials inventory, Jan. 1, 2011	$15	Purchases of direct materials	$325
Work-in-process inventory, Jan. 1, 2011	10	Direct manufacturing labor	100
Finished goods inventory, Jan. 1, 2011	70	Depreciation—plant and equipment	80
Direct materials inventory, Dec. 31, 2011	20	Plant supervisory salaries	5
Work-in-process inventory, Dec. 31, 2011	5	Miscellaneous plant overhead	35
Finished goods inventory, Dec. 31, 2011	55	Revenues	950
		Marketing, distribution, and customer-service costs	240
		Plant supplies used	10
		Plant utilities	30
		Indirect manufacturing labor	60

Required Prepare an income statement and a supporting schedule of cost of goods manufactured for the year ended December 31, 2011. (For additional questions regarding these facts, see the next problem.)

2-35 Interpretation of statements (continuation of 2-34).

Required

1. How would the answer to Problem 2-34 be modified if you were asked for a schedule of cost of goods manufactured and sold instead of a schedule of cost of goods manufactured? Be specific.
2. Would the sales manager's salary (included in marketing, distribution, and customer-service costs) be accounted for any differently if the Howell Corporation were a merchandising-sector company instead of a manufacturing-sector company? Using the flow of manufacturing costs outlined in Exhibit 2-9 (p. 42), describe how the wages of an assembler in the plant would be accounted for in this manufacturing company.
3. Plant supervisory salaries are usually regarded as manufacturing overhead costs. When might some of these costs be regarded as direct manufacturing costs? Give an example.
4. Suppose that both the direct materials used and the plant and equipment depreciation are related to the manufacture of 1 million units of product. What is the unit cost for the direct materials assigned to those units? What is the unit cost for plant and equipment depreciation? Assume that yearly plant and equipment depreciation is computed on a straight-line basis.
5. Assume that the implied cost-behavior patterns in requirement 4 persist. That is, direct material costs behave as a variable cost, and plant and equipment depreciation behaves as a fixed cost. Repeat the

computations in requirement 4, assuming that the costs are being predicted for the manufacture of 1.2 million units of product. How would the total costs be affected?

6. As a management accountant, explain concisely to the president why the unit costs differed in requirements 4 and 5.

2-36 Income statement and schedule of cost of goods manufactured. The following items (in millions) pertain to Calendar Corporation:

For Specific Date		For Year 2011	
Work-in-process inventory, Jan. 1, 2011	$18	Plant utilities	$ 9
Direct materials inventory, Dec. 31, 2011	8	Indirect manufacturing labor	27
Finished goods inventory, Dec. 31, 2011	11	Depreciation—plant and equipment	6
Accounts payable, Dec. 31, 2011	24	Revenues	355
Accounts receivable, Jan. 1, 2011	52	Miscellaneous manufacturing overhead	15
Work-in-process inventory, Dec. 31, 2011	3	Marketing, distribution, and customer-service costs	94
Finished goods inventory, Jan 1, 2011	47	Direct materials purchased	84
Accounts receivable, Dec. 31, 2011	38	Direct manufacturing labor	42
Accounts payable, Jan. 1, 2011	49	Plant supplies used	4
Direct materials inventory, Jan. 1, 2011	32	Property taxes on plant	2

Calendar's manufacturing costing system uses a three-part classification of direct materials, direct manufacturing labor, and manufacturing overhead costs.

Prepare an income statement and a supporting schedule of cost of goods manufactured. (For additional questions regarding these facts, see the next problem.) **Required**

2-37 Terminology, interpretation of statements (continuation of 2-36).

1. Calculate total prime costs and total conversion costs.
2. Calculate total inventoriable costs and period costs.
3. Design costs and R&D costs are not considered product costs for financial statement purposes. When might some of these costs be regarded as product costs? Give an example.
4. Suppose that both the direct materials used and the depreciation on plant and equipment are related to the manufacture of 2 million units of product. Determine the unit cost for the direct materials assigned to those units and the unit cost for depreciation on plant and equipment. Assume that yearly depreciation is computed on a straight-line basis.
5. Assume that the implied cost-behavior patterns in requirement 4 persist. That is, direct material costs behave as a variable cost and depreciation on plant and equipment behaves as a fixed cost. Repeat the computations in requirement 4, assuming that the costs are being predicted for the manufacture of 3 million units of product. Determine the effect on total costs.
6. Assume that depreciation on the equipment (but not the plant) is computed based on the number of units produced because the equipment deteriorates with units produced. The depreciation rate on equipment is $1 per unit. Calculate the depreciation on equipment assuming (a) 2 million units of product are produced and (b) 3 million units of product are produced.

2-38 Labor cost, overtime, and idle time. Jim Anderson works in the production department of Midwest Steelworks as a machine operator. Jim, a long-time employee of Midwest, is paid on an hourly basis at a rate of $20 per hour. Jim works five 8-hour shifts per week Monday–Friday (40 hours). Any time Jim works over and above these 40 hours is considered overtime for which he is paid at a rate of time and a half ($30 per hour). If the overtime falls on weekends, Jim is paid at a rate of double time ($40 per hour). Jim is also paid an additional $20 per hour for any holidays worked, even if it is part of his regular 40 hours.

Jim is paid his regular wages even if the machines are down (not operating) due to regular machine maintenance, slow order periods, or unexpected mechanical problems. These hours are considered "idle time."

During December Jim worked the following hours:

	Hours worked including machine downtime	Machine downtime
Week 1	44	3.5
Week 2	43	6.4
Week 3	48	5.8
Week 4	46	2

Included in the total hours worked are two company holidays (Christmas Eve and Christmas Day) during Week 4. All overtime worked by Jim was Monday–Friday, except for the hours worked in Week 3. All of the Week 3 overtime hours were worked on a Saturday.

Required

1. Calculate (a) direct manufacturing labor, (b) idle time, (c) overtime and holiday premium, and (d) total earnings for Jim in December.
2. Is idle time and overtime premium a direct or indirect cost of the products that Jim worked on in December? Explain.

2-39 Missing records, computing inventory costs. Ron Williams recently took over as the controller of Johnson Brothers Manufacturing. Last month, the previous controller left the company with little notice and left the accounting records in disarray. Ron needs the ending inventory balances to report first quarter numbers.

For the previous month (March 2011) Ron was able to piece together the following information:

Direct materials purchased	$ 240,000
Work-in-process inventory, 3/1/2011	$ 70,000
Direct materials inventory, 3/1/2011	$ 25,000
Finished goods inventory, 3/1/2011	$ 320,000
Conversion Costs	$ 660,000
Total manufacturing costs added during the period	$ 840,000
Cost of goods manufactured	4 times direct materials used
Gross margin as a percentage of revenues	20%
Revenues	$1,037,500

Required Calculate the cost of:

1. Finished goods inventory, 3/31/2011
2. Work-in-process inventory, 3/31/2011
3. Direct materials inventory, 3/31/2011

2-40 Comprehensive problem on unit costs, product costs. Denver Office Equipment manufactures and sells metal shelving. It began operations on January 1, 2011. Costs incurred for 2011 are as follows (V stands for variable; F stands for fixed):

Direct materials used	$147,600 V
Direct manufacturing labor costs	38,400 V
Plant energy costs	2,000 V
Indirect manufacturing labor costs	14,000 V
Indirect manufacturing labor costs	19,000 F
Other indirect manufacturing costs	11,000 V
Other indirect manufacturing costs	14,000 F
Marketing, distribution, and customer-service costs	128,000 V
Marketing, distribution, and customer-service costs	48,000 F
Administrative costs	56,000 F

Variable manufacturing costs are variable with respect to units produced. Variable marketing, distribution, and customer-service costs are variable with respect to units sold.

Inventory data are as follows:

	Beginning: January 1, 2011	Ending: December 31, 2011
Direct materials	0 lb	2,400 lbs
Work in process	0 units	0 units
Finished goods	0 units	? units

Production in 2011 was 123,000 units. Two pounds of direct materials are used to make one unit of finished product.

Revenues in 2011 were $594,000. The selling price per unit and the purchase price per pound of direct materials were stable throughout the year. The company's ending inventory of finished goods is carried at the average unit manufacturing cost for 2011. Finished-goods inventory at December 31, 2011, was $26,000.

1. Calculate direct materials inventory, total cost, December 31, 2011.
2. Calculate finished-goods inventory, total units, December 31, 2011.
3. Calculate selling price in 2011.
4. Calculate operating income for 2011.

Required

2-41 Cost Classification; Ethics. Scott Hewitt, the new Plant Manager of Old World Manufacturing Plant Number 7, has just reviewed a draft of his year-end financial statements. Hewitt receives a year-end bonus of 10% of the plant's operating income before tax. The year-end income statement provided by the plant's controller was disappointing to say the least. After reviewing the numbers, Hewitt demanded that his controller go back and "work the numbers" again. Hewitt insisted that if he didn't see a better operating income number the next time around he would be forced to look for a new controller.

Old World Manufacturing classifies all costs directly related to the manufacturing of its product as product costs. These costs are inventoried and later expensed as costs of goods sold when the product is sold. All other expenses, including finished goods warehousing costs of $3,250,000 are classified as period expenses. Hewitt had suggested that warehousing costs be included as product costs because they are "definitely related to our product." The company produced 200,000 units during the period and sold 180,000 units.

As the controller reworked the numbers he discovered that if he included warehousing costs as product costs, he could improve operating income by $325,000. He was also sure these new numbers would make Hewitt happy.

1. Show numerically how operating income would improve by $325,000 just by classifying the preceding costs as product costs instead of period expenses?
2. Is Hewitt correct in his justification that these costs "are definitely related to our product."
3. By how much will Hewitt profit personally if the controller makes the adjustments in requirement 1.
4. What should the plant controller do?

Required

Collaborative Learning Problem

2-42 Finding unknown amounts. An auditor for the Internal Revenue Service is trying to reconstruct some partially destroyed records of two taxpayers. For each of the cases in the accompanying list, find the unknowns designated by the letters A through D.

	Case 1	Case 2
	(in thousands)	
Accounts receivable, 12/31	$ 6,000	$ 2,100
Cost of goods sold	A	20,000
Accounts payable, 1/1	3,000	1,700
Accounts payable, 12/31	1,800	1,500
Finished goods inventory, 12/31	B	5,300
Gross margin	11,300	C
Work-in-process inventory, 1/1	0	800
Work-in-process inventory, 12/31	0	3,000
Finished goods inventory, 1/1	4,000	4,000
Direct materials used	8,000	12,000
Direct manufacturing labor	3,000	5,000
Manufacturing overhead costs	7,000	D
Purchases of direct materials	9,000	7,000
Revenues	32,000	31,800
Accounts receivable, 1/1	2,000	1,400

3 Cost-Volume-Profit Analysis

3 Cost-Volume-Profit Analysis

► Learning Objectives

1. Explain the features of cost-volume-profit (CVP) analysis

2. Determine the breakeven point and output level needed to achieve a target operating income

3. Understand how income taxes affect CVP analysis

4. Explain how managers use CVP analysis in decision making

5. Explain how sensitivity analysis helps managers cope with uncertainty

6. Use CVP analysis to plan variable and fixed costs

7. Apply CVP analysis to a company producing multiple products

All managers want to know how profits will change as the units sold of a product or service change.

Home Depot managers, for example, might wonder how many units of a new product must be sold to break even or make a certain amount of profit. Procter & Gamble managers might ask themselves how expanding their business into a particular foreign market would affect costs, selling price, and profits. These questions have a common "what-if" theme. Examining the results of these what-if possibilities and alternatives helps managers make better decisions.

Managers must also decide how to price their products and understand the effect of their pricing decisions on revenues and profits. The following article explains how the Irish rock band U2 recently decided whether it should decrease the prices on some of its tickets during its recent world tour. Does lowering ticket price sound like a wise strategy to you?

How the "The Biggest Rock Show Ever" Turned a Big Profit[1]

When U2 embarked on its recent world tour, *Rolling Stone* magazine called it "the biggest rock show ever." Visiting large stadiums across the United States and Europe, the Irish quartet performed on an imposing 164-foot high stage that resembled a spaceship, complete with a massive video screen and footbridges leading to ringed catwalks.

With an ambitious 48-date trek planned, U2 actually had three separate stages leapfrogging its global itinerary—each one costing nearly $40 million dollars. As a result, the tour's success was dependent not only on each night's concert, but also recouping its tremendous fixed costs—costs that do not change with the number of fans in the audience.

To cover its high fixed costs and make a profit, U2 needed to sell a lot of tickets. To maximize revenue, the tour employed a unique in-the-round stage configuration, which boosted stadium capacity by roughly 20%, and sold tickets for as little as $30, far less than most large outdoor concerts.

The band's plan worked—despite a broader music industry slump and global recession, U2 shattered attendance records in most of the venues it played. By the end of the tour, the band played to over

---

[1] *Source*: Gundersen, Edna. 2009. U2 turns 360 stadium into attendance-shattering sellouts. *USA Today*, October 4. *www.usatoday.com/life/music/news/2009-10-04-u2-stadium-tour_N.htm*

3 million fans, racking up almost $300 million in ticket and merchandise sales and turning a profit. As you read this chapter, you will begin to understand how and why U2 made the decision to lower prices.

Many capital intensive companies, such as US Airways and United Airlines in the airlines industry and Global Crossing and WorldCom in the telecommunications industry, have high fixed costs. They must generate sufficient revenues to cover these costs and turn a profit. When revenues declined at these companies during 2001 and 2002 and fixed costs remained high, these companies declared bankruptcy. The methods of CVP analysis described in this chapter help managers minimize such risks.

Essentials of CVP Analysis

In Chapter 2, we discussed total revenues, total costs, and income. **Cost-volume-profit (CVP) analysis** studies the behavior and relationship among these elements as changes occur in the units sold, the selling price, the variable cost per unit, or the fixed costs of a product. Let's consider an example to illustrate CVP analysis.

> Example: Emma Frost is considering selling GMAT Success, a test prep book and software package for the business school admission test, at a college fair in Chicago. Emma knows she can purchase this package from a wholesaler at $120 per package, with the privilege of returning all unsold packages and receiving a full $120 refund per package. She also knows that she must pay $2,000 to the organizers for the booth rental at the fair. She will incur no other costs. She must decide whether she should rent a booth.

Emma, like most managers who face such a situation, works through a series of steps.

1. **Identify the problem and uncertainties.** The decision to rent the booth hinges critically on how Emma resolves two important uncertainties—the price she can charge and the number of packages she can sell at that price. Every decision deals with selecting a course of action. Emma must decide knowing that the outcome of the chosen action is uncertain and will only be known in the future. The more confident Emma is about selling a large number of packages at a good price, the more willing she will be to rent the booth.

2. **Obtain information.** When faced with uncertainty, managers obtain information that might help them understand the uncertainties better. For example, Emma gathers information about the type of individuals likely to attend the fair and other test-prep packages that might be sold at the fair. She also gathers data on her past experiences selling GMAT Success at fairs very much like the Chicago fair.

3. **Make predictions about the future.** Using all the information available to them, managers make predictions. Emma predicts that she can charge a price of $200 for GMAT Success. At that price she is reasonably confident that she will be able to sell at least 30 packages and possibly as many as 60. In making these predictions, Emma like most managers, must be realistic and exercise careful judgment. If her predictions are excessively optimistic, Emma will rent the booth when she should not. If they are unduly pessimistic, Emma will not rent the booth when she should.

   Emma's predictions rest on the belief that her experience at the Chicago fair will be similar to her experience at the Boston fair four months earlier. Yet, Emma is uncertain about several aspects of her prediction. Is the comparison between Boston and Chicago appropriate? Have conditions and circumstances changed over the last four months? Are there any biases creeping into her thinking? She is keen on selling at the Chicago fair because sales in the last couple of months have been lower than expected. Is this experience making her predictions overly optimistic? Has she ignored some of the competitive risks? Will the other test prep vendors at the fair reduce their prices?

   Emma reviews her thinking. She retests her assumptions. She also explores these questions with John Mills, a close friend, who has extensive experience selling test-prep packages like GMAT Success. In the end, she feels quite confident that her predictions are reasonable, accurate, and carefully thought through.

4. **Make decisions by choosing among alternatives.** Emma uses the CVP analysis that follows, and decides to rent the booth at the Chicago fair.

5. **Implement the decision, evaluate performance, and learn.** Thoughtful managers never stop learning. They compare their actual performance to predicted performance to understand why things worked out the way they did and what they might learn. At the end of the Chicago fair, for example, Emma would want to evaluate whether her predictions about price and the number of packages she could sell were correct. Such feedback would be very helpful to Emma as she makes decisions about renting booths at subsequent fairs.

How does Emma use CVP analysis in Step 4 to make her decision? Emma begins by identifying which costs are fixed and which costs are variable and then calculates *contribution margin*.

Contribution Margins

The booth-rental cost of $2,000 is a fixed cost because it will not change no matter how many packages Emma sells. The cost of the package itself is a variable cost because it increases in proportion to the number of packages sold. Emma will incur a cost of $120 for each package that she sells. To get an idea of how operating income will change as a result of selling different quantities of packages, Emma calculates operating income if sales are 5 packages and if sales are 40 packages.

	5 packages sold	**40 packages sold**
Revenues	$ 1,000 ($200 per package × 5 packages)	$8,000 ($200 per package × 40 packages)
Variable purchase costs	600 ($120 per package × 5 packages)	4,800 ($120 per package × 40 packages)
Fixed costs	2,000	2,000
Operating income	$(1,600)	$1,200

The only numbers that change from selling different quantities of packages are *total revenues* and *total variable costs*. The difference between total revenues and total variable costs is called **contribution margin**. That is,

Contribution margin = Total revenues − Total variable costs

Contribution margin indicates why operating income changes as the number of units sold changes. The contribution margin when Emma sells 5 packages is $400 ($1,000 in total revenues minus $600 in total variable costs); the contribution margin when Emma sells

40 packages is $3,200 ($8,000 in total revenues minus $4,800 in total variable costs). When calculating the contribution margin, be sure to subtract all variable costs. For example, if Emma had variable selling costs because she paid a commission to salespeople for each package they sold at the fair, variable costs would include the cost of each package plus the sales commission.

Contribution margin per unit is a useful tool for calculating contribution margin and operating income. It is defined as,

$$\text{Contribution margin per unit} = \text{Selling price} - \text{Variable cost per unit}$$

In the GMAT Success example, contribution margin per package, or per unit, is $200 − $120 = $80. Contribution margin per unit recognizes the tight coupling of selling price and variable cost per unit. Unlike fixed costs, Emma will only incur the variable cost per unit of $120 when she sells a unit of GMAT Success for $200.

Contribution margin per unit provides a second way to calculate contribution margin:

$$\text{Contribution margin} = \text{Contribution margin per unit} \times \text{Number of units sold}$$

For example, when 40 packages are sold, contribution margin = $80 per unit × 40 units = $3,200.

Even before she gets to the fair, Emma incurs $2,000 in fixed costs. Because the contribution margin per unit is $80, Emma will recover $80 for each package that she sells at the fair. Emma hopes to sell enough packages to fully recover the $2,000 she spent for renting the booth and to then start making a profit.

Exhibit 3-1 presents contribution margins for different quantities of packages sold. The income statement in Exhibit 3-1 is called a **contribution income statement** because it groups costs into variable costs and fixed costs to highlight contribution margin. Each additional package sold from 0 to 1 to 5 increases contribution margin by $80 per package, recovering more of the fixed costs and reducing the operating loss. If Emma sells 25 packages, contribution margin equals $2,000 ($80 per package × 25 packages), exactly recovering fixed costs and resulting in $0 operating income. If Emma sells 40 packages, contribution margin increases by another $1,200 ($3,200 − $2,000), all of which becomes operating income. As you look across Exhibit 3-1 from left to right, you see that the increase in contribution margin exactly equals the increase in operating income (or the decrease in operating loss).

Instead of expressing contribution margin as a dollar amount per unit, we can express it as a percentage called **contribution margin percentage** (or **contribution margin ratio**):

$$\text{Contribution margin percentage (or contribution margin ratio)} = \frac{\text{Contribution margin per unit}}{\text{Selling price}}$$

In our example,

$$\text{Contribution margin percentage} = \frac{\$80}{\$200} = 0.40, \text{ or } 40\%$$

Contribution margin percentage is the contribution margin per dollar of revenue. Emma earns 40% of each dollar of revenue (equal to 40 cents).

	Home	Insert	Page Layout	Formulas	Data	Review	View	
	A	B	C	D	E	F	G	H
1				**Number of Packages Sold**				
2				0	1	5	25	40
3	Revenues	$ 200	per package	$ 0	$ 200	$ 1,000	$5,000	$8,000
4	Variable costs	$ 120	per package	0	120	600	3,000	4,800
5	Contribution margin	$ 80	per package	0	80	400	2,000	3,200
6	Fixed costs	$2,000		2,000	2,000	2,000	2,000	2,000
7	Operating income			$(2,000)	$(1,920)	$(1,600)	$ 0	$1,200

Exhibit 3-1

Contribution Income Statement for Different Quantities of GMAT Success Packages Sold

Most companies have multiple products. As we shall see later in this chapter, calculating contribution margin per unit when there are multiple products is more cumbersome. In practice, companies routinely use contribution margin percentage as a handy way to calculate contribution margin for different dollar amounts of revenue:

$$\text{Contribution margin} = \text{Contribution margin percentage} \times \text{Revenues (in dollars)}$$

For example, in Exhibit 3-1, if Emma sells 40 packages, revenues will be $8,000 and contribution margin will equal 40% of $8,000, or 0.40 × $8,000 = $3,200. Emma earns operating income of $1,200 ($3,200 − Fixed costs, $2,000) by selling 40 packages for $8,000.

Expressing CVP Relationships

How was the Excel spreadsheet in Exhibit 3-1 constructed? Underlying the Exhibit are some equations that express the CVP relationships. To make good decisions using CVP analysis, we must understand these relationships and the structure of the contribution income statement in Exhibit 3-1. There are three related ways (we will call them methods) to think more deeply about and model CVP relationships:

1. The equation method
2. The contribution margin method
3. The graph method

The equation method and the contribution margin method are most useful when managers want to determine operating income at few specific levels of sales (for example 5, 15, 25, and 40 units sold). The graph method helps managers visualize the relationship between units sold and operating income over a wide range of quantities of units sold. As we shall see later in the chapter, different methods are useful for different decisions.

Equation Method

Each column in Exhibit 3-1 is expressed as an equation.

$$\text{Revenues} - \text{Variable costs} - \text{Fixed costs} = \text{Operating income}$$

How are revenues in each column calculated?

$$\text{Revenues} = \text{Selling price } (SP) \times \text{Quantity of units sold } (Q)$$

How are variable costs in each column calculated?

$$\text{Variable costs} = \text{Variable cost per unit } (VCU) \times \text{Quantity of units sold } (Q)$$

So,

$$\left[\left(\begin{matrix} \text{Selling} \\ \text{price} \end{matrix} \times \begin{matrix} \text{Quantity of} \\ \text{units sold} \end{matrix} \right) - \left(\begin{matrix} \text{Variable cost} \\ \text{per unit} \end{matrix} \times \begin{matrix} \text{Quantity of} \\ \text{units sold} \end{matrix} \right) \right] - \begin{matrix} \text{Fixed} \\ \text{costs} \end{matrix} = \begin{matrix} \text{Operating} \\ \text{income} \end{matrix} \qquad \textbf{(Equation 1)}$$

Equation 1 becomes the basis for calculating operating income for different quantities of units sold. For example, if you go to cell F7 in Exhibit 3-1, the calculation of operating income when Emma sells 5 packages is

$$(\$200 \times 5) - (\$120 \times 5) - \$2,000 = \$1,000 - \$600 - \$2,000 = -\$1,600$$

Contribution Margin Method

Rearranging equation 1,

$$\left[\left(\begin{matrix} \text{Selling} \\ \text{price} \end{matrix} - \begin{matrix} \text{Variable cost} \\ \text{per unit} \end{matrix} \right) \times \left(\begin{matrix} \text{Quantity of} \\ \text{units sold} \end{matrix} \right) \right] - \begin{matrix} \text{Fixed} \\ \text{costs} \end{matrix} = \begin{matrix} \text{Operating} \\ \text{income} \end{matrix}$$

$$\left(\begin{matrix} \text{Contribution margin} \\ \text{per unit} \end{matrix} \times \begin{matrix} \text{Quantity of} \\ \text{units sold} \end{matrix} \right) - \begin{matrix} \text{Fixed} \\ \text{costs} \end{matrix} = \begin{matrix} \text{Operating} \\ \text{income} \end{matrix} \qquad \textbf{(Equation 2)}$$

In our GMAT Success example, contribution margin per unit is $80 ($200 − $120), so when Emma sells 5 packages,

$$\text{Operating income} = (\$80 \times 5) - \$2,000 = -\$1,600$$

Equation 2 expresses the basic idea we described earlier—each unit sold helps Emma recover $80 (in contribution margin) of the $2,000 in fixed costs.

Graph Method

In the graph method, we represent total costs and total revenues graphically. Each is shown as a line on a graph. Exhibit 3-2 illustrates the graph method for GMAT Success. Because we have assumed that total costs and total revenues behave in a linear fashion, we need only two points to plot the line representing each of them.

1. **Total costs line.** The total costs line is the sum of fixed costs and variable costs. Fixed costs are $2,000 for all quantities of units sold within the relevant range. To plot the total costs line, use as one point the $2,000 fixed costs at zero units sold (point A) because variable costs are $0 when no units are sold. Select a second point by choosing any other convenient output level (say, 40 units sold) and determine the corresponding total costs. Total variable costs at this output level are $4,800 (40 units × $120 per unit). Remember, fixed costs are $2,000 at all quantities of units sold within the relevant range, so total costs at 40 units sold equal $6,800 ($2,000 + $4,800), which is point B in Exhibit 3-2. The total costs line is the straight line from point A through point B.

2. **Total revenues line.** One convenient starting point is $0 revenues at 0 units sold, which is point C in Exhibit 3-2. Select a second point by choosing any other convenient output level and determining the corresponding total revenues. At 40 units sold, total revenues are $8,000 ($200 per unit × 40 units), which is point D in Exhibit 3-2. The total revenues line is the straight line from point C through point D.

    Profit or loss at any sales level can be determined by the vertical distance between the two lines at that level in Exhibit 3-2. For quantities fewer than 25 units sold, total costs exceed total revenues, and the purple area indicates operating losses. For quantities greater than 25 units sold, total revenues exceed total costs, and the blue-green area indicates operating incomes. At 25 units sold, total revenues equal total costs. Emma will break even by selling 25 packages.

◄ Decision Point

How can CVP analysis assist managers?

Exhibit 3-2

Cost-Volume Graph for GMAT Success

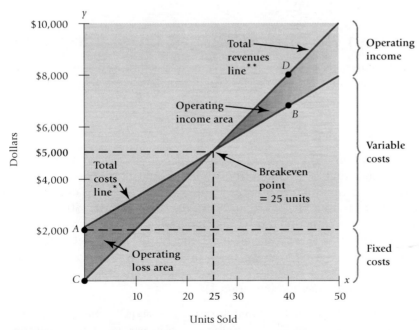

*Slope of the total costs line is the variable cost per unit = $120
**Slope of the total revenues line is the selling price = $200

Cost-Volume-Profit Assumptions

Now that you have seen how CVP analysis works, think about the following assumptions we made during the analysis:

1. Changes in the levels of revenues and costs arise only because of changes in the number of product (or service) units sold. The number of units sold is the only revenue driver and the only cost driver. Just as a cost driver is any factor that affects costs, a **revenue driver** is a variable, such as volume, that causally affects revenues.

2. Total costs can be separated into two components: a fixed component that does not vary with units sold and a variable component that changes with respect to units sold.

3. When represented graphically, the behaviors of total revenues and total costs are linear (meaning they can be represented as a straight line) in relation to units sold within a relevant range (and time period).

4. Selling price, variable cost per unit, and total fixed costs (within a relevant range and time period) are known and constant.

As the CVP assumptions make clear, an important feature of CVP analysis is distinguishing fixed from variable costs. Always keep in mind, however, that whether a cost is variable or fixed depends on the time period for a decision.

The shorter the time horizon, the higher the percentage of total costs considered fixed. For example, suppose an American Airlines plane will depart from its gate in the next hour and currently has 20 seats unsold. A potential passenger arrives with a transferable ticket from a competing airline. The variable costs (such as one more meal) to American of placing one more passenger in an otherwise empty seat is negligible At the time of this decision, with only an hour to go before the flight departs, virtually all costs (such as crew costs and baggage-handling costs) are fixed.

Alternatively, suppose American Airlines must decide whether to keep this flight in its flight schedule. This decision will have a one-year planning horizon. If American Airlines decides to cancel this flight because very few passengers during the last year have taken this flight, many more costs, including crew costs, baggage-handling costs, and airport fees, would be considered variable. That's because over this longer horizon, these costs would not have to be incurred if the flight were no longer operating. Always consider the relevant range, the length of the time horizon, and the specific decision situation when classifying costs as variable or fixed.

Breakeven Point and Target Operating Income

Managers and entrepreneurs like Emma always want to know how much they must sell to earn a given amount of income. Equally important, they want to know how much they must sell to avoid a loss.

Breakeven Point

The **breakeven point (BEP)** is that quantity of output sold at which total revenues equal total costs—that is, the quantity of output sold that results in $0 of operating income. We have already seen how to use the graph method to calculate the breakeven point. Recall from Exhibit 3-1 that operating income was $0 when Emma sold 25 units, the breakeven point. But by understanding the equations underlying the calculations in Exhibit 3-1, we can calculate the breakeven point directly for GMAT Success rather than trying out different quantities and checking when operating income equals $0.

Recall the equation method (equation 1):

$$\left(\begin{array}{c}\text{Selling}\\\text{price}\end{array} \times \begin{array}{c}\text{Quantity of}\\\text{units sold}\end{array}\right) - \left(\begin{array}{c}\text{Variable cost}\\\text{per unit}\end{array} \times \begin{array}{c}\text{Quantity of}\\\text{units sold}\end{array}\right) - \begin{array}{c}\text{Fixed}\\\text{costs}\end{array} = \begin{array}{c}\text{Operating}\\\text{income}\end{array}$$

Setting operating income equal to $0 and denoting quantity of output units that must be sold by Q,

$$(\$200 \times Q) - (\$120 \times Q) - \$2,000 = \$0$$
$$\$80 \times Q = \$2,000$$
$$Q = \$2,000 \div \$80 \text{ per unit } = 25 \text{ units}$$

If Emma sells fewer than 25 units, she will incur a loss; if she sells 25 units, she will break even; and if she sells more than 25 units, she will make a profit. While this breakeven point is expressed in units, it can also be expressed in revenues: 25 units × $200 selling price = $5,000.

Recall the contribution margin method (equation 2):

$$\left(\begin{array}{c} \text{Contribution} \\ \text{margin per unit} \end{array} \times \begin{array}{c} \text{Quantity of} \\ \text{units sold} \end{array} \right) - \text{Fixed costs} = \text{Operating income}$$

At the breakeven point, operating income is by definition $0 and so,

$$\text{Contribution margin per unit} \times \text{Breakeven number of units} = \text{Fixed cost} \quad \textbf{(Equation 3)}$$

Rearranging equation 3 and entering the data,

$$\begin{array}{c} \text{Breakeven} \\ \text{number of units} \end{array} = \frac{\text{Fixed costs}}{\text{Contribution margin per unit}} = \frac{\$2,000}{\$80 \text{ per unit}} = 25 \text{ units}$$

$$\text{Breakeven revenues} = \text{Breakeven number of units} \times \text{Selling price}$$
$$= 25 \text{ units} \times \$200 \text{ per unit} = \$5,000$$

In practice (because they have multiple products), companies usually calculate breakeven point directly in terms of revenues using contribution margin percentages. Recall that in the GMAT Success example,

$$\begin{array}{c} \text{Contribution margin} \\ \text{percentage} \end{array} = \frac{\text{Contribution margin per unit}}{\text{Selling price}} = \frac{\$80}{\$200} = 0.40, \text{ or } 40\%$$

That is, 40% of each dollar of revenue, or 40 cents, is contribution margin. To break even, contribution margin must equal fixed costs of $2,000. To earn $2,000 of contribution margin, when $1 of revenue earns $0.40 of contribution margin, revenues must equal $2,000 ÷ 0.40 = $5,000.

$$\begin{array}{c} \text{Breakeven} \\ \text{revenues} \end{array} = \frac{\text{Fixed costs}}{\text{Contribution margin \%}} = \frac{\$2,000}{0.40} = \$5,000$$

While the breakeven point tells managers how much they must sell to avoid a loss, managers are equally interested in how they will achieve the operating income targets underlying their strategies and plans. In our example, selling 25 units at a price of $200 assures Emma that she will not lose money if she rents the booth. This news is comforting, but we next describe how Emma determines how much she needs to sell to achieve a targeted amount of operating income.

Target Operating Income

We illustrate target operating income calculations by asking the following question: How many units must Emma sell to earn an operating income of $1,200? One approach is to keep plugging in different quantities into Exhibit 3-1 and check when operating income equals $1,200. Exhibit 3-1 shows that operating income is $1,200 when 40 packages are sold. A more convenient approach is to use equation 1 from page 66.

$$\left[\left(\begin{array}{c} \text{Selling} \\ \text{price} \end{array} \times \begin{array}{c} \text{Quantity of} \\ \text{units sold} \end{array} \right) - \left(\begin{array}{c} \text{Variable cost} \\ \text{per unit} \end{array} \times \begin{array}{c} \text{Quantity of} \\ \text{units sold} \end{array} \right) \right] - \begin{array}{c} \text{Fixed} \\ \text{costs} \end{array} = \begin{array}{c} \text{Operating} \\ \text{income} \end{array} \quad \textbf{(Equation 1)}$$

We denote by Q the unknown quantity of units Emma must sell to earn an operating income of $1,200. Selling price is $200, variable cost per package is $120, fixed costs are

$2,000, and target operating income is $1,200. Substituting these values into equation 1, we have

$$(\$200 \times Q) - (\$120 \times Q) - \$2,000 = \$1,200$$
$$\$80 \times Q = \$2,000 + \$1,200 = \$3,200$$
$$Q = \$3,200 \div \$80 \text{ per unit} = 40 \text{ units}$$

Alternatively, we could use equation 2,

$$\left(\begin{array}{c} \text{Contribution margin} \\ \text{per unit} \end{array} \times \begin{array}{c} \text{Quantity of} \\ \text{units sold} \end{array} \right) - \begin{array}{c} \text{Fixed} \\ \text{costs} \end{array} = \begin{array}{c} \text{Operating} \\ \text{income} \end{array} \qquad \textbf{(Equation 2)}$$

Given a target operating income ($1,200 in this case), we can rearrange terms to get equation 4.

$$\frac{\text{Quantity of units}}{\text{required to be sold}} = \frac{\text{Fixed costs} + \text{Target operating income}}{\text{Contribution margin per unit}} \qquad \textbf{(Equation 4)}$$

$$\frac{\text{Quantity of units}}{\text{required to be sold}} = \frac{\$2,000 + \$1,200}{\$80 \text{ per unit}} = 40 \text{ units}$$

Proof:

Revenues, $200 per unit × 40 units	$8,000
Variable costs, $120 per unit × 40 units	4,800
Contribution margin, $80 per unit × 40 units	3,200
Fixed costs	2,000
Operating income	$1,200

The revenues needed to earn an operating income of $1,200 can also be calculated directly by recognizing (1) that $3,200 of contribution margin must be earned (fixed costs of $2,000 plus operating income of $1,200) and (2) that $1 of revenue earns $0.40 (40 cents) of contribution margin. To earn $3,200 of contribution margin, revenues must equal $3,200 ÷ 0.40 = $8,000.

$$\text{Revenues needed to earn operating income of \$1,200} = \frac{\$2,000 + \$1,200}{0.40} = \frac{\$3,200}{0.40} = \$8,000$$

The graph in Exhibit 3-2 is very difficult to use to answer the question: How many units must Emma sell to earn an operating income of $1,200? Why? Because it is not easy to determine from the graph the precise point at which the difference between the total revenues line and the total costs line equals $1,200. However, recasting Exhibit 3-2 in the form of a profit-volume (PV) graph makes it easier to answer this question.

A **PV graph** shows how changes in the quantity of units sold affect operating income. Exhibit 3-3 is the PV graph for GMAT Success (fixed costs, $2,000; selling price, $200; and variable cost per unit, $120). The PV line can be drawn using two points. One convenient point (M) is the operating loss at 0 units sold, which is equal to the fixed costs of $2,000, shown at –$2,000 on the vertical axis. A second convenient point (N) is the breakeven point, which is 25 units in our example (see p. 69). The PV line is the straight line from point M through point N. To find the number of units Emma must sell to earn an operating income of $1,200, draw a horizontal line parallel to the x-axis corresponding to $1,200 on the vertical axis (that's the y-axis). At the point where this line intersects the PV line, draw a vertical line down to the horizontal axis (that's the x-axis). The vertical line intersects the x-axis at 40 units, indicating that by selling 40 units Emma will earn an operating income of $1,200.

(see p. 69)

Target Net Income and Income Taxes

Net income is operating income plus nonoperating revenues (such as interest revenue) minus nonoperating costs (such as interest cost) minus income taxes. For simplicity, throughout this chapter we assume nonoperating revenues and nonoperating costs are zero. Thus,

$$\text{Net income} = \text{Operating income} - \text{Income taxes}$$

Until now, we have ignored the effect of income taxes in our CVP analysis. In many companies, the income targets for managers in their strategic plans are expressed in terms of

---

Decision Point ▶

How can managers determine the breakeven point or the output needed to achieve a target operating income?

Learning Objective 3

Understand how income taxes affect CVP analysis

. . . focus on net income

Exhibit 3-3

Profit-Volume Graph for
GMAT Success

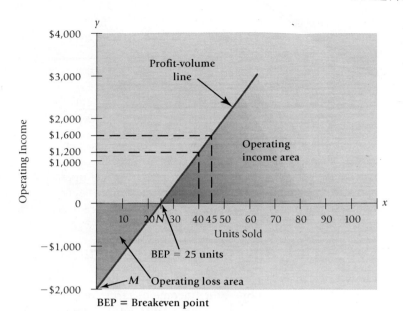

BEP = Breakeven point

net income. That's because top management wants subordinate managers to take into account the effects their decisions have on operating income after income taxes. Some decisions may not result in large operating incomes, but they may have favorable tax consequences, making them attractive on a net income basis—the measure that drives shareholders' dividends and returns.

To make net income evaluations, CVP calculations for target income must be stated in terms of target net income instead of target operating income. For example, Emma may be interested in knowing the quantity of units she must sell to earn a net income of $960, assuming an income tax rate of 40%.

$$\text{Target net income} = \left(\begin{array}{c}\text{Target} \\ \text{operating income}\end{array}\right) - \left(\begin{array}{c}\text{Target} \\ \text{operating income}\end{array} \times \text{Tax rate}\right)$$

$$\text{Target net income} = (\text{Target operating income}) \times (1 - \text{Tax rate})$$

$$\text{Target operating income} = \frac{\text{Target net income}}{1 - \text{Tax rate}} = \frac{\$960}{1 - 0.40} = \$1,600$$

In other words, to earn a target net income of $960, Emma's target operating income is $1,600.

Proof:

Target operating income	$1,600
Tax at 40% (0.40 × $1,600)	640
Target net income	$ 960

The key step is to take the target net income number and convert it into the corresponding target operating income number. We can then use equation 1 for target operating income and substitute numbers from our GMAT Success example.

$$\left[\left(\begin{array}{c}\text{Selling} \\ \text{price}\end{array} \times \begin{array}{c}\text{Quantity of} \\ \text{units sold}\end{array}\right) - \left(\begin{array}{c}\text{Variable cost} \\ \text{per unit}\end{array} \times \begin{array}{c}\text{Quantity of} \\ \text{units sold}\end{array}\right)\right] - \begin{array}{c}\text{Fixed} \\ \text{costs}\end{array} = \begin{array}{c}\text{Operating} \\ \text{income}\end{array} \quad \textbf{(Equation 1)}$$

$$(\$200 \times Q) - (\$120 \times Q) - \$2,000 = \$1,600$$
$$\$80 \times Q = \$3,600$$
$$Q = \$3,600 \div \$80 \text{ per unit} = 45 \text{ units}$$

Alternatively we can calculate the number of units Emma must sell by using the contribution margin method and equation 4:

$$\begin{array}{c}\text{Quantity of units} \\ \text{required to be sold}\end{array} = \frac{\text{Fixed costs} + \text{Target operating income}}{\text{Contribution margin per unit}} \quad \textbf{(Equation 4)}$$

$$= \frac{\$2,000 + \$1,600}{\$80 \text{ per unit}} = 45 \text{ units}$$

Proof:	Revenues, $200 per unit × 45 units	$9,000
	Variable costs, $120 per unit × 45 units	5,400
	Contribution margin	3,600
	Fixed costs	2,000
	Operating income	1,600
	Income taxes, $1,600 × 0.40	640
	Net income	$ 960

▶ **Decision Point**

How can managers incorporate income taxes into CVP analysis?

Emma can also use the PV graph in Exhibit 3-3. To earn target operating income of $1,600, Emma needs to sell 45 units.

Focusing the analysis on target net income instead of target operating income will not change the breakeven point. That's because, by definition, operating income at the breakeven point is $0, and no income taxes are paid when there is no operating income.

Using CVP Analysis for Decision Making

Learning Objective 4

Explain how managers use CVP analysis in decision making

. . . choose the alternative that maximizes operating income

We have seen how CVP analysis is useful for calculating the units that need to be sold to break even, or to achieve a target operating income or target net income. Managers also use CVP analysis to guide other decisions, many of them strategic decisions. Consider a decision about choosing additional features for an existing product. Different choices can affect selling prices, variable cost per unit, fixed costs, units sold, and operating income. CVP analysis helps managers make product decisions by estimating the expected profitability of these choices.

Strategic decisions invariably entail risk. CVP analysis can be used to evaluate how operating income will be affected if the original predicted data are not achieved—say, if sales are 10% lower than estimated. Evaluating this risk affects other strategic decisions a company might make. For example, if the probability of a decline in sales seems high, a manager may take actions to change the cost structure to have more variable costs and fewer fixed costs. We return to our GMAT Success example to illustrate how CVP analysis can be used for strategic decisions concerning advertising and selling price.

Decision to Advertise

Suppose Emma anticipates selling 40 units at the fair. Exhibit 3-3 indicates that Emma's operating income will be $1,200. Emma is considering placing an advertisement describing the product and its features in the fair brochure. The advertisement will be a fixed cost of $500. Emma thinks that advertising will increase sales by 10% to 44 packages. Should Emma advertise? The following table presents the CVP analysis.

	40 Packages Sold with No Advertising (1)	**44 Packages Sold with Advertising (2)**	**Difference (3) = (2) – (1)**
Revenues ($200 × 40; $200 × 44)	$8,000	$8,800	$ 800
Variable costs ($120 × 40; $120 × 44)	4,800	5,280	480
Contribution margin ($80 × 40; $80 × 44)	3,200	3,520	320
Fixed costs	2,000	2,500	500
Operating income	$1,200	$1,020	$(180)

Operating income will decrease from $1,200 to $1,020, so Emma should not advertise. Note that Emma could focus only on the difference column and come to the same conclusion: If Emma advertises, contribution margin will increase by $320 (revenues, $800 – variable costs, $480), and fixed costs will increase by $500, resulting in a $180 decrease in operating income.

As you become more familiar with CVP analysis, try evaluating decisions based on differences rather than mechanically working through the contribution income statement. Analyzing differences gets to the heart of CVP analysis and sharpens intuition by focusing only on the revenues and costs that will change as a result of a decision.

Decision to Reduce Selling Price

Having decided not to advertise, Emma is contemplating whether to reduce the selling price to $175. At this price, she thinks she will sell 50 units. At this quantity, the test-prep package wholesaler who supplies GMAT Success will sell the packages to Emma for $115 per unit instead of $120. Should Emma reduce the selling price?

Contribution margin from lowering price to $175: ($175 − $115) per unit × 50 units	$3,000
Contribution margin from maintaining price at $200: ($200 − $120) per unit × 40 units	3,200
Change in contribution margin from lowering price	$ (200)

Decreasing the price will reduce contribution margin by $200 and, because the fixed costs of $2,000 will not change, it will also reduce operating income by $200. Emma should not reduce the selling price.

Determining Target Prices

Emma could also ask "At what price can I sell 50 units (purchased at $115 per unit) and continue to earn an operating income of $1,200?" The answer is $179, as the following calculations show.

	Target operating income	$1,200
	Add fixed costs	2,000
	Target contribution margin	$3,200
	Divided by number of units sold	÷ 50 units
	Target contribution margin per unit	$ 64
	Add variable cost per unit	115
	Target selling price	$ 179
Proof:	Revenues, $179 per unit × 50 units	$8,950
	Variable costs, $115 per unit × 50 units	5,750
	Contribution margin	3,200
	Fixed costs	2,000
	Operating income	$1,200

Emma should also examine the effects of other decisions, such as simultaneously increasing advertising costs and lowering prices. In each case, Emma will compare the changes in contribution margin (through the effects on selling prices, variable costs, and quantities of units sold) to the changes in fixed costs, and she will choose the alternative that provides the highest operating income.

Sensitivity Analysis and Margin of Safety

Before choosing strategies and plans about how to implement strategies, managers frequently analyze the sensitivity of their decisions to changes in underlying assumptions. **Sensitivity analysis** is a "what-if" technique that managers use to examine how an outcome will change if the original predicted data are not achieved or if an underlying assumption changes. In the context of CVP analysis, sensitivity analysis answers questions such as, "What will operating income be if the quantity of units sold decreases by 5% from the original prediction?" and "What will operating income be if variable cost per unit increases by 10%?" Sensitivity analysis broadens managers' perspectives to possible outcomes that might occur *before* costs are committed.

Electronic spreadsheets, such as Excel, enable managers to conduct CVP-based sensitivity analyses in a systematic and efficient way. Using spreadsheets, managers can conduct sensitivity analysis to examine the effect and interaction of changes in selling price, variable cost per unit, fixed costs, and target operating income. Exhibit 3-4 displays a spreadsheet for the GMAT Success example.

Using the spreadsheet, Emma can immediately see how many units she needs to sell to achieve particular operating-income levels, given alternative levels of fixed costs and variable cost per unit that she may face. For example, 32 units must be sold to earn an

◀ **Decision Point**

How do managers use CVP analysis to make decisions?

Learning Objective 5

Explain how sensitivity analysis helps managers cope with uncertainty

. . . determine the effect on operating income of different assumptions

Exhibit 3-4

Spreadsheet Analysis
of CVP Relationships
for GMAT Success

| | | Number of units required to be sold at $200 | | | |
| | | Selling Price to Earn Target Operating Income of | | | |
		A	B	C	D	E	F
	Variable Costs	$0	$1,200	$1,600	$2,000
Fixed Costs	per Unit	(Breakeven point)			
$2,000	$100	20	32[a]	36	40
$2,000	$120	25	40	45	50
$2,000	$150	40	64	72	80
$2,400	$100	24	36	40	44
$2,400	$120	30	45	50	55
$2,400	$150	48	72	80	88
$2,800	$100	28	40	44	48
$2,800	$120	35	50	55	60
$2,800	$150	56	80	88	96

D5 ▾ fx =($A5+D$3)/(F1-$B5)

$$^a\frac{\text{Number of units}}{\text{required to be sold}} = \frac{\text{Fixed costs} + \text{Target operating income}}{\text{Contribution margin per unit}} = \frac{\$2,000 + \$1,200}{\$200 - \$100} = 32$$

operating income of $1,200 if fixed costs are $2,000 and variable cost per unit is $100. Emma can also use Exhibit 3-4 to determine that she needs to sell 56 units to break even if fixed cost of the booth rental at the Chicago fair is raised to $2,800 and if the variable cost per unit charged by the test-prep package supplier increases to $150. Emma can use information about costs and sensitivity analysis, together with realistic predictions about how much she can sell to decide if she should rent a booth at the fair.

Another aspect of sensitivity analysis is **margin of safety**:

$$\text{Margin of safety} = \text{Budgeted (or actual) revenues} - \text{Breakeven revenues}$$
$$\text{Margin of safety (in units)} = \text{Budgeted (or actual) sales quantity} - \text{Breakeven quantity}$$

The margin of safety answers the "what-if" question: If budgeted revenues are above breakeven and drop, how far can they fall below budget before the breakeven point is reached? Sales might decrease as a result of a competitor introducing a better product, or poorly executed marketing programs, and so on. Assume that Emma has fixed costs of $2,000, a selling price of $200, and variable cost per unit of $120. From Exhibit 3-1, if Emma sells 40 units, budgeted revenues are $8,000 and budgeted operating income is $1,200. The breakeven point is 25 units or $5,000 in total revenues.

$$\text{Margin of safety} = \frac{\text{Budgeted}}{\text{revenues}} - \frac{\text{Breakeven}}{\text{revenues}} = \$8,000 - \$5,000 = \$3,000$$

$$\frac{\text{Margin of}}{\text{safety (in units)}} = \frac{\text{Budgeted}}{\text{sales (units)}} - \frac{\text{Breakeven}}{\text{sales (units)}} = 40 - 25 = 15 \text{ units}$$

Sometimes margin of safety is expressed as a percentage:

$$\text{Margin of safety percentage} = \frac{\text{Margin of safety in dollars}}{\text{Budgeted (or actual) revenues}}$$

In our example, margin of safety percentage $= \dfrac{\$3,000}{\$8,000} = 37.5\%$

This result means that revenues would have to decrease substantially, by 37.5%, to reach breakeven revenues. The high margin of safety gives Emma confidence that she is unlikely to suffer a loss.

If, however, Emma expects to sell only 30 units, budgeted revenues would be $6,000 ($200 per unit × 30 units) and the margin of safety would equal:

$$\text{Budgeted revenues} - \text{Breakeven revenues} = \$6,000 - \$5,000 = \$1,000$$

$$\frac{\text{Margin of}}{\text{safety percentage}} = \frac{\text{Margin of safety in dollars}}{\text{Budgeted (or actual) revenues}} = \frac{\$1,000}{\$6,000} = 16.67\%$$

The analysis implies that if revenues decrease by more than 16.67%, Emma would suffer a loss. A low margin of safety increases the risk of a loss. If Emma does not have the tolerance for this level of risk, she will prefer not to rent a booth at the fair.

Sensitivity analysis is a simple approach to recognizing **uncertainty**, which is the possibility that an actual amount will deviate from an expected amount. Sensitivity analysis gives managers a good feel for the risks involved. A more comprehensive approach to recognizing uncertainty is to compute expected values using probability distributions. This approach is illustrated in the appendix to this chapter.

◀ **Decision Point**

What can managers do to cope with uncertainty or changes in underlying assumptions?

Cost Planning and CVP

Managers have the ability to choose the levels of fixed and variable costs in their cost structures. This is a strategic decision. In this section, we describe various factors that managers and management accountants consider as they make this decision.

Learning Objective 6

Use CVP analysis to plan variable and fixed costs

. . . compare risk of losses versus higher returns

Alternative Fixed-Cost/Variable-Cost Structures

CVP-based sensitivity analysis highlights the risks and returns as fixed costs are substituted for variable costs in a company's cost structure. In Exhibit 3-4, compare line 6 and line 11.

	Fixed Cost	Variable Cost	Number of units required to be sold at $200 selling price to earn target operating income of	
			$0 (Breakeven point)	$2,000
Line 6	$2,000	$120	25	50
Line 11	$2,800	$100	28	48

Compared to line 6, line 11, with higher fixed costs, has more risk of loss (has a higher breakeven point) but requires fewer units to be sold (48 versus 50) to earn operating income of $2,000. CVP analysis can help managers evaluate various fixed-cost/variable-cost structures. We next consider the effects of these choices in more detail. Suppose the Chicago college fair organizers offer Emma three rental alternatives:

Option 1: $2,000 fixed fee

Option 2: $800 fixed fee plus 15% of GMAT Success revenues

Option 3: 25% of GMAT Success revenues with no fixed fee

Emma's variable cost per unit is $120. Emma is interested in how her choice of a rental agreement will affect the income she earns and the risks she faces. Exhibit 3-5 graphically depicts the profit-volume relationship for each option. The line representing the relationship between units sold and operating income for Option 1 is the same as the line in the PV graph shown in Exhibit 3-3 (fixed costs of $2,000 and contribution margin per unit of $80). The line representing Option 2 shows fixed costs of $800 and a contribution margin per unit of $50 [selling price, $200, minus variable cost per unit, $120, minus variable rental fees per unit, $30, (0.15 × $200)]. The line representing Option 3 has fixed costs of $0 and a contribution margin per unit of $30 [$200 − $120 − $50 (0.25 × $200)].

Option 3 has the lowest breakeven point (0 units), and Option 1 has the highest breakeven point (25 units). Option 1 has the highest risk of loss if sales are low, but it also has the highest contribution margin per unit ($80) and hence the highest operating income when sales are high (greater than 40 units).

The choice among Options 1, 2, and 3 is a strategic decision that Emma faces. As in most strategic decisions, what she decides now will significantly affect her operating

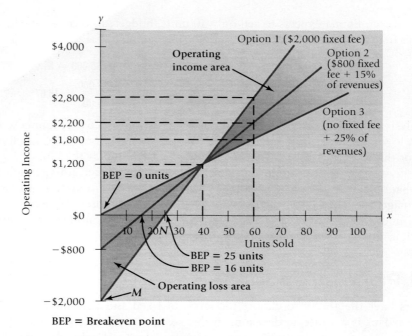

income (or loss), depending on the demand for GMAT Success. Faced with this uncertainty, Emma's choice will be influenced by her confidence in the level of demand for GMAT Success and her willingness to risk losses if demand is low. For example, if Emma's tolerance for risk is high, she will choose Option 1 with its high potential rewards. If, however, Emma is averse to taking risk, she will prefer Option 3, where the rewards are smaller if sales are high but where she never suffers a loss if sales are low.

Operating Leverage

The risk-return trade-off across alternative cost structures can be measured as *operating leverage*. **Operating leverage** describes the effects that fixed costs have on changes in operating income as changes occur in units sold and contribution margin. Organizations with a high proportion of fixed costs in their cost structures, as is the case under Option 1, have high operating leverage. The line representing Option 1 in Exhibit 3-5 is the steepest of the three lines. Small increases in sales lead to large increases in operating income. Small decreases in sales result in relatively large decreases in operating income, leading to a greater risk of operating losses. *At any given level of sales,*

$$\frac{\text{Degree of}}{\text{operating leverage}} = \frac{\text{Contribution margin}}{\text{Operating income}}$$

The following table shows the **degree of operating leverage** at sales of 40 units for the three rental options.

	Option 1	Option 2	Option 3
1. Contribution margin per unit (p. 75)	$ 80	$ 50	$ 30
2. Contribution margin (row 1 × 40 units)	$3,200	$2,000	$1,200
3. Operating income (from Exhibit 3-5)	$1,200	$1,200	$1,200
4. Degree of operating leverage (row 2 ÷ row 3)	$\frac{\$3,200}{\$1,200} = 2.67$	$\frac{\$2,000}{\$1,200} = 1.67$	$\frac{\$1,200}{\$1,200} = 1.00$

These results indicate that, when sales are 40 units, a percentage change in sales and contribution margin will result in 2.67 times that percentage change in operating income for Option 1, but the same percentage change (1.00) in operating income for Option 3. Consider, for example, a sales increase of 50% from 40 to 60 units. Contribution margin will increase by 50% under each option. Operating income, however, will increase by 2.67 × 50% = 133% from $1,200 to $2,800 in Option 1, but it will increase by only $1.00 \times 50\% = 50\%$ from $1,200 to $1,800 in Option 3 (see Exhibit 3-5). The degree of operating leverage at a given level of sales helps managers calculate the effect of sales fluctuations on operating income.

Keep in mind that, in the presence of fixed costs, the degree of operating leverage is different at different levels of sales. For example, at sales of 60 units, the degree of operating leverage under each of the three options is as follows:

	Option 1	Option 2	Option 3
1. Contribution margin per unit (p. 75)	$ 80	$ 50	$ 30
2. Contribution margin (row 1 × 60 units)	$4,800	$3,000	$1,800
3. Operating income (from Exhibit 3-5)	$2,800	$2,200	$1,800
4. Degree of operating leverage (row 2 ÷ row 3)	$\dfrac{\$4,800}{\$2,800} = 1.71$	$\dfrac{\$3,000}{\$2,200} = 1.36$	$\dfrac{\$1,800}{\$1,800} = 1.00$

The degree of operating leverage decreases from 2.67 (at sales of 40 units) to 1.71 (at sales of 60 units) under Option 1 and from 1.67 to 1.36 under Option 2. In general, whenever there are fixed costs, the degree of operating leverage decreases as the level of sales increases beyond the breakeven point. If fixed costs are $0 as in Option 3, contribution margin equals operating income, and the degree of operating leverage equals 1.00 at all sales levels.

But why must managers monitor operating leverage carefully? Again, consider companies such as General Motors, Global Crossing, US Airways, United Airlines, and WorldCom. Their high operating leverage was a major reason for their financial problems. Anticipating high demand for their services, these companies borrowed money to acquire assets, resulting in high fixed costs. As sales declined, these companies suffered losses and could not generate sufficient cash to service their interest and debt, causing them to seek bankruptcy protection. Managers and management accountants should always evaluate how the level of fixed costs and variable costs they choose will affect the risk-return trade-off. See Concepts in Action, page 78, for another example of the risks of high fixed costs.

What actions are managers taking to reduce their fixed costs? Many companies are moving their manufacturing facilities from the United States to lower-cost countries, such as Mexico and China. To substitute high fixed costs with lower variable costs, companies are purchasing products from lower-cost suppliers instead of manufacturing products themselves. These actions reduce both costs and operating leverage. More recently, General Electric and Hewlett-Packard began outsourcing service functions, such as post-sales customer service, by shifting their customer call centers to countries, such as India, where costs are lower. These decisions by companies are not without controversy. Some economists argue that outsourcing helps to keep costs, and therefore prices, low and enables U.S. companies to remain globally competitive. Others argue that outsourcing reduces job opportunities in the United States and hurts working-class families.

◄ **Decision Point**

How should managers choose among different variable-cost/ fixed-cost structures?

Effects of Sales Mix on Income

Sales mix is the quantities (or proportion) of various products (or services) that constitute total unit sales of a company. Suppose Emma is now budgeting for a subsequent college fair in New York. She plans to sell two different test-prep packages—GMAT Success and GRE Guarantee—and budgets the following:

Learning Objective 7

Apply CVP analysis to a company producing multiple products

. . . assume sales mix of products remains constant as total units sold changes

	GMAT Success	GRE Guarantee	Total
Expected sales	60	40	100
Revenues, $200 and $100 per unit	$12,000	$4,000	$16,000
Variable costs, $120 and $70 per unit	7,200	2,800	10,000
Contribution margin, $80 and $30 per unit	$ 4,800	$1,200	6,000
Fixed costs			4,500
Operating income			$ 1,500

Concepts in Action

Fixed Costs, Variable Costs, and the Future of Radio

Building up too much fixed costs can be hazardous to a company's health. Because fixed costs, unlike variable costs, do not automatically decrease as volume declines, companies with too much fixed costs can lose a considerable amount of money during lean times. Sirius XM, the satellite radio broadcaster, learned this lesson the hard way.

To begin broadcasting in 2001, both Sirius Satellite Radio and XM Satellite Radio—the two companies now comprising Sirius XM—spent billions of dollars on broadcasting licenses, space satellites, and other technology infrastructure. Once operational, the companies also spent billions on other fixed items such as programming and content (including Howard Stern and Major League Baseball), satellite transmission, and R&D. In contrast, variable costs were minimal, consisting mainly of artist-royalty fees and customer service and billing. In effect, this created a business model with a high operating leverage—that is, the companies' cost structure had a very significant proportion of fixed costs. As such, profitability could only be achieved by amassing millions of paid subscribers and selling advertising.

The competitive disadvantage of this highly-leveraged business model was nearly disastrous. Despite amassing more than 14 million subscribers, over the years Sirius and XM rang up $3 billion in debt and tallied cumulative operating losses in excess of $10 billion. Operating leverage, and the threat of bankruptcy, forced the merger of Sirius and XM in 2007, and since then the combined entity has struggled to cut costs, refinance its sizable debt, and reap the profits from over 18 million monthly subscribers.

While satellite radio has struggled under the weight of too much fixed cost, Internet radio had the opposite problem—too much variable costs. But "How?" you ask. Don't variable costs only increase as revenues increase? Yes, but if the revenue earned is less than the variable cost, an increase in revenue can lead to bankruptcy. This is almost what happened to Pandora, the Internet radio service.

Pandora launched in 2005 with only $9.3 million in venture capital. Available free over the Internet, Pandora earned revenue in three ways: advertising on its Web site, subscription fees from users who wanted to opt-out of advertising, and affiliate fees from iTunes and Amazon.com. Pandora had low fixed costs but high variable costs for streaming and performance royalties. Over time, as Pandora's popular service attracted millions of loyal listeners, its costs for performance royalties—set by the Copyright Royalty Board on a per song basis—far exceeded its revenues from advertising and subscriptions. As a result, even though royalty rates were only a fraction of a cent, Pandora lost more and more money each time it played another song!

In 2009, Pandora avoided bankruptcy by renegotiating a lower per-song royalty rate in exchange for at least 25% of its U.S. revenue annually. Further, Pandora began charging its most frequent users a small fee and also started increasing its advertising revenue.

Sources: Birger, Jon. 2009. Mel Karmazian fights to rescue Sirius. *Fortune*, March 16; Clifford, Stephanie. 2007. Pandora's long strange trip. *Inc.*, October 1; Pandora: Royalties kill the web radio star? (A). Harvard Business School Case No. 9-310-026; Satellite radio: An industry case study. Kellogg School of Management, Northwestern University. Case No. 5-206-255; XM satellite radio (A). Harvard Business School Case No. 9-504-009.

What is the breakeven point? In contrast to the single-product (or service) situation, the total number of units that must be sold to break even in a multiproduct company depends on the sales mix—the combination of the number of units of GMAT Success sold and the number of units of GRE Guarantee sold. We assume that the budgeted sales mix (60 units of GMAT Success sold for every 40 units of GRE Guarantee sold, that is, a ratio of 3:2) will not change at different levels of total unit sales. That is, we think of Emma selling a bundle of 3 units of GMAT Success and 2 units of GRE Guarantee. (Note that this does not mean that Emma physically bundles the two products together into one big package.)

Each bundle yields a contribution margin of $300 calculated as follows:

	Number of Units of GMAT Success and GRE Guarantee in Each Bundle	Contribution Margin per Unit for GMAT Success and GRE Guarantee	Contribution Margin of the Bundle
GMAT Success	3	$80	$240
GRE Guarantee	2	30	60
Total			$300

To compute the breakeven point, we calculate the number of bundles Emma needs to sell.

$$\text{Breakeven point in bundles} = \frac{\text{Fixed costs}}{\text{Contribution margin per bundle}} = \frac{\$4,500}{\$300 \text{ per bundle}} = 15 \text{ bundles}$$

Breakeven point in units of GMAT Success and GRE Guarantee is as follows:

GMAT Success: 15 bundles × 3 units of GMAT Success per bundle	45 units
GRE Guarantee: 15 bundles × 2 units of GRE Guarantee per bundle	30 units
Total number of units to break even	75 units

Breakeven point in dollars for GMAT Success and GRE Guarantee is as follows:

GMAT Success: 45 units × $200 per unit	$ 9,000
GRE Guarantee: 30 units × $100 per unit	3,000
Breakeven revenues	$12,000

When there are multiple products, it is often convenient to use contribution margin percentage. Under this approach, Emma first calculates the revenues from selling a bundle of 3 units of GMAT Success and 2 units of GRE Guarantee:

	Number of Units of GMAT Success and GRE Guarantee in Each Bundle	Selling Price for GMAT Success and GRE Guarantee	Revenue of the Bundle
GMAT Success	3	$200	$600
GRE Guarantee	2	100	200
Total			$800

$$\text{Contribution margin percentage for the bundle} = \frac{\text{Contribution margin of the bundle}}{\text{Revenue of the bundle}} = \frac{\$300}{\$800} = 0.375 \text{ or } 37.5\%$$

$$\text{Breakeven revenues} = \frac{\text{Fixed costs}}{\text{Contribution margin \% for the bundle}} = \frac{\$4,500}{0.375} = \$12,000$$

$$\text{Number of bundles required to be sold to break even} = \frac{\text{Breakeven revenues}}{\text{Revenue per bundle}} = \frac{\$12,000}{\$800 \text{ per bundle}} = 15 \text{ bundles}$$

The breakeven point in units and dollars for GMAT Success and GRE Guarantee are as follows:

GMAT Success: 15 bundles × 3 units of GMAT Success per bundle = 45 units × $200 per unit = $9,000

GRE Guarantee: 15 bundles × 2 units of GRE Guarantee per bundle = 30 units × $100 per unit = $3,000

Recall that in all our calculations we have assumed that the budgeted sales mix (3 units of GMAT Success for every 2 units of GRE Guarantee) will not change at different levels of total unit sales.

Of course, there are many different sales mixes (in units) that result in a contribution margin of $4,500 and cause Emma to break even, as the following table shows:

Sales Mix (Units)		Contribution Margin from		
GMAT Success (1)	GRE Guarantee (2)	GMAT Success (3) = $80 × (1)	GRE Guarantee (4) = $30 × (2)	Total Contribution Margin (5) = (3) + (4)
48	22	$3,840	$ 660	$4,500
36	54	2,880	1,620	4,500
30	70	2,400	2,100	4,500

If for example, the sales mix changes to 3 units of GMAT Success for every 7 units of GRE Guarantee, the breakeven point increases from 75 units to 100 units, comprising 30 units of GMAT Success and 70 units of GRE Guarantee. The breakeven quantity increases because the sales mix has shifted toward the lower-contribution-margin product, GRE Guarantee ($30 per unit compared to GMAT Success's $80 per unit). In general, for any given total quantity of units sold, as the sales mix shifts toward units with lower contribution margins (more units of GRE Guarantee compared to GMAT Success), operating income will be lower.

How do companies choose their sales mix? They adjust their mix to respond to demand changes. For example, as gasoline prices increase and customers want smaller cars, auto companies shift their production mix to produce smaller cars.

The multi-product case has two cost drivers, GMAT Success and GRE Guarantee. It shows how CVP and breakeven analysis can be adapted to the case of multiple cost drivers. The key point is that many different combinations of cost drivers can result in a given contribution margin.

Decision Point ▶

How can CVP analysis be applied to a company producing multiple products?

CVP Analysis in Service and Nonprofit Organizations

Thus far, our CVP analysis has focused on a merchandising company. CVP can also be applied to decisions by manufacturing companies like BMW, service companies like Bank of America, and nonprofit organizations like the United Way. To apply CVP analysis in service and nonprofit organizations, we need to focus on measuring their output, which is different from the tangible units sold by manufacturing and merchandising companies. Examples of output measures in various service and nonprofit industries are as follows:

Industry	Measure of Output
Airlines	Passenger miles
Hotels/motels	Room-nights occupied
Hospitals	Patient days
Universities	Student credit-hours

Consider an agency of the Massachusetts Department of Social Welfare with a $900,000 budget appropriation (its revenues) for 2011. This nonprofit agency's purpose is to assist handicapped people seeking employment. On average, the agency supplements each person's income by $5,000 annually. The agency's only other costs are fixed costs of rent and administrative salaries equal to $270,000. The agency manager wants to know how many people could be assisted in 2011. We can use CVP analysis here by setting operating income to $0. Let Q be the number of handicapped people to be assisted:

$$\text{Revenues} - \text{Variable costs} - \text{Fixed costs} = 0$$
$$\$900,000 - \$5,000\,Q - \$270,000 = 0$$
$$\$5,000\,Q = \$900,000 - \$270,000 = \$630,000$$
$$Q = \$630,000 \div \$5,000 \text{ per person} = 126 \text{ people}$$

Suppose the manager is concerned that the total budget appropriation for 2012 will be reduced by 15% to $900,000 × (1 − 0.15) = $765,000. The manager wants to know how many handicapped people could be assisted with this reduced budget. Assume the same amount of monetary assistance per person:

$$\$765,000 - \$5,000\,Q - \$270,000 = 0$$
$$\$5,000\,Q = \$765,000 - \$270,000 = \$495,000$$
$$Q = \$495,000 \div \$5,000 \text{ per person} = 99 \text{ people}$$

Note the following two characteristics of the CVP relationships in this nonprofit situation:

1. The percentage drop in the number of people assisted, $(126 - 99) \div 126$, or 21.4%, is greater than the 15% reduction in the budget appropriation. It is greater because the \$270,000 in fixed costs still must be paid, leaving a proportionately lower budget to assist people. The percentage drop in service exceeds the percentage drop in budget appropriation.

2. Given the reduced budget appropriation (revenues) of \$765,000, the manager can adjust operations to stay within this appropriation in one or more of three basic ways: (a) reduce the number of people assisted from the current 126, (b) reduce the variable cost (the extent of assistance per person) from the current \$5,000 per person, or (c) reduce the total fixed costs from the current \$270,000.

Contribution Margin Versus Gross Margin

In the following equations, we clearly distinguish contribution margin, which provides information for CVP analysis, from gross margin, a measure of competitiveness, as defined in Chapter 2.

$$\text{Gross margin} = \text{Revenues} - \text{Cost of goods sold}$$
$$\text{Contribution margin} = \text{Revenues} - \text{All variable costs}$$

Gross margin measures how much a company can charge for its products over and above the cost of acquiring or producing them. Companies, such as branded pharmaceuticals, have high gross margins because their products provide unique and distinctive benefit to consumers. Products such as televisions that operate in competitive markets have low gross margins. Contribution margin indicates how much of a company's revenues are available to cover fixed costs. It helps in assessing risk of loss. Risk of loss is low (high) if, when sales are low, contribution margin exceeds (is less than) fixed costs. Gross margin and contribution margin are related but give different insights. For example, a company operating in a competitive market with a low gross margin will have a low risk of loss if its fixed costs are small.

Consider the distinction between gross margin and contribution margin in the context of manufacturing companies. In the manufacturing sector, contribution margin and gross margin differ in two respects: fixed manufacturing costs and variable nonmanufacturing costs. The following example (figures assumed) illustrates this difference:

Contribution Income Statement Emphasizing Contribution Margin (in 000s)			Financial Accounting Income Statement Emphasizing Gross Margin (in 000s)	
Revenues		$1,000	Revenues	$1,000
Variable manufacturing costs	$250		Cost of goods sold (variable manufacturing costs, $250 + fixed manufacturing costs, $160)	410
Variable nonmanufacturing costs	270	520		
Contribution margin		480	Gross margin	590
Fixed manufacturing costs	160		Nonmanufacturing costs	
Fixed nonmanufacturing costs	138	298	(variable, $270 + fixed $138)	408
Operating income		$ 182	Operating income	$ 182

Fixed manufacturing costs of \$160,000 are not deducted from revenues when computing contribution margin but are deducted when computing gross margin. Cost of goods sold in a manufacturing company includes all variable manufacturing costs and all fixed manufacturing costs ($250,000 + $160,000). Variable nonmanufacturing costs (such as commissions paid to salespersons) of $270,000 are deducted from revenues when computing contribution margin but are not deducted when computing gross margin.

Like contribution margin, gross margin can be expressed as a total, as an amount per unit, or as a percentage. For example, the **gross margin percentage** is the gross margin divided by revenues—59% ($590 ÷ $1,000) in our manufacturing-sector example.

One reason why gross margin and contribution margin are confused with each other is that the two are identical in the case of merchandising companies. That's because cost of goods sold equals the variable cost of goods purchased (and subsequently sold).

Problem for Self-Study

Wembley Travel Agency specializes in flights between Los Angeles and London. It books passengers on United Airlines at $900 per round-trip ticket. Until last month, United paid Wembley a commission of 10% of the ticket price paid by each passenger. This commission was Wembley's only source of revenues. Wembley's fixed costs are $14,000 per month (for salaries, rent, and so on), and its variable costs are $20 per ticket purchased for a passenger. This $20 includes a $15 per ticket delivery fee paid to Federal Express. (To keep the analysis simple, we assume each round-trip ticket purchased is delivered in a separate package. Thus, the $15 delivery fee applies to each ticket.)

United Airlines has just announced a revised payment schedule for all travel agents. It will now pay travel agents a 10% commission per ticket up to a maximum of $50. Any ticket costing more than $500 generates only a $50 commission, regardless of the ticket price.

Required

1. Under the old 10% commission structure, how many round-trip tickets must Wembley sell each month (a) to break even and (b) to earn an operating income of $7,000?
2. How does United's revised payment schedule affect your answers to (a) and (b) in requirement 1?

Solution

1. Wembley receives a 10% commission on each ticket: 10% × $900 = $90. Thus,

$$\text{Selling price} = \$90 \text{ per ticket}$$
$$\text{Variable cost per unit} = \$20 \text{ per ticket}$$
$$\text{Contribution margin per unit} = \$90 - \$20 = \$70 \text{ per ticket}$$
$$\text{Fixed costs} = \$14,000 \text{ per month}$$

a. $\dfrac{\text{Breakeven number}}{\text{of tickets}} = \dfrac{\text{Fixed costs}}{\text{Contribution margin per unit}} = \dfrac{\$14,000}{\$70 \text{ per ticket}} = 200 \text{ tickets}$

b. When target operating income = $7,000 per month,

$$\dfrac{\text{Quantity of tickets}}{\text{required to be sold}} = \dfrac{\text{Fixed costs} + \text{Target operating income}}{\text{Contribution margin per unit}}$$
$$= \dfrac{\$14,000 + \$7,000}{\$70 \text{ per ticket}} = \dfrac{\$21,000}{\$70 \text{ per ticket}} = 300 \text{ tickets}$$

2. Under the new system, Wembley would receive only $50 on the $900 ticket. Thus,

$$\text{Selling price} = \$50 \text{ per ticket}$$
$$\text{Variable cost per unit} = \$20 \text{ per ticket}$$
$$\text{Contribution margin per unit} = \$50 - \$20 = \$30 \text{ per ticket}$$
$$\text{Fixed costs} = \$14,000 \text{ per month}$$

a. $\dfrac{\text{Breakeven number}}{\text{of tickets}} = \dfrac{\$14,000}{\$30 \text{ per ticket}} = 467 \text{ tickets (rounded up)}$

b. $\dfrac{\text{Quantity of tickets}}{\text{required to be sold}} = \dfrac{\$21{,}000}{\$30 \text{ per ticket}} = 700 \text{ tickets}$

The $50 cap on the commission paid per ticket causes the breakeven point to more than double (from 200 to 467 tickets) and the tickets required to be sold to earn $7,000 per month to also more than double (from 300 to 700 tickets). As would be expected, travel agents reacted very negatively to the United Airlines announcement to change commission payments. Unfortunately for travel agents, other airlines also changed their commission structure in similar ways.

Decision Points

The following question-and-answer format summarizes the chapter's learning objectives. Each decision presents a key question related to a learning objective. The guidelines are the answer to that question.

Decision	Guidelines
1. How can CVP analysis assist managers?	CVP analysis assists managers in understanding the behavior of a product's or service's total costs, total revenues, and operating income as changes occur in the output level, selling price, variable costs, or fixed costs.
2. How can managers determine the breakeven point or the output needed to achieve a target operating income?	The breakeven point is the quantity of output at which total revenues equal total costs. The three methods for computing the breakeven point and the quantity of output to achieve target operating income are the equation method, the contribution margin method, and the graph method. Each method is merely a restatement of the others. Managers often select the method they find easiest to use in the specific decision situation.
3. How can managers incorporate income taxes into CVP analysis?	Income taxes can be incorporated into CVP analysis by using target net income to calculate the corresponding target operating income. The breakeven point is unaffected by income taxes because no income taxes are paid when operating income equals zero.
4. How do managers use CVP analysis to make decisions?	Managers compare how revenues, costs, and contribution margins change across various alternatives. They then choose the alternative that maximizes operating income.
5. What can managers do to cope with uncertainty or changes in underlying assumptions?	Sensitivity analysis, a "what-if" technique, examines how an outcome will change if the original predicted data are not achieved or if an underlying assumption changes. When making decisions, managers use CVP analysis to compare contribution margins and fixed costs under different assumptions. Managers also calculate the margin of safety equal to budgeted revenues minus breakeven revenues.
6. How should managers choose between different variable-cost/fixed-cost structures?	Choosing the variable-cost/fixed-cost structure is a strategic decision for companies. CVP analysis highlights the risk of losses when revenues are low and the upside profits when revenues are high for different proportions of variable and fixed costs in a company's cost structure.
7. How can CVP analysis be applied to a company producing multiple products?	CVP analysis can be applied to a company producing multiple products by assuming the sales mix of products sold remains constant as the total quantity of units sold changes.

Appendix

Decision Models and Uncertainty

This appendix explores the characteristics of uncertainty, describes an approach managers can use to make decisions in a world of uncertainty, and illustrates the insights gained when uncertainty is recognized in CVP analysis.

Coping with Uncertainty[2]

In the face of uncertainty, managers rely on decision models to help them make the right choices.

Role of a Decision Model

Uncertainty is the possibility that an actual amount will deviate from an expected amount. In the GMAT Success example, Emma might forecast sales at 42 units, but actual sales might turn out to be 30 units or 60 units. A decision model helps managers deal with such uncertainty. It is a formal method for making a choice, commonly involving both quantitative and qualitative analyses. The quantitative analysis usually includes the following steps:

Step 1: **Identify a choice criterion.** A **choice criterion** is an objective that can be quantified such as maximize income or minimize costs. Managers use the choice criterion to choose the best alternative action. Emma's choice criterion is to maximize expected operating income at the Chicago college fair.

Step 2: **Identify the set of alternative actions that can be taken.** We use the letter a with subscripts $_1$, $_2$, and $_3$ to distinguish each of Emma's three possible actions:

$$a_1 = \text{Pay \$2,000 fixed fee}$$
$$a_2 = \text{Pay \$800 fixed fee plus 15\% of GMAT Success revenues}$$
$$a_3 = \text{Pay 25\% of GMAT Success revenues with no fixed fee}$$

Step 3: **Identify the set of events that can occur.** An **event** is a possible relevant occurrence, such as the actual number of GMAT Success packages Emma might sell at the fair. The set of events should be mutually exclusive and collectively exhaustive. Events are mutually exclusive if they cannot occur at the same time. Events are collectively exhaustive if, taken together, they make up the entire set of possible relevant occurrences (no other event can occur). Examples of mutually exclusive and collectively exhaustive events are growth, decline, or no change in industry demand, and increase, decrease, or no change in interest rates. Only one event out of the entire set of mutually exclusive and collectively exhaustive events will actually occur.

Suppose Emma's only uncertainty is the number of units of GMAT Success that she can sell. For simplicity, suppose Emma estimates that sales will be either 30 or 60 units. This set of events is mutually exclusive because clearly sales of 30 units and 60 units cannot both occur at the same time. It is collectively exhaustive because under our assumptions, sales cannot be anything other than 30 or 60 units. We use the letter x with subscripts $_1$ and $_2$ to distinguish the set of mutually exclusive and collectively exhaustive events:

$$x_1 = \text{30 units}$$
$$x_2 = \text{60 units}$$

Step 4: **Assign a probability to each event that can occur.** A **probability** is the likelihood or chance that an event will occur. The decision model approach to coping with uncertainty assigns probabilities to events. A **probability distribution** describes the likelihood, or the probability, that each of the mutually exclusive and collectively exhaustive set of events will occur. In some cases, there will be much evidence to guide the assignment of probabilities. For example, the probability of obtaining heads in the toss of a coin is 1/2 and that of drawing a particular playing card from a standard, well-shuffled deck is 1/52. In business, the probability of having a specified percentage of defective units may be assigned with great confidence on the basis of production experience with thousands of units. In other cases, there will be little evidence supporting estimated probabilities—for example, expected sales of a new pharmaceutical product next year.

Suppose that Emma, on the basis of past experience, assesses a 60% chance, or a 6/10 probability, that she will sell 30 units and a 40% chance, or a 4/10 probability, that she will sell 60 units. Using P(x) as the notation for the probability of an event, the probabilities are as follows:

$$P(x_1) = 6/10 = 0.60$$
$$P(x_2) = 4/10 = 0.40$$

The sum of these probabilities must equal 1.00 because these events are mutually exclusive and collectively exhaustive.

[2] The presentation here draws (in part) from teaching notes prepared by R. Williamson.

Exhibit 3-6 Decision Table for GMAT Success

	A	B	C	D	E	F	G	H	I
							Operating Income		
1		Selling price = $200							
2		Package cost = $120				**Under Each Possible Event**			
3			Percentage						
4		**Fixed**	**of Fair**	**Event x_1: Units Sold = 30**			**Event x_2: Units Sold = 60**		
5	**Actions**	**Fee**	**Revenues**	**Probability(x_1) = 0.60**			**Probability(x_2) = 0.40**		
6	a_1: Pay $2,000 fixed fee	$2,000	0%	$400[l]			$2,800[m]		
7	a_2: Pay $800 fixed fee plus 15% of revenues	$ 800	15%	$700[n]			$2,200[p]		
8	a_3: Pay 25% of revenues with no fixed fee	$ 0	25%	$900[q]			$1,800[r]		
9									
10	[l]Operating income = ($200 – $120)(30) – $2,000	=	$ 400						
11	[m]Operating income = ($200 – $120)(60) – $2,000	=	$2,800						
12	[n]Operating income = ($200 – $120 – 15% × $200)(30) – $800	=	$ 700						
13	[p]Operating income = ($200 – $120 – 15% × $200)(60) – $800	=	$2,200						
14	[q]Operating income = ($200 – $120 – 25% × $200)(30)	=	$ 900						
15	[r]Operating income = ($200 – $120 – 25% × $200)(60)	=	$1,800						

Step 5: Identify the set of possible outcomes. Outcomes specify, in terms of the choice criterion, the predicted economic results of the various possible combinations of actions and events. In the GMAT Success example, the outcomes are the six possible operating incomes displayed in the decision table in Exhibit 3-6. A **decision table** is a summary of the alternative actions, events, outcomes, and probabilities of events.

Distinguish among actions, events, and outcomes. Actions are decision choices available to managers—for example, the particular rental alternatives that Emma can choose. Events are the set of all relevant occurrences that can happen—for example, the different quantities of GMAT Success packages that may be sold at the fair. The outcome is operating income, which depends both on the action the manager selects (rental alternative chosen) and the event that occurs (the quantity of packages sold).

Exhibit 3-7 presents an overview of relationships among a decision model, the implementation of a chosen action, its outcome, and a subsequent performance evaluation. Thoughtful managers step back and evaluate what happened and learn from their experiences. This learning serves as feedback for adapting the decision model for future actions.

Expected Value

An **expected value** is the weighted average of the outcomes, with the probability of each outcome serving as the weight. When the outcomes are measured in monetary terms, expected value is often called **expected monetary value.** Using information in Exhibit 3-6, the expected monetary value of each booth-rental alternative denoted by $E(a_1)$, $E(a_2)$, and $E(a_3)$ is as follows:

Pay $2,000 fixed fee:	$E(a_1) = (0.60 \times \$400) + (0.40 \times \$2,800) = \$1,360$
Pay $800 fixed fee plus 15% of revenues:	$E(a_2) = (0.60 \times \$700) + (0.40 \times \$2,200) = \$1,300$
Pay 25% of revenues with no fixed fee:	$E(a_3) = (0.60 \times \$900) + (0.40 \times \$1,800) = \$1,260$

Exhibit 3-7 A Decision Model and Its Link to Performance Evaluation

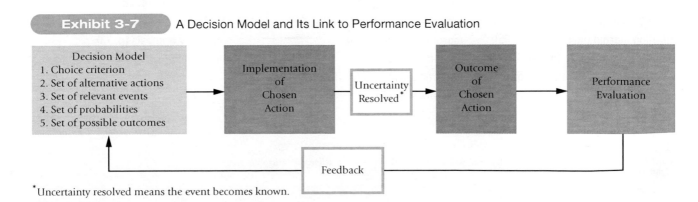

[*]Uncertainty resolved means the event becomes known.

To maximize expected operating income, Emma should select action a_1—pay the fair organizers a $2,000 fixed fee.

To interpret the expected value of selecting action a_1, imagine that Emma attends many fairs, each with the probability distribution of operating incomes given in Exhibit 3-6. For a specific fair, Emma will earn operating income of either $400, if she sells 30 units, or $2,800, if she sells 60 units. But if Emma attends 100 fairs, she will expect to earn $400 operating income 60% of the time (at 60 fairs), and $2,800 operating income 40% of the time (at 40 fairs), for a total operating income of $136,000 ($400 × 60 + $2,800 × 40). The expected value of $1,360 is the operating income per fair that Emma will earn when averaged across all fairs ($136,000 ÷ 100). Of course, in many real-world situations, managers must make one-time decisions under uncertainty. Even in these cases, expected value is a useful tool for choosing among alternatives.

Consider the effect of uncertainty on the preferred action choice. If Emma were certain she would sell only 30 units (that is, $P(x_1) = 1$), she would prefer alternative a_3—pay 25% of revenues with no fixed fee. To follow this reasoning, examine Exhibit 3-6. When 30 units are sold, alternative a_3 yields the maximum operating income of $900. Because fixed costs are $0, booth-rental costs are lower, equal to $1,500 (25% of revenues = 0.25 × $200 per unit × 30 units), when sales are low.

However, if Emma were certain she would sell 60 packages (that is, $P(x_2) = 1$), she would prefer alternative a_1—pay a $2,000 fixed fee. Exhibit 3-6 indicates that when 60 units are sold, alternative a_1 yields the maximum operating income of $2,800. Rental payments under a_2 and a_3 increase with units sold but are fixed under a_1.

Despite the high probability of selling only 30 units, Emma still prefers to take action a_1, which is to pay a fixed fee of $2,000. That's because the high risk of low operating income (the 60% probability of selling only 30 units) is more than offset by the high return from selling 60 units, which has a 40% probability. If Emma were more averse to risk (measured in our example by the difference between operating incomes when 30 versus 60 units are sold), she might have preferred action a_2 or a_3. For example, action a_2 ensures an operating income of at least $700, greater than the operating income of $400 that she would earn under action a_1 if only 30 units were sold. Of course, choosing a_2 limits the upside potential to $2,200 relative to $2,800 under a_1, if 60 units are sold. If Emma is very concerned about downside risk, however, she may be willing to forgo some upside benefits to protect against a $400 outcome by choosing a_2.[3]

Good Decisions and Good Outcomes

Always distinguish between a good decision and a good outcome. One can exist without the other. Suppose you are offered a one-time-only gamble tossing a coin. You will win $20 if the event is heads, but you will lose $1 if the event is tails. As a decision maker, you proceed through the logical phases: gathering information, assessing outcomes, and making a choice. You accept the bet. Why? Because the expected value is $9.50 [0.5($20) + 0.5(−$1)]. The coin is tossed and the event is tails. You lose. From your viewpoint, this was a good decision but a bad outcome.

A decision can be made only on the basis of information that is available at the time of evaluating and making the decision. By definition, uncertainty rules out guaranteeing that the best outcome will always be obtained. As in our example, it is possible that bad luck will produce bad outcomes even when good decisions have been made. A bad outcome does not mean a bad decision was made. The best protection against a bad outcome is a good decision.

Terms to Learn

This chapter and the Glossary at the end of the book contain definitions of the following important terms:

breakeven point (BEP) (**p. 68**)

choice criterion (**p. 84**)

contribution income statement (**p. 65**)

contribution margin (**p. 64**)

contribution margin per unit (**p. 65**)

contribution margin percentage (**p. 65**)

contribution margin ratio (**p. 65**)

cost-volume-profit (CVP) analysis (**p. 63**)

decision table (**p. 85**)

degree of operating leverage (**p. 76**)

event (**p. 84**)

expected monetary value (**p. 85**)

expected value (**p. 85**)

gross margin percentage (**p. 82**)

margin of safety (**p. 74**)

net income (**p. 70**)

operating leverage (**p. 76**)

outcomes (**p. 85**)

probability (**p. 84**)

probability distribution (**p. 84**)

PV graph (**p. 70**)

revenue driver (**p. 68**)

sales mix (**p. 77**)

sensitivity analysis (**p. 73**)

uncertainty (**p. 75**)

---

[3] For more formal approaches, refer to Moore, J. and L. Weatherford. 2001. *Decision modeling with Microsoft Excel*, 6th ed. Upper Saddle River, NJ: Prentice Hall.

Assignment Material

Note: To underscore the basic CVP relationships, the assignment material ignores income taxes unless stated otherwise.

Questions

3-1 Define cost-volume-profit analysis.

3-2 Describe the assumptions underlying CVP analysis.

3-3 Distinguish between operating income and net income.

3-4 Define contribution margin, contribution margin per unit, and contribution margin percentage.

3-5 Describe three methods that can be used to express CVP relationships.

3-6 Why is it more accurate to describe the subject matter of this chapter as CVP analysis rather than as breakeven analysis?

3-7 "CVP analysis is both simple and simplistic. If you want realistic analysis to underpin your decisions, look beyond CVP analysis." Do you agree? Explain.

3-8 How does an increase in the income tax rate affect the breakeven point?

3-9 Describe sensitivity analysis. How has the advent of the electronic spreadsheet affected the use of sensitivity analysis?

3-10 Give an example of how a manager can decrease variable costs while increasing fixed costs.

3-11 Give an example of how a manager can increase variable costs while decreasing fixed costs.

3-12 What is operating leverage? How is knowing the degree of operating leverage helpful to managers?

3-13 "There is no such thing as a fixed cost. All costs can be 'unfixed' given sufficient time." Do you agree? What is the implication of your answer for CVP analysis?

3-14 How can a company with multiple products compute its breakeven point?

3-15 "In CVP analysis, gross margin is a less-useful concept than contribution margin." Do you agree? Explain briefly.

Exercises

3-16 **CVP computations.** Fill in the blanks for each of the following independent cases.

Case	Revenues	Variable Costs	Fixed Costs	Total Costs	Operating Income	Contribution Margin Percentage
a.		$500		$ 800	$1,200	
b.	$2,000		$300		$ 200	
c.	$1,000	$700		$1,000		
d.	$1,500		$300			40%

3-17 **CVP computations.** Garrett Manufacturing sold 410,000 units of its product for $68 per unit in 2011. Variable cost per unit is $60 and total fixed costs are $1,640,000.

Required

1. Calculate (a) contribution margin and (b) operating income.
2. Garrett's current manufacturing process is labor intensive. Kate Schoenen, Garrett's production manager, has proposed investing in state-of-the-art manufacturing equipment, which will increase the annual fixed costs to $5,330,000. The variable costs are expected to decrease to $54 per unit. Garrett expects to maintain the same sales volume and selling price next year. How would acceptance of Schoenen's proposal affect your answers to (a) and (b) in requirement 1?
3. Should Garrett accept Schoenen's proposal? Explain.

3-18 **CVP analysis, changing revenues and costs.** Sunny Spot Travel Agency specializes in flights between Toronto and Jamaica. It books passengers on Canadian Air. Sunny Spot's fixed costs are $23,500 per month. Canadian Air charges passengers $1,500 per round-trip ticket.

Required

Calculate the number of tickets Sunny Spot must sell each month to (a) break even and (b) make a target operating income of $17,000 per month in each of the following independent cases.

1. Sunny Spot's variable costs are $43 per ticket. Canadian Air pays Sunny Spot 6% commission on ticket price.
2. Sunny Spot's variable costs are $40 per ticket. Canadian Air pays Sunny Spot 6% commission on ticket price.
3. Sunny Spot's variable costs are $40 per ticket. Canadian Air pays $60 fixed commission per ticket to Sunny Spot. Comment on the results.
4. Sunny Spot's variable costs are $40 per ticket. It receives $60 commission per ticket from Canadian Air. It charges its customers a delivery fee of $5 per ticket. Comment on the results.

3-19 **CVP exercises.** The Super Donut owns and operates six doughnut outlets in and round Kansas City. You are given the following corporate budget data for next year:

Revenues	$10,000,000
Fixed costs	$ 1,800,000
Variable costs	$ 8,000,000

Variable costs change with respect to the number of doughnuts sold.

Required

Compute the budgeted operating income for each of the following deviations from the original budget data. (Consider each case independently.)

1. A 10% increase in contribution margin, holding revenues constant
2. A 10% decrease in contribution margin, holding revenues constant
3. A 5% increase in fixed costs
4. A 5% decrease in fixed costs
5. An 8% increase in units sold
6. An 8% decrease in units sold
7. A 10% increase in fixed costs and a 10% increase in units sold
8. A 5% increase in fixed costs and a 5% decrease in variable costs

3-20 **CVP exercises.** The Doral Company manufactures and sells pens. Currently, 5,000,000 units are sold per year at $0.50 per unit. Fixed costs are $900,000 per year. Variable costs are $0.30 per unit.

Required

Consider each case separately:

1a. What is the current annual operating income?
 b. What is the present breakeven point in revenues?

Compute the new operating income for each of the following changes:

2. A $0.04 per unit increase in variable costs
3. A 10% increase in fixed costs and a 10% increase in units sold
4. A 20% decrease in fixed costs, a 20% decrease in selling price, a 10% decrease in variable cost per unit, and a 40% increase in units sold

Compute the new breakeven point in units for each of the following changes:

5. A 10% increase in fixed costs
6. A 10% increase in selling price and a $20,000 increase in fixed costs

3-21 **CVP analysis, income taxes.** Brooke Motors is a small car dealership. On average, it sells a car for $27,000, which it purchases from the manufacturer for $23,000. Each month, Brooke Motors pays $48,200 in rent and utilities and $68,000 for salespeople's salaries. In addition to their salaries, salespeople are paid a commission of $600 for each car they sell. Brooke Motors also spends $13,000 each month for local advertisements. Its tax rate is 40%.

Required

1. How many cars must Brooke Motors sell each month to break even?
2. Brooke Motors has a target monthly net income of $51,000. What is its target monthly operating income? How many cars must be sold each month to reach the target monthly net income of $51,000?

3-22 **CVP analysis, income taxes.** The Express Banquet has two restaurants that are open 24-hours a day. Fixed costs for the two restaurants together total $459,000 per year. Service varies from a cup of coffee to full meals. The average sales check per customer is $8.50. The average cost of food and other variable costs for each customer is $3.40. The income tax rate is 30%. Target net income is $107,100.

Required

1. Compute the revenues needed to earn the target net income.
2. How many customers are needed to break even? To earn net income of $107,100?
3. Compute net income if the number of customers is 170,000.

3-23 **CVP analysis, sensitivity analysis.** Hoot Washington is the newly elected leader of the Republican Party. Media Publishers is negotiating to publish Hoot's Manifesto, a new book that promises to be an instant best-seller. The fixed costs of producing and marketing the book will be $500,000. The variable costs of producing and marketing will be $4.00 per copy sold. These costs are before any payments to Hoot. Hoot negotiates an up-front payment of $3 million, plus a 15% royalty rate on the net sales price of each book. The net sales price is the listed bookstore price of $30, minus the margin paid to the bookstore to sell the book. The normal bookstore margin of 30% of the listed bookstore price is expected to apply.

Required

1. Prepare a PV graph for Media Publishers.
2. How many copies must Media Publishers sell to (a) break even and (b) earn a target operating income of $2 million?
3. Examine the sensitivity of the breakeven point to the following changes:

   a. Decreasing the normal bookstore margin to 20% of the listed bookstore price of $30
   b. Increasing the listed bookstore price to $40 while keeping the bookstore margin at 30%
   c. Comment on the results

3-24 CVP analysis, margin of safety. Suppose Doral Corp.'s breakeven point is revenues of $1,100,000. Fixed costs are $660,000.

Required

1. Compute the contribution margin percentage.
2. Compute the selling price if variable costs are $16 per unit.
3. Suppose 95,000 units are sold. Compute the margin of safety in units and dollars.

3-25 Operating leverage. Color Rugs is holding a two-week carpet sale at Jerry's Club, a local warehouse store. Color Rugs plans to sell carpets for $500 each. The company will purchase the carpets from a local distributor for $350 each, with the privilege of returning any unsold units for a full refund. Jerry's Club has offered Color Rugs two payment alternatives for the use of space.

▪ Option 1: A fixed payment of $5,000 for the sale period
▪ Option 2: 10% of total revenues earned during the sale period

Assume Color Rugs will incur no other costs.

Required

1. Calculate the breakeven point in units for (a) option 1 and (b) option 2.
2. At what level of revenues will Color Rugs earn the same operating income under either option?
   a. For what range of unit sales will Color Rugs prefer option 1?
   b. For what range of unit sales will Color Rugs prefer option 2?
3. Calculate the degree of operating leverage at sales of 100 units for the two rental options.
4. Briefly explain and interpret your answer to requirement 3.

3-26 CVP analysis, international cost structure differences. Global Textiles, Inc., is considering three possible countries for the sole manufacturing site of its newest area rug: Singapore, Brazil, and the United States. All area rugs are to be sold to retail outlets in the United States for $250 per unit. These retail outlets add their own markup when selling to final customers. Fixed costs and variable cost per unit (area rug) differ in the three countries.

Country	Sales Price to Retail Outlets	Annual Fixed Costs	Variable Manufacturing Cost per Area Rug	Variable Marketing & Distribution Cost per Area Rug
Singapore	$250.00	$ 9,000,000	$75.00	$25.00
Brazil	250.00	9,400,000	60.00	15.00
United States	250.00	12,400,000	82.50	12.50

Required

1. Compute the breakeven point for Global Textiles, Inc., in each country in (a) units sold and (b) revenues.
2. If Global Textiles, Inc., plans to produce and sell 75,000 rugs in 2011, what is the budgeted operating income for each of the three manufacturing locations? Comment on the results.

3-27 Sales mix, new and upgrade customers. Data 1-2-3 is a top-selling electronic spreadsheet product. Data is about to release version 5.0. It divides its customers into two groups: new customers and upgrade customers (those who previously purchased Data 1-2-3, 4.0 or earlier versions). Although the same physical product is provided to each customer group, sizable differences exist in selling prices and variable marketing costs:

	New Customers		Upgrade Customers	
Selling price		$275		$100
Variable costs				
Manufacturing	$35		$35	
Marketing	65	100	15	50
Contribution margin		$175		$ 50

The fixed costs of Data 1-2-3, 5.0 are $15,000,000. The planned sales mix in units is 60% new customers and 40% upgrade customers.

Required

1. What is the Data 1-2-3, 5.0 breakeven point in units, assuming that the planned 60%:40% sales mix is attained?
2. If the sales mix is attained, what is the operating income when 220,000 total units are sold?
3. Show how the breakeven point in units changes with the following customer mixes:
   a. New 40% and Upgrade 60%
   b. New 80% and Upgrade 20%
   c. Comment on the results

3-28 Sales mix, three products. Bobbie's Bagel Shop sells only coffee and bagels. Bobbie estimates that every time she sells one bagel, she sells four cups of coffee. The budgeted cost information for Bobbie's products for 2011 follows:

	Coffee	Bagels
Selling Price	$2.50	$3.75
Product ingredients	$0.25	$0.50
Hourly sales staff (cost per unit)	$0.50	$1.00
Packaging	$0.50	$0.25
Fixed Costs		
Rent on store and equipment	$5,000	
Marketing and advertising cost	$2,000	

Required

1. How many cups of coffee and how many bagels must Bobbie sell in order to break even assuming the sales mix of four cups of coffee to one bagel, given previously?
2. If the sales mix is four cups of coffee to one bagel, how many units of each product does Bobbie need to sell to earn operating income before tax of $28,000?
3. Assume that Bobbie decides to add the sale of muffins to her product mix. The selling price for muffins is $3.00 and the related variable costs are $0.75. Assuming a sales mix of three cups of coffee to two bagels to one muffin, how many units of each product does Bobbie need to sell in order to break even? Comment on the results.

3-29 CVP, Not for profit. Monroe Classical Music Society is a not-for-profit organization that brings guest artists to the community's greater metropolitan area. The Music Society just bought a small concert hall in the center of town to house its performances. The mortgage payments on the concert hall are expected to be $2,000 per month. The organization pays its guest performers $1,000 per concert and anticipates corresponding ticket sales to be $2,500 per event. The Music Society also incurs costs of approximately $500 per concert for marketing and advertising. The organization pays its artistic director $50,000 per year and expects to receive $40,000 in donations in addition to its ticket sales.

Required

1. If the Monroe Classical Music Society just breaks even, how many concerts does it hold?
2. In addition to the organization's artistic director, the Music Society would like to hire a marketing director for $40,000 per year. What is the breakeven point? The Music Society anticipates that the addition of a marketing director would allow the organization to increase the number of concerts to 60 per year. What is the Music Society's operating income/(loss) if it hires the new marketing director?
3. The Music Society expects to receive a grant that would provide the organization with an additional $20,000 toward the payment of the marketing director's salary. What is the breakeven point if the Music Society hires the marketing director and receives the grant?

3-30 Contribution margin, decision making. Lurvey Men's Clothing's revenues and cost data for 2011 are as follows:

Revenues		$600,000
Cost of goods sold		300,000
Gross margin		300,000
Operating costs:		
Salaries fixed	$170,000	
Sales commissions (10% of sales)	60,000	
Depreciation of equipment and fixtures	20,000	
Store rent ($4,500 per month)	54,000	
Other operating costs	45,000	349,000
Operating income (loss)		$ (49,000)

Mr. Lurvey, the owner of the store, is unhappy with the operating results. An analysis of other operating costs reveals that it includes $30,000 variable costs, which vary with sales volume, and $15,000 (fixed) costs.

Required

1. Compute the contribution margin of Lurvey Men's Clothing.
2. Compute the contribution margin percentage.
3. Mr. Lurvey estimates that he can increase revenues by 15% by incurring additional advertising costs of $13,000. Calculate the impact of the additional advertising costs on operating income.

3-31 Contribution margin, gross margin, and margin of safety. Mirabella Cosmetics manufactures and sells a face cream to small ethnic stores in the greater New York area. It presents the monthly operating income statement shown here to George Lopez, a potential investor in the business. Help Mr. Lopez understand Mirabella's cost structure.

	A	B	C	D
	Home	Insert	Page Layout	Formulas	Data	Review	View
1	Mirabella Cosmetics			
2	Operating Income Statement, June 2011			
3	Units sold			10,000
4	Revenues			$100,000
5	Cost of goods sold			
6	Variable manufacturing costs		$55,000	
7	Fixed manufacturing costs		20,000	
8	Total			75,000
9	Gross margin			25,000
10	Operating costs			
11	Variable marketing costs		$ 5,000	
12	Fixed marketing & administration costs		10,000	
13	Total operating costs			15,000
14	Operating income			$ 10,000

1. Recast the income statement to emphasize contribution margin.
2. Calculate the contribution margin percentage and breakeven point in units and revenues for June 2011.
3. What is the margin of safety (in units) for June 2011?
4. If sales in June were only 8,000 units and Mirabella's tax rate is 30%, calculate its net income.

3-32 Uncertainty and expected costs. Foodmart Corp, an international retail giant, is considering implementing a new business to business (B2B) information system for processing purchase orders. The current system costs Foodmart $2,500,000 per month and $50 per order. Foodmart has two options, a partially automated B2B and a fully automated B2B system. The partially automated B2B system will have a fixed cost of $10,000,000 per month and a variable cost of $40 per order. The fully automated B2B system has a fixed cost of $20,000,000 per month and $25 per order.

Based on data from the last two years, Foodmart has determined the following distribution on monthly orders:

Monthly Number of Orders	Probability
350,000	0.15
450,000	0.20
550,000	0.35
650,000	0.20
750,000	0.10

1. Prepare a table showing the cost of each plan for each quantity of monthly orders.
2. What is the expected cost of each plan?
3. In addition to the information systems costs, what other factors should Foodmart consider before deciding to implement a new B2B system?

Problems

3-33 CVP analysis, service firm. Lifetime Escapes generates average revenue of $5,000 per person on its five-day package tours to wildlife parks in Kenya. The variable costs per person are as follows:

Airfare	$1,400
Hotel accommodations	1,100
Meals	300
Ground transportation	100
Park tickets and other costs	800
Total	$3,700

Annual fixed costs total $520,000.

Required

1. Calculate the number of package tours that must be sold to break even.
2. Calculate the revenue needed to earn a target operating income of $91,000.
3. If fixed costs increase by $32,000, what decrease in variable cost per person must be achieved to maintain the breakeven point calculated in requirement 1?

3-34 CVP, target operating income, service firm. Snow Leopard Daycare provides daycare for children Mondays through Fridays. Its monthly variable costs per child are as follows:

Lunch and snacks	$150
Educational supplies	60
Other supplies (paper products, toiletries, etc.)	20
Total	$230

Monthly fixed costs consist of the following:

Rent	$2,150
Utilities	200
Insurance	250
Salaries	2,350
Miscellaneous	650
Total	$5,600

Snow Leopard charges each parent $580 per child.

Required

1. Calculate the breakeven point.
2. Snow Leopard's target operating income is $10,500 per month. Compute the number of children who must be enrolled to achieve the target operating income.
3. Snow Leopard lost its lease and had to move to another building. Monthly rent for the new building is $3,150. At the suggestion of parents, Snow Leopard plans to take children on field trips. Monthly costs of the field trips are $1,300. By how much should Snow Leopard increase fees per child to meet the target operating income of $10,500 per month, assuming the same number of children as in requirement 2?

3-35 CVP analysis, margin of safety. (CMA, adapted) Technology Solutions sells a ready-to-use software product for small businesses. The current selling price is $300. Projected operating income for 2011 is $490,000 based on a sales volume of 10,000 units. Variable costs of producing the software are $120 per unit sold plus an additional cost of $5 per unit for shipping and handling. Technology Solutions annual fixed costs are $1,260,000.

Required

1. Calculate Technology Solutions breakeven point and margin of safety in units.
2. Calculate the company's operating income for 2011 if there is a 10% increase in unit sales.
3. For 2012, management expects that the per unit production cost of the software will increase by 30%, but the shipping and handling costs per unit will decrease by 20%. Calculate the sales revenue Technology Solutions must generate for 2012 to maintain the current year's operating income if the selling price remains unchanged, assuming all other data as in the original problem.

3-36 CVP analysis, income taxes. (CMA, adapted) R. A. Ro and Company, a manufacturer of quality handmade walnut bowls, has had a steady growth in sales for the past five years. However, increased competition has led Mr. Ro, the president, to believe that an aggressive marketing campaign will be necessary next year to maintain the company's present growth. To prepare for next year's marketing campaign, the company's controller has prepared and presented Mr. Ro with the following data for the current year, 2011:

Variable cost (per bowl)	
Direct materials	$ 3.25
Direct manufacturing labor	8.00
Variable overhead (manufacturing, marketing, distribution, and customer service)	2.50
Total variable cost per bowl	$ 13.75
Fixed costs	
Manufacturing	$ 25,000
Marketing, distribution, and customer service	110,000
Total fixed costs	$135,000
Selling price	25.00
Expected sales, 20,000 units	$500,000
Income tax rate	40%

1. What is the projected net income for 2011?
2. What is the breakeven point in units for 2011?
3. Mr. Ro has set the revenue target for 2012 at a level of $550,000 (or 22,000 bowls). He believes an additional marketing cost of $11,250 for advertising in 2012, with all other costs remaining constant, will be necessary to attain the revenue target. What is the net income for 2012 if the additional $11,250 is spent and the revenue target is met?
4. What is the breakeven point in revenues for 2012 if the additional $11,250 is spent for advertising?
5. If the additional $11,250 is spent, what are the required 2012 revenues for 2012 net income to equal 2011 net income?
6. At a sales level of 22,000 units, what maximum amount can be spent on advertising if a 2012 net income of $60,000 is desired?

3-37 CVP, sensitivity analysis. The Brown Shoe Company produces its famous shoe, the Divine Loafer that sells for $60 per pair. Operating income for 2011 is as follows:

Sales revenue ($60 per pair)	$300,000
Variable cost ($25 per pair)	125,000
Contribution margin	175,000
Fixed cost	100,000
Operating income	$ 75,000

Brown Shoe Company would like to increase its profitability over the next year by at least 25%. To do so, the company is considering the following options:

1. Replace a portion of its variable labor with an automated machining process. This would result in a 20% decrease in variable cost per unit, but a 15% increase in fixed costs. Sales would remain the same.
2. Spend $30,000 on a new advertising campaign, which would increase sales by 20%.
3. Increase both selling price by $10 per unit and variable costs by $7 per unit by using a higher quality leather material in the production of its shoes. The higher priced shoe would cause demand to drop by approximately 10%.
4. Add a second manufacturing facility which would double Brown's fixed costs, but would increase sales by 60%.

Evaluate each of the alternatives considered by Brown Shoes. Do any of the options meet or exceed Brown's targeted increase in income of 25%? What should Brown do?

3-38 CVP analysis, shoe stores. The WalkRite Shoe Company operates a chain of shoe stores that sell 10 different styles of inexpensive men's shoes with identical unit costs and selling prices. A unit is defined as a pair of shoes. Each store has a store manager who is paid a fixed salary. Individual salespeople receive a fixed salary and a sales commission. WalkRite is considering opening another store that is expected to have the revenue and cost relationships shown here:

	Home	Insert	Page Layout	Formulas	Data	Review	View	
	A		B		C	D		E
1	Unit Variable Data (per pair of shoes)					Annual Fixed Costs		
2	Selling price		$30.00			Rent		$ 60,000
3	Cost of shoes		$19.50			Salaries		200,000
4	Sales commission		1.50			Advertising		80,000
5	Variable cost per unit		$21.00			Other fixed costs		20,000
6						Total fixed costs		$360,000

Consider each question independently:

1. What is the annual breakeven point in (a) units sold and (b) revenues?
2. If 35,000 units are sold, what will be the store's operating income (loss)?
3. If sales commissions are discontinued and fixed salaries are raised by a total of $81,000, what would be the annual breakeven point in (a) units sold and (b) revenues?
4. Refer to the original data. If, in addition to his fixed salary, the store manager is paid a commission of $0.30 per unit sold, what would be the annual breakeven point in (a) units sold and (b) revenues?
5. Refer to the original data. If, in addition to his fixed salary, the store manager is paid a commission of $0.30 *per unit in excess of the breakeven point*, what would be the store's operating income if 50,000 units were sold?

3-39 CVP analysis, shoe stores (continuation of 3-38). Refer to requirement 3 of Problem 3-38. In this problem, assume the role of the owner of WalkRite.

Required

1. Calculate the number of units sold at which the owner of WalkRite would be indifferent between the original salary-plus-commissions plan for salespeople and the higher fixed-salaries-only plan.
2. As owner, which sales compensation plan would you choose if forecasted annual sales of the new store were at least 55,000 units? What do you think of the motivational aspect of your chosen compensation plan?
3. Suppose the target operating income is $168,000. How many units must be sold to reach the target operating income under (a) the original salary-plus-commissions plan and (b) the higher-fixed-salaries-only plan?
4. You open the new store on January 1, 2011, with the original salary-plus-commission compensation plan in place. Because you expect the cost of the shoes to rise due to inflation, you place a firm bulk order for 50,000 shoes and lock in the $19.50 price per unit. But, toward the end of the year, only 48,000 shoes are sold, and you authorize a markdown of the remaining inventory to $18 per unit. Finally, all units are sold. Salespeople, as usual, get paid a commission of 5% of revenues. What is the annual operating income for the store?

3-40 Alternate cost structures, uncertainty, and sensitivity analysis. Stylewise Printing Company currently leases its only copy machine for $1,000 a month. The company is considering replacing this leasing agreement with a new contract that is entirely commission based. Under the new agreement Stylewise would pay a commission for its printing at a rate of $10 for every 500 pages printed. The company currently charges $0.15 per page to its customers. The paper used in printing costs the company $.03 per page and other variable costs, including hourly labor amount to $.04 per page.

Required

1. What is the company's breakeven point under the current leasing agreement? What is it under the new commission based agreement?
2. For what range of sales levels will Stylewise prefer (a) the fixed lease agreement (b) the commission agreement?
3. Do this question only if you have covered the chapter appendix in your class. Stylewise estimates that the company is equally likely to sell 20,000; 40,000; 60,000; 80,000; or 100,000 pages of print. Using information from the original problem, prepare a table that shows the expected profit at each sales level under the fixed leasing agreement and under the commission based agreement. What is the expected value of each agreement? Which agreement should Stylewise choose?

3-41 CVP, alternative cost structures. PC Planet has just opened its doors. The new retail store sells refurbished computers at a significant discount from market prices. The computers cost PC Planet $100 to purchase and require 10 hours of labor at $15 per hour. Additional variable costs, including wages for sales personnel, are $50 per computer. The newly refurbished computers are resold to customers for $500. Rent on the retail store costs the company $4,000 per month.

Required

1. How many computers does PC Planet have to sell each month to break even?
2. If PC Planet wants to earn $5,000 per month after all expenses, how many computers does the company need to sell?
3. PC Planet can purchase already refurbished computers for $200. This would mean that all labor required to refurbish the computers could be eliminated. What would PC Planet's new breakeven point be if it decided to purchase the computers already refurbished?
4. Instead of paying the monthly rental fee for the retail space, PC Planet has the option of paying its landlord a 20% commission on sales. Assuming the original facts in the problem, at what sales level would PC Planet be indifferent between paying a fixed amount of monthly rent and paying a 20% commission on sales?

3-42 CVP analysis, income taxes, sensitivity. (CMA, adapted) Agro Engine Company manufactures and sells diesel engines for use in small farming equipment. For its 2012 budget, Agro Engine Company estimates the following:

Selling price	$ 3,000
Variable cost per engine	$ 500
Annual fixed costs	$3,000,000
Net income	$1,500,000
Income tax rate	25%

The first quarter income statement, as of March 31, reported that sales were not meeting expectations. During the first quarter, only 300 units had been sold at the current price of $3,000. The income statement showed that variable and fixed costs were as planned, which meant that the 2012 annual net income projection would not be met unless management took action. A management committee was formed and presented the following mutually exclusive alternatives to the president:

a. Reduce the selling price by 20%. The sales organization forecasts that at this significantly reduced price, 2,000 units can be sold during the remainder of the year. Total fixed costs and variable cost per unit will stay as budgeted.

b. Lower variable cost per unit by $50 through the use of less-expensive direct materials. The selling price will also be reduced by $250, and sales of 1,800 units are expected for the remainder of the year.

c. Reduce fixed costs by 20% and lower the selling price by 10%. Variable cost per unit will be unchanged. Sales of 1,700 units are expected for the remainder of the year.

1. If no changes are made to the selling price or cost structure, determine the number of units that Agro Engine Company must sell (a) to break even and (b) to achieve its net income objective. **Required**

2. Determine which alternative Agro Engine should select to achieve its net income objective. Show your calculations.

3-43 Choosing between compensation plans, operating leverage. (CMA, adapted) Marston Corporation manufactures pharmaceutical products that are sold through a network of external sales agents. The agents are paid a commission of 18% of revenues. Marston is considering replacing the sales agents with its own salespeople, who would be paid a commission of 10% of revenues and total salaries of $2,080,000. The income statement for the year ending December 31, 2011, under the two scenarios is shown here.

	Home	Insert	Page Layout	Formulas	Data	Review	View
	A		B	C	D	E	

	A	B	C	D	E
1		Marston Corporation			
2		Income Statement			
3		For the Year Ended December 31, 2011			
4		Using Sales Agents		Using Own Sales Force	
5	Revenues		$26,000,000		$26,000,000
6	Cost of goods sold				
7	Variable	$11,700,000		$11,700,000	
8	Fixed	2,870,000	14,570,000	2,870,000	14,570,000
9	Gross margin		11,430,000		11,430,000
10	Marketing costs				
11	Commissions	$ 4,680,000		$ 2,600,000	
12	Fixed costs	3,420,000	8,100,000	5,500,000	8,100,000
13	Operating income		$ 3,330,000		$ 3,330,000

1. Calculate Marston's 2011 contribution margin percentage, breakeven revenues, and degree of operating leverage under the two scenarios. **Required**

2. Describe the advantages and disadvantages of each type of sales alternative.

3. In 2012, Marston uses its own salespeople, who demand a 15% commission. If all other cost behavior patterns are unchanged, how much revenue must the salespeople generate in order to earn the same operating income as in 2011?

3-44 Sales mix, three products. The Ronowski Company has three product lines of belts—A, B, and C—with contribution margins of $3, $2, and $1, respectively. The president foresees sales of 200,000 units in the coming period, consisting of 20,000 units of A, 100,000 units of B, and 80,000 units of C. The company's fixed costs for the period are $255,000.

1. What is the company's breakeven point in units, assuming that the given sales mix is maintained? **Required**

2. If the sales mix is maintained, what is the total contribution margin when 200,000 units are sold? What is the operating income?

3. What would operating income be if 20,000 units of A, 80,000 units of B, and 100,000 units of C were sold? What is the new breakeven point in units if these relationships persist in the next period?

3-45 Multiproduct CVP and decision making. Pure Water Products produces two types of water filters. One attaches to the faucet and cleans all water that passes through the faucet. The other is a pitcher-cum-filter that only purifies water meant for drinking.

The unit that attaches to the faucet is sold for $80 and has variable costs of $20.
The pitcher-cum-filter sells for $90 and has variable costs of $25.

Pure Water sells two faucet models for every three pitchers sold. Fixed costs equal $945,000.

Required

1. What is the breakeven point in unit sales and dollars for each type of filter at the current sales mix?
2. Pure Water is considering buying new production equipment. The new equipment will increase fixed cost by $181,400 per year and will decrease the variable cost of the faucet and the pitcher units by $5 and $9 respectively. Assuming the same sales mix, how many of each type of filter does Pure Water need to sell to break even?
3. Assuming the same sales mix, at what total sales level would Pure Water be indifferent between using the old equipment and buying the new production equipment? If total sales are expected to be 30,000 units, should Pure Water buy the new production equipment?

3-46 Sales mix, two products. The Stackpole Company retails two products: a standard and a deluxe version of a luggage carrier. The budgeted income statement for next period is as follows:

	Standard Carrier	Deluxe Carrier	Total
Units sold	187,500	62,500	250,000
Revenues at $28 and $50 per unit	$5,250,000	$3,125,000	$8,375,000
Variable costs at $18 and $30 per unit	3,375,000	1,875,000	5,250,000
Contribution margins at $10 and $20 per unit	$1,875,000	$1,250,000	3,125,000
Fixed costs			2,250,000
Operating income			$ 875,000

Required

1. Compute the breakeven point in units, assuming that the planned sales mix is attained.
2. Compute the breakeven point in units (a) if only standard carriers are sold and (b) if only deluxe carriers are sold.
3. Suppose 250,000 units are sold but only 50,000 of them are deluxe. Compute the operating income. Compute the breakeven point in units. Compare your answer with the answer to requirement 1. What is the major lesson of this problem?

3-47 Gross margin and contribution margin. The Museum of America is preparing for its annual appreciation dinner for contributing members. Last year, 525 members attended the dinner. Tickets for the dinner were $24 per attendee. The profit report for last year's dinner follows.

Ticket sales	$12,600
Cost of dinner	15,300
Gross margin	(2,700)
Invitations and paperwork	2,500
Profit (loss)	$(5,200)

This year the dinner committee does not want to lose money on the dinner. To help achieve its goal, the committee analyzed last year's costs. Of the $15,300 cost of the dinner, $9,000 were fixed costs and $6,300 were variable costs. Of the $2,500 cost of invitations and paperwork, $1,975 were fixed and $525 were variable.

Required

1. Prepare last year's profit report using the contribution margin format.
2. The committee is considering expanding this year's dinner invitation list to include volunteer members (in addition to contributing members). If the committee expands the dinner invitation list, it expects attendance to double. Calculate the effect this will have on the profitability of the dinner assuming fixed costs will be the same as last year.

3-48 Ethics, CVP analysis. Allen Corporation produces a molded plastic casing, LX201, for desktop computers. Summary data from its 2011 income statement are as follows:

Revenues	$5,000,000
Variable costs	3,000,000
Fixed costs	2,160,000
Operating income	$ (160,000)

Jane Woodall, Allen's president, is very concerned about Allen Corporation's poor profitability. She asks Max Lemond, production manager, and Lester Bush, controller, to see if there are ways to reduce costs.

After two weeks, Max returns with a proposal to reduce variable costs to 52% of revenues by reducing the costs Allen currently incurs for safe disposal of wasted plastic. Lester is concerned that this would expose the company to potential environmental liabilities. He tells Max, "We would need to estimate some of these potential environmental costs and include them in our analysis." "You can't do that," Max replies. "We are not violating any laws. There is some possibility that we may have to incur environmental costs in the future, but if we bring it up now, this proposal will not go through because our senior management always assumes these costs to be larger than they turn out to be. The market is very tough, and we are in danger of shutting down the company and costing all of us our jobs. The only reason our competitors are making money is because they are doing exactly what I am proposing."

Required

1. Calculate Allen Corporation's breakeven revenues for 2011.
2. Calculate Allen Corporation's breakeven revenues if variable costs are 52% of revenues.
3. Calculate Allen Corporation's operating income for 2011 if variable costs had been 52% of revenues.
4. Given Max Lemond's comments, what should Lester Bush do?

Collaborative Learning Problem

3-49 Deciding where to produce. (CMA, adapted) The Domestic Engines Co. produces the same power generators in two Illinois plants, a new plant in Peoria and an older plant in Moline. The following data are available for the two plants:

	Home Insert Page Layout Formulas Data Review View				
	A	B	C	D	E
1		**Peoria**		**Moline**	
2	Selling price		$150.00		$150.00
3	Variable manufacturing cost per unit	$72.00		$88.00	
4	Fixed manufacturing cost per unit	30.00		15.00	
5	Variable marketing and distribution cost per unit	14.00		14.00	
6	Fixed marketing and distribution cost per unit	19.00		14.50	
7	Total cost per unit		135.00		131.50
8	Operating income per unit		$ 15.00		$ 18.50
9	Production rate per day	400	units	320	units
10	Normal annual capacity usage	240	days	240	days
11	Maximum annual capacity	300	days	300	days

All fixed costs per unit are calculated based on a normal capacity usage consisting of 240 working days. When the number of working days exceeds 240, overtime charges raise the variable manufacturing costs of additional units by $3.00 per unit in Peoria and $8.00 per unit in Moline.

Domestic Engines Co. is expected to produce and sell 192,000 power generators during the coming year. Wanting to take advantage of the higher operating income per unit at Moline, the company's production manager has decided to manufacture 96,000 units at each plant, resulting in a plan in which Moline operates at capacity (320 units per day × 300 days) and Peoria operates at its normal volume (400 units per day × 240 days).

Required

1. Calculate the breakeven point in units for the Peoria plant and for the Moline plant.
2. Calculate the operating income that would result from the production manager's plan to produce 96,000 units at each plant.
3. Determine how the production of 192,000 units should be allocated between the Peoria and Moline plants to maximize operating income for Domestic Engines. Show your calculations.

4

Job Costing

Job Costing

It's fair to say that no one likes to lose money.

Whether a company is a new startup venture providing marketing consulting services or an established manufacturer of custom-built motorcycles, knowing how to job cost—how much it costs to produce an individual product—is critical if a profit is to be generated. As the following article shows, Nexamp, a clean-energy company, knows this all too well.

Job Costing and Nexamp's Next Generation Energy and Carbon Solutions[1]

Making a profit on a project depends on pricing it correctly. At Nexamp, a leading renewable-energy systems provider in Massachusetts, a team of managers and employees is responsible for the costing and pricing of its solar, geothermal, wind, and biomass installation jobs for homeowners and businesses.

For each project, account managers carefully examine and verify job costs as part of a competitive bidding process. Using a computer model developed from previous projects, a company executive double-checks all the numbers, watching for costs that could wreak havoc with the net profit on the job. Projects of a certain size, such as a recent $20 million government stimulus contract to install solar panels, require the approval of a company vice president or other high-ranking officer. This type of approval ensures that Nexamp does not approve jobs that could lose money.

Nexamp holds a weekly project management meeting where managers report on the status of each job approved and scheduled. Once a project is underway, on-site project managers provide weekly reports on the progress of each phase of installation. Nexamp project managers are also responsible for identifying any potential problems with each project and determining any alterations necessary to ensure high quality, on-time delivery within the original project budget.

At Nexamp, job costing includes three key elements: direct costs of a job, indirect costs of a job, and general administrative costs. Direct costs are costs traceable to a specific job such as costs of solar panels, electricity converters, mounting systems, and

---

[1] *Sources*: Conversations with Nexamp management. June 4, 2010. Noblett, Jackie. 2010. Nexamp lands $20M stimulus contract. *Boston Business Journal*, February 5.

subcontractor payments. All materials are purchased through a formal procurement process, which helps Nexamp carefully manage and control material costs. Another key element of direct costs is direct labor. Besides the actual wages paid to employees, direct labor costs include costs of workers' compensation insurance, health insurance, vacations and holidays, sick days, and paid days off.

Indirect costs of a job are allocated to each project. These include cost of supervisory labor, company-owned equipment, construction supplies, and safety equipment. Finally, Nexamp allocates general and administrative costs, such as office rent, utilities, and general insurance to each job.

Just like at Nexamp, managers at Nissan need to know how much it costs to manufacture its new Leaf electric car, and managers at Ernst & Young need to know what it costs to audit Whole Foods, the organic grocer. Knowing the costs and profitability of jobs helps managers pursue their business strategies, develop pricing plans, and meet external reporting requirements. Of course, when making decisions, managers combine cost information with noncost information, such as personal observations of operations, and nonfinancial performance measures, such as quality and customer satisfaction.

Building-Block Concepts of Costing Systems

Before we begin our discussion of costing systems, let's review Chapter 2's cost-related terms and introduce the new terms that we will need for our primary discussion.

Learning Objective 1

Describe the building-block concepts of costing systems

. . . the building blocks are cost object, direct costs, indirect costs, cost pools, and cost-allocation bases

1. *Cost object*—anything for which a measurement of costs is desired—for example, a product, such as an iMac computer, or a service, such as the cost of repairing an iMac computer.
2. *Direct costs of a cost object*—costs related to a particular cost object that can be traced to that cost object in an economically feasible (cost-effective) way—for example the cost of purchasing the main computer board or the cost of parts used to make an iMac computer.
3. *Indirect costs of a cost object*—costs related to a particular cost object that cannot be traced to that cost object in an economically feasible (cost-effective) way—for example, the costs of supervisors who oversee multiple products, one of which is the iMac, or the rent paid for the repair facility that repairs many different Apple computer products besides the iMac. Indirect costs are allocated to the cost object using a cost-allocation method.

Recall that *cost assignment* is a general term for assigning costs, whether direct or indirect, to a cost object. *Cost tracing* is a specific term for assigning direct costs; *cost allocation* refers to assigning indirect costs. The relationship among these three concepts can be graphically represented as

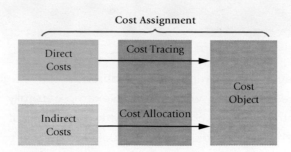

Throughout this chapter, the costs assigned to a cost object, for example, a product such as a Mini Cooper or a service such as an audit of MTV, include both variable costs and costs that are fixed in the short run. Managers cost products and services to guide long-run strategic decisions (for example, what mix of products and services to produce and sell and what prices to charge for them). In the long run, managers want revenues to exceed total costs.

We also need to introduce and explain two more terms before discussing costing systems:

4. **Cost pool.** A **cost pool** is a grouping of individual indirect cost items. Cost pools can range from broad, such as all manufacturing-plant costs, to narrow, such as the costs of operating metal-cutting machines. Cost pools are often organized in conjunction with cost-allocation bases.

5. **Cost-allocation base.** How should a company allocate costs to operate metal-cutting machines among different products? One way to allocate costs is based on the number of machine-hours used to produce different products. The **cost-allocation base** (number of machine-hours) is a systematic way to link an indirect cost or group of indirect costs (operating costs of all metal-cutting machines) to cost objects (different products). For example, if indirect costs of operating metal-cutting machines is $500,000 based on running these machines for 10,000 hours, the cost allocation rate is $500,000 ÷ 10,000 hours = $50 per machine-hour, where machine-hours is the cost allocation base. If a product uses 800 machine-hours, it will be allocated $40,000, $50 per machine-hour × 800 machine-hours. The ideal cost-allocation base is the cost driver of the indirect costs, because there is a cause-and-effect relationship between the cost allocation base and the indirect costs. A cost-allocation base can be either financial (such as direct labor costs) or nonfinancial (such as the number of machine-hours). When the cost object is a job, product, or customer, the cost-allocation base is also called a **cost-application base.**

Decision Point ▶

What are the building block concepts of a costing system?

The concepts represented by these five terms constitute the building blocks that we will use to design the costing systems described in this chapter.

Job-Costing and Process-Costing Systems

Management accountants use two basic types of costing systems to assign costs to products or services:

1. **Job-costing system.** In this system, the cost object is a unit or multiple units of a distinct product or service called a **job**. Each job generally uses different amounts of resources. The product or service is often a single unit, such as a specialized machine made at Hitachi, a construction project managed by Bechtel Corporation, a repair job done at an Audi Service Center, or an advertising campaign produced by Saatchi & Saatchi. Each special machine made by Hitachi is unique and distinct. An advertising campaign for one client at Saatchi and Saatchi is unique and distinct from advertising campaigns for other clients. Job costing is also used by companies such as Ethan Allen

Learning Objective 2

Distinguish job costing

. . . job costing is used to cost a distinct product from process costing

. . . process costing is used to cost masses of identical or similar units

to cost multiple identical units of distinct furniture products. Because the products and services are distinct, job-costing systems accumulate costs separately for each product or service.

2. **Process-costing system.** In this system, the cost object is masses of identical or similar units of a product or service. For example, Citibank provides the same service to all its customers when processing customer deposits. Intel provides the same product (say, a Pentium 4 chip) to each of its customers. All Minute Maid consumers receive the same frozen orange juice product. In each period, process-costing systems divide the total costs of producing an identical or similar product or service by the total number of units produced to obtain a per-unit cost. This per-unit cost is the average unit cost that applies to each of the identical or similar units produced in that period.

Exhibit 4-1 presents examples of job costing and process costing in the service, merchandising, and manufacturing sectors. These two types of costing systems are best considered as opposite ends of a continuum; in between, one type of system can blur into the other to some degree.

Many companies have costing systems that are neither pure job costing nor pure process costing but have elements of both. Costing systems need to be tailored to the underlying operations. For example, Kellogg Corporation uses job costing to calculate the total cost to manufacture each of its different and distinct types of products—such as Corn Flakes, Crispix, and Froot Loops—and process costing to calculate the per-unit cost of producing each identical box of Corn Flakes. In this chapter, we focus on job-costing systems. Chapters 17 and 18 discuss process-costing systems.

Decision Point

How do you distinguish job costing from process costing?

Exhibit 4-1

Examples of Job Costing and Process Costing in the Service, Merchandising, and Manufacturing Sectors

	Service Sector	Merchandising Sector	Manufacturing Sector
Job Costing Used	• Audit engagements done by Price Waterhouse Coopers • Consulting engagements done by McKinsey & Co. • Advertising-agency campaigns run by Ogilvy & Mather • Individual legal cases argued by Hale & Dorr • Computer-repair jobs done by CompUSA • Movies produced by Universal Studios	• L. L. Bean sending individual items by mail order • Special promotion of new products by Wal-Mart	• Assembly of individual aircrafts at Boeing • Construction of ships at Litton Industries
Process Costing Used	• Bank-check clearing at Bank of America • Postal delivery (standard items) by U.S. Postal Service	• Grain dealing by Arthur Daniel Midlands • Lumber dealing by Weyerhauser	• Oil refining by Shell Oil • Beverage production by PepsiCo

Job Costing: Evaluation and Implementation

We illustrate job costing using the example of Robinson Company, a company that manufactures and installs specialized machinery for the paper-making industry. In early 2011, Robinson receives a request to bid for the manufacturing and installation of a new paper-making machine for the Western Pulp and Paper Company (WPP). Robinson had never made a machine quite like this one, and its managers wonder what to bid for the job. Robinson's management team works through the five-step decision-making process.

1. **Identify the problems and uncertainties.** The decision of whether and how much to bid for the WPP job depends on how management resolves two critical uncertainties: what it will cost to complete the job and the prices that its competitors are likely to bid.

2. **Obtain information.** Robinson's managers first evaluate whether doing the WPP job is consistent with the company's strategy. Do they want to do more of these kinds of jobs? Is this an attractive segment of the market? Will Robinson be able to develop a competitive advantage over its competitors and satisfy customers? Robinson's managers conclude that the WPP job fits well with the company's strategy.

   Robinson's managers study the drawings and engineering specifications provided by WPP and decide on technical details of the machine. They compare the specifications of this machine to similar machines they have made in the past, identify competitors who might bid on the job, and gather information on what these bids might be.

3. **Make predictions about the future.** Robinson's managers estimate the cost of direct materials, direct manufacturing labor, and overhead for the WPP job. They also consider qualitative factors and risk factors and think through any biases they might have. For example, do engineers and employees working on the WPP job have the necessary skills and technical competence? Would they find the experience valuable and challenging? How accurate are the cost estimates, and what is the likelihood of cost overruns? What biases do Robinson's managers have to be careful about? Remember, Robinson has not made a machine quite like this one. Robinson's managers need to be careful not to draw inappropriate analogies and to seek the most relevant information when making their judgments.

4. **Make decisions by choosing among alternatives.** Robinson bids $15,000 for the WPP job. This bid is based on a manufacturing cost estimate of $10,000 and a markup of 50% over manufacturing cost. The $15,000 price takes into account likely bids by competitors, the technical and business risks, and qualitative factors. Robinson's managers are very confident that they have obtained the best possible information in reaching their decision.

5. **Implement the decision, evaluate performance, and learn.** Robinson wins the bid for the WPP job. As Robinson works on the WPP job, it keeps careful track of all the costs it has incurred (which are detailed later in this chapter). Ultimately, Robinson's managers compare the predicted amounts against actual costs to evaluate how well they did on the WPP job.

In its job-costing system, Robinson accumulates costs incurred on a job in different parts of the value chain, such as manufacturing, marketing, and customer service. We focus here on Robinson's manufacturing function (which also includes product installation). To make a machine, Robinson purchases some components from outside suppliers and makes others itself. Each of Robinson's jobs also has a service element: installing a machine at a customer's site, integrating it with the customer's other machines and processes, and ensuring the machine meets customer expectations.

One form of a job-costing system that Robinson can use is actual costing. **Actual costing** is a costing system that traces direct costs to a cost object by using the actual direct-cost rates times the actual quantities of the direct-cost inputs. It allocates indirect costs based on the actual indirect-cost rates times the actual quantities of the cost-allocation bases. The *actual indirect-cost rate* is calculated by dividing actual total indirect costs by the actual total quantity of the cost-allocation base. As its name suggests, actual costing systems calculate the actual costs of jobs. Yet, actual costing systems are not commonly found in practice because actual costs cannot be computed in a *timely* manner. The problem is not with computing direct-cost rates for direct materials and direct manufacturing labor. For example, Robinson records the actual prices paid for materials. As it uses these materials, the prices paid serve as actual direct-cost rates for charging material costs to jobs. As we discuss next, calculating actual indirect-cost rates on a timely basis each week or each month is, however, a problem. Robinson can only calculate actual indirect-cost rates at the end of the fiscal year and Robinson's managers are unwilling to wait that long to learn the costs of various jobs.

Time Period Used to Compute Indirect-Cost Rates

There are two reasons for using longer periods, such as a year, to calculate indirect-cost rates.

1. **The numerator reason (indirect-cost pool).** The shorter the period, the greater the influence of seasonal patterns on the amount of costs. For example, if indirect-cost rates were calculated each month, costs of heating (included in the numerator) would be charged to production only during the winter months. An annual period incorporates the effects of all four seasons into a single, annual indirect-cost rate.

   Levels of total indirect costs are also affected by nonseasonal erratic costs. Examples of nonseasonal erratic costs include costs incurred in a particular month that benefit operations during future months, such as costs of repairs and maintenance of equipment, and costs of vacation and holiday pay. If monthly indirect-cost rates were calculated, jobs done in a month with high, nonseasonal erratic costs would be charged with these costs. Pooling all indirect costs together over the course of a full year and calculating a single annual indirect-cost rate helps smooth some of the erratic bumps in costs associated with shorter periods.

2. **The denominator reason (quantity of the cost-allocation base).** Another reason for longer periods is to avoid spreading monthly fixed indirect costs over fluctuating levels of monthly output and fluctuating quantities of the cost-allocation base. Consider the following example.

Reardon and Pane are tax accountants whose work follows a highly seasonal pattern with very busy months during tax season and less busy months at other times. Assume the following mix of variable indirect costs (such as supplies, food, power, and indirect support labor) that vary with the quantity of the cost-allocation base (direct professional labor-hours) and fixed indirect costs (depreciation and general administrative support) that do not vary with short-run fluctuations in the quantity of the cost-allocation base:

	Indirect Costs			Direct	Allocation Rate per Direct
	Variable	Fixed	Total	Professional Labor-Hours	Professional Labor-Hour
	(1)	(2)	(3)	(4)	(5) = (3) ÷ (4)
High-output month	$40,000	$60,000	$100,000	3,200	$31.25
Low-output month	10,000	60,000	70,000	800	87.50

You can see that variable indirect costs change in proportion to changes in direct professional labor-hours. Therefore, the variable indirect-cost rate is the same in both the high-output months and the low-output months ($40,000 ÷ 3,200 labor-hours = $12.50 per labor-hour; $10,000 ÷ 800 labor-hours = $12.50 per labor-hour). Sometimes overtime payments can cause the variable indirect-cost rate to be higher in high-output months. In such cases, variable indirect costs will be allocated at a higher rate to production in high-output months relative to production in low-output months.

Consider now the fixed costs of $60,000. The fixed costs cause monthly total indirect-cost rates to vary considerably—from $31.25 per hour to $87.50 per hour. Few managers believe that identical jobs done in different months should be allocated indirect-cost charges per hour that differ so significantly ($87.50 ÷ $31.25 = 2.80, or 280%) because of fixed costs. Furthermore, if fees for preparing tax returns are based on costs, fees would be high in low-output months leading to lost business, when in fact management wants to accept more bids to utilize idle capacity. Reardon and Pane chose a specific level of capacity based on a time horizon far beyond a mere month. An average, annualized rate based on the relationship of total annual indirect costs to the total annual level of output smoothes the effect of monthly variations in output levels and is more representative of the total costs and total output that management considered when choosing the level of capacity and, hence, fixed costs. Another denominator reason for using annual overhead rates is that the calculation of monthly indirect-cost rates is affected by the number of Monday-to-Friday workdays in a month. The number of workdays per month varies from 20 to 23 during a year. If separate rates are computed each month, jobs in February would bear a greater share of indirect costs (such as depreciation and property taxes) than jobs in other months, because February has the fewest workdays (and consequently labor-hours) in a month. Many managers believe such results to be an unrepresentative and unreasonable way to assign indirect costs to jobs. An annual period reduces the effect that the number of working days per month has on unit costs.

Decision Point ▶

What is the main challenge in implementing job-costing systems?

Normal Costing

The difficulty of calculating actual indirect-cost rates on a weekly or monthly basis means managers cannot calculate the actual costs of jobs as they are completed. However, managers, including those at Robinson, want a close approximation of the costs of various jobs regularly during the year, not just at the end of the fiscal year. Managers want to know manufacturing costs (and other costs, such as marketing costs) for ongoing uses, including pricing jobs, monitoring and managing costs, evaluating the success of the job, learning about what worked and what didn't, bidding on new jobs, and preparing interim financial statements. Because of the need for immediate access to job costs, few companies wait to allocate overhead costs until year-end when the actual manufacturing overhead is finally known. Instead, a *predetermined* or *budgeted* indirect-cost rate is calculated for each cost pool at the beginning of a fiscal year, and overhead costs are allocated to jobs as work progresses. For the numerator and denominator reasons already described, the **budgeted indirect-cost rate** for each cost pool is computed as follows:

$$\frac{\text{Budgeted indirect}}{\text{cost rate}} = \frac{\text{Budgeted annual indirect costs}}{\text{Budgeted annual quantity of the cost-allocation base}}$$

Using budgeted indirect-cost rates gives rise to normal costing.

Normal costing is a costing system that (1) traces direct costs to a cost object by using the actual direct-cost rates times the actual quantities of the direct-cost inputs and (2) allocates indirect costs based on the *budgeted* indirect-cost rates times the actual quantities of the cost-allocation bases.

We illustrate normal costing for the Robinson Company example using the following seven steps to assign costs to an individual job. This approach is commonly used by companies in the manufacturing, merchandising, and service sectors.

General Approach to Job Costing

Learning Objective 4

Outline the seven-step approach to normal costing

. . . the seven-step approach is used to compute direct and indirect costs of a job

Step 1: Identify the Job That Is the Chosen Cost Object. The cost object in the Robinson Company example is Job WPP 298, manufacturing a paper-making machine for Western Pulp and Paper (WPP) in 2011. Robinson's managers and management accountants gather information to cost jobs through source documents. A **source document** is an original record (such as a labor time card on which an employee's work hours are recorded) that supports journal entries in an accounting system. The main source document for Job WPP 298 is a job-cost record. A **job-cost record**, also called a **job-cost sheet**, records and accumulates all the costs assigned to a specific job, starting when work begins. Exhibit 4-2 shows the job-cost record for the paper-making machine ordered by WPP. Follow the various steps in costing Job WPP 298 on the job-cost record in Exhibit 4-2.

Exhibit 4-2	Source Documents at Robinson Company: Job-Cost Record

	Home	Insert	Page Layout	Formulas	Data	Review	View	
	A	B	C	D	E		
1			JOB-COST RECORD				
2	JOB NO:	WPP 298		CUSTOMER:	Western Pulp and Paper		
3	Date Started:	Feb. 7, 2011		Date Completed	Feb. 28, 2011		
4							
5							
6	DIRECT MATERIALS						
7	Date	Materials		Quantity	Unit	Total	
8	Received	Requisition No.	Part No.	Used	Cost	Costs	
9	Feb. 7, 2011	2011: 198	MB 468-A	8	$14	$ 112	
10	Feb. 7, 2011	2011: 199	TB 267-F	12	63	756	
11						●	
12						●	
13	Total					$ 4,606	
14							
15	DIRECT MANUFACTURING LABOR						
16	Period	Labor Time	Employee	Hours	Hourly	Total	
17	Covered	Record No.	No.	Used	Rate	Costs	
18	Feb. 7-13, 2011	LT 232	551-87-3076	25	$18	$ 450	
19	Feb. 7-13, 2011	LT 247	287-31-4671	5	19	95	
20						●	
21						●	
22	Total					$ 1,579	
23							
24	MANUFACTURING OVERHEAD*						
25		Cost Pool		Allocation Base	Allocation-	Total	
26	Date	Category	Allocation Base	Quantity Used	Base Rate	Costs	
27	Dec. 31, 2011	Manufacturing	Direct Manufacturing	88 hours	$40	$ 3,520	
28			Labor-Hours				
29							
30	Total					$ 3,520	
31	TOTAL MANUFACTURING COST OF JOB					$ 9,705	
32							
33							
34	*The Robinson Company uses a single manufacturing-overhead cost pool. The use of multiple overhead cost pools						
35	would mean multiple entries in the "Manufacturing Overhead" section of the job-cost record.						
36							

Step 2: Identify the Direct Costs of the Job. Robinson identifies two direct-manufacturing cost categories: direct materials and direct manufacturing labor.

■ **Direct materials:** On the basis of the engineering specifications and drawings provided by WPP, a manufacturing engineer orders materials from the storeroom. The order is placed using a basic source document called a **materials-requisition record,** which contains information about the cost of direct materials used on a specific job and in a specific department. Exhibit 4-3, Panel A, shows a materials-requisition record for the Robinson Company. See how the record specifies the job for which the material is requested (WPP 298), the description of the material (Part Number MB 468-A, metal brackets), the actual quantity (8), the actual unit cost ($14), and the actual total cost ($112). The $112 actual total cost also appears on the job-cost record in Exhibit 4-2. If we add the cost of all material requisitions, the total actual direct material cost is $4,606, which is shown in the Direct Materials panel of the job-cost record in Exhibit 4-2.

■ **Direct manufacturing labor:** The accounting for direct manufacturing labor is similar to the accounting described for direct materials. The source document for direct manufacturing labor is a **labor-time sheet,** which contains information about the amount of labor time used for a specific job in a specific department. Exhibit 4-3, Panel B, shows a typical weekly labor-time sheet for a particular employee (G. L. Cook). Each day Cook records the time spent on individual jobs (in this case WPP 298 and JL 256), as well as the time spent on other tasks, such as maintenance of machines or cleaning, that are not related to a specific job.

The 25 hours that Cook spent on Job WPP 298 appears on the job-cost record in Exhibit 4-2 at a cost of $450 (25 hours × $18 per hour). Similarly, the job-cost record for Job JL 256 will carry a cost of $216 (12 hours × $18 per hour). The three hours of time spent on maintenance and cleaning at $18 per hour equals $54. This cost is part of indirect manufacturing costs because it is not traceable to any particular job. This indirect cost is included as part of the manufacturing-overhead cost pool allocated to jobs. The total direct manufacturing labor costs of $1,579 for the paper-making machine that appears in the Direct Manufacturing Labor panel of the job-cost record in Exhibit 4-2 is the sum of all the direct manufacturing labor costs charged to this job by different employees.

All costs other than direct materials and direct manufacturing labor are classified as indirect costs.

Step 3:   Select the Cost-Allocation Bases to Use for Allocating Indirect Costs to the Job. Indirect manufacturing costs are costs that are necessary to do a job but that cannot be traced to a specific job. It would be impossible to complete a job without incurring indirect costs such as supervision, manufacturing engineering, utilities, and repairs. Because these costs cannot be traced to a specific job, they must be allocated to all jobs in a systematic way. Different jobs require different quantities of indirect resources. The objective is to allocate the costs of indirect resources in a systematic way to their related jobs.

Companies often use multiple cost-allocation bases to allocate indirect costs because different indirect costs have different cost drivers. For example, some indirect costs such as depreciation and repairs of machines are more closely related to machine-hours. Other indirect costs such as supervision and production support are more closely related to direct manufacturing labor-hours. Robinson, however, chooses direct manufacturing labor-hours as the sole allocation base for linking all indirect manufacturing costs to jobs. That's because, in its labor-intensive environment, Robinson believes that the number of direct manufacturing labor-hours drives the manufacturing overhead resources (such as salaries paid to supervisors, engineers, production support staff, and quality management staff) required by individual jobs. (We will see in Chapter 5 that, in many manufacturing

| Exhibit 4-3 | Source Documents at Robinson Company: Materials Requisition Record and Labor-Time Sheet |

PANEL A:

MATERIALS-REQUISITION RECORD				
Materials-Requisition Record No.			2011: 198	
Job No. WPP 298		Date:	FEB. 7, 2011	
Part No.	Part Description	Quantity	Unit Cost	Total Cost
MB 468-A	Metal Brackets	8	$14	$112
Issued By: B. Clyde		Date:	Feb. 7, 2011	
Received By: L. Daley		Date:	Feb. 7, 2011	

PANEL B:

LABOR-TIME SHEET								
Labor-Time Record No:			LT 232					
Employee Name: G. L. Cook			Employee No: 551-87-3076					
Employee Classification Code:			Grade 3 Machinist					
Hourly Rate: $18								
Week Start: Feb. 7, 2011			Week End: Feb. 13, 2011					
Job. No.	M	T	W	Th	F	S	Su	Total
WPP 298	4	8	3	6	4	0	0	25
JL 256	3	0	4	2	3	0	0	12
Maintenance	1	0	1	0	1	0	0	3
Total	8	8	8	8	8	0	0	40
Supervisor: R. Stuart		Date: Feb. 13, 2011						

environments, we need to broaden the set of cost drivers.) In 2011, Robinson budgets 28,000 direct manufacturing labor-hours.

Step 4: Identify the Indirect Costs Associated with Each Cost-Allocation Base. Because Robinson believes that a single cost-allocation base—direct manufacturing labor-hours— can be used to allocate indirect manufacturing costs to jobs, Robinson creates a single cost pool called manufacturing overhead costs. This pool represents all indirect costs of the Manufacturing Department that are difficult to trace directly to individual jobs. In 2011, budgeted manufacturing overhead costs total $1,120,000.

As we saw in Steps 3 and 4, managers first identify cost-allocation bases and then identify the costs related to each cost-allocation base, not the other way around. They choose this order because managers must first understand the cost driver, the reasons why costs are being incurred (for example, setting up machines, moving materials, or designing jobs), before they can determine the costs associated with each cost driver. Otherwise, there is nothing to guide the creation of cost pools. Of course, Steps 3 and 4 are often done almost simultaneously.

Step 5: Compute the Rate per Unit of Each Cost-Allocation Base Used to Allocate Indirect Costs to the Job. For each cost pool, the budgeted indirect-cost rate is calculated by dividing budgeted total indirect costs in the pool (determined in Step 4) by the budgeted total quantity of the cost-allocation base (determined in Step 3). Robinson calculates the allocation rate for its single manufacturing overhead cost pool as follows:

$$\text{Budgeted manufacturing overhead rate} = \frac{\text{Budgeted manufacturing overhead costs}}{\text{Budgeted total quantity of cost-allocation base}}$$

$$= \frac{\$1,120,000}{28,000 \text{ direct manufacturing labor-hours}}$$

$$= \$40 \text{ per direct manufacturing labor-hour}$$

Step 6: Compute the Indirect Costs Allocated to the Job. The indirect costs of a job are calculated by multiplying the *actual* quantity of each different allocation base (one allocation base for each cost pool) associated with the job by the *budgeted* indirect cost rate of each allocation base (computed in Step 5). Recall that Robinson's managers selected direct manufacturing labor-hours as the only cost-allocation base. Robinson uses 88 direct manufacturing labor-hours on the WPP 298 job. Manufacturing overhead costs allocated to WPP 298 equal $3,520 ($40 per direct manufacturing labor-hour × 88 hours) and appear in the Manufacturing Overhead panel of the WPP 298 job-cost record in Exhibit 4-2.

Step 7: Compute the Total Cost of the Job by Adding All Direct and Indirect Costs Assigned to the Job. Exhibit 4-2 shows that the total manufacturing costs of the WPP job are $9,705.

Direct manufacturing costs		
Direct materials	$4,606	
Direct manufacturing labor	1,579	$ 6,185
Manufacturing overhead costs		
($40 per direct manufacturing labor-hour × 88 hours)		3,520
Total manufacturing costs of job WPP 298		$9,705

Recall that Robinson bid a price of $15,000 for the job. At that revenue, the normal-costing system shows a gross margin of $5,295 ($15,000 − $9,705) and a gross-margin percentage of 35.3% ($5,295 ÷ $15,000 = 0.353).

Robinson's manufacturing managers and sales managers can use the gross margin and gross-margin percentage calculations to compare the profitability of different jobs to try to understand the reasons why some jobs show low profitability. Have direct materials been wasted? Was direct manufacturing labor too high? Were there ways to improve the efficiency of these jobs? Were these jobs simply underpriced? Job-cost analysis provides the information needed for judging the performance of manufacturing and sales managers and for making future improvements (see Concepts in Action on p. 108).

Concepts in Action   Job Costing on Cowboys Stadium

Over the years, fans of the National Football League have identified the Dallas Cowboys as "America's Team." Since 2009, however, the team known for winning five Super Bowls has become just as recognized for its futuristic new home, Cowboys Stadium in Arlington, Texas.

When the Cowboys take the field, understanding each week's game plan is critical for success. But for Manhattan Construction, the company that managed the development of the $1.2 billion Cowboys Stadium project, understanding costs is just as critical for making successful pricing decisions, winning contracts, and ensuring that each project is profitable. Each job is estimated individually because the unique end-products, whether a new stadium or an office building, demand different quantities of Manhattan Construction's resources.

In 2006, the Dallas Cowboys selected Manhattan Construction to lead the construction of its 73,000 seat, 3 million-square-foot stadium. To be completed in three years, the stadium design featured two monumental arches spanning about a quarter-mile in length over the dome, a retractable roof, the largest retractable glass doors in the world (in each end zone), canted glass exterior walls, 325 private suites, and a 600-ton JumboTron hovering 90 feet above the field.

With only 7% of football fans ever setting foot in a professional stadium, "Our main competition is the home media center," Cowboys owner Jerry Jones said in unveiling the stadium design in 2006. "We wanted to offer a real experience that you can't have at home, but to see it with the technology that you do have at home."

Generally speaking, the Cowboys Stadium project had five stages: (1) conceptualization, (2) design and planning, (3) preconstruction, (4) construction, and (5) finalization and delivery. During this 40-month process, Manhattan Construction hired architects and subcontractors, created blueprints, purchased and cleared land, developed the stadium—ranging from excavation to materials testing to construction—built out and finished interiors, and completed last-minute changes before the stadium's grand opening in mid-2009.

While most construction projects have distinct stages, compressed timeframes and scope changes required diligent management by Manhattan Construction. Before the first game was played, Manhattan Construction successfully navigated nearly 3,000 change requests and a constantly evolving budget.

To ensure proper allocation and accounting of resources, Manhattan Construction project managers used a job-costing system. The system first calculated the budgeted cost of more than 500 line items of direct materials and labor costs. It then allocated estimated overhead costs (supervisor salaries, rent, materials handling, and so on) to the job using direct material costs and direct labor-hours as allocation bases. Manhattan Construction's job-costing system allowed managers to track project variances on a weekly basis. Manhattan Construction continually estimated the profitability of the Cowboys Stadium project based on the percentage of work completed, insight gleaned from previous stadium projects, and revenue earned. Managers used the job-costing system to actively manage costs, while the Dallas Cowboys had access to clear, concise, and transparent costing data.

Just like quarterback Tony Romo navigating opposing defenses, Manhattan Construction was able to leverage its job-costing system to ensure the successful construction of a stadium as iconic as the blue star on the Cowboys' helmets.

Sources: Dillon, David. 2009. New Cowboys Stadium has grand design, but discipline isn't compromised *The Dallas Morning News*, June 3. http://www.dallasnews.com/sharedcontent/dws/ent/stories/DN-stadiumarchitecture_03gd.ART.State.Edition2.5125e7c.html; Knudson, Brooke. 2008. Profile: Dallas Cowboys Stadium. *Construction Today*, December 22. http://www.construction-today.com/cms1/content/view/1175/139/1/0/; Lacayo, Richard. 2009. Inside the new Dallas Cowboys stadium. *Time*, September 21. http://www.time.com/time/nation/article/0,8599,1924535,00.html; Penny, Mark, Project Manager, Manhattan Construction Co. 2010. Interview. January 12.

Exhibit 4-4 is an overview of Robinson Company's job-costing system. This exhibit represents the concepts comprising the five building blocks—cost object, direct costs of a cost object, indirect (overhead) costs of a cost object, indirect-cost pool, and cost-allocation base—of job-costing systems that were first introduced at the beginning of this chapter. Costing-system overviews such as Exhibit 4-4 are important learning tools. We urge you to sketch one when you need to understand a costing system in manufacturing, merchandising, or service companies. (The symbols in Exhibit 4-4 are used consistently in the costing-system overviews presented in this book. A triangle always identifies a direct

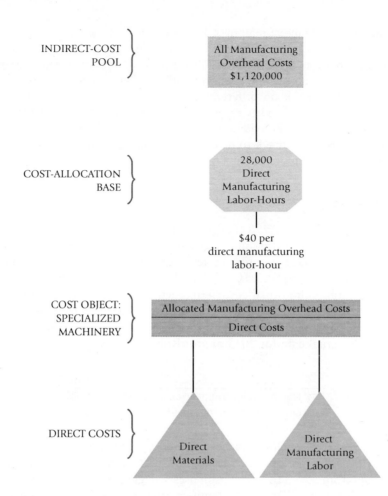

INDIRECT-COST POOL

All Manufacturing Overhead Costs $1,120,000

COST-ALLOCATION BASE

28,000 Direct Manufacturing Labor-Hours

$40 per direct manufacturing labor-hour

COST OBJECT: SPECIALIZED MACHINERY

Allocated Manufacturing Overhead Costs

Direct Costs

DIRECT COSTS

Direct Materials

Direct Manufacturing Labor

Exhibit 4-4

Job-Costing Overview for Determining Manufacturing Costs of Jobs at Robinson Company

cost, a rectangle represents the indirect-cost pool, and an octagon describes the cost-allocation base.) Note the parallel between the overview diagram and the cost of the WPP 298 job described in Step 7. Exhibit 4-4 shows two direct-cost categories (direct materials and direct manufacturing labor) and one indirect-cost category (manufacturing overhead) used to allocate indirect costs. The costs in Step 7 also have three dollar amounts, each corresponding respectively to the two direct-cost and one indirect-cost categories.

Decision Point

How do you implement a normal-costing system?

The Role of Technology

To improve the efficiency of their operations, managers use costing information about products and jobs to control materials, labor, and overhead costs. Modern information technology provides managers with quick and accurate product-cost information, making it easier to manage and control jobs. For example, in many costing systems, source documents exist only in the form of computer records. Bar coding and other forms of online information recording reduce human intervention and improve the accuracy of materials and labor time records for individual jobs.

Consider, for example, direct materials charged to jobs for product-costing purposes. Managers control these costs as materials are purchased and used. Using Electronic Data Interchange (EDI) technology, companies like Robinson order materials from their suppliers by clicking a few keys on a computer keyboard. EDI, an electronic computer link between a company and its suppliers, ensures that the order is transmitted quickly and accurately with minimum paperwork and costs. A bar code scanner records the receipt of incoming materials. The computer matches the receipt with the order, prints out a check to the supplier, and records the material received. When an operator on the production floor transmits a request for materials via a computer terminal, the computer prepares a materials-requisition record, instantly recording the issue of materials in the materials and job-cost records. Each day, the computer sums the materials-requisition records charged to a particular job or manufacturing department. A performance report is then prepared monitoring actual costs of direct materials. Direct material usage can be reported hourly—if the benefits exceed the cost of such frequent reporting.

Similarly, information about direct manufacturing labor is obtained as employees log into computer terminals and key in the job numbers, their employee numbers, and start and end times of their work on different jobs. The computer automatically prints the labor time record and, using hourly rates stored for each employee, calculates the direct manufacturing labor costs of individual jobs. Information technology also provides managers with instantaneous feedback to help control manufacturing overhead costs, jobs in process, jobs completed, and jobs shipped and installed at customer sites.

Actual Costing

How would the cost of Job WPP 298 change if Robinson had used actual costing rather than normal costing? Both actual costing and normal costing trace direct costs to jobs in the same way because source documents identify the actual quantities and actual rates of direct materials and direct manufacturing labor for a job as the work is being done. The only difference between costing a job with normal costing and actual costing is that normal costing uses *budgeted* indirect-cost rates, whereas actual costing uses *actual* indirect-cost rates calculated annually at the end of the year. Exhibit 4-5 distinguishes actual costing from normal costing.

The following actual data for 2011 are for Robinson's manufacturing operations:

	Actual
Total manufacturing overhead costs	$1,215,000
Total direct manufacturing labor-hours	27,000

Steps 1 and 2 are exactly as before: Step 1 identifies WPP 298 as the cost object; Step 2 calculates actual direct material costs of $4,606, and actual direct manufacturing labor costs of $1,579. Recall from Step 3 that Robinson uses a single cost-allocation base, direct manufacturing labor-hours, to allocate all manufacturing overhead costs to jobs. The actual quantity of direct manufacturing labor-hours for 2011 is 27,000 hours. In Step 4, Robinson groups all actual indirect manufacturing costs of $1,215,000 into a single manufacturing overhead cost pool. In Step 5, the **actual indirect-cost rate** is calculated by dividing actual total indirect costs in the pool (determined in Step 4) by the actual total quantity of the cost-allocation base (determined in Step 3). Robinson calculates the actual manufacturing overhead rate in 2011 for its single manufacturing overhead cost pool as follows:

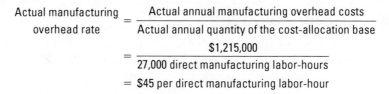

$$\begin{aligned} \text{Actual manufacturing overhead rate} &= \frac{\text{Actual annual manufacturing overhead costs}}{\text{Actual annual quantity of the cost-allocation base}} \\ &= \frac{\$1,215,000}{27,000 \text{ direct manufacturing labor-hours}} \\ &= \$45 \text{ per direct manufacturing labor-hour} \end{aligned}$$

In Step 6, under an actual-costing system,

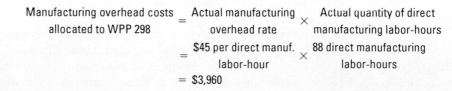

$$\begin{aligned} \text{Manufacturing overhead costs allocated to WPP 298} &= \text{Actual manufacturing overhead rate} \times \text{Actual quantity of direct manufacturing labor-hours} \\ &= \$45 \text{ per direct manuf. labor-hour} \times 88 \text{ direct manufacturing labor-hours} \\ &= \$3,960 \end{aligned}$$

	Actual Costing	Normal Costing
Direct Costs	Actual direct-cost rates × actual quantities of direct-cost inputs	Actual direct-cost rates × actual quantities of direct-cost inputs
Indirect Costs	Actual indirect-cost rates × actual quantities of cost-allocation bases	Budgeted indirect-cost rates × actual quantities of cost-allocation bases

In Step 7, the cost of the job under actual costing is $10,145, calculated as follows:

Direct manufacturing costs		
Direct materials	$4,606	
Direct manufacturing labor	1,579	$ 6,185
Manufacturing overhead costs		
($45 per direct manufacturing labor-hour × 88 actual		
direct manufacturing labor-hours)		3,960
Total manufacturing costs of job		$10,145

The manufacturing cost of the WPP 298 job is higher by $440 under actual costing ($10,145) than it is under normal costing ($9,705) because the actual indirect-cost rate is $45 per hour, whereas the budgeted indirect-cost rate is $40 per hour. That is, ($45 – $40) × 88 actual direct manufacturing labor-hours = $440.

As we discussed previously, manufacturing costs of a job are available much earlier under a normal-costing system. Consequently, Robinson's manufacturing and sales managers can evaluate the profitability of different jobs, the efficiency with which the jobs are done, and the pricing of different jobs as soon as the jobs are completed, while the experience is still fresh in everyone's mind. Another advantage of normal costing is that corrective actions can be implemented much sooner. At the end of the year, though, costs allocated using normal costing will not, in general, equal actual costs incurred. If material, adjustments will need to be made so that the cost of jobs and the costs in various inventory accounts are based on actual rather that normal costing. We describe these adjustments later in the chapter.

Decision Point

How do you distinguish actual costing from normal costing?

A Normal Job-Costing System in Manufacturing

We now explain how a normal job-costing system operates in manufacturing. Continuing with the Robinson Company example, the following illustration considers events that occurred in February 2011. Before getting into details, study Exhibit 4-6, which provides a broad framework for understanding the flow of costs in job costing.

The upper part of Exhibit 4-6 shows the flow of inventoriable costs from the purchase of materials and other manufacturing inputs, to their conversion into work-in-process and finished goods, to the sale of finished goods.

Direct materials used and direct manufacturing labor can be easily traced to jobs. They become part of work-in-process inventory on the balance sheet because direct manufacturing labor transforms direct materials into another asset, work-in-process inventory. Robinson also incurs manufacturing overhead costs (including indirect materials and indirect manufacturing labor) to convert direct materials into work-in-process inventory. The overhead (indirect) costs, however, cannot be easily traced to individual jobs.

Learning Objective 6

Track the flow of costs in a job-costing system

. . . from purchase of materials to sale of finished goods

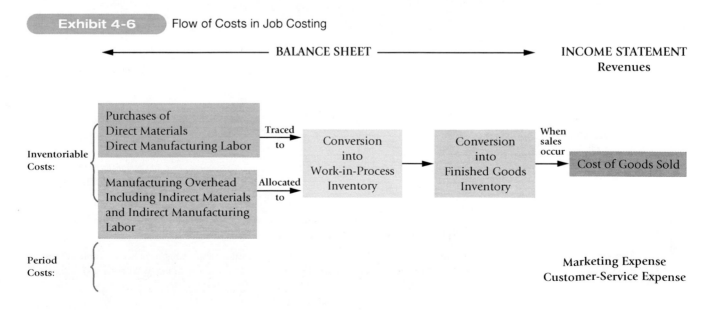

Exhibit 4-6 Flow of Costs in Job Costing

Manufacturing overhead costs, therefore, are first accumulated in a manufacturing over-head account and later allocated to individual jobs. As manufacturing overhead costs are allocated, they become part of work-in-process inventory.

As individual jobs are completed, work-in-process inventory becomes another balance sheet asset, finished goods inventory. Only when finished goods are sold is an expense, cost of goods sold, recognized in the income statement and matched against revenues earned.

The lower part of Exhibit 4-6 shows the period costs—marketing and customer-service costs. These costs do not create any assets on the balance sheet because they are not incurred to transform materials into a finished product. Instead, they are expensed in the income statement, as they are incurred, to best match revenues.

We next describe the entries made in the general ledger.

General Ledger

You know by this point that a job-costing system has a separate job-cost record for each job. A summary of the job-cost record is typically found in a subsidiary ledger. The general ledger account Work-in-Process Control presents the total of these separate job-cost records pertaining to all unfinished jobs. The job-cost records and Work-in-Process Control account track job costs from when jobs start until they are complete.

Exhibit 4-7 shows T-account relationships for Robinson Company's general ledger. The general ledger gives a "bird's-eye view" of the costing system. The amounts shown in

| Exhibit 4-7 | Manufacturing Job-Costing System Using Normal Costing: Diagram of General Ledger Relationships for February 2011 |

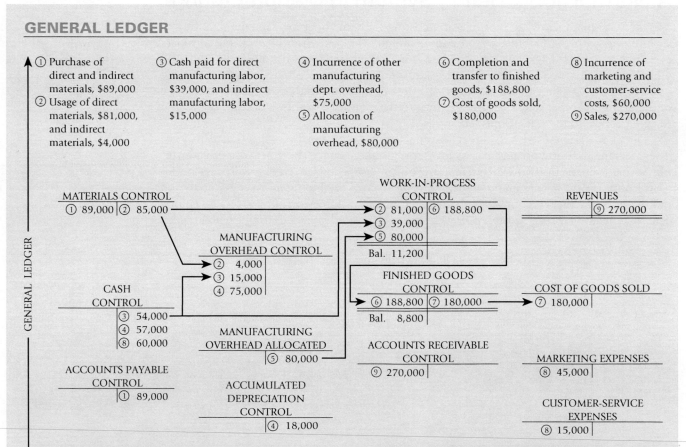

GENERAL LEDGER

① Purchase of direct and indirect materials, $89,000
② Usage of direct materials, $81,000, and indirect materials, $4,000

③ Cash paid for direct manufacturing labor, $39,000, and indirect manufacturing labor, $15,000

④ Incurrence of other manufacturing dept. overhead, $75,000
⑤ Allocation of manufacturing overhead, $80,000

⑥ Completion and transfer to finished goods, $188,800
⑦ Cost of goods sold, $180,000

⑧ Incurrence of marketing and customer-service costs, $60,000
⑨ Sales, $270,000

GENERAL LEDGER

MATERIALS CONTROL
① 89,000 | ② 85,000

MANUFACTURING OVERHEAD CONTROL
② 4,000
③ 15,000
④ 75,000

CASH CONTROL
③ 54,000
④ 57,000
⑧ 60,000

ACCOUNTS PAYABLE CONTROL
① 89,000

MANUFACTURING OVERHEAD ALLOCATED
⑤ 80,000

ACCUMULATED DEPRECIATION CONTROL
④ 18,000

WORK-IN-PROCESS CONTROL
② 81,000 | ⑥ 188,800
③ 39,000
⑤ 80,000
Bal. 11,200

FINISHED GOODS CONTROL
⑥ 188,800 | ⑦ 180,000
Bal. 8,800

ACCOUNTS RECEIVABLE CONTROL
⑨ 270,000

REVENUES
⑨ 270,000

COST OF GOODS SOLD
⑦ 180,000

MARKETING EXPENSES
⑧ 45,000

CUSTOMER-SERVICE EXPENSES
⑧ 15,000

The debit balance of $11,200 in the Work-in-Process Control account represents the total cost of all jobs that have not been completed as of the end of February 2011. There were no incomplete jobs as of the beginning of February 2011.

The debit balance of $8,800 in the Finished Goods Control account represents the cost of all jobs that have been completed but not sold as of the end of February 2011. There were no jobs completed but not sold as of the beginning of February 2011.

Exhibit 4-7 are based on the transactions and journal entries that follow. As you go through each journal entry, use Exhibit 4-7 to see how the various entries being made come together. General ledger accounts with "Control" in the titles (for example, Materials Control and Accounts Payable Control) have underlying subsidiary ledgers that contain additional details, such as each type of material in inventory and individual suppliers that Robinson must pay.

Some companies simultaneously make entries in the general ledger and subsidiary ledger accounts. Others, such as Robinson, make entries in the subsidiary ledger when transactions occur and entries in the general ledger less frequently, on a monthly basis.

A general ledger should be viewed as only one of many tools that assist management in planning and control. To control operations, managers rely on not only the source documents used to record amounts in the subsidiary ledgers, but also on nonfinancial information such as the percentage of jobs requiring rework.

Explanations of Transactions

We next look at a summary of Robinson Company's transactions for February 2011 and the corresponding journal entries for those transactions.

1. Purchases of materials (direct and indirect) on credit, $89,000

Materials Control	89,000	
Accounts Payable Control		89,000

2. Usage of direct materials, $81,000, and indirect materials, $4,000

Work-in-Process Control	81,000	
Manufacturing Overhead Control	4,000	
Materials Control		85,000

3. Manufacturing payroll for February: direct labor, $39,000, and indirect labor, $15,000, paid in cash

Work-in-Process Control	39,000	
Manufacturing Overhead Control	15,000	
Cash Control		54,000

4. Other manufacturing overhead costs incurred during February, $75,000, consisting of supervision and engineering salaries, $44,000 (paid in cash); plant utilities, repairs, and insurance, $13,000 (paid in cash); and plant depreciation, $18,000

Manufacturing Overhead Control	75,000	
Cash Control		57,000
Accumulated Depreciation Control		18,000

5. Allocation of manufacturing overhead to jobs, $80,000

Work-in-Process Control	80,000	
Manufacturing Overhead Allocated		80,000

Under normal costing, **manufacturing overhead allocated**—also called **manufacturing overhead applied**—is the amount of manufacturing overhead costs allocated to individual jobs based on the budgeted rate multiplied by actual quantity used of the allocation base. Keep in mind the distinct difference between transactions 4 and 5. In transaction 4, all actual overhead costs incurred throughout the month are added (debited) to the Manufacturing Overhead Control account. These costs are *not* debited to Work-in-Process Control because, unlike direct costs, they cannot be traced to individual jobs. Manufacturing overhead costs are added (debited) to individual jobs and to Work-in-Process Control *only when* manufacturing overhead costs are allocated in Transaction 5. At the time these costs are allocated, Manufacturing Overhead Control is, *in effect*, decreased (credited) via its contra account, Manufacturing Overhead Allocated. Recall that under normal costing, the budgeted manufacturing overhead rate of $40 per direct manufacturing labor-hour is calculated at the beginning of the year on the basis of predictions of annual manufacturing overhead costs and the annual quantity of the cost-allocation base. Almost certainly, the overhead allocated will differ from the actual overhead incurred. In a later section, we discuss what to do with this difference.

6. Completion and transfer of individual jobs to finished goods, $188,800

Finished Goods Control	188,800	
Work-in-Process Control		188,800

7. Cost of goods sold, $180,000

Cost of Goods Sold	180,000	
Finished Goods Control		180,000

8. Marketing costs for February, $45,000, and customer service costs for February, $15,000, paid in cash

Marketing Expenses	45,000	
Customer Service Expenses	15,000	
Cash Control		60,000

9. Sales revenues, all on credit, $270,000

Accounts Receivable Control	270,000	
Revenues		270,000

Subsidiary Ledgers

Exhibits 4-8 and 4-9 present subsidiary ledgers that contain the underlying details—the "worm's-eye view" that helps Robinson's managers keep track of the WPP 298 job, as opposed to the "bird's-eye view" of the general ledger. The sum of all entries in

---

Exhibit 4-8 Subsidiary Ledger for Materials, Labor, and Manufacturing Department Overhead[1]

PANEL A: Materials Records by Type of Materials

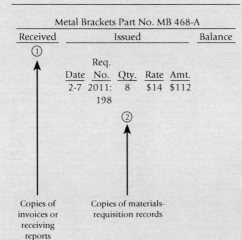

Metal Brackets Part No. MB 468-A

Received	Issued				Balance
①					
	Date	Req. No.	Qty.	Rate	Amt.
	2-7 2011:	198	8	$14	$112
		②			

Copies of invoices or receiving reports

Copies of materials-requisition records

Total cost of all types of materials received in February, $89,000

Total cost of all types of materials issued in February, $85,000

PANEL B: Labor Records by Employee

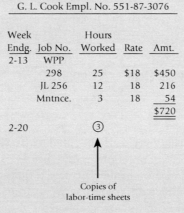

G. L. Cook Empl. No. 551-87-3076

Week Endg.	Job No.	Hours Worked	Rate	Amt.
2-13	WPP			
	298	25	$18	$450
	JL 256	12	18	216
	Mntnce.	3	18	54
				$720
2-20	③			

Copies of labor-time sheets

Total cost of all direct and indirect manufacturing labor incurred in February, $54,000 ($39,000 + $15,000)

PANEL C: Manufacturing Department Overhead Records by Month

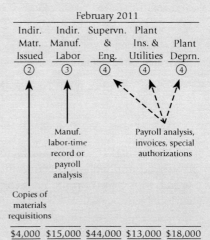

February 2011

Indir. Matr. Issued	Indir. Manuf. Labor	Supervn. & Eng.	Plant Ins. & Utilities	Plant Deprn.
②	③	④	④	④
	Manuf. labor-time record or payroll analysis		Payroll analysis, invoices, special authorizations	
$4,000	$15,000	$44,000	$13,000	$18,000

Copies of materials requisitions

Other manufacturing overhead costs incurred in February, $75,000

[1]The arrows show how the supporting documentation (for example, copies of materials requisition records) results in the journal entry number shown in circles (for example, journal entry number 2) that corresponds to the entries in Exhibit 4-7.

| Exhibit 4-9 | Subsidiary Ledger for Individual Jobs[1] |

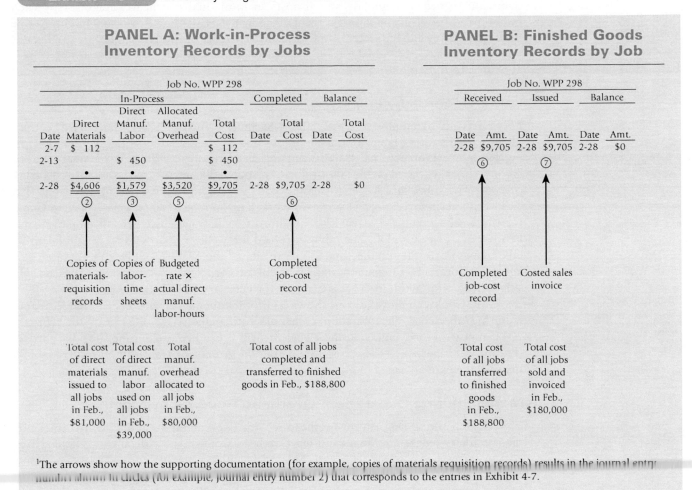

PANEL A: Work-in-Process Inventory Records by Jobs

PANEL B: Finished Goods Inventory Records by Job

[1]The arrows show how the supporting documentation (for example, copies of materials requisition records) results in the journal entry number shown in circles (for example, journal entry number 2) that corresponds to the entries in Exhibit 4-7.

underlying subsidiary ledgers equals the total amount in the corresponding general ledger control accounts.

Material Records by Type of Materials

The subsidiary ledger for materials at Robinson Company—called *Materials Records*—keeps a continuous record of quantity received, quantity issued to jobs, and inventory balances for each type of material. Panel A of Exhibit 4-8 shows the Materials Record for Metal Brackets (Part No. MB 468-A). In many companies, the source documents supporting the receipt and issue of materials (the material requisition record in Exhibit 4-3, Panel A, p. 106) are scanned into a computer. Software programs then automatically update the Materials Records and make all the necessary accounting entries in the subsidiary and general ledgers. The cost of materials received across all types of direct and indirect material records for February 2011 is $89,000 (Exhibit 4-8, Panel A). The cost of materials issued across all types of direct and indirect material records for February 2011 is $85,000 (Exhibit 4-8, Panel A).

As direct materials are used, they are recorded as issued in the Materials Records (see Exhibit 4-8, Panel A, for a record of the Metal Brackets issued for the WPP machine job). Direct materials are also charged to Work-in-Process Inventory Records for Jobs, which are the subsidiary ledger accounts for the Work-in-Process Control account in the general ledger. For example, the metal brackets used in the WPP machine job appear as direct material costs of $112 in the subsidiary ledger under the work-in-process inventory record for WPP 298 (Exhibit 4-9, Panel A, based on the job-cost record source document in Exhibit 4-2, p. 105.). The cost of direct materials used across all job-cost records for February 2011 is $81,000 (Exhibit 4-9, Panel A).

As indirect materials (for example, lubricants) are used, they are charged to the Manufacturing Department overhead records (Exhibit 4-8, Panel C), which comprise the subsidiary ledger for Manufacturing Overhead Control. The Manufacturing Department overhead records accumulate actual costs in individual overhead categories by each indirect-cost-pool account in the general ledger. Recall that Robinson has only one indirect-cost pool: Manufacturing Overhead. The cost of indirect materials used is not added directly to individual job records. Instead, the cost of these indirect materials is allocated to individual job records as a part of manufacturing overhead.

Labor Records by Employee

Labor records by employee (see Exhibit 4-8, Panel B for G. L. Cook) are used to trace direct manufacturing labor to individual jobs and to accumulate the indirect manufacturing labor in Manufacturing Department overhead records (Exhibit 4-8, Panel C). The labor records are based on the labor-time sheet source documents (see Exhibit 4-3, Panel B, p. 106). The subsidiary ledger for employee labor records shows the different jobs that G. L. Cook, Employee No. 551-87-3076 worked on and the $720 of wages owed to Cook, for the week ending February 13. The sum of total wages owed to all employees for February 2011 is $54,000. The job-cost record for WPP 298 shows direct manufacturing labor costs of $450 for the time Cook spent on the WPP machine job (Exhibit 4-9, Panel A). Total direct manufacturing labor costs recorded in all job-cost records (the subsidiary ledger for Work-in-Process Control) for February 2011 is $39,000.

G. L. Cook's employee record shows $54 for maintenance, which is an indirect manufacturing labor cost. The total indirect manufacturing labor costs of $15,000 for February 2011 appear in the Manufacturing Department overhead records in the subsidiary ledger (Exhibit 4-8, Panel C). These costs, by definition, cannot be traced to an individual job. Instead, they are allocated to individual jobs as a part of manufacturing overhead.

Manufacturing Department Overhead Records by Month

The Manufacturing Department overhead records (see Exhibit 4-8, Panel C) that make up the subsidiary ledger for Manufacturing Overhead Control show details of different categories of overhead costs such as indirect materials, indirect manufacturing labor, supervision and engineering, plant insurance and utilities, and plant depreciation. The source documents for these entries include invoices (for example, a utility bill) and special schedules (for example, a depreciation schedule) from the responsible accounting officer. Manufacturing department overhead for February 2011 is indirect materials, $4,000; indirect manufacturing labor, $15,000; and other manufacturing overhead, $75,000 (Exhibit 4-8, Panel C).

Work-in-Process Inventory Records by Jobs

As we have already discussed, the job-cost record for each individual job in the subsidiary ledger is debited by the actual cost of direct materials and direct manufacturing labor used by individual jobs. In Robinson's normal-costing system, the job-cost record for each individual job in the subsidiary ledger is also debited for manufacturing overhead allocated based on the budgeted manufacturing overhead rate times the actual direct manufacturing labor-hours used in that job. For example, the job-cost record for Job WPP 298 (Exhibit 4-9, Panel A) shows Manufacturing Overhead Allocated of $3,520 (budgeted rate of $40 per labor-hour × 88 actual direct manufacturing labor-hours used). For the 2,000 actual direct manufacturing labor-hours used for all jobs in February 2011, total manufacturing overhead allocated equals $40 per labor-hour × 2,000 direct manufacturing labor-hours = $80,000.

Finished Goods Inventory Records by Jobs

Exhibit 4-9, Panel A, shows that Job WPP 298 was completed at a cost of $9,705. Job WPP 298 also simultaneously appears in the finished goods records of the subsidiary ledger. The total cost of all jobs completed and transferred to finished goods in February 2011 is $188,800 (Exhibit 4-9, Panels A and B). Exhibit 4-9, Panel B, indicates that Job WPP 298 was sold and delivered to the customer on February 28, 2011, at which time $9,705 was transferred from finished goods to cost of goods sold. The total cost of all jobs sold and invoiced in February 2011 is $180,000 (Exhibit 4-9, Panel B).

Revenues		$270,000
Cost of goods sold ($180,000 + $14,000[1])		194,000
Gross margin		76,000
Operating costs		
Marketing costs	$45,000	
Customer-service costs	15,000	
Total operating costs		60,000
Operating income		$ 16,000

[1]Cost of goods sold has been increased by $14,000, the difference between the Manufacturing overhead control account ($94,000) and the Manufacturing overhead allocated ($80,000). In a later section of this chapter, we discuss this adjustment, which represents the amount by which actual manufacturing overhead cost exceeds the manufacturing overhead allocated to jobs during February 2011.

Other Subsidiary Records

Just as in manufacturing payroll, Robinson maintains employee labor records in subsidiary ledgers for marketing and customer service payroll as well as records for different types of advertising costs (print, television, and radio). An accounts receivable subsidiary ledger is also used to record the February 2011 amounts due from each customer, including the $15,000 due from the sale of Job WPP 298.

At this point, pause and review the nine entries in this illustration. Exhibit 4-7 is a handy summary of all nine general-ledger entries presented in T-account form. Be sure to trace each journal entry, step-by-step, to T-accounts in the general ledger presented in Exhibit 4-7.

Exhibit 4-10 provides Robinson's income statement for February 2011 using information from entries 7, 8, and 9. If desired, the cost of goods sold calculations can be further subdivided and presented in the format of Exhibit 2-8, page 40.

Nonmanufacturing Costs and Job Costing

Chapter 2 (pp. 45–47) pointed out that companies use product costs for different purposes. The product costs reported as inventoriable costs to shareholders may differ from product costs reported for government contracting and may also differ from product costs reported to managers for guiding pricing and product-mix decisions. We emphasize that even though marketing and customer-service costs are expensed when incurred for financial accounting purposes, companies often trace or allocate these costs to individual jobs for pricing, product-mix, and cost-management decisions.

To identify marketing and customer-service costs of individual jobs, Robinson can use the same approach to job costing described earlier in this chapter in the context of manufacturing. Robinson can trace the direct marketing costs and customer-service costs to jobs. Assume marketing and customer-service costs have the same cost-allocation base, revenues, and are included in a single cost pool. Robinson can then calculate a budgeted indirect-cost rate by dividing budgeted indirect marketing costs plus budgeted indirect customer-service costs by budgeted revenues. Robinson can use this rate to allocate these indirect costs to jobs. For example, if this rate were 15% of revenues, Robinson would allocate $2,250 to Job WPP 298 (0.15 × $15,000, the revenue from the job). By assigning both manufacturing costs and nonmanufacturing costs to jobs, Robinson can compare all costs against the revenues that different jobs generate.

Decision Point

How are transactions recorded in a manufacturing job-costing system?

Budgeted Indirect Costs and End-of-Accounting-Year Adjustments

Using budgeted indirect-cost rates and normal costing instead of actual costing has the advantage that indirect costs can be assigned to individual jobs on an ongoing and timely basis, rather than only at the end of the fiscal year when actual costs are known. However, budgeted rates are unlikely to equal actual rates because they are based on

Learning Objective 7

Dispose of under- or overallocated manufacturing overhead costs at the end of the fiscal year using alternative methods

. . . for example, writing off this amount to the Cost of Goods Sold account

estimates made up to 12 months before actual costs are incurred. We now consider adjustments that are needed when, at the end of the fiscal year, indirect costs allocated differ from actual indirect costs incurred. Recall that for the numerator and denominator reasons discussed earlier (pp. 103–104), we do *not* expect actual overhead costs incurred each month to equal overhead costs allocated each month.

Underallocated and Overallocated Direct Costs

Underallocated indirect costs occur when the allocated amount of indirect costs in an accounting period is less than the actual (incurred) amount. **Overallocated indirect costs** occur when the allocated amount of indirect costs in an accounting period is greater than the actual (incurred) amount.

$$\text{Underallocated (overallocated) indirect costs} =$$
$$\text{Actual indirect costs incurred} - \text{Indirect costs allocated}$$

Underallocated (overallocated) indirect costs are also called **underapplied (overapplied) indirect costs** and **underabsorbed (overabsorbed) indirect costs**.

Consider the manufacturing overhead cost pool at Robinson Company. There are two indirect-cost accounts in the general ledger that have to do with manufacturing overhead:

1. Manufacturing Overhead Control, the record of the actual costs in all the individual overhead categories (such as indirect materials, indirect manufacturing labor, supervision, engineering, utilities, and plant depreciation)

2. Manufacturing Overhead Allocated, the record of the manufacturing overhead allocated to individual jobs on the basis of the budgeted rate multiplied by actual direct manufacturing labor-hours

At the end of the year, the overhead accounts show the following amounts.

Manufacturing Overhead Control		Manufacturing Overhead Allocated	
Bal. Dec. 31, 2011	1,215,000	Bal. Dec. 31, 2011	1,080,000

The $1,080,000 credit balance in Manufacturing Overhead Allocated results from multiplying the 27,000 actual direct manufacturing labor-hours worked on all jobs in 2011 by the budgeted rate of $40 per direct manufacturing labor-hour.

The $135,000 ($1,215,000 – $1,080,000) difference (a net debit) is an underallocated amount because actual manufacturing overhead costs are greater than the allocated amount. This difference arises from two reasons related to the computation of the $40 budgeted hourly rate:

1. **Numerator reason (indirect-cost pool).** Actual manufacturing overhead costs of $1,215,000 are greater than the budgeted amount of $1,120,000.

2. **Denominator reason (quantity of allocation base).** Actual direct manufacturing labor-hours of 27,000 are fewer than the budgeted 28,000 hours.

There are three main approaches to accounting for the $135,000 underallocated manufacturing overhead caused by Robinson underestimating manufacturing overhead costs and overestimating the quantity of the cost-allocation base: (1) adjusted allocation-rate approach, (2) proration approach, and (3) write-off to cost of goods sold approach.

Adjusted Allocation-Rate Approach

The **adjusted allocation-rate approach** restates all overhead entries in the general ledger and subsidiary ledgers using actual cost rates rather than budgeted cost rates. First, the actual manufacturing overhead rate is computed at the end of the fiscal year. Then, the manufacturing overhead costs allocated to every job during the year are recomputed using the actual manufacturing overhead rate (rather than the budgeted manufacturing overhead rate). Finally, end-of-year closing entries are made. The result is that at year-end, every job-cost record and finished goods record—as well as the ending Work-in-Process Control, Finished Goods Control, and Cost of Goods Sold accounts—represent actual manufacturing overhead costs incurred.

The widespread adoption of computerized accounting systems has greatly reduced the cost of using the adjusted allocation-rate approach. In our Robinson example, the actual manufacturing overhead ($1,215,000) exceeds the manufacturing overhead allocated ($1,080,000) by 12.5% [($1,215,000 – $1,080,000) ÷ $1,080,000]. At year-end, Robinson could increase the manufacturing overhead allocated to each job in 2011 by 12.5% using a single software command. The command would adjust both the subsidiary ledgers and the general ledger.

Consider the Western Pulp and Paper machine job, WPP 298. Under normal costing, the manufacturing overhead allocated to the job is $3,520 (the budgeted rate of $40 per direct manufacturing labor-hour × 88 hours). Increasing the manufacturing overhead allocated by 12.5%, or $440 ($3,520 × 0.125), means the adjusted amount of manufacturing overhead allocated to Job WPP 298 equals $3,960 ($3,520 + $440). Note from page 110 that using actual costing, manufacturing overhead allocated to this job is $3,960 (the actual rate of $45 per direct manufacturing labor-hour × 88 hours). Making this adjustment under normal costing for each job in the subsidiary ledgers ensures that all $1,215,000 of manufacturing overhead is allocated to jobs.

The adjusted allocation-rate approach yields the benefits of both the *timeliness and convenience of normal costing during the year and the allocation of actual manufacturing overhead costs at year-end.* Each individual job-cost record and the end-of-year account balances for inventories and cost of goods sold are adjusted to actual costs. After-the-fact analysis of actual profitability of individual jobs provides managers with accurate and useful insights for future decisions about job pricing, which jobs to emphasize, and ways to manage job costs.

Proration Approach

Proration spreads underallocated overhead or overallocated overhead among ending work-in-process inventory, finished goods inventory, and cost of goods sold. Materials inventory is not included in this proration, because no manufacturing overhead costs have been allocated to it. In our Robinson example, end-of-year proration is made to the ending balances in Work-in-Process Control, Finished Goods Control, and Cost of Goods Sold. Assume the following actual results for Robinson Company in 2011:

	Home Insert Page Layout Formulas Data		
	A	B	C
1	Account	Account Balance (Before Proration)	Allocated Manufacturing Overhead Included in Each Account Balance (Before Proration)
2	Work-in-process control	$ 50,000	$ 16,200
3	Finished goods control	75,000	31,320
4	Cost of goods sold	2,375,000	1,032,480
5		$2,500,000	$1,080,000

How should Robinson prorate the underallocated $135,000 of manufacturing overhead at the end of 2011?

Robinson prorates underallocated or overallocated amounts on the basis of the total amount of manufacturing overhead allocated in 2011 (before proration) in the ending balances of Work-in-Process Control, Finished Goods Control, and Cost of Goods Sold. The $135,000 underallocated overhead is prorated over the three affected accounts in proportion to the total amount of manufacturing overhead allocated (before proration) in column 2 of the following table, resulting in the ending balances (after proration) in column 5 at actual costs.

	Home	Insert	Page Layout	Formulas	Data	Review	View		
	A	B	C	D	E		F	G	

10		Account Balance (Before Proration)	Allocated Manufacturing Overhead Included in Each Account Balance (Before Proration)	Allocated Manufacturing Overhead Included in Each Account Balance as a Percent of Total	Proration of $135,000 of Underallocated Manufacturing Overhead		Account Balance (After Proration)
11	Account	(1)	(2)	(3) = (2) / $1,080,000	(4) = (3) x $135,000		(5) = (1) + (4)
12	Work-in-process control	$ 50,000	$ 16,200	1.5%	0.015 x $135,000 =	$ 2,025	$ 52,025
13	Finished goods control	75,000	31,320	2.9%	0.029 x 135,000 =	3,915	78,915
14	Cost of goods sold	2,375,000	1,032,480	95.6%	0.956 x 135,000 =	129,060	2,504,060
15	Total	$2,500,000	$1,080,000	100.0%		$135,000	$2,635,000

Prorating on the basis of the manufacturing overhead allocated (before proration) results in allocating manufacturing overhead based on actual manufacturing overhead costs. Recall that the actual manufacturing overhead ($1,215,000) in 2011 exceeds the manufacturing overhead allocated ($1,080,000) in 2011 by 12.5%. The proration amounts in column 4 can also be derived by multiplying the balances in column 2 by 0.125. For example, the $3,915 proration to Finished Goods is 0.125 × $31,320. Adding these amounts effectively means allocating manufacturing overhead at 112.5% of what had been allocated before. The journal entry to record this proration is as follows:

Work-in-Process Control	2,025	
Finished Goods Control	3,915	
Cost of Goods Sold	129,060	
Manufacturing Overhead Allocated	1,080,000	
Manufacturing Overhead Control		1,215,000

If manufacturing overhead had been overallocated, the Work-in-Process Control, Finished Goods Control, and Cost of Goods Sold accounts would be decreased (credited) instead of increased (debited).

This journal entry closes (brings to zero) the manufacturing overhead-related accounts and restates the 2011 ending balances for Work-in-Process Control, Finished Goods Control, and Cost of Goods Sold to what they would have been if actual manufacturing overhead rates had been used rather than budgeted manufacturing overhead rates. This method reports the same 2011 ending balances in the general ledger as the adjusted allocation-rate approach. However, unlike the adjusted allocation-rate approach, the sum of the amounts shown in the subsidiary ledgers will not match the amounts shown in the general ledger after proration. That's because the amounts in the subsidiary ledgers will still show allocated overhead based on budgeted manufacturing overhead rates. The proration approach only adjusts the general ledger and not the subsidiary ledgers to actual manufacturing overhead rates.

Some companies use the proration approach but base it on the ending balances of Work-in-Process Control, Finished Goods Control, and Cost of Goods Sold before proration (column 1 of the preceding table). The following table shows that prorations based on ending account balances are not the same as the more accurate prorations calculated earlier based on the amount of manufacturing overhead allocated to the accounts because the proportions of manufacturing overhead costs to total costs in these accounts are not the same.

| | Home | Insert | Page Layout | Formulas | Data | Review | View | | |

	A	B	C	D	E	F
1		Account Balance (Before Proration)	Account Balance as a Percent of Total	Proration of $135,000 of Underallocated Manufacturing Overhead		Account Balance (After Proration)
2	Account	(1)	(2) = (1) / $2,500,000	(3) = (2) x $135,000		(4) = (1) + (3)
3	Work-in-process control	$ 50,000	2.0%	0.02 x $135,000 =	$ 2,700	$ 52,700
4	Finished goods control	75,000	3.0%	0.03 x 135,000 =	4,050	79,050
5	Cost of goods sold	2,375,000	95.0%	0.95 x 135,000 =	128,250	2,503,250
6	Total	$2,500,000	100.0%		$135,000	$2,635,000

However, proration based on ending balances is frequently justified as being an expedient way of approximating the more accurate results from using manufacturing overhead costs allocated.

Write-Off to Cost of Goods Sold Approach

Under this approach, the total under- or overallocated manufacturing overhead is included in this year's Cost of Goods Sold. For Robinson, the journal entry would be as follows:

Cost of Goods Sold	135,000	
Manufacturing Overhead Allocated	1,080,000	
Manufacturing Overhead Control		1,215,000

Robinson's two Manufacturing Overhead accounts are closed with the difference between them included in cost of goods sold. The Cost of Goods Sold account after the write-off equals $2,510,000, the balance before the write-off of $2,375,000 *plus the underallocated* manufacturing overhead amount of $135,000.

Choice Among Approaches

Which of these three approaches is the best one to use? In making this decision, managers should be guided by the causes for underallocation or overallocation and the purpose of the adjustment. The most common purpose is to state the balance sheet and income statement amounts based on actual rather than budgeted manufacturing overhead rates.

Many management accountants, industrial engineers, and managers argue that to the extent that the under- or overallocated overhead cost measures inefficiency during the period, it should be written off to Cost of Goods Sold instead of being prorated. This line of reasoning argues for applying a combination of the write-off and proration methods. For example, the portion of the underallocated overhead cost that is due to inefficiency (say, because of excessive spending) and that could have been avoided should be written off to Cost of Goods Sold, whereas the portion that is unavoidable should be prorated. Unlike full proration, this approach avoids carrying the costs of inefficiency as part of inventory assets.

Proration should be based on the manufacturing overhead allocated component in the ending balances of Work-in-Process Control, Finished Goods Control, and Cost of Goods Sold. Prorating to each individual job (as in the adjusted allocation-rate approach) is only done if the goal is to develop the most accurate record of individual job costs for profitability analysis purposes.

For balance sheet and income statement reporting purposes, the write-off to Cost of Goods Sold is the simplest approach for dealing with under- or overallocated overhead. If the amount of under- or overallocated overhead is small—in comparison with total operating income or some other measure of materiality—the write-off to Cost of Goods Sold approach yields a good approximation to more accurate, but more complex, approaches. Companies are also becoming increasingly conscious of inventory control, and quantities of inventories are lower than they were in earlier years. As a result, cost of goods sold tends to be higher in relation to the dollar amount of work-in-process and finished goods inventories. Also, the inventory balances of job-costing companies are usually small

Decision Point

How should managers dispose of under- or overallocated manufacturing overhead costs at the end of the fiscal year?

because goods are often made in response to customer orders. Consequently, as is true in our Robinson example, writing off, instead of prorating, under- or overallocated overhead is unlikely to result in significant distortions in financial statements.

The Robinson Company illustration assumed that a single manufacturing overhead cost pool with direct manufacturing labor-hours as the cost-allocation base was appropriate for allocating all manufacturing overhead costs to jobs. Had Robinson used multiple cost-allocation bases, such as direct manufacturing labor-hours and machine-hours, it would have created two cost pools and calculated two budgeted overhead rates: one based on direct manufacturing labor-hours and the other based on machine-hours to allocate overhead costs to jobs. The general ledger would contain Manufacturing Overhead Control and Manufacturing Overhead Allocated amounts for each cost pool. End-of-year adjustments for under- or overallocated overhead costs would then be made separately for each cost pool.

Variations from Normal Costing: A Service-Sector Example

Job costing is also very useful in service industries such as accounting and consulting firms, advertising agencies, auto repair shops, and hospitals. In an accounting firm, each audit is a job. The costs of each audit are accumulated in a job-cost record, much like the document used by Robinson Company, based on the seven-step approach described earlier. On the basis of labor-time sheets, direct labor costs of the professional staff—audit partners, audit managers, and audit staff—are traced to individual jobs. Other direct costs, such as travel, out-of-town meals and lodging, phone, fax, and copying, are also traced to jobs. The costs of secretarial support, office staff, rent, and depreciation of furniture and equipment are indirect costs because these costs cannot be traced to jobs in an economically feasible way. Indirect costs are allocated to jobs, for example, using a cost-allocation base such as number of professional labor-hours.

In some service organizations, a variation from normal costing is helpful because actual direct-labor costs—the largest component of total costs—can be difficult to trace to jobs as they are completed. For example, in our audit illustration, the actual direct-labor costs may include bonuses that become known only at the end of the year (a numerator reason). Also, the hours worked each period might vary significantly depending on the number of working days each month and the demand from clients (a denominator reason). In situations like these, a company needing timely information during the progress of an audit (and not wanting to wait until the end of the fiscal year) will use budgeted rates for some direct costs and budgeted rates for indirect costs. All budgeted rates are calculated at the start of the fiscal year. In contrast, normal costing uses actual cost rates for all direct costs and budgeted cost rates only for indirect costs.

The mechanics of using budgeted rates for direct costs are similar to the methods employed when using budgeted rates for indirect costs in normal costing. We illustrate this for Donahue and Associates, a public accounting firm. For 2011, Donahue budgets total direct-labor costs of $14,400,000, total indirect costs of $12,960,000, and total direct (professional) labor-hours of 288,000. In this case,

$$\text{Budgeted direct-labor cost rate} = \frac{\text{Budgeted total direct-labor costs}}{\text{Budgeted total direct-labor hours}}$$

$$= \frac{\$14,400,000}{288,000 \text{ direct labor-hours}} = \$50 \text{ per direct labor-hour}$$

Assuming only one indirect-cost pool and total direct-labor costs as the cost-allocation base,

$$\text{Budgeted indirect cost rate} = \frac{\text{Budgeted total costs in indirect cost pool}}{\text{Budgeted total quantity of cost-allocation base (direct-labor costs)}}$$

$$= \frac{\$12,960,000}{\$14,400,000} = 0.90, \text{ or } 90\% \text{ of direct-labor costs}$$

Suppose that in March 2011, an audit of Hanley Transport, a client of Donahue, uses 800 direct labor-hours. Donahue calculates the direct-labor costs of the Hanley Transport audit by multiplying the budgeted direct-labor cost rate, $50 per direct labor-hour, by

800, the actual quantity of direct labor-hours. The indirect costs allocated to the Hanley Transport audit are determined by multiplying the budgeted indirect-cost rate (90%) by the direct-labor costs assigned to the job ($40,000). Assuming no other direct costs for travel and the like, the cost of the Hanley Transport audit is as follows:

Direct-labor costs, $50 × 800	$40,000
Indirect costs allocated, 90% × $40,000	36,000
Total	$76,000

At the end of the fiscal year, the direct costs traced to jobs using budgeted rates will generally not equal actual direct costs because the actual rate and the budgeted rate are developed at different times using different information. End-of-year adjustments for under- or overallocated direct costs would need to be made in the same way that adjustments are made for under- or overallocated indirect costs.

The Donahue and Associates example illustrates that all costing systems do not exactly match either the actual-costing system or the normal-costing system described earlier in the chapter. As another example, engineering consulting firms often have some actual direct costs (cost of making blueprints or fees paid to outside experts), other direct costs (professional labor costs) assigned to jobs using a budgeted rate, and indirect costs (engineering and office-support costs) allocated to jobs using a budgeted rate. Therefore, users of costing systems should be aware of the different systems that they may encounter.

◄ Decision Point

What are some variations from normal costing?

Problem for Self-Study

You are asked to bring the following incomplete accounts of Endeavor Printing, Inc., up-to-date through January 31, 2012. Consider the data that appear in the T-accounts as well as the following information in items (a) through (j).

Endeavor's normal-costing system has two direct-cost categories (direct material costs and direct manufacturing labor costs) and one indirect-cost pool (manufacturing overhead costs, which are allocated using direct manufacturing labor costs).

Materials Control		Wages Payable Control	
12-31-2011 Bal. 15,000			1-31-2012 Bal. 3,000

Work-in-Process Control		Manufacturing Overhead Control	
		1-31-2012 Bal. 57,000	

Finished Goods Control		Costs of Goods Sold	
12-31-2011 Bal. 20,000			

Additional information follows:

a. Manufacturing overhead is allocated using a budgeted rate that is set every December. Management forecasts next year's manufacturing overhead costs and next year's direct manufacturing labor costs. The budget for 2012 is $600,000 for manufacturing overhead costs and $400,000 for direct manufacturing labor costs.

b. The only job unfinished on January 31, 2012, is No. 419, on which direct manufacturing labor costs are $2,000 (125 direct manufacturing labor-hours) and direct material costs are $8,000.

c. Total direct materials issued to production during January 2012 are $90,000.

d. Cost of goods completed during January is $180,000.

e. Materials inventory as of January 31, 2012, is $20,000.

f. Finished goods inventory as of January 31, 2012, is $15,000.

g. All plant workers earn the same wage rate. Direct manufacturing labor-hours used for January total 2,500 hours. Other labor costs total $10,000.

h. The gross plant payroll paid in January equals $52,000. Ignore withholdings.

i. All "actual" manufacturing overhead incurred during January has already been posted.

j. All materials are direct materials.

Required   Calculate the following:

1. Materials purchased during January
2. Cost of Goods Sold during January
3. Direct manufacturing labor costs incurred during January
4. Manufacturing Overhead Allocated during January
5. Balance, Wages Payable Control, December 31, 2011
6. Balance, Work-in-Process Control, January 31, 2012
7. Balance, Work-in-Process Control, December 31, 2011
8. Manufacturing Overhead Underallocated or Overallocated for January 2012

Solution

Amounts from the T-accounts are labeled "(T)."

1. From Materials Control T-account, Materials purchased: $90,000 (c) + $20,000 (e) − $15,000 (T) = $95,000
2. From Finished Goods Control T-account, Cost of Goods Sold: $20,000 (T) + $180,000 (d) − $15,000 (f) = $185,000
3. Direct manufacturing wage rate: $2,000 (b) ÷ 125 direct manufacturing labor-hours (b) = $16 per direct manufacturing labor-hour
      Direct manufacturing labor costs: 2,500 direct manufacturing labor-hours (g) × $16 per hour = $40,000
4. Manufacturing overhead rate: $600,000 (a) ÷ $400,000 (a) = 150%

Manufacturing Overhead Allocated: 150% of $40,000 = 1.50 × $40,000 (see 3) = $60,000

5. From Wages Payable Control T-account, Wages Payable Control, December 31, 2011: $52,000 (h) + $3,000 (T) − $40,000 (see 3) − $10,000 (g) = $5,000
6. Work-in-Process Control, January 31, 2012: $8,000 (b) + $2,000 (b) + 150% of $2,000 (b) = $13,000 (This answer is used in item 7.)
7. From Work-in-Process Control T-account, Work-in-Process Control, December 31, 2011: $180,000 (d) + $13,000 (see 6) − $90,000 (c) − $40,000 (see 3) − $60,000 (see 4) = $3,000
8. Manufacturing overhead overallocated: $60,000 (see 4) − $57,000 (T) = $3,000.

Letters alongside entries in T-accounts correspond to letters in the preceding additional information. Numbers alongside entries in T-accounts correspond to numbers in the preceding requirements.

Materials Control

December 31, 2011, Bal.	(given)	15,000			
	(1)	95,000*		(c)	90,000
January 31, 2012, Bal.	(e)	20,000			

Work-in-Process Control

December 31, 2011, Bal.	(7)	3,000		(d)	180,000
Direct materials	(c)	90,000			
Direct manufacturing labor	(b) (g) (3)	40,000			
Manufacturing overhead allocated	(3) (a) (4)	60,000			
January 31, 2012, Bal.	(b) (6)	13,000			

Finished Goods Control

December 31, 2011, Bal.	(given)	20,000		(2)	185,000
	(d)	180,000			
January 31, 2012, Bal.	(f)	15,000			

*Can be computed only after all other postings in the account have been made.

Wages Payable Control

(h)	52,000	December 31, 2011, Bal.	(5)	5,000
			(g) (3)	40,000
			(g)	10,000
		January 31, 2012	(given)	3,000

Manufacturing Overhead Control

Total January charges	(given)	57,000	

Manufacturing Overhead Allocated

	(3) (a) (4)	60,000

Cost of Goods Sold

(d) (f) (2)	185,000	

Decision Points

The following question-and-answer format summarizes the chapter's learning objectives. Each decision presents a key question related to a learning objective. The guidelines are the answer to that question.

Decision	Guidelines
1. What are the building-block concepts of a costing system?	The building-block concepts of a costing system are cost object, direct costs of a cost object, indirect costs of a cost object, cost pool, and cost-allocation base. Costing system overview diagrams represent these concepts in a systematic way. Costing systems aim to report cost numbers that reflect the way chosen cost objects (such as products or services) use the resources of an organization.
2. How do you distinguish job costing from process costing?	Job-costing systems assign costs to distinct units of a product or service. Process-costing systems assign costs to masses of identical or similar units and compute unit costs on an average basis. These two costing systems represent opposite ends of a continuum. The costing systems of many companies combine some elements of both job costing and process costing.
3. What is the main challenge of implementing job-costing systems?	The main challenge of implementing job-costing systems is estimating actual costs of jobs in a timely manner.
4. How do you implement a normal-costing system?	A general seven-step approach to normal costing requires identifying (1) the job, (2) the actual direct costs, (3) the budgeted cost-allocation bases, (4) the budgeted indirect cost pools, (5) the budgeted cost-allocation rates, (6) the allocated indirect costs (budgeted rate times actual quantity), and (7) the total direct and indirect costs of a job.
5. How do you distinguish actual costing from normal costing?	Actual costing and normal costing differ in the type of indirect-cost rates used:

	Actual Costing	**Normal Costing**
Direct-cost rates	Actual rates	Actual rates
Indirect-cost rates	Actual rates	Budgeted rates

Both systems use actual quantities of inputs for tracing direct costs and actual quantities of the allocation bases for allocating indirect costs.

6. How are transactions recorded in a manufacturing job-costing system?	A job-costing system in manufacturing records the flow of inventoriable costs in the general and subsidiary ledgers for (a) acquisition of materials and other manufacturing inputs, (b) their conversion into work in process, (c) their conversion into finished goods, and (d) the sale of finished goods. The job costing system also expenses period costs, such as marketing costs, as they are incurred.
7. How should managers dispose of under- or over-allocated manufacturing overhead costs at the end of the fiscal year?	The two theoretically correct approaches to disposing of under- or overallocated manufacturing overhead costs at the end of the fiscal year for correctly stating balance sheet and income statement amounts are (1) to adjust the allocation rate and (2) to prorate on the basis of the total amount of the allocated manufacturing overhead cost in the ending balances of Work-in-Process Control, Finished Goods Control, and Cost of Goods Sold. Many companies, however, simply write off amounts of under- or overallocated manufacturing overhead to Cost of Goods Sold when amounts are immaterial.
8. What are some variations from normal costing?	In some variations from normal costing, organizations use budgeted rates to assign direct costs, as well as indirect costs, to jobs.

Terms to Learn

This chapter and the Glossary at the end of the book contain definitions of the following important terms:

actual costing (**p. 102**)
actual indirect-cost rate (**p. 110**)
adjusted allocation-rate approach (**p. 118**)
budgeted indirect-cost rate (**p. 104**)
cost-allocation base (**p. 100**)
cost-application base (**p. 100**)
cost pool (**p. 100**)
job (**p. 100**)
job-cost record (**p. 104**)

job-cost sheet (**p. 104**)
job-costing system (**p. 100**)
labor-time sheet (**p. 106**)
manufacturing overhead allocated (**p. 113**)
manufacturing overhead applied (**p. 113**)
materials-requisition record (**p. 105**)
normal costing (**p. 104**)

overabsorbed indirect costs (**p. 118**)
overallocated indirect costs (**p. 118**)
overapplied indirect costs (**p. 118**)
process-costing system (**p. 101**)
proration (**p. 119**)
source document (**p. 104**)
underabsorbed indirect costs (**p. 118**)
underallocated indirect costs (**p. 118**)
underapplied indirect costs (**p. 118**)

Assignment Material

MyAccountingLab

Questions

4-1 Define cost pool, cost tracing, cost allocation, and cost-allocation base.
4-2 How does a job-costing system differ from a process-costing system?
4-3 Why might an advertising agency use job costing for an advertising campaign by Pepsi, whereas a bank might use process costing to determine the cost of checking account deposits?
4-4 Describe the seven steps in job costing.
4-5 Give examples of two cost objects in companies using job costing?
4-6 Describe three major source documents used in job-costing systems.
4-7 What is the advantage of using computerized source documents to prepare job-cost records?
4-8 Give two reasons why most organizations use an annual period rather than a weekly or monthly period to compute budgeted indirect-cost rates.
4-9 Distinguish between actual costing and normal costing.
4-10 Describe two ways in which a house construction company may use job-cost information.
4-11 Comment on the following statement: "In a normal-costing system, the amounts in the Manufacturing Overhead Control account will always equal the amounts in the Manufacturing Overhead Allocated account."
4-12 Describe three different debit entries to the Work-in-Process Control T-account under normal costing.
4-13 Describe three alternative ways to dispose of under- or overallocated overhead costs.
4-14 When might a company use budgeted costs rather than actual costs to compute direct-labor rates?
4-15 Describe briefly why Electronic Data Interchange (EDI) is helpful to managers.

Exercises

4-16 Job costing, process costing. In each of the following situations, determine whether job costing or process costing would be more appropriate.

a. A CPA firm
b. An oil refinery
c. A custom furniture manufacturer
d. A tire manufacturer
e. A textbook publisher
f. A pharmaceutical company
g. An advertising agency
h. An apparel manufacturing plant
i. A flour mill
j. A paint manufacturer
k. A medical care facility

l. A landscaping company
m. A cola-drink-concentrate producer
n. A movie studio
o. A law firm
p. A commercial aircraft manufacturer
q. A management consulting firm
r. A breakfast-cereal company
s. A catering service
t. A paper mill
u. An auto repair shop

4-17 Actual costing, normal costing, accounting for manufacturing overhead. Destin Products uses a job-costing system with two direct-cost categories (direct materials and direct manufacturing labor) and one manufacturing overhead cost pool. Destin allocates manufacturing overhead costs using direct manufacturing labor costs. Destin provides the following information:

	Budget for 2011	Actual Results for 2011
Direct material costs	$2,000,000	$1,900,000
Direct manufacturing labor costs	1,500,000	1,450,000
Manufacturing overhead costs	2,700,000	2,755,000

Required

1. Compute the actual and budgeted manufacturing overhead rates for 2011.
2. During March, the job-cost record for Job 626 contained the following information:

Direct materials used	$40,000
Direct manufacturing labor costs	$30,000

Compute the cost of Job 626 using (a) actual costing and (b) normal costing.
3. At the end of 2011, compute the under- or overallocated manufacturing overhead under normal costing. Why is there no under- or overallocated overhead under actual costing?

4-18 Job costing, normal and actual costing. Amesbury Construction assembles residential houses. It uses a job-costing system with two direct-cost categories (direct materials and direct labor) and one indirect-cost pool (assembly support). Direct labor-hours is the allocation base for assembly support costs. In December 2010, Amesbury budgets 2011 assembly-support costs to be $8,300,000 and 2011 direct labor-hours to be 166,000.

At the end of 2011, Amesbury is comparing the costs of several jobs that were started and completed in 2011.

	Laguna Model	Mission Model
Construction period	Feb–June 2011	May–Oct 2011
Direct material costs	$106,760	$127,550
Direct labor costs	$ 36,950	$ 41,320
Direct labor-hours	960	1,050

Direct materials and direct labor are paid for on a contract basis. The costs of each are known when direct materials are used or when direct labor-hours are worked. The 2011 actual assembly-support costs were $6,520,000, and the actual direct labor-hours were 163,000.

Required

1. Compute the (a) budgeted indirect-cost rate and (b) actual indirect-cost rate. Why do they differ?
2. What are the job costs of the Laguna Model and the Mission Model using (a) normal costing and (b) actual costing?
3. Why might Amesbury Construction prefer normal costing over actual costing?

4-19 Budgeted manufacturing overhead rate, allocated manufacturing overhead. Gammaro Company uses normal costing. It allocates manufacturing overhead costs using a budgeted rate per machine-hour. The following data are available for 2011:

Budgeted manufacturing overhead costs	$4,200,000
Budgeted machine-hours	175,000
Actual manufacturing overhead costs	$4,050,000
Actual machine-hours	170,000

Required

1. Calculate the budgeted manufacturing overhead rate.
2. Calculate the manufacturing overhead allocated during 2011.
3. Calculate the amount of under- or overallocated manufacturing overhead.

4-20 Job costing, accounting for manufacturing overhead, budgeted rates. The Lynn Company uses a normal job-costing system at its Minneapolis plant. The plant has a machining department and an assembly department. Its job-costing system has two direct-cost categories (direct materials and direct manufacturing labor) and two manufacturing overhead cost pools (the machining department overhead, allocated to jobs based on actual machine-hours, and the assembly department overhead, allocated to jobs based on actual direct manufacturing labor costs). The 2011 budget for the plant is as follows:

	Machining Department	Assembly Department
Manufacturing overhead	$1,800,000	$3,600,000
Direct manufacturing labor costs	$1,400,000	$2,000,000
Direct manufacturing labor-hours	100,000	200,000
Machine-hours	50,000	200,000

Required

1. Present an overview diagram of Lynn's job-costing system. Compute the budgeted manufacturing overhead rate for each department.
2. During February, the job-cost record for Job 494 contained the following:

	Machining Department	Assembly Department
Direct materials used	$45,000	$70,000
Direct manufacturing labor costs	$14,000	$15,000
Direct manufacturing labor-hours	1,000	1,500
Machine-hours	2,000	1,000

Compute the total manufacturing overhead costs allocated to Job 494.
3. At the end of 2011, the actual manufacturing overhead costs were $2,100,000 in machining and $3,700,000 in assembly. Assume that 55,000 actual machine-hours were used in machining and that actual direct manufacturing labor costs in assembly were $2,200,000. Compute the over- or underallocated manufacturing overhead for each department.

4-21 Job costing, consulting firm. Turner & Associates, a consulting firm, has the following condensed budget for 2011:

Revenues		$21,250,000
Total costs:		
Direct costs		
Professional Labor	$ 5,312,500	
Indirect costs		
Client support	13,600,000	18,912,500
Operating income		$ 2,337,500

Turner has a single direct-cost category (professional labor) and a single indirect-cost pool (client support). Indirect costs are allocated to jobs on the basis of professional labor costs.

Required

1. Prepare an overview diagram of the job-costing system. Calculate the 2011 budgeted indirect-cost rate for Turner & Associates.
2. The markup rate for pricing jobs is intended to produce operating income equal to 11% of revenues. Calculate the markup rate as a percentage of professional labor costs.
3. Turner is bidding on a consulting job for Tasty Chicken, a fast-food chain specializing in poultry meats. The budgeted breakdown of professional labor on the job is as follows:

Professional Labor Category	Budgeted Rate per Hour	Budgeted Hours
Director	$198	4
Partner	101	17
Associate	49	42
Assistant	36	153

Calculate the budgeted cost of the Tasty Chicken job. How much will Turner bid for the job if it is to earn its target operating income of 11% of revenues?

4-22 Time period used to compute indirect cost rates. Splash Manufacturing produces outdoor wading and slide pools. The company uses a normal-costing system and allocates manufacturing overhead on the basis of direct manufacturing labor-hours. Most of the company's production and sales occur in the first and second quarters of the year. The company is in danger of losing one of its larger customers, Sotco Wholesale, due to large fluctuations in price. The owner of Splash has requested an analysis of the manufacturing cost per unit in the second and third quarters. You have been provided the following budgeted information for the coming year:

	Quarter			
	1	2	3	4
Pools manufactured and sold	700	500	150	150

It takes 0.5 direct manufacturing labor-hour to make each pool. The actual direct material cost is $7.50 per pool. The actual direct manufacturing labor rate is $16 per hour. The budgeted variable manufacturing overhead rate is $12 per direct manufacturing labor-hour. Budgeted fixed manufacturing overhead costs are $10,500 each quarter.

1. Calculate the total manufacturing cost per unit for the second and third quarter assuming the company allocates manufacturing overhead costs based on the budgeted manufacturing overhead rate determined for each quarter.   **Required**
2. Calculate the total manufacturing cost per unit for the second and third quarter assuming the company allocates manufacturing overhead costs based on an annual budgeted manufacturing overhead rate.
3. Splash Manufacturing prices its pools at manufacturing cost plus 30%. Why might Sotco Wholesale be seeing large fluctuations in the prices of pools? Which of the methods described in requirements 1 and 2 would you recommend Splash use? Explain.

4-23 Accounting for manufacturing overhead. Consider the following selected cost data for the Pittsburgh Forging Company for 2011.

Budgeted manufacturing overhead costs	$7,500,000
Budgeted machine-hours	250,000
Actual manufacturing overhead costs	$7,300,000
Actual machine-hours	245,000

The company uses normal costing. Its job-costing system has a single manufacturing overhead cost pool. Costs are allocated to jobs using a budgeted machine-hour rate. Any amount of under- or overallocation is written off to Cost of Goods Sold.

1. Compute the budgeted manufacturing overhead rate.   **Required**
2. Prepare the journal entries to record the allocation of manufacturing overhead.
3. Compute the amount of under- or overallocation of manufacturing overhead. Is the amount material? Prepare a journal entry to dispose of this amount.

4-24 Job costing, journal entries. The University of Chicago Press is wholly owned by the university. It performs the bulk of its work for other university departments, which pay as though the press were an outside business enterprise. The press also publishes and maintains a stock of books for general sale. The press uses normal costing to cost each job. Its job-costing system has two direct-cost categories (direct materials and direct manufacturing labor) and one indirect-cost pool (manufacturing overhead, allocated on the basis of direct manufacturing labor costs).

The following data (in thousands) pertain to 2011:

Direct materials and supplies purchased on credit	$ 800
Direct materials used	710
Indirect materials issued to various production departments	100
Direct manufacturing labor	1,300
Indirect manufacturing labor incurred by various production departments	900
Depreciation on building and manufacturing equipment	400
Miscellaneous manufacturing overhead* incurred by various production departments (ordinarily would be detailed as repairs, photocopying, utilities, etc.)	550
Manufacturing overhead allocated at 160% of direct manufacturing labor costs	?
Cost of goods manufactured	4,120
Revenues	8,000
Cost of goods sold (before adjustment for under- or overallocated manufacturing overhead)	4,020
Inventories, December 31, 2010 (not 2011):	

---

* The term manufacturing overhead is not used uniformly. Other terms that are often encountered in printing companies include job overhead and shop overhead.

Materials Control	100
Work-in-Process Control	60
Finished Goods Control	500

Required

1. Prepare an overview diagram of the job-costing system at the University of Chicago Press.
2. Prepare journal entries to summarize the 2011 transactions. As your final entry, dispose of the year-end under- or overallocated manufacturing overhead as a write-off to Cost of Goods Sold. Number your entries. Explanations for each entry may be omitted.
3. Show posted T-accounts for all inventories, Cost of Goods Sold, Manufacturing Overhead Control, and Manufacturing Overhead Allocated.

4-25 **Journal entries, T-accounts, and source documents.** Production Company produces gadgets for the coveted small appliance market. The following data reflect activity for the year 2011:

Costs incurred:	
Purchases of direct materials (net) on credit	$124,000
Direct manufacturing labor cost	80,000
Indirect labor	54,500
Depreciation, factory equipment	30,000
Depreciation, office equipment	7,000
Maintenance, factory equipment	20,000
Miscellaneous factory overhead	9,500
Rent, factory building	70,000
Advertising expense	90,000
Sales commissions	30,000

Inventories:

	January 1, 2011	December 31, 2011
Direct materials	$ 9,000	$11,000
Work in process	6,000	21,000
Finished goods	69,000	24,000

Production Co. uses a normal costing system and allocates overhead to work in process at a rate of $2.50 per direct manufacturing labor dollar. Indirect materials are insignificant so there is no inventory account for indirect materials.

Required

1. Prepare journal entries to record the transactions for 2011 including an entry to close out over- or underallocated overhead to cost of goods sold. For each journal entry indicate the source document that would be used to authorize each entry. Also note which subsidiary ledger, if any, should be referenced as backup for the entry.
2. Post the journal entries to T-accounts for all of the inventories, Cost of Goods Sold, the Manufacturing Overhead Control Account, and the Manufacturing Overhead Allocated Account.

4-26 **Job costing, journal entries.** Donnell Transport assembles prestige manufactured homes. Its job costing system has two direct-cost categories (direct materials and direct manufacturing labor) and one indirect-cost pool (manufacturing overhead allocated at a budgeted $30 per machine-hour in 2011). The following data (in millions) pertain to operations for 2011:

Materials Control, beginning balance, January 1, 2011	$ 12
Work-in-Process Control, beginning balance, January 1, 2011	2
Finished Goods Control, beginning balance, January 1, 2011	6
Materials and supplies purchased on credit	150
Direct materials used	145
Indirect materials (supplies) issued to various production departments	10
Direct manufacturing labor	90
Indirect manufacturing labor incurred by various production departments	30
Depreciation on plant and manufacturing equipment	19
Miscellaneous manufacturing overhead incurred (ordinarily would be detailed as repairs, utilities, etc., with a corresponding credit to various liability accounts)	9
Manufacturing overhead allocated, 2,100,000 actual machine-hours	?
Cost of goods manufactured	294
Revenues	400
Cost of goods sold	292

Required

1. Prepare an overview diagram of Donnell Transport's job-costing system.
2. Prepare journal entries. Number your entries. Explanations for each entry may be omitted. Post to T-accounts. What is the ending balance of Work-in-Process Control?
3. Show the journal entry for disposing of under- or overallocated manufacturing overhead directly as a year-end write-off to Cost of Goods Sold. Post the entry to T-accounts.

4-27 Job costing, unit cost, ending work in process. Rafael Company produces pipes for concert-quality organs. Each job is unique. In April 2011, it completed all outstanding orders, and then, in May 2011, it worked on only two jobs, M1 and M2:

	Home	Insert	Page Layout	Formulas	Data
		A		B	C
1	**Rafael Company, May 2011**		**Job M1**	**Job M2**	
2	Direct materials		$ 78,000	$ 51,000	
3	Direct manufacturing labor		273,000	208,000	

Direct manufacturing labor is paid at the rate of $26 per hour. Manufacturing overhead costs are allocated at a budgeted rate of $20 per direct manufacturing labor-hour. Only Job M1 was completed in May.

Required

1. Calculate the total cost for Job M1.
2. 1,100 pipes were produced for Job M1. Calculate the cost per pipe.
3. Prepare the journal entry transferring Job M1 to finished goods.
4. What is the ending balance in the Work-in-Process Control account?

4-28 Job costing; actual, normal, and variation from normal costing. Chico & Partners, a Quebec-based public accounting partnership, specializes in audit services. Its job-costing system has a single direct-cost category (professional labor) and a single indirect-cost pool (audit support, which contains all costs of the Audit Support Department). Audit support costs are allocated to individual jobs using actual professional labor-hours. Chico & Partners employs 10 professionals to perform audit services.
     Budgeted and actual amounts for 2011 are as follows:

	Home	Insert	Page Layout	Formulas	Data
		A		B	C
1	**Chico & Partners**				
2	**Budget for 2011**				
3	Professional labor compensation		$990,000		
4	Audit support department costs		$774,000		
5	Professional labor-hours billed to clients		18,000	hours	
6					
7	**Actual results for 2011**				
8	Audit support department costs		$735,000		
9	Professional labor-hours billed to clients		17,500		
10	Actual professional labor cost rate		$ 59	per hour	

Required

1. Compute the direct-cost rate and the indirect-cost rate per professional labor-hour for 2011 under (a) actual costing, (b) normal costing, and (c) the variation from normal costing that uses budgeted rates for direct costs.
2. Chico's 2011 audit of Pierre & Co. was budgeted to take 150 hours of professional labor time. The actual professional labor time spent on the audit was 160 hours. Compute the cost of the Pierre & Co. audit using (a) actual costing, (b) normal costing, and (c) the variation from normal costing that uses budgeted rates for direct costs. Explain any differences in the job cost.

4-29 Job costing; actual, normal, and variation from normal costing. Braden Brothers, Inc., is an architecture firm specializing in high-rise buildings. Its job-costing system has a single direct-cost category (architectural labor) and a single indirect-cost pool, which contains all costs of supporting the office. Support costs are allocated to individual jobs using architect labor-hours. Braden Brothers employs 15 architects.

Budgeted and actual amounts for 2010 are as follows:

Braden Brothers, Inc.

Budget for 2010	
Architect labor cost	$2,880,000
Office support costs	$1,728,000
Architect labor-hours billed to clients	32,000 hours
Actual results for 2010	
Office support costs	$1,729,500
Architect labor-hours billed to clients	34,590 hours
Actual architect labor cost rate	$ 92 per hour

Required

1. Compute the direct-cost rate and the indirect-cost rate per architectural labor-hour for 2010 under (a) actual costing, (b) normal costing, and (c) the variation from normal costing that uses budgeted rates for direct costs.
2. Braden Brother's architectural sketches for Champ Tower in Houston was budgeted to take 275 hours of architectural labor time. The actual architectural labor time spent on the job was 250 hours. Compute the cost of the Champ Tower sketches using (a) actual costing, (b) normal costing, and (c) the variation from normal costing that uses budgeted rates for direct costs.

4-30 Proration of overhead. The Ride-On-Wave Company (ROW) produces a line of non-motorized boats. ROW uses a normal-costing system and allocates manufacturing overhead using direct manufacturing labor cost. The following data are for 2011:

Budgeted manufacturing overhead cost	$125,000
Budgeted direct manufacturing labor cost	$250,000
Actual manufacturing overhead cost	$117,000
Actual direct manufacturing labor cost	$228,000

Inventory balances on December 31, 2011, were as follows:

Account	Ending balance	2011 direct manufacturing labor cost in ending balance
Work in process	$ 50,700	$ 20,520
Finished goods	245,050	59,280
Cost of goods sold	549,250	148,200

Required

1. Calculate the manufacturing overhead allocation rate.
2. Compute the amount of under- or overallocated manufacturing overhead.
3. Calculate the ending balances in work in process, finished goods, and cost of goods sold if under-overallocated manufacturing overhead is as follows:
   a. Written off to cost of goods sold
   b. Prorated based on ending balances (before proration) in each of the three accounts
   c. Prorated based on the overhead allocated in 2011 in the ending balances (before proration) in each of the three accounts
4. Which method makes the most sense? Justify your answer.

MyAccountingLab▐▌▌

Problems

4-31 Job costing, accounting for manufacturing overhead, budgeted rates. The Fasano Company uses a job-costing system at its Dover, Delaware, plant. The plant has a machining department and a finishing department. Fasano uses normal costing with two direct-cost categories (direct materials and direct manufacturing labor) and two manufacturing overhead cost pools (the machining department with machine-hours as the allocation base, and the finishing department with direct manufacturing labor costs as the allocation base). The 2011 budget for the plant is as follows:

	Machining Department	Finishing Department
Manufacturing overhead costs	$10,660,000	$7,372,000
Direct manufacturing labor costs	$ 940,000	$3,800,000
Direct manufacturing labor-hours	36,000	145,000
Machine-hours	205,000	32,000

1. Prepare an overview diagram of Fasano's job-costing system.
2. What is the budgeted manufacturing overhead rate in the machining department? In the finishing department?
3. During the month of January, the job-cost record for Job 431 shows the following:

	Machining Department	Finishing Department
Direct materials used	$15,500	$ 5,000
Direct manufacturing labor costs	$ 400	$1,1,00
Direct manufacturing labor-hours	50	50
Machine-hours	130	20

Compute the total manufacturing overhead cost allocated to Job 431.
4. Assuming that Job 431 consisted of 400 units of product, what is the cost per unit?
5. Amounts at the end of 2011 are as follows:

	Machining Department	Finishing Department
Manufacturing overhead incurred	$11,070,000	$8,236,000
Direct manufacturing labor costs	$ 1,000,000	$4,400,000
Machine-hours	210,000	31,000

Compute the under- or overallocated manufacturing overhead for each department and for the Dover plant as a whole.
6. Why might Fasano use two different manufacturing overhead cost pools in its job-costing system?

4-32 Service industry, job costing, law firm. Keating & Associates is a law firm specializing in labor relations and employee-related work. It employs 25 professionals (5 partners and 20 associates) who work directly with its clients. The average budgeted total compensation per professional for 2011 is $104,000. Each professional is budgeted to have 1,600 billable hours to clients in 2011. All professionals work for clients to their maximum 1,600 billable hours available. All professional labor costs are included in a single direct-cost category and are traced to jobs on a per-hour basis. All costs of Keating & Associates other than professional labor costs are included in a single indirect-cost pool (legal support) and are allocated to jobs using professional labor-hours as the allocation base. The budgeted level of indirect costs in 2011 is $2,200,000.

1. Prepare an overview diagram of Keating's job-costing system.
2. Compute the 2011 budgeted direct-cost rate per hour of professional labor.
3. Compute the 2011 budgeted indirect-cost rate per hour of professional labor.
4. Keating & Associates is considering bidding on two jobs:
   a. Litigation work for Richardson, Inc., which requires 100 budgeted hours of professional labor
   b. Labor contract work for Punch, Inc., which requires 150 budgeted hours of professional labor
   Prepare a cost estimate for each job.

4-33 Service industry, job costing, two direct- and two indirect-cost categories, law firm (continuation of 4-32). Keating has just completed a review of its job-costing system. This review included a detailed analysis of how past jobs used the firm's resources and interviews with personnel about what factors drive the level of indirect costs. Management concluded that a system with two direct-cost categories (professional partner labor and professional associate labor) and two indirect-cost categories (general support and secretarial support) would yield more accurate job costs. Budgeted information for 2011 related to the two direct-cost categories is as follows:

	Professional Partner Labor	Professional Associate Labor
Number of professionals	5	20
Hours of billable time per professional	1,600 per year	1,600 per year
Total compensation (average per professional)	$200,000	$80,000

Budgeted information for 2011 relating to the two indirect-cost categories is as follows:

	General Support	Secretarial Support
Total costs	$1,800,000	$400,000
Cost-allocation base	Professional labor-hours	Partner labor-hours

1. Compute the 2011 budgeted direct-cost rates for (a) professional partners and (b) professional associates.
2. Compute the 2011 budgeted indirect-cost rates for (a) general support and (b) secretarial support.

3. Compute the budgeted costs for the Richardson and Punch jobs, given the following information:

	Richardson, Inc.	Punch, Inc.
Professional partners	60 hours	30 hours
Professional associates	40 hours	120 hours

4. Comment on the results in requirement 3. Why are the job costs different from those computed in Problem 4-32?

4-34 Proration of overhead. (Z. Iqbal, adapted) The Zaf Radiator Company uses a normal-costing system with a single manufacturing overhead cost pool and machine-hours as the cost-allocation base. The following data are for 2011:

Budgeted manufacturing overhead costs	$4,800,000
Overhead allocation base	Machine-hours
Budgeted machine-hours	80,000
Manufacturing overhead costs incurred	$4,900,000
Actual machine-hours	75,000

Machine-hours data and the ending balances (before proration of under- or overallocated overhead) are as follows:

	Actual Machine-Hours	2011 End-of-Year Balance
Cost of Goods Sold	60,000	$8,000,000
Finished Goods Control	11,000	1,250,000
Work-in-Process Control	4,000	750,000

Required

1. Compute the budgeted manufacturing overhead rate for 2011.
2. Compute the under- or overallocated manufacturing overhead of Zaf Radiator in 2011. Dispose of this amount using the following:
   a. Write-off to Cost of Goods Sold
   b. Proration based on ending balances (before proration) in Work-in-Process Control, Finished Goods Control, and Cost of Goods Sold
   c. Proration based on the overhead allocated in 2011 (before proration) in the ending balances of Work-in-Process Control, Finished Goods Control, and Cost of Goods Sold
3. Which method do you prefer in requirement 2? Explain.

4-35 Normal costing, overhead allocation, working backward. Gibson Manufacturing uses normal costing for its job-costing system, which has two direct-cost categories (direct materials and direct manufacturing labor) and one indirect-cost category (manufacturing overhead). The following information is obtained for 2011:

- Total manufacturing costs, $8,000,000
- Manufacturing overhead allocated, $3,600,000 (allocated at a rate of 200% of direct manufacturing labor costs)
- Work-in-process inventory on January 1, 2011, $320,000
- Cost of finished goods manufactured, $7,920,000

Required

1. Use information in the first two bullet points to calculate (a) direct manufacturing labor costs in 2011 and (b) cost of direct materials used in 2011.
2. Calculate the ending work-in-process inventory on December 31, 2011.

4-36 Proration of overhead with two indirect cost pools. New Rise, Inc., produces porcelain figurines. The production is semi-automated where the figurine is molded almost entirely by operator-less machines and then individually hand-painted. The overhead in the molding department is allocated based on machine-hours and the overhead in the painting department is allocated based on direct manufacturing labor-hours. New Rise, Inc., uses a normal-costing system and reported actual overhead for the month of May of $17,248 and $31,485 for the molding and painting departments, respectively. The company reported the following information related to its inventory accounts and cost of goods sold for the month of May:

	Work in Process	Finished Goods	Cost of Goods Sold
Balance before proration	$27,720	$15,523.20	$115,156.80
Molding Department Overhead Allocated	$ 4,602	$ 957.00	$ 12,489.00
Painting Department Overhead Allocated	$ 2,306	$ 1,897.00	$ 24,982.00

1. Calculate the over- or underallocated overhead for each of the Molding and Painting departments for May.
2. Calculate the ending balances in work in process, finished goods, and cost of goods sold if the under- or overallocated overhead amounts in *each* department are as follows:
   a. Written off to cost of goods sold
   b. Prorated based on the ending balance (before proration) in each of the three accounts
   c. Prorated based on the overhead allocated in May (before proration) in the ending balances in each of the three accounts
3. Which method would you choose? Explain.

4-37 General ledger relationships, under- and overallocation. (S. Sridhar, adapted) Needham Company uses normal costing in its job-costing system. Partially completed T-accounts and additional information for Needham for 2011 are as follows:

Direct Materials Control			Work-in-Process Control		Finished Goods Control		
1-1-2011	30,000	380,000	1-1-2011	20,000	1-1-2011	10,000	900,000
	400,000		Dir. manuf.			940,000	
			labor	360,000			

Manufacturing Overhead Control	Manufacturing Overhead Allocated	Cost of Goods Sold
540,000		

Additional information follows:

a. Direct manufacturing labor wage rate was $15 per hour.
b. Manufacturing overhead was allocated at $20 per direct manufacturing labor-hour.
c. During the year, sales revenues were $1,090,000, and marketing and distribution costs were $140,000.

1. What was the amount of direct materials issued to production during 2011?
2. What was the amount of manufacturing overhead allocated to jobs during 2011?
3. What was the total cost of jobs completed during 2011?
4. What was the balance of work-in-process inventory on December 31, 2011?
5. What was the cost of goods sold before proration of under- or overallocated overhead?
6. What was the under- or overallocated manufacturing overhead in 2011?
7. Dispose of the under- or overallocated manufacturing overhead using the following:
   a. Write-off to Cost of Goods Sold
   b. Proration based on ending balances (before proration) in Work-in-Process Control, Finished Goods Control, and Cost of Goods Sold
8. Using each of the approaches in requirement 7, calculate Needham's operating income for 2011.
9. Which approach in requirement 7 do you recommend Needham use? Explain your answer briefly.

4-38 Overview of general ledger relationships. Brady Company uses normal costing in its job-costing system. The company produces custom bikes for toddlers. The beginning balances (December 1) and ending balances (as of December 30) in their inventory accounts are as follows:

	Beginning Balance 12/1	Ending Balance 12/30
Materials Control	$1,200	$ 7,600
Work-in-Process Control	5,800	8,100
Manufacturing Department Overhead Control	—	94,070
Finished Goods Control	3,500	18,500

Additional information follows:

a. Direct materials purchased during December were $65,400.
b. Cost of goods manufactured for December was $225,000.
c. No direct materials were returned to suppliers.
d. No units were started or completed on December 31.
e. The manufacturing labor costs for the December 31 working day: direct manufacturing labor, $3,850, and indirect manufacturing labor, $950.
f. Manufacturing overhead has been allocated at 120% of direct manufacturing labor costs through December 30.

Required
1. Prepare journal entries for the December 31 payroll.
2. Use T-accounts to compute the following:
   a. The total amount of materials requisitioned into work in process during December
   b. The total amount of direct manufacturing labor recorded in work in process during December (Hint: You have to solve requirements **2b** and **2c** simultaneously)
   c. The total amount of manufacturing overhead recorded in work in process during December
   d. Ending balance in work in process, December 31
   e. Cost of goods sold for December before adjustments for under- or overallocated manufacturing overhead
3. Prepare closing journal entries related to manufacturing overhead. Assume that all under- or overallocated manufacturing overhead is closed directly to Cost of Goods Sold.

4-39 Allocation and proration of overhead. Tamden, Inc., prints custom marketing materials. The business was started January 1, 2010. The company uses a normal-costing system. It has two direct cost pools, materials and labor and one indirect cost pool, overhead. Overhead is charged to printing jobs on the basis of direct labor cost. The following information is available for 2010.

Budgeted direct labor costs	$150,000
Budgeted overhead costs	$180,000
Costs of actual material used	$126,500
Actual direct labor costs	$148,750
Actual overhead costs	$176,000

There were two jobs in process on December 31, 2010: Job 11 and Job 12. Costs added to each job as of December 31 are as follows:

	Direct materials	Direct labor
Job 11	$3,620	$4,500
Job 12	$6,830	$7,250

Tamden, Inc., has no finished goods inventories because all printing jobs are transferred to cost of goods sold when completed.

Required
1. Compute the overhead allocation rate.
2. Calculate the balance in ending work in process and cost of goods sold before any adjustments for under- or overallocated overhead.
3. Calculate under- or overallocated overhead.
4. Calculate the ending balances in work in process and cost of goods sold if the under- or overallocated overhead amount is as follows:
   a. Written off to cost of goods sold
   b. Prorated using the ending balance (before proration) in cost of goods sold and work-in-process control accounts
5. Which of the methods in requirement 4 would you choose? Explain.

4-40 Job costing, contracting, ethics. Kingston Company manufactures modular homes. The company has two main products that it sells commercially: a 1,000 square foot, one-bedroom model and a 1,500 square foot, two-bedroom model. The company recently began providing emergency housing (huts) to FEMA. The emergency housing is similar to the 1,000 square foot model.

FEMA has requested Kingston to create a bid for 150 emergency huts to be sent for flood victims in the south. Your boss has asked that you prepare this bid. In preparing the bid, you find a recent invoice to FEMA for 200 huts provided after hurricane Katrina. You also have a standard cost sheet for the 1,000 square foot model sold commercially. Both are provided as follows:

Standard cost sheet: 1,000 sq. ft. one-bedroom model

Direct materials		$ 8,000
Direct manufacturing labor	30 hours	600
Manufacturing overhead*	$3 per direct labor dollar	1,800
Total cost		$10,400
Retail markup on total cost		20%
Retail price		$12,480

---
*Overhead cost pool includes inspection labor ($15 per hour), setup labor ($12 per hour), and other indirect costs associated with production.

INVOICE:
DATE: September 15, 2005
BILL TO: FEMA
FOR: 200 Emergency Huts
SHIP TO: New Orleans, Louisiana

Direct materials	$1,840,000
Direct manufacturing labor**	138,400
Manufacturing overhead	415,200
Total cost	2,393,600
Government contract markup on total cost	15%
Total due	$2,752,640

**Direct manufacturing labor includes 28 production hours per unit, 4 inspection hours per unit, and 6 setup hours per unit

Required

1. Calculate the total bid if you base your calculations on the standard cost sheet assuming a cost plus 15% government contract.
2. Calculate the total bid if you base your calculations on the September 15, 2005, invoice assuming a cost plus 15% government contract.
3. What are the main discrepancies between the bids you calculated in #1 and #2?
4. What bid should you present to your boss? What principles from the IMA *Standards of Ethical Conduct for Practitioners of Management Accounting and Financial Management* should guide your decision?

Collaborative Learning Problem

4-41 **Job costing—service industry.** Cam Cody schedules book signings for science fiction authors and creates e-books and books on CD to sell at each signing. Cody uses a normal-costing system with two direct cost pools, labor and materials, and one indirect cost pool, general overhead. General overhead is allocated to each signing based on 80% of labor cost. Actual overhead equaled allocated overhead in March 2010. Actual overhead in April was $1,980. All costs incurred during the planning stage for a signing and during the signing are gathered in a balance sheet account called "Signings in Progress (SIP)." When a signing is completed, the costs are transferred to an income statement account called "Cost of Completed Signings (CCS)." Following is cost information for April 2010:

Author	From Beginning SIP		Incurred in April	
	Materials	Labor	Materials	Labor
N. Asher	$425	$750	$ 90	$225
T. Bucknell	710	575	150	75
S. Brown	200	550	320	450
S. King	—	—	650	400
D. Sherman	—	—	150	200

The following information relates to April 2010.

As of April 1, there were three signings in progress, *N. Asher, T. Bucknell,* and *S. Brown.* Signings for *S. King* and *D. Sherman* were started during April. The signings for *T. Bucknell* and *S. King* were completed during April.

Required

1. Calculate SIP at the end of April.
2. Calculate CCS for April.
3. Calculate under/overallocated overhead at the end of April.
4. Calculate the ending balances in SIP and CCS if the under/overallocated overhead amount is as follows:
   a. Written off to CCS
   b. Prorated based on the ending balances (before proration) in SIP and CCS
   c. Prorated based on the overhead allocated in April in the ending balances of SIP and CCS (before proration)
5. Which of the methods in requirement 4 would you choose?

5 Activity-Based Costing and Activity-Based Management

5 Activity-Based Costing and Activity-Based Management

A good mystery never fails to capture the imagination.

Money is stolen or lost, property disappears, or someone meets with foul play. On the surface, what appears unremarkable to the untrained eye can turn out to be quite a revelation once the facts and details are uncovered. Getting to the bottom of the case, understanding what happened and why, and taking action can make the difference between a solved case and an unsolved one. Business and organizations are much the same. Their costing systems are often mysteries with unresolved questions: Why are we bleeding red ink? Are we pricing our products accurately? Activity-based costing can help unravel the mystery and result in improved operations, as LG Electronics discovers in the following article.

LG Electronics Reduces Costs and Inefficiencies Through Activity-Based Costing[1]

LG Electronics is one of the world's largest manufacturers of flat-screen televisions and mobile phones. In 2009, the Seoul, South Korea-based company sold 16 million liquid crystal display televisions and 117 million mobile phones worldwide.

To make so many electronic devices, LG Electronics spends nearly $40 billion annually on the procurement of semiconductors, metals, connectors, and other materials. Costs for many of these components have soared in recent years. Until 2008, however, LG Electronics did not have a centralized procurement system to leverage its scale and to control supply costs. Instead, the company had a decentralized system riddled with wasteful spending and inefficiencies.

To respond to these challenges, LG Electronics hired its first chief procurement officer who turned to activity-based costing ("ABC") for answers. ABC analysis of the company's procurement system revealed that most company resources were applied to administrative and not strategic tasks. Furthermore, the administrative tasks were done manually and at a very high cost.

The ABC analysis led LG Electronics to change many of its procurement practices and processes, improve efficiency and focus

[1] *Sources:* Carbone, James. 2009. LG Electronics centralizes purchasing to save. *Purchasing*, April. http://www.purchasing.com/article/217108-LG_Electronics_centralizes_purchasing_to_save.php; Linton's goals. 2009. Supply Management, May 12. http://www.supplymanagement.com/analysis/features/2009/lintons-goals/; Yoou-chul, Kim. 2009. CPO expects to save $1 billion in procurement. *The Korea Times*, April 1. http://www.koreatimes.co.kr/www/news/biz/2009/04/123_42360.html

on the highest-value tasks such as managing costs of commodity products and negotiating with suppliers. Furthermore, the company developed a global procurement strategy for its televisions, mobile phones, computers, and home theatre systems by implementing competitive bidding among suppliers, standardizing parts across product lines, and developing additional buying capacity in China.

The results so far have been staggering. In 2008 alone, LG Electronics reduced its materials costs by 16%, and expects to further reduce costs by $5 billion by the end of 2011.

Most companies—such as Dell, Oracle, JP Morgan Chase, and Honda—offer more than one product (or service). Dell Computer, for example, produces desktops, laptops, and servers. The three basic activities for manufacturing computers are (a) designing computers, (b) ordering component parts, and (c) assembly. The different products, however, require different quantities of the three activities. For example, a server has a more complex design, many more parts, and a more complex assembly than a desktop.

To measure the cost of producing each product, Dell separately tracks activity costs for each product. In this chapter, we describe activity-based costing systems and how they help companies make better decisions about pricing and product mix. And, just as in the case of LG Electronics, we show how ABC systems assist in cost management decisions by improving product designs, processes, and efficiency.

Broad Averaging and Its Consequences

Historically, companies (such as television and automobile manufacturers) produced a limited variety of products. Indirect (or overhead) costs were a relatively small percentage of total costs. Using simple costing systems to allocate costs broadly was easy, inexpensive, and reasonably accurate. However, as product diversity and indirect costs have increased, broad averaging has resulted in greater inaccuracy of product costs. For example, the use of a single, plant-wide manufacturing overhead rate to allocate costs to products often produces unreliable cost data. The term *peanut-butter costing* (yes, that's what it's called) describes a particular costing approach that uses broad averages for assigning (or spreading, as in spreading peanut butter) the cost of resources uniformly to cost

Learning Objective 1

Explain how broad averaging undercosts and overcosts products or services

. . . this problem arises when reported costs of products do not equal their actual costs

objects (such as products or services) when the individual products or services, may in fact, use those resources in nonuniform ways.

Undercosting and Overcosting

The following example illustrates how averaging can result in inaccurate and misleading cost data. Consider the cost of a restaurant bill for four colleagues who meet monthly to discuss business developments. Each diner orders separate entrees, desserts, and drinks. The restaurant bill for the most recent meeting is as follows:

	Emma	James	Jessica	Matthew	Total	Average
Entree	$11	$20	$15	$14	$ 60	$15
Dessert	0	8	4	4	16	4
Drinks	4	14	8	6	32	8
Total	$15	$42	$27	$24	$108	$27

If the $108 total restaurant bill is divided evenly, $27 is the average cost per diner. This cost-averaging approach treats each diner the same. Emma would probably object to paying $27 because her actual cost is only $15; she ordered the lowest-cost entree, had no dessert, and had the lowest-cost drink. When costs are averaged across all four diners, both Emma and Matthew are overcosted, James is undercosted, and Jessica is (by coincidence) accurately costed.

Broad averaging can lead to undercosting or overcosting of products or services:

■ **Product undercosting**—a product consumes a high level of resources but is reported to have a low cost per unit (James's dinner).

■ **Product overcosting**—a product consumes a low level of resources but is reported to have a high cost per unit (Emma's dinner).

What are the strategic consequences of product undercosting and overcosting? Think of a company that uses cost information about its products to guide pricing decisions. Undercosted products will be underpriced and may even lead to sales that actually result in losses—sales bring in less revenue than the cost of resources they use. Overcosted products lead to overpricing, causing these products to lose market share to competitors producing similar products. Worse still, product undercosting and overcosting causes managers to focus on the wrong products, drawing attention to overcosted products whose costs may in fact be perfectly reasonable and ignoring undercosted products that in fact consume large amounts of resources.

Product-Cost Cross-Subsidization

Product-cost cross-subsidization means that if a company undercosts one of its products, it will overcost at least one of its other products. Similarly, if a company overcosts one of its products, it will undercost at least one of its other products. Product-cost cross-subsidization is very common in situations in which a cost is uniformly spread—meaning it is broadly averaged—across multiple products without recognizing the amount of resources consumed by each product.

In the restaurant-bill example, the amount of cost cross-subsidization of each diner can be readily computed *because all cost items can be traced as direct costs to each diner*. If all diners pay $27, Emma is paying $12 more than her actual cost of $15. She is cross-subsidizing James who is paying $15 less than his actual cost of $42. Calculating the amount of cost cross-subsidization takes more work when there are indirect costs to be considered. Why? Because when the resources represented by indirect costs are used by two or more diners, we need to find a way to allocate costs to each diner. Consider, for example, a $40 bottle of wine whose cost is shared equally. Each diner would pay $10 ($40 ÷ 4). Suppose Matthew drinks 2 glasses of wine while Emma, James, and Jessica drink one glass each for a total of 5 glasses. Allocating the cost of the bottle of wine on the basis of the glasses of wine that each diner drinks would result in Matthew paying $16 ($40 × 2/5) and each of the others $8 ($40 × 1/5). In this case, by sharing the cost equally, Emma, James, and Jessica are each paying $2 ($10 – $8) more and are cross-subsidizing Matthew who is paying $6 ($16 – $10) less for the wine he consumes.

To see the effects of broad averaging on direct and indirect costs, we consider Plastim Corporation's costing system.

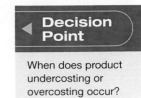

Decision Point

When does product undercosting or overcosting occur?

Simple Costing System at Plastim Corporation

Plastim Corporation manufactures lenses for the rear taillights of automobiles. A lens, made from black, red, orange, or white plastic, is the part of the lamp visible on the automobile's exterior. Lenses are made by injecting molten plastic into a mold to give the lamp its desired shape. The mold is cooled to allow the molten plastic to solidify, and the lens is removed.

Under its contract with Giovanni Motors, a major automobile manufacturer, Plastim makes two types of lenses: a complex lens, CL5, and a simple lens, S3. The complex lens is a large lens with special features, such as multicolor molding (when more than one color is injected into the mold) and a complex shape that wraps around the corner of the car. Manufacturing CL5 lenses is more complex because various parts in the mold must align and fit precisely. The S3 lens is simpler to make because it has a single color and few special features.

Design, Manufacturing, and Distribution Processes

The sequence of steps to design, produce, and distribute lenses, whether simple or complex, is as follows:

- **Design products and processes.** Each year Giovanni Motors specifies some modifications to the simple and complex lenses. Plastim's design department designs the molds from which the lenses will be made and specifies the processes needed (that is, details of the manufacturing operations).
- **Manufacture lenses.** The lenses are molded, finished, cleaned, and inspected.
- **Distribute lenses.** Finished lenses are packed and sent to Giovanni Motors.

Plastim is operating at capacity and incurs very low marketing costs. Because of its high-quality products, Plastim has minimal customer-service costs. Plastim's business environment is very competitive with respect to simple lenses. At a recent meeting, Giovanni's purchasing manager indicated that a new supplier, Bandix, which makes only simple lenses, is offering to supply the S3 lens to Giovanni at a price of $53, well below the $63 price that Plastim is currently projecting and budgeting for 2011. Unless Plastim can lower its selling price, it will lose the Giovanni business for the simple lens for the upcoming model year. Fortunately, the same competitive pressures do not exist for the complex lens, which Plastim currently sells to Giovanni at $137 per lens.

Plastim's management has two primary options:

- Plastim can give up the Giovanni business in simple lenses if selling simple lenses is unprofitable. Bandix makes only simple lenses and perhaps, therefore, uses simpler technology and processes than Plastim. The simpler operations may give Bandix a cost advantage that Plastim cannot match. If so, it is better for Plastim to not supply the S3 lens to Giovanni.
- Plastim can reduce the price of the simple lens and either accept a lower margin or aggressively seek to reduce costs.

To make these long-run strategic decisions, management needs to first understand the costs to design, make, and distribute the S3 and CL5 lenses.

While Bandix makes only simple lenses and can fairly accurately calculate the cost of a lens by dividing total costs by units produced, Plastim's costing environment is more challenging. The processes to make both simple and complex lenses are more complicated than the processes required to make only simple lenses. Plastim needs to find a way to allocate costs to each type of lens.

In computing costs, Plastim assigns both variable costs and costs that are fixed in the short run to the S3 and CL5 lenses. Managers cost products and services to guide long-run strategic decisions (for example, what mix of products and services to produce and sell and what prices to charge for them). In the long-run, managers want revenues to exceed total costs (variable and fixed) to design, make, and distribute the lenses.

To guide their pricing and cost-management decisions, Plastim's managers assign all costs, both manufacturing and nonmanufacturing, to the S3 and CL5 lenses. If managers had wanted to calculate the cost of inventory, Plastim's management accountants would have assigned only manufacturing costs to the lenses, as required by generally accepted accounting principles. Surveys of company practice across the globe overwhelmingly indicate that the vast majority of companies use costing systems not just for inventory costing but also for strategic purposes such as pricing and product-mix decisions and decisions about cost reduction, process improvement, design, and planning and budgeting. As a result, even merchandising-sector companies (for whom inventory costing is straight-forward) and service-sector companies (who have no inventory) expend considerable resources in designing and operating their costing systems. In this chapter, we take this more strategic focus and allocate costs in all functions of the value chain to the S3 and CL5 lenses.

Simple Costing System Using a Single Indirect-Cost Pool

Plastim has historically had a simple costing system that allocates indirect costs using a single indirect-cost rate, the type of system described in Chapter 4. We calculate budgeted costs for each type of lens in 2011 using Plastim's simple costing system and later contrast it with activity-based costing. (Note that instead of jobs, as in Chapter 4, we now have products as the cost objects.) Exhibit 5-1 shows an overview of Plastim's simple costing system. Use this exhibit as a guide as you study the following steps, each of which is marked in Exhibit 5-1.

Exhibit 5-1

Overview of Plastim's
Simple Costing System

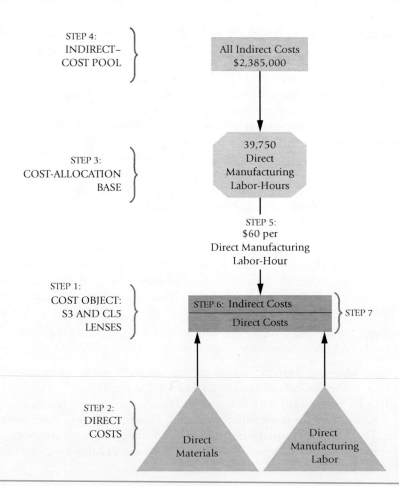

Step 1: Identify the Products That Are the Chosen Cost Objects. The cost objects are the 60,000 simple S3 lenses and the 15,000 complex CL5 lenses that Plastim will produce in 2011. Plastim's goal is to first calculate the total costs and then the unit cost of designing, manufacturing, and distributing these lenses.

Step 2: Identify the Direct Costs of the Products. Plastim identifies the direct costs—direct materials and direct manufacturing labor—of the lenses. Exhibit 5-2 shows the direct and indirect costs for the S3 and the CL5 lenses using the simple costing system. The direct cost calculations appear on lines 5, 6, and 7 of Exhibit 5-2. Plastim classifies all other costs as indirect costs.

Step 3: Select the Cost-Allocation Bases to Use for Allocating Indirect (or Overhead) Costs to the Products. A majority of the indirect costs consist of salaries paid to supervisors, engineers, manufacturing support, and maintenance staff, all supporting direct manufacturing labor. Plastim uses direct manufacturing labor-hours as the only allocation base to allocate all manufacturing and nonmanufacturing indirect costs to S3 and CL5. In 2011, Plastim plans to use 39,750 direct manufacturing labor-hours.

Step 4: Identify the Indirect Costs Associated with Each Cost-Allocation Base. Because Plastim uses only a single cost-allocation base, Plastim groups all budgeted indirect costs of $2,385,000 for 2011 into a single overhead cost pool.

Step 5: Compute the Rate per Unit of Each Cost-Allocation Base.

$$\text{Budgeted indirect-cost rate} = \frac{\text{Budgeted total costs in indirect-cost pool}}{\text{Budgeted total quantity of cost-allocation base}}$$

$$= \frac{\$2,385,000}{39,750 \text{ direct manufacturing labor-hours}}$$

$$= \$60 \text{ per direct manufacturing labor-hour}$$

Step 6: Compute the Indirect Costs Allocated to the Products. Plastim expects to use 30,000 total direct manufacturing labor-hours to make the 60,000 S3 lenses and 9,750 total direct manufacturing labor-hours to make the 15,000 CL5 lenses. Exhibit 5-2 shows indirect costs of $1,800,000 ($60 per direct manufacturing labor-hour × 30,000 direct manufacturing labor-hours) allocated to the simple lens and $585,000 ($60 per direct manufacturing labor-hour × 9,750 direct manufacturing labor-hours) allocated to the complex lens.

Step 7: Compute the Total Cost of the Products by Adding All Direct and Indirect Costs Assigned to the Products. Exhibit 5-2 presents the product costs for the simple and complex lenses. The direct costs are calculated in Step 2 and the indirect costs in Step 6. Be sure you see the parallel between the simple costing system overview diagram (Exhibit 5-1)

Exhibit 5-2　　Plastim's Product Costs Using the Simple Costing System

	Home	Insert	Page Layout	Formulas	Data	Review	View		
	A		B	C	D	E		F	G
1			60,000			15,000			
2			Simple Lenses (S3)			Complex Lenses (CL5)			
3			Total	per Unit		Total	per Unit		Total
4			(1)	(2) = (1) ÷ 60,000		(3)	(4) = (3) ÷ 15,000		(5) = (1) + (3)
5	Direct materials		$1,125,000	$18.75		$ 675,000	$45.00		$1,800,000
6	Direct manufacturing labor		600,000	10.00		195,000	13.00		795,000
7	Total direct costs (Step 2)		1,725,000	28.75		870,000	58.00		2,595,000
8	Indirect costs allocated (Step 6)		1,800,000	30.00		585,000	39.00		2,385,000
9	Total costs (Step 7)		$3,525,000	$58.75		$1,455,000	$97.00		$4,980,000
10									

and the costs calculated in Step 7. Exhibit 5-1 shows two direct-cost categories and one indirect-cost category. Hence, the budgeted cost of each type of lens in Step 7 (Exhibit 5-2) has three line items: two for direct costs and one for allocated indirect costs. The budgeted cost per S3 lens is $58.75, well above the $53 selling price quoted by Bandix. The budgeted cost per CL5 lens is $97.

Applying the Five-Step Decision-Making Process at Plastim

To decide how it should respond to the threat that Bandix poses to its S3 lens business, Plastim's management works through the five-step decision-making process introduced in Chapter 1.

Step 1: Identify the problem and uncertainties. The problem is clear: If Plastim wants to retain the Giovanni business for S3 lenses and make a profit, it must find a way to reduce the price and costs of the S3 lens. The two major uncertainties Plastim faces are (1) whether Plastim's technology and processes for the S3 lens are competitive with Bandix's and (2) whether the S3 lens is overcosted by the simple costing system.

Step 2: Obtain information. Management asks a team of its design and process engineers to analyze and evaluate the design, manufacturing, and distribution operations for the S3 lens. The team is very confident that the technology and processes for the S3 lens are not inferior to those of Bandix and other competitors because Plastim has many years of experience in manufacturing and distributing the S3 with a history and culture of continuous process improvements. If anything, the team is less certain about Plastim's capabilities in manufacturing and distributing complex lenses, because it only recently started making this type of lens. Given these doubts, management is happy that Giovanni Motors considers the price of the CL5 lens to be competitive. It is somewhat of a puzzle, though, how at the currently budgeted prices, Plastim is expected to earn a very large profit margin percentage (operating income ÷ revenues) on the CL5 lenses and a small profit margin on the S3 lenses:

| | 60,000 Simple Lenses (S3) | | 15,000 Complex Lenses (CL5) | | |
| | Total | per Unit | Total | per Unit | Total |
	(1)	(2) = (1) ÷ 60,000	(3)	(4) = (3) ÷ 15,000	(5) = (1) + (3)
Revenues	$3,780,000	$63.00	$2,055,000	$137.00	$5,835,000
Total costs	3,525,000	58.75	1,455,000	97.00	4,980,000
Operating income	$ 255,000	$ 4.25	$ 600,000	$ 40.00	$ 855,000
Profit margin percentage		6.75%		29.20%	

As it continues to gather information, Plastim's management begins to ponder why the profit margins (and process) are under so much pressure for the S3 lens, where the company has strong capabilities, but high on the newer, less-established CL5 lens. Plastim is not deliberately charging a low price for S3, so management starts to believe that perhaps the problem lies with its costing system. Plastim's simple costing system may be overcosting the simple S3 lens (assigning too much cost to it) and undercosting the complex CL5 lens (assigning too little cost to it).

Step 3: Make predictions about the future. Plastim's key challenge is to get a better estimate of what it will cost to design, make, and distribute the S3 and CL5 lenses. Management is fairly confident about the direct material and direct manufacturing labor costs of each lens because these costs are easily traced to the lenses. But management is quite concerned about how accurately the simple costing system measures the indirect resources used by each type of lens. It believes it can do much better.

At the same time, management wants to ensure that no biases enter its thinking. In particular, it wants to be careful that the desire to be competitive on the S3 lens should not lead to assumptions that bias in favor of lowering costs of the S3 lens.

Step 4: Make decisions by choosing among alternatives. On the basis of predicted costs, and taking into account how Bandix might respond, Plastim's managers must decide whether they should bid for Giovanni Motors' S3 lens business and if they do bid, what price they should offer.

Step 5: Implement the decision, evaluate performance, and learn. If Plastim bids and wins Giovanni's S3 lens business, it must compare actual costs, as it makes and ships S3 lenses, to predicted costs and learn why actual costs deviate from predicted costs. Such evaluation and learning form the basis for future improvements.

The next few sections focus on Steps 3, 4, and 5—how Plastim improves the allocation of indirect costs to the S3 and CL5 lenses, how it uses these predictions to bid for the S3 lens business, and how it makes product design and process improvements.

Refining a Costing System

A **refined costing system** reduces the use of broad averages for assigning the cost of resources to cost objects (such as jobs, products, and services) and provides better measurement of the costs of indirect resources used by different cost objects—no matter how differently various cost objects use indirect resources.

Reasons for Refining a Costing System

There are three principal reasons that have accelerated the demand for such refinements.

1. **Increase in product diversity.** The growing demand for customized products has led companies to increase the variety of products and services they offer. Kanthal, the Swedish manufacturer of heating elements, for example, produces more than 10,000 different types of electrical heating wires and thermostats. Banks, such as the Cooperative Bank in the United Kingdom, offer many different types of accounts and services: special passbook accounts, ATMs, credit cards, and electronic banking. These products differ in the demands they place on the resources needed to produce them, because of differences in volume, process, and complexity. The use of broad averages is likely to lead to distorted and inaccurate cost information.

2. **Increase in indirect costs.** The use of product and process technology such as computer-integrated manufacturing (CIM) and flexible manufacturing systems (FMS), has led to an increase in indirect costs and a decrease in direct costs, particularly direct manufacturing labor costs. In CIM and FMS, computers on the manufacturing floor give instructions to set up and run equipment quickly and automatically. The computers accurately measure hundreds of production parameters and directly control the manufacturing processes to achieve high-quality output. Managing more complex technology and producing very diverse products also requires committing an increasing amount of resources for various support functions, such as production scheduling, product and process design, and engineering. Because direct manufacturing labor is not a cost driver of these costs, allocating indirect costs on the basis of direct manufacturing labor (which was the common practice) does not accurately measure how resources are being used by different products.

3. **Competition in product markets.** As markets have become more competitive, managers have felt the need to obtain more accurate cost information to help them make important strategic decisions, such as how to price products and which products to sell. Making correct pricing and product mix decisions is critical in competitive markets because competitors quickly capitalize on a company's mistakes.

   Whereas the preceding factors point to reasons for the increase in *demand* for refined cost systems, *advances in information technology* have enabled companies to implement these refinements. Costing system refinements require more data gathering and more analysis, and improvements in information technology have drastically reduced the costs to gather, validate, store, and analyze vast quantities of data.

Learning Objective 2

Present three guidelines for refining a costing system

. . . classify more costs as direct costs, expand the number of indirect-cost pools, and identify cost drivers

Guidelines for Refining a Costing System

There are three main guidelines for refining a costing system. In the following sections, we delve more deeply into each in the context of the Plastim example.

1. **Direct-cost tracing.** Identify as many direct costs as is economically feasible. This guideline aims to reduce the amount of costs classified as indirect, thereby minimizing the extent to which costs have to be allocated, rather than traced.

2. **Indirect-cost pools.** Expand the number of indirect-cost pools until each pool is more homogeneous. All costs in a *homogeneous cost pool* have the same or a similar cause-and-effect (or benefits-received) relationship with a single cost driver that is used as the cost-allocation base. Consider, for example, a single indirect-cost pool containing both indirect machining costs and indirect distribution costs that are allocated to products using machine-hours. This pool is not homogeneous because machine-hours are a cost driver of machining costs but not of distribution costs, which has a different cost driver, number of shipments. If, instead, machining costs and distribution costs are separated into two indirect-cost pools (with machine-hours as the cost-allocation base for the machining cost pool and number of shipments as the cost-allocation base for the distribution cost pool), each indirect-cost pool would become homogeneous.

3. **Cost-allocation bases.** As we describe later in the chapter, whenever possible, use the cost driver (the cause of indirect costs) as the cost-allocation base for each homogenous indirect-cost pool (the effect).

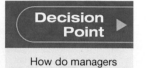

Decision Point ▶

How do managers refine a costing system?

Learning Objective 3

Distinguish between simple and activity-based costing systems

. . . unlike simple systems, ABC systems calculate costs of individual activities to cost products

Activity-Based Costing Systems

One of the best tools for refining a costing system is activity-based costing. **Activity-based costing (ABC)** refines a costing system by identifying individual activities as the fundamental cost objects. An **activity** is an event, task, or unit of work with a specified purpose—for example, designing products, setting up machines, operating machines, and distributing products. More informally, activities are verbs; they are things that a firm does. To help make strategic decisions, ABC systems identify activities in all functions of the value chain, calculate costs of individual activities, and assign costs to cost objects such as products and services on the basis of the mix of activities needed to produce each product or service.[2]

Fundamental Cost Objects

Assignment to Other Cost Objects

Activities → Costs of Activities → Costs of
• Products
• Services
• Customers

Plastim's ABC System

After reviewing its simple costing system and the potential miscosting of product costs, Plastim decides to implement an ABC system. Direct material costs and direct manufacturing labor costs can be traced to products easily, so the ABC system focuses on refining the assignment of indirect costs to departments, processes, products, or other cost objects. Plastim's ABC system identifies various activities that help explain why Plastim incurs the costs it currently classifies as indirect in its simple costing system. In other words, it breaks up the current indirect cost pool into finer pools of costs related to various activities. To identify these activities, Plastim organizes a team comprised of managers from design, manufacturing, distribution, accounting, and administration.

---

[2] For more details on ABC systems, see R. Cooper and R. S. Kaplan, *The Design of Cost Management Systems* (Upper Saddle River, NJ: Prentice Hall, 1999); G. Cokins, *Activity-Based Cost Management: An Executive's Guide* (Hoboken, NJ: John Wiley & Sons, 2001); and R. S. Kaplan and S. Anderson, *Time-Driven Activity-Based Costing: A Simpler and More Powerful Path to Higher Profits* (Boston: Harvard Business School Press, 2007).

Defining activities is not a simple matter. The team evaluates hundreds of tasks performed at Plastim before choosing the activities that form the basis of its ABC system. For example, it decides if maintenance of molding machines, operations of molding machines, and process control should each be regarded as a separate activity or should be combined into a single activity. An activity-based costing system with many activities becomes overly detailed and unwieldy to operate. An activity-based costing system with too few activities may not be refined enough to measure cause-and-effect relationships between cost drivers and various indirect costs. Plastim's team focuses on activities that account for a sizable fraction of indirect costs and combines activities that have the same cost driver into a single activity. For example, the team decides to combine maintenance of molding machines, operations of molding machines, and process control into a single activity—molding machine operations—because all these activities have the same cost driver: molding machine-hours.

The team identifies the following seven activities by developing a flowchart of all the steps and processes needed to design, manufacture, and distribute S3 and CL5 lenses.

a. Design products and processes

b. Set up molding machines to ensure that the molds are properly held in place and parts are properly aligned before manufacturing starts

c. Operate molding machines to manufacture lenses

d. Clean and maintain the molds after lenses are manufactured

e. Prepare batches of finished lenses for shipment

f. Distribute lenses to customers

g. Administer and manage all processes at Plastim

These activity descriptions form the basis of the activity-based costing system—sometimes called an *activity list* or *activity dictionary*. Compiling the list of tasks, however, is only the first step in implementing activity-based costing systems. Plastim must also identify the cost of each activity and the related cost driver. To do so, Plastim uses the three guidelines for refining a costing system described on page 146.

1. **Direct-cost tracing.** Plastim's ABC system subdivides the single indirect cost pool into seven smaller cost pools related to the different activities. The costs in the cleaning and maintenance activity cost pool (item d) consist of salaries and wages paid to workers who clean the mold. These costs are direct costs, because they can be economically traced to a specific mold and lens.

2. **Indirect-cost pools.** The remaining six activity cost pools are indirect cost pools. Unlike the single indirect cost pool of Plastim's simple costing system, each of the activity-related cost pools is homogeneous. That is, each activity cost pool includes only those narrow and focused set of costs that have the same cost driver. For example, the distribution cost pool includes only those costs (such as wages of truck drivers) that, over time, increase as the cost driver of distribution costs, cubic feet of packages delivered, increases. In the simple costing system, all indirect costs were lumped together and the cost-allocation base, direct manufacturing labor-hours, was not a cost driver of the indirect costs.

   Determining costs of activity pools requires assigning and reassigning costs accumulated in support departments, such as human resources and information systems, to each of the activity cost pools on the basis of how various activities use support department resources. This is commonly referred to as *first-stage allocation*, a topic which we discuss in detail in Chapters 14 and 15. We focus here on the *second-stage allocation*, the allocation of costs of activity cost pools to products.

3. **Cost-allocation bases.** For each activity cost pool, the cost driver is used (whenever possible) as the cost-allocation base. To identify cost drivers, Plastim's managers consider various alternatives and use their knowledge of operations to choose among them. For example, Plastim's managers choose setup-hours rather than the number of setups as the cost driver of setup costs, because Plastim's managers believe that more complex setups take more time and are more costly. Over time, Plastim's managers can use data to test their beliefs. (Chapter 10 discusses several methods to estimate the relationship between a cost driver and costs.)

The logic of ABC systems is twofold. First, structuring activity cost pools more finely with cost drivers for each activity cost pool as the cost-allocation base leads to more accurate costing of activities. Second, allocating these costs to products by measuring the cost-allocation bases of different activities used by different products leads to more accurate product costs. We illustrate this logic by focusing on the setup activity at Plastim.

Setting up molding machines frequently entails trial runs, fine-tuning, and adjustments. Improper setups cause quality problems such as scratches on the surface of the lens. The resources needed for each setup depend on the complexity of the manufacturing operation. Complex lenses require more setup resources (setup-hours) per setup than simple lenses. Furthermore, complex lenses can be produced only in small batches because the molds for complex lenses need to be cleaned more often than molds for simple lenses. Thus, relative to simple lenses, complex lenses not only use more setup-hours per setup, but they also require more frequent setups.

Setup data for the simple S3 lens and the complex CL5 lens are as follows:

		Simple S3 Lens	Complex CL5 Lens	Total
1	Quantity of lenses produced	60,000	15,000	
2	Number of lenses produced per batch	240	50	
3 = (1) ÷ (2)	Number of batches	250	300	
4	Setup time per batch	2 hours	5 hours	
5 = (3) × (4)	Total setup-hours	500 hours	1,500 hours	2,000 hours

Of the $2,385,000 in the total indirect-cost pool, Plastim identifies the total costs of setups (consisting mainly of depreciation on setup equipment and allocated costs of process engineers, quality engineers, and supervisors) to be $300,000. Recall that in its simple costing system, Plastim uses direct manufacturing labor-hours to allocate all indirect costs to products. The following table compares how setup costs allocated to simple and complex lenses will be different if Plastim allocates setup costs to lenses based on setup-hours rather than direct manufacturing labor-hours. Of the $60 total rate per direct manufacturing labor-hour (p. 143), the setup cost per direct manufacturing labor-hour amounts to $7.54717 ($300,000 ÷ 39,750 total direct manufacturing labor-hours). The setup cost per setup-hour equals $150 ($300,000 ÷ 2,000 total setup-hours).

	Simple S3 Lens	Complex CL5 Lens	Total
Setup cost allocated using direct manufacturing labor-hours:			
$7.54717 × 30,000; $7.54717 × 9,750	$226,415	$ 73,585	$300,000
Setup cost allocated using setup-hours:			
$150 × 500; $150 × 1,500	$ 75,000	$225,000	$300,000

As we have already discussed when presenting guidelines 2 and 3, setup-hours, not direct manufacturing labor-hours, are the cost driver of setup costs.. The CL5 lens uses substantially more setup-hours than the S3 lens (1,500 hours ÷ 2,000 hours = 75% of the total setup-hours) because the CL5 requires a greater number of setups (batches) and each setup is more challenging and requires more setup-hours.

The ABC system therefore allocates substantially more setup costs to CL5 than to S3. When direct manufacturing labor-hours rather than setup-hours are used to allocate setup costs in the simple costing system, it is the S3 lens that is allocated a very large share of the setup costs because the S3 lens uses a larger proportion of direct manufacturing labor-hours (30,000 ÷ 39,750 = 75.47%). As a result, the simple costing system overcosts the S3 lens with regard to setup costs.

Note that setup-hours are related to batches (or groups) of lenses made, not the number of individual lenses. Activity-based costing attempts to identify the most relevant cause-and-effect relationship for each activity pool, without restricting the cost driver to only units of output or variables related to units of output (such as direct manufacturing labor-hours). As our discussion of setups illustrates, limiting cost-allocation bases in this manner weakens the cause-and-effect relationship between the cost-allocation base and the costs in a cost pool.

Decision Point ▶

What is the difference between the design of a simple costing system and an activity-based costing (ABC) system?

Cost Hierarchies

A **cost hierarchy** categorizes various activity cost pools on the basis of the different types of cost drivers, or cost-allocation bases, or different degrees of difficulty in determining cause-and-effect (or benefits-received) relationships. ABC systems commonly use a cost hierarchy with four levels—output unit-level costs, batch-level costs, product-sustaining costs, and facility-sustaining costs—to identify cost-allocation bases that are cost drivers of the activity cost pools.

Output unit-level costs are the costs of activities performed on each individual unit of a product or service. Machine operations costs (such as the cost of energy, machine depreciation, and repair) related to the activity of running the automated molding machines are output unit-level costs. They are output unit-level costs because, over time, the cost of this activity increases with additional units of output produced (or machine-hours used). Plastim's ABC system uses molding machine-hours—an output-unit level cost-allocation base—to allocate machine operations costs to products.

Batch-level costs are the costs of activities related to a group of units of a product or service rather than each individual unit of product or service. In the Plastim example, setup costs are batch-level costs because, over time, the cost of this setup activity increases with setup-hours needed to produce batches (groups) of lenses. As described in the table on page 148, the S3 lens requires 500 setup-hours (2 setup-hours per batch × 250 batches). The CL5 lens requires 1,500 setup-hours (5 setup-hours per batch × 300 batches). The total setup costs allocated to S3 and CL5 depend on the total setup-hours required by each type of lens, not on the number of units of S3 and CL5 produced. (Setup costs being a batch-level cost cannot be avoided by producing one less unit of S3 or CL5.) Plastim's ABC system uses setup-hours—a batch-level cost-allocation base—to allocate setup costs to products. Other examples of batch-level costs are material-handling and quality-inspection costs associated with batches (not the quantities) of products produced, and costs of placing purchase orders, receiving materials, and paying invoices related to the number of purchase orders placed rather than the quantity or value of materials purchased.

Product-sustaining costs (**service-sustaining costs**) are the costs of activities undertaken to support individual products or services regardless of the number of units or batches in which the units are produced. In the Plastim example, design costs are product-sustaining costs. Over time, design costs depend largely on the time designers spend on designing and modifying the product, the mold, and the process. These design costs are a function of the complexity of the mold, measured by the number of parts in the mold multiplied by the area (in square feet) over which the molten plastic must flow (12 parts × 2.5 square feet, or 30 parts-square feet for the S3 lens, and 14 parts × 5 square feet, or 70 parts-square feet for the CL5 lens). As a result, the total design costs allocated to S3 and CL5 depend on the complexity of the mold, regardless of the number of units or batches of production. Design costs cannot be avoided by producing fewer units or running fewer batches. Plastim's ABC system uses parts-square feet—a product-sustaining cost-allocation base—to allocate design costs to products. Other examples of product-sustaining costs are product research and development costs, costs of making engineering changes, and marketing costs to launch new products.

Facility-sustaining costs are the costs of activities that cannot be traced to individual products or services but that support the organization as a whole. In the Plastim example, the general administration costs (including top management compensation, rent, and building security) are facility-sustaining costs. It is usually difficult to find a good cause-and-effect relationship between these costs and the cost-allocation base. This lack of a cause-and-effect relationship causes some companies not to allocate these costs to products and instead to deduct them as a separate lump-sum amount from operating income. Other companies, such as Plastim, allocate facility-sustaining costs to products on some basis—for example, direct manufacturing labor-hours—because management believes all costs should be allocated to products. Allocating all costs to products or services becomes important when management wants to set selling prices on the basis of an amount of cost that includes all costs.

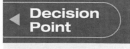

Implementing Activity-Based Costing

Now that you understand the basic concepts of ABC, let's use it to refine Plastim's simple costing system, compare it to alternative costing systems, and examine what managers look for when deciding whether or not to develop ABC systems.

Implementing ABC at Plastim

In order to apply ABC to Plastim's costing system, we follow the seven-step approach to
costing and the three guidelines for refining costing systems (increasing direct-cost tracing, creating homogeneous indirect-cost pools, and identifying cost-allocation bases that
have cause-and-effect relationships with costs in the cost pool). Exhibit 5-3 shows an
overview of Plastim's ABC system. Use this exhibit as a guide as you study the following
steps, each of which is marked in Exhibit 5-3.

Step 1: **Identify the Products That Are the Chosen Cost Objects.** The cost objects are the
60,000 S3 and the 15,000 CL5 lenses that Plastim will produce in 2011. Plastim's goal is
to first calculate the total costs and then the per-unit cost of designing, manufacturing,
and distributing these lenses.

Step 2: **Identify the Direct Costs of the Products.** Plastim identifies as direct costs of the
lenses: direct material costs, direct manufacturing labor costs, and mold cleaning and maintenance costs because these costs can be economically traced to a specific lens or mold.

Exhibit 5-5 shows the direct and indirect costs for the S3 and CL5 lenses using the
ABC system. The direct costs calculations appear on lines 6, 7, 8, and 9 of Exhibit 5-5.
Plastim classifies all other costs as indirect costs, as we will see in Exhibit 5-4.

Step 3: **Select the Activities and Cost-Allocation Bases to Use for Allocating Indirect
Costs to the Products.** Following guidelines 2 and 3 for refining a costing system, Plastim
identifies six activities—(a) design, (b) molding machine setups, (c) machine operations,
(d) shipment setup, (e) distribution, and (f) administration—for allocating indirect costs
to products. Exhibit 5-4, column 2, shows the cost hierarchy category, and column 4

Exhibit 5-3 Overview of Plastim's Activity-Based Costing System

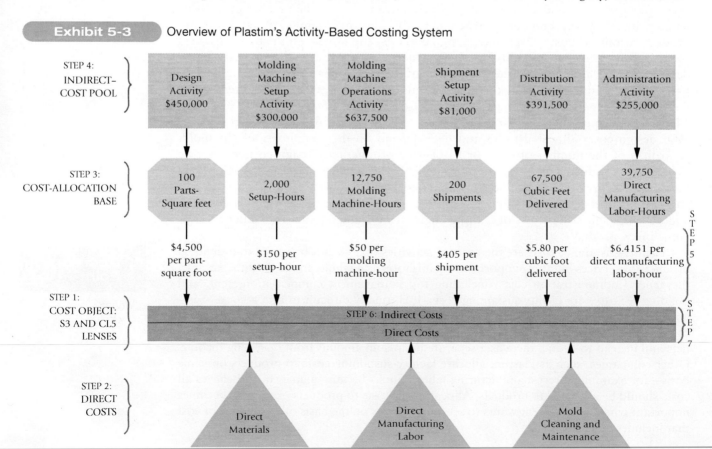

Exhibit 5-4 Activity-Cost Rates for Indirect-Cost Pools

	Home	Insert	Page Layout	Formulas	Data	Review	View	
	A	B	C	D	E	F	G	H
1			(Step 4)	(Step 3)		(Step 5)		
2	Activity	Cost Hierarchy Category	Total Budgeted Indirect Costs	Budgeted Quantity of Cost-Allocation Base		Budgeted Indirect Cost Rate		Cause-and-Effect Relationship Between Allocation Base and Activity Cost
3	(1)	(2)	(3)	(4)		(5) = (3) ÷ (4)		(6)
4	Design	Product-sustaining	$450,000	100	parts-square feet	$ 4,500	per part-square foot	Design Department indirect costs increase with more complex molds (more parts, larger surface area).
5	Setup molding machines	Batch-level	$300,000	2,000	setup-hours	$ 150	per setup-hour	Indirect setup costs increase with setup-hours.
6	Machine operations	Output unit-level	$637,500	12,750	molding machine-hours	$ 50	per molding machine-hour	Indirect costs of operating molding machines increases with molding machine-hours.
7	Shipment setup	Batch-level	$ 81,000	200	shipments	$ 405	per shipment	Shipping costs incurred to prepare batches for shipment increase with the number of shipments.
8	Distribution	Output-unit-level	$391,500	67,500	cubic feet delivered	$ 5.80	per cubic foot delivered	Distribution costs increase with the cubic feet of packages delivered.
9	Administration	Facility sustaining	$255,000	39,750	direct manuf. labor-hours	$6.4151	per direct manuf. labor-hour	The demand for administrative resources increases with direct manufacturing labor-hours.

shows the cost-allocation base and the budgeted quantity of the cost-allocation base for each activity described in column 1.

Identifying the cost-allocation bases defines the number of activity pools into which costs must be grouped in an ABC system. For example, rather than define the design activities of product design, process design, and prototyping as separate activities, Plastim defines these three activities together as a combined "design" activity and forms a homogeneous design cost pool. Why? Because the same cost driver, the complexity of the mold, drives costs of each design activity. A second consideration for choosing a cost-allocation base is the availability of reliable data and measures. For example, in its ABC system, Plastim measures mold complexity in terms of the number of parts in the mold and the surface area of the mold (parts-square feet). If these data are difficult to obtain or measure, Plastim may be forced to use some other measure of complexity, such as the amount of material flowing through the mold that may only be weakly related to the cost of the design activity.

Step 4: Identify the Indirect Costs Associated with Each Cost-Allocation Base. In this step, Plastim assigns budgeted indirect costs for 2011 to activities (see Exhibit 5-4, column 3), to the extent possible, on the basis of a cause-and-effect relationship between the cost-allocation base for an activity and the cost. For example, all costs that have a cause-and-effect relationship to cubic feet of packages moved are assigned to the distribution cost pool. Of course, the strength of the cause-and-effect relationship between the cost-allocation base and the cost of an activity varies across cost pools. For example, the cause-and-effect relationship between direct manufacturing labor-hours and administration activity costs is not as strong as the relationship between setup-hours and setup activity costs.

Some costs can be directly identified with a particular activity. For example, cost of materials used when designing products, salaries paid to design engineers, and depreciation of equipment used in the design department are directly identified with the design activity. Other costs need to be allocated across activities. For example, on the basis of interviews or time records, manufacturing engineers and supervisors estimate the time they will spend on design, molding machine setup, and machine operations. The time to be spent on these activities serves as a basis for allocating each manufacturing engineer's and supervisor's salary

Exhibit 5-5 Plastim's Product Costs Using Activity-Based Costing System

	A	B	C	D	E	F	G
1		60,000			15,000		
2		Simple Lenses (S3)			Complex Lenses (CL5)		
3		Total	per Unit		Total	per Unit	Total
4	Cost Description	(1)	(2) = (1) ÷ 60,000		(3)	(4) = (3) ÷ 15,000	(5) = (1) + (3)
5	Direct costs						
6	Direct materials	$1,125,000	$18.75		$ 675,000	$ 45.00	$1,800,000
7	Direct manufacturing labor	600,000	10.00		195,000	13.00	795,000
8	Direct mold cleaning and maintenance costs	120,000	2.00		150,000	10.00	270,000
9	Total direct costs (Step 2)	1,845,000	30.75		1,020,000	68.00	2,865,000
10	Indirect Costs of Activities						
11	Design						
12	S3, 30 parts-sq.ft. × $4,500	135,000	2.25				} 450,000
13	CL5, 70 parts-sq.ft. × $4,500				315,000	21.00	
14	Setup of molding machines						
15	S3, 500 setup-hours × $150	75,000	1.25				} 300,000
16	CL5, 1,500 setup-hours × $150				225,000	15.00	
17	Machine operations						
18	S3, 9,000 molding machine-hours × $50	450,000	7.50				} 637,500
19	CL5, 3,750 molding machine-hours × $50				187,500	12.50	
20	Shipment setup						
21	S3, 100 shipments × $405	40,500	0.67				} 81,000
22	CL5, 100 shipments × $405				40,500	2.70	
23	Distribution						
24	S3, 45,000 cubic feet delivered × $5.80	261,000	4.35				} 391,500
25	CL5, 22,500 cubic feet delivered × $5.80				130,500	8.70	
26	Administration						
27	S3, 30,000 dir. manuf. labor-hours × $6.4151	192,453	3.21				} 255,000
28	CL5, 9,750 dir. manuf. labor-hours × $6.4151				62,547	4.17	
29	Total indirect costs allocated (Step 6)	1,153,953	19.23		961,047	64.07	2,115,000
30	Total Costs (Step 7)	$2,998,953	$49.98		$1,981,047	$132.07	$4,980,000
31							

costs to various activities. Still other costs are allocated to activity-cost pools using allocation bases that measure how these costs support different activities. For example, rent costs are allocated to activity cost pools on the basis of square-feet area used by different activities.

The point here is that all costs do not fit neatly into activity categories. Often, costs may first need to be allocated to activities (Stage 1 of the 2-stage cost-allocation model) before the costs of the activities can be allocated to products (Stage 2).

Step 5: Compute the Rate per Unit of Each Cost-Allocation Base. Exhibit 5-4, column 5, summarizes the calculation of the budgeted indirect cost rates using the budgeted quantity of the cost-allocation base from Step 3 and the total budgeted indirect costs of each activity from Step 4.

Step 6: Compute the Indirect Costs Allocated to the Products. Exhibit 5-5 shows total budgeted indirect costs of $1,153,953 allocated to the simple lens and $961,047 allocated to the complex lens. Follow the budgeted indirect cost calculations for each lens in Exhibit 5-5. For each activity, Plastim's operations personnel indicate the total quantity of the cost-allocation base that will be used by each type of lens (recall that Plastim operates at capacity). For example, lines 15 and 16 of Exhibit 5-5 show that of the 2,000 total setup-hours, the S3 lens is budgeted to use 500 hours and the CL5 lens 1,500 hours. The budgeted indirect cost rate is $150 per setup-hour (Exhibit 5-4, column 5, line 5). Therefore, the total budgeted cost of the setup activity allocated to the S3 lens is $75,000 (500 setup-hours × $150 per setup-hour) and to the CL5 lens is $225,000 (1,500 setup-hours × $150 per setup-hour). Budgeted setup cost per unit equals $1.25 ($75,000 ÷ 60,000 units) for the S3 lens and $15 ($225,000 ÷ 15,000 units) for the CL5 lens.

Step 7: Compute the Total Cost of the Products by Adding All Direct and Indirect Costs Assigned to the Products. Exhibit 5-5 presents the product costs for the simple and complex lenses. The direct costs are calculated in Step 2, and the indirect costs are calculated in Step 6. The ABC system overview in Exhibit 5-3 shows three direct-cost categories and six indirect-cost categories. The budgeted cost of each lens type in Exhibit 5-5 has nine line items, three for direct costs and six for indirect costs. The differences between the ABC product costs of S3 and CL5 calculated in Exhibit 5-5 highlight how each of these products uses different amounts of direct and indirect costs in each activity area.

We emphasize two features of ABC systems. First, these systems identify all costs used by products, whether the costs are variable or fixed in the short run. When making long-run strategic decisions using ABC information, managers want revenues to exceed total costs. Second, recognizing the hierarchy of costs is critical when allocating costs to products. It is easiest to use the cost hierarchy to first calculate the total costs of each product. The per-unit costs can then be derived by dividing total costs by the number of units produced.

Decision Point

How do managers cost products or services using ABC systems?

Comparing Alternative Costing Systems

Exhibit 5-6 compares the simple costing system using a single indirect-cost pool (Exhibit 5-1 and Exhibit 5-2) Plastim had been using and the ABC system (Exhibit 5-3 and Exhibit 5-5). Note three points in Exhibit 5-6, consistent with the guidelines for

Exhibit 5-6

Comparing Alternative Costing Systems

	Simple Costing System Using a Single Indirect-Cost Pool (1)	ABC System (2)	Difference (3) = (2) − (1)
Direct-cost categories	2	3	1
	Direct materials	Direct materials	
	Direct manufacturing labor	Direct manufacturing labor	
		Direct mold cleaning and maintenance labor	
Total direct costs	$2,595,000	$2,865,000	$270,000
Indirect-cost pools	1	6	5
	Single indirect-cost pool allocated using direct manufacturing labor-hours	Design (parts-square feet)[1]	
		Molding machine setup (setup-hours)	
		Machine operations (molding machine-hours)	
		Shipment setup (number of shipments)	
		Distribution (cubic feet delivered)	
		Administration (direct manufacturing labor-hours)	
Total indirect costs	$2,385,000	$2,115,000	($270,000)
Total costs assigned to simple (S3) lens	$3,525,000	$2,998,953	($526,047)
Cost per unit of simple (S3) lens	$58.75	$49.98	($8.77)
Total costs assigned to complex (CL5) lens	$1,455,000	$1,981,047	$526,047
Cost per unit of complex (CL5) lens	$97.00	$132.07	$35.07

[1]Cost drivers for the various indirect-cost pools are shown in parentheses.

refining a costing system: (1) ABC systems trace more costs as direct costs; (2) ABC systems create homogeneous cost pools linked to different activities; and (3) for each activity-cost pool, ABC systems seek a cost-allocation base that has a cause-and-effect relationship with costs in the cost pool.

The homogeneous cost pools and the choice of cost-allocation bases, tied to the cost hierarchy, give Plastim's managers greater confidence in the activity and product cost numbers from the ABC system. The bottom part of Exhibit 5-6 shows that allocating costs to lenses using only an output unit-level allocation base—direct manufacturing labor-hours, as in the single indirect-cost pool system used prior to ABC—overcosts the simple S3 lens by $8.77 per unit and undercosts the complex CL5 lens by $35.07 per unit. The CL5 lens uses a disproportionately larger amount of output unit-level, batch-level, and product-sustaining costs than is represented by the direct manufacturing labor-hour cost-allocation base. The S3 lens uses a disproportionately smaller amount of these costs.

The benefit of an ABC system is that it provides information to make better decisions. But this benefit must be weighed against the measurement and implementation costs of an ABC system.

Considerations in Implementing Activity-Based-Costing Systems

Managers choose the level of detail to use in a costing system by evaluating the expected costs of the system against the expected benefits that result from better decisions. There are telltale signs of when an ABC system is likely to provide the most benefits. Here are some of these signs:

- Significant amounts of indirect costs are allocated using only one or two cost pools.
- All or most indirect costs are identified as output unit-level costs (few indirect costs are described as batch-level costs, product-sustaining costs, or facility-sustaining costs).
- Products make diverse demands on resources because of differences in volume, process steps, batch size, or complexity.
- Products that a company is well-suited to make and sell show small profits; whereas products that a company is less suited to produce and sell show large profits.
- Operations staff has substantial disagreement with the reported costs of manufacturing and marketing products and services.

When a company decides to implement ABC, it must make important choices about the level of detail to use. Should it choose many finely specified activities, cost drivers, and cost pools, or would a few suffice? For example, Plastim could identify a different molding machine-hour rate for each different type of molding machine. In making such choices, managers weigh the benefits against the costs and limitations of implementing a more detailed costing system.

The main costs and limitations of an ABC system are the measurements necessary to implement it. ABC systems require management to estimate costs of activity pools and to identify and measure cost drivers for these pools to serve as cost-allocation bases. Even basic ABC systems require many calculations to determine costs of products and services. These measurements are costly. Activity cost rates also need to be updated regularly.

As ABC systems get very detailed and more cost pools are created, more allocations are necessary to calculate activity costs for each cost pool. This increases the chances of misidentifying the costs of different activity cost pools. For example, supervisors are more prone to incorrectly identify the time they spent on different activities if they have to allocate their time over five activities rather than only two activities.

At times, companies are also forced to use allocation bases for which data are readily available rather than allocation bases they would have liked to use. For example, a company might be forced to use the number of loads moved, instead of the degree of difficulty and distance of different loads moved, as the allocation base for

Concepts in Action   Successfully Championing ABC

Successfully implementing ABC systems requires more than an understanding of the technical details. ABC implementation often represents a significant change in the costing system and, as the chapter indicates, it requires a manager to make major choices with respect to the definition of activities and the level of detail. What then are some of the behavioral issues that the management accountant must be sensitive to?

1. **Gaining support of top management and creating a sense of urgency for the ABC effort.** This requires management accountants to lay out the vision for the ABC project and to clearly communicate its strategic benefits (for example, the resulting improvements in product and process design). It also requires selling the idea to end users and working with members of other departments as business partners of the managers in the various areas affected by the ABC project. For example, at USAA Federal Savings Bank, project managers demonstrated how the information gained from ABC would provide insights into the efficiency of bank operations, which was previously unavailable. Now the finance area communicates regularly with operations about new reports and proposed changes to the financial reporting package that managers receive.

2. **Creating a guiding coalition of managers throughout the value chain for the ABC effort.** ABC systems measure how the resources of an organization are used. Managers responsible for these resources have the best knowledge about activities and cost drivers. Getting managers to cooperate and take the initiative for implementing ABC is essential for gaining the required expertise, the proper credibility, and the necessary leadership.

   Gaining wider participation among managers has other benefits. Managers who feel more involved in the process are likely to commit more time to and be less skeptical of the ABC effort. Engaging managers throughout the value chain also creates greater opportunities for coordination and cooperation across the different functions, for example, design and manufacturing.

3. **Educating and training employees in ABC as a basis for employee empowerment.** Disseminating information about ABC throughout an organization allows workers in all areas of a business to use their knowledge of ABC to make improvements. For example, WS Industries, an Indian manufacturer of insulators, not only shared ABC information with its workers but also established an incentive plan that gave employees a percentage of the cost savings. The results were dramatic because employees were empowered and motivated to implement numerous cost-saving projects.

4. **Seeking small short-run successes as proof that the ABC implementation is yielding results.** Too often, managers and management accountants seek big results and major changes far too quickly. In many situations, achieving a significant change overnight is difficult. However, showing how ABC information has helped improve a process and save costs, even if only in small ways, motivates the team to stay on course and build momentum. The credibility gained from small victories leads to additional and bigger improvements involving larger numbers of people and different parts of the organization. Eventually ABC and ABM become rooted in the culture of the organization. Sharing short-term successes may also help motivate employees to be innovative. At USAA Federal Savings Bank, managers created a "process improvement" mailbox in Microsoft Outlook to facilitate the sharing of process improvement ideas.

5. **Recognizing that ABC information is not perfect because it balances the need for better information against the costs of creating a complex system that few managers and employees can understand.** The management accountant must help managers recognize both the value and the limitations of ABC and not oversell it. Open and honest communication about ABC ensures that managers use ABC thoughtfully to make good decisions. Critical judgments can then be made without being adversarial, and tough questions can be asked to help drive better decisions about the system.

material-handling costs, because data on degree of difficulty and distance of moves are difficult to obtain. When erroneous cost-allocation bases are used, activity-cost information can be misleading. For example, if the cost per load moved decreases, a company may conclude that it has become more efficient in its materials-handling operations. In fact, the lower cost per load move may have resulted solely from moving many lighter loads over shorter distances.

Many companies, such as Kanthal, the Swedish manufacturer of heating elements, have found the strategic and operational benefits of a less-detailed ABC system to be good enough to not warrant incurring the costs and challenges of operating a more-detailed system. Other organizations, such as Hewlett-Packard, implement ABC in chosen divisions or functions. As improvements in information technology and accompanying

Decision Point ▶

What should managers consider when deciding to implement ABC systems?

declines in measurement costs continue, more-detailed ABC systems have become a practical alternative in many companies. As such trends persist, more detailed ABC systems will be better able to pass the cost–benefit test.

Global surveys of company practice suggest that ABC implementation varies among companies. Nevertheless, its framework and ideas provide a standard for judging whether any simple costing system is good enough for a particular management's purposes. Any contemplated changes in a simple costing system will inevitably be improved by ABC thinking. The Concepts in Action box on page 155 describes some of the behavioral issues that management accountants must be sensitive to as they seek to immerse an organization in ABC thinking.

Using ABC Systems for Improving Cost Management and Profitability

Learning Objective 7

Explain how activity-based costing systems are used in activity-based management

. . . such as pricing decisions, product-mix decisions, and cost reduction

The emphasis of this chapter so far has been on the role of ABC systems in obtaining better product costs. However, Plastim's managers must now use this information to make decisions (Step 4 of the 5-step decision process, p. 145) and to implement the decision, evaluate performance, and learn (Step 5, p. 145). **Activity-based management (ABM)** is a method of management decision making that uses activity-based costing information to improve customer satisfaction and profitability. We define ABM broadly to include decisions about pricing and product mix, cost reduction, process improvement, and product and process design.

Pricing and Product-Mix Decisions

An ABC system gives managers information about the costs of making and selling diverse products. With this information, managers can make pricing and product-mix decisions. For example, the ABC system indicates that Plastim can match its competitor's price of $53 for the S3 lens and still make a profit because the ABC cost of S3 is $49.98 (see Exhibit 5-5).

Plastim's managers offer Giovanni Motors a price of $52 for the S3 lens. Plastim's managers are confident that they can use the deeper understanding of costs that the ABC system provides to improve efficiency and further reduce the cost of the S3 lens. Without information from the ABC system, Plastim managers might have erroneously concluded that they would incur an operating loss on the S3 lens at a price of $53. This incorrect conclusion would have probably caused Plastim to reduce its business in simple lenses and focus instead on complex lenses, where its single indirect-cost-pool system indicated it is very profitable.

Focusing on complex lenses would have been a mistake. The ABC system indicates that the cost of making the complex lens is much higher—$132.07 versus $97 indicated by the direct manufacturing labor-hour-based costing system Plastim had been using. As Plastim's operations staff had thought all along, Plastim has no competitive advantage in making CL5 lenses. At a price of $137 per lens for CL5, the profit margin is very small ($137.00 – $132.07 = $4.93). As Plastim reduces its prices on simple lenses, it would need to negotiate a higher price for complex lenses with Giovanni Motors.

Cost Reduction and Process Improvement Decisions

Manufacturing and distribution personnel use ABC systems to focus on how and where to reduce costs. Managers set cost reduction targets in terms of reducing the cost per unit of the cost-allocation base in different activity areas. For example, the supervisor of the distribution activity area at Plastim could have a performance target of decreasing distribution cost per cubic foot of products delivered from $5.80 to $5.40 by reducing distribution labor and warehouse rental costs. The goal is to reduce these costs by improving the way work is done without compromising customer service or the actual or perceived value (usefulness) customers obtain from the product or service. That is, Plastim will attempt to take out only those costs that are *nonvalue added*. Controlling physical cost drivers, such as setup-hours or cubic feet delivered, is another fundamental way that operating personnel manage costs. For example, Plastim can decrease distribution costs by packing the lenses in a way that reduces the bulkiness of the packages delivered.

The following table shows the reduction in distribution costs of the S3 and CL5 lenses as a result of actions that lower cost per cubic foot delivered (from $5.80 to $5.40) and total cubic feet of deliveries (from 45,000 to 40,000 for S3 and 22,500 to 20,000 for CL5).

	60,000 (S3) Lenses		15,000 (CL5) Lenses	
	Total (1)	per Unit (2) = (1) ÷ 60,000	Total (3)	per Unit (4) = (3) ÷ 15,000
Distribution costs (from Exhibit 5-5)				
S3, 45,000 cubic feet × $5.80/cubic foot	$261,000	$4.35		
CL5, 22,500 cubic feet × $5.80/cubic foot			$130,500	$8.70
Distribution costs as a result of process improvements				
S3, 40,000 cubic feet × $5.40/cubic foot	216,000	3.60		
CL5, 20,000 cubic feet × $5.40/cubic foot			108,000	7.20
Savings in distribution costs from process improvements	$ 45,000	$0.75	$ 22,500	$1.50

In the long run, total distribution costs will decrease from $391,500 ($261,000 + $130,500) to $324,000 ($216,000 + $108,000). In the short run, however, distribution costs may be fixed and may not decrease. Suppose all $391,500 of distribution costs are fixed costs in the short run. The efficiency improvements (using less distribution labor and space) mean that the same $391,500 of distribution costs can now be used to distribute $72,500 \left(\dfrac{\$391,500}{\$5.40 \text{ per cubic feet}} \right)$ cubic feet of lenses. In this case, how should costs be allocated to the S3 and CL5 lenses?

ABC systems distinguish *costs incurred* from *resources used* to design, manufacture, and deliver products and services. For the distribution activity, after process improvements,

$$\text{Costs incurred} = \$391,500$$

$$\text{Resources used} = \$216,000 \text{ (for S3 lens)} + \$108,000 \text{ (for CL5 lens)} = \$324,000$$

On the basis of the resources used by each product, Plastim's ABC system allocates $216,000 to S3 and $108,000 to CL5 for a total of $324,000. The difference of $67,500 ($391,500 – $324,000) is shown as costs of unused but available distribution capacity. Plastim's ABC system does not allocate the costs of unused capacity to products so as not to burden the product costs of S3 and CL5 with the cost of resources not used by these products. Instead, the system highlights the amount of unused capacity as a separate line item to signal to managers the need to reduce these costs, such as by redeploying labor to other uses or laying off workers. Chapter 9 discusses issues related to unused capacity in more detail.

Design Decisions

Management can evaluate how its current product and process designs affect activities and costs as a way of identifying new designs to reduce costs. For example, design decisions that decrease complexity of the mold reduce costs of design, materials, labor, machine setups, machine operations, and mold cleaning and maintenance. Plastim's customers may be willing to give up some features of the lens in exchange for a lower price. Note that Plastim's previous costing system, which used direct manufacturing labor-hours as the cost-allocation base for all indirect costs, would have mistakenly signaled that Plastim choose those designs that most reduce direct manufacturing labor-hours when, in fact, there is a weak cause-and-effect relationship between direct manufacturing labor-hours and indirect costs.

Planning and Managing Activities

Many companies implementing ABC systems for the first time analyze actual costs to identify activity-cost pools and activity-cost rates. To be useful for planning, making decisions, and managing activities, companies calculate a budgeted cost rate for each activity and use these budgeted cost rates to cost products as we saw in the Plastim example. At year-end, budgeted costs and actual costs are compared to provide feedback on how well activities were managed and to make adjustments for underallocated or overallocated indirect costs for each activity using methods described in Chapter 4. As activities and processes are changed, new activity-cost rates are calculated.

We will return to activity-based management in later chapters. Management decisions that use activity-based costing information are described in Chapter 6, in which we discuss activity-based budgeting; Chapter 11, in which we discuss outsourcing and adding or dropping business segments; in Chapter 12, in which we evaluate alternative design choices to improve efficiency and reduce nonvalue-added costs; in Chapter 13, in which we cover reengineering and downsizing; in Chapter 14, in which we explore managing customer profitability; in Chapter 19, in which we explain quality improvements; and in Chapter 20, in which we describe how to evaluate suppliers.

Decision Point ▶

How can ABC systems be used to manage better?

Activity-Based Costing and Department Costing Systems

Companies often use costing systems that have features of ABC systems—such as multiple cost pools and multiple cost-allocation bases—but that do not emphasize individual activities. Many companies have evolved their costing systems from using a single indirect cost rate system to using separate indirect cost rates for each department (such as design, manufacturing, distribution, and so on) or each subdepartment (such as machining and assembly departments within manufacturing) that can be thought of as representing broad tasks. ABC systems, with its focus on specific activities, are a further refinement of department costing systems. In this section, we compare ABC systems and department costing systems.

Plastim uses the design department indirect cost rate to cost its design activity. Plastim calculates the design activity rate by dividing total design department costs by total parts-square feet, a measure of the complexity of the mold and the driver of design department costs. Plastim does not find it worthwhile to calculate separate activity rates within the design department for the different design activities, such as designing products, making temporary molds, and designing processes. Why? Because complexity of a mold is an appropriate cost-allocation base for costs incurred in each design activity. Design department costs are homogeneous with respect to this cost-allocation base.

In contrast, the manufacturing department identifies two activity cost pools—a setup cost pool and a machine operations cost pool—instead of a single manufacturing department overhead cost pool. It identifies these activity cost pools for two reasons. First, each of these activities within manufacturing incurs significant costs and has a different cost driver, setup-hours for the setup cost pool and machine-hours for the machine operations cost pool. Second, the S3 and CL5 lenses do not use resources from these two activity areas in the same proportion. For example, CL5 uses 75% (1,500 ÷ 2,000) of the setup-hours but only 29.4% (3,750 ÷ 12,750) of the machine-hours. Using only machine-hours, say, to allocate all manufacturing department costs at Plastim would result in CL5 being undercosted because it would not be charged for the significant amounts of setup resources it actually uses.

Based on what we just explained, using department indirect cost rates to allocate costs to products results in similar information as activity cost rates if (1) a single activity accounts for a sizable proportion of the department's costs; or (2) significant costs are incurred on different activities within a department, but each activity has the same cost driver and hence cost-allocation base (as was the case in Plastim's design department). From a purely product costing standpoint, department and activity indirect cost rates

Learning Objective 8

Compare activity-based costing systems and department costing systems

. . . activity-based costing systems are a refinement of department costing systems into more-focused and homogenous cost pools

will also result in the same product costs if (1) significant costs are incurred for different activities with different cost-allocation bases within a department but (2) different products use resources from the different activity areas in the same proportions (for example, if CL5 had used 65%, say, of the setup-hours and 65% of the machine-hours). In this case, though, not identifying activities and cost drivers within departments conceals activity cost information that would be valuable for cost management and design and process improvements.

We close this section with a note of caution. Do not assume that because department costing systems require the creation of multiple indirect cost pools that they properly recognize the drivers of costs within departments as well as how resources are used by products. As we have indicated, in many situations, department costing systems can be refined using ABC. Emphasizing activities leads to more-focused and homogeneous cost pools, aids in identifying cost-allocation bases for activities that have a better cause-and-effect relationship with the costs in activity cost pools, and leads to better design and process decisions. But these benefits of an ABC system would need to be balanced against its costs and limitations.

◀ **Decision Point**

When can department costing systems be used instead of ABC systems?

ABC in Service and Merchandising Companies

Although many of the early examples of ABC originated in manufacturing, ABC has many applications in service and merchandising companies. In addition to manufacturing activities, the Plastim example includes the application of ABC to a service activity—design—and to a merchandising activity—distribution. Companies such as the Cooperative Bank, Braintree Hospital, BCTel in the telecommunications industry, and Union Pacific in the railroad industry have implemented some form of ABC system to identify profitable product mixes, improve efficiency, and satisfy customers. Similarly, many retail and wholesale companies—for example, Supervalu, a retailer and distributor of grocery store products, and Owens and Minor, a medical supplies distributor—have used ABC systems. Finally, as we describe in Chapter 14, a large number of financial services companies (as well as other companies) employ variations of ABC systems to analyze and improve the profitability of their customer interactions.

The widespread use of ABC systems in service and merchandising companies reinforces the idea that ABC systems are used by managers for strategic decisions rather than for inventory valuation. (Inventory valuation is fairly straightforward in merchandising companies and not needed in service companies.) Service companies, in particular, find great value from ABC because a vast majority of their cost structure comprises indirect costs. After all, there are few direct costs when a bank makes a loan, or when a representative answers a phone call at a call center. As we have seen, a major benefit of ABC is its ability to assign indirect costs to cost objects by identifying activities and cost drivers. As a result, ABC systems provide greater insight than traditional systems into the management of these indirect costs. The general approach to ABC in service and merchandising companies is similar to the ABC approach in manufacturing.

The Cooperative Bank followed the approach described in this chapter when it implemented ABC in its retail banking operations. It calculated the costs of various activities, such as performing ATM transactions, opening and closing accounts, administering mortgages, and processing Visa transactions. It then used the activity cost rates to calculate costs of various products, such as checking accounts, mortgages, and Visa cards and the costs of supporting different customers. ABC information helped the Cooperative Bank to improve its processes and to identify profitable products and customer segments. The Concepts in Action feature on page 160 describes how Charles Schwab has similarly benefited from using ABC analysis.

Activity-based costing raises some interesting issues when it is applied to a public service institution such as the U.S. Postal Service. The costs of delivering mail to remote locations are far greater than the costs of delivering mail within urban areas. However, for fairness and community-building reasons, the Postal Service cannot charge higher prices to customers in remote areas. In this case, activity-based costing is valuable for understanding, managing, and reducing costs but not for pricing decisions.

Concepts in Action

Time-Driven Activity-Based Costing at Charles Schwab

Time-driven activity-based costing ("TDABC") helps Charles Schwab, the leading stock brokerage, with strategic-analysis, measurement, and management of its stock trading activity across multiple channels such as branches, call centers, and the Internet. Because the costs for each channel are different, TDABC helps answer questions such as the following: What are the total costs of branch transactions versus online transactions? Which channels help reduce overall costs? How can Charles Schwab price its services to drive changes in customer behavior?

TDABC assigns all of the company's resource costs to cost objects using a framework that requires two sets of estimates. TDABC first calculates the cost of supplying resource capacity, such as broker time. The total cost of resources including personnel, management, occupancy, technology, and supplies is divided by the available capacity—the time available for brokers to do the work—to obtain the capacity cost rate. Next, TDABC uses the capacity cost rate to drive resource costs to cost objects, such as stock trades executed through brokers at a branch, by estimating the demand for resource capacity (time) that the cost object requires.

Realizing that trades executed online cost much less than trades completed through brokers, Charles Schwab developed a fee structure for trading of mutual funds to stimulate the use of cheaper channels. Charles Schwab also used TDABC information to lower process costs by several hundred million dollars annually and to better align product pricing and account management to the company's diverse client segments. The company is working on other opportunities, including priority-call routing and email marketing, to further reduce costs while maintaining or enhancing Charles Schwab's already top-rated customer service.

Sources: Kaplan, R. S. and S. R., Anderson. 2007. The innovation of time-driven activity-based costing. *Cost Management*, March–April: 5–15; Kaplan R. S. and S.R. Anderson. 2007. *Time-driven activity-based costing.* Boston, MA: Harvard Business School Press; Martinez-Jerez, F. Asis. 2007. Understanding customer profitability at Charles Schwab. Harvard Business School Case Study No. 9-106-102, January.

Problem for Self-Study

Family Supermarkets (FS) has decided to increase the size of its Memphis store. It wants information about the profitability of individual product lines: soft drinks, fresh produce, and packaged food. FS provides the following data for 2011 for each product line:

	Soft Drinks	Fresh Produce	Packaged Food
Revenues	$317,400	$840,240	$483,960
Cost of goods sold	$240,000	$600,000	$360,000
Cost of bottles returned	$ 4,800	$ 0	$ 0
Number of purchase orders placed	144	336	144
Number of deliveries received	120	876	264
Hours of shelf-stocking time	216	2,160	1,080
Items sold	50,400	441,600	122,400

FS also provides the following information for 2011:

Activity (1)	Description of Activity (2)	Total Support Costs (3)	Cost-Allocation Base (4)
1. Bottle returns	Returning of empty bottles to store	$ 4,800	Direct tracing to soft-drink line
2. Ordering	Placing of orders for purchases	$ 62,400	624 purchase orders
3. Delivery	Physical delivery and receipt of merchandise	$100,800	1,260 deliveries
4. Shelf-stocking	Stocking of merchandise on store shelves and ongoing restocking	$ 69,120	3,456 hours of shelf-stocking time
5. Customer support	Assistance provided to customers, including checkout and bagging	$122,880	614,400 items sold
Total		$360,000	

Required

1. Family Supermarkets currently allocates store support costs (all costs other than cost of goods sold) to product lines on the basis of cost of goods sold of each product line. Calculate the operating income and operating income as a percentage of revenues for each product line.
2. If Family Supermarkets allocates store support costs (all costs other than cost of goods sold) to product lines using an ABC system, calculate the operating income and operating income as a percentage of revenues for each product line.
3. Comment on your answers in requirements 1 and 2.

Solution

1. The following table shows the operating income and operating income as a percentage of revenues for each product line. All store support costs (all costs other than cost of goods sold) are allocated to product lines using cost of goods sold of each product line as the cost-allocation base. Total store support costs equal $360,000 (cost of bottles returned, $4,800 + cost of purchase orders, $62,400 + cost of deliveries, $100,800 + cost of shelf-stocking, $69,120 + cost of customer support, $122,880). The allocation rate for store support costs = $360,000 ÷ $1,200,000 (soft drinks $240,000 + fresh produce $600,000 + packaged food, $360,000) = 30% of cost of goods sold. To allocate support costs to each product line, FS multiplies the cost of goods sold of each product line by 0.30.

	Soft Drinks	Fresh Produce	Packaged Food	Total
Revenues	$317,400	$840,240	$483,960	$1,641,600
Cost of goods sold	240,000	600,000	360,000	1,200,000
Store support cost				
($240,000; $600,000; $360,000) × 0.30	72,000	180,000	108,000	360,000
Total costs	312,000	780,000	468,000	1,560,000
Operating income	$ 5,400	$ 60,240	$ 15,960	$ 81,600
Operating income ÷ Revenues	1.70%	7.17%	3.30%	4.97%

2. Under an ABC system, FS identifies bottle-return costs as a direct cost because these costs can be traced to the soft drink product line. FS then calculates cost-allocation rates for each activity area (as in Step 5 of the seven-step costing system, described in the chapter, p. 152). The activity rates are as follows:

Activity (1)	Cost Hierarchy (2)	Total Costs (3)	Quantity of Cost-Allocation Base (4)	Overhead Allocation Rate (5) = (3) ÷ (4)
Ordering	Batch-level	$ 62,400	624 purchase orders	$100 per purchase order
Delivery	Batch-level	$100,800	1,260 deliveries	$80 per delivery
Shelf-stocking	Output unit-level	$ 69,120	3,456 shelf-stocking-hours	$20 per stocking-hour
Customer support	Output unit-level	$122,880	614,400 items sold	$0.20 per item sold

Store support costs for each product line by activity are obtained by multiplying the total quantity of the cost-allocation base for each product line by the activity cost rate. Operating income and operating income as a percentage of revenues for each product line are as follows:

	Soft Drinks	Fresh Produce	Packaged Food	Total
Revenues	$317,400	$840,240	$483,960	$1,641,600
Cost of goods sold	240,000	600,000	360,000	1,200,000
Bottle-return costs	4,800	0	0	4,800
Ordering costs				
(144; 336; 144) purchase orders × $100	14,400	33,600	14,400	62,400
Delivery costs				
(120; 876; 264) deliveries × $80	9,600	70,080	21,120	100,800
Shelf-stocking costs				
(216; 2,160; 1,080) stocking-hours × $20	4,320	43,200	21,600	69,120
Customer-support costs				
(50,400; 441,600; 122,400) items sold × $0.20	10,080	88,320	24,480	122,880
Total costs	283,200	835,200	441,600	1,560,000
Operating income	$ 34,200	$ 5,040	$ 42,360	$ 81,600
Operating income ÷ Revenues	10.78%	0.60%	8.75%	4.97%

3. Managers believe the ABC system is more credible than the simple costing system. The ABC system distinguishes the different types of activities at FS more precisely. It also tracks more accurately how individual product lines use resources. Rankings of relative profitability—operating income as a percentage of revenues—of the three product lines under the simple costing system and under the ABC system are as follows:

Simple Costing System		ABC System	
1. Fresh produce	7.17%	1. Soft drinks	10.78%
2. Packaged food	3.30%	2. Packaged food	8.75%
3. Soft drinks	1.70%	3. Fresh produce	0.60%

The percentage of revenues, cost of goods sold, and activity costs for each product line are as follows:

	Soft Drinks	Fresh Produce	Packaged Food
Revenues	19.34%	51.18%	29.48%
Cost of goods sold	20.00	50.00	30.00
Bottle returns	100.00	0	0
Activity areas:			
Ordering	23.08	53.84	23.08
Delivery	9.53	69.52	20.95
Shelf-stocking	6.25	62.50	31.25
Customer-support	8.20	71.88	19.92

Soft drinks have fewer deliveries and require less shelf-stocking time and customer support than either fresh produce or packaged food. Most major soft-drink suppliers deliver merchandise to the store shelves and stock the shelves themselves. In contrast, the fresh produce area has the most deliveries and consumes a large percentage of shelf-stocking time. It also has the highest number of individual sales items and so requires the most customer support. The simple costing system assumed that each product line used the resources in each activity area in the same ratio as their respective individual cost of goods sold to total cost of goods sold. Clearly, this assumption is incorrect. Relative to cost of goods sold, soft drinks and packaged food use fewer resources while fresh produce uses more resources. As a result, the ABC system reduces the costs assigned to soft drinks and packaged food and increases the costs assigned to fresh produce. The simple costing system is an example of averaging that is too broad.

FS managers can use the ABC information to guide decisions such as how to allocate a planned increase in floor space. An increase in the percentage of space allocated to soft drinks is warranted. Note, however, that ABC information should be but one input into decisions about shelf-space allocation. FS may have minimum limits on the shelf space allocated to fresh produce because of shoppers' expectations that supermarkets will carry products from this product line. In many situations, companies cannot make product decisions in isolation but must consider the effect that dropping or deemphasizing a product might have on customer demand for other products.

Pricing decisions can also be made in a more informed way with ABC information. For example, suppose a competitor announces a 5% reduction in soft-drink prices. Given the 10.78% margin FS currently earns on its soft-drink product line, it has flexibility to reduce prices and still make a profit on this product line. In contrast, the simple costing system erroneously implied that soft drinks only had a 1.70% margin, leaving little room to counter a competitor's pricing initiatives.

Decision Points

The following question-and-answer format summarizes the chapter's learning objectives. Each decision presents a key question related to a learning objective. The guidelines are the answer to that question.

Decision	Guidelines
1. When does product under-costing or overcosting occur?	Product undercosting (overcosting) occurs when a product or service consumes a high (low) level of resources but is reported to have a low (high) cost. Broad averaging, or peanut-butter costing, a common cause of undercosting or over-costing, is the result of using broad averages that uniformly assign, or spread, the cost of resources to products when the individual products use those resources in a nonuniform way. Product-cost cross-subsidization exists when one undercosted (overcosted) product results in at least one other product being overcosted (undercosted).
2. How do managers refine a costing system?	Refining a costing system means making changes that result in cost numbers that better measure the way different cost objects, such as products, use different amounts of resources of the company. These changes can require additional direct-cost tracing, the choice of more-homogeneous indirect cost pools, or the use of cost drivers as cost-allocation bases.
3. What is the difference between the design of a simple costing system and an activity-based costing (ABC) system?	The ABC system differs from the simple system by its fundamental focus on activities. The ABC system typically has more-homogeneous indirect-cost pools than the simple system, and more cost drivers are used as cost-allocation bases.

4. What is a cost hierarchy?

A cost hierarchy categorizes costs into different cost pools on the basis of the different types of cost-allocation bases or different degrees of difficulty in determining cause-and-effect (or benefits-received) relationships. A four-part hierarchy to cost products consists of output unit-level costs, batch-level costs, product-sustaining or service-sustaining costs, and facility-sustaining costs.

5. How do managers cost products or services using ABC systems?

In ABC, costs of activities are used to assign costs to other cost objects such as products or services based on the activities the products or services consume.

6. What should managers consider when deciding to implement ABC systems?

ABC systems are likely to yield the most decision-making benefits when indirect costs are a high percentage of total costs or when products and services make diverse demands on indirect resources. The main costs of ABC systems are the difficulties of the measurements necessary to implement and update the systems.

7. How can ABC systems be used to manage better?

Activity-based management (ABM) is a management method of decision making that uses ABC information to satisfy customers and improve profits. ABC systems are used for such management decisions as pricing, product-mix, cost reduction, process improvement, product and process redesign, and planning and managing activities.

8. When can department costing systems be used instead of ABC systems?

Activity-based costing systems are a refinement of department costing systems into more-focused and homogeneous cost pools. Cost information in department costing systems approximates cost information in ABC systems only when each department has a single activity (or a single activity accounts for a significant proportion of department costs), a single cost driver for different activities, or when different products use the different activities of the department in the same proportions.

Terms to Learn

This chapter and the Glossary at the end of this book contain definitions of the following important terms:

activity (**p. 146**)
activity-based costing (ABC) (**p. 146**)
activity-based management (ABM) (**p. 156**)
batch-level costs (**p. 149**)

cost hierarchy (**p. 149**)
facility-sustaining costs (**p. 149**)
output unit-level costs (**p. 149**)
product-cost cross-subsidization (**p. 140**)

product overcosting (**p. 140**)
product-sustaining costs (**p. 149**)
product undercosting (**p. 140**)
refined costing system (**p. 145**)
service-sustaining costs (**p. 149**)

Assignment Material

MyAccountingLab

Questions

5-1 What is broad averaging and what consequences can it have on costs?
5-2 Why should managers worry about product overcosting or undercosting?
5-3 What is costing system refinement? Describe three guidelines for refinement.
5-4 What is an activity-based approach to designing a costing system?
5-5 Describe four levels of a cost hierarchy.
5-6 Why is it important to classify costs into a cost hierarchy?
5-7 What are the key reasons for product cost differences between simple costing systems and ABC systems?
5-8 Describe four decisions for which ABC information is useful.
5-9 "Department indirect-cost rates are never activity-cost rates." Do you agree? Explain.
5-10 Describe four signs that help indicate when ABC systems are likely to provide the most benefits.

5-11 What are the main costs and limitations of implementing ABC systems?

5-12 "ABC systems only apply to manufacturing companies." Do you agree? Explain.

5-13 "Activity-based costing is the wave of the present and the future. All companies should adopt it." Do you agree? Explain.

5-14 "Increasing the number of indirect-cost pools is guaranteed to sizably increase the accuracy of product or service costs." Do you agree? Why?

5-15 The controller of a retail company has just had a $50,000 request to implement an ABC system quickly turned down. A senior vice president, in rejecting the request, noted, "Given a choice, I will always prefer a $50,000 investment in improving things a customer sees or experiences, such as our shelves or our store layout. How does a customer benefit by our spending $50,000 on a supposedly better accounting system?" How should the controller respond?

Exercises

5-16 Cost hierarchy. Hamilton, Inc., manufactures boom boxes (music systems with radio, cassette, and compact disc players) for several well-known companies. The boom boxes differ significantly in their complexity and their manufacturing batch sizes. The following costs were incurred in 2011:

a. Indirect manufacturing labor costs such as supervision that supports direct manufacturing labor, $1,450,000

b. Procurement costs of placing purchase orders, receiving materials, and paying suppliers related to the number of purchase orders placed, $850,000

c. Cost of indirect materials, $275,000

d. Costs incurred to set up machines each time a different product needs to be manufactured, $630,000

e. Designing processes, drawing process charts, making engineering process changes for products, $775,000

f. Machine-related overhead costs such as depreciation, maintenance, production engineering, $1,500,000 (These resources relate to the activity of running the machines.)

g. Plant management, plant rent, and plant insurance, $925,000

Required

1. Classify each of the preceding costs as output unit-level, batch-level, product-sustaining, or facility-sustaining. Explain each answer.

2. Consider two types of boom boxes made by Hamilton, Inc. One boom box is complex to make and is produced in many batches. The other boom box is simple to make and is produced in few batches. Suppose that Hamilton needs the same number of machine-hours to make each type of boom box and that Hamilton allocates all overhead costs using machine-hours as the only allocation base. How, if at all, would the boom boxes be miscosted? Briefly explain why.

3. How is the cost hierarchy helpful to Hamilton in managing its business?

5-17 ABC, cost hierarchy, service. (CMA, adapted) Vineyard Test Laboratories does heat testing (HT) and stress testing (ST) on materials and operates at capacity. Under its current simple costing system, Vineyard aggregates all operating costs of $1,190,000 into a single overhead cost pool. Vineyard calculates a rate per test-hour of $17 ($1,190,000 ÷ 70,000 total test-hours). HT uses 40,000 test-hours, and ST uses 30,000 test-hours. Gary Celeste, Vineyard's controller, believes that there is enough variation in test procedures and cost structures to establish separate costing and billing rates for HT and ST. The market for test services is becoming competitive. Without this information, any miscosting and mispricing of its services could cause Vineyard to lose business. Celeste divides Vineyard's costs into four activity-cost categories.

a. Direct-labor costs, $146,000. These costs can be directly traced to HT, $100,000, and ST, $46,000.

b. Equipment-related costs (rent, maintenance, energy, and so on), $350,000. These costs are allocated to HT and ST on the basis of test-hours.

c. Setup costs, $430,000. These costs are allocated to HT and ST on the basis of the number of setup-hours required. HT requires 13,600 setup-hours, and ST requires 3,600 setup-hours.

d. Costs of designing tests, $264,000. These costs are allocated to HT and ST on the basis of the time required for designing the tests. HT requires 3,000 hours, and ST requires 1,400 hours.

Required

1. Classify each activity cost as output unit-level, batch-level, product- or service-sustaining, or facility-sustaining. Explain each answer.

2. Calculate the cost per test-hour for HT and ST. Explain briefly the reasons why these numbers differ from the $17 per test-hour that Vineyard calculated using its simple costing system.

3. Explain the accuracy of the product costs calculated using the simple costing system and the ABC system. How might Vineyard's management use the cost hierarchy and ABC information to better manage its business?

5-18 Alternative allocation bases for a professional services firm. The Walliston Group (WG) provides tax advice to multinational firms. WG charges clients for (a) direct professional time (at an hourly rate) and (b) support services (at 30% of the direct professional costs billed). The three professionals in WG and their rates per professional hour are as follows:

Professional	Billing Rate per Hour
Max Walliston	$640
Alexa Boutin	220
Jacob Abbington	100

WG has just prepared the May 2011 bills for two clients. The hours of professional time spent on each client are as follows:

	Hours per Client	
Professional	San Antonio Dominion	Amsterdam Enterprises
Walliston	26	4
Boutin	5	14
Abbington	39	52
Total	70	70

Required

1. What amounts did WG bill to San Antonio Dominion and Amsterdam Enterprises for May 2011?
2. Suppose support services were billed at $75 per professional labor-hour (instead of 30% of professional labor costs). How would this change affect the amounts WG billed to the two clients for May 2011? Comment on the differences between the amounts billed in requirements 1 and 2.
3. How would you determine whether professional labor costs or professional labor-hours is the more appropriate allocation base for WG's support services?

5-19 Plant-wide, department, and ABC indirect cost rates. Automotive Products (AP) designs and produces automotive parts. In 2011, actual variable manufacturing overhead is $308,600. AP's simple costing system allocates variable manufacturing overhead to its three customers based on machine-hours and prices its contracts based on full costs. One of its customers has regularly complained of being charged noncompetitive prices, so AP's controller Devon Smith realizes that it is time to examine the consumption of overhead resources more closely. He knows that there are three main departments that consume overhead resources: design, production, and engineering. Interviews with the department personnel and examination of time records yield the following detailed information:

			Home Insert Page Layout Formulas Data Review View		
	A	B	C	D	E	F
				Usage of Cost Drivers by Customer Contract		
1			Variable Manufacturing Overhead in 2011	United Motors	Holden Motors	Leland Vehicle
2	Department	Cost Driver				
3	Design	CAD-design-hours	$ 39,000	110	200	80
4	Production	Engineering-hours	29,600	70	60	240
5	Engineering	Machine-hours	240,000	120	2,800	1,080
6	Total		$308,600			

Required

1. Compute the variable manufacturing overhead allocated to each customer in 2011 using the simple costing system that uses machine-hours as the allocation base.
2. Compute the variable manufacturing overhead allocated to each customer in 2011 using department-based variable manufacturing overhead rates.
3. Comment on your answers in requirements 1 and 2. Which customer do you think was complaining about being overcharged in the simple system? If the new department-based rates are used to price contracts, which customer(s) will be unhappy? How would you respond to these concerns?

4. How else might AP use the information available from its department-by-department analysis of variable manufacturing overhead costs?

5. AP's managers are wondering if they should further refine the department-by-department costing system into an ABC system by identifying different activities within each department. Under what conditions would it not be worthwhile to further refine the department costing system into an ABC system?

5-20 Plant-wide, department, and activity-cost rates. Tarquin's Trophies makes trophies and plaques and operates at capacity. Tarquin does large custom orders, such as the participant trophies for the Mishawaka Little League. The controller has asked you to compare plant-wide, department, and activity-based cost allocation.

Tarquin's Trophies
Budgeted Information
For the Year Ended November 30, 2011

Forming Department	Trophies	Plaques	Total
Direct materials	$13,000	$11,250	$24,250
Direct labor	15,600	9,000	24,600
Overhead Costs			
Setup			12,000
Supervision			10,386

Assembly Department	Trophies	Plaques	Total
Direct materials	$ 2,600	$ 9,375	$11,975
Direct labor	7,800	10,500	18,300
Overhead costs			
Setup			23,000
Supervision			10,960

Other information follows:

Setup costs vary with the number of batches processed in each department. The budgeted number of batches for each product line in each department is as follows:

	Trophies	Plaques
Forming department	40	116
Assembly department	43	103

Supervision costs vary with direct labor costs in each department.

1. Calculate the budgeted cost of trophies and plaques based on a single plant-wide overhead rate, if total overhead is allocated based on total direct costs.   **Required**

2. Calculate the budgeted cost of trophies and plaques based on departmental overhead rates, where forming department overhead costs are allocated based on direct labor costs of the forming department, and assembly department overhead costs are allocated based on total direct costs of the assembly department.

3. Calculate the budgeted cost of trophies and plaques if Tarquin allocates overhead costs in each department using activity-based costing.

4. Explain how the disaggregation of information could improve or reduce decision quality.

5-21 ABC, process costing. Parker Company produces mathematical and financial calculators and operates at capacity. Data related to the two products are presented here:

	Mathematical	Financial
Annual production in units	50,000	100,000
Direct material costs	$150,000	$300,000
Direct manufacturing labor costs	$ 50,000	$100,000
Direct manufacturing labor-hours	2,500	5,000
Machine-hours	25,000	50,000
Number of production runs	50	50
Inspection hours	1,000	500

Total manufacturing overhead costs are as follows:

	Total
Machining costs	$375,000
Setup costs	120,000
Inspection costs	105,000

Required

1. Choose a cost driver for each overhead cost pool and calculate the manufacturing overhead cost per unit for each product.

2. Compute the manufacturing cost per unit for each product.

5-22 Activity-based costing, service company. Quikprint Corporation owns a small printing press that prints leaflets, brochures, and advertising materials. Quikprint classifies its various printing jobs as standard jobs or special jobs. Quikprint's simple job-costing system has two direct-cost categories (direct materials and direct labor) and a single indirect-cost pool. Quikprint operates at capacity and allocates all indirect costs using printing machine-hours as the allocation base.

Quikprint is concerned about the accuracy of the costs assigned to standard and special jobs and therefore is planning to implement an activity-based costing system. Quikprint's ABC system would have the same direct-cost categories as its simple costing system. However, instead of a single indirect-cost pool there would now be six categories for assigning indirect costs: design, purchasing, setup, printing machine operations, marketing, and administration. To see how activity-based costing would affect the costs of standard and special jobs, Quikprint collects the following information for the fiscal year 2011 that just ended.

	Home	Insert	Page Layout	Formulas	Data	Review	View	
	A	B	C	D	E F G H			
1		Standard Job	Special Job	Total	Cause-and-Effect Relationship Between Allocation Base and Activity Cost			
2	Number of printing jobs	400	200					
3	Price per job	$1,200	$ 1,500					
4	Cost of supplies per job	$ 200	$ 250					
5	Direct labor costs per job	$ 180	$ 200					
6	Printing machine-hours per job	10	10					
7	Cost of printing machine operations			$150,000	Indirect costs of operating printing machines			
8					increase with printing machine hours			
9	Setup-hours per job	4	7					
10	Setup costs			$ 90,000	Indirect setup costs increase with setup hours			
11	Total number of purchase orders	400	500					
12	Purchase order costs			$ 36,000	Indirect purchase order costs increase with			
13					number of purchase orders			
14	Design costs	$8,000	$32,000	$ 40,000	Design costs are allocated to standard and special			
15					jobs based on a special study of the design department			
16	Marketing costs as a percentage of revenues	5%	5%	$ 39,000				
17	Administration costs			$ 48,000	Demand for administrative resources increases with direct labor costs			

Required

1. Calculate the cost of a standard job and a special job under the simple costing system.
2. Calculate the cost of a standard job and a special job under the activity-based costing system.
3. Compare the costs of a standard job and a special job in requirements 1 and 2. Why do the simple and activity-based costing systems differ in the cost of a standard job and a special job?
4. How might Quikprint use the new cost information from its activity-based costing system to better manage its business?

5-23 Activity-based costing, manufacturing. Open Doors, Inc., produces two types of doors, interior and exterior. The company's simple costing system has two direct cost categories (materials and labor) and one indirect cost pool. The simple costing system allocates indirect costs on the basis of machine-hours. Recently, the owners of Open Doors have been concerned about a decline in the market share for their interior doors, usually their biggest seller. Information related to Open Doors production for the most recent year follows:

	Interior	Exterior
Units sold	3,200	1,800
Selling price	$ 125	$ 200
Direct material cost per unit	$ 30	$ 45
Direct manufacturing labor cost per hour	$ 16	$ 16
Direct manufacturing labor-hours per unit	1.50	2.25
Production runs	40	85
Material moves	72	168
Machine setups	45	155
Machine-hours	5,500	4,500
Number of inspections	250	150

The owners have heard of other companies in the industry that are now using an activity-based costing system and are curious how an ABC system would affect their product costing decisions. After analyzing the indirect cost pool for Open Doors, six activities were identified as generating indirect costs: production scheduling, material handling, machine setup, assembly, inspection, and marketing. Open Doors collected the following data related to the indirect cost activities:

Activity	Activity Cost	Activity Cost Driver
Production scheduling	$95,000	Production runs
Material handling	$45,000	Material moves
Machine setup	$25,000	Machine setups
Assembly	$60,000	Machine-hours
Inspection	$ 8,000	Number of inspections

Marketing costs were determined to be 3% of the sales revenue for each type of door.

1. Calculate the cost of an interior door and an exterior door under the existing simple costing system.
2. Calculate the cost of an interior door and an exterior door under an activity-based costing system.
3. Compare the costs of the doors in requirements 1 and 2. Why do the simple and activity-based costing systems differ in the cost of an interior and exterior door?
4. How might Open Door, Inc., use the new cost information from its activity-based costing system to address the declining market share for interior doors?

Required

5-24 ABC, retail product-line profitability. Family Supermarkets (FS) operates at capacity and decides to apply ABC analysis to three product lines: baked goods, milk and fruit juice, and frozen foods. It identifies four activities and their activity cost rates as follows:

Ordering	$100 per purchase order
Delivery and receipt of merchandise	$ 80 per delivery
Shelf-stocking	$ 20 per hour
Customer support and assistance	$ 0.20 per item sold

The revenues, cost of goods sold, store support costs, the activities that account for the store support costs, and activity-area usage of the three product lines are as follows:

	Baked Goods	Milk and Fruit Juice	Frozen Products
Financial data			
Revenues	$57,000	$63,000	$52,000
Cost of goods sold	$38,000	$47,000	$35,000
Store support	$11,400	$14,100	$10,500
Activity-area usage (cost-allocation base)			
Ordering (purchase orders)	30	25	13
Delivery (deliveries)	98	36	28
Shelf-stocking (hours)	183	166	24
Customer support (items sold)	15,500	20,500	7,900

Under its simple costing system, FS allocated support costs to products at the rate of 30% of cost of goods sold.

1. Use the simple costing system to prepare a product-line profitability report for FS.
2. Use the ABC system to prepare a product-line profitability report for FS.
3. What new insights does the ABC system in requirement 2 provide to FS managers?

5-25 ABC, wholesale, customer profitability. Ramirez Wholesalers operates at capacity and sells furniture items to four department-store chains (customers). Mr. Ramirez commented, "We apply ABC to determine product-line profitability. The same ideas apply to customer profitability, and we should find out our customer profitability as well." Ramirez Wholesalers sends catalogs to corporate purchasing departments on a monthly basis. The customers are entitled to return unsold merchandise within a six-month period from the purchase date and receive a full purchase price refund. The following data were collected from last year's operations:

| | Chain | | | |
	1	2	3	4
Gross sales	$55,000	$25,000	$100,000	$75,000
Sales returns:				
Number of items	101	25	65	35
Amount	$11,000	$ 3,500	$ 7,000	$ 6,500
Number of orders:				
Regular	45	175	52	75
Rush	11	48	11	32

Ramirez has calculated the following activity rates:

Activity	Cost-Driver Rate
Regular order processing	$25 per regular order
Rush order processing	$125 per rush order
Returned items processing	$15 per item
Catalogs and customer support	$1,100 per customer

Customers pay the transportation costs. The cost of goods sold averages 70% of sales.

Determine the contribution to profit from each chain last year. Comment on your solution.

5-26 ABC, activity area cost-driver rates, product cross-subsidization. Idaho Potatoes (IP) operates at capacity and processes potatoes into potato cuts at its highly automated Pocatello plant. It sells potatoes to the retail consumer market and to the institutional market, which includes hospitals, cafeterias, and university dormitories.

IP's simple costing system, which does not distinguish between potato cuts processed for retail and institutional markets, has a single direct-cost category (direct materials, i.e. raw potatoes) and a single indirect-cost pool (production support). Support costs, which include packaging materials, are allocated on the basis of pounds of potato cuts processed. The company uses 1,200,000 pounds of raw potatoes to process 1,000,000 pounds of potato cuts. At the end of 2011, IP unsuccessfully bid for a large institutional contract. Its bid was reported to be 30% above the winning bid. This feedback came as a shock because IP included only a minimum profit margin on its bid and the Pocatello plant was acknowledged as the most efficient in the industry.

As a result of its review process of the lost contract bid, IP decided to explore ways to refine its costing system. The company determined that 90% of the direct materials (raw potatoes) related to the retail market and 10% to the institutional market. In addition, the company identified that packaging materials could be directly traced to individual jobs ($180,000 for retail and $8,000 for institutional). Also, the company used ABC to identify three main activity areas that generated support costs: cleaning, cutting, and packaging.

- **Cleaning Activity Area**—The cost-allocation base is pounds of raw potatoes cleaned.

- **Cutting Activity Area**—The production line produces (a) 250 pounds of retail potato cuts per cutting-hour and (b) 400 pounds of institutional potato cuts per cutting-hour. The cost-allocation base is cutting-hours on the production line.

- **Packaging Activity Area**—The packaging line packages (a) 25 pounds of retail potato cuts per packaging-hour and (b) 100 pounds of institutional potato cuts per packaging-hour. The cost-allocation base is packaging-hours on the production line.

The following table summarizes the actual costs for 2011 before and after the preceding cost analysis:

	Before the cost analysis	After the cost analysis			
		Production Support	Retail	Institutional	Total
Direct materials used					
Potatoes	$ 150,000		$135,000	$15,000	$ 150,000
Packaging			180,000	8,000	188,000
Production support	983,000				
Cleaning		$120,000			120,000
Cutting		231,000			231,000
Packaging		444,000			444,000
Total	$1,133,000	$795,000	$315,000	$23,000	$1,133,000

1. Using the simple costing system, what is the cost per pound of potato cuts produced by IP?
2. Calculate the cost rate per unit of the cost driver in the (a) cleaning, (b) cutting, and (c) packaging activity areas.
3. Suppose IP uses information from its activity cost rates to calculate costs incurred on retail potato cuts and institutional potato cuts. Using the ABC system, what is the cost per pound of (a) retail potato cuts and (b) institutional potato cuts?
4. Comment on the cost differences between the two costing systems in requirements 1 and 3. How might IP use the information in requirement 3 to make better decisions?

5-27 Activity-based costing. The job costing system at Smith's Custom Framing has five indirect cost pools (purchasing, material handling, machine maintenance, product inspection, and packaging). The company is in the process of bidding on two jobs; Job 215, an order of 15 intricate personalized frames, and Job 325, an order of 6 standard personalized frames. The controller wants you to compare overhead allocated under the current simple job-costing system and a newly-designed activity-based job-costing system. Total budgeted costs in each indirect cost pool and the budgeted quantity of activity driver are as follows:

	Budgeted Overhead	Activity Driver	Budgeted Quantity of Activity Driver
Purchasing	$ 70,000	Purchase orders processed	2,000
Material handling	87,500	Material moves	5,000
Machine maintenance	237,300	Machine-hours	10,500
Product inspection	18,900	Inspections	1,200
Packaging	39,900	Units produced	3,800
	$453,600		

Information related to Job 215 and Job 325 follows. Job 215 incurs more batch-level costs because it uses more types of materials that need to be purchased, moved, and inspected relative to Job 325.

	Job 215	Job 325
Number of purchase orders	25	8
Number of material moves	10	4
Machine-hours	40	60
Number of inspections	9	3
Units produced	15	6

1. Compute the total overhead allocated to each job under a simple costing system, where overhead is allocated based on machine-hours.
2. Compute the total overhead allocated to each job under an activity-based costing system using the appropriate activity drivers.
3. Explain why Smith's Custom Framing might favor the ABC job-costing system over the simple job-costing system, especially in its bidding process.

5-28 ABC, product costing at banks, cross-subsidization. National Savings Bank (NSB) is examining the profitability of its Premier Account, a combined savings and checking account. Depositors receive a 7% annual interest rate on their average deposit. NSB earns an interest rate spread of 3% (the difference between the rate at which it lends money and the rate it pays depositors) by lending money for home loan purposes at 10%. Thus, NSB would gain $60 on the interest spread if a depositor had an average Premier Account balance of $2,000 in 2011 ($2,000 × 3% = $60).

The Premier Account allows depositors unlimited use of services such as deposits, withdrawals, checking accounts, and foreign currency drafts. Depositors with Premier Account balances of $1,000 or more receive unlimited free use of services. Depositors with minimum balances of less than $1,000 pay a $22-a-month service fee for their Premier Account.

NSB recently conducted an activity-based costing study of its services. It assessed the following costs for six individual services. The use of these services in 2011 by three customers is as follows:

	Activity-Based Cost per "Transaction"	Account Usage		
		Holt	Turner	Graham
Deposit/withdrawal with teller	$ 2.30	42	48	5
Deposit/withdrawal with automatic teller machine (ATM)	0.70	7	19	17
Deposit/withdrawal on prearranged monthly basis	0.40	0	13	62
Bank checks written	8.40	11	1	3
Foreign currency drafts	12.40	4	2	6
Inquiries about account balance	1.40	12	20	9
Average Premier Account balance for 2011		$1,100	$700	$24,600

Assume Holt and Graham always maintain a balance above $1,000, whereas Turner always has a balance below $1,000.

Required

1. Compute the 2011 profitability of the Holt, Turner, and Graham Premier Accounts at NSB.
2. Why might NSB worry about the profitability of individual customers if the Premier Account product offering is profitable as a whole?
3. What changes would you recommend for NSB's Premier Account?

MyAccountingLab

Problems

5-29 Job costing with single direct-cost category, single indirect-cost pool, law firm. Wigan Associates is a recently formed law partnership. Ellery Hanley, the managing partner of Wigan Associates, has just finished a tense phone call with Martin Offiah, president of Widnes Coal. Offiah strongly complained about the price Wigan charged for some legal work done for Widnes Coal.

Hanley also received a phone call from its only other client (St. Helen's Glass), which was very pleased with both the quality of the work and the price charged on its most recent job.

Wigan Associates operates at capacity and uses a cost-based approach to pricing (billing) each job. Currently it uses a simple costing system with a single direct-cost category (professional labor-hours) and a single indirect-cost pool (general support). Indirect costs are allocated to cases on the basis of professional labor-hours per case. The job files show the following:

	Widnes Coal	St. Helen's Glass
Professional labor	104 hours	96 hours

Professional labor costs at Wigan Associates are $70 an hour. Indirect costs are allocated to cases at $105 an hour. Total indirect costs in the most recent period were $21,000.

Required

1. Why is it important for Wigan Associates to understand the costs associated with individual jobs?
2. Compute the costs of the Widnes Coal and St. Helen's Glass jobs using Wigan's simple costing system.

5-30 Job costing with multiple direct-cost categories, single indirect-cost pool, law firm (continuation of 5-29). Hanley asks his assistant to collect details on those costs included in the $21,000 indirect-cost pool that can be traced to each individual job. After analysis, Wigan is able to reclassify $14,000 of the $21,000 as direct costs:

Other Direct Costs	Widnes Coal	St. Helen's Glass
Research support labor	$1,600	$ 3,400
Computer time	500	1,300
Travel and allowances	600	4,400
Telephones/faxes	200	1,000
Photocopying	250	750
Total	$3,150	$10,850

Hanley decides to calculate the costs of each job as if Wigan had used six direct cost-pools and a single indirect-cost pool. The single indirect-cost pool would have $7,000 of costs and would be allocated to each case using the professional labor-hours base.

Required

1. What is the revised indirect-cost allocation rate per professional labor-hour for Wigan Associates when total indirect costs are $7,000?
2. Compute the costs of the Widnes and St. Helen's jobs if Wigan Associates had used its refined costing system with multiple direct-cost categories and one indirect-cost pool.
3. Compare the costs of Widnes and St. Helen's jobs in requirement 2 with those in requirement 2 of Problem 5-29. Comment on the results.

5-31 Job costing with multiple direct-cost categories, multiple indirect-cost pools, law firm (continuation of 5-29 and 5-30). Wigan has two classifications of professional staff: partners and associates. Hanley asks his assistant to examine the relative use of partners and associates on the recent Widnes Coal and St. Helen's jobs. The Widnes job used 24 partner-hours and 80 associate-hours. The St. Helen's job used 56 partner-hours and 40 associate-hours. Therefore, totals of the two jobs together were 80 partner-hours and 120 associate-hours. Hanley decides to examine how using separate direct-cost rates for partners and associates and using separate indirect-cost pools for partners and associates would have affected the costs of the Widnes and St. Helen's jobs. Indirect costs in each indirect-cost pool would be allocated on the basis of total hours of that category of professional labor. From the total indirect cost-pool of $7,000, $4,600 is attributable to the activities of partners, and $2,400 is attributable to the activities of associates.

The rates per category of professional labor are as follows:

Category of Professional Labor	Direct Cost per Hour	Indirect Cost per Hour
Partner	$100.00	$4,600 ÷ 80 hours = $57.50
Associate	50.00	$2,400 ÷ 120 hours = $20.00

Required

1. Compute the costs of the Widnes and St. Helen's cases using Wigan's further refined system, with multiple direct-cost categories and multiple indirect-cost pools.
2. For what decisions might Wigan Associates find it more useful to use this job-costing approach rather than the approaches in Problem 5-29 or 5-30?

5-32 Plant-wide, department, and activity-cost rates. Allen's Aero Toys makes two models of toy airplanes, fighter jets, and cargo planes. The fighter jets are more detailed and require smaller batch sizes. The controller has asked you to compare plant-wide, department, and activity-based cost allocations.

Allen's Aero Toys
Budgeted Information per unit
For the Year Ended 30 November 2010

Assembly Department	Fighters	Cargo	Total
Direct materials	$2.50	$3.75	$ 6.25
Direct manufacturing labor	3.50	2.00	5.50
Total direct cost per unit	$6.00	$5.75	$11.75

Painting Department	Fighters	Cargo	
Direct materials	$0.50	$1.00	$ 1.50
Direct manufacturing labor	2.25	1.50	3.75
Total direct cost per unit	$2.75	$2.50	$ 5.25
Number of units produced	800	740	

The budgeted overhead cost for each department is as follows:

	Assembly Department	Painting Department	Total
Materials handling	$1,700	$ 900	$ 2,600
Quality inspection	2,750	1,150	3,900
Utilities	2,580	2,100	4,680
	$7,030	$4,150	$11,180

Other information follows:

Materials handling and quality inspection costs vary with the number of batches processed in each department. The budgeted number of batches for each product line in each department is as follows:

	Fighters	Cargo	Total
Assembly department	150	48	198
Painting department	100	32	132
Total	250	80	330

Utilities costs vary with direct manufacturing labor cost in each department.

Required

1. Calculate the budgeted cost per unit for fighter jets and cargo planes based on a single plant-wide overhead rate, if total overhead is allocated based on total direct costs.
2. Calculate the budgeted cost per unit for fighter jets and cargo planes based on departmental overhead rates, where assembly department overhead costs are allocated based on direct manufacturing labor costs of the assembly department and painting department overhead costs are allocated based on total direct costs of the painting department.
3. Calculate the budgeted cost per unit for fighter jets and cargo planes if Allen's Aero Toys allocates overhead costs using activity-based costing.
4. Explain how activity-based costing could improve or reduce decision quality.

5-33 Department and activity-cost rates, service sector. Roxbury's Radiology Center (RRC) performs X-rays, ultrasounds, CT scans, and MRIs. RRC has developed a reputation as a top Radiology Center in the state. RRC has achieved this status because it constantly reexamines its processes and procedures. RRC has been using a single, facility-wide overhead allocation rate. The VP of Finance believes that RRC can make better process improvements if it uses more disaggregated cost information. She says, "We have state of the art medical imaging technology. Can't we have state of the art accounting technology?"

Roxbury's Radiology Center
Budgeted Information
For the Year Ended May 30, 2011

	X-rays	Ultrasound	CT scan	MRI	Total
Technician labor	$ 64,000	$104,000	$119,000	$106,000	$ 393,000
Depreciation	136,800	231,000	400,200	792,000	1560,000
Materials	22,400	16,500	23,900	30,800	93,600
Administration					19,000
Maintenance					260,000
Sanitation					267,900
Utilities					121,200
	$223,200	$351,500	$543,100	$928,800	$2,714,700
Number of procedures	2,555	4,760	3,290	2,695	
Minutes to clean after each procedure	10	10	20	40	
Minutes for each procedure	5	20	15	40	

RRC operates at capacity. The proposed allocation bases for overhead are as follows:

Administration	Number of procedures
Maintenance (including parts)	Capital cost of the equipment (use Depreciation)
Sanitation	Total cleaning minutes
Utilities	Total procedure minutes

Required

1. Calculate the budgeted cost per service for X-rays, Ultrasounds, CT scans, and MRIs using direct technician labor costs as the allocation basis.
2. Calculate the budgeted cost per service of X-rays, Ultrasounds, CT scans, and MRIs if RRC allocated overhead costs using activity-based costing.
3. Explain how the disaggregation of information could be helpful to RRC's intention to continuously improve its services.

5-34 Choosing cost drivers, activity-based costing, activity-based management. Annie Warbucks runs a dance studio with childcare and adult fitness classes. Annie's budget for the upcoming year is as follows:

Annie Warbuck's Dance Studio
Budgeted Costs and Activities
For the Year Ended June 30, 2010

Dance teacher salaries	$62,100	
Child care teacher salaries	24,300	
Fitness instructor salaries	39,060	
Total salaries		$125,460
Supplies (art, dance accessories, fitness)		21,984
Rent, maintenance, and utilities		97,511
Administration salaries		50,075
Marketing expenses		21,000
Total		$316,030

Other budget information follows:

	Dance	Childcare	Fitness	Total
Square footage	6,000	3,150	2,500	11,650
Number of participants	1,485	450	270	2,205
Teachers per hour	3	3	1	7
Number of advertisements	26	24	20	70

1. Determine which costs are direct costs and which costs are indirect costs of different programs.
2. Choose a cost driver for the indirect costs and calculate the budgeted cost per unit of the cost driver. Explain briefly your choice of cost driver.
3. Calculate the budgeted costs of each program.
4. How can Annie use this information for pricing? What other factors should she consider?

Required

5-35 Activity-based costing, merchandising. Pharmacare, Inc., a distributor of special pharmaceutical products, operates at capacity and has three main market segments:

a. General supermarket chains
b. Drugstore chains
c. Mom-and-Pop single-store pharmacies

Rick Flair, the new controller of Pharmacare, reported the following data for 2011:

	Home Insert Page Layout Formulas Data Review View			
	A	B	C	D	E
---	---	---	---	---	---
1					
2	Pharmacare, 2011	General			
3		Supermarket	Drugstore	Mom-and-Pop	
4		Chains	Chains	Single Stores	Pharmacare
5	Revenues	$3,708,000	$3,150,000	$1,980,000	$8,838,000
6	Cost of goods sold	3,600,000	3,000,000	1,800,000	8,400,000
7	Gross margin	$ 108,000	$ 150,000	$ 180,000	438,000
8	Other operating costs				301,080
9	Operating income				$ 136,920

For many years, Pharmacare has used gross margin percentage [(Revenue – Cost of goods sold) ÷ Revenue] to evaluate the relative profitability of its market segments. But, Flair recently attended a seminar on activity-based costing and is considering using it at Pharmacare to analyze and allocate "other operating costs." He meets with all the key managers and several of his operations and sales staff and they agree that there are five key activities that drive other operating costs at Pharmacare:

Activity Area	Cost Driver
Order processing	Number of customer purchase orders
Line-item processing	Number of line items ordered by customers
Delivering to stores	Number of store deliveries
Cartons shipped to store	Number of cartons shipped
Stocking of customer store shelves	Hours of shelf-stocking

Each customer order consists of one or more line items. A line item represents a single product (such as Extra-Strength Tylenol Tablets). Each product line item is delivered in one or more separate cartons. Each store delivery entails the delivery of one or more cartons of products to a customer. Pharmacare's staff stacks cartons directly onto display shelves in customers' stores. Currently, there is no additional charge to the customer for shelf-stocking and not all customers use Pharmacare for this activity. The level of each activity in the three market segments and the total cost incurred for each activity in 2011 is as follows:

	Home	Insert	Page Layout	Formulas	Data	Review	View	
	A		B	C	D		E	
13								
14	**Activity-based Cost Data**			**Activity Level**				
15	**Pharmacare 2011**		**General**				**Total Cost**	
16			**Supermarket**	**Drugstore**	**Mom-and-Pop**		**of Activity**	
17	**Activity**		**Chains**	**Chains**	**Single Stores**		**in 2011**	
18	Orders processed (number)		140	360	1,500		$ 80,000	
19	Line-items ordered (number)		1,960	4,320	15,000		63,840	
20	Store deliveries made (number)		120	360	1,000		71,000	
21	Cartons shipped to stores (number)		36,000	24,000	16,000		76,000	
22	Shelf stocking (hours)		360	180	100		10,240	
23							$301,080	

Required

1. Compute the 2011 gross-margin percentage for each of Pharmacare's three market segments.
2. Compute the cost driver rates for each of the five activity areas.
3. Use the activity-based costing information to allocate the $301,080 of "other operating costs" to each of the market segments. Compute the operating income for each market segment.
4. Comment on the results. What new insights are available with the activity-based costing information?

5-36 Choosing cost drivers, activity-based costing, activity-based management. Pumpkin Bags (PB) is a designer of high quality backpacks and purses. Each design is made in small batches. Each spring, PB comes out with new designs for the backpack and for the purse. The company uses these designs for a year, and then moves on to the next trend. The bags are all made on the same fabrication equipment that is expected to operate at capacity. The equipment must be switched over to a new design and set up to prepare for the production of each new batch of products. When completed, each batch of products is immediately shipped to a wholesaler. Shipping costs vary with the number of shipments. Budgeted information for the year is as follows:

Pumpkin Bags
Budget for costs and Activities
For the Year Ended February 28, 2011

Direct materials—purses	$ 379,290
Direct materials—backpacks	412,920
Direct manufacturing labor—purses	98,000
Direct manufacturing labor—backpacks	120,000
Setup	65,930
Shipping	73,910
Design	166,000
Plant utilities and administration	243,000
Total	$1,559,050

Other budget information follows:

	Backpacks	Purses	Total
Number of bags	6,050	3,350	9,400
Hours of production	1,450	2,600	4,050
Number of batches	130	60	190
Number of designs	2	2	4

Required

1. Identify the cost hierarchy level for each cost category.
2. Identify the most appropriate cost driver for each cost category. Explain briefly your choice of cost driver.
3. Calculate the budgeted cost per unit of cost driver for each cost category.
4. Calculate the budgeted total costs and cost per unit for each product line.
5. Explain how you could use the information in requirement 4 to reduce costs.

5-37 ABC, health care. Uppervale Health Center runs two programs: drug addict rehabilitation and aftercare (counseling and support of patients after release from a mental hospital). The center's budget for 2010 follows:

Professional salaries:		
4 physicians × $150,000	$600,000	
12 psychologists × $75,000	900,000	
16 nurses × $30,000	480,000	$1,980,000
Medical supplies		220,000
Rent and clinic maintenance		126,000
Administrative costs to manage patient charts, food, laundry		440,000
Laboratory services		84,000
Total		$2,850,000

Muriel Clayton, the director of the center, is keen on determining the cost of each program. Clayton compiled the following data describing employee allocations to individual programs:

	Drug	Aftercare	Total Employees
Physicians	4		4
Psychologists	4	8	12
Nurses	6	10	16

Clayton has recently become aware of activity-based costing as a method to refine costing systems. She asks her accountant, Huey Deluth, how she should apply this technique. Deluth obtains the following budgeted information for 2010:

	Drug	Aftercare	Total
Square feet of space occupied by each program	9,000	12,000	21,000
Patient-years of service	50	60	110
Number of laboratory tests	1,400	700	2,100

Required

1. **a.** Selecting cost-allocation bases that you believe are the most appropriate for allocating indirect costs to programs, calculate the budgeted indirect cost rates for medical supplies; rent and clinic maintenance; administrative costs for patient charts, food, and laundry; and laboratory services.
   b. Using an activity-based costing approach to cost analysis, calculate the budgeted cost of each program and the budgeted cost per patient-year of the drug program.
   c. What benefits can Uppervale Health Center obtain by implementing the ABC system?
2. What factors, other than cost, do you think Uppervale Health Center should consider in allocating resources to its programs?

5-38 Unused capacity, activity-based costing, activity-based management. Nivag's Netballs is a manufacturer of high quality basketballs and volleyballs. Setup costs are driven by the number of batches. Equipment and maintenance costs increase with the number of machine-hours, and lease rent is paid per square foot. Capacity of the facility is 12,000 square feet and Nivag is using only 70% of this capacity. Nivag records the cost of unused capacity as a separate line item, and not as a product cost. The following is the budgeted information for Nivag:

Nivag's Netballs
Budgeted Costs and Activities
For the Year Ended August 31, 2012

Direct materials—basketballs	$ 209,750
Direct materials—volleyballs	358,290
Direct manufacturing labor—basketballs	107,333
Direct manufacturing labor—volleyballs	102,969
Setup	143,500
Equipment and maintenance costs	109,900
Lease rent	216,000
Total	$1,247,742

Other budget information follows:

	Basketballs	Volleyballs
Number of balls	66,000	100,000
Machine-hours	11,000	12,500
Number of batches	300	400
Square footage of production space used	3,360	5,040

Required

1. Calculate the budgeted cost per unit of cost driver for each indirect cost pool.
2. What is the budgeted cost of unused capacity?
3. What is the budgeted total cost and the cost per unit of resources used to produce (a) basketballs and (b) volleyballs?
4. What factors should Nivag consider if it has the opportunity to manufacture a new line of footballs?

5-39 **Activity-based job costing, unit-cost comparisons.** The Tracy Corporation has a machining facility specializing in jobs for the aircraft-components market. Tracy's previous simple job-costing system had two direct-cost categories (direct materials and direct manufacturing labor) and a single indirect-cost pool (manufacturing overhead, allocated using direct manufacturing labor-hours). The indirect cost-allocation rate of the simple system for 2010 would have been $115 per direct manufacturing labor-hour.

Recently a team with members from product design, manufacturing, and accounting used an ABC approach to refine its job-costing system. The two direct-cost categories were retained. The team decided to replace the single indirect-cost pool with five indirect-cost pools. The cost pools represent five activity areas at the plant, each with its own supervisor and budget responsibility. Pertinent data are as follows:

Activity Area	Cost-Allocation Base	Cost-Allocation Rate
Materials handling	Parts	$ 0.40
Lathe work	Lathe turns	0.20
Milling	Machine-hours	20.00
Grinding	Parts	0.80
Testing	Units tested	15.00

Information-gathering technology has advanced to the point at which the data necessary for budgeting in these five activity areas are collected automatically.

Two representative jobs processed under the ABC system at the plant in the most recent period had the following characteristics:

	Job 410	Job 411
Direct material cost per job	$ 9,700	$59,900
Direct manufacturing labor cost per job	$750	$11,250
Number of direct manufacturing labor-hours per job	25	375
Parts per job	500	2,000
Lathe turns per job	20,000	59,250
Machine-hours per job	150	1,050
Units per job (all units are tested)	10	200

Required

1. Compute the manufacturing cost per unit for each job under the previous simple job-costing system.
2. Compute the manufacturing cost per unit for each job under the activity-based costing system.
3. Compare the per-unit cost figures for Jobs 410 and 411 computed in requirements 1 and 2. Why do the simple and the activity-based costing systems differ in the manufacturing cost per unit for each job? Why might these differences be important to Tracy Corporation?
4. How might Tracy Corporation use information from its ABC system to better manage its business?

5-40 **ABC, implementation, ethics.** (CMA, adapted) Applewood Electronics, a division of Elgin Corporation, manufactures two large-screen television models: the Monarch, which has been produced since 2006 and sells for $900, and the Regal, a newer model introduced in early 2009 that sells for $1,140. Based on the following income statement for the year ended November 30, 2010, senior management at Elgin have decided to concentrate Applewood's marketing resources on the Regal model and to begin to phase out the Monarch model because Regal generates a much bigger operating income per unit.

Applewood Electronics
Income Statement
For the Fiscal Year Ended November 30, 2010

	Monarch	Regal	Total
Revenues	$19,800,000	$4,560,000	$24,360,000
Cost of goods sold	12,540,000	3,192,000	15,732,000
Gross margin	7,260,000	1,368,000	8,628,000
Selling and administrative expense	5,830,000	978,000	6,808,000
Operating income	$ 1,430,000	$ 390,000	$ 1,820,000
Units produced and sold	22,000	4,000	
Operating income per unit sold	$65.00	$97.50	

Details for cost of goods sold for Monarch and Regal are as follows:

	Monarch		Regal	
	Total	Per unit	Total	Per unit
Direct materials	$ 4,576,000	$208	$2,336,000	$584
Direct manufacturing labor[a]	396,000	18	168,000	42
Machine costs[b]	3,168,000	144	288,000	72
Total direct costs	$ 8,140,000	$370	$2,792,000	$698
Manufacturing overhead costs[c]	$ 4,400,000	$200	$ 400,000	$100
Total cost of goods sold	$12,540,000	$570	$3,192,000	$798

[a] Monarch requires 1.5 hours per unit and Regal requires 3.5 hours per unit. The direct manufacturing labor cost is $12 per hour.
[b] Machine costs include lease costs of the machine, repairs, and maintenance. Monarch requires 8 machine-hours per unit and Regal requires 4 machine-hours per unit. The machine hour rate is $18 per hour.
[c] Manufacturing overhead costs are allocated to products based on machine-hours at the rate of $25 per hour.

Applewood's controller, Susan Benzo, is advocating the use of activity-based costing and activity-based management and has gathered the following information about the company's manufacturing overhead costs for the year ended November 30, 2010.

	Total Activity	Units of the Cost-Allocation Base		
Activity Center (Cost-Allocation Base)	Costs	Monarch	Regal	Total
Soldering (number of solder points)	$ 942,000	1,185,000	385,000	1,570,000
Shipments (number of shipments)	860,000	16,200	3,800	20,000
Quality control (number of inspections)	1,240,000	56,200	21,300	77,500
Purchase orders (number of orders)	950,400	80,100	109,980	190,080
Machine power (machine-hours)	57,600	176,000	16,000	192,000
Machine setups (number of setups)	750,000	16,000	14,000	30,000
Total manufacturing overhead	$4,800,000			

After completing her analysis, Benzo shows the results to Fred Duval, the Applewood division president. Duval does not like what he sees. "If you show headquarters this analysis, they are going to ask us to phase out the Regal line, which we have just introduced. This whole costing stuff has been a major problem for us. First Monarch was not profitable and now Regal."

"Looking at the ABC analysis, I see two problems. First, we do many more activities than the ones you have listed. If you had included all activities, maybe your conclusions would be different. Second, you used number of setups and number of inspections as allocation bases. The numbers would be different had you used setup-hours and inspection-hours instead. I know that measurement problems precluded you from using these other cost-allocation bases, but I believe you ought to make some adjustments to our current numbers to compensate for these issues. I know you can do better. We can't afford to phase out either product."

Benzo knows that her numbers are fairly accurate. As a quick check, she calculates the profitability of Regal and Monarch using more and different allocation bases. The set of activities and activity rates she had used results in numbers that closely approximate those based on more detailed analyses. She is confident that headquarters, knowing that Regal was introduced only recently, will not ask Applewood to phase it out. She is also aware that a sizable portion of Duval's bonus is based on division revenues. Phasing out either product would adversely affect his bonus. Still, she feels some pressure from Duval to do something.

Required

1. Using activity-based costing, calculate the gross margin per unit of the Regal and Monarch models.
2. Explain briefly why these numbers differ from the gross margin per unit of the Regal and Monarch models calculated using Applewood's existing simple costing system.
3. Comment on Duval's concerns about the accuracy and limitations of ABC.
4. How might Applewood find the ABC information helpful in managing its business?
5. What should Susan Benzo do in response to Duval's comments?

Collaborative Learning Problem

5-41 **Activity-based costing, activity-based management, merchandising.** Super Bookstore (SB) is a large city bookstore that sells books and music CDs, and has a café. SB operates at capacity and allocates selling, general, and administration (S, G & A) costs to each product line using the cost of merchandise of each product line. SB wants to optimize the pricing and cost management of each product line. SB is wondering if its accounting system is providing it with the best information for making such decisions.

Super Bookstore
Product Line Information
For the Year Ended December 31, 2010

	Books	CDs	Café
Revenues	$3,720,480	$2,315,360	$736,216
Cost of merchandise	$2,656,727	$1,722,311	$556,685
Cost of café cleaning	—	—	$ 18,250
Number of purchase orders placed	2,800	2,500	2,000
Number of deliveries received	1,400	1,700	1,600
Hours of shelf stocking time	15,000	14,000	10,000
Items sold	124,016	115,768	368,108

Super Bookstore incurs the following selling, general, and administration costs:

Super Bookstore
Selling, General, & Administration (S, G & A) Costs
For the Year Ended December 31, 2010

Purchasing department expenses	$ 474,500
Receiving department expenses	432,400
Shelf stocking labor expense	487,500
Customer support expense (cashiers and floor employees)	91,184
	$1,485,584

Required

1. Suppose Super Bookstore uses cost of merchandise to allocate all S, G & A costs. Prepare product line and total company income statements.
2. Identify an improved method for allocating costs to the three product lines. Explain. Use the method for allocating S, G & A costs that you propose to prepare new product line and total company income statements. Compare your results to the results in requirement 1.
3. Write a memo to Super Bookstore's management describing how the improved system might be useful for managing Super Bookstore.

6

Master Budget and Responsibility Accounting

6

Master Budget and Responsibility Accounting

Amid the recent recession, one of the hottest innovations was the growth of Web sites that enable users to get an aggregate picture of their financial data and to set up budgets to manage their spending and other financial decisions online. (Mint.com, a pioneer in this market, was acquired by Intuit for $170 million in September 2009.)

Budgets play a similar crucial role in businesses. Without budgets, it's difficult for managers and their employees to know whether they're on target for their growth and spending goals. You might think a budget is only for companies that are in financial difficulty (such as Citigroup) or whose profit margins are slim—Wal-Mart, for example. As the following article shows, even companies that sell high-dollar value goods and services adhere to budgets.

"Scrimping" at the Ritz: Master Budgets

"Ladies and gentlemen serving ladies and gentlemen." That's the motto of the Ritz-Carlton. With locations ranging from South Beach (Miami) to South Korea, the grand hotel chain is known for its indulgent luxury and sumptuous surroundings. However, the aura of the chain's old-world elegance stands in contrast to its rather heavy emphasis—behind the scenes, of course—on cost control and budgets. It is this very approach, however, that makes it possible for the Ritz to offer the legendary grandeur its guests expect during their stay.

A Ritz hotel's performance is the responsibility of its general manager and controller at each location worldwide. Local forecasts and budgets are prepared annually and are the basis of subsequent performance evaluations for the hotel and people who work there.

The preparation of a hotel's budget begins with the hotel's sales director, who is responsible for all hotel revenues. Sources of revenue include hotel rooms, conventions, weddings, meeting facilities, merchandise, and food and beverage. The controller then seeks input about costs. Standard costs, based on cost per occupied room, are used to build the budget for guest room stays. Other standard costs are used to calculate costs for meeting rooms and food and beverages. The completed sales budget and annual operating budget are sent to corporate headquarters. From there, the hotel's actual monthly performance is monitored against the approved budget.

The managers of each hotel meet daily to review the hotel's performance to date relative to plan. They have the ability to adjust prices in the reservation system if they so choose. Adjusting prices can be particularly important if a hotel experiences unanticipated changes in occupancy rates.

Each month, the hotel's actual performance is monitored against the approved budget. The controller of each hotel receives a report from corporate headquarters that shows how the hotel performed against budget, as well as against the actual performance of other Ritz hotels. Any ideas for boosting revenues and reducing costs are regularly shared among hotel controllers.

Why does a successful company feel the need to watch its spending so closely? In many profitable companies, a strict budget is actually a key to their success. As the Ritz-Carlton example illustrates, budgeting is a critical function in organizations. Southwest Airlines, for example, uses budgets to monitor and manage fuel costs. Wal-Mart depends on its budget to maintain razor-thin margins as it competes with Target. Gillette uses budgets to plan marketing campaigns for its razors and blades.

Budgeting is a common accounting tool that companies use for implementing strategy. Management uses budgets to communicate directions and goals throughout a company. Budgets turn managers' perspectives forward and aid in planning and controlling the actions managers must undertake to satisfy their customers and succeed in the marketplace. Budgets provide measures of the financial results a company expects from its planned activities and help define objectives and timelines against which progress can be measured. Through budgeting, managers learn to anticipate and avoid potential problems. Interestingly, even when it comes to entrepreneurial activities, business planning has been shown to increase a new venture's probability of survival, as well as its product development and venture organizing activities.[1] As the old adage goes: "If you fail to plan, you plan to fail."

---

[1] For more details, take a look at F. Delmar and S. Shane, "Does Business Planning Facilitate the Development of New Ventures?" *Strategic Management Journal*, December 2003.

Budgets and the Budgeting Cycle

A *budget* is (a) the quantitative expression of a proposed plan of action by management for a specified period and (b) an aid to coordinate what needs to be done to implement that plan. A budget generally includes both financial and nonfinancial aspects of the plan, and it serves as a blueprint for the company to follow in an upcoming period. A financial budget quantifies management's expectations regarding income, cash flows, and financial position. Just as financial statements are prepared for past periods, financial statements can be prepared for future periods—for example, a budgeted income statement, a budgeted statement of cash flows, and a budgeted balance sheet. Underlying these financial budgets are nonfinancial budgets for, say, units manufactured or sold, number of employees, and number of new products being introduced to the marketplace.

Strategic Plans and Operating Plans

Budgeting is most useful when it is integrated with a company's strategy. *Strategy* specifies how an organization matches its own capabilities with the opportunities in the marketplace to accomplish its objectives. In developing successful strategies, managers consider questions such as the following:

- What are our objectives?
- How do we create value for our customers while distinguishing ourselves from our competitors?
- Are the markets for our products local, regional, national, or global? What trends affect our markets? How are we affected by the economy, our industry, and our competitors?
- What organizational and financial structures serve us best?
- What are the risks and opportunities of alternative strategies, and what are our contingency plans if our preferred plan fails?

A company, such as Home Depot, can have a strategy of providing quality products or services at a low price. Another company, such as Pfizer or Porsche, can have a strategy of providing a unique product or service that is priced higher than the products or services of competitors. Exhibit 6-1 shows that strategic plans are expressed through long-run budgets and operating plans are expressed via short-run budgets. But there is more to the story! The exhibit shows arrows pointing backward as well as forward. The backward arrows are a way of graphically indicating that budgets can lead to changes in plans and strategies. Budgets help managers assess strategic risks and opportunities by providing them with feedback about the likely effects of their strategies and plans. Sometimes the feedback signals to managers that they need to revise their plans and possibly their strategies.

Boeing's experience with the 747-8 program illustrates how budgets can help managers rework their operating plans. Boeing viewed updating its 747 jumbo jet by sharing design synergies with the ongoing 787 Dreamliner program as a relatively inexpensive way to take sales from Airbus' A380 superjumbo jet. However, continued cost overruns and delays have undermined that strategy: The 747-8 program is already $2 billion over budget and a year behind schedule. The company recently revealed that it expects to earn no profit on virtually any of the 105 747-8 planes on its order books. With the budget for 2010 revealing higher-than-expected costs in design, rework, and production, Boeing has postponed plans to accelerate the jumbo's production to 2013. Some aerospace experts are urging Boeing to consider more dramatic steps, including discontinuing the passenger aircraft version of the 747-8 program.

Exhibit 6-1

Strategy, Planning, and Budgets

Budgeting Cycle and Master Budget

Well-managed companies usually cycle through the following budgeting steps during the course of the fiscal year:

1. Working together, managers and management accountants plan the performance of the company as a whole and the performance of its subunits (such as departments or divisions). Taking into account past performance and anticipated changes in the future, managers at all levels reach a common understanding on what is expected.

2. Senior managers give subordinate managers a frame of reference, a set of specific financial or nonfinancial expectations against which actual results will be compared.

3. Management accountants help managers investigate variations from plans, such as an unexpected decline in sales. If necessary, corrective action follows, such as a reduction in price to boost sales or cutting of costs to maintain profitability.

4. Managers and management accountants take into account market feedback, changed conditions, and their own experiences as they begin to make plans for the next period. For example, a decline in sales may cause managers to make changes in product features for the next period.

The preceding four steps describe the ongoing budget process. The working document at the core of this process is called the *master budget*. The **master budget** expresses management's operating and financial plans for a specified period (usually a fiscal year), and it includes a set of budgeted financial statements. The master budget is the initial plan of what the company intends to accomplish in the budget period. The master budget evolves from both operating and financing decisions made by managers.

- Operating decisions deal with how to best use the limited resources of an organization.
- Financing decisions deal with how to obtain the funds to acquire those resources.

The terminology used to describe budgets varies among companies. For example, budgeted financial statements are sometimes called **pro forma statements**. Some companies, such as Hewlett-Packard, refer to budgeting as *targeting*. And many companies, such as Nissan Motor Company and Owens Corning, refer to the budget as a *profit plan*. Microsoft refers to goals as *commitments* and distributes firm-level goals across the company, connecting them to organizational, team, and ultimately individual commitments.

This book's focus centers on how management accounting helps managers make operating decisions, which is why this chapter emphasizes operating budgets. Managers spend a significant part of their time preparing and analyzing budgets. The many advantages of budgeting make spending time on the budgeting process a worthwhile investment of managers' energies.

Advantages of Budgets

Budgets are an integral part of management control systems. When administered thoughtfully by managers, budgets do the following:

- Promote coordination and communication among subunits within the company
- Provide a framework for judging performance and facilitating learning
- Motivate managers and other employees

Coordination and Communication

Coordination is meshing and balancing all aspects of production or service and all departments in a company in the best way for the company to meet its goals. *Communication* is making sure those goals are understood by all employees.

Coordination forces executives to think of relationships among individual departments within the company, as well as between the company and its supply chain partners. Consider budgeting at Pace, a United Kingdom-based manufacturer of electronic products. A key product is Pace's digital set-top box for decoding satellite broadcasts. The production manager can achieve more timely production by coordinating and

Decision Point

What is the master budget and why is it useful?

Learning Objective 2

Describe the advantages of budgets

. . . advantages include coordination, communication, performance evaluation, and managerial motivation

communicating with the company's marketing team to understand when set-top boxes will be needed. In turn, the marketing team can make better predictions of future demand for set-top boxes by coordinating and communicating with Pace's customers.

Suppose BSkyB, one of Pace's largest customers, is planning to launch a new high-definition personal video recorder service. If Pace's marketing group is able to obtain information about the launch date for the service, it can share this information with Pace's manufacturing group. The manufacturing group must then coordinate and communicate with Pace's materials-procurement group, and so on. The point to understand is that Pace is more likely to have satisfied customers (by having personal video recorders in the demanded quantities at the times demanded) if Pace coordinates and communicates both within its business functions and with its suppliers and customers during the budgeting process as well as during the production process.

Framework for Judging Performance and Facilitating Learning

Budgets enable a company's managers to measure actual performance against predicted performance. Budgets can overcome two limitations of using past performance as a basis for judging actual results. One limitation is that past results often incorporate past miscues and substandard performance. Consider a cellular telephone company (Mobile Communications) examining the current-year (2012) performance of its sales force. Suppose the performance for 2011 incorporated the efforts of many salespeople who have since left Mobile because they did not have a good understanding of the marketplace. (The president of Mobile said, "They could not sell ice cream in a heat wave.") Using the sales record of those departed employees would set the performance bar for 2012 much too low.

The other limitation of using past performance is that future conditions can be expected to differ from the past. Consider again Mobile Communications. Suppose, in 2012, Mobile had a 20% revenue increase, compared with a 10% revenue increase in 2011. Does this increase indicate outstanding sales performance? Before you say yes, consider the following facts. In November 2011, an industry trade association forecasts that the 2012 growth rate in industry revenues will be 40%, which also turned out to be the actual growth rate. As a result, Mobile's 20% actual revenue gain in 2012 takes on a negative connotation, even though it exceeded the 2011 actual growth rate of 10%. Using the 40% budgeted sales growth rate provides a better measure of the 2012 sales performance than using the 2011 actual growth rate of 10%.

It is important to remember that a company's budget should not be the only benchmark used to evaluate performance. Many companies also consider performance relative to peers as well as improvement over prior years. The problem with evaluating performance relative only to a budget is it creates an incentive for subordinates to set a target that is relatively easy to achieve.[2] Of course, managers at all levels recognize this incentive, and therefore work to make the budget more challenging to achieve for the individuals who report to them. Negotiations occur among managers at each of these levels to understand what is possible and what is not. The budget is the end product of these negotiations.

One of the most valuable benefits of budgeting is that it helps managers gather relevant information for improving future performance. When actual outcomes fall short of budgeted or planned results, it prompts thoughtful senior managers to ask questions about what happened and why, and how this knowledge can be used to ensure that such shortfalls do not occur again. This probing and learning is one of the most important reasons why budgeting helps improve performance.

Motivating Managers and Other Employees

Research shows that challenging budgets improve employee performance because employees view falling short of budgeted numbers as a failure. Most employees are motivated to work more intensely to avoid failure than to achieve success. As employees get

---

[2] For several examples, see J. Hope and R. Fraser, *Beyond Budgeting* (Boston, MA: Harvard Business School Press, 2003). The authors also criticize the tendency for managers to administer budgets rigidly even when changing market conditions have rendered the budget obsolete.

closer to a goal, they work harder to achieve it. Therefore, many executives like to set demanding but achievable goals for their subordinate managers and employees.[3] Creating a little anxiety improves performance, but overly ambitious and unachievable budgets increase anxiety without motivation because employees see little chance of avoiding failure. General Electric's former CEO, Jack Welch, describes challenging, yet achievable, budgets as energizing, motivating, and satisfying for managers and other employees, and capable of unleashing out-of-the-box and creative thinking.

Challenges in Administering Budgets

The budgeting process involves all levels of management. Top managers want lower-level managers to participate in the budgeting process because lower-level managers have more specialized knowledge and first-hand experience with day-to-day aspects of running the business. Participation creates greater commitment and accountability toward the budget among lower-level managers. This is the bottom-up aspect of the budgeting process.

The budgeting process, however, is a time-consuming one. It has been estimated that senior managers spend about 10% to 20% of their time on budgeting, and finance planning departments spend as much as 50% of their time on it.[4] For most organizations, the annual budget process is a months-long exercise that consumes a tremendous amount of resources. Despite his admiration for setting challenging targets, Jack Welch has also referred to the budgeting process as "the most ineffective process in management," and as "the bane of corporate America."

The widespread prevalence of budgets in companies ranging from major multinational corporations to small local businesses indicates that the advantages of budgeting systems outweigh the costs. To gain the benefits of budgeting, management at all levels of a company should understand and support the budget and all aspects of the management control system. This is critical for obtaining lower-level management's participation in the formulation of budgets and for successful administration of budgets. Lower-level managers who feel that top management does not "believe" in a budget are unlikely to be active participants in a budget process.

Budgets should not be administered rigidly. Attaining the budget is not an end in itself, especially when conditions change dramatically. A manager may commit to a budget, but if a situation arises in which some unplanned repairs or an unplanned advertising program would serve the long-run interests of the company, the manager should undertake the additional spending. On the flip side, the dramatic decline in consumer demand during the recent recession led designers such as Gucci to slash their ad budgets and put on hold planned new boutiques. Macy's and other retailers, stuck with shelves of merchandise ordered before the financial crisis, had no recourse but to slash prices and cut their workforce. JCPenney eventually missed its sales projections for 2008–09 by $2 billion. However, its aggressive actions during the year enabled it to survive the recession and emerge with sophisticated new inventory management plans to profit from the next holiday season.

◀ Decision Point

When should a company prepare budgets? What are the advantages of preparing budgets?

Developing an Operating Budget

Budgets are typically developed for a set period, such as a month, quarter, year, and so on. The set period can itself be broken into subperiods. For example, a 12-month cash budget may be broken into 12 monthly periods so that cash inflows and outflows can be better coordinated.

Learning Objective 3

Prepare the operating budget

. . . the budgeted income statement

Time Coverage of Budgets

The motive for creating a budget should guide a manager in choosing the period for the budget. For example, consider budgeting for a new Harley-Davidson 500-cc motorcycle. If the purpose is to budget for the total profitability of this new model, a five-year period (or more) may be suitable and long enough to cover the product from design through to manufacture, sales, and after-sales support. In contrast, consider budgeting for a school

and its supporting schedules

. . . such as cost of goods sold and nonmanufacturing costs

---

[3] For a detailed discussion and several examples of the merits of setting specific hard goals, see G. Latham, "The Motivational Benefits of Goal-Setting," *Academy of Management Executive* 18, no. 4, (2004).
[4] See P. Horvath and R. Sauter, "Why Budgeting Fails: One Management System is Not Enough," Balanced Scorecard Report, (September 2004).

play. If the purpose is to estimate all cash outlays, a six-month period from the planning stage to the final performance may suffice.

The most frequently used budget period is one year, which is often subdivided into months and quarters. The budgeted data for a year are frequently revised as the year goes on. At the end of the second quarter, management may change the budget for the next two quarters in light of new information obtained during the first six months. For example, Amerigroup, a health insurance firm, had to make substantial revisions to its third-quarter and annual cost projections for 2009 because of higher-than-expected costs related to the H1N1 virus.

Businesses are increasingly using rolling budgets. A **rolling budget**, also called a **continuous budget**, is a budget that is always available for a specified future period. It is created by continually adding a month, quarter, or year to the period that just ended. Consider Electrolux, the global appliance company, which has a three- to five-year strategic plan and a four-quarter rolling budget. A four-quarter rolling budget for the April 2011 to March 2012 period is superseded in the next quarter—that is in June 2011—by a four-quarter rolling budget for July 2011 to June 2012, and so on. There is always a 12-month budget (for the next year) in place. Rolling budgets constantly force Electrolux's management to think about the forthcoming 12 months, regardless of the quarter at hand. Some companies prepare rolling financial forecasts that look ahead five quarters. Examples are Borealis, Europe's leading polyolefin plastics manufacturer; Millipore, a life sciences research and manufacturing firm headquartered in Massachusetts; and Nordea, the largest financial services group in the Nordic and Baltic Sea region. Others, such as EMC Corporation, the information infrastructure giant, employ a six-quarter rolling-forecast process so that budget allocations can be constantly adjusted to meet changing market conditions.

Steps in Preparing an Operating Budget

The best way to explain how to prepare an operating budget is by walking through the steps a company would take to do so. Consider Stylistic Furniture, a company that makes two types of granite-top coffee tables: Casual and Deluxe. It is late 2011 and Stylistic's CEO, Rex Jordan, is very concerned about how he is going to respond to the board of directors' mandate to increase profits by 10% in the coming year. Jordan goes through the five-step decision-making process introduced in Chapter 1.

1. **Identify the problem and uncertainties.** The problem is to identify a strategy and to build a budget to achieve a 10% profit growth. There are several uncertainties. Can Stylistic dramatically increase sales for its more profitable Deluxe tables? What price pressures is Stylistic likely to face? Will the cost of materials increase? Can costs be reduced through efficiency improvements?

2. **Obtain information.** Stylistic's managers gather information about sales of Deluxe tables in the current year. They are delighted to learn that sales have been stronger than expected. Moreover, one of the key competitors in Stylistic's Casual tables line has had quality problems that are unlikely to be resolved until early 2012. Unfortunately, they also discover that the prices of direct materials have increased slightly during 2011.

3. **Make predictions about the future.** Stylistic's managers feel confident that with a little more marketing, they will be able to grow the Deluxe tables business and even increase prices slightly relative to 2011. They also do not expect significant price pressures on Casual tables in the early part of the year, because of the quality problems faced by a key competitor. They are concerned, however, that when the competitor does start selling again, pressure on prices could increase.

The purchasing manager anticipates that prices of direct materials will be about the same as in 2011. The manufacturing manager believes that efficiency improvements would allow costs of manufacturing tables to be maintained at 2011 costs despite an increase in the prices of other inputs. Achieving these efficiency improvements is important if Stylistic is to maintain its 12% operating margin (that is, operating income ÷ sales = 12%) and to grow sales and operating income.

4. **Make decisions by choosing among alternatives.** Jordan and his managers feel confident in their strategy of pushing sales of Deluxe tables. This decision has some risks but is easily the best option available for Stylistic to increase profits by 10%.

5. **Implement the decision, evaluate performance, and learn.** As we will discuss in Chapters 7 and 8, managers compare actual to predicted performance to learn about why things turned out the way they did and how to do things better. Stylistic's managers would want to know whether their predictions about prices of Casual and Deluxe tables were correct. Did prices of direct materials increase more or less than anticipated? Did efficiency improvements occur? Such learning would be very helpful as Stylistic plans its budgets in subsequent years.

Stylistic's managers begin their work toward the 2012 budget. Exhibit 6-2 shows a diagram of the various parts of the *master budget*. The master budget comprises the financial projections of all the individual budgets for a company for a specified period, usually a fiscal year. The light, medium, and dark purple boxes in Exhibit 6-2 represent the budgeted income statement and its supporting budget schedules—together called the **operating budget**.

We show the revenues budget box in a light purple color to indicate that it is often the starting point of the operating budget. The supporting schedules—shown in medium purple— quantify the budgets for various business functions of the value chain, from research and development to distribution costs. These schedules build up to the budgeted income statement—the key summary statement in the operating budget—shown in dark purple.

The light and dark blue boxes in the exhibit are the **financial budget**, which is that part of the master budget made up of the capital expenditures budget, the cash budget, the budgeted balance sheet, and the budgeted statement of cash flows. A financial budget focuses on how operations and planned capital outlays affect cash—shown in light blue.

The cash budget and the budgeted income statement can then be used to prepare two other summary financial statements—the budgeted balance sheet and the budgeted statement of cash flows—shown in dark blue. The master budget is finalized only after several rounds of discussions between top management and managers responsible for various business functions in the value chain.

We next present the steps in preparing an operating budget for Stylistic Furniture for 2012. Use Exhibit 6-2 as a guide for the steps that follow. The appendix to this chapter presents Stylistic's cash budget, which is another key component of the master budget. Details needed to prepare the budget follow:

- Stylistic sells two models of granite-top coffee tables: Casual and Deluxe. Revenue unrelated to sales, such as interest income, is zero.
- Work-in-process inventory is negligible and is ignored.
- Direct materials inventory and finished goods inventory are costed using the first-in, first-out (FIFO) method. Unit costs of direct materials purchased and unit costs of finished goods sold remain unchanged throughout each budget year but can change from year to year.
- There are two types of direct materials: red oak (RO) and granite slabs (GS). Direct material costs are variable with respect to units of output—coffee tables.
- Direct manufacturing labor workers are hired on an hourly basis; no overtime is worked.
- There are two cost drivers for manufacturing overhead costs—direct manufacturing labor-hours and setup labor-hours.
- Direct manufacturing labor-hours is the cost driver for the variable portion of manufacturing operations overhead. The fixed component of manufacturing operations overhead is tied to the manufacturing capacity of 300,000 direct manufacturing labor-hours that Stylistic has planned for 2012.
- Setup labor-hours is the cost driver for the variable portion of machine setup overhead. The fixed component of machine setup overhead is tied to the setup capacity of 15,000 setup labor-hours that Stylistic has planned for 2012.
- For computing inventoriable costs, Stylistic allocates all (variable and fixed) manufacturing operations overhead costs using direct manufacturing labor-hours and machine setup overhead costs using setup labor-hours.

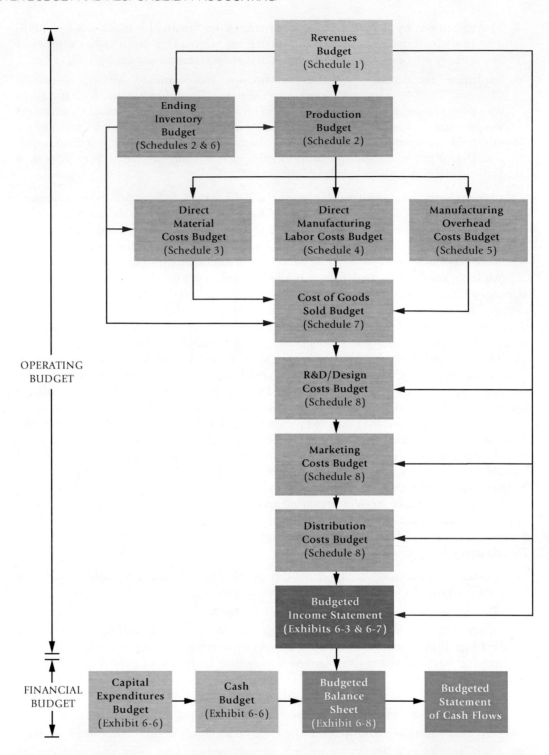

Exhibit 6-2

Overview of the Master
Budget for Stylistic
Furniture

OPERATING
BUDGET

FINANCIAL
BUDGET

■ Nonmanufacturing costs consist of product design, marketing, and distribution costs.
All product design costs are fixed costs for 2012. The variable component of marketing costs equals the 6.5% sales commission on revenues paid to salespeople. The variable portion of distribution costs varies with cubic feet of tables moved.

The following data are available for the 2012 budget:

Direct materials	
Red Oak	$ 7 per board foot (b.f.) (same as in 2011)
Granite	$10 per square foot (sq. ft.) (same as in 2011)
Direct manufacturing labor	$20 per hour

Content of Each Product Unit

	Product	
	Casual Granite Table	**Deluxe Granite Table**
Red Oak	12 board feet	12 board feet
Granite	6 square feet	8 square feet
Direct manufacturing labor	4 hours	6 hours

	Product	
	Casual Granite Table	**Deluxe Granite Table**
Expected sales in units	50,000	10,000
Selling price	$ 600	$ 800
Target ending inventory in units	11,000	500
Beginning inventory in units	1,000	500
Beginning inventory in dollars	$384,000	$262,000

	Direct Materials	
	Red Oak	**Granite**
Beginning inventory	70,000 b.f.	60,000 sq. ft.
Target ending inventory	80,000 b.f.	20,000 sq. ft.

Stylistic bases its budgeted cost information on the costs it predicts it will incur to support its revenue budget, taking into account the efficiency improvements it expects to make in 2012. Recall from Step 3 in the decision-making process (p. 188) that efficiency improvements are critical to offset anticipated increases in the cost of inputs and to maintain Stylistic's 12% operating margin. Some companies rely heavily on past results when developing budgeted amounts; others rely on detailed engineering studies. Companies differ in how they compute their budgeted amounts.

Most companies have a budget manual that contains a company's particular instructions and relevant information for preparing its budgets. Although the details differ among companies, the following basic steps are common for developing the operating budget for a manufacturing company. Beginning with the revenues budget, each of the other budgets follows step-by-step in logical fashion.

Step 1: **Prepare the Revenues Budget.** A revenues budget, calculated in Schedule 1, is the usual starting point for the operating budget. That's because the production level and the inventory level—and therefore manufacturing costs—as well as nonmanufacturing costs, generally depend on the forecasted level of unit sales or revenues. Many factors influence the sales forecast, including the sales volume in recent periods, general economic and industry conditions, market research studies, pricing policies, advertising and sales promotions, competition, and regulatory policies. In Stylistic's case, the revenues budget for 2012 reflects Stylistic's strategy to grow revenues by increasing sales of Deluxe tables from 8,000 tables in 2011 to 10,000 tables in 2012.

Schedule 1: Revenues Budget
For the Year Ending December 31, 2012

	Units	Selling Price	Total Revenues
Casual	50,000	$600	$30,000,000
Deluxe	10,000	800	8,000,000
Total			$38,000,000

The $38,000,000 is the amount of revenues in the budgeted income statement. The revenues budget is often the result of elaborate information gathering and discussions among sales managers and sales representatives who have a detailed understanding of customer needs, market potential, and competitors' products. This information is often gathered through a customer response management (CRM) or sales management system. Statistical approaches such as regression and trend analysis can also help in sales forecasting. These techniques use indicators of economic activity and past sales data to forecast future sales. Managers should use statistical analysis only as one input to forecast sales. In the final analysis, the sales forecast should represent the collective experience and judgment of managers.

The usual starting point for Step 1 is to base revenues on expected demand. Occasionally, a factor other than demand limits budgeted revenues. For example, when demand is greater than available production capacity or a manufacturing input is in short supply, the revenues budget would be based on the maximum units that could be produced. Why? Because sales would be limited by the amount produced.

Step 2:   Prepare the Production Budget (in Units). After revenues are budgeted, the manufacturing manager prepares the production budget, which is calculated in Schedule 2. The total finished goods units to be produced depend on budgeted unit sales and expected changes in units of inventory levels:

$$\begin{matrix} \text{Budget} \\ \text{production} \\ \text{(units)} \end{matrix} = \begin{matrix} \text{Budget} \\ \text{sales} \\ \text{(units)} \end{matrix} + \begin{matrix} \text{Target ending} \\ \text{finished goods} \\ \text{inventory} \\ \text{(units)} \end{matrix} - \begin{matrix} \text{Beginning} \\ \text{finished goods} \\ \text{inventory} \\ \text{(units)} \end{matrix}$$

Schedule 2: Production Budget (in Units)
For the Year Ending December 31, 2012

	Product	
	Casual	Deluxe
Budgeted unit sales (Schedule 1)	50,000	10,000
Add target ending finished goods inventory	11,000	500
Total required units	61,000	10,500
Deduct beginning finished goods inventory	1,000	500
Units of finished goods to be produced	60,000	10,000

Step 3:   Prepare the Direct Material Usage Budget and Direct Material Purchases Budget. The number of units to be produced, calculated in Schedule 2, is the key to computing the usage of direct materials in quantities and in dollars. The direct material quantities used depend on the efficiency with which materials are consumed to produce a table. In determining budgets, managers are constantly anticipating ways to make process improvements that increase quality and reduce waste, thereby reducing direct material usage and costs.

Like many companies, Stylistic has a *bill of materials*, stored and updated in its computer systems. This document identifies how each product is manufactured, specifying all materials (and components), the sequence in which the materials are used, the quantity of materials in each finished unit, and the work centers where the operations are performed. For example, the bill of materials would indicate that 12 board feet of red oak and 6 square feet of granite are needed to produce each Casual coffee table, and 12 board feet of red oak and 8 square feet of granite to produce each Deluxe coffee table. This information is then used to calculate the amounts in Schedule 3A.

Schedule 3A: Direct Material Usage Budget in Quantity and Dollars
For the Year Ending December 31, 2012

	Material		Total
	Red Oak	Granite	
Physical Units Budget			
Direct materials required for Casual tables (60,000 units × 12 b.f. and 6 sq. ft.)	720,000 b.f.	360,000 sq. ft.	
Direct materials required for Deluxe tables (10,000 units × 12 b.f. and 8 sq. ft.)	120,000 b.f.	80,000 sq. ft.	
Total quantity of direct materials to be used	840,000 b.f.	440,000 sq. ft.	
Cost Budget			
Available from beginning direct materials inventory (under a FIFO cost-flow assumption)			
Red Oak: 70,000 b.f. × $7 per b.f.	$ 490,000		
Granite: 60,000 sq. ft. × $10 per sq. ft.		$ 600,000	
To be purchased this period			
Red Oak: (840,000 – 70,000) b.f. × $7 per b.f.	5,390,000		
Granite: (440,000 – 60,000) sq. ft. × $10 per sq. ft.		3,800,000	
Direct materials to be used this period	$5,880,000	$4,400,000	$10,280,000

The purchasing manager prepares the budget for direct material purchases, calculated in Schedule 3B, based on the budgeted direct materials to be used, the beginning inventory of direct materials, and the target ending inventory of direct materials:

$$\begin{matrix} \text{Purchases} \\ \text{of direct} \\ \text{materials} \end{matrix} = \begin{matrix} \text{Direct} \\ \text{materials} \\ \text{used in} \\ \text{production} \end{matrix} + \begin{matrix} \text{Target ending} \\ \text{inventory} \\ \text{of direct} \\ \text{materials} \end{matrix} - \begin{matrix} \text{Beginning} \\ \text{inventory} \\ \text{of direct} \\ \text{materials} \end{matrix}$$

Schedule 3B: Direct Material Purchases Budget
For the Year Ending December 31, 2012

| | Material | | |
	Red Oak	Granite	Total
Physical Units Budget			
To be used in production (from Schedule 3A)	840,000 b.f.	440,000 sq. ft.	
Add target ending inventory	80,000 b.f.	20,000 sq. ft.	
Total requirements	920,000 b.f.	460,000 sq. ft.	
Deduct beginning inventory	70,000 b.f.	60,000 sq. ft.	
Purchases to be made	850,000 b.f.	400,000 sq. ft.	
Cost Budget			
Red Oak: 850,000 b.f. × $7 per b.f.	$5,950,000		
Granite: 400,000 sq. ft. × $10 per sq. ft.		$4,000,000	
Purchases	$5,950,000	$4,000,000	$9,950,000

Step 4: Prepare the Direct Manufacturing Labor Costs Budget. In this step, manufacturing managers use *labor standards*, the time allowed per unit of output, to calculate the direct manufacturing labor costs budget in Schedule 4. These costs depend on wage rates, production methods, process and efficiency improvements, and hiring plans.

Schedule 4: Direct Manufacturing Labor Costs Budget
For the Year Ending December 31, 2012

	Output Units Produced (Schedule 2)	Direct Manufacturing Labor-Hours per Unit	Total Hours	Hourly Wage Rate	Total
Casual	60,000	4	240,000	$20	$4,800,000
Deluxe	10,000	6	60,000	20	1,200,000
Total			300,000		$6,000,000

Step 5: Prepare the Manufacturing Overhead Costs Budget. As we described earlier, direct manufacturing labor-hours is the cost driver for the variable portion of manufacturing operations overhead and setup labor-hours is the cost driver for the variable portion of machine setup overhead costs. The use of activity-based cost drivers such as these gives rise to *activity-based budgeting*. **Activity-based budgeting (ABB)** focuses on the budgeted cost of the activities necessary to produce and sell products and services.

For the 300,000 direct manufacturing labor-hours, Stylistic's manufacturing managers estimate various line items of overhead costs that constitute manufacturing operations overhead (that is, all costs for which direct manufacturing labor-hours is the cost driver). Managers identify opportunities for process improvements and determine budgeted manufacturing operations overhead costs in the operating department. They also determine the resources that they will need from the two support departments—kilowatt hours of energy from the power department and hours of maintenance service from the maintenance department. The support department managers, in turn, plan the costs of personnel and supplies that they will need in order to provide the operating department with the support services it requires. The costs of the support departments are then allocated (first-stage cost allocation) as part of manufacturing operations overhead. Chapter 15 describes how the allocation of support department costs to operating departments is done when support departments provide services to each other and to operating departments. The upper half of Schedule 5 shows the various line items of costs that constitute manufacturing operations overhead costs—that is, all overhead costs that are caused by the 300,000 direct manufacturing labor-hours (the cost driver).

Stylistic's managers determine how setups should be done for the Casual and Deluxe line of tables, taking into account past experiences and potential improvements in setup efficiency. For example, managers consider the following:

- Increasing the length of the production run per batch so that fewer batches (and therefore fewer setups) are needed for the budgeted production of tables
- Decreasing the setup time per batch
- Reducing the supervisory time needed, for instance by increasing the skill base of workers

Stylistic's managers forecast the following setup information for the Casual and Deluxe tables:

	Casual Tables	Deluxe Tables	Total
1. Quantity of tables to be produced	60,000 tables	10,000 tables	
2. Number of tables to be produced per batch	50 tables/batch	40 tables/batch	
3. Number of batches (1) ÷ (2)	1,200 batches	250 batches	
4. Setup time per batch	10 hours/batch	12 hours/batch	
5. Total setup-hours (3) × (4)	12,000 hours	3,000 hours	15,000 hours
6. Setup-hours per table (5) ÷ (1)	0.2 hour	0.3 hour	

Using an approach similar to the one described for manufacturing operations overhead costs, Stylistic's managers estimate various line items of costs that comprise machine setup overhead costs—that is, all costs that are caused by the 15,000 setup labor-hours (the cost driver). Note how using activity-based cost drivers provide additional and detailed information that improves decision making compared with budgeting based solely on output-based cost drivers. Of course, managers must always evaluate whether the expected benefit of adding more cost drivers exceeds the expected cost.[5] The bottom half of Schedule 5 summarizes these costs.

Schedule 5: Manufacturing Overhead Costs Budget
For the Year Ending December 31, 2012
Manufacturing Operations Overhead Costs

Variable costs		
Supplies	$1,500,000	
Indirect manufacturing labor	1,680,000	
Power (support department costs)	2,100,000	
Maintenance (support department costs)	1,200,000	$6,480,000
Fixed costs (to support capacity of 300,000 direct manufacturing labor-hours)		
Depreciation	1,020,000	
Supervision	390,000	
Power (support department costs)	630,000	
Maintenance (support department costs)	480,000	2,520,000
Total manufacturing operations overhead costs		$9,000,000

Machine Setup Overhead Costs

Variable costs		
Supplies	$ 390,000	
Indirect manufacturing labor	840,000	
Power (support department costs)	90,000	$ 1,320,000
Fixed costs (to support capacity of 15,000 setup labor-hours)		
Depreciation	603,000	
Supervision	1,050,000	
Power (support department costs)	27,000	1,680,000
Total machine setup overhead costs		$ 3,000,000
Total manufacturing operations overhead costs		$12,000,000

[5] The Stylistic example illustrates ABB using setup costs included in Stylistic's manufacturing overhead costs budget. ABB implementations in practice include costs in many parts of the value chain. For an example, see S. Borjesson, "A Case Study on Activity-Based Budgeting," *Journal of Cost Management* 10, no. 4: 7–18.

Step 6: Prepare the Ending Inventories Budget. The management accountant prepares the ending inventories budget, calculated in Schedules 6A and 6B. In accordance with generally accepted accounting principles, Stylistic treats both variable and fixed manufacturing overhead as inventoriable (product) costs. Stylistic is budgeted to operate at capacity. Manufacturing operations overhead costs are allocated to finished goods inventory at the budgeted rate of $30 per direct manufacturing labor-hour (total budgeted manufacturing operations overhead, $9,000,000 ÷ 300,000 budgeted direct manufacturing labor-hours). Machine setup overhead costs are allocated to finished goods inventory at the budgeted rate of $200 per setup-hour (total budgeted machine setup overhead, $3,000,000 ÷ 15,000 budgeted setup labor-hours). Schedule 6A shows the computation of the unit cost of coffee tables started and completed in 2012.

Schedule 6A: Unit Costs of Ending Finished Goods Inventory
December 31, 2012

		Product				
		Casual Tables			Deluxe Tables	
	Cost per Unit of Input	Input per Unit of Output	Total		Input per Unit of Output	Total
Red Oak	$ 7	12 b.f.	$ 84		12 b.f.	$ 84
Granite	10	6 sq. ft.	60		8 sq. ft.	80
Direct manufacturing labor	20	4 hrs.	80		6 hrs.	120
Manufacturing overhead	30	4 hrs.	120		6 hrs.	180
Machine setup overhead	200	0.2 hrs.	40		0.3 hrs.	60
Total			$384			$524

Under the FIFO method, this unit cost is used to calculate the cost of target ending inventories of finished goods in Schedule 6B.

Schedule 6B: Ending Inventories Budget
December 31, 2012

	Quantity	Cost per Unit		Total	
Direct materials					
Red Oak	80,000*	$ 7	$ 560,000		
Granite	20,000*	10	200,000	$ 760,000	
Finished goods					
Casual	11,000**	$384***	$4,224,000		
Deluxe	500**	524***	262,000	4,486,000	
Total ending inventory				$5,246,000	

*Data are from page 191. **Data are from page 191 ***From Schedule 6A, this is based on 2012 costs of manufacturing finished goods because under the FIFO costing method, the units in finished goods ending inventory consists of units that are produced during 2012.

Step 7: Prepare the Cost of Goods Sold Budget. The manufacturing and purchase managers, together with the management accountant, use information from Schedules 3 through 6 to prepare Schedule 7.

Schedule 7: Cost of Goods Sold Budget
For the Year Ending December 31, 2012

	From Schedule		Total
Beginning finished goods inventory, January 1, 2012	Given*		$ 646,000
Direct materials used	3A	$10,280,000	
Direct manufacturing labor	4	6,000,000	
Manufacturing overhead	5	12,000,000	
Cost of goods manufactured			28,280,000
Cost of goods available for sale			28,926,000
Deduct ending finished goods inventory, December 31, 2012	6B		4,486,000
Cost of goods sold			$24,440,000

*Given in the description of basic data and requirements (Casual, $384,000, Deluxe $262,000).

Step 8:   Prepare the Nonmanufacturing Costs Budget. Schedules 2 through 7 cover budgeting for Stylistic's production function of the value chain. For brevity, other parts of the value chain—product design, marketing, and distribution—are combined into a single schedule. Just as in the case of manufacturing costs, managers in other functions of the value chain build in process and efficiency improvements and prepare nonmanufacturing cost budgets on the basis of the quantities of cost drivers planned for 2012.

Product design costs are fixed costs, determined on the basis of the product design work anticipated for 2012. The variable component of budgeted marketing costs is the commissions paid to sales people equal to 6.5% of revenues. The fixed component of budgeted marketing costs equal to $1,330,000 is tied to the marketing capacity for 2012. The cost driver of the variable component of budgeted distribution costs is cubic feet of tables moved (Casual: 18 cubic feet × 50,000 tables + Deluxe: 24 cubic feet × 10,000 tables = 1,140,000 cubic feet). Variable distribution costs equal $2 per cubic foot. The fixed component of budgeted distribution costs equals $1,596,000 and is tied to the distribution capacity for 2012. Schedule 8 shows the product design, marketing, and distribution costs budget for 2012.

Schedule 8: Nonmanufacturing Costs Budget
For the Year Ending December 31, 2012

Business Function	Variable Costs	Fixed Costs	Total Costs
Product design	—	$1,024,000	$1,024,000
Marketing (Variable cost: $38,000,000 × 0.065)	$2,470,000	1,330,000	3,800,000
Distribution (Variable cost: $2 × 1,140,000 cu. ft.)	2,280,000	1,596,000	3,876,000
	$4,750,000	$3,950,000	$8,700,000

Step 9:   Prepare the Budgeted Income Statement. The CEO and managers of various business functions, with help from the management accountant, use information in Schedules 1, 7, and 8 to finalize the budgeted income statement, shown in Exhibit 6-3. The style used in Exhibit 6-3 is typical, but more details could be included in the income statement; the more details that are put in the income statement, the fewer supporting schedules that are needed for the income statement.

Budgeting is a cross-functional activity. Top management's strategies for achieving revenue and operating income goals influence the costs planned for the different business functions of the value chain. For example, a budgeted increase in sales based on spending more for marketing must be matched with higher production costs to ensure that there is an adequate supply of tables and with higher distribution costs to ensure timely delivery of tables to customers.

Rex Jordan, the CEO of Stylistic Furniture, is very pleased with the 2012 budget. It calls for a 10% increase in operating income compared with 2011. The keys to achieving a higher operating income are a significant increase in sales of Deluxe tables, and process improvements and efficiency gains throughout the value chain. As Rex studies the budget

Exhibit 6-3

Budgeted Income Statement for Stylistic Furniture

	A	B	C	D
	Home Insert Page Layout Formulas Data Review View			
1	Budgeted Income Statement for Stylistic Furniture			
2	For the Year Ending December 31, 2012			
3	Revenues	Schedule 1		$38,000,000
4	Cost of goods sold	Schedule 7		24,440,000
5	Gross margin			13,560,000
6	Operating costs			
7	Product design costs	Schedule 8	$1,024,000	
8	Marketing costs	Schedule 8	3,800,000	
9	Distribution costs	Schedule 8	3,876,000	8,700,000
10	Operating income			$ 4,860,000

more carefully, however, he is struck by two comments appended to the budget: First, to achieve the budgeted number of tables sold, Stylistic may need to reduce its selling prices by 3% to $582 for Casual tables and to $776 for Deluxe tables. Second, a supply shortage in direct materials may result in a 5% increase in the prices of direct materials (red oak and granite) above the material prices anticipated in the 2012 budget. If direct materials prices increase, however, no reduction in selling prices is anticipated. He asks Tina Larsen, the management accountant, to use Stylistic's financial planning model to evaluate how these outcomes will affect budgeted operating income.

Decision Point

What is the operating budget and what are its components?

Financial Planning Models and Sensitivity Analysis

Financial planning models are mathematical representations of the relationships among operating activities, financing activities, and other factors that affect the master budget. Companies can use computer-based systems, such as Enterprise Resource Planning (ERP) systems, to perform calculations for these planning models. Companies that use ERP systems, and other such budgeting tools, find that these systems simplify budgeting and reduce the computational burden and time required to prepare budgets. The Concepts in Action box on page 198 provides an example of one such company. ERP systems store vast quantities of information about the materials, machines and equipment, labor, power, maintenance, and setups needed to manufacture different products. Once sales quantities for different products have been identified, the software can quickly compute the budgeted costs for manufacturing these products.

Software packages typically have a module on sensitivity analysis to assist managers in their planning and budgeting activities. *Sensitivity analysis* is a "what-if" technique that examines how a result will change if the original predicted data are not achieved or if an underlying assumption changes.

To see how sensitivity analysis works, we consider two scenarios identified as possibly affecting Stylistic Furniture's budget model for 2012.

Learning Objective 4

Use computer-based financial planning models in sensitivity analysis

. . . for example, understand the effects of changes in selling prices and direct material prices on budgeted income

> **Scenario 1:** A 3% decrease in the selling price of the Casual table and a 3% decrease in the selling price of the Deluxe table.

> **Scenario 2:** A 5% increase in the price per board foot of red oak and a 5% increase in the price per square foot of granite.

Exhibit 6-4 presents the budgeted operating income for the two scenarios.

Note that under Scenario 1, a change in selling prices per table affects revenues (Schedule 1) as well as variable marketing costs (sales commissions, Schedule 8). The Problem for Self-Study at the end of the chapter shows the revised schedules for Scenario 1. Similarly, a change in the price of direct materials affects the direct material usage budget (Schedule 3A), the unit cost of ending finished goods inventory (Schedule 6A), the ending

Exhibit 6-4 Effect of Changes in Budget Assumptions on Budgeted Operating Income for Stylistic Furniture

	Home	Insert	Page Layout	Formulas	Data	Review	View		
	A	B	C	D	E	F	G	H	I
1	Key Assumptions								
2		Units Sold		Selling Price		Direct Material Cost		Budgeted Operating Income	
3	What-If Scenario	Casual	Deluxe	Casual	Deluxe	Red Oak	Granite	Dollars	Change from Master Budget
4	Master budget	50,000	10,000	$600	$800	$7.00	$10.00	$4,860,000	
5	Scenario 1	50,000	10,000	582	776	$7.00	$10.00	3,794,100	22% decrease
6	Scenario 2	50,000	10,000	600	800	$7.35	$10.50	4,483,800	8% decrease

Concepts in Action

Web-Enabled Budgeting and Hendrick Motorsports

In recent years, an increasing number of companies have implemented comprehensive software packages that manage budgeting and forecasting functions across the organization. One such option is Microsoft Forecaster, which was originally designed by FRx Software for businesses looking to gain control over their budgeting and forecasting process within a fully integrated Web-based environment.

Among the more unique companies implementing Web-enabled budgeting is Hendrick Motorsports. Featuring champion drivers Jeff Gordon and Jimmie Johnson, Hendrick is the premier NASCAR Sprint Cup stock car racing organization. According to Forbes magazine, Hendrick is NASCAR's most valuable team, with an estimated value of $350 million. Headquartered on a 12 building, 600,000-square-foot campus near Charlotte, North Carolina, Hendrick operates four full-time teams in the Sprint Cup series, which runs annually from February through November and features 36 races at 22 speedways across the United States. The Hendrick organization has annual revenues of close to $195 million and more than 500 employees, with tasks ranging from accounting and marketing to engine building and racecar driving. Such an environment features multiple functional areas and units, varied worksites, and ever-changing circumstances. Patrick Perkins, director of marketing, noted, "Racing is a fast business. It's just as fast off the track as it is on it. With the work that we put into development of our teams and technologies, and having to respond to change as well as anticipate change, I like to think of us in this business as change experts."

Microsoft Forecaster, Hendrick's Web-enabled budgeting package, has allowed Hendrick's financial managers to seamlessly manage the planning and budgeting process. Authorized users from each functional area or team sign on to the application through the corporate intranet. Security on the system is tight: Access is limited to only the accounts that a manager is authorized to budget. (For example, Jeff Gordon's crew chief is not able to see what Jimmie Johnson's team members are doing.) Forecaster also allows users at the racetrack to access the application remotely, which allows mangers to receive or update real-time "actuals" from the system. This way, team managers know their allotted expenses for each race. Forecaster also provides users with additional features, including seamless links with general ledger accounts and the option to perform what-if (sensitivity) analyses. Scott Lampe, chief financial officer, said, "Forecaster allows us to change our forecasts to respond to changes, either rule changes [such as changes in the series' points system] or technology changes [such as pilot testing NASCAR's new, safer "Car of Tomorrow"] throughout the racing season."

Hendrick's Web-enabled budgeting system frees the finance department so it can work on strategy, analysis, and decision making. It also allows Hendrick to complete its annual budgeting process in only six weeks, a 50% reduction in the time spent budgeting and planning, which is critical given NASCAR's extremely short off-season. Patrick Pearson from Hendrick Motorsports believes the system gives the organization a competitive advantage: "In racing, the team that wins is not only the team with the fastest car, but the team that is the most disciplined and prepared week in and week out. Forecaster allows us to respond to that changing landscape."

Sources: Gage, Jack. 2009. Nascar's most valuable teams. Forbes.com, June 3. http://www.forbes.com/2009/06/03/nascar-most-valuable-teams-business-sports-nascar.html; Goff, John. 2004. In the fast lane. *CFO Magazine*, December 1; Hendrick Motorsports. 2010. About Hendrick Motorsports. Hendrick Motorsports Web site, May 28. www.hendrickmotorsports.com; Lampe, Scott. 2003. NASCAR racing team stays on track with FRx Software's comprehensive budget planning solution. *DM Review*, July 1; Microsoft Corporation. 2009. Microsoft Forecaster: Hendrick Motorsports customer video. October 8. http://www.microsoft.com/BusinessSolutions/frx_hendrick_video.mspx; Ryan, Nate. 2006. Hendrick empire strikes back with three contenders in chase for the Nextel Cup. *USA Today*, September 17.

finished goods inventories budget (in Schedule 6B) and the cost of goods sold budget (Schedule 7). Sensitivity analysis is especially useful in incorporating such interrelationships into budgeting decisions by managers.

Exhibit 6-4 shows a substantial decrease in operating income as a result of decreases in selling prices but a smaller decline in operating income if direct material prices increase by 5%. The sensitivity analysis prompts Stylistic's managers to put in place contingency plans. For example, should selling prices decline in 2012, Stylistic may choose to postpone some product development programs that it had included in its 2012 budget but that could be deferred to a later year. More generally, when the success or viability of a venture is highly dependent on attaining one or more targets, managers should frequently update their budgets as uncertainty is resolved. These updated budgets can help managers to adjust expenditure levels as circumstances change.

Instructors and students who, at this point, want to explore the cash budget and the budgeted balance sheet for the Stylistic Furniture example can skip ahead to the appendix on page 206.

on page 206.

Decision Point

How can managers plan for changes in the assumptions underlying the budget?

Budgeting and Responsibility Accounting

To attain the goals described in the master budget, a company must coordinate the efforts of all its employees—from the top executive through all levels of management to every supervised worker. Coordinating the company's efforts means assigning responsibility to managers who are accountable for their actions in planning and controlling human and other resources. How each company structures its own organization significantly shapes how the company's efforts will be coordinated.

Learning Objective 5

Describe responsibility centers

. . . a part of an organization that a manager is accountable for

and responsibility accounting

. . . measurement of plans and actual results that a manager is accountable for

Organization Structure and Responsibility

Organization structure is an arrangement of lines of responsibility within the organization. A company such as ExxonMobil is organized by business function—exploration, refining, marketing, and so on—with the president of each business-line company having decision-making authority over his or her function. Another company, such as Procter & Gamble, the household-products giant, is organized primarily by product line or brand. The managers of the individual divisions (toothpaste, soap, and so on) would each have decision-making authority concerning all the business functions (manufacturing, marketing, and so on) within that division.

Each manager, regardless of level, is in charge of a responsibility center. A **responsibility center** is a part, segment, or subunit of an organization whose manager is accountable for a specified set of activities. The higher the manager's level, the broader the responsibility center and the larger the number of his or her subordinates. **Responsibility accounting** is a system that measures the plans, budgets, actions, and actual results of each responsibility center. Four types of responsibility centers are as follows:

1. **Cost center**—the manager is accountable for costs only.
2. **Revenue center**—the manager is accountable for revenues only.
3. **Profit center**—the manager is accountable for revenues and costs.
4. **Investment center**—the manager is accountable for investments, revenues, and costs.

The maintenance department of a Marriott hotel is a cost center because the maintenance manager is responsible only for costs, so this budget is based on costs. The sales department is a revenue center because the sales manager is responsible primarily for revenues, so this budget is based on revenues. The hotel manager is in charge of a profit center because the manager is accountable for both revenues and costs, so this budget is based on revenues and costs. The regional manager responsible for determining the amount to be invested in new hotel projects and for revenues and costs generated from these investments is in charge of an investment center, so this budget is based on revenues, costs, and the investment base.

A responsibility center can be structured to promote better alignment of individual and company goals. For example, until recently, OPD, an office products distributor, operated its sales department as a revenue center. Each salesperson received a commission of 3% of the revenues per order, regardless of its size, the cost of processing it, or the cost of delivering the office products. An analysis of customer profitability at OPD found that many customers were unprofitable. The main reason was the high ordering and delivery costs of small orders. OPD's managers decided to make the sales department a profit center, accountable for revenues and costs, and to change the incentive system for salespeople to 15% of the monthly profits per customer. The costs for each customer included the ordering and delivery costs. The effect of this change was immediate. The sales department began charging customers for ordering and delivery, and salespeople at OPD actively encouraged customers to consolidate their purchases into fewer orders. As a result, each order began producing larger revenues. Customer profitability increased because of a 40% reduction in ordering and delivery costs in one year.

Feedback

Budgets coupled with responsibility accounting provide feedback to top management about the performance relative to the budget of different responsibility center managers.

Differences between actual results and budgeted amounts—called *variances*—if properly used, can help managers implement and evaluate strategies in three ways:

1. *Early warning.* Variances alert managers early to events not easily or immediately evident. Managers can then take corrective actions or exploit the available opportunities. For example, after observing a small decline in sales this period, managers may want to investigate if this is an indication of an even steeper decline to follow later in the year.

2. *Performance evaluation.* Variances prompt managers to probe how well the company has performed in implementing its strategies. Were materials and labor used efficiently? Was R&D spending increased as planned? Did product warranty costs decrease as planned?

3. *Evaluating strategy.* Variances sometimes signal to managers that their strategies are ineffective. For example, a company seeking to compete by reducing costs and improving quality may find that it is achieving these goals but that it is having little effect on sales and profits. Top management may then want to reevaluate the strategy.

Responsibility and Controllability

Controllability is the degree of influence that a specific manager has over costs, revenues, or related items for which he or she is responsible. A **controllable cost** is any cost that is primarily subject to the influence of a given *responsibility center manager* for a given *period.* A responsibility accounting system could either exclude all uncontrollable costs from a manager's performance report or segregate such costs from the controllable costs. For example, a machining supervisor's performance report might be confined to direct materials, direct manufacturing labor, power, and machine maintenance costs and might exclude costs such as rent and taxes paid on the plant.

In practice, controllability is difficult to pinpoint for at least two reasons:

1. Few costs are clearly under the sole influence of one manager. For example, prices of direct materials may be influenced by a purchasing manager, but these prices also depend on market conditions beyond the manager's control. Quantities used may be influenced by a production manager, but quantities used also depend on the quality of materials purchased. Moreover, managers often work in teams. Think about how difficult it is to evaluate individual responsibility in a team situation.

2. With a long enough time span, all costs will come under somebody's control. However, most performance reports focus on periods of a year or less. A current manager may benefit from a predecessor's accomplishments or may inherit a predecessor's problems and inefficiencies. For example, present managers may have to work under undesirable contracts with suppliers or labor unions that were negotiated by their predecessors. How can we separate what the current manager actually controls from the results of decisions made by others? Exactly what is the current manager accountable for? Answers may not be clear-cut.

Executives differ in how they embrace the controllability notion when evaluating those reporting to them. Some CEOs regard the budget as a firm commitment that subordinates must meet. Failure to meet the budget is viewed unfavorably. Other CEOs believe a more risk-sharing approach with managers is preferable, in which noncontrollable factors and performance relative to competitors are taken into account when judging the performance of managers who fail to meet their budgets.

Managers should avoid overemphasizing controllability. Responsibility accounting is more far-reaching. It focuses on gaining *information and knowledge*, not only on control. *Responsibility accounting helps managers to first focus on whom they should ask to obtain information and not on whom they should blame.* For example, if actual revenues at a Marriott hotel are less than budgeted revenues, the managers of the hotel may be tempted to blame the sales manager for the poor performance. The fundamental purpose of responsibility accounting, however, is not to fix blame but to gather information to enable future improvement.

Managers want to know who can tell them the most about the specific item in question, regardless of that person's ability to exert personal control over that item. For instance, purchasing managers may be held accountable for total purchase costs, not because of their ability to control market prices, but because of their ability to predict uncontrollable prices and to explain uncontrollable price changes. Similarly, managers at a Pizza Hut unit may be held responsible for operating income of their units, even though they (a) do not fully control selling prices or the costs of many food items and (b) have minimal flexibility about what items to sell or the ingredients in the items they sell. They are, however, in the best position to explain differences between their actual operating incomes and their budgeted operating incomes.

Performance reports for responsibility centers are sometimes designed to change managers' behavior in the direction top management desires. A cost-center manager may emphasize efficiency and deemphasize the pleas of sales personnel for faster service and rush orders. When evaluated as a profit center, the manager will more likely consider ways to influence activities that affect sales and weigh the impact of decisions on costs and revenues rather than on costs alone. To induce that change, some companies have changed the accountability of a cost center to a profit center. Call centers are an interesting example of this trend. As firms continue to differentiate on customer service while attempting to control operating expenses, driving efficiency wherever possible in the call centers has become a critical issue—as has driving revenue through this unique channel. There is increasing pressure for customer service representatives to promote new offers through upsell and cross-sell tactics. Microsoft, Oracle, and others offer software platforms that seek to evolve the call center from cost center to profit center. The new adage is, "Every service call is a sales call."

Decision Point

How do companies use responsibility centers? Should performance reports of responsibility center managers include only costs the manager can control?

Human Aspects of Budgeting

Why did we discuss the two major topics, the master budget and responsibility accounting, in the same chapter? Primarily to emphasize that human factors are crucial in budgeting. Too often, budgeting is thought of as a mechanical tool as the budgeting techniques themselves are free of emotion. However, the administration of budgeting requires education, persuasion, and intelligent interpretation.

Learning Objective 6

Recognize the human aspects of budgeting

. . . to engage subordinate managers in the budgeting process

Budgetary Slack

As we discussed earlier in this chapter, budgeting is most effective when lower-level managers actively participate and meaningfully engage in the budgeting process. Participation adds credibility to the budgeting process and creates greater commitment and accountability toward the budget. But participation requires "honest" communication about the business from subordinates and lower-level managers to their bosses.

At times, subordinates may try to "play games" and build in *budgetary slack*. **Budgetary slack** describes the practice of underestimating budgeted revenues, or overestimating budgeted costs, to make budgeted targets more easily achievable. It frequently occurs when budget variances (the differences between actual results and budgeted amounts) are used to evaluate performance. Line managers are also unlikely to be fully honest in their budget communications if top management mechanically institutes across-the-board cost reductions (say, a 10% reduction in all areas) in the face of projected revenue reductions.

Budgetary slack provides managers with a hedge against unexpected adverse circumstances. But budgetary slack also misleads top management about the true profit potential of the company, which leads to inefficient resource planning and allocation and poor coordination of activities across different parts of the company.

To avoid problems of budgetary slack, some companies use budgets primarily for planning purposes. They evaluate managerial performance using multiple indicators that take into account various factors such as the prevailing business environment and performance relative to competitors. Evaluating performance in this way takes time and requires careful exercise of judgment. Other companies use budgets for both planning and performance evaluation and use different approaches to obtain accurate information.

To explain one approach, let's consider the plant manager of a beverage bottler who is suspected by top management of understating the productivity potential of the bottling lines in his forecasts for the coming year. His presumed motivation is to increase the likelihood of meeting next year's production bonus targets. Suppose top management could purchase a consulting firm's study that reports productivity levels—such as the number of bottles filled per hour—at a number of comparable plants owned by other bottling companies. This report shows that its own plant manager's productivity forecasts are well below the actual productivity levels being achieved at other comparable plants.

Top management could share this independent information source with the plant manager and ask him to explain why his productivity differs from that at other similar plants. Management could also base part of the plant manager's compensation on his plant's productivity in comparison with other "benchmark" plants rather than on the forecasts he provided. Using external benchmark performance measures reduces a manager's ability to set budget levels that are easy to achieve.[6]

Another approach to reducing budgetary slack is for managers to involve themselves regularly in understanding what their subordinates are doing. Such involvement should not result in managers dictating the decisions and actions of subordinates. Rather, a manager's involvement should take the form of providing support, challenging in a motivational way the assumptions subordinates make, and enhancing mutual learning about the operations. Regular interaction with subordinates allows managers to become knowledgeable about the operations and diminishes the ability of subordinates to create slack in their budgets.

Part of top management's responsibility is to promote commitment among the employees to a set of core values and norms. These values and norms describe what constitutes acceptable and unacceptable behavior. For example, Johnson & Johnson (J&J) has a credo that describes its responsibilities to doctors, patients, employees, communities, and shareholders. Employees are trained in the credo to help them understand the behavior that is expected of them. Managers are often promoted from within and are therefore very familiar with the work of the employees reporting to them. Managers also have the responsibility to interact with and mentor their subordinates. These values and practices create a culture at J&J that discourages budgetary slack.

Some companies, such as IBM and Kodak, have designed innovative performance evaluation measures that reward managers based on the subsequent accuracy of the forecasts used in preparing budgets. For example, the *higher and more accurate* the budgeted profit forecasts of division managers, the higher their incentive bonuses.

Many of the best performing companies, such as General Electric, Microsoft, and Novartis, set "stretch" targets. Stretch targets are challenging but achievable levels of expected performance, intended to create a little discomfort and to motivate employees to exert extra effort and attain better performance. Organizations such as Goldman Sachs also use "horizontal" stretch goal initiatives. The aim is to enhance professional development of employees by asking them to take on significantly different responsibilities or roles outside their comfort zone.

Many managers regard budgets negatively. To them, the word budget is about as popular as, say, *downsizing, layoff,* or *strike.* Top managers must convince their subordinates that the budget is a tool designed to help them set and reach goals. Whatever the manager's perspective on budgets—pro or con—budgets are not remedies for weak management talent, faulty organization, or a poor accounting system.

---

[6] For an excellent discussion of these issues, see Chapter 14 ("Formal Models in Budgeting and Incentive Contracts") of R. S. Kaplan and A. A. Atkinson, *Advanced Management Accounting,* 3rd ed. (Upper Saddle River, NJ: Prentice Hall, 1998).

The management style of executives is a factor in how budgets are perceived in companies. Some CEOs argue that "numbers always tell the story." An executive once noted, "You can miss your plan once, but you wouldn't want to miss it twice." Other CEOs believe "too much focus on making the numbers in a budget" can lead to poor decision making and unethical practices.

Kaizen Budgeting

Chapter 1 noted the importance of continuous improvement, or *kaizen* in Japanese. **Kaizen budgeting** explicitly incorporates continuous improvement anticipated during the budget period into the budget numbers. Many companies that have cost reduction as a strategic focus, including General Electric in the United States and Citizens Watch and Toyota in Japan, use kaizen budgeting to continuously reduce costs. Much of the cost reduction associated with kaizen budgeting arises from many small improvements rather than "quantum leaps."

A significant aspect of kaizen budgeting is employee suggestions. Companies implementing kaizen budgeting believe that employees who actually do the job, whether in manufacturing, sales, or distribution, have the best information and knowledge of how the job can be done better. These companies create a culture in which employee suggestions are valued, recognized, and rewarded.

As an example, throughout our nine budgeting steps for Stylistic Furniture, we assumed four hours of direct labor time to manufacture each Casual coffee table. A kaizen budgeting approach would incorporate continuous improvement resulting from, for example, employee suggestions for doing the work faster or reducing idle time. The kaizen budget might then prescribe 4.00 direct manufacturing labor-hours per table for the first quarter of 2012, 3.95 hours for the second quarter, 3.90 hours for the third quarter, and so on. The implications of these reductions would be lower direct manufacturing labor costs, as well as lower variable manufacturing overhead costs, because direct manufacturing labor is the driver of these costs. If these continuous improvement goals are not met, Stylistic's managers will explore the reasons behind it and either adjust the targets or implement process changes that will accelerate continuous improvement.

Kaizen budgeting can also be applied to activities such as setups with the goal of reducing setup time and setup costs, or distribution with the goal of reducing the cost of moving each cubic foot of table. Kaizen budgeting and budgeting for specific activities are key building blocks of the master budget. Interestingly, companies are not the only ones interested in kaizen techniques. A growing number of cash-strapped states in the United States are bringing together government workers, regulators, and end users of government processes to identify ways to attack inefficiencies arising from bureaucratic procedures. Environmental regulators, whose cumbersome processes have long been the targets of business developers, have taken particular interest in kaizen. By the end of 2008, 29 state environmental agencies had conducted a kaizen session or were planning one.[7] How successful these efforts will be depends heavily on human factors such as the commitment and engagement of the individuals involved.

◄ Decision Point

Why are human factors crucial in budgeting?

Budgeting in Multinational Companies

Multinational companies, such as Federal Express, Kraft, and Pfizer, have operations in many countries. An international presence carries with it positives—access to new markets and resources—and negatives—operating in less-familiar business environments and exposure to currency fluctuations. For example, multinational companies earn revenues and incur expenses in many different currencies, and they must translate their operating performance into a single currency (say, U.S. dollars) for reporting results to their shareholders each quarter. This translation is based on the average exchange rates that prevail during the quarter. That is, in addition to budgeting in different currencies, management accountants in multinational companies also need to budget for foreign exchange rates. This is difficult because management accountants need to anticipate potential changes

Learning Objective 7

Appreciate the special challenges of budgeting in multinational companies

... exposure to currency fluctuations and to different legal, political, and economic environments

---

[7] For details, see "State governments, including Ohio's, embrace Kaizen to seek efficiency via Japanese methods," www.cleveland.com, (December 12, 2008).

that might take place during the year. Exchange rates are constantly fluctuating, so to reduce the possible negative impact on performance caused by unfavorable exchange rate movements, finance managers will frequently use sophisticated techniques such as forward, future, and option contracts to minimize exposure to foreign currency fluctuations. Besides currency issues, multinational companies need to understand the political, legal, and, in particular, economic environments of the different countries in which they operate. For example, in countries such as Zimbabwe, Iraq, and Guinea, annual inflation rates are very high, resulting in sharp declines in the value of the local currency. Issues related to differences in tax regimes are also critical, especially when the company transfers goods or services across the many countries in which it operates.

Multinational companies find budgeting to be a valuable tool when operating in very uncertain environments. As circumstances and conditions change, companies revise their budgets. The purpose of budgeting in such environments is not to evaluate performance relative to budgets, which is a meaningless comparison when conditions are so volatile, but to help managers throughout the organization to learn and to adapt their plans to the changing conditions and to communicate and coordinate the actions that need to be taken throughout the company. Senior managers evaluate performance more subjectively, based on how well subordinate managers have managed in these uncertain environments.

Decision Point

What are the special challenges involved in budgeting at multinational companies?

Problem for Self-Study

Consider the Stylistic Furniture example described earlier. Suppose that to maintain its sales quantities, Stylistic needs to decrease selling prices to $582 per Casual table and $776 per Deluxe table, a 3% decrease in the selling prices used in the chapter illustration. All other data are unchanged.

Required Prepare a budgeted income statement, including all necessary detailed supporting budget schedules that are different from the schedules presented in the chapter. Indicate those schedules that will remain unchanged.

Solution

Schedules 1 and 8 will change. Schedule 1 changes because a change in selling price affects revenues. Schedule 8 changes because revenues are a cost driver of marketing costs (sales commissions). The remaining schedules will not change because a change in selling price has no effect on manufacturing costs. The revised schedules and the new budgeted income statement follow:

Schedule 1: Revenue Budget
For the Year Ending December 31, 2012

	Selling Price	Units	Total Revenues
Casual tables	$582	50,000	$29,100,000
Deluxe tables	776	10,000	7,760,000
Total			$36,860,000

Schedule 8: Nonmanufacturing Costs Budget
For the Year Ending December 31, 2012

Business Function	Variable Costs	Fixed Costs (as in Schedule 8, p. 196)	Total Costs
Product design		$1,024,000	$1,024,000
Marketing (Variable cost: $36,860,000 × 0.065)	$2,395,900	1,330,000	3,725,900
Distribution (Variable cost: $2 × 1,140,000 cu. ft.)	2,280,000	1,596,000	3,876,000
	$4,675,900	$3,950,000	$8,625,900

Stylistic Furniture
Budgeted Income Statement
For the Year Ending December 31, 2012

Revenues	Schedule 1		$36,860,000
Cost of goods sold	Schedule 7		24,440,000
Gross margin			12,420,000
Operating costs			
Product design	Schedule 8	$1,024,000	
Marketing costs	Schedule 8	3,725,900	
Distribution costs	Schedule 8	3,876,000	8,625,900
Operating income			$ 3,794,100

Decision Points

The following question-and-answer format summarizes the chapter's learning objectives. Each decision presents a key question related to a learning objective. The guidelines are the answer to that question.

Decision	Guidelines
1. What is the master budget and why is it useful?	The master budget summarizes the financial projections of all the company's budgets. It expresses management's operating and financing plans—the formalized outline of the company's financial objectives and how they will be attained. Budgets are tools that, by themselves, are neither good nor bad. Budgets are useful when administered skillfully.
2. When should a company prepare budgets? What are the advantages of preparing budgets?	Budgets should be prepared when their expected benefits exceed their expected costs. The advantages of budgets include the following: (a) they compel strategic analysis and planning, (b) they promote coordination and communication among subunits of the company, (c) they provide a framework for judging performance and facilitating learning, and (d) they motivate managers and other employees.
3. What is the operating budget and what are its components?	The operating budget is the budgeted income statement and its supporting budget schedules. The starting point for the operating budget is generally the revenues budget. The following supporting schedules are derived from the revenues budget and the activities needed to support the revenues budget: production budget, direct material usage budget, direct material purchases budget, direct manufacturing labor cost budget, manufacturing overhead costs budget, ending inventories budget, cost of goods sold budget, R&D/product design cost budget, marketing cost budget, distribution cost budget, and customer-service cost budget.
4. How can managers plan for changes in the assumptions underlying the budget?	Managers can use financial planning models—mathematical statements of the relationships among operating activities, financing activities, and other factors that affect the budget. These models make it possible for management to conduct what-if (sensitivity) analysis of the effects that changes in the original predicted data or changes in underlying assumptions would have on the master budget and to develop plans to respond to changed conditions.

5. How do companies use responsibility centers? Should performance reports of responsibility center managers include only costs the manager can control?

A responsibility center is a part, segment, or subunit of an organization whose manager is accountable for a specified set of activities. Four types of responsibility centers are cost centers, revenue centers, profit centers, and investment centers. Responsibility accounting systems are useful because they measure the plans, budgets, actions, and actual results of each responsibility center. Controllable costs are costs primarily subject to the influence of a given responsibility center manager for a given time period. Performance reports of responsibility center managers often include costs, revenues, and investments that the managers cannot control. Responsibility accounting associates financial items with managers on the basis of which manager has the most knowledge and information about the specific items, regardless of the manager's ability to exercise full control.

6. Why are human factors crucial in budgeting?

The administration of budgets requires education, participation, persuasion, and intelligent interpretation. When wisely administered, budgets create commitment, accountability, and honest communication, and can be used as the basis for continuous improvement efforts. When badly managed, budgeting can lead to game-playing and budgetary slack—the practice of making budget targets more easily achievable.

7. What are the special challenges involved in budgeting at multinational companies?

Budgeting is a valuable tool for multinational companies but is made difficult by the enormous uncertainties inherent in operating in multiple countries. In addition to budgeting in different currencies, management accountants in multinational companies also need to budget for foreign exchange rates. Besides currency issues, multinational companies need to understand the political, legal, and economic environments of the different countries in which they operate.

Appendix

The Cash Budget

The chapter illustrated the operating budget, which is one part of the master budget. The other part is the financial budget, which comprises the capital expenditures budget, the cash budget, the budgeted balance sheet, and the budgeted statement of cash flows. This appendix focuses on the cash budget and the budgeted balance sheet. Capital budgeting is discussed in Chapter 21. The budgeted statement of cash flows is beyond the scope of this book, and generally is covered in financial accounting and corporate finance courses.

Suppose Stylistic Furniture had the balance sheet for the year ended December 31, 2011, shown in Exhibit 6-5. The budgeted cash flows for 2012 are as follows:

	Quarters			
	1	**2**	**3**	**4**
Collections from customers	$9,136,600	$10,122,000	$10,263,200	$8,561,200
Disbursements				
Direct materials	2,947,605	2,714,612	2,157,963	2,155,356
Payroll	3,604,512	2,671,742	2,320,946	2,562,800
Manufacturing overhead costs	2,109,018	1,530,964	1,313,568	1,463,450
Nonmanufacturing costs	1,847,750	1,979,000	1,968,250	1,705,000
Machinery purchase	—	—	758,000	—
Income taxes	725,000	400,000	400,000	400,000

The quarterly data are based on the budgeted cash effects of the operations formulated in Schedules 1 through 8 in the chapter, but the details of that formulation are not shown here to keep this illustration as brief and as focused as possible.

The company wants to maintain a $350,000 minimum cash balance at the end of each quarter. The company can borrow or repay money at an interest rate of 12% per year. Management does not want to borrow any more short-term cash than is necessary. By special arrangement, interest is computed and paid when the principal is repaid.

Exhibit 6-5

Balance Sheet for
Stylistic Furniture,
December 31, 2011

	A	B	C	D
	Home Insert Page Layout Formulas Data Review View			
1	Stylistic Furniture			
1	Balance Sheet			
2	December 31, 2011			
3	Assets			
4	Current assets			
5	Cash		$ 300,000	
6	Accounts receivable		1,711,000	
7	Direct materials inventory		1,090,000	
8	Finished goods inventory		646,000	$ 3,747,000
9	Property, plant, and equipment:			
10	Land		2,000,000	
11	Building and equipment	$22,000,000		
12	Accumulated depreciation	(6,900,000)	15,100,000	17,100,000
13	Total			$20,847,000
14	Liabilities and Stockholders' Equity			
15	Current liabilities			
16	Accounts payable		$ 904,000	
17	Income taxes payable		325,000	$ 1,229,000
18	Stockholders' equity			
19	Common stock, no-par,			
20	25,000 shares outstanding		3,500,000	
21	Retained earnings		16,118,000	19,618,000
22	Total			$20,847,000

Assume, for simplicity, that borrowing takes place at the beginning and repayment at the end of the quarter under consideration (in multiples of $1,000). Interest is computed to the nearest dollar.

Suppose the management accountant at Stylistic is given the preceding data and the other data contained in the budgets in the chapter (pp. 189–197). She is instructed as follows:

1. Prepare a cash budget for 2012 by quarter. That is, prepare a statement of cash receipts and disbursements by quarter, including details of borrowing, repayment, and interest.

2. Prepare a budgeted income statement for the year ending December 31, 2012. This statement should include interest expense and income taxes (at a rate of 40% of operating income).

3. Prepare a budgeted balance sheet on December 31, 2012.

Preparation of Budgets

1. The **cash budget** (Exhibit 6-6) is a schedule of expected cash receipts and disbursements. It predicts the effects on the cash position at the given level of operations. Exhibit 6-6 presents the cash budget by quarters to show the impact of cash flow timing on bank loans and their repayment. In practice, monthly—and sometimes weekly or even daily—cash budgets are critical for cash planning and control. Cash budgets help avoid unnecessary idle cash and unexpected cash deficiencies. They thus keep cash balances in line with needs. Ordinarily, the cash budget has these main sections:

   a. **Cash available for needs (before any financing).** The beginning cash balance plus cash receipts equals the total cash available for needs before any financing. Cash receipts depend on collections of accounts receivable, cash sales, and miscellaneous recurring sources, such as rental or royalty receipts. Information on the expected collectibility of accounts receivable is needed for accurate predictions. Key factors include bad-debt (uncollectible accounts) experience (not an issue in the Stylistic case because Stylistic sells to only a few large wholesalers) and average time lag between sales and collections.

   b. **Cash disbursements.** Cash disbursements by Stylistic Furniture include the following:
      i. *Direct material purchases.* Suppliers are paid in full three weeks after the goods are delivered.

Exhibit 6-6   Cash Budget for Stylistic Furniture for the Year Ending December 31, 2012

	A	B	C	D	E	F
1		Stylistic Furniture				
2		Cash Budget				
3		For Year Ending December 31, 2012				
4				Quarters		Year as a
5		1	2	3	4	Whole
6	Cash balance, beginning	$ 300,000	$ 350,715	$ 350,657	$ 350,070	$ 300,000
7	Add receipts					
8	Collections from customers	9,136,600	10,122,000	10,263,200	8,561,200	38,083,000
9	Total cash available for needs (x)	9,436,600	10,472,715	10,613,857	8,911,270	38,383,000
10	Deduct disbursements					
11	Direct materials	2,947,605	2,714,612	2,157,963	2,155,356	9,975,536
12	Payroll	3,604,512	2,671,742	2,320,946	2,562,800	11,160,000
13	Manufacturing overhead costs	2,109,018	1,530,964	1,313,568	1,463,450	6,417,000
14	Nonmanufacturing costs	1,847,750	1,979,000	1,968,250	1,705,000	7,500,000
15	Machinery purchase			758,000		758,000
16	Income taxes	725,000	400,000	400,000	400,000	1,925,000
17	Total disbursements (y)	11,233,885	9,296,318	8,918,727	8,286,606	37,735,536
18	Minimum cash balance desired	350,000	350,000	350,000	350,000	350,000
19	Total cash needed	11,583,885	9,646,318	9,268,727	8,636,606	38,085,536
20	Cash excess (deficiency)*	$(2,147,285)	$ 826,397	$ 1,345,130	$ 274,664	$ 297,464
21	Financing					
22	Borrowing (at beginning)	$ 2,148,000	$ 0	$ 0	$ 0	$ 2,148,000
23	Repayment (at end)	0	(779,000)	(1,234,000)	(135,000)	(2,148,000)
24	Interest (at 12% per year)**	0	(46,740)	(111,060)	(16,200)	(174,000)
25	Total effects of financing (z)	$ 2,148,000	$ (825,740)	$ (1,345,060)	$ (151,200)	$ (174,000)
26	Cash balance, ending***	$ 350,715	$ 350,657	$ 350,070	$ 473,464	$ 473,464
27	*Excess of total cash available for needs − Total cash needed before financing.					
28	**Note that the short-term interest payments pertain only to the amount of principal being repaid at the end of a quarter. The specific computations regarding interest are $779,000 × 0.12 × 0.5 = $46,740; $1,234,000 × 0.12 × 0.75 = $111,060; $135,000 × 0.12 = $16,200. Also note that *depreciation does not require a cash outlay.*					
29	***Ending cash balance = Total cash available for needs (x) − Total disbursements (y) + Total effects of financing (z)					

ii. *Direct labor and other wage and salary outlays.* All payroll-related costs are paid in the month in which the labor effort occurs.

iii. *Other costs.* These depend on timing and credit terms. (In the Stylistic case, all other costs are paid in the month in which the cost is incurred.) *Note, depreciation does not require a cash outlay.*

iv. *Other disbursements.* These include outlays for property, plant, equipment, and other long-term investments.

v. Income tax payments.

c. **Financing effects.** Short-term financing requirements depend on how the total cash available for needs [keyed as (x) in Exhibit 6-6] compares with the total cash disbursements [keyed as (y)], plus the minimum ending cash balance desired. The financing plans will depend on the relationship between total cash available for needs and total cash needed. If there is a deficiency of cash, loans will be obtained. If there is excess cash, any outstanding loans will be repaid.

d. **Ending cash balance.** The cash budget in Exhibit 6-6 shows the pattern of short-term "self-liquidating" cash loans. In quarter 1, Stylistic budgets a $2,147,285 cash deficiency. Hence, it undertakes short-term borrowing of $2,148,000 that it pays off over the course of the year. Seasonal peaks of production or sales often result in heavy cash disbursements for purchases, payroll, and other operating outlays as the products are produced and sold. Cash receipts from customers typically lag behind sales. The loan is *self-liquidating* in the sense that the borrowed money is used to acquire resources that are used to produce and sell finished goods, and the proceeds from sales are used to repay the loan. This self-liquidating cycle is the movement from cash to inventories to receivables and back to cash.

2. The budgeted income statement is presented in Exhibit 6-7. It is merely the budgeted operating income statement in Exhibit 6-3 (p. 196) expanded to include interest expense and income taxes.

3. The budgeted balance sheet is presented in Exhibit 6-8. Each item is projected in light of the details of the business plan as expressed in all the previous budget schedules. For example, the ending balance of accounts receivable of $1,628,000 is computed by adding the budgeted revenues of $38,000,000 (from Schedule 1 on page 191) to the beginning balance of accounts receivable of $1,711,000 (from Exhibit 6-5) and subtracting cash receipts of $38,083,000 (from Exhibit 6-6).

For simplicity, the cash receipts and disbursements were given explicitly in this illustration. Usually, the receipts and disbursements are calculated based on the lags between the items reported on the accrual basis of accounting in an income statement and balance sheet and their related cash receipts and disbursements. Consider accounts receivable. In the first three quarters, Stylistic estimates that 80% of all sales made in a quarter are collected in the same quarter and 20% are collected in the following quarter. Estimated collections from customers each quarter are calculated in the following table (assuming sales by quarter of $9,282,000; $10,332,000; $10,246,000; and $8,140,000 that equal 2012 budgeted sales of $38,000,000).

Schedule of Cash Collections

| | Quarters | | | |
	1	2	3	4
Accounts receivable balance on 1-1-2012 (p. 207)				
(Fourth quarter sales from prior year collected in first quarter of 2012)	$1,711,000			
From first-quarter 2012 sales (9,282,000 × 0.80; 9,282,000 × 0.20)	7,425,600	$ 1,856,400		
From second-quarter 2012 sales (10,332,000 × 0.80; 10,332,000 × 0.20)		8,265,600	$ 2,066,400	
From third-quarter 2012 sales (10,246,000 × 0.80; 10,246,000 × 0.20)			8,196,800	$2,049,200
From fourth-quarter 2012 sales (8,140,000 × 0.80)				6,512,000
Total collections	$9,136,600	$10,122,000	$10,263,200	$8,561,200

Note that the quarterly cash collections from customers calculated in this schedule equal the cash collections by quarter shown on page 206. Furthermore, the difference between fourth-quarter sales and the cash collected from fourth-quarter sales, $8,140,000 – $6,512,000 = $1,628,000 appears as accounts receivable in the budgeted balance sheet as of December 31, 2012 (see Exhibit 6-8).

Exhibit 6-7

Budgeted Income Statement for Stylistic Furniture for the Year Ending December 31, 2012

	A	B	C	D
1		Stylistic Furniture		
2		Budgeted Income Statement		
3		For the Year Ending December 31, 2012		
4	Revenues	Schedule 1		$38,000,000
5	Cost of goods sold	Schedule 7		24,440,000
6	Gross margin			13,560,000
7	Operating costs			
8	Product design costs	Schedule 8	$1,024,000	
9	Marketing costs	Schedule 8	3,800,000	
10	Distribution costs	Schedule 8	3,876,000	8,700,000
11	Operating income			4,860,000
12	Interest expense	Exhibit 6-6		174,000
13	Income before income taxes			4,686,000
14	Income taxes (at 40%)			1,874,400
15	Net income			$ 2,811,600

Exhibit 6-8   Budgeted Balance Sheet for Stylistic Furniture, December 31, 2012

	A	B	C	D
	Home Insert Page Layout Formulas Data Review View			
1	Stylistic Furniture			
2	Budgeted Balance Sheet			
3	December 31, 2012			
4	Assets			
5	Current assets			
6	Cash (from Exhibit 6-6)		$ 473,464	
7	Accounts receivable (1)		1,628,000	
8	Direct materials inventory (2)		760,000	
9	Finished goods inventory (2)		4,486,000	$ 7,347,464
10	Property, plant, and equipment			
11	Land (3)		2,000,000	
12	Building and equipment (4)	$22,758,000		
13	Accumulated depreciation (5)	(8,523,000)	14,235,000	16,235,000
14	Total			$23,582,464
15	Liabilities and Stockholders' Equity			
16	Current liabilities			
17	Accounts payable (6)		$ 878,464	
18	Income taxes payable (7)		274,400	$ 1,152,864
19	Stockholders' equity			
20	Common stock, no-par, 25,000 shares outstanding (8)		3,500,000	
21	Retained earnings (9) ·		18,929,600	22,429,600
22	Total			$23,582,464
23				
24	Notes:			
25	Beginning balances are used as the starting point for most of the following computations:			
26	(1) $1,711,000 + $38,000,000 revenues − $38,083,000 receipts (Exhibit 6-6) = $1,628,000			
27	(2) From Schedule 6B, p. 195			
28	(3) From beginning balance sheet, p. 207			
29	(4) $22,000,000 ÷ $758,000 purchases = $22,758,0000			
30	(5) $6,900,000 + $1,020,000 + $603,000 depreciation from Schedule 5, p. 194			
31	(6) $904,000 + $9,950,000 (Schedule 3B) − $9,975,536 (Exhibit 6-6) = $878,464			
32	There are no other current liabilities. Cash flows for payroll, manufacturing overhead and nonmanufacturing costs totaling $25,077,000 on the cash budget (Exhibit 6-6) consists of direct manufacturing labor costs of $6,000,000 from Schedule 4 + cash manufacturing overhead costs of $10,377,000 ($12,000,000 − depreciation of $1,623,000) from Schedule 5 + cash nonmanufacturing costs of $8,700,000 from Schedule 8.			
33	(7) $325,000 + $1,874,400 current year − $1,925,0000 payment = $274,400.			
34	(8) From beginning balance sheet.			
35	(9) $16,118,000 + $2,811,600 net income per Exhibit 6-7 = $18,929,600			

Sensitivity Analysis and Cash Flows

Exhibit 6-4 (p. 197) shows how differing assumptions about selling prices of coffee tables and direct material prices led to differing amounts for budgeted operating income for Stylistic Furniture. A key use of sensitivity analysis is to budget cash flow. Exhibit 6-9 outlines the short-term borrowing implications of the two combinations examined in Exhibit 6-4. Scenario 1, with the lower selling prices per table ($582 for the Casual table and $776 for the Deluxe table), requires $2,352,000 of short-term borrowing in quarter 1 that cannot be fully repaid as of December 31, 2012. Scenario 2, with the 5% higher direct material costs, requires $2,250,000 borrowing by Stylistic Furniture that also cannot be repaid by December 31, 2012. Sensitivity analysis helps managers anticipate such outcomes and take steps to minimize the effects of expected reductions in cash flows from operations.

Exhibit 6-9 Sensitivity Analysis: Effects of Key Budget Assumptions in Exhibit 6-4 on 2012 Short-Term Borrowing for Stylistic Furniture

	Home	Insert	Page Layout	Formulas	Data	Review	View			
	A	B	C	D	E	F	G	H	I	J
1				Direct Material			Short-Term Borrowing and Repayment by Quarter			
2		Selling Price		Purchase Costs		Budgeted	Quarters			
3	Scenario	Casual	Deluxe	Red Oak	Granite	Operating Income	1	2	3	4
4	1	$582	$776	$7.00	$10.00	$3,794,100	$2,352,000	($511,000)	($ 969,000)	($ 30,000)
5	2	$600	$800	7.35	10.50	4,483,800	2,250,000	(651,000)	(1,134,000)	(149,000)

Terms to Learn

The chapter and the Glossary at the end of the book contain definitions of the following important terms:

activity-based budgeting (ABB) (**p. 193**)
budgetary slack (**p. 201**)
cash budget (**p. 207**)
continuous budget (**p. 188**)
controllability (**p. 200**)
controllable cost (**p. 200**)
cost center (**p. 199**)

financial budget (**p. 189**)
financial planning models (**p. 197**)
investment center (**p. 199**)
kaizen budgeting (**p. 203**)
master budget (**p. 185**)
operating budget (**p. 189**)
organization structure (**p. 199**)

pro forma statements (**p. 185**)
profit center (**p. 199**)
responsibility accounting (**p. 199**)
responsibility center (**p. 199**)
revenue center (**p. 199**)
rolling budget (**p. 188**)

Assignment Material

Questions

6-1 What are the four elements of the budgeting cycle?
6-2 Define master budget.
6-3 "Strategy, plans, and budgets are unrelated to one another." Do you agree? Explain.
6-4 "Budgeted performance is a better criterion than past performance for judging managers." Do you agree? Explain.
6-5 "Production managers and marketing managers are like oil and water. They just don't mix." How can a budget assist in reducing battles between these two areas?
6-6 "Budgets meet the cost-benefit test. They force managers to act differently." Do you agree? Explain.
6-7 Define rolling budget. Give an example.
6-8 Outline the steps in preparing an operating budget.
6-9 "The sales forecast is the cornerstone for budgeting." Why?
6-10 How can sensitivity analysis be used to increase the benefits of budgeting?
6-11 Define kaizen budgeting.
6-12 Describe how nonoutput-based cost drivers can be incorporated into budgeting.
6-13 Explain how the choice of the type of responsibility center (cost, revenue, profit, or investment) affects behavior.
6-14 What are some additional considerations that arise when budgeting in multinational companies?
6-15 "Cash budgets must be prepared before the operating income budget." Do you agree? Explain.

Exercises

6-16 **Sales budget, service setting.** In 2011, Rouse & Sons, a small environmental-testing firm, performed 12,200 radon tests for $290 each and 16,400 lead tests for $240 each. Because newer homes are being built with lead-free pipes, lead-testing volume is expected to decrease by 10% next year. However, awareness of radon-related health hazards is expected to result in a 6% increase in radon-test volume each year in the near future. Jim Rouse feels that if he lowers his price for lead testing to $230 per test, he will have to face only a 7% decline in lead-test sales in 2012.

1. Prepare a 2012 sales budget for Rouse & Sons assuming that Rouse holds prices at 2011 levels.
2. Prepare a 2012 sales budget for Rouse & Sons assuming that Rouse lowers the price of a lead test to $230. Should Rouse lower the price of a lead test in 2012 if its goal is to maximize sales revenue?

6-17 Sales and production budget. The Mendez Company expects sales in 2012 of 200,000 units of serving trays. Mendez's beginning inventory for 2012 is 15,000 trays and its target ending inventory is 25,000 trays. Compute the number of trays budgeted for production in 2012.

6-18 Direct material budget. Inglenook Co. produces wine. The company expects to produce 2,500,000 two-liter bottles of Chablis in 2012. Inglenook purchases empty glass bottles from an outside vendor. Its target ending inventory of such bottles is 80,000; its beginning inventory is 50,000. For simplicity, ignore breakage. Compute the number of bottles to be purchased in 2012.

6-19 Budgeting material purchases. The Mahoney Company has prepared a sales budget of 45,000 finished units for a three-month period. The company has an inventory of 16,000 units of finished goods on hand at December 31 and has a target finished goods inventory of 18,000 units at the end of the succeeding quarter.

It takes three gallons of direct materials to make one unit of finished product. The company has an inventory of 60,000 gallons of direct materials at December 31 and has a target ending inventory of 50,000 gallons at the end of the succeeding quarter. How many gallons of direct materials should be purchased during the three months ending March 31?

6-20 Revenues and production budget. Purity, Inc., bottles and distributes mineral water from the company's natural springs in northern Oregon. Purity markets two products: twelve-ounce disposable plastic bottles and four-gallon reusable plastic containers.

Required

1. For 2012, Purity marketing managers project monthly sales of 400,000 twelve-ounce bottles and 100,000 four-gallon containers. Average selling prices are estimated at $0.25 per twelve-ounce bottle and $1.50 per four-gallon container. Prepare a revenues budget for Purity, Inc., for the year ending December 31, 2012.
2. Purity begins 2012 with 900,000 twelve-ounce bottles in inventory. The vice president of operations requests that twelve-ounce bottles ending inventory on December 31, 2012, be no less than 600,000 bottles. Based on sales projections as budgeted previously, what is the minimum number of twelve-ounce bottles Purity must produce during 2012?
3. The VP of operations requests that ending inventory of four-gallon containers on December 31, 2012, be 200,000 units. If the production budget calls for Purity to produce 1,300,000 four-gallon containers during 2012, what is the beginning inventory of four-gallon containers on January 1, 2012?

6-21 Budgeting; direct material usage, manufacturing cost and gross margin. Xerxes Manufacturing Company manufactures blue rugs, using wool and dye as direct materials. One rug is budgeted to use 36 skeins of wool at a cost of $2 per skein and 0.8 gallons of dye at a cost of $6 per gallon. All other materials are indirect. At the beginning of the year Xerxes has an inventory of 458,000 skeins of wool at a cost of $961,800 and 4,000 gallons of dye at a cost of $23,680. Target ending inventory of wool and dye is zero. Xerxes uses the FIFO inventory cost flow method.

Xerxes blue rugs are very popular and demand is high, but because of capacity constraints the firm will produce only 200,000 blue rugs per year. The budgeted selling price is $2,000 each. There are no rugs in beginning inventory. Target ending inventory of rugs is also zero.

Xerxes makes rugs by hand, but uses a machine to dye the wool. Thus, overhead costs are accumulated in two cost pools—one for weaving and the other for dyeing. Weaving overhead is allocated to products based on direct manufacturing labor-hours (DMLH). Dyeing overhead is allocated to products based on machine-hours (MH).

There is no direct manufacturing labor cost for dyeing. Xerxes budgets 62 direct manufacturing labor-hours to weave a rug at a budgeted rate of $13 per hour. It budgets 0.2 machine-hours to dye each skein in the dyeing process.

The following table presents the budgeted overhead costs for the dyeing and weaving cost pools:

	Dyeing (based on 1,440,000 MH)	Weaving (based on 12,400,000 DMLH)
Variable costs		
Indirect materials	$ 0	$15,400,000
Maintenance	6,560,000	5,540,000
Utilities	7,550,000	2,890,000
Fixed costs		
Indirect labor	347,000	1,700,000
Depreciation	2,100,000	274,000
Other	723,000	5,816,000
Total budgeted costs	$17,280,000	$31,620,000

Required

1. Prepare a direct material usage budget in both units and dollars.

2. Calculate the budgeted overhead allocation rates for weaving and dyeing.
3. Calculate the budgeted unit cost of a blue rug for the year.
4. Prepare a revenue budget for blue rugs for the year, assuming Xerxes sells (a) 200,000 or (b) 185,000 blue rugs (that is, at two different sales levels).
5. Calculate the budgeted cost of goods sold for blue rugs under each sales assumption.
6. Find the budgeted gross margin for blue rugs under each sales assumption.

6-22 Revenues, production, and purchases budgets. The Suzuki Co. in Japan has a division that manufactures two-wheel motorcycles. Its budgeted sales for Model G in 2013 is 900,000 units. Suzuki's target ending inventory is 80,000 units, and its beginning inventory is 100,000 units. The company's budgeted selling price to its distributors and dealers is 400,000 yen (¥) per motorcycle.

Suzuki buys all its wheels from an outside supplier. No defective wheels are accepted. (Suzuki's needs for extra wheels for replacement parts are ordered by a separate division of the company.) The company's target ending inventory is 60,000 wheels, and its beginning inventory is 50,000 wheels. The budgeted purchase price is 16,000 yen (¥) per wheel.

Required

1. Compute the budgeted revenues in yen.
2. Compute the number of motorcycles to be produced.
3. Compute the budgeted purchases of wheels in units and in yen.

6-23 Budgets for production and direct manufacturing labor. (CMA, adapted) Roletter Company makes and sells artistic frames for pictures of weddings, graduations, and other special events. Bob Anderson, the controller, is responsible for preparing Roletter's master budget and has accumulated the following information for 2013:

	2013				
	January	February	March	April	May
Estimated sales in units	10,000	12,000	8,000	9,000	9,000
Selling price	$54.00	$51.50	$51.50	$51.50	$51.50
Direct manufacturing labor-hours per unit	2.0	2.0	1.5	1.5	1.5
Wage per direct manufacturing labor-hour	$10.00	$10.00	$10.00	$11.00	$11.00

In addition to wages, direct manufacturing labor-related costs include pension contributions of $0.50 per hour, worker's compensation insurance of $0.15 per hour, employee medical insurance of $0.40 per hour, and Social Security taxes. Assume that as of January 1, 2013, the Social Security tax rates are 7.5% for employers and 7.5% for employees. The cost of employee benefits paid by Roletter on its employees is treated as a direct manufacturing labor cost.

Roletter has a labor contract that calls for a wage increase to $11 per hour on April 1, 2013. New labor-saving machinery has been installed and will be fully operational by March 1, 2013. Roletter expects to have 16,000 frames on hand at December 31, 2012, and it has a policy of carrying an end-of-month inventory of 100% of the following month's sales plus 50% of the second following month's sales.

Required

Prepare a production budget and a direct manufacturing labor budget for Roletter Company by month and for the first quarter of 2013. Both budgets may be combined in one schedule. The direct manufacturing labor budget should include labor-hours, and show the details for each labor cost category.

6-24 Activity-based budgeting. The Chelsea store of Family Supermarket (FS), a chain of small neighborhood grocery stores, is preparing its activity-based budget for January 2011. FS has three product categories: soft drinks, fresh produce, and packaged food. The following table shows the four activities that consume indirect resources at the Chelsea store, the cost drivers and their rates, and the cost-driver amount budgeted to be consumed by each activity in January 2011.

	Home	Insert	Page Layout	Formulas	Data	Review	View		
	A		B		C	D	E	F	
1					January 2011	January 2011 Budgeted			
2					Budgeted	Amount of Cost Driver Used			
3	**Activity**		**Cost Driver**		Cost-Driver Rate	Soft Drinks	Fresh Produce	Packaged Food	
4	Ordering		Number of purchase orders		$90	14	24	14	
5	Delivery		Number of deliveries		$82	12	62	19	
6	Shelf stocking		Hours of stocking time		$21	16	172	94	
7	Customer support		Number of items sold		$ 0.18	4,600	34,200	10,750	

Required

1. What is the total budgeted indirect cost at the Chelsea store in January 2011? What is the total budgeted cost of each activity at the Chelsea store for January 2011? What is the budgeted indirect cost of each product category for January 2011?
2. Which product category has the largest fraction of total budgeted indirect costs?
3. Given your answer in requirement 2, what advantage does FS gain by using an activity-based approach to budgeting over, say, allocating indirect costs to products based on cost of goods sold?

6-25 Kaizen approach to activity-based budgeting (continuation of 6-24). Family Supermarkets (FS) has a kaizen (continuous improvement) approach to budgeting monthly activity costs for each month of 2011. Each successive month, the budgeted cost-driver rate decreases by 0.4% relative to the preceding month. So, for example, February's budgeted cost-driver rate is 0.996 times January's budgeted cost-driver rate, and March's budgeted cost-driver rate is 0.996 times the budgeted February 2011 rate. FS assumes that the budgeted amount of cost-driver usage remains the same each month.

Required

1. What is the total budgeted cost for each activity and the total budgeted indirect cost for March 2011?
2. What are the benefits of using a kaizen approach to budgeting? What are the limitations of this approach, and how might FS management overcome them?

6-26 Responsibility and controllability. Consider each of the following independent situations for Anderson Forklifts. Anderson manufactures and sells forklifts. The company also contracts to service both its own and other brands of forklifts. Anderson has a manufacturing plant, a supply warehouse that supplies both the manufacturing plant and the service technicians (who often need parts to repair forklifts) and 10 service vans. The service technicians drive to customer sites to service the forklifts. Anderson owns the vans, pays for the gas, and supplies forklift parts, but the technicians own their own tools.

1. In the manufacturing plant the production manager is not happy with the engines that the purchasing manager has been purchasing. In May the production manager stops requesting engines from the supply warehouse, and starts purchasing them directly from a different engine manufacturer. Actual materials costs in May are higher than budgeted.
2. Overhead costs in the manufacturing plant for June are much higher than budgeted. Investigation reveals a utility rate hike in effect that was not figured into the budget.
3. Gasoline costs for each van are budgeted based on the service area of the van and the amount of driving expected for the month. The driver of van 3 routinely has monthly gasoline costs exceeding the budget for van 3. After investigating, the service manager finds that the driver has been driving the van for personal use.
4. At Bigstore Warehouse, one of Anderson's forklift service customers, the service people are only called in for emergencies and not for routine maintenance. Thus, the materials and labor costs for these service calls exceeds the monthly budgeted costs for a contract customer.
5. Anderson's service technicians are paid an hourly wage, with overtime pay if they exceed 40 hours per week, excluding driving time. Fred Snert, one of the technicians, frequently exceeds 40 hours per week. Service customers are happy with Fred's work, but the service manager talks to him constantly about working more quickly. Fred's overtime causes the actual costs of service to exceed the budget almost every month.
6. The cost of gasoline has increased by 50% this year, which caused the actual gasoline costs to greatly exceed the budgeted costs for the service vans.

Required

For each situation described, determine where (that is, with whom) (a) responsibility and (b) controllability lie. Suggest what might be done to solve the problem or to improve the situation.

6-27 Cash flow analysis, sensitivity analysis. Game Guys is a retail store selling video games. Sales are uniform for most of the year, but pick up in June and December, both because new releases come out and because games are purchased in anticipation of summer or winter holidays. Game Guys also sells and repairs game systems. The forecast of sales and service revenue for the second quarter of 2012 is as follows:

Sales and Service Revenue Budget
Second Quarter, 2012

Month	Expected Sales Revenue	Expected Service Revenue	Total Revenue
April	$ 5,500	$1,000	$ 6,500
May	6,200	1,400	7,600
June	9,700	2,600	12,300
Total	$21,400	$5,000	$26,400

Almost all the service revenue is paid for by bank credit card, so Game Guys budgets this as 100% bank card revenue. The bank cards charge an average fee of 3% of the total. Half of the sales revenue is also paid for by bank credit card, for which the fee is also 3% on average. About 10% of the sales are paid in cash, and the rest (the remaining 40%) are carried on a store account. Although the store tries to give store credit only to the best customers, it still averages about 2% for uncollectible accounts; 90% of store accounts are paid in the month following the purchase, and 8% are paid two months after purchase.

1. Calculate the cash that Game Guys expects to collect in May and in June of 2012. Show calculations for each month. **Required**
2. Game Guys has budgeted expenditures for May of $4,350 for the purchase of games and game systems, $1,400 for rent and utilities and other costs, and $1,000 in wages for the two part time employees.
   a. Given your answer to requirement 1, will Game Guys be able to cover its payments for May?
   b. The projections for May are a budget. Assume (independently for each situation) that May revenues might also be 5% less and 10% less, and that costs might be 8% higher. Under each of those three scenarios show the total net cash for May and the amount Game Guys would have to borrow if cash receipts are less than cash payments. Assume the beginning cash balance for May is $100.
3. Suppose the costs for May are as described in requirement 2, but the expected cash receipts for May are $6,200 and beginning cash balance is $100. Game Guys has the opportunity to purchase the games and game systems on account in May, but the supplier offers the company credit terms of 2/10 net 30, which means if Game Guys pays within 10 days (in May) it will get a 2% discount on the price of the merchandise. Game Guys can borrow money at a rate of 24%. Should Game Guys take the purchase discount?

Problems

MyAccountingLab

6-28 **Budget schedules for a manufacturer.** Logo Specialties manufactures, among other things, woolen blankets for the athletic teams of the two local high schools. The company sews the blankets from fabric and sews on a logo patch purchased from the licensed logo store site. The teams are as follows:

■ Knights, with red blankets and the Knights logo

■ Raiders, with black blankets and the Raider logo

Also, the black blankets are slightly larger than the red blankets.

The budgeted direct-cost inputs for each product in 2012 are as follows:

	Knights Blanket	Raiders Blanket
Red wool fabric	3 yards	0
Black wool fabric	0	3.3 yards
Knight logo patches	1	0
Raider logo patches	0	1
Direct manufacturing labor	1.5 hours	2 hours

Unit data pertaining to the direct materials for March 2012 are as follows:

Actual Beginning Direct Materials Inventory (3/1/2012)

	Knights Blanket	Raiders Blanket
Red wool fabric	30 yards	0
Black wool fabric	0	10 yards
Knight logo patches	40	0
Raider logo patches	0	55

Target Ending Direct Materials Inventory (3/31/2012)

	Knights Blanket	Raiders Blanket
Red wool fabric	20 yards	0
Black wool fabric	0	20 yards
Knight logo patches	20	0
Raider logo patches	0	20

Unit cost data for direct-cost inputs pertaining to February 2012 and March 2012 are as follows:

	February 2012 (actual)	March 2012 (budgeted)
Red wool fabric (per yard)	$8	$9
Black wool fabric (per yard)	10	9
Knight logo patches (per patch)	6	6
Raider logo patches (per patch)	5	7
Manufacturing labor cost per hour	25	26

Manufacturing overhead (both variable and fixed) is allocated to each blanket on the basis of budgeted direct manufacturing labor-hours per blanket. The budgeted variable manufacturing overhead rate for March 2012 is $15 per direct manufacturing labor-hour. The budgeted fixed manufacturing overhead for March 2012 is $9,200. Both variable and fixed manufacturing overhead costs are allocated to each unit of finished goods.

Data relating to finished goods inventory for March 2012 are as follows:

	Knights Blankets	Raiders Blankets
Beginning inventory in units	10	15
Beginning inventory in dollars (cost)	$1,210	$2,235
Target ending inventory in units	20	25

Budgeted sales for March 2012 are 120 units of the Knights blankets and 180 units of the Raiders blankets. The budgeted selling prices per unit in March 2012 are $150 for the Knights blankets and $175 for the Raiders blankets. Assume the following in your answer:

- Work-in-process inventories are negligible and ignored.

- Direct materials inventory and finished goods inventory are costed using the FIFO method.

- Unit costs of direct materials purchased and finished goods are constant in March 2012.

Required

1. Prepare the following budgets for March 2012:
   a. Revenues budget
   b. Production budget in units
   c. Direct material usage budget and direct material purchases budget
   d. Direct manufacturing labor budget
   e. Manufacturing overhead budget
   f. Ending inventories budget (direct materials and finished goods)
   g. Cost of goods sold budget

2. Suppose Logo Specialties decides to incorporate continuous improvement into its budgeting process. Describe two areas where it could incorporate continuous improvement into the budget schedules in requirement 1.

6-29 Budgeted costs; kaizen improvements. DryPool T-Shirt Factory manufactures plain white and solid colored T-shirts. Inputs include the following:

	Price	Quantity	Cost per unit of output
Fabric	$ 6 per yard	1 yard per unit	$6 per unit
Labor	$12 per DMLH	0.25 DMLH per unit	$3 per unit

Additionally, the colored T-shirts require 3 ounces of dye per shirt at a cost of $0.20 per ounce. The shirts sell for $15 each for white and $20 each for colors. The company expects to sell 12,000 white T-shirts and 60,000 colored T-shirts uniformly over the year.

DryPool has the opportunity to switch from using the dye it currently uses to using an environmentally friendly dye that costs $1.00 per ounce. The company would still need three ounces of dye per shirt. DryPool is reluctant to change because of the increase in costs (and decrease in profit) but the Environmental Protection Agency has threatened to fine them $102,000 if they continue to use the harmful but less expensive dye.

Required

1. Given the preceding information, would DryPool be better off financially by switching to the environmentally friendly dye? (Assume all other costs would remain the same.)

2. Assume DryPool chooses to be environmentally responsible regardless of cost, and it switchs to the new dye. The production manager suggests trying Kaizen costing. If DryPool can reduce fabric and labor costs each by 1% per month, how close will it be at the end of 12 months to the gross profit it would have earned before switching to the more expensive dye? (Round to the nearest dollar for calculating cost reductions)

3. Refer to requirement 2. How could the reduction in material and labor costs be accomplished? Are there any problems with this plan?

6-30 Revenue and production budgets. (CPA, adapted) The Scarborough Corporation manufactures and sells two products: Thingone and Thingtwo. In July 2011, Scarborough's budget department gathered the following data to prepare budgets for 2012:

2012 Projected Sales

Product	Units	Price
Thingone	60,000	$165
Thingtwo	40,000	$250

2012 Inventories in Units

	Expected Target	
Product	**January 1, 2012**	**December 31, 2012**
Thingone	20,000	25,000
Thingtwo	8,000	9,000

The following direct materials are used in the two products:

		Amount Used per Unit	
Direct Material	**Unit**	**Thingone**	**Thingtwo**
A	pound	4	5
B	pound	2	3
C	each	0	1

Projected data for 2012 with respect to direct materials are as follows:

Direct Material	**Anticipated Purchase Price**	**Expected Inventories January 1, 2012**	**Target Inventories December 31, 2012**
A	$12	32,000 lb.	36,000 lb.
B	5	29,000 lb.	32,000 lb.
C	3	6,000 units	7,000 units

Projected direct manufacturing labor requirements and rates for 2012 are as follows:

Product	**Hours per Unit**	**Rate per Hour**
Thingone	2	$12
Thingtwo	3	16

Manufacturing overhead is allocated at the rate of $20 per direct manufacturing labor-hour.

Based on the preceding projections and budget requirements for Thingone and Thingtwo, prepare the following budgets for 2012.   **Required**

1. Revenues budget (in dollars)
2. Production budget (in units)
3. Direct material purchases budget (in quantities)
4. Direct material purchases budget (in dollars)
5. Direct manufacturing labor budget (in dollars)
6. Budgeted finished goods inventory at December 31, 2012 (in dollars)

6-31 Budgeted income statement. (CMA, adapted) Easecom Company is a manufacturer of videoconferencing products. Regular units are manufactured to meet marketing projections, and specialized units are made after an order is received. Maintaining the videoconferencing equipment is an important area of customer satisfaction. With the recent downturn in the computer industry, the videoconferencing equipment segment has suffered, leading to a decline in Easecom's financial performance. The following income statement shows results for 2011:

Easecom Company
Income Statement
For the Year Ended December 31, 2011 (in thousands)

Revenues:		
Equipment	$6,000	
Maintenance contracts	1,800	
Total revenues		$7,800
Cost of goods sold		4,600
Gross margin		3,200
Operating costs		
Marketing	600	
Distribution	150	
Customer maintenance	1,000	
Administration	900	
Total operating costs		2,650
Operating income		$ 550

Easecom's management team is in the process of preparing the 2012 budget and is studying the following information:

1. Selling prices of equipment are expected to increase by 10% as the economic recovery begins. The selling price of each maintenance contract is expected to remain unchanged from 2011.
2. Equipment sales in units are expected to increase by 6%, with a corresponding 6% growth in units of maintenance contracts.
3. Cost of each unit sold is expected to increase by 3% to pay for the necessary technology and quality improvements.
4. Marketing costs are expected to increase by $250,000, but administration costs are expected to remain at 2011 levels.
5. Distribution costs vary in proportion to the number of units of equipment sold.
6. Two maintenance technicians are to be hired at a total cost of $130,000, which covers wages and related travel costs. The objective is to improve customer service and shorten response time.
7. There is no beginning or ending inventory of equipment.

Required   Prepare a budgeted income statement for the year ending December 31, 2012.

6-32   **Responsibility in a restaurant.** Barney Briggs owns a restaurant franchise that is part of a chain of "southern homestyle" restaurants. One of the chain's popular breakfast items is biscuits and gravy. Central Warehouse makes and freezes the biscuit dough, which is then sold to the franchise stores; there, it is thawed and baked in the individual stores by the cook. Each franchise also has a purchasing agent who orders the biscuits (and other items) based on expected demand. In March, 2012, one of the freezers in Central Warehouse breaks down and biscuit production is reduced by 25% for three days. During those three days, Barney's franchise runs out of biscuits but demand does not slow down. Barney's franchise cook, Janet Trible, sends one of the kitchen helpers to the local grocery store to buy refrigerated ready-to-bake biscuits. Although the customers are kept happy, the refrigerated biscuits cost Barney's franchise three times the cost of the Central Warehouse frozen biscuits, and the franchise loses money on this item for those three days. Barney is angry with the purchasing agent for not ordering enough biscuits to avoid running out of stock, and with Janet for spending too much money on the replacement biscuits.

Required   Who is responsible for the cost of the biscuits? At what level is the cost controllable? Do you agree that Barney should be angry with the purchasing agent? With Janet? Why or why not?

6-33   **Comprehensive problem with ABC costing.** Pet Luggage Company makes two pet carriers, the Cat-allac and the Dog-eriffic. They are both made of plastic with metal doors, but the Cat-allac is smaller. Information for the two products for the month of April is given in the following tables:

Input Prices
Direct materials

Plastic	$ 4 per pound
Metal	$ 3 per pound
Direct manufacturing labor	$14 per direct manufacturing labor-hour

Input Quantities per Unit of Output

	Cat-allac	Dog-eriffic
Direct materials		
Plastic	3 pounds	5 pounds
Metal	0.5 pounds	1 pound
Direct manufacturing labor-hours (DMLH)	3 hours	5 hours
Machine-hours (MH)	13 MH	20 MH

Inventory Information, Direct Materials

	Plastic	Metal
Beginning inventory	230 pounds	70 pounds
Target ending inventory	400 pounds	65 pounds
Cost of beginning inventory	$874	$224

Pet Luggage accounts for direct materials using a FIFO cost flow assumption.

Sales and Inventory Information, Finished Goods

	Cat-allac	Dog-eriffic
Expected sales in units	580	240
Selling price	$ 190	$ 275
Target ending inventory in units	45	25
Beginning inventory in units	25	40
Beginning inventory in dollars	$2,500	$7,440

Pet Luggage uses a FIFO cost flow assumption for finished goods inventory.

Pet Luggage uses an activity-based costing system and classifies overhead into three activity pools: Setup, Processing, and Inspection. Activity rates for these activities are $130 per setup-hour, $5 per machine-hour, and $20 per inspection-hour, respectively. Other information follows:

Cost Driver Information

	Cat-allac	Dog-eriffic
Number of units per batch	25	13
Setup time per batch	1.25 hours	2.00 hours
Inspection time per batch	0.5 hour	0.6 hour

Nonmanufacturing fixed costs for March equal $32,000, of which half are salaries. Salaries are expected to increase 5% in April. The only variable nonmanufacturing cost is sales commission, equal to 1% of sales revenue.

Prepare the following for April:

Required

1. Revenues budget
2. Production budget in units
3. Direct material usage budget and direct material purchases budget
4. Direct manufacturing labor cost budget
5. Manufacturing overhead cost budgets for each of the three activities
6. Budgeted unit cost of ending finished goods inventory and ending inventories budget
7. Cost of goods sold budget
8. Nonmanufacturing costs budget
9. Budgeted income statement (ignore income taxes)

6-34 Cash budget (continuation of 6-33). Refer to the information in Problem 6-33.

Assume the following: Pet Luggage (PL) does not make any sales on credit. PL sells only to the public, and accepts cash and credit cards; 90% of its sales are to customers using credit cards, for which PL gets the cash right away less a 2% transaction fee.

Purchases of materials are on account. PL pays for half the purchases in the period of the purchase, and the other half in the following period. At the end of March, PL owes suppliers $8,400.

PL plans to replace a machine in April at a net cash cost of $13,800.

Labor, other manufacturing costs, and nonmanufacturing costs are paid in cash in the month incurred except of course, depreciation, which is not a cash flow. $22,000 of the manufacturing cost and $12,800 of the nonmanufacturing cost for April is depreciation.

PL currently has a $2,600 loan at an annual interest rate of 24%. The interest is paid at the end of each month. If PL has more than $10,000 cash at the end of April it will pay back the loan. PL owes $5,400 in income taxes that need to be remitted in April. PL has cash of $5,200 on hand at the end of March.

Prepare a cash budget for April for Pet Luggage.

Required

6-35 Comprehensive operating budget, budgeted balance sheet. Slopes, Inc., manufactures and sells snowboards. Slopes manufactures a single model, the Pipex. In the summer of 2011, Slopes' management accountant gathered the following data to prepare budgets for 2012:

Materials and Labor Requirements

Direct materials	
Wood	5 board feet (b.f.) per snowboard
Fiberglass	6 yards per snowboard
Direct manufacturing labor	5 hours per snowboard

Slopes' CEO expects to sell 1,000 snowboards during 2012 at an estimated retail price of $450 per board. Further, the CEO expects 2012 beginning inventory of 100 snowboards and would like to end 2012 with 200 snowboards in stock.

Direct Materials Inventories

	Beginning Inventory 1/1/2012	Ending Inventory 12/31/2012
Wood	2,000 b.f.	1,500 b.f.
Fiberglass	1,000 yards	2,000 yards

Variable manufacturing overhead is $7 per direct manufacturing labor-hour. There are also $66,000 in fixed manufacturing overhead costs budgeted for 2012. Slopes combines both variable and fixed manufacturing overhead into a single rate based on direct manufacturing labor-hours. Variable marketing costs are allocated at the rate of $250 per sales visit. The marketing plan calls for 30 sales visits during 2012. Finally, there are $30,000 in fixed nonmanufacturing costs budgeted for 2012.

Other data include the following:

	2011 Unit Price	2012 Unit Price
Wood	$28.00 per b.f.	$30.00 per b.f.
Fiberglass	$ 4.80 per yard	$ 5.00 per yard
Direct manufacturing labor	$24.00 per hour	$25.00 per hour

The inventoriable unit cost for ending finished goods inventory on December 31, 2011, is $374.80. Assume Slopes uses a FIFO inventory method for both direct materials and finished goods. Ignore work in process in your calculations.

Budgeted balances at December 31, 2012, in the selected accounts are as follows:

Cash	$ 10,000
Property, plant, and equipment (net)	850,000
Current liabilities	17,000
Long-term liabilities	178,000
Stockholders' equity	800,000

Required

1. Prepare the 2012 revenues budget (in dollars).
2. Prepare the 2012 production budget (in units).
3. Prepare the direct material usage and purchases budgets for 2012.
4. Prepare a direct manufacturing labor budget for 2012.
5. Prepare a manufacturing overhead budget for 2012.
6. What is the budgeted manufacturing overhead rate for 2012?
7. What is the budgeted manufacturing overhead cost per output unit in 2012?
8. Calculate the cost of a snowboard manufactured in 2012.
9. Prepare an ending inventory budget for both direct materials and finished goods for 2012.
10. Prepare a cost of goods sold budget for 2012.
11. Prepare the budgeted income statement for Slopes, Inc., for the year ending December 31, 2012.
12. Prepare the budgeted balance sheet for Slopes, Inc., as of December 31, 2012.

6-36 Cash budgeting. Retail outlets purchase snowboards from Slopes, Inc., throughout the year. However, in anticipation of late summer and early fall purchases, outlets ramp up inventories from May through August. Outlets are billed when boards are ordered. Invoices are payable within 60 days. From past experience, Slopes' accountant projects 20% of invoices will be paid in the month invoiced, 50% will be paid in the following month, and 30% of invoices will be paid two months after the month of invoice. The average selling price per snowboard is $450.

To meet demand, Slopes increases production from April through July, because the snowboards are produced a month prior to their projected sale. Direct materials are purchased in the month of production and are paid for during the following month (terms are payment in full within 30 days of the invoice date). During this period there is no production for inventory, and no materials are purchased for inventory.

Direct manufacturing labor and manufacturing overhead are paid monthly. Variable manufacturing overhead is incurred at the rate of $7 per direct manufacturing labor-hour. Variable marketing costs are driven by the number of sales visits. However, there are no sales visits during the months studied. Slopes, Inc., also incurs fixed manufacturing overhead costs of $5,500 per month and fixed nonmanufacturing overhead costs of $2,500 per month.

Projected Sales

May 80 units	August 100 units
June 120 units	September 60 units
July 200 units	October 40 units

Direct Materials and Direct Manufacturing Labor Utilization and Cost

	Units per Board	Price per Unit	Unit
Wood	5	$30	board feet
Fiberglass	6	5	yard
Direct manufacturing labor	5	25	hour

The beginning cash balance for July 1, 2012, is $10,000. On October 1, 2011, Slopes had a cash crunch and borrowed $30,000 on a 6% one-year note with interest payable monthly. The note is due October 1, 2012. Using the information provided, you will need to determine whether Slopes will be in a position to pay off this short-term debt on October 1, 2012.

1. Prepare a cash budget for the months of July through September 2012. Show supporting schedules for the calculation of receivables and payables. **Required**

2. Will Slopes be in a position to pay off the $30,000 one-year note that is due on October 1, 2012? If not, what actions would you recommend to Slopes' management?

3. Suppose Slopes is interested in maintaining a minimum cash balance of $10,000. Will the company be able to maintain such a balance during all three months analyzed? If not, suggest a suitable cash management strategy.

6-37 Cash budgeting. On December 1, 2011, the Itami Wholesale Co. is attempting to project cash receipts and disbursements through January 31, 2012. On this latter date, a note will be payable in the amount of $100,000. This amount was borrowed in September to carry the company through the seasonal peak in November and December.

Selected general ledger balances on December 1 are as follows:

Cash	$ 88,000	
Inventory	65,200	
Accounts payable		136,000

Sales terms call for a 3% discount if payment is made within the first 10 days of the month after sale, with the balance due by the end of the month after sale. Experience has shown that 50% of the billings will be collected within the discount period, 30% by the end of the month after purchase, and 14% in the following month. The remaining 6% will be uncollectible. There are no cash sales.

The average selling price of the company's products is $100 per unit. Actual and projected sales are as follows:

October actual	$ 280,000
November actual	320,000
December estimated	330,000
January estimated	250,000
February estimated	240,000
Total estimated for year ending June 30, 2012	$2,400,000

All purchases are payable within 15 days. Approximately 60% of the purchases in a month are paid that month, and the rest the following month. The average unit purchase cost is $80. Target ending inventories are 500 units plus 10% of the next month's unit sales.

Total budgeted marketing, distribution, and customer-service costs for the year are $600,000. Of this amount, $120,000 are considered fixed (and include depreciation of $30,000). The remainder varies with sales. Both fixed and variable marketing, distribution, and customer-service costs are paid as incurred.

Prepare a cash budget for December 2011 and January 2012. Supply supporting schedules for collections of receivables; payments for merchandise; and marketing, distribution, and customer-service costs. **Required**

6-38 Comprehensive problem; ABC manufacturing, two products. Follete Inc. operates at capacity and makes plastic combs and hairbrushes. Although the combs and brushes are a matching set, they are sold individually and so the sales mix is not 1:1. Follette Inc. is planning its annual budget for fiscal year 2011. Information for 2011 follows:

Input Prices
Direct materials
    Plastic $ 0.20 per ounce
    Bristles $ 0.50 per bunch
Direct manufacturing labor $12 per direct manufacturing labor-hour

Input Quantities per Unit of Output

	Combs	Brushes
Direct materials		
Plastic	5 ounces	8 ounces
Bristles	—	16 bunches
Direct manufacturing labor	0.05 hours	0.2 hours
Machine-hours (MH)	0.025 MH	0.1 MH

Inventory Information, Direct Materials

	Plastic	Bristles
Beginning inventory	1,600 ounces	1,820 bunches
Target ending inventory	1,766 ounces	2,272 bunches
Cost of beginning inventory	$304	$946

Folette Inc. accounts for direct materials using a FIFO cost flow.

Sales and Inventory Information, Finished Goods

	Combs	Brushes
Expected sales in units	12,000	14,000
Selling price	$ 6	$ 20
Target ending inventory in units	1,200	1,400
Beginning inventory in units	600	1,200
Beginning inventory in dollars	$ 1,800	$18,120

Folette Inc. uses a FIFO cost flow assumption for finished goods inventory.

Combs are manufactured in batches of 200, and brushes are manufactured in batches of 100. It takes 20 minutes to set up for a batch of combs, and one hour to set up for a batch of brushes.

Folette Inc. uses activity-based costing and has classified all overhead costs as shown in the following table:

Cost Type	Budgeted Variable	Budgeted Fixed	Cost Driver/Allocation Base
Manufacturing:			
Materials handling	$11,490	$15,000	Number of ounces of plastic used
Setup	6,830	11,100	Setup-hours
Processing	7,760	20,000	Machine-hours
Inspection	7,000	1,040	Number of units produced
Nonmanufacturing:			
Marketing	14,100	60,000	Sales revenue
Distribution	0	780	Number of deliveries

Delivery trucks transport units sold in delivery sizes of 1,000 combs or 1,000 brushes.

Required Do the following for the year 2011:

1. Prepare the revenues budget.
2. Use the revenue budget to
   a. find the budgeted allocation rate for marketing costs.
   b. find the budgeted number of deliveries and allocation rate for distribution costs.
3. Prepare the production budget in units.
4. Use the production budget to
   a. find the budgeted number of setups, setup-hours, and the allocation rate for setup costs.
   b. find the budgeted total machine-hours and the allocation rate for processing costs.
   c. find the budgeted total units produced and the allocation rate for inspection costs.
5. Prepare the direct material usage budget and the direct material purchases budgets in both units and dollars; round to whole dollars.
6. Use the direct material usage budget to find the budgeted allocation rate for materials handling costs.
7. Prepare the direct manufacturing labor cost budget.
8. Prepare the manufacturing overhead cost budget for materials handling, setup, and processing.
9. Prepare the budgeted unit cost of ending finished goods inventory and ending inventories budget.

10. Prepare the cost of goods sold budget.
11. Prepare the nonmanufacturing overhead costs budget for marketing and distribution.
12. Prepare a budgeted income statement (ignore income taxes).

6-39 **Budgeting and ethics.** Delma Company manufactures a variety of products in a variety of departments, and evaluates departments and departmental managers by comparing actual cost and output relative to the budget. Departmental managers help create the budgets, and usually provide information about input quantities for materials, labor, and overhead costs.

Wert Mimble is the manager of the department that produces product Z. Wert has estimated these inputs for product Z:

Input	Budget Quantity per Unit of Output
Direct material	4 pounds
Direct manufacturing labor	15 minutes
Machine time	12 minutes

The department produces about 100 units of product Z each day. Wert's department always gets excellent evaluations, sometimes exceeding budgeted production quantities. Each 100 units of product Z uses, on average, about 24 hours of direct manufacturing labor (four people working six hours each), 395 pounds of material, and 19.75 machine-hours.

Top management of Delma Company has decided to implement budget standards that will challenge the workers in each department, and it has asked Wert to design more challenging input standards for product Z. Wert provides top management with the following input quantities:

Input	Budget Quantity per Unit of Output
Direct material	3.95 pounds
Direct manufacturing labor	14.5 minutes
Machine time	11.8 minutes

Discuss the following:

Required

1. Are these standards challenging standards for the department that produces product Z?
2. Why do you suppose Wert picked these particular standards?
3. What steps can Delma Company's top management take to make sure Wert's standards really meet the goals of the firm?

6-40 **Human Aspects of Budgeting in a Service Firm.** Jag Meerkat owns three upscale hair salons: Hair Suite I, II, and III. Each of the salons has a manager and 10 stylists who rent space in the salons as independent contractors and who pay a fee of 10% of each week's revenue to the salon as rent. In exchange they get to use the facility and utilities, but must bring their own equipment.

The manager of each salon schedules each customer appointment to last an hour, and then allows the stylist 10 minutes between appointments to clean up, rest, and prepare for the next appointment. The salons are open from 10 A.M. to 6 P.M., so each stylist can serve seven customers per day. Stylists each work five days a week on a staggered schedule, so the salon is open seven days a week. Everyone works on Saturdays, but some stylists have Sunday and Monday off, some have Tuesday and Wednesday off, and some have Thursday and Friday off.

Jag Meerkat knows that utility costs are rising. Jag wants to increase revenues to cover at least some part of rising utility costs, so Jag tells each of the managers to find a way to increase productivity in the salons so that the stylists will pay more to the salons. Jag does not want to increase the rental fee above 10% of revenue for fear the stylists will leave, and each salon has only 10 stations, so he feels each salon cannot hire more than 10 full-time stylists.

The manager of Hair Suite I attacks the problem by simply telling the stylists that, from now on, customers will be scheduled for 40 minute appointments and breaks will be five minutes. This will allow each stylist to add one more customer per day.

The manager of Hair Suite II asks the stylists on a voluntary basis to work one extra hour per day, from 10 A.M. to 7 P.M., to add an additional customer per stylist per day.

The manager of Hair Suite III sits down with the stylists and discusses the issue. After considering shortening the appointment and break times, or lengthening the hours of operation, one of the stylists says, "I know we rent stations in your store, but I am willing to share my station. You could hire an eleventh stylist, who will simply work at whatever station is vacant during our days off. Since we use our own equipment, this will not be a problem for me as long as there is a secure place I can leave my equipment on my days off." Most of the other stylists agree that this is a good solution.

Required

1. Which manager's style do you think is most effective? Why?
2. How do you think the stylists will react to the managers of salons I and II? What can they do to indicate their displeasure, assuming they are displeased?
3. In Hair Suite III, if the stylists did not want to share their stations with another party, how else could they find a way to increase revenues?
4. Refer again to the action that the manager of Hair Suite I has chosen. How does this relate to the concept of stretch targets?

Collaborative Learning Problem

6-41 Comprehensive budgeting problem; activity based costing, operating and financial budgets. Borkenstick makes a very popular undyed cloth sandal in one style, but in Regular and Deluxe. The Regular sandals have cloth soles and the Deluxe sandals have cloth covered wooden soles. Borkenstick is preparing its budget for June 2012, and has estimated sales based on past experience.

Other information for the month of June follows:

Input Prices

Direct materials	
Cloth	$3.50 per yard
Wood	$5.00 per board foot
Direct manufacturing labor	$10 per direct manufacturing labor-hour

Input Quantities per Unit of Output (per pair of sandals)

	Regular	Deluxe
Direct materials		
Cloth	1.3 yards	1.5 yards
Wood	0	2 b.f.
Direct manufacturing labor-hours (DMLH)	5 hours	7 hours
Setup-hours per batch	2 hours	3 hours

Inventory Information, Direct Materials

	Cloth	Wood
Beginning inventory	610 yards	800 b.f.
Target ending inventory	386 yards	295 b.f.
Cost of beginning inventory	$2,146	$4,040

Borkenstick accounts for direct materials using a FIFO cost flow assumption.

Sales and Inventory Information, Finished Goods

	Regular	Deluxe
Expected sales in units (pairs of sandals)	2,000	3,000
Selling price	$ 80	$ 130
Target ending inventory in units	400	600
Beginning inventory in units	250	650
Beginning inventory in dollars	$15,500	$61,750

Borkenstick uses a FIFO cost flow assumption for finished goods inventory.

All the sandals are made in batches of 50 pairs of sandals. Borkenstick incurs manufacturing overhead costs, marketing and general administration, and shipping costs. Besides materials and labor, manufacturing costs include setup, processing, and inspection costs. Borkenstick ships 40 pairs of sandals per shipment. Borkenstick uses activity-based costing and has classified all overhead costs for the month of June as shown in the following chart:

Cost type	Denominator Activity	Rate
Manufacturing:		
Setup	Setup-hours	$12 per setup-hour
Processing	Direct manufacturing labor-hours	$1.20 per DMLH
Inspection	Number of pairs of sandals	$0.90 per pair
Nonmanufacturing:		
Marketing and general administration	Sales revenue	8%
Shipping	Number of shipments	$10 per shipment

1. Prepare each of the following for June:

   a. Revenues budget
   b. Production budget in units
   c. Direct material usage budget and direct material purchases budget in both units and dollars; round to dollars
   d. Direct manufacturing labor cost budget
   e. Manufacturing overhead cost budgets for processing and setup activities
   f. Budgeted unit cost of ending finished goods inventory and ending inventories budget
   g. Cost of goods sold budget
   h. Marketing and general administration costs budget

2. Borkenstick's balance sheet for May 31 follows. Use it and the following information to prepare a cash budget for Borkenstick for June. Round to dollars.

   ■ All sales are on account; 60% are collected in the month of the sale, 38% are collected the following month, and 2% are never collected and written off as bad debts.

   ■ All purchases of materials are on account. Borkenstick pays for 80% of purchases in the month of purchase and 20% in the following month.

   ■ All other costs are paid in the month incurred, including the declaration and payment of a $10,000 cash dividend in June.

   ■ Borkenstick is making monthly interest payments of 0.5% (6% per year) on a $100,000 long term loan.

   ■ Borkenstick plans to pay the $7,200 of taxes owed as of May 31 in the month of June. Income tax expense for June is zero.

   ■ 30% of processing and setup costs, and 10% of marketing and general administration costs are depreciation.

Borkenstick
Balance Sheet
as of May 31

Assets		
Cash		$ 6,290
Accounts receivable	$216,000	
Less: Allowance for bad debts	10,800	205,200
Inventories		
Direct materials		6,186
Finished goods		77,250
Fixed assets	$580,000	
Less: Accumulated depreciation	90,890	489,110
Total assets		$784,036

Liabilities and Equity	
Accounts payable	$ 10,400
Taxes payable	7,200
Interest payable	500
Long-term debt	100,000
Common stock	200,000
Retained earnings	465,936
Total liabilities and equity	$784,036

3. Prepare a budgeted income statement for June and a budgeted balance sheet for Borkenstick as of June 30.

7

Flexible Budgets, Direct-Cost Variances, and Management Control

Professional sports leagues thrive on providing excitement for their fans.

It seems that no expense is spared to entertain spectators and keep them occupied before, during, and after games. Professional basketball has been at the forefront of this trend, popularizing such crowd-pleasing distractions as pregame pyrotechnics, pumped-in noise, fire-shooting scoreboards, and T-shirt-shooting cheerleaders carrying air guns. What is the goal of investing millions in such "game presentation" activities? Such showcasing attracts and maintains the loyalty of younger fans. But eventually, every organization, regardless of its growth, has to step back and take a hard look at the wisdom of its spending choices. And when customers are affected by a recession, the need for an organization to employ budgeting and variance analysis tools for cost control becomes especially critical, as the following article shows.

The NBA: Where Frugal Happens[1]

For more than 20 years, the National Basketball Association (NBA) flew nearly as high as one of LeBron James's slam dunks. The league expanded from 24 to 30 teams, negotiated lucrative TV contracts, and made star players like Kobe Bryant and Dwayne Wade household names and multimillionaires. The NBA was even advertised as "where amazing happens." While costs for brand new arenas and player contracts increased, fans continued to pay escalating ticket prices to see their favorite team. But when the economy nosedived in 2008, the situation changed dramatically.

In the season that followed (2008–2009), more than half of the NBA's franchises lost money. Fans stopped buying tickets and many companies could no longer afford pricy luxury suites. NBA commissioner David Stern announced that overall league revenue for the 2009–2010 season was expected to fall by an additional 5% over the previous disappointing campaign. With revenues dwindling and operating profits tougher to achieve, NBA teams began to heavily emphasize cost control and operating-variance reduction for the first time since the 1980s.

Some of the changes were merely cosmetic. The Charlotte Bobcats stopped paying for halftime entertainment, which cost up to

---

[1] *Sources:* Arnold, Gregory. 2009. NBA teams cut rosters, assistants, scouts to reduce costs. *The Oregonian,* October 26; Biderman, David. 2009. The NBA: Where frugal happens. *Wall Street Journal,* October 27.

$15,000 per game, while the Cleveland Cavaliers saved $40,000 by switching from paper holiday cards to electronic ones. Many other teams—including the Dallas Mavericks, Indiana Pacers, and Miami Heat—reduced labor costs by laying off front-office staff.

Other changes, however, affected play on the court. While NBA teams were allowed to have 15 players on their respective rosters, 10 teams chose to save money by employing fewer players. For example, the Memphis Grizzlies eliminated its entire scouting department, which provided important information on upcoming opponents and potential future players, while the New Jersey Nets traded away most of its high-priced superstars and chose to play with lower-salaried younger players. Each team cutting costs experienced different results. The Grizzlies were a playoff contender, but the Nets were on pace for one of the worst seasons in NBA history.

Just as companies like General Electric and Bank of America have to manage costs and analyze variances for long-term sustainability, so, too, do sports teams. "The NBA is a business just like any other business," Sacramento Kings co-owner Joe Maloof said. "We have to watch our costs and expenses, especially during this trying economic period. It's better to be safe and watch your expenses and make sure you keep your franchise financially strong."

In Chapter 6, you saw how budgets help managers with their planning function. We now explain how budgets, specifically flexible budgets, are used to compute variances, which assist managers in their control function. Flexible budgets and variances enable managers to make meaningful comparisons of actual results with planned performance, and to obtain insights into why actual results differ from planned performance. They form the critical final function in the five-step decision-making process, by making it possible for managers to *evaluate performance and learn* after decisions are implemented. In this chapter and the next, we explain how.

Static Budgets and Variances

A **variance** is the difference between actual results and expected performance. The expected performance is also called **budgeted performance**, which is a point of reference for making comparisons.

The Use of Variances

Variances lie at the point where the planning and control functions of management come together. They assist managers in implementing their strategies by enabling **management by exception**. This is the practice of focusing management attention on areas that are not

Learning Objective 1

Understand static budgets

. . . the master budget based on output planned at start of period

and static-budget variances

. . . the difference between the actual result and the corresponding budgeted amount in the static budget

operating as expected (such as a large shortfall in sales of a product) and devoting less time to areas operating as expected. In other words, by highlighting the areas that have deviated most from expectations, variances enable managers to focus their efforts on the most critical areas. Consider scrap and rework costs at a Maytag appliances plant. If actual costs are much higher than budgeted, the variances will guide managers to seek explanations and to take early corrective action, ensuring that future operations result in less scrap and rework. Sometimes a large positive variance may occur, such as a significant decrease in manufacturing costs of a product. Managers will try to understand the reasons for this decrease (better operator training or changes in manufacturing methods for example), so these practices can be appropriately continued and transferred to other divisions within the organization.

Variances are also used in performance evaluation and to motivate managers. Production-line managers at Maytag may have quarterly efficiency incentives linked to achieving a budgeted amount of operating costs.

Sometimes variances suggest that the company should consider a change in strategy. For example, large negative variances caused by excessive defect rates for a new product may suggest a flawed product design. Managers may then want to investigate the product design and potentially change the mix of products being offered.

Variance analysis contributes in many ways to making the five-step decision-making process more effective. It allows managers to evaluate performance and learn by providing a framework for correctly assessing current performance. In turn, managers take corrective actions to ensure that decisions are implemented correctly and that previously budgeted results are attained. Variances also enable managers to generate more informed predictions about the future, and thereby improve the quality of the five-step decision-making process.

The benefits of variance analysis are not restricted to companies. In today's difficult economic environment, public officials have realized that the ability to make timely tactical alterations based on variance information guards against having to make more draconian adjustments later. For example, the city of Scottsdale, Arizona, monitors its tax and fee performance against expenditures monthly. Why? One of the city's goals is to keep its water usage rates stable. By monitoring the extent to which water revenues are meeting current expenses and obligations, while simultaneously building up funds for future infrastructure projects, the city can avoid rate spikes and achieve long-run rate stability.[2]

How important is variance analysis? A survey by the United Kingdom's Chartered Institute of Management Accountants in July 2009 found that variance analysis was easily the most popular costing tool in practice, and retained that distinction across organizations of all sizes.

Static Budgets and Static-Budget Variances

We will take a closer look at variances by examining one company's accounting system. Note as you study the exhibits in this chapter that "level" followed by a number denotes the amount of detail shown by a variance analysis. Level 1 reports the least detail; level 2 offers more information; and so on.

Consider Webb Company, a firm that manufactures and sells jackets. The jackets require tailoring and many other hand operations. Webb sells exclusively to distributors, who in turn sell to independent clothing stores and retail chains. For simplicity, we assume that Webb's only costs are in the manufacturing function; Webb incurs no costs in other value-chain functions, such as marketing and distribution. We also assume that all units manufactured in April 2011 are sold in April 2011. Therefore, all direct materials are purchased and used in the same budget period, and there is no direct materials inventory at either the beginning or the end of the period. No work-in-process or finished goods inventories exist at either the beginning or the end of the period.

---

[2] For an excellent discussion and other related examples from governmental settings, see S. Kavanagh and C. Swanson, "Tactical Financial Management: Cash Flow and Budgetary Variance Analysis," *Government Finance Review* (October 1, 2009).

Webb has three variable-cost categories. The budgeted variable cost per jacket for each category is as follows:

Cost Category	Variable Cost per Jacket
Direct material costs	$60
Direct manufacturing labor costs	16
Variable manufacturing overhead costs	12
Total variable costs	$88

The *number of units manufactured* is the cost driver for direct materials, direct manufacturing labor, and variable manufacturing overhead. The relevant range for the cost driver is from 0 to 12,000 jackets. Budgeted and actual data for April 2011 follow:

Budgeted fixed costs for production between 0 and 12,000 jackets	$276,000
Budgeted selling price	$ 120 per jacket
Budgeted production and sales	12,000 jackets
Actual production and sales	10,000 jackets

The **static budget**, or master budget, is based on the level of output planned at the start of the budget period. The master budget is called a static budget because the budget for the period is developed around a single (static) planned output level. Exhibit 7-1, column 3, presents the static budget for Webb Company for April 2011 that was prepared at the end of 2010. For each line item in the income statement, Exhibit 7-1, column 1, displays data for the actual April results. For example, actual revenues are $1,250,000, and the actual selling price is $1,250,000 ÷ 10,000 jackets = $125 per jacket—compared with the budgeted selling price of $120 per jacket. Similarly, actual direct material costs are $621,600, and the direct material cost per jacket is $621,600 ÷ 10,000 = $62.16 per jacket—compared with the budgeted direct material cost per jacket of $60. We describe potential reasons and explanations for these differences as we discuss different variances throughout the chapter.

The **static-budget variance** (see Exhibit 7-1, column 2) is the difference between the actual result and the corresponding budgeted amount in the static budget.

A **favorable variance**—denoted F in this book—has the effect, when considered in isolation, of increasing operating income relative to the budgeted amount. For revenue

Exhibit 7-1

Static-Budget-Based Variance Analysis for Webb Company for April 2011

Level 1 Analysis

	Actual Results (1)	Static-Budget Variances (2) = (1) – (3)	Static Budget (3)
Units sold	10,000	2,000 U	12,000
Revenues	$ 1,250,000	$190,000 U	$1,440,000
Variable costs			
Direct materials	621,600	98,400 F	720,000
Direct manufacturing labor	198,000	6,000 U	192,000
Variable manufacturing overhead	130,500	13,500 F	144,000
Total variable costs	950,100	105,900 F	1,056,000
Contribution margin	299,900	84,100 U	384,000
Fixed costs	285,000	9,000 U	276,000
Operating income	$ 14,900	$ 93,100 U	$ 108,000

$ 93,100 U

Static-budget variance

items, F means actual revenues exceed budgeted revenues. For cost items, F means actual costs are less than budgeted costs. An **unfavorable variance**—denoted U in this book—has the effect, when viewed in isolation, of decreasing operating income relative to the budgeted amount. Unfavorable variances are also called *adverse variances* in some countries, such as the United Kingdom.

The unfavorable static-budget variance for operating income of $93,100 in Exhibit 7-1 is calculated by subtracting static-budget operating income of $108,000 from actual operating income of $14,900:

$$\begin{array}{c}\text{Static-budget} \\ \text{variance for} \\ \text{operating income}\end{array} = \begin{array}{c}\text{Actual} \\ \text{result}\end{array} - \begin{array}{c}\text{Static-budget} \\ \text{amount}\end{array}$$

$$= \$14,900 - \$108,000$$

$$= \$93,100 \text{ U}.$$

The analysis in Exhibit 7-1 provides managers with additional information on the static-budget variance for operating income of $93,100 U. The more detailed breakdown indicates how the line items that comprise operating income—revenues, individual variable costs, and fixed costs—add up to the static-budget variance of $93,100.

Remember, Webb produced and sold only 10,000 jackets, although managers anticipated an output of 12,000 jackets in the static budget. *Managers want to know how much of the static-budget variance is because of inaccurate forecasting of output units sold and how much is due to Webb's performance in manufacturing and selling 10,000 jackets.* Managers, therefore, create a flexible budget, which enables a more in-depth understanding of deviations from the static budget.

Decision Point

What are static budgets and static-budget variances?

Flexible Budgets

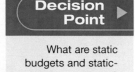

Learning Objective 2

Examine the concept of a flexible budget

. . . the budget that is adjusted (flexed) to recognize the actual output level

and learn how to develop it

. . . proportionately increase variable costs; keep fixed costs the same

A **flexible budget** calculates budgeted revenues and budgeted costs based on *the actual output in the budget period.* The flexible budget is prepared at the end of the period (April 2011), after the actual output of 10,000 jackets is known. The flexible budget is the *hypothetical* budget that Webb would have prepared at the start of the budget period if it had correctly forecast the actual output of 10,000 jackets. In other words, the flexible budget is not the plan Webb initially had in mind for April 2011 (remember Webb planned for an output of 12,000 jackets instead). Rather, it is the budget Webb *would have* put together for April if it knew in advance that the output for the month would be 10,000 jackets. In preparing the flexible budget, note that:

■ The budgeted selling price is the same $120 per jacket used in preparing the static budget.

■ The budgeted unit variable cost is the same $88 per jacket used in the static budget.

■ The budgeted *total* fixed costs are the same static-budget amount of $276,000. Why? Because the 10,000 jackets produced falls within the relevant range of 0 to 12,000 jackets. Therefore, Webb would have budgeted the same amount of fixed costs, $276,000, whether it anticipated making 10,000 or 12,000 jackets.

The *only* difference between the static budget and the flexible budget is that the static budget is prepared for the planned output of 12,000 jackets, whereas the flexible budget is based on the actual output of 10,000 jackets. The static budget is being "flexed," or adjusted, from 12,000 jackets to 10,000 jackets.[3] The flexible budget for 10,000 jackets assumes that all costs are either completely variable or completely fixed with respect to the number of jackets produced.

Webb develops its flexible budget in three steps.

Step 1: Identify the Actual Quantity of Output. In April 2011, Webb produced and sold 10,000 jackets.

---

[3] Suppose Webb, when preparing its next year's budget at the end of 2010, had perfectly anticipated that its output in April 2011 would equal 10,000 jackets. Then, the flexible budget for April 2011 would be identical to the static budget.

Step 2: Calculate the Flexible Budget for Revenues Based on Budgeted Selling Price and Actual Quantity of Output.

$$\text{Flexible-budget revenues} = \$120 \text{ per jacket} \times 10,000 \text{ jackets}$$

$$= \$1,200,000$$

Step 3: Calculate the Flexible Budget for Costs Based on Budgeted Variable Cost per Output Unit, Actual Quantity of Output, and Budgeted Fixed Costs.

Flexible-budget variable costs	
Direct materials, $60 per jacket × 10,000 jackets	$ 600,000
Direct manufacturing labor, $16 per jacket × 10,000 jackets	160,000
Variable manufacturing overhead, $12 per jacket × 10,000 jackets	120,000
Total flexible-budget variable costs	880,000
Flexible-budget fixed costs	276,000
Flexible-budget total costs	$1,156,000

These three steps enable Webb to prepare a flexible budget, as shown in Exhibit 7-2, column 3. The flexible budget allows for a more detailed analysis of the $93,100 unfavorable static-budget variance for operating income.

Decision Point

How can managers develop a flexible budget and why is it useful to do so?

Flexible-Budget Variances and Sales-Volume Variances

Exhibit 7-2 shows the flexible-budget-based variance analysis for Webb, which subdivides the $93,100 unfavorable static-budget variance for operating income into two parts: a flexible-budget variance of $29,100 U and a sales-volume variance of $64,000 U. The **sales-volume variance** is the difference between a flexible-budget amount and the corresponding static-budget amount. The **flexible-budget variance** is the difference between an actual result and the corresponding flexible-budget amount.

Exhibit 7-2   Level 2 Flexible-Budget-Based Variance Analysis for Webb Company for April 2011[a]

Level 2 Analysis

	Actual Results (1)	Flexible-Budget Variances (2) = (1) − (3)	Flexible Budget (3)	Sales-Volume Variances (4) = (3) − (5)	Static Budget (5)
Units sold	10,000	0	10,000	2,000 U	12,000
Revenues	$1,250,000	$50,000 F	$1,200,000	$240,000 U	$1,440,000
Variable costs					
Direct materials	621,600	21,600 U	600,000	120,000 F	720,000
Direct manufacturing labor	198,000	38,000 U	160,000	32,000 F	192,000
Variable manufacturing overhead	130,500	10,500 U	120,000	24,000 F	144,000
Total variable costs	950,100	70,100 U	880,000	176,000 F	1,056,000
Contribution margin	299,900	20,100 U	320,000	64,000 U	384,000
Fixed manufacturing costs	285,000	9,000 U	276,000	0	276,000
Operating income	$ 14,900	$29,100 U	$ 44,000	$ 64,000 U	$ 108,000
Level 2	↑	$29,100 U	↑	$ 64,000 U	↑
		Flexible-budget variance		Sales-volume variance	
Level 1	↑		$93,100 U		↑
			Static-budget variance		

[a]F = favorable effect on operating income; U = unfavorable effect on operating income.

Sales-Volume Variances

Keep in mind that the flexible-budget amounts in column 3 of Exhibit 7-2 and the static-budget amounts in column 5 are both computed using budgeted selling prices, budgeted variable cost per jacket, and budgeted fixed costs. The difference between the static-budget and the flexible-budget amounts is called the sales-volume variance because it arises *solely* from the difference between the 10,000 actual quantity (or volume) of jackets sold and the 12,000 quantity of jackets expected to be sold in the static budget.

$$\text{Sales-volume variance for operating income} = \text{Flexible-budget amount} - \text{Static-budget amount}$$

$$= \$44,000 - \$108,000$$

$$= \$64,000 \text{ U}$$

The sales-volume variance in operating income for Webb measures the change in budgeted contribution margin because Webb sold only 10,000 jackets rather than the budgeted 12,000.

$$\text{Sales-volume variance for operating income} = \left(\begin{array}{c}\text{Budgeted contribution}\\\text{margin per unit}\end{array}\right) \times \left(\begin{array}{c}\text{Actual units}\\\text{sold}\end{array} - \begin{array}{c}\text{Static-budget}\\\text{units sold}\end{array}\right)$$

$$= \left(\begin{array}{c}\text{Budgeted selling}\\\text{price}\end{array} - \begin{array}{c}\text{Budgeted variable}\\\text{cost per unit}\end{array}\right) \times \left(\begin{array}{c}\text{Actual units}\\\text{sold}\end{array} - \begin{array}{c}\text{Static-budget}\\\text{units sold}\end{array}\right)$$

$$= (\$120 \text{ per jacket} - \$88 \text{ per jacket}) \times (10,000 \text{ jackets} - 12,000 \text{ jackets})$$

$$= \$32 \text{ per jacket} \times (-2,000 \text{ jackets})$$

$$= \$64,000 \text{ U}$$

Exhibit 7-2, column 4, shows the components of this overall variance by identifying the sales-volume variance for each of the line items in the income statement. Webb's managers determine that the unfavorable sales-volume variance in operating income could be because of one or more of the following reasons:

1. The overall demand for jackets is not growing at the rate that was anticipated.
2. Competitors are taking away market share from Webb.
3. Webb did not adapt quickly to changes in customer preferences and tastes.
4. Budgeted sales targets were set without careful analysis of market conditions.
5. Quality problems developed that led to customer dissatisfaction with Webb's jackets.

How Webb responds to the unfavorable sales-volume variance will be influenced by what management believes to be the cause of the variance. For example, if Webb's managers believe the unfavorable sales-volume variance was caused by market-related reasons (reasons 1, 2, 3, or 4), the sales manager would be in the best position to explain what happened and to suggest corrective actions that may be needed, such as sales promotions or market studies. If, however, managers believe the unfavorable sales-volume variance was caused by quality problems (reason 5), the production manager would be in the best position to analyze the causes and to suggest strategies for improvement, such as changes in the manufacturing process or investments in new machines. The appendix shows how to further analyze the sales volume variance to identify the reasons behind the unfavorable outcome.

The static-budget variances compared actual revenues and costs for 10,000 jackets against budgeted revenues and costs for 12,000 jackets. A portion of this difference, the sales-volume variance, reflects the effects of inaccurate forecasting of output units sold.

By removing this component from the static-budget variance, managers can compare actual revenues earned and costs incurred for April 2011 against the flexible budget—the revenues and costs Webb would have budgeted for the 10,000 jackets actually produced and sold. *These flexible-budget variances are a better measure of operating performance than static-budget variances because they compare actual revenues to budgeted revenues and actual costs to budgeted costs for the same 10,000 jackets of output.*

Flexible-Budget Variances

The first three columns of Exhibit 7-2 compare actual results with flexible-budget amounts. Flexible-budget variances are in column 2 for each line item in the income statement:

$$\frac{\text{Flexible-budget}}{\text{variance}} = \frac{\text{Actual}}{\text{result}} - \frac{\text{Flexible-budget}}{\text{amount}}$$

The operating income line in Exhibit 7-2 shows the flexible-budget variance is $29,100 U ($14,900 – $44,000). The $29,100 U arises because actual selling price, actual variable cost per unit, and actual fixed costs differ from their budgeted amounts. The actual results and budgeted amounts for the selling price and variable cost per unit are as follows:

	Actual Result	Budgeted Amount
Selling price	$125.00 ($1,250,000 ÷ 10,000 jackets)	$120.00 ($1,200,000 ÷ 10,000 jackets)
Variable cost per jacket	$ 95.01 ($ 950,100 ÷ 10,000 jackets)	$ 88.00 ($ 880,000 ÷ 10,000 jackets)

The flexible-budget variance for revenues is called the **selling-price variance** because it arises solely from the difference between the actual selling price and the budgeted selling price:

$$\frac{\text{Selling-price}}{\text{variance}} = \left(\frac{\text{Actual}}{\text{selling price}} - \frac{\text{Budgeted}}{\text{selling price}} \right) \times \frac{\text{Actual}}{\text{units sold}}$$

$$= (\$125 \text{ per jacket} - \$120 \text{ per jacket}) \times 10,000 \text{ jackets}$$

$$= \$50,000 \text{ F}$$

Webb has a favorable selling-price variance because the $125 actual selling price exceeds the $120 budgeted amount, which increases operating income. Marketing managers are generally in the best position to understand and explain the reason for this selling price difference. For example, was the difference due to better quality? Or was it due to an overall increase in market prices? Webb's managers concluded it was due to a general increase in prices.

The flexible-budget variance for total variable costs is unfavorable ($70,100 U) for the actual output of 10,000 jackets. It's unfavorable because of one or both of the following:

- Webb used greater quantities of inputs (such as direct manufacturing labor-hours) compared to the budgeted quantities of inputs.

- Webb incurred higher prices per unit for the inputs (such as the wage rate per direct manufacturing labor-hour) compared to the budgeted prices per unit of the inputs.

Higher input quantities and/or higher input prices relative to the budgeted amounts could be the result of Webb deciding to produce a better product than what was planned or the result of inefficiencies in Webb's manufacturing and purchasing, or both. *You should always think of variance analysis as providing suggestions for further investigation rather than as establishing conclusive evidence of good or bad performance.*

The actual fixed costs of $285,000 are $9,000 more than the budgeted amount of $276,000. This unfavorable flexible-budget variance reflects unexpected increases in the cost of fixed indirect resources, such as factory rent or supervisory salaries.

In the rest of this chapter, we will focus on variable direct-cost input variances. Chapter 8 emphasizes indirect (overhead) cost variances.

◄ **Decision Point**

How are flexible-budget and sales-volume variances calculated?

Price Variances and Efficiency Variances for Direct-Cost Inputs

To gain further insight, almost all companies subdivide the flexible-budget variance for direct-cost inputs into two more-detailed variances:

1. A price variance that reflects the difference between an actual input price and a budgeted input price

2. An efficiency variance that reflects the difference between an actual input quantity and a budgeted input quantity

The information available from these variances (which we call level 3 variances) helps managers to better understand past performance and take corrective actions to implement superior strategies in the future. Managers generally have more control over efficiency variances than price variances because the quantity of inputs used is primarily affected by factors inside the company (such as the efficiency with which operations are performed), while changes in the price of materials or in wage rates may be largely dictated by market forces outside the company (see the Concepts in Action feature on p. 237).

Obtaining Budgeted Input Prices and Budgeted Input Quantities

Learning Objective 4

Explain why standard costs are often used in variance analysis

. . . standard costs exclude past inefficiencies and take into account expected future changes

To calculate price and efficiency variances, Webb needs to obtain budgeted input prices and budgeted input quantities. Webb's three main sources for this information are past data, data from similar companies, and standards.

1. **Actual input data from past periods.** Most companies have past data on actual input prices and actual input quantities. These historical data could be analyzed for trends or patterns (using some of the techniques we will discuss in Chapter 10) to obtain estimates of budgeted prices and quantities. The advantage of past data is that they represent quantities and prices that are real rather than hypothetical and can serve as benchmarks for continuous improvement. Another advantage is that past data are typically available at low cost. However, there are limitations to using past data. Past data can include inefficiencies such as wastage of direct materials. They also do not incorporate any changes expected for the budget period.

2. **Data from other companies that have similar processes.** The benefit of using data from peer firms is that the budget numbers represent competitive benchmarks from other companies. For example, Baptist Healthcare System in Louisville, Kentucky, maintains detailed flexible budgets and benchmarks its labor performance against hospitals that provide similar types of services and volumes and are in the upper quartile of a national benchmark. The main difficulty of using this source is that input-price and input quantity data from other companies are often not available or may not be comparable to a particular company's situation. Consider American Apparel, which makes over 1 million articles of clothing a week. At its sole factory, in Los Angeles, workers receive hourly wages, piece rates, and medical benefits well in excess of those paid by its competitors, virtually all of whom are offshore. Moreover, because sourcing organic cotton from overseas results in too high of a carbon footprint, American Apparel purchases more expensive domestic cotton in keeping with its sustainability programs.

3. **Standards developed by Webb.** A **standard** is a carefully determined price, cost, or quantity that is used as a benchmark for judging performance. Standards are usually expressed on a per-unit basis. Consider how Webb determines its direct manufacturing labor standards. Webb conducts engineering studies to obtain a detailed breakdown of the steps required to make a jacket. Each step is assigned a standard time based on work performed by a *skilled* worker using equipment operating in an *efficient* manner. There are two advantages of using standard times: (i) They aim to exclude past inefficiencies and (ii) they aim to take into account changes expected to occur in the budget period. An example of (ii) is the decision by Webb, for strategic reasons, to lease new

sewing machines that operate at a faster speed and enable output to be produced with lower defect rates. Similarly, Webb determines the standard quantity of square yards of cloth required by a skilled operator to make each jacket.

The term "standard" refers to many different things. Always clarify its meaning and how it is being used. A **standard input** is a carefully determined quantity of input—such as square yards of cloth or direct manufacturing labor-hours—required for one unit of output, such as a jacket. A **standard price** is a carefully determined price that a company expects to pay for a unit of input. In the Webb example, the standard wage rate that Webb expects to pay its operators is an example of a standard price of a direct manufacturing labor-hour. A **standard cost** is a carefully determined cost of a unit of output—for example, the standard direct manufacturing labor cost of a jacket at Webb.

$$\begin{array}{c}\text{Standard cost per output unit for}\\ \text{each variable direct-cost input}\end{array} = \begin{array}{c}\text{Standard input allowed}\\ \text{for one output unit}\end{array} \times \begin{array}{c}\text{Standard price}\\ \text{per input unit}\end{array}$$

Standard direct material cost per jacket: 2 square yards of cloth input allowed per output unit (jacket) manufactured, at $30 standard price per square yard

Standard direct material cost per jacket = 2 square yards $\times$ $30 per square yard = $60

Standard direct manufacturing labor cost per jacket: 0.8 manufacturing labor-hour of input allowed per output unit manufactured, at $20 standard price per hour

Standard direct manufacturing labor cost per jacket = 0.8 labor-hour $\times$ $20 per labor-hour = $16

How are the words "budget" and "standard" related? Budget is the broader term. To clarify, budgeted input prices, input quantities, and costs need *not* be based on standards. As we saw previously, they could be based on past data or competitive benchmarks, for example. However, when standards *are* used to obtain budgeted input quantities and prices, the terms "standard" and "budget" are used interchangeably. The standard cost of each input required for one unit of output is determined by the standard quantity of the input required for one unit of output and the standard price per input unit. See how the standard-cost computations shown previously for direct materials and direct manufacturing labor result in the budgeted direct material cost per jacket of $60 and the budgeted direct manufacturing labor cost of $16 referred to earlier (p. 229).

In its standard costing system, Webb uses standards that are attainable through efficient operations but that allow for normal disruptions. An alternative is to set more-challenging standards that are more difficult to attain. As we discussed in Chapter 6, setting challenging standards can increase motivation and performance. If, however, standards are regarded by workers as essentially unachievable, it can increase frustration and hurt performance.

Data for Calculating Webb's Price Variances and Efficiency Variances

Consider Webb's two direct-cost categories. The actual cost for each of these categories for the 10,000 jackets manufactured and sold in April 2011 is as follows:

Direct Materials Purchased and Used[4]

1. Square yards of cloth input purchased and used	22,200
2. Actual price incurred per square yard	$ 28
3. Direct material costs (22,200 × $28) [shown in Exhibit 7-2, column 1]	$621,600

Direct Manufacturing Labor

1. Direct manufacturing labor-hours	9,000
2. Actual price incurred per direct manufacturing labor-hour	$ 22
3. Direct manufacturing labor costs (9,000 × $22) [shown in Exhibit 7-2, column 1]	$198,000

---

[4] The Problem for Self-Study (pp. 246–247) relaxes the assumption that the quantity of direct materials used equals the quantity of direct materials purchased.

◄ **Decision Point**

What is a standard cost and what are its purposes?

Learning Objective 5

Compute price variances

. . . each price variance is the difference between an actual input price and a budgeted input price

and efficiency variances

. . . each efficiency variance is the difference between an actual input quantity and a budgeted input quantity for actual output

for direct-cost categories

Let's use the Webb Company data to illustrate the price variance and the efficiency variance for direct-cost inputs.

A **price variance** is the difference between actual price and budgeted price, multiplied by actual input quantity, such as direct materials purchased or used. A price variance is sometimes called an **input-price variance** or **rate variance**, especially when referring to a price variance for direct manufacturing labor. An **efficiency variance** is the difference between actual input quantity used—such as square yards of cloth of direct materials—and budgeted input quantity allowed for actual output, multiplied by budgeted price. An efficiency variance is sometimes called a **usage variance**. Let's explore price and efficiency variances in greater detail so we can see how managers use these variances to improve their future performance.

Price Variances

The formula for computing the price variance is as follows:

$$\text{Price variance} = \left(\begin{array}{c} \text{Actual price} \\ \text{of input} \end{array} - \begin{array}{c} \text{Budgeted price} \\ \text{of input} \end{array} \right) \times \begin{array}{c} \text{Actual quantity} \\ \text{of input} \end{array}$$

Price variances for Webb's two direct-cost categories are as follows:

Direct-Cost Category	(Actual price of input − Budgeted price of input) ×	Actual quantity of input	Price = Variance
Direct materials	($28 per sq. yard − $30 per sq. yard) ×	22,200 square yards	= $44,400 F
Direct manufacturing labor	($22 per hour − $20 per hour) ×	9,000 hours	= $18,000 U

The direct materials price variance is favorable because actual price of cloth is less than budgeted price, resulting in an increase in operating income. The direct manufacturing labor price variance is unfavorable because actual wage rate paid to labor is more than the budgeted rate, resulting in a decrease in operating income.

Always consider a broad range of possible causes for a price variance. For example, Webb's favorable direct materials price variance could be due to one or more of the following:

■ Webb's purchasing manager negotiated the direct materials prices more skillfully than was planned for in the budget.

■ The purchasing manager changed to a lower-price supplier.

■ Webb's purchasing manager ordered larger quantities than the quantities budgeted, thereby obtaining quantity discounts.

■ Direct material prices decreased unexpectedly because of, say, industry oversupply.

■ Budgeted purchase prices of direct materials were set too high without careful analysis of market conditions.

■ The purchasing manager received favorable prices because he was willing to accept unfavorable terms on factors other than prices (such as lower-quality material).

Webb's response to a direct materials price variance depends on what is believed to be the cause of the variance. Assume Webb's managers attribute the favorable price variance to the purchasing manager ordering in larger quantities than budgeted, thereby receiving quantity discounts. Webb could examine if purchasing in these larger quantities resulted in higher storage costs. If the increase in storage and inventory holding costs exceeds the quantity discounts, purchasing in larger quantities is not beneficial. Some companies have reduced their materials storage areas to prevent their purchasing managers from ordering in larger quantities.

Efficiency Variance

For any actual level of output, the efficiency variance is the difference between actual quantity of input used and the budgeted quantity of input allowed for that output level, multiplied by the budgeted input price:

$$\text{Efficiency Variance} = \left(\begin{array}{c} \text{Actual} \\ \text{quantity of} \\ \text{input used} \end{array} - \begin{array}{c} \text{Budgeted quantity} \\ \text{of input allowed} \\ \text{for actual output} \end{array} \right) \times \begin{array}{c} \text{Budgeted price} \\ \text{of input} \end{array}$$

Concepts in Action

Starbucks Reduces Direct-Cost Variances to Brew a Turnaround

Along with coffee, Starbucks brewed profitable growth for many years. From Seattle to Singapore, customers lined up to buy $4 lattes and Frappuccinos. Walking around with a coffee drink from Starbucks became an affordable-luxury status symbol. But when consumers tightened their purse strings amid the recession, the company was in serious trouble. With customers cutting back and lower-priced competition—from Dunkin' Donuts and McDonald's among others—increasing, Starbucks' profit margins were under attack.

For Starbucks, profitability depends on making each high-quality beverage at the lowest possible costs. As a result, an intricate understanding of direct costs is critical. Variance analysis helps managers assess and maintain profitability at desired levels. In each Starbucks store, the two key direct costs are materials and labor.

Materials costs at Starbucks include coffee beans, milk, flavoring syrups, pastries, paper cups, and lids. To reduce budgeted costs for materials, Starbucks focused on two key inputs: coffee and milk. For coffee, Starbucks sought to avoid waste and spoilage by no longer brewing decaffeinated and darker coffee blends in the afternoon and evening, when store traffic is slower. Instead, baristas were instructed to brew a pot only when a customer ordered it. With milk prices rising (and making up around 10% of Starbucks' cost of sales), the company switched to 2% milk, which is healthier and costs less, and redoubled efforts to reduce milk-related spoilage.

Labor costs at Starbucks, which cost 24% of company revenue annually, were another area of variance focus. Many stores employed fewer baristas. In other stores, Starbucks adopted many "lean" production techniques. With 30% of baristas' time involved in walking around behind the counter, reaching for items, and blending drinks, Starbucks sought to make its drink-making processes more efficient. While the changes seem small—keeping bins of coffee beans on top of the counter so baristas don't have to bend over, moving bottles of flavored syrups closer to where drinks are made, and using colored tape to quickly differentiate between pitchers of soy, nonfat, and low-fat milk—some stores experienced a 10% increase in transactions using the same number of workers or fewer.

The company took additional steps to align labor costs with its pricing. Starbucks cut prices on easier-to-make drinks like drip coffee, while lifting prices by as much as 30 cents for larger and more complex drinks, such as a venti caramel macchiato.

Starbucks' focus on reducing year-over-year variances paid off. In fiscal year 2009, the company reduced its store operating expenses by $320 million, or 8.5%. Continued focus on direct-cost variances will be critical to the company's future success in any economic climate.

Sources: Adamy, Janet. 2009. Starbucks brews up new cost cuts by putting lid on afternoon decaf. *Wall Street Journal,* January 28; Adamy, Janet. 2008. New Starbucks brew attracts customers, flak. *Wall Street Journal*, July 1; Harris, Craig. 2007. Starbucks slips; lattes rise. *Seattle Post Intelligencer*, July 23; Jargon, Julie. 2010. Starbucks growth revives, perked by Via. *Wall Street Journal*, January 21; Jargon, Julie. 2009. Latest Starbucks buzzword: 'Lean' Japanese techniques. *Wall Street Journal*, August 4; Kesmodel, David. 2009. Starbucks sees demand stirring again. *Wall Street Journal*, November 6.

The idea here is that a company is inefficient if it uses a larger quantity of input than the budgeted quantity for its actual level of output; the company is efficient if it uses a smaller quantity of input than was budgeted for that output level.

The efficiency variances for each of Webb's direct-cost categories are as follows:

Direct-Cost Category	$\left(\begin{array}{c}\text{Actual} \\ \text{quantity of} \\ \text{input used}\end{array} - \begin{array}{c}\text{Budgeted quantity} \\ \text{of input allowed} \\ \text{for actual output}\end{array}\right)$	$\times$	Budgeted price of input	$=$	Efficiency Variance
Direct materials	[22,200 sq. yds. – (10,000 units × 2 sq. yds./unit)]	×	$30 per sq. yard		
	= (22,200 sq. yds. – 20,000 sq. yds.)	×	$30 per sq. yard	=	$66,000 U
Direct manufacturing labor	[9,000 hours – (10,000 units × 0.8 hour/unit)]	×	$20 per hour		
	= (9,000 hours – 8,000 hours)	×	$20 per hour	=	20,000 U

The two manufacturing efficiency variances—direct materials efficiency variance and direct manufacturing labor efficiency variance—are each unfavorable because more input was used than was budgeted for the actual output, resulting in a decrease in operating income.

As with price variances, there is a broad range of possible causes for these efficiency variances. For example, Webb's unfavorable efficiency variance for direct manufacturing labor could be because of one or more of the following:

- Webb's personnel manager hired underskilled workers.
- Webb's production scheduler inefficiently scheduled work, resulting in more manufacturing labor time than budgeted being used per jacket.
- Webb's maintenance department did not properly maintain machines, resulting in more manufacturing labor time than budgeted being used per jacket.
- Budgeted time standards were set too tight without careful analysis of the operating conditions and the employees' skills.

Decision Point ▶

Why should a company calculate price and efficiency variances?

Suppose Webb's managers determine that the unfavorable variance is due to poor machine maintenance. Webb may then establish a team consisting of plant engineers and machine operators to develop a maintenance schedule that will reduce future breakdowns and thereby prevent adverse effects on labor time and product quality.

Exhibit 7-3 provides an alternative way to calculate price and efficiency variances. It also illustrates how the price variance and the efficiency variance subdivide the flexible-budget variance. Consider direct materials. The direct materials flexible-budget variance of $21,600 U is the difference between actual costs incurred (actual input quantity × actual price) of $621,600 shown in column 1 and the flexible budget (budgeted input quantity allowed for actual output × budgeted price) of $600,000 shown in column 3. Column 2 (actual input quantity × budgeted price) is inserted between column 1 and column 3. The difference between columns 1 and 2 is the price variance of $44,400 F. This price variance occurs because the same actual input quantity (22,200 sq. yds.) is multiplied by *actual price* ($28) in column 1 and *budgeted price* ($30) in column 2. The difference between columns 2 and 3 is the efficiency variance of $66,000 U because the same budgeted price ($30) is multiplied by *actual input quantity* (22,200 sq. yds) in column 2

Exhibit 7-3 Columnar Presentation of Variance Analysis: Direct Costs for Webb Company for April 2011[a]

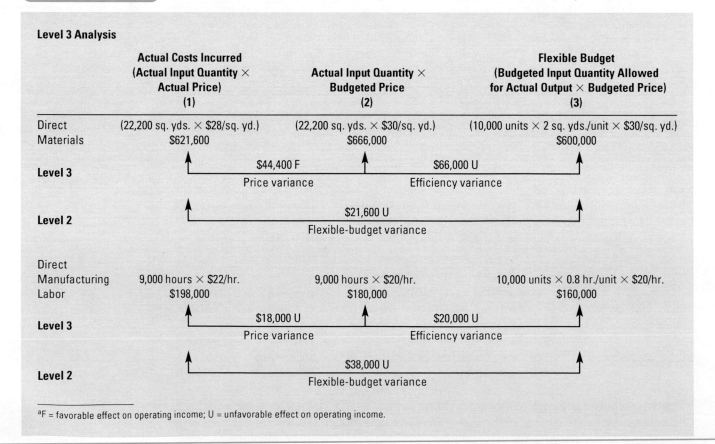

[a]F = favorable effect on operating income; U = unfavorable effect on operating income.

and *budgeted input quantity allowed for actual output* (20,000 sq. yds.) in column 3. The sum of the direct materials price variance, $44,400 F, and the direct materials efficiency variance, $66,000 U, equals the direct materials flexible budget variance, $21,600 U.

Summary of Variances

Exhibit 7-4 provides a summary of the different variances. Note how the variances at each higher level provide disaggregated and more detailed information for evaluating performance.

The following computations show why actual operating income is $14,900 when the static-budget operating income is $108,000. The numbers in the computations can be found in Exhibits 7-2 and 7-3.

Static-budget operating income			$108,000
Unfavorable sales-volume variance for operating income			(64,000)
Flexible-budget operating income			44,000
Flexible-budget variances for operating income:			
Favorable selling-price variance		$50,000	
Direct materials variances:			
Favorable direct materials price variance	$ 44,400		
Unfavorable direct materials efficiency variance	(66,000)		
Unfavorable direct materials variance		(21,600)	
Direct manufacturing labor variances:			
Unfavorable direct manufacturing labor price variance	(18,000)		
Unfavorable direct manufacturing labor efficiency variance	(20,000)		
Unfavorable direct manufacturing labor variance		(38,000)	
Unfavorable variable manufacturing overhead variance		(10,500)	
Unfavorable fixed manufacturing overhead variance		(9,000)	
Unfavorable flexible-budget variance for operating income			(29,100)
Actual operating income			$ 14,900

The summary of variances highlights three main effects:

1. Webb sold 2,000 fewer units than budgeted, resulting in an unfavorable sales volume variance of $64,000. Sales declined because of quality problems and new styles of jackets introduced by Webb's competitors.

2. Webb sold units at a higher price than budgeted, resulting in a favorable selling-price variance of $50,000. Webb's prices, however, were lower than the prices charged by Webb's competitors.

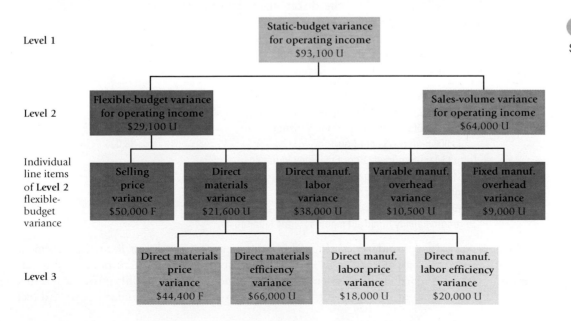

Exhibit 7-4

Summary of Level 1, 2, and 3 Variance Analyses

3. Manufacturing costs for the actual output produced were higher than budgeted—direct materials by $21,600, direct manufacturing labor by $38,000, variable manufacturing overhead by $10,500, and fixed overhead by $9,000 because of poor quality of cloth, poor maintenance of machines, and underskilled workers.

We now present Webb's journal entries under its standard costing system.

Journal Entries Using Standard Costs

Chapter 4 illustrated journal entries when normal costing is used. We will now illustrate journal entries for Webb Company using standard costs. Our focus is on direct materials and direct manufacturing labor. All the numbers included in the following journal entries are found in Exhibit 7-3.

Note: In each of the following entries, unfavorable variances are always debits (they decrease operating income), and favorable variances are always credits (they increase operating income).

JOURNAL ENTRY 1A: Isolate the direct materials price variance at the time of purchase by increasing (debiting) Direct Materials Control at standard prices. This is the earliest time possible to isolate this variance.

1a. Direct Materials Control

(22,200 square yards × $30 per square yard)	666,000	
Direct Materials Price Variance		
(22,200 square yards × $2 per square yard)		44,400
Accounts Payable Control		
(22,200 square yards × $28 per square yard)		621,600
To record direct materials purchased.		

JOURNAL ENTRY 1B: Isolate the direct materials efficiency variance at the time the direct materials are used by increasing (debiting) Work-in-Process Control at standard quantities allowed for actual output units manufactured times standard prices.

1b. Work-in-Process Control

(10,000 jackets × 2 yards per jacket × $30 per square yard)	600,000	
Direct Materials Efficiency Variance		
(2,200 square yards × $30 per square yard)	66,000	
Direct Materials Control		
(22,200 square yards × $30 per square yard)		666,000
To record direct materials used.		

JOURNAL ENTRY 2: Isolate the direct manufacturing labor price variance and efficiency variance at the time this labor is used by increasing (debiting) Work-in-Process Control at standard quantities allowed for actual output units manufactured at standard prices. Note that Wages Payable Control measures the actual amounts payable to workers based on actual hours worked and actual wage rates.

2. Work-in-Process Control

(10,000 jackets × 0.80 hour per jacket × $20 per hour)	160,000	
Direct Manufacturing Labor Price Variance		
(9,000 hours × $2 per hour)	18,000	
Direct Manufacturing Labor Efficiency Variance		
(1,000 hours × $20 per hour)	20,000	
Wages Payable Control		
(9,000 hours × $22 per hour)		198,000
To record liability for direct manufacturing labor costs.		

We have seen how standard costing and variance analysis help to focus management attention on areas not operating as expected. The journal entries here point to another advantage of standard costing systems—that is, standard costs simplify product costing. As each unit is manufactured, costs are assigned to it using the standard cost of direct materials, the standard cost of direct manufacturing labor and, as you will see in Chapter 8, standard manufacturing overhead cost.

From the perspective of control, all variances are isolated at the earliest possible time. For example, by isolating the direct materials price variance at the time of purchase, corrective actions—such as seeking cost reductions from the current supplier or obtaining price quotes from other potential suppliers—can be taken immediately when a large unfavorable variance is first known rather than waiting until after the materials are used in production.

At the end of the fiscal year, the variance accounts are written off to cost of goods sold if they are immaterial in amount. For simplicity, we assume that the balances in the different direct cost variance accounts as of April 2011 are also the balances at the end of 2011 and therefore immaterial in total. Webb would record the following journal entry to write off the direct cost variance accounts to Cost of Goods Sold.

Cost of Goods Sold	59,600	
Direct Materials Price Variance	44,400	
Direct Materials Efficiency Variance		66,000
Direct Manufacturing Labor Price Variance		18,000
Direct Manufacturing Labor Efficiency Variance		20,000

Alternatively, assuming Webb has inventories at the end of the fiscal year, and the variances are material in their amounts, the variance accounts are prorated between cost of goods sold and various inventory accounts using the methods described in Chapter 4 (pp. 117–122). For example, Direct Materials Price Variance is prorated among Materials Control, Work-in-Process Control, Finished Goods Control and Cost of Goods Sold on the basis of the standard costs of direct materials in each account's ending balance. Direct Materials Efficiency Variance is prorated among Work-in-Process Control, Finished Goods Control, and Cost of Goods Sold on the basis of the direct material costs in each account's ending balance (after proration of the direct materials price variance).

Many accountants, industrial engineers, and managers maintain that to the extent that variances measure inefficiency or abnormal efficiency during the year, they should be written off instead of being prorated among inventories and cost of goods sold. This reasoning argues for applying a combination of the write-off and proration methods for each individual variance. Consider the efficiency variance. The portion of the efficiency variance that is due to inefficiency and could have been avoided should be written off to cost of goods sold while the portion that is unavoidable should be prorated. If another variance, such as the direct materials price variance, is considered unavoidable because it is entirely caused by general market conditions, it should be prorated. Unlike full proration, this approach avoids carrying the costs of inefficiency as part of inventoriable costs.

Implementing Standard Costing

Standard costing provides valuable information for the management and control of materials, labor, and other activities related to production.

Standard Costing and Information Technology

Modern information technology promotes the increased use of standard costing systems for product costing and control. Companies such as Dell and Sandoz store standard prices and standard quantities in their computer systems. A bar code scanner records the receipt of materials, immediately costing each material using its stored standard price. The receipt of materials is then matched with the purchase order to record accounts payable and to isolate the direct materials price variance.

The direct materials efficiency variance is calculated as output is completed by comparing the standard quantity of direct materials that should have been used with the computerized request for direct materials submitted by an operator on the production floor. Labor variances are calculated as employees log into production-floor terminals and punch in their employee numbers, start and end times, and the quantity of product they helped produce. Managers use this instantaneous feedback from variances to initiate immediate corrective action, as needed.

Wide Applicability of Standard Costing

Companies that have implemented total quality management and computer-integrated manufacturing (CIM) systems, as well as companies in the service sector, find standard costing to be a useful tool. Companies implementing total quality management programs use standard costing to control materials costs. Service-sector companies such as McDonald's are labor intensive and use standard costs to control labor costs. Companies that have implemented CIM, such as Toyota, use flexible budgeting and standard costing to manage activities such as materials handling and setups. The growing use of Enterprise Resource Planning (ERP) systems, as described in Chapter 6, has made it easy for firms to keep track of standard, average, and actual costs for inventory items and to make real-time assessments of variances. Managers use variance information to identify areas of the firm's manufacturing or purchasing process that most need attention.

Management Uses of Variances

Managers and management accountants use variances to evaluate performance after decisions are implemented, to trigger organization learning, and to make continuous improvements. Variances serve as an early warning system to alert managers to existing problems or to prospective opportunities. Variance analysis enables managers to evaluate the effectiveness of the actions and performance of personnel in the current period, as well as to fine-tune strategies for achieving improved performance in the future. To make sure that managers interpret variances correctly and make appropriate decisions based on them, managers need to recognize that variances can have multiple causes.

Multiple Causes of Variances

Managers must not interpret variances in isolation of each other. The causes of variances in one part of the value chain can be the result of decisions made in another part of the value chain. Consider an unfavorable direct materials efficiency variance on Webb's production line. Possible operational causes of this variance across the value chain of the company are as follows:

1. Poor design of products or processes
2. Poor work on the production line because of underskilled workers or faulty machines
3. Inappropriate assignment of labor or machines to specific jobs
4. Congestion due to scheduling a large number of rush orders from Webb's sales representatives
5. Webb's suppliers not manufacturing cloth materials of uniformly high quality

Item 5 offers an even broader reason for the cause of the unfavorable direct materials efficiency variance by considering inefficiencies in the supply chain of companies—in this case, by the cloth suppliers for Webb's jackets. Whenever possible, managers must attempt to understand the root causes of the variances.

When to Investigate Variances

Managers realize that a standard is not a single measure but rather a range of possible acceptable input quantities, costs, output quantities, or prices. Consequently, they expect small variances to arise. A variance within an acceptable range is considered to be an "in control occurrence" and calls for no investigation or action by managers. So when would managers need to investigate variances?

Frequently, managers investigate variances based on subjective judgments or rules of thumb. For critical items, such as product defects, even a small variance may prompt investigations and actions. For other items, such as direct material costs, labor costs, and repair costs, companies generally have rules such as "investigate all variances exceeding $5,000 or 25% of the budgeted cost, whichever is lower." The idea is that a 4% variance in direct material costs of $1 million—a $40,000 variance—deserves more attention than a 20% variance in repair costs of $10,000—a $2,000 variance. Variance analysis is subject to the same cost-benefit test as all other phases of a management control system.

Performance Measurement Using Variances

Managers often use variance analysis when evaluating the performance of their subordinates. Two attributes of performance are commonly evaluated:

1. **Effectiveness**: the degree to which a predetermined objective or target is met—for example, sales, market share and customer satisfaction ratings of Starbucks' new VIA® Ready Brew line of instant coffees.

2. **Efficiency**: the relative amount of inputs used to achieve a given output level—the smaller the quantity of Arabica beans used to make a given number of VIA packets or the greater the number of VIA packets made from a given quantity of beans, the greater the efficiency.

As we discussed earlier, managers must be sure they understand the causes of a variance before using it for performance evaluation. Suppose a Webb purchasing manager has just negotiated a deal that results in a favorable price variance for direct materials. The deal could have achieved a favorable variance for any or all of the following reasons:

1. The purchasing manager bargained effectively with suppliers.

2. The purchasing manager secured a discount for buying in bulk with fewer purchase orders. However, buying larger quantities than necessary for the short run resulted in excessive inventory.

3. The purchasing manager accepted a bid from the lowest-priced supplier after only minimal effort to check quality amid concerns about the supplier's materials.

If the purchasing manager's performance is evaluated solely on price variances, then the evaluation will be positive. Reason 1 would support this favorable conclusion: The purchasing manager bargained effectively. Reasons 2 and 3 have short-run gains, buying in bulk or making only minimal effort to check the supplier's quality-monitoring procedures. However, these short-run gains could be offset by higher inventory storage costs or higher inspection costs and defect rates on Webb's production line, leading to unfavorable direct manufacturing labor and direct materials efficiency variances. Webb may ultimately lose more money because of reasons 2 and 3 than it gains from the favorable price variance.

Bottom line: Managers should not automatically interpret a favorable variance as "good news."

Managers benefit from variance analysis because it highlights individual aspects of performance. However, if any single performance measure (for example, a labor efficiency variance or a consumer rating report) receives excessive emphasis, managers will tend to make decisions that will cause the particular performance measure to look good. These actions may conflict with the company's overall goals, inhibiting the goals from being achieved. This faulty perspective on performance usually arises when top management designs a performance evaluation and reward system that does not emphasize total company objectives.

Organization Learning

The goal of variance analysis is for managers to understand why variances arise, to learn, and to improve future performance. For instance, to reduce the unfavorable direct materials efficiency variance, Webb's managers may seek improvements in product design, in the commitment of workers to do the job right the first time, and in the quality of supplied materials, among other improvements. Sometimes an unfavorable direct materials efficiency variance may signal a need to change product strategy, perhaps because the product cannot be made at a low enough cost. Variance analysis should not be a tool to "play the blame game" (that is, seeking a person to blame for every unfavorable variance). Rather, it should help the company learn about what happened and how to perform better in the future.

Managers need to strike a delicate balance between the two uses of variances we have discussed: performance evaluation and organization learning. Variance analysis is helpful for performance evaluation, but an overemphasis on performance evaluation and meeting individual variance targets can undermine learning and continuous improvement. Why? Because achieving the standard becomes an end in and of itself. As a result, managers will seek targets that are easy to attain rather than targets that are challenging and that require creativity and resourcefulness. For example, if performance evaluation is overemphasized, Webb's manufacturing manager will prefer an easy standard that allows workers ample time to manufacture a jacket; he will then have little incentive to improve processes and methods to reduce manufacturing time and cost.

An overemphasis on performance evaluation may also cause managers to take actions to achieve the budget and avoid an unfavorable variance, even if such actions could hurt the company in the long run. For example, the manufacturing manager may push workers to produce jackets within the time allowed, even if this action could lead to poorer quality jackets being produced, which could later hurt revenues. Such negative impacts are less likely to occur if variance analysis is seen as a way of promoting organization learning.

Continuous Improvement

Managers can also use variance analysis to create a virtuous cycle of continuous improvement. How? By repeatedly identifying causes of variances, initiating corrective actions, and evaluating results of actions. Improvement opportunities are often easier to identify when products are first produced. Once the easy opportunities have been identified ("the low-hanging fruit picked"), much more ingenuity may be required to identify successive improvement opportunities. Some companies use kaizen budgeting (Chapter 6, p. 203) to specifically target reductions in budgeted costs over successive periods. The advantage of kaizen budgeting is that it makes continuous improvement goals explicit.

Financial and Nonfinancial Performance Measures

Almost all companies use a combination of financial and nonfinancial performance measures for planning and control rather than relying exclusively on either type of measure. To control a production process, supervisors cannot wait for an accounting report with variances reported in dollars. Instead, timely nonfinancial performance measures are frequently used for control purposes in such situations. For example, a Nissan plant compiles data such as defect rates and production-schedule attainment and broadcasts them in ticker-tape fashion on screens throughout the plant.

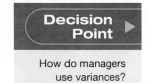

Decision Point ▶

How do managers use variances?

In Webb's cutting room, cloth is laid out and cut into pieces, which are then matched and assembled. Managers exercise control in the cutting room by observing workers and by focusing on *nonfinancial measures*, such as number of square yards of cloth used to produce 1,000 jackets or percentage of jackets started and completed without requiring any rework. Webb production workers find these nonfinancial measures easy to understand. At the same time, Webb production managers will also use *financial measures* to evaluate the overall cost efficiency with which operations are being run and to help guide decisions about, say, changing the mix of inputs used in manufacturing jackets. Financial measures are often critical in a company because they indicate the economic impact of diverse physical activities. This knowledge allows managers to make trade-offs—increase the costs of one physical activity (say, cutting) to reduce the costs of another physical measure (say, defects).

Benchmarking and Variance Analysis

Learning Objective 7

Describe benchmarking and explain its role in cost management

. . . benchmarking compares actual performance against the best levels of performance

The budgeted amounts in the Webb Company illustration are based on analysis of operations within their own respective companies. We now turn to the situation in which companies develop standards based on an analysis of operations at other companies. **Benchmarking** is the continuous process of comparing the levels of performance in producing products and services and executing activities against the best levels of performance in competing companies or in companies having similar processes. When benchmarks are used as standards, managers and management accountants know that the company will be competitive in the marketplace if it can attain the standards.

Companies develop benchmarks and calculate variances on items that are the most important to their businesses. Consider the cost per available seat mile (ASM) for United Airlines; ASMs equal the total seats in a plane multiplied by the distance traveled, and are a measure of airline size. Assume United uses data from each of seven competing U.S. airlines in its benchmark cost comparisons. Summary data are in Exhibit 7-5. The benchmark

Exhibit 7-5 Available Seat Mile (ASM) Benchmark Comparison of United Airlines with Seven Other Airlines

| | Home | Insert | Page Layout | Formulas | Data | Review | View | | |

	A	Operating Cost per ASM (1)	Operating Revenue per ASM (2)	Operating Income per ASM (3) = (2) − (1)	Fuel Cost per ASM (4)	Labor Cost per ASM (5)	Total ASMs (Millions) (6)
3	Airline						
4							
5	United Airlines	$0.1574	$0.1258	−$0.0315	$0.0568	$0.0317	135,861
6	Airlines used as benchmarks:						
7	JetBlue Airways	$0.1011	$0.1045	$0.0034	$0.0417	$0.0214	32,422
8	Southwest Airlines	$0.1024	$0.1067	$0.0043	$0.0360	$0.0323	103,271
9	Continental Airlines	$0.1347	$0.1319	−$0.0027	$0.0425	$0.0258	115,511
10	Alaska Airlines	$0.1383	$0.1330	−$0.0053	$0.0480	$0.0319	24,218
11	American Airlines	$0.1387	$0.1301	−$0.0086	$0.0551	$0.0407	163,532
12	U.S. Airways	$0.1466	$0.1263	−$0.0203	$0.0488	$0.0301	74,151
13	Delta/Northwest Airlines	$0.1872	$0.1370	−$0.0502	$0.0443	$0.0290	165,639
14	Average of airlines						
15	used as benchmarks	$0.1356	$0.1242	−$0.0113	$0.0452	$0.0302	96,963
16							
17							
18	Source: Individual companies' 10-K reports for the year ending December 31, 2008						

companies are ranked from lowest to highest operating cost per ASM in column 1. Also reported in Exhibit 7-5 are operating revenue per ASM, operating income per ASM, labor cost per ASM, fuel cost per ASM, and total available seat miles. The impact of the recession on the travel industry is evident in the fact that only two airlines—JetBlue and Southwest—have positive levels of operating income.

How well did United manage its costs? The answer depends on which specific benchmark is being used for comparison. United's actual operating cost of $0.1574 per ASM is above the average operating cost of $0.1356 per ASM of the seven other airlines. Moreover, United's operating cost per ASM is 55.7% higher than JetBlue Airways, the lowest-cost competitor at $0.1011 per ASM [($0.1574 − $0.1011) ÷ $0.1011 = 55.7%]. So why is United's operating cost per ASM so high? Columns E and F suggest that both fuel cost and labor cost are possible reasons. These benchmarking data alert management at United that it needs to become more efficient in its use of both material and labor inputs to become more cost competitive.

Using benchmarks such as those in Exhibit 7-5 is not without problems. Finding appropriate benchmarks is a major issue in implementing benchmarking. Many companies purchase benchmark data from consulting firms. Another problem is ensuring the benchmark numbers are comparable. In other words, there needs to be an "apples to apples" comparison. Differences can exist across companies in their strategies, inventory costing methods, depreciation methods, and so on. For example, JetBlue serves fewer cities and has mostly long-haul flights compared with United, which serves almost all major U.S. cities and several international cities and has both long-haul and short-haul flights. Southwest Airlines differs from United because it specializes in short-haul direct flights and offers fewer services on board its planes. Because United's strategy is different from the strategies of JetBlue and Southwest, one might expect its cost per ASM to be different too. United's strategy is more comparable to the strategies of American, Continental, Delta, and U.S. Airways. Note that its costs per ASM are relatively more competitive with these airlines. But United competes head-to-head with JetBlue and Southwest in several cities and markets, so it still needs to benchmark against these carriers as well.

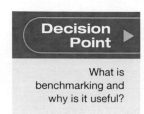

Decision Point

What is benchmarking and why is it useful?

United's management accountants can use benchmarking data to address several questions. How do factors such as plane size and type, or the duration of flights, affect the cost per ASM? Do airlines differ in their fixed cost/variable cost structures? Can performance be improved by rerouting flights, using different types of aircraft on different routes, or changing the frequency or timing of specific flights? What explains revenue differences per ASM across airlines? Is it differences in perceived quality of service or differences in competitive power at specific airports? Management accountants are more valuable to managers when they use benchmarking data to provide insight into *why* costs or revenues differ across companies, or within plants of the same company, as distinguished from simply reporting the magnitude of such differences.

Problem for Self-Study

O'Shea Company manufactures ceramic vases. It uses its standard costing system when developing its flexible-budget amounts. In April 2012, 2,000 finished units were produced. The following information relates to its two direct manufacturing cost categories: direct materials and direct manufacturing labor.

Direct materials used were 4,400 kilograms (kg). The standard direct materials input allowed for one output unit is 2 kilograms at $15 per kilogram. O'Shea purchased 5,000 kilograms of materials at $16.50 per kilogram, a total of $82,500. (This Problem for Self-Study illustrates how to calculate direct materials variances when the quantity of materials *purchased* in a period differs from the quantity of materials *used* in that period.)

Actual direct manufacturing labor-hours were 3,250, at a total cost of $66,300. Standard manufacturing labor time allowed is 1.5 hours per output unit, and the standard direct manufacturing labor cost is $20 per hour.

Required

1. Calculate the direct materials price variance and efficiency variance, and the direct manufacturing labor price variance and efficiency variance. Base the direct materials price variance on a flexible budget for *actual quantity purchased*, but base the direct materials efficiency variance on a flexible budget for *actual quantity used*.
2. Prepare journal entries for a standard costing system that isolates variances at the earliest possible time.

Solution

1. Exhibit 7-6 shows how the columnar presentation of variances introduced in Exhibit 7-3 can be adjusted for the difference in timing between purchase and use of materials. Note, in particular, the two sets of computations in column 2 for direct materials—the $75,000 for direct materials purchased and the $66,000 for direct materials used. The direct materials price variance is calculated on purchases so that managers responsible for the purchase can immediately identify and isolate reasons for the variance and initiate any desired corrective action. The efficiency variance is the responsibility of the production manager, so this variance is identified only at the time materials are used.

2.

Materials Control (5,000 kg × $15 per kg)	75,000	
Direct Materials Price Variance (5,000 kg × $1.50 per kg)	7,500	
Accounts Payable Control (5,000 kg × $16.50 per kg)		82,500
Work-in-Process Control (2,000 units × 2 kg per unit × $15 per kg)	60,000	
Direct Materials Efficiency Variance (400 kg × $15 per kg)	6,000	
Materials Control (4,400 kg × $15 per kg)		66,000
Work-in-Process Control (2,000 units × 1.5 hours per unit × $20 per hour)	60,000	
Direct Manufacturing Labor Price Variance (3,250 hours × $0.40 per hour)	1,300	
Direct Manufacturing Labor Efficiency Variance (250 hours × $20 per hour)	5,000	
Wages Payable Control (3,250 hours × $20.40 per hour)		66,300

Note: All the variances are debits because they are unfavorable and therefore reduce operating income.

| Exhibit 7-6 | Columnar Presentation of Variance Analysis for O'Shea Company: Direct Materials and Direct Manufacturing Labor for April 2012[a] |

Level 3 Analysis

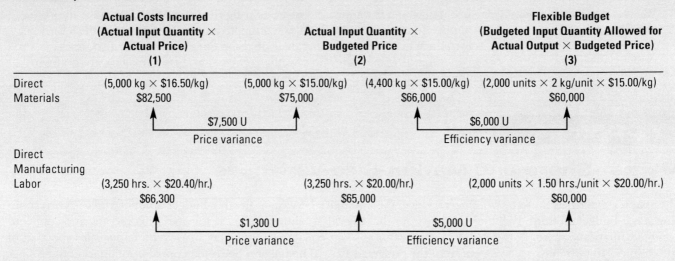

	Actual Costs Incurred (Actual Input Quantity × Actual Price) (1)	Actual Input Quantity × Budgeted Price (2)	Flexible Budget (Budgeted Input Quantity Allowed for Actual Output × Budgeted Price) (3)
Direct Materials	(5,000 kg × $16.50/kg) $82,500	(5,000 kg × $15.00/kg) $75,000 (4,400 kg × $15.00/kg) $66,000	(2,000 units × 2 kg/unit × $15.00/kg) $60,000
	↑ $7,500 U ↑ Price variance	↑ $6,000 U ↑ Efficiency variance	
Direct Manufacturing Labor	(3,250 hrs. × $20.40/hr.) $66,300	(3,250 hrs. × $20.00/hr.) $65,000	(2,000 units × 1.50 hrs./unit × $20.00/hr.) $60,000
	↑ $1,300 U ↑ Price variance	↑ $5,000 U ↑ Efficiency variance	

[a]F = favorable effect on operating income; U = unfavorable effect on operating income.

Decision Points

The following question-and-answer format summarizes the chapter's learning objectives. Each decision presents a key question related to a learning objective. The guidelines are the answer to that question.

Decision	Guidelines
1. What are static budgets and static-budget variances?	A static budget is based on the level of output planned at the start of the budget period. The static-budget variance is the difference between the actual result and the corresponding budgeted amount in the static budget.
2. How can managers develop a flexible budget and why is it useful to do so?	A flexible budget is adjusted (flexed) to recognize the actual output level of the budget period. Managers use a three-step procedure to develop a flexible budget. When all costs are either variable with respect to output units or fixed, these three steps require only information about budgeted selling price, budgeted variable cost per output unit, budgeted fixed costs, and actual quantity of output units. Flexible budgets help managers gain more insight into the causes of variances than is available from static budgets.
3. How are flexible-budget and sales-volume variances calculated?	The static-budget variance can be subdivided into a flexible-budget variance (the difference between an actual result and the corresponding flexible-budget amount) and a sales-volume variance (the difference between the flexible-budget amount and the corresponding static-budget amount).
4. What is a standard cost and what are its purposes?	A standard cost is a carefully determined cost used as a benchmark for judging performance. The purposes of a standard cost are to exclude past inefficiencies and to take into account changes expected to occur in the budget period.
5. Why should a company calculate price and efficiency variables?	The computation of price and efficiency variances helps managers gain insight into two different—but not independent—aspects of performance. The price variance focuses on the difference between actual input price and budgeted input price. The efficiency variance focuses on the difference between actual quantity of input and budgeted quantity of input allowed for actual output.

6. How do managers use variances?

Managers use variances for control, decision implementation, performance evaluation, organization learning, and continuous improvement. When using variances for these purposes, managers consider several variances together rather than focusing only on an individual variance.

7. What is benchmarking and why is it useful?

Benchmarking is the process of comparing the level of performance in producing products and services and executing activities against the best levels of performance in competing companies or companies with similar processes. Benchmarking measures how well a company and its managers are doing in comparison to other organizations.

Appendix

Market-Share and Market-Size Variances

The chapter described the sales-volume variance, the difference between a flexible-budget amount and the corresponding static-budget amount. Exhibit 7-2 points out that the sales-volume variances for operating income and contribution margin are the same. In the Webb example, this amount equals 64,000 U, because Webb had a sales shortfall of 2,000 units (10,000 units sold compared to the budgeted 12,000 units), at a budgeted contribution margin of $32 per jacket. Webb's managers can gain more insight into the sales-volume variance by subdividing it. We explore one such analysis here.

Recall that Webb sells a single product, jackets, using a single distribution channel. In this case, the sales-volume variance is also called the *sales-quantity variance*.[5] Sales depend on overall demand for jackets, as well as Webb's share of the market. Assume that Webb derived its total unit sales budget for April 2011 from a management estimate of a 20% market share and a budgeted industry market size of 60,000 units (0.20 × 60,000 units = 12,000 units). For April 2011, actual market size was 62,500 units and actual market share was 16% (10,000 units ÷ 62,500 units = 0.16 or 16%). Exhibit 7-7 shows the columnar presentation of how Webb's sales-quantity variance can be decomposed into market-share and market-size variances.

Exhibit 7-7   Market-Share and Market-Size Variance Analysis of Webb Company for April 2011[a]

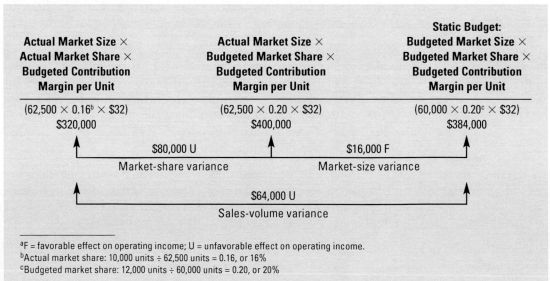

[a]F = favorable effect on operating income; U = unfavorable effect on operating income.
[b]Actual market share: 10,000 units ÷ 62,500 units = 0.16, or 16%
[c]Budgeted market share: 12,000 units ÷ 60,000 units = 0.20, or 20%

---

[5] Chapter 14 examines more complex settings with multiple products and multiple distribution channels. In those cases, the sales-quantity variance is one of the components of the sales-volume variance; the other portion has to do with the mix of products/channels used by the firm for generating sales revenues.

Market-Share Variance

The **market-share variance** is the difference in budgeted contribution margin for actual market size in units caused solely by *actual market share* being different from *budgeted market share*. The formula for computing the market-share variance is as follows:

$$\text{Market-share variance} = \text{Actual market size in units} \times \left(\text{Actual market share} - \text{Budgeted market share}\right) \times \text{Budgeted contribution margin per unit}$$

$$= 62{,}500 \text{ units} \times (0.16 - 0.20) \times \$32 \text{ per unit}$$

$$= \$80{,}000 \text{ U}$$

Webb lost 4.0 market-share percentage points—from the 20% budgeted share to the actual share of 16%. The $80,000 U market-share variance is the decline in contribution margin as a result of those lost sales.

Market-Size Variance

The **market-size variance** is the difference in budgeted contribution margin at budgeted market share caused solely by *actual market size in units* being different from *budgeted market size in units*. The formula for computing the market-size variance is as follows:

$$\text{Market-size variance} = \left(\text{Actual market size} - \text{Budgeted market size}\right) \times \text{Budgeted market share} \times \text{Budgeted contribution margin per unit}$$

$$= (62{,}500 \text{ units} - 60{,}000 \text{ units}) \times 0.20 \times \$32 \text{ per unit}$$

$$= \$16{,}000 \text{ F}$$

The market-size variance is favorable because actual market size increased 4.17% [(62,500 − 60,000) ÷ 60,000 = 0.417, or 4.17%] compared to budgeted market size.

Managers should probe the reasons for the market-size and market-share variances for April 2011. Is the $16,000 F market-size variance because of an increase in market size that can be expected to continue in the future? If yes, Webb has much to gain by attaining or exceeding its budgeted 20% market share. Was the $80,000 unfavorable market-share variance because of competitors providing better offerings or greater value to customers? We saw earlier that Webb was able to charge a higher selling price than expected, resulting in a favorable selling-price variance. However, competitors introduced new styles of jackets that stimulated market demand and enabled them to charge higher prices than Webb. Webb's products also experienced quality-control problems that were the subject of negative media coverage, leading to a significant drop in market share, even as overall industry sales were growing.

Some companies place more emphasis on the market-share variance than the market-size variance when evaluating their managers. That's because they believe the market-size variance is influenced by economy-wide factors and shifts in consumer preferences that are outside the managers' control, whereas the market-share variance measures how well managers performed relative to their peers.

Be cautious when computing the market-size variance and the market-share variance. Reliable information on market size and market share is available for some, but not all, industries. The automobile, computer, and television industries are cases in which market-size and market-share statistics are widely available. In other industries, such as management consulting and personal financial planning, information about market size and market share is far less reliable.

Terms to Learn

This chapter and the Glossary at the end of the book contain definitions of the following important terms:

benchmarking **(p. 244)**
budgeted performance **(p. 227)**
effectiveness **(p. 243)**
efficiency **(p. 243)**
efficiency variance **(p. 236)**
favorable variance **(p. 229)**
flexible budget **(p. 230)**
flexible-budget variance **(p. 231)**
input-price variance **(p. 236)**
management by exception **(p. 227)**
market-share variance **(p. 249)**
market-size variance **(p. 249)**
price variance **(p. 236)**
rate variance **(p. 236)**
sales-volume variance **(p. 231)**
selling-price variance **(p. 233)**
standard **(p. 234)**
standard cost **(p. 235)**

standard input **(p. 235)**   static-budget variance **(p. 229)**   usage variance **(p. 236)**
standard price **(p. 235)**   unfavorable variance **(p. 230)**   variance **(p. 227)**
static budget **(p. 229)**

Assignment Material

Questions

7-1 What is the relationship between management by exception and variance analysis?
7-2 What are two possible sources of information a company might use to compute the budgeted amount in variance analysis?
7-3 Distinguish between a favorable variance and an unfavorable variance.
7-4 What is the key difference between a static budget and a flexible budget?
7-5 Why might managers find a flexible-budget analysis more informative than a static-budget analysis?
7-6 Describe the steps in developing a flexible budget.
7-7 List four reasons for using standard costs.
7-8 How might a manager gain insight into the causes of a flexible-budget variance for direct materials?
7-9 List three causes of a favorable direct materials price variance.
7-10 Describe three reasons for an unfavorable direct manufacturing labor efficiency variance.
7-11 How does variance analysis help in continuous improvement?
7-12 Why might an analyst examining variances in the production area look beyond that business function for explanations of those variances?
7-13 Comment on the following statement made by a plant manager: "Meetings with my plant accountant are frustrating. All he wants to do is pin the blame on someone for the many variances he reports."
7-14 How can the sales-volume variance be decomposed further to obtain useful information?
7-15 "Benchmarking against other companies enables a company to identify the lowest-cost producer. This amount should become the performance measure for next year." Do you agree?

Exercises

7-16 Flexible budget. Brabham Enterprises manufactures tires for the Formula I motor racing circuit. For August 2012, it budgeted to manufacture and sell 3,000 tires at a variable cost of $74 per tire and total fixed costs of $54,000. The budgeted selling price was $110 per tire. Actual results in August 2012 were 2,800 tires manufactured and sold at a selling price of $112 per tire. The actual total variable costs were $229,600, and the actual total fixed costs were $50,000.

Required
1. Prepare a performance report (akin to Exhibit 7-2, p. 231) that uses a flexible budget and a static budget.
2. Comment on the results in requirement 1.

7-17 Flexible budget. Connor Company's budgeted prices for direct materials, direct manufacturing labor, and direct marketing (distribution) labor per attaché case are $40, $8, and $12, respectively. The president is pleased with the following performance report:

	Actual Costs	Static Budget	Variance
Direct materials	$364,000	$400,000	$36,000 F
Direct manufacturing labor	78,000	80,000	2,000 F
Direct marketing (distribution) labor	110,000	120,000	10,000 F

Actual output was 8,800 attaché cases. Assume all three direct-cost items shown are variable costs.

Required Is the president's pleasure justified? Prepare a revised performance report that uses a flexible budget and a static budget.

7-18 Flexible-budget preparation and analysis. Bank Management Printers, Inc., produces luxury checkbooks with three checks and stubs per page. Each checkbook is designed for an individual customer and is ordered through the customer's bank. The company's operating budget for September 2012 included these data:

Number of checkbooks	15,000
Selling price per book	$ 20
Variable cost per book	$ 8
Fixed costs for the month	$145,000

The actual results for September 2012 were as follows:

Number of checkbooks produced and sold	12,000
Average selling price per book	$ 21
Variable cost per book	$ 7
Fixed costs for the month	$150,000

The executive vice president of the company observed that the operating income for September was much lower than anticipated, despite a higher-than-budgeted selling price and a lower-than-budgeted variable cost per unit. As the company's management accountant, you have been asked to provide explanations for the disappointing September results.

Bank Management develops its flexible budget on the basis of budgeted per-output-unit revenue and per-output-unit variable costs without detailed analysis of budgeted inputs.

1. Prepare a static-budget-based variance analysis of the September performance.
2. Prepare a flexible-budget-based variance analysis of the September performance.
3. Why might Bank Management find the flexible-budget-based variance analysis more informative than the static-budget-based variance analysis? Explain your answer.

Required

7-19 Flexible budget, working backward. The Clarkson Company produces engine parts for car manufacturers. A new accountant intern at Clarkson has accidentally deleted the calculations on the company's variance analysis calculations for the year ended December 31, 2012. The following table is what remains of the data.

	A	B	C	D	E	F
		Home Insert Page Layout Formulas Data Review View				
1	Performance Report, Year Ended December 31, 2012					
2						
3		Actual Results	Flexible-Budget Variances	Flexible Budget	Sales-Volume Variances	Static Budget
4	Units sold	130,000				120,000
5	Revenues (sales)	$715,000				$420,000
6	Variable costs	515,000				240,000
7	Contribution margin	200,000				180,000
8	Fixed costs	140,000				120,000
9	Operating income	$ 60,000				$ 60,000

1. Calculate all the required variances. (If your work is accurate, you will find that the total static-budget variance is $0.)
2. What are the actual and budgeted selling prices? What are the actual and budgeted variable costs per unit?
3. Review the variances you have calculated and discuss possible causes and potential problems. What is the important lesson learned here?

Required

7-20 Flexible-budget and sales volume variances, market-share and market-size variances. Marron, Inc., produces the basic fillings used in many popular frozen desserts and treats—vanilla and chocolate ice creams, puddings, meringues, and fudge. Marron uses standard costing and carries over no inventory from one month to the next. The ice-cream product group's results for June 2012 were as follows:

	A	B	C
	Home Insert Page Layout Formulas Data		
1	Performance Report, June 2012		
2		Actual Results	Static Budget
3	Units (pounds)	355,000	345,000
4	Revenues	$1,917,000	$1,880,250
5	Variable manufacturing costs	1,260,250	1,207,500
6	Contribution margin	$ 656,750	$ 672,750

Ted Levine, the business manager for ice-cream products, is pleased that more pounds of ice cream were sold than budgeted and that revenues were up. Unfortunately, variable manufacturing costs went up too. The bottom line is that contribution margin declined by $16,000, which is less than 1% of the budgeted revenues of $1,880,250. Overall, Levine feels that the business is running fine.

Levine would also like to analyze how the company is performing compared to the overall market for ice-cream products. He knows that the expected total market for ice-cream products was 1,150,000 pounds and that the actual total market was 1,109,375 pounds.

Required

1. Calculate the static-budget variance in units, revenues, variable manufacturing costs, and contribution margin. What percentage is each static-budget variance relative to its static-budget amount?
2. Break down each static-budget variance into a flexible-budget variance and a sales-volume variance.
3. Calculate the selling-price variance.
4. Calculate the market-share and market-size variances.
5. Assume the role of management accountant at Marron. How would you present the results to Ted Levine? Should he be more concerned? If so, why?

7-21 Price and efficiency variances. Peterson Foods manufactures pumpkin scones. For January 2012, it budgeted to purchase and use 15,000 pounds of pumpkin at $0.89 a pound. Actual purchases and usage for January 2012 were 16,000 pounds at $0.82 a pound. Peterson budgeted for 60,000 pumpkin scones. Actual output was 60,800 pumpkin scones.

Required

1. Compute the flexible-budget variance.
2. Compute the price and efficiency variances.
3. Comment on the results for requirements 1 and 2 and provide a possible explanation for them.

7-22 Materials and manufacturing labor variances. Consider the following data collected for Great Homes, Inc.:

	Direct Materials	Direct Manufacturing Labor
Cost incurred: Actual inputs × actual prices	$200,000	$90,000
Actual inputs × standard prices	214,000	86,000
Standard inputs allowed for actual output × standard prices	225,000	80,000

Required

Compute the price, efficiency, and flexible-budget variances for direct materials and direct manufacturing labor.

7-23 Direct materials and direct manufacturing labor variances. GloriaDee, Inc., designs and manufactures T-shirts. It sells its T-shirts to brand-name clothes retailers in lots of one dozen. GloriaDee's May 2011 static budget and actual results for direct inputs are as follows:

Static Budget	
Number of T-shirt lots (1 lot = 1 dozen)	500

Per Lot of T-shirts:	
Direct materials	12 meters at $1.50 per meter = $18.00
Direct manufacturing labor	2 hours at $8.00 per hour = $16.00

Actual Results	
Number of T-shirt lots sold	550

Total Direct Inputs:	
Direct materials	7,260 meters at $1.75 per meter = $12,705.00
Direct manufacturing labor	1,045 hours at $8.10 per hour = $8,464.50

GloriaDee has a policy of analyzing all input variances when they add up to more than 10% of the total cost of materials and labor in the flexible budget, and this is true in May 2011. The production manager discusses the sources of the variances: "A new type of material was purchased in May. This led to faster cutting and sewing, but the workers used more material than usual as they learned to work with it. For now, the standards are fine."

Required

1. Calculate the direct materials and direct manufacturing labor price and efficiency variances in May 2011. What is the total flexible-budget variance for both inputs (direct materials and direct manufacturing labor) combined? What percentage is this variance of the total cost of direct materials and direct manufacturing labor in the flexible budget?

2. Gloria Denham, the CEO, is concerned about the input variances. But, she likes the quality and feel of the new material and agrees to use it for one more year. In May 2012, GloriaDee again produces 550 lots of T-shirts. Relative to May 2011, 2% less direct material is used, direct material price is down 5%, and 2% less direct manufacturing labor is used. Labor price has remained the same as in May 2011. Calculate the direct materials and direct manufacturing labor price and efficiency variances in May 2012. What is the total flexible-budget variance for both inputs (direct materials and direct manufacturing labor) combined? What percentage is this variance of the total cost of direct materials and direct manufacturing labor in the flexible budget?

3. Comment on the May 2012 results. Would you continue the "experiment" of using the new material?

7-24 Price and efficiency variances, journal entries. The Monroe Corporation manufactures lamps. It has set up the following standards per finished unit for direct materials and direct manufacturing labor:

Direct materials: 10 lb. at $4.50 per lb.	$45.00
Direct manufacturing labor: 0.5 hour at $30 per hour	15.00

The number of finished units budgeted for January 2012 was 10,000; 9,850 units were actually produced. Actual results in January 2012 were as follows:

Direct materials: 98,055 lb. used	
Direct manufacturing labor: 4,900 hours	$154,350

Assume that there was no beginning inventory of either direct materials or finished units.

During the month, materials purchased amounted to 100,000 lb., at a total cost of $465,000. Input price variances are isolated upon purchase. Input-efficiency variances are isolated at the time of usage.

1. Compute the January 2012 price and efficiency variances of direct materials and direct manufacturing labor. **Required**

2. Prepare journal entries to record the variances in requirement 1.

3. Comment on the January 2012 price and efficiency variances of Monroe Corporation.

4. Why might Monroe calculate direct materials price variances and direct materials efficiency variances with reference to different points in time?

7-25 Continuous improvement (continuation of 7-24). The Monroe Corporation sets monthly standard costs using a continuous-improvement approach. In January 2012, the standard direct material cost is $45 per unit and the standard direct manufacturing labor cost is $15 per unit. Due to more efficient operations, the standard quantities for February 2012 are set at 0.980 of the standard quantities for January. In March 2012, the standard quantities are set at 0.990 of the standard quantities for February 2012. Assume the same information for March 2012 as in Exercise 7-24, except for these revised standard quantities.

1. Compute the March 2012 standard quantities for direct materials and direct manufacturing labor (to three decimal places). **Required**

2. Compute the March 2012 price and efficiency variances for direct materials and direct manufacturing labor (round to the nearest dollar).

7-26 Materials and manufacturing labor variances, standard costs. Dunn, Inc., is a privately held furniture manufacturer. For August 2012, Dunn had the following standards for one of its products, a wicker chair:

Standards per Chair	
Direct materials	2 square yards of input at $5 per square yard
Direct manufacturing labor	0.5 hour of input at $10 per hour

The following data were compiled regarding *actual performance*: actual output units (chairs) produced, 2,000; square yards of input purchased and used, 3,700; price per square yard, $5.10; direct manufacturing labor costs, $8,820; actual hours of input, 900; labor price per hour, $9.80.

1. Show computations of price and efficiency variances for direct materials and direct manufacturing labor. Give a plausible explanation of why each variance occurred.

2. Suppose 6,000 square yards of materials were purchased (at $5.10 per square yard), even though only 3,700 square yards were used. Suppose further that variances are identified at their most timely control point; accordingly, direct materials price variances are isolated and traced at the time of purchase to the purchasing department rather than to the production department. Compute the price and efficiency variances under this approach.

7-27 Journal entries and T-accounts (continuation of 7-26). Prepare journal entries and post them to T-accounts for all transactions in Exercise 7-26, including requirement 2. Summarize how these journal entries differ from the normal-costing entries described in Chapter 4, pages 112–114.

7-28 Flexible budget. (Refer to data in Exercise 7-26). Suppose the static budget was for 2,500 units of output. Actual output was 2,000 units. The variances are shown in the following report:

	Actual Results	Static Budget	Variance
Direct materials	$18,870	$25,000	$6,130F
Direct manufacturing labor	$ 8,820	$12,500	$3,680F

Required

What are the price, efficiency, and sales-volume variances for direct materials and direct manufacturing labor? Based on your results, explain why the static budget was not achieved.

7-29 Market-Share and Market-Size Variances. Rhaden Company produces sweat-resistant headbands for joggers. Information pertaining to Rhaden's operations for May 2011 follows:

	Actual	Budget
Units sold	230,550	220,000
Sales revenue	$3,412,140	$3,300,000
Variable cost ratio	68%	64%
Market size in units	4,350,000	4,400,000

Required

1. Compute the sales volume variance for May 2011.
2. Compute the market-share and market-size variances for May 2011.
3. Comment on possible reasons for the variances you computed in requirement 2.

MyAccountingLab

Problems

7-30 Flexible budget, direct materials, and direct manufacturing labor variances. Tuscany Statuary manufactures bust statues of famous historical figures. All statues are the same size. Each unit requires the same amount of resources. The following information is from the static budget for 2011:

Expected production and sales	6,000 units
Direct materials	72,000 pounds
Direct manufacturing labor	21,000 hours
Total fixed costs	$1,200,000

Standard quantities, standard prices, and standard unit costs follow for direct materials and direct manufacturing labor:

	Standard Quantity	Standard Price	Standard Unit Cost
Direct materials	12 pounds	$10 per pound	$120
Direct manufacturing labor	3.5 hours	$50 per hour	$175

During 2011, actual number of units produced and sold was 5,500. Actual cost of direct materials used was $668,800, based on 70,400 pounds purchased at $9.50 per pound. Direct manufacturing labor-hours actually used were 18,500, at the rate of $51.50 per hour. As a result, actual direct manufacturing labor costs were $952,750. Actual fixed costs were $1,180,000. There were no beginning or ending inventories.

Required

1. Calculate the sales-volume variance and flexible-budget variance for operating income.
2. Compute price and efficiency variances for direct materials and direct manufacturing labor.

7-31 Variance analysis, nonmanufacturing setting. Stevie McQueen has run Lightning Car Detailing for the past 10 years. His static budget and actual results for June 2011 are provided next. Stevie has one employee who has been with him for all 10 years that he has been in business. In addition, at any given time he also employs two other less experienced workers. It usually takes each employee 2 hours to detail a vehicle, regardless of his or her experience. Stevie pays his experienced employee $40 per vehicle and the other two employees $20 per vehicle. There were no wage increases in June.

Lightning Car Detailing
Actual and Budgeted Income Statements
For the Month Ended June 30, 2011

	Budget	Actual
Cars detailed	200	225
Revenue	$30,000	$39,375
Variable costs		
Costs of supplies	1,500	2,250
Labor	5,600	6,000
Total variable costs	7,100	8,250
Contribution margin	22,900	31,125
Fixed costs	9,500	9,500
Operating income	$13,400	$21,625

1. How many cars, on average, did Stevie budget for each employee? How many cars did each employee actually detail? **Required**
2. Prepare a flexible budget for June 2011.
3. Compute the sales price variance and the labor efficiency variance for each labor type.
4. What information, in addition to that provided in the income statements, would you want Stevie to gather, if you wanted to improve operational efficiency?

7-32 Comprehensive variance analysis, responsibility issues. (CMA, adapted) Styles, Inc., manufactures a full line of well-known sunglasses frames and lenses. Styles uses a standard costing system to set attainable standards for direct materials, labor, and overhead costs. Styles reviews and revises standards annually, as necessary. Department managers, whose evaluations and bonuses are affected by their department's performance, are held responsible to explain variances in their department performance reports.

Recently, the manufacturing variances in the Image prestige line of sunglasses have caused some concern. For no apparent reason, unfavorable materials and labor variances have occurred. At the monthly staff meeting, Jack Barton, manager of the Image line, will be expected to explain his variances and suggest ways of improving performance. Barton will be asked to explain the following performance report for 2011:

	Actual Results	Static-Budget Amounts
Units sold	7,275	7,500
Revenues	$596,550	$600,000
Variable manufacturing costs	351,965	324,000
Fixed manufacturing costs	108,398	112,500
Gross margin	136,187	163,500

Barton collected the following information:

Three items comprised the standard variable manufacturing costs in 2011:

■ Direct materials: Frames. Static budget cost of $49,500. The standard input for 2011 is 3.00 ounces per unit.

■ Direct materials: Lenses. Static budget costs of $139,500. The standard input for 2011 is 6.00 ounces per unit.

■ Direct manufacturing labor: Static budget costs of $135,000. The standard input for 2011 is 1.20 hours per unit.

Assume there are no variable manufacturing overhead costs.

The actual variable manufacturing costs in 2011 were as follows:

■ Direct materials: Frames. Actual costs of $55,872. Actual ounces used were 3.20 ounces per unit.

■ Direct materials: Lenses. Actual costs of $150,738. Actual ounces used were 7.00 ounces per unit.

■ Direct manufacturing labor: Actual costs of $145,355. The actual labor rate was $14.80 per hour.

1. Prepare a report that includes the following: **Required**
   a. Selling-price variance
   b. Sales-volume variance and flexible-budget variance for operating income in the format of the analysis in Exhibit 7-2

c. Price and efficiency variances for the following:
- ■ Direct materials: frames
- ■ Direct materials: lenses
- ■ Direct manufacturing labor

2. Give three possible explanations for each of the three price and efficiency variances at Styles in requirement 1c.

7-33 Possible causes for price and efficiency variances. You are a student preparing for a job interview with a *Fortune* 100 consumer products manufacturer. You are applying for a job in the finance department. This company is known for its rigorous case-based interview process. One of the students who successfully obtained a job with them upon graduation last year advised you to "know your variances cold!" When you inquired further, she told you that she had been asked to pretend that she was investigating wage and materials variances. Per her advice, you have been studying the causes and consequences of variances. You are excited when you walk in and find that the first case deals with variance analysis. You are given the following data for May for a detergent bottling plant located in Mexico:

Actual	
Bottles filled	340,000
Direct materials used in production	6,150,000 oz.
Actual direct material cost	2,275,500 pesos
Actual direct manufacturing labor-hours	26,000 hours
Actual direct labor cost	784,420 pesos

Standards	
Purchase price of direct materials	0.36 pesos/oz
Bottle size	15 oz.
Wage rate	29.25 pesos/hour
Bottles per minute	0.50

Required

Please respond to the following questions as if you were in an interview situation:

1. Calculate the materials efficiency and price variance, and the wage and labor efficiency variances for the month of May.

2. You are given the following context: "Union organizers are targeting our detergent bottling plant in Puebla, Mexico, for a union." Can you provide a better explanation for the variances that you have calculated on the basis of this information?

7-34 Material cost variances, use of variances for performance evaluation. Katharine Stanley is the owner of Better Bikes, a company that produces high quality cross-country bicycles. Better Bikes participates in a supply chain that consists of suppliers, manufacturers, distributors, and elite bicycle shops. For several years Better Bikes has purchased titanium from suppliers in the supply chain. Better Bikes uses titanium for the bicycle frames because it is stronger and lighter than other metals and therefore increases the quality of the bicycle. Earlier this year, Better Bikes hired Michael Scott, a recent graduate from State University, as purchasing manager. Michael believed that he could reduce costs if he purchased titanium from an online marketplace at a lower price.

Better Bikes established the following standards based upon the company's experience with previous suppliers. The standards are as follows:

Cost of titanium	$22 per pound
Titanium used per bicycle	8 lb.

Actual results for the first month using the online supplier of titanium are as follows:

Bicycles produced	800
Titanium purchased	8,400 lb. for $159,600
Titanium used in production	7,900 lb.

Required

1. Compute the direct materials price and efficiency variances.

2. What factors can explain the variances identified in requirement 1? Could any other variances be affected?

3. Was switching suppliers a good idea for Better Bikes? Explain why or why not.

4. Should Michael Scott's performance evaluation be based solely on price variances? Should the production manager's evaluation be based solely on efficiency variances? Why it is important for Katharine Stanley to understand the causes of a variance before she evaluates performance?

5. Other than performance evaluation, what reasons are there for calculating variances?

6. What future problems could result from Better Bikes' decision to buy a lower quality of titanium from the online marketplace?

7-35 **Direct manufacturing labor and direct materials variances, missing data.** (CMA, heavily adapted) Morro Bay Surfboards manufactures fiberglass surfboards. The standard cost of direct materials and direct manufacturing labor is $225 per board. This includes 30 pounds of direct materials, at the budgeted price of $3 per pound, and 9 hours of direct manufacturing labor, at the budgeted rate of $15 per hour. Following are additional data for the month of July:

Units completed	5,500 units
Direct material purchases	190,000 pounds
Cost of direct material purchases	$579,500
Actual direct manufacturing labor-hours	49,000 hours
Actual direct labor cost	$739,900
Direct materials efficiency variance	$ 1,500 F

There were no beginning inventories.

Required

1. Compute direct manufacturing labor variances for July.
2. Compute the actual pounds of direct materials used in production in July.
3. Calculate the actual price per pound of direct materials purchased.
4. Calculate the direct materials price variance.

7-36 **Direct materials and manufacturing labor variances, solving unknowns.** (CPA, adapted) On May 1, 2012, Bovar Company began the manufacture of a new paging machine known as Dandy. The company installed a standard costing system to account for manufacturing costs. The standard costs for a unit of Dandy follow:

Direct materials (3 lb. at $5 per lb.)	$15.00
Direct manufacturing labor (1/2 hour at $20 per hour)	10.00
Manufacturing overhead (75% of direct manufacturing labor costs)	7.50
	$32.50

The following data were obtained from Bovar's records for the month of May:

	Debit	Credit
Revenues		$125,000
Accounts payable control (for May's purchases of direct materials)		68,250
Direct materials price variance	33,250	
Direct materials efficiency variance	2,500	
Direct manufacturing labor price variance	1,900	
Direct manufacturing labor efficiency variance		2,000

Actual production in May was 4,000 units of Dandy, and actual sales in May were 2,500 units.

The amount shown for direct materials price variance applies to materials purchased during May. There was no beginning inventory of materials on May 1, 2012.

Compute each of the following items for Bovar for the month of May. Show your computations.

Required

1. Standard direct manufacturing labor-hours allowed for actual output produced
2. Actual direct manufacturing labor-hours worked
3. Actual direct manufacturing labor wage rate
4. Standard quantity of direct materials allowed (in pounds)
5. Actual quantity of direct materials used (in pounds)
6. Actual quantity of direct materials purchased (in pounds)
7. Actual direct materials price per pound

7-37 **Direct materials and manufacturing labor variances, journal entries.** Shayna's Smart Shawls, Inc., is a small business that Shayna developed while in college. She began hand-knitting shawls for her dorm friends to wear while studying. As demand grew, she hired some workers and began to manage the operation. Shayna's shawls require wool and labor. She experiments with the type of wool that she uses, and she has great variety in the shawls she produces. Shayna has bimodal turnover in her labor. She has some employees who have been with her for a very long time and others who are new and inexperienced.

Shayna uses standard costing for her shawls. She expects that a typical shawl should take 4 hours to produce, and the standard wage rate is $10.00 per hour. An average shawl uses 12 skeins of wool. Shayna shops around for good deals, and expects to pay $3.50 per skein.

Shayna uses a just-in-time inventory system, as she has clients tell her what type and color of wool they would like her to use.

For the month of April, Shayna's workers produced 235 shawls using 925 hours and 3,040 skeins of wool. Shayna bought wool for $10,336 (and used the entire quantity), and incurred labor costs of $9,620.

Required 1. Calculate the price and efficiency variances for the wool, and the price and efficiency variances for direct manufacturing labor.
2. Record the journal entries for the variances incurred.
3. Discuss logical explanations for the combination of variances that Shayna experienced.

7-38 Use of materials and manufacturing labor variances for benchmarking. You are a new junior accountant at Clearview Corporation, maker of lenses for eyeglasses. Your company sells generic-quality lenses for a moderate price. Your boss, the Controller, has given you the latest month's report for the lens trade association. This report includes information related to operations for your firm and three of your competitors within the trade association. The report also includes information related to the industry benchmark for each line item in the report. You do not know which firm is which, except that you know you are Firm A.

Unit Variable Costs
Member Firms
For the Month Ended September 30, 2012

	Firm A	Firm B	Firm C	Firm D	Industry Benchmark
Materials input	2.00	1.95	2.15	2.50	2.0 oz. of glass
Materials price	$ 4.90	$ 5.60	$ 5.00	$ 4.50	$ 5.00 per oz.
Labor-hours used	1.10	1.15	0.95	1.00	1.00 hours
Wage rate	$15.00	$15.50	$16.50	$15.90	$13.00 per DLH
Variable overhead rate	$ 9.00	$13.50	$ 7.50	$11.25	$12.00 per DLH

Required 1. Calculate the total variable cost per unit for each firm in the trade association. Compute the percent of total for the material, labor, and variable overhead components.
2. Using the trade association's industry benchmark, calculate direct materials and direct manufacturing labor price and efficiency variances for the four firms. Calculate the percent over standard for each firm and each variance.
3. Write a brief memo to your boss outlining the advantages and disadvantages of belonging to this trade association for benchmarking purposes. Include a few ideas to improve productivity that you want your boss to take to the department heads' meeting.

7-39 Comprehensive variance analysis review. Sonnet, Inc., has the following budgeted standards for the month of March 2011:

Average selling price per diskette	$	6.00
Total direct material cost per diskette	$	1.50
Direct manufacturing labor		
Direct manufacturing labor cost per hour	$	12.00
Average labor productivity rate (diskettes per hour)		300
Direct marketing cost per unit	$	0.30
Fixed overhead	$800,000	

Sales of 1,500,000 units are budgeted for March. The expected total market for this product was 7,500,000 diskettes. Actual March results are as follows:

- Unit sales and production totaled 95% of plan.
- Actual average selling price increased to $6.10.
- Productivity dropped to 250 diskettes per hour.
- Actual direct manufacturing labor cost is $12.20 per hour.
- Actual total direct material cost per unit increased to $1.60.
- Actual direct marketing costs were $0.25 per unit.
- Fixed overhead costs were $10,000 above plan.
- Actual market size was 8,906,250 diskettes.

Required Calculate the following:

1. Static-budget and actual operating income
2. Static-budget variance for operating income
3. Flexible-budget operating income
4. Flexible-budget variance for operating income
5. Sales-volume variance for operating income
6. Market share and market size variances
7. Price and efficiency variances for direct manufacturing labor
8. Flexible-budget variance for direct manufacturing labor

7-40 Comprehensive variance analysis. (CMA) Iceland, Inc., is a fast-growing ice-cream maker. The company's new ice-cream flavor, Cherry Star, sells for $9 per pound. The standard monthly production level is 300,000 pounds, and the standard inputs and costs are as follows:

	Home	Insert	Page Layout	Formulas	Data	Review	
		A		B	C	D	E
1				**Quantity per**		**Standard**	
2		**Cost Item**		**Pound of Ice Cream**		**Unit Costs**	
3	Direct materials						
4		Cream		12	oz.	$ 0.03	/oz.
5		Vanilla extract		4	oz.	0.12	/oz.
6		Cherry		1	oz.	0.45	/oz.
7							
8	Direct manufacturing labor[a]						
9		Preparing		1.2	min.	14.40	/hr.
10		Stirring		1.8	min.	18.00	/hr.
11							
12	Variable overhead[b]			3	min.	32.40	/hr.
13							
14	[a] Direct manufacturing labor rates include employee benefits.						
15	[b] Allocated on the basis of direct manufacturing labor-hours.						

Molly Cates, the CFO, is disappointed with the results for May 2011, prepared based on these standard costs.

	Home	Insert	Page Layout	Formulas	Data	Review	View		
	A		B	C	D	E		F	G
17			**Performance Report, May 2011**						
18			**Actual**		**Budget**			**Variance**	
19	Units (pounds)		275,000		300,000			25,000	U
20	Revenues		$2,502,500		$2,700,000			$197,500	U
21	Direct materials		432,500		387,000			45,500	U
22	Direct manufacturing labor		174,000		248,400			74,400	F

Cates notes that despite a sizable increase in the pounds of ice cream sold in May, Cherry Star's contribution to the company's overall profitability has been lower than expected. Cates gathers the following information to help analyze the situation:

	Home	Insert	Page Layout	Formulas	Data	Review	
		A		B	C	D	
25		**Usage Report, May 2011**					
26		**Cost Item**		**Quantity**		**Actual Cost**	
27	Direct materials						
28		Cream		3,120,000	oz.	$124,800	
29		Vanilla extract		1,230,000	oz.	184,500	
30		Cherry		325,000	oz.	133,250	
31							
32	Direct manufacturing labor						
33		Preparing		310,000	min.	77,500	
34		Stirring		515,000	min.	154,500	

Required Compute the following variances. Comment on the variances, with particular attention to the variances that may be related to each other and the controllability of each variance:

1. Selling-price variance
2. Direct materials price variance
3. Direct materials efficiency variance
4. Direct manufacturing labor efficiency variance

7-41 Price and efficiency variances, problems in standard-setting, and benchmarking. Stuckey, Inc., manufactures industrial 55 gallon drums for storing chemicals used in the mining industry. The body of the drums is made from aluminum and the lid is made of chemical resistant plastic. Andy Jorgenson, the controller, is becoming increasingly disenchanted with Stuckey's standard costing system. The budgeted information for direct materials and direct manufacturing labor for June 2011 were as follows:

	Budget
Drums and lids produced	5,200
Direct materials price per sq. ft.	
Aluminum	$ 3.00
Plastic	$ 1.50
Direct materials per unit	
Aluminum (sq. ft.)	20
Plastic (sq. ft.)	7
Direct labor-hours per unit	2.3
Direct labor cost per hour	$12.00

The actual number of drums and lids produced was 4,920. The actual cost of aluminum and plastic was $283,023 (95,940 sq. ft.) and $50,184 (33,456 sq. ft.), respectively. The actual direct labor cost incurred was $118,572 (9,840 hours). There were no beginning or ending inventories of materials.

Standard costs are based on a study of the operations conducted by an independent consultant six months earlier. Jorgenson observes that since that study he has rarely seen an unfavorable variance of any magnitude. He notes that even at their current output levels, the workers seem to have a lot of time for sitting around and gossiping. Jorgenson is concerned that the production manager, Charlie Fenton, is aware of this but does not want to tighten up the standards because the lax standards make his performance look good.

Required

1. Compute the price and efficiency variances of Stuckey, Inc., for each direct material and direct manufacturing labor in June 2011.
2. Describe the types of actions the employees at Stuckey, Inc., may have taken to reduce the accuracy of the standards set by the independent consultant. Why would employees take those actions? Is this behavior ethical?
3. If Jorgenson does nothing about the standard costs, will his behavior violate any of the Standards of Ethical Conduct for Management Accountants described in Exhibit 1-7 on page 16?
4. What actions should Jorgenson take?
5. Jorgenson can obtain benchmarking information about the estimated costs of Stuckey's major competitors from Benchmarking Clearing House (BCH). Discuss the pros and cons of using the BCH information to compute the variances in requirement 1.

Collaborative Learning Problem

7-42 Comprehensive variance analysis. Sol Electronics, a fast-growing electronic device producer, uses a standard costing system, with standards set at the beginning of each year.

In the second quarter of 2011, Sol faced two challenges: It had to negotiate and sign a new short-term labor agreement with its workers' union, and it also had to pay a higher rate to its suppliers for direct materials. The new labor contract raised the cost of direct manufacturing labor relative to the company's 2011 standards. Similarly, the new rate for direct materials exceeded the company's 2011 standards. However, the materials were of better quality than expected, so Sol's management was confident that there would be less waste and less rework in the manufacturing process. Management also speculated that the per-unit direct manufacturing labor cost might decline as a result of the materials' improved quality.

At the end of the second quarter, Sol's CFO, Terence Shaw, reviewed the following results:

	Home	Insert	Page Layout	Formulas	Data	Review	View

	A	B	C	D	E	F	G	H	I	J	K	L	M	N	O	P	Q	R	S
1							Variable Costs Per Unit												
2	Per Unit Variable Costs			Standard				First Quarter 2011 Actual Results						Second Quarter 2011 Actual Results					
3	Direct materials	2.2	lb.	at	$5.70	per lb.	$12.54	2.3	lb.	at	$ 5.80	per lb.	$13.34	2.0	lb.	at	$ 6.00	per lb.	$12.00
4	Direct manufacturing labor	0.5	hrs.	at	$ 12	per hr.	$ 6.00	0.52	hrs.	at	$ 12	per hr.	$ 6.24	0.45	hrs.	at	$ 14	per hr.	$ 6.30
5	Other variable costs						$10.00						$10.00						$ 9.85
6							$28.54						$29.58						$28.15

	Home	Insert	Page Layout	Formulas	Data	Review	View

	U	V	W	X
1				
2		Static Budget for Each Quarter Based on 2011	First Quarter 2011 Results	Second Quarter 2011 Results
3	Units	4,000	4,400	4,800
4	Selling price	$ 70	$ 72	$ 71.50
5	Sales	$280,000	$316,800	$343,200
6	Variable costs			
7	Direct materials	50,160	58,696	57,600
8	Direct manufacturing labor	24,000	27,456	30,240
9	Other variable costs	40,000	44,000	47,280
10	Total variable costs	114,160	130,152	135,120
11	Contribution margin	165,840	186,648	208,080
12	Fixed costs	68,000	66,000	68,400
13	Operating income	$ 97,840	$120,648	$139,680

Shaw was relieved to see that the anticipated savings in material waste and rework seemed to have materialized. But, he was concerned that the union would press hard for higher wages given that actual unit costs came in below standard unit costs and operating income continued to climb.

Required

1. Prepare a detailed variance analysis of the second quarter results relative to the static budget. Show how much of the improvement in operating income arose due to changes in sales volume and how much arose for other reasons. Calculate variances that isolate the effects of price and usage changes in direct materials and direct manufacturing labor.
2. Use the results of requirement 1 to prepare a rebuttal to the union's anticipated demands in light of the second quarter results.
3. Terence Shaw thinks that the company can negotiate better if it changes the standards. Without performing any calculations, discuss the pros and cons of immediately changing the standards.

8

Flexible Budgets, Overhead Cost Variances, and Management Control

8

Flexible Budgets, Overhead Cost Variances, and Management Control

What do this week's weather forecast and organization performance have in common?

Most of the time, reality doesn't match expectations. Cloudy skies that cancel a little league game may suddenly let the sun shine through just as the vans are packed. Jubilant business owners may change their tune when they tally their monthly bills and discover that skyrocketing operation costs have significantly reduced their profits. Differences, or variances, are all around us.

For organizations, variances are of great value because they highlight the areas where performance most lags expectations. By using this information to make corrective adjustments, companies can achieve significant savings, as the following article shows.

Overhead Cost Variances Force Macy's to Shop for Changes in Strategy[1]

Managers frequently review the differences, or variances, in overhead costs and make changes in the operations of a business. Sometimes staffing levels are increased or decreased, while at other times managers identify ways to use fewer resources like, say, office supplies and travel for business meetings that don't add value to the products and services that customers buy.

At the department-store chain Macy's, however, managers analyzed overhead cost variances and changed the way the company purchased the products it sells. In 2005, when Federated Department Stores and the May Department Store Company merged, Macy's operated seven buying offices across the United States. Each of these offices was responsible for purchasing some of the clothes, cosmetics, jewelry, and many other items Macy's sells. But overlapping responsibilities, seasonal buying patterns (clothes are generally purchased in the spring and fall) and regional differences in costs and salaries (for example, it costs more for employees and rent in San Francisco than Cincinnati) led to frequent and significant variances in overhead costs.

These overhead costs weighed on the company as the retailer struggled with disappointing sales after the merger. As a result, Macy's leaders felt pressured to reduce its costs that were not directly related to selling merchandise in stores and online.

---

[1] *Sources*: Boyle, Matthew. 2009. A leaner Macy's tries to cater to local tastes. *BusinessWeek.com*, September 3; Kapner, Suzanne. 2009. Macy's looking to cut costs. *Fortune*, January 14. http://money.cnn.com/2009/01/14/news/companies/macys_consolidation.fortune/; *Macy's 2009 Corporate Fact Book*. 2009. Cincinnati: Macy's, Inc., 7.

In early 2009, the company announced plans to consolidate its network of seven buying offices into one location in New York. With all centralized buying and merchandise planning in one location, Macy's buying structure and overhead costs were in line with how many other large chains operate, including JCPenney and Kohl's. All told, the move to centralized buying would generate $100 million in annualized cost savings for the company.

While centralized buying was applauded by industry experts and shareholders, Macy's CEO Terry Lundgren was concerned about keeping a "localized flavor" in his stores. To ensure that nationwide buying accommodated local tastes, a new team of merchants was formed in each Macy's market to gauge local buying habits. That way, the company could reduce its overhead costs while ensuring that Macy's stores near water parks had extra swimsuits.

Companies such as DuPont, International Paper, and LLG Steel, which invest heavily in capital equipment, or Amazon.com and Yahoo!, which invest large amounts in software, have high overhead costs. As the Macy's example suggests, understanding the behavior of overhead costs, planning for them, performing variance analysis, and acting appropriately on the results are critical for a company.

In this chapter, we will examine how flexible budgets and variance analysis can help managers plan and control overhead costs. Chapter 7 emphasized the direct-cost categories of direct materials and direct manufacturing labor. In this chapter, we focus on the indirect-cost categories of variable manufacturing overhead and fixed manufacturing overhead. Finally, we explain why managers should be careful when interpreting variances based on overhead-cost concepts developed primarily for financial reporting purposes.

Planning of Variable and Fixed Overhead Costs

We'll use the Webb Company example again to illustrate the planning and control of variable and fixed overhead costs. Recall that Webb manufactures jackets that are sold to distributors who in turn sell to independent clothing stores and retail chains. For simplicity, we assume Webb's only costs are *manufacturing* costs. For ease of exposition, we use the term overhead costs instead of manufacturing overhead costs. Variable (manufacturing) overhead costs for Webb include energy, machine maintenance, engineering support, and indirect materials. Fixed (manufacturing) overhead costs include plant leasing costs, depreciation on plant equipment, and the salaries of the plant managers.

Planning Variable Overhead Costs

To effectively plan variable overhead costs for a product or service, managers must focus attention on the activities that create a superior product or service for their customers and eliminate activities that do not add value. Webb's managers examine how each of their variable overhead costs relates to delivering a superior product or service to customers. For example, customers expect Webb's jackets to last, so managers at Webb consider sewing to be an essential activity. Therefore, maintenance activities for sewing machines—included in Webb's variable overhead costs—are also essential activities for which management must plan. In addition, such maintenance should be done in a cost-effective way, such as by scheduling periodic equipment maintenance rather than waiting for sewing machines to break down. For many companies today, it is critical to plan for ways to become more efficient in the use of energy, a rapidly growing component of variable overhead costs. Webb installs smart meters in order to monitor energy use in real time and steer production operations away from peak consumption periods.

Planning Fixed Overhead Costs

Effective planning of fixed overhead costs is similar to effective planning for variable overhead costs—planning to undertake only essential activities and then planning to be efficient in that undertaking. But in planning fixed overhead costs, there is one more strategic issue that managers must take into consideration: choosing the appropriate level of capacity or investment that will benefit the company in the long run. Consider Webb's leasing of sewing machines, each having a fixed cost per year. Leasing more machines than necessary—if Webb overestimates demand—will result in additional fixed leasing costs on machines not fully used during the year. Leasing insufficient machine capacity—say, because Webb underestimates demand or because of limited space in the plant—will result in an inability to meet demand, lost sales of jackets, and unhappy customers. Consider the example of AT&T, which did not foresee the iPhone's appeal or the proliferation of "apps" and did not upgrade its network sufficiently to handle the resulting data traffic. AT&T has since had to impose limits on how customers can use the iPhone (such as by curtailing tethering and the streaming of Webcasts). In December 2009, AT&T had the lowest customer satisfaction ratings among all major carriers.

The planning of fixed overhead costs differs from the planning of variable overhead costs in one important respect: timing. At the start of a budget period, management will have made most of the decisions that determine the level of fixed overhead costs to be incurred. But, it's the day-to-day, ongoing operating decisions that mainly determine the level of variable overhead costs incurred in that period. In health care settings, for example, variable overhead, which includes disposable supplies, unit doses of medication, suture packets, and medical waste disposal costs, is a function of the number and nature of procedures carried out, as well as the practice patterns of the physicians. However, the majority of the cost of providing hospital service is related to buildings, equipment, and salaried labor, which are fixed overhead items, unrelated to the volume of activity.[2]

▶ **Decision Point**

How do managers plan variable overhead costs and fixed overhead costs?

Standard Costing at Webb Company

Learning Objective 2

Develop budgeted variable overhead cost rates

. . . budgeted variable costs divided by quantity of cost-allocation base

and budgeted fixed overhead cost rates

. . . budgeted fixed costs divided by quantity of cost-allocation base

Webb uses standard costing. The development of standards for Webb's direct manufacturing costs was described in Chapter 7. This chapter discusses the development of standards for Webb's manufacturing overhead costs. **Standard costing** is a costing system that (a) traces direct costs to output produced by multiplying the standard prices or rates by the standard quantities of inputs allowed for actual outputs produced and (b) allocates overhead costs on the basis of the standard overhead-cost rates times the standard quantities of the allocation bases allowed for the actual outputs produced.

---

[2] Related to this, free-standing surgery centers have thrived because they have an economic advantage of lower fixed overhead when compared to a traditional hospital. For an enlightening summary of costing issues in health care, see A. Macario, "What Does One Minute of Operating Room Time Cost?" Stanford University School of Medicine (2009).

The standard cost of Webb's jackets can be computed at the start of the budget period. This feature of standard costing simplifies record keeping because no record is needed of the actual overhead costs or of the actual quantities of the cost-allocation bases used for making the jackets. What is needed are the standard overhead cost rates for variable and fixed overhead. Webb's management accountants calculate these cost rates based on the planned amounts of variable and fixed overhead and the standard quantities of the allocation bases. We describe these computations next. Note that once standards have been set, the costs of using standard costing are low relative to the costs of using actual costing or normal costing.

Developing Budgeted Variable Overhead Rates

Budgeted variable overhead cost-allocation rates can be developed in four steps. We use the Webb example to illustrate these steps. Throughout the chapter, we use the broader term "budgeted rate" rather than "standard rate" to be consistent with the term used in describing normal costing in earlier chapters. In standard costing, the budgeted rates are standard rates.

Step 1: Choose the Period to Be Used for the Budget. Webb uses a 12-month budget period. Chapter 4 (p. 103) provides two reasons for using annual overhead rates rather than, say, monthly rates. The first relates to the numerator (such as reducing the influence of seasonality on the cost structure) and the second to the denominator (such as reducing the effect of varying output and number of days in a month). In addition, setting overhead rates once a year saves management the time it would need 12 times during the year if budget rates had to be set monthly.

Step 2: Select the Cost-Allocation Bases to Use in Allocating Variable Overhead Costs to Output Produced. Webb's operating managers select machine-hours as the cost-allocation base because they believe that machine-hours is the only cost driver of variable overhead. Based on an engineering study, Webb estimates it will take 0.40 of a machine-hour per actual output unit. For its budgeted output of 144,000 jackets in 2011, Webb budgets 57,600 (0.40 × 144,000) machine-hours.

Step 3: Identify the Variable Overhead Costs Associated with Each Cost-Allocation Base. Webb groups all of its variable overhead costs, including costs of energy, machine maintenance, engineering support, indirect materials, and indirect manufacturing labor in a single cost pool. Webb's total budgeted variable overhead costs for 2011 are $1,728,000.

Step 4: Compute the Rate per Unit of Each Cost-Allocation Base Used to Allocate Variable Overhead Costs to Output Produced. Dividing the amount in Step 3 ($1,728,000) by the amount in Step 2 (57,600 machine-hours), Webb estimates a rate of $30 per standard machine-hour for allocating its variable overhead costs.

In standard costing, the variable overhead rate per unit of the cost-allocation base ($30 per machine-hour for Webb) is generally expressed as a standard rate per output unit. Webb calculates the budgeted variable overhead cost rate per output unit as follows:

$$
\begin{array}{ccc}
\text{Budgeted variable} & \text{Budgeted input} & \text{Budgeted variable} \\
\text{overhead cost rate} = & \text{allowed per} \times & \text{overhead cost rate} \\
\text{per output unit} & \text{output unit} & \text{per input unit}
\end{array}
$$

$$= 0.40 \text{ hour per jacket} \times \$30 \text{ per hour}$$

$$= \$12 \text{ per jacket}$$

Webb uses $12 per jacket as the budgeted variable overhead cost rate in both its static budget for 2011 and in the monthly performance reports it prepares during 2011.

The $12 per jacket represents the amount by which Webb's variable overhead costs are expected to change with respect to output units for planning and control purposes. Accordingly, as the number of jackets manufactured increases, variable overhead costs are allocated to output units (for the inventory costing purpose) at the same rate of $12 per jacket. Of course, this presents an overall picture of total variable overhead costs, which in reality consist of many items, including energy, repairs, indirect labor, and so on. Managers help control variable overhead costs by budgeting each line item and then investigating possible causes for any significant variances.

Developing Budgeted Fixed Overhead Rates

Fixed overhead costs are, by definition, a lump sum of costs that remains unchanged in total for a given period, despite wide changes in the level of total activity or volume related to those overhead costs. Fixed costs are included in flexible budgets, but they remain the same total amount within the relevant range of activity regardless of the output level chosen to "flex" the variable costs and revenues. Recall from Exhibit 7-2, page 231 and the steps in developing a flexible budget, that the fixed-cost amount is the same $276,000 in the static budget and in the flexible budget. Do not assume, however, that fixed overhead costs can never be changed. Managers can reduce fixed overhead costs by selling equipment or by laying off employees. But they are fixed in the sense that, unlike variable costs such as direct material costs, fixed costs do not *automatically* increase or decrease with the level of activity within the relevant range.

The process of developing the budgeted fixed overhead rate is the same as that detailed earlier for calculating the budgeted variable overhead rate. The four steps are as follows:

Step 1: **Choose the Period to Use for the Budget.** As with variable overhead costs, the budget period for fixed overhead costs is typically 12 months to help smooth out seasonal effects.

Step 2: **Select the Cost-Allocation Bases to Use in Allocating Fixed Overhead Costs to Output Produced.** Webb uses machine-hours as the only cost-allocation base for fixed overhead costs. Why? Because Webb's managers believe that, in the long run, fixed overhead costs will increase or decrease to the levels needed to support the amount of machine-hours. Therefore, in the long run, the amount of machine-hours used is the only cost driver of fixed overhead costs. The number of machine-hours is the denominator in the budgeted fixed overhead rate computation and is called the **denominator level** or, in manufacturing settings, the **production-denominator level.** For simplicity, we assume Webb expects to operate at capacity in fiscal year 2011—with a budgeted usage of 57,600 machine-hours for a budgeted output of 144,000 jackets.[3]

Step 3: **Identify the Fixed Overhead Costs Associated with Each Cost-Allocation Base.** Because Webb identifies only a single cost-allocation base—machine-hours—to allocate fixed overhead costs, it groups all such costs into a single cost pool. Costs in this pool include depreciation on plant and equipment, plant and equipment leasing costs, and the plant manager's salary. Webb's fixed overhead budget for 2011 is $3,312,000.

Step 4: **Compute the Rate per Unit of Each Cost-Allocation Base Used to Allocate Fixed Overhead Costs to Output Produced.** Dividing the $3,312,000 from Step 3 by the 57,600 machine-hours from Step 2, Webb estimates a fixed overhead cost rate of $57.50 per machine-hour:

$$\begin{array}{c}\text{Budgeted fixed}\\\text{overhead cost per}\\\text{unit of cost-allocation}\\\text{base}\end{array} = \dfrac{\begin{array}{c}\text{Budgeted total costs}\\\text{in fixed overhead cost pool}\end{array}}{\begin{array}{c}\text{Budgeted total quantity of}\\\text{cost-allocation base}\end{array}} = \dfrac{\$3,312,000}{57,600} = \$57.50 \text{ per machine-hour}$$

In standard costing, the $57.50 fixed overhead cost per machine-hour is usually expressed as a standard cost per output unit. Recall that Webb's engineering study estimates that it will take 0.40 machine-hour per output unit. Webb can now calculate the budgeted fixed overhead cost per output unit as follows:

$$\begin{array}{c}\text{Budgeted fixed}\\\text{overhead cost per}\\\text{output unit}\end{array} = \begin{array}{c}\text{Budgeted quantity of}\\\text{cost-allocation}\\\text{base allowed per}\\\text{output unit}\end{array} \times \begin{array}{c}\text{Budgeted fixed}\\\text{overhead cost}\\\text{per unit of}\\\text{cost-allocation base}\end{array}$$

$$= 0.40 \text{ of a machine-hour per jacket} \times \$57.50 \text{ per machine-hour}$$

$$= \$23.00 \text{ per jacket}$$

---

[3] Because Webb plans its capacity over multiple periods, anticipated demand in 2011 could be such that budgeted output for 2011 is less than capacity. Companies vary in the denominator levels they choose; some may choose budgeted output and others may choose capacity. In either case, the basic approach and analysis presented in this chapter is unchanged. Chapter 9 discusses choosing a denominator level and its implications in more detail.

When preparing monthly budgets for 2011, Webb divides the $3,312,000 annual total fixed costs into 12 equal monthly amounts of $276,000.

Variable Overhead Cost Variances

We now illustrate how the budgeted variable overhead rate is used in computing Webb's variable overhead cost variances. The following data are for April 2011, when Webb produced and sold 10,000 jackets:

	Actual Result	Flexible-Budget Amount
1. Output units (jackets)	10,000	10,000
2. Machine-hours per output unit	0.45	0.40
3. Machine-hours (1 × 2)	4,500	4,000
4. Variable overhead costs	$130,500	$120,000
5. Variable overhead costs per machine-hour (4 ÷ 3)	$ 29.00	$ 30.00
6. Variable overhead costs per output unit (4 ÷ 1)	$ 13.05	$ 12.00

As we saw in Chapter 7, the flexible budget enables Webb to highlight the differences between actual costs and actual quantities versus budgeted costs and budgeted quantities for the actual output level of 10,000 jackets.

Flexible-Budget Analysis

The **variable overhead flexible-budget variance** measures the difference between actual variable overhead costs incurred and flexible-budget variable overhead amounts.

$$\frac{\text{Variable overhead}}{\text{flexible-budget variance}} = \frac{\text{Actual costs}}{\text{incurred}} - \frac{\text{Flexible-budget}}{\text{amount}}$$

$$= \$130,500 - \$120,000$$

$$= \$10,500 \text{ U}$$

This $10,500 unfavorable flexible-budget variance means Webb's actual variable overhead exceeded the flexible-budget amount by $10,500 for the 10,000 jackets actually produced and sold. Webb's managers would want to know why actual costs exceeded the flexible-budget amount. Did Webb use more machine-hours than planned to produce the 10,000 jackets? If so, was it because workers were less skilled than expected in using machines? Or did Webb spend more on variable overhead costs, such as maintenance?

Just as we illustrated in Chapter 7 with the flexible-budget variance for direct-cost items, Webb's managers can get further insight into the reason for the $10,500 unfavorable variance by subdividing it into the efficiency variance and spending variance.

Variable Overhead Efficiency Variance

The **variable overhead efficiency variance** is the difference between actual quantity of the cost-allocation base used and budgeted quantity of the cost-allocation base that should have been used to produce actual output, multiplied by budgeted variable overhead cost per unit of the cost-allocation base.

$$\text{Variable overhead efficiency variance} = \left(\begin{array}{c} \text{Actual quantity of} \\ \text{variable overhead} \\ \text{cost-allocation base} \\ \text{used for actual} \\ \text{output} \end{array} - \begin{array}{c} \text{Budgeted quantity of} \\ \text{variable overhead} \\ \text{cost-allocation base} \\ \text{allowed for} \\ \text{actual output} \end{array} \right) \times \begin{array}{c} \text{Budgeted variable} \\ \text{overhead cost per unit} \\ \text{of cost-allocation base} \end{array}$$

$$= (4,500 \text{ hours} - 0.40 \text{ hr./unit} \times 10,000 \text{ units}) \times \$30 \text{ per hour}$$

$$= (4,500 \text{ hours} - 4,000 \text{ hours}) \times \$30 \text{ per hour}$$

$$= \$15,000 \text{ U}$$

Decision Point

How are budgeted variable overhead and fixed overhead cost rates calculated?

Learning Objective 3

Compute the variable overhead flexible-budget variance,

... difference between actual variable overhead costs and flexible-budget variable overhead amounts

the variable overhead efficiency variance,

... difference between actual quantity of cost-allocation base and budgeted quantity of cost-allocation base

and the variable overhead spending variance

... difference between actual variable overhead cost rate and budgeted variable overhead cost rate

Columns 2 and 3 of Exhibit 8-1 depict the variable overhead efficiency variance. Note the variance arises solely because of the difference between actual quantity (4,500 hours) and budgeted quantity (4,000 hours) of the cost-allocation base. The variable overhead efficiency variance is computed the same way the efficiency variance for direct-cost items is (Chapter 7, pp. 236–239). However, the interpretation of the variance is quite different. Efficiency variances for direct-cost items are based on differences between actual inputs used and budgeted inputs allowed for actual output produced. For example, a forensic laboratory (the kind popularized by television shows such as *CSI* and *Dexter*) would calculate a direct labor efficiency variance based on whether the lab used more or fewer hours than the standard hours allowed for the actual number of DNA tests. In contrast, the efficiency variance for variable overhead cost is based on the efficiency with which *the cost-allocation base* is used. Webb's unfavorable variable overhead efficiency variance of $15,000 means that the actual machine-hours (the cost-allocation base) of 4,500 hours turned out to be higher than the budgeted machine-hours of 4,000 hours allowed to manufacture 10,000 jackets.

The following table shows possible causes for Webb's actual machine-hours exceeding budgeted machine-hours and management's potential responses to each of these causes.

Possible Causes for Exceeding Budget	Potential Management Responses
1. Workers were less skilled than expected in using machines.	1. Encourage the human resources department to implement better employee-hiring practices and training procedures.
2. Production scheduler inefficiently scheduled jobs, resulting in more machine-hours used than budgeted.	2. Improve plant operations by installing production scheduling software.
3. Machines were not maintained in good operating condition.	3. Ensure preventive maintenance is done on all machines.
4. Webb's sales staff promised a distributor a rush delivery, which resulted in more machine-hours used than budgeted.	4. Coordinate production schedules with sales staff and distributors and share information with them.
5. Budgeted machine time standards were set too tight.	5. Commit more resources to develop appropriate standards.

Management would assess the cause(s) of the $15,000 U variance in April 2011 and respond accordingly. Note how, depending on the cause(s) of the variance, corrective actions may need to be taken not just in manufacturing but also in other business functions of the value chain, such as sales and distribution.

Exhibit 8-1   Columnar Presentation of Variable Overhead Variance Analysis: Webb Company for April 2011[a]

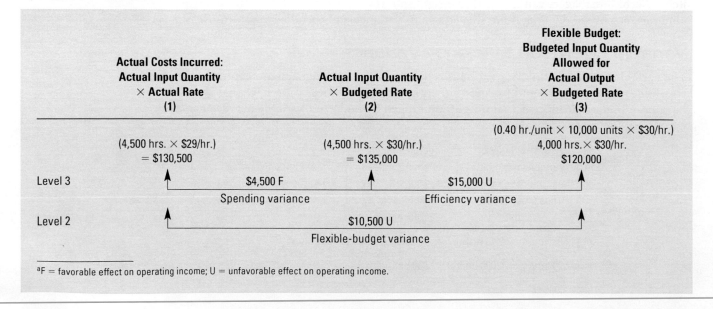

[a]F = favorable effect on operating income; U = unfavorable effect on operating income.

Webb's managers discovered that one reason the machines operated below budgeted efficiency levels in April 2011 was insufficient maintenance performed in the prior two months. A former plant manager delayed maintenance in a presumed attempt to meet monthly budget cost targets. As we discussed in Chapter 6, managers should not be focused on meeting short-run budget targets if they are likely to result in harmful long-run consequences. Webb is now strengthening its internal maintenance procedures so that failure to do monthly maintenance as needed will raise a "red flag" that must be immediately explained to management. Another reason for actual machine-hours exceeding budgeted machine-hours was the use of underskilled workers. As a result, Webb is initiating steps to improve hiring and training practices.

Variable Overhead Spending Variance

The **variable overhead spending variance** is the difference between actual variable overhead cost per unit of the cost-allocation base and budgeted variable overhead cost per unit of the cost-allocation base, multiplied by the actual quantity of variable overhead cost-allocation base used for actual output.

$$\begin{matrix} \text{Variable} \\ \text{overhead} \\ \text{spending} \\ \text{variance} \end{matrix} = \left(\begin{matrix} \text{Actual variable} \\ \text{overhead cost per unit} \\ \text{of cost-allocation base} \end{matrix} - \begin{matrix} \text{Budgeted variable} \\ \text{overhead cost per unit} \\ \text{of cost-allocation base} \end{matrix} \right) \times \begin{matrix} \text{Actual quantity of} \\ \text{variable overhead} \\ \text{cost-allocation base} \\ \text{used for actual output} \end{matrix}$$

$$= (\$29 \text{ per machine-hour} - \$30 \text{ per machine-hour}) \times 4,500 \text{ machine-hours}$$

$$= (-\$1 \text{ per machine-hour}) \times 4,500 \text{ machine-hours}$$

$$= \$4,500 \text{ F}$$

Since Webb operated in April 2011 with a lower-than-budgeted variable overhead cost per machine-hour, there is a favorable variable overhead spending variance. Columns 1 and 2 in Exhibit 9-1 depict this variance.

To understand the favorable variable overhead spending variance and its implications, Webb's managers need to recognize why *actual* variable overhead cost per unit of the cost-allocation base (\$29 per machine-hour) is *lower* than the *budgeted* variable overhead cost per unit of the cost-allocation base (\$30 per machine-hour). Overall, Webb used 4,500 machine-hours, which is 12.5% greater than the flexible-budget amount of 4,000 machine hours. However, actual variable overhead costs of \$130,500 are only 8.75% greater than the flexible-budget amount of \$120,000. Thus, relative to the flexible budget, the percentage increase in actual variable overhead costs is *less* than the percentage increase in machine-hours. Consequently, actual variable overhead cost per machine-hour is lower than the budgeted amount, resulting in a favorable variable overhead spending variance.

Recall that variable overhead costs include costs of energy, machine maintenance, indirect materials, and indirect labor. Two possible reasons why the percentage increase in actual variable overhead costs is less than the percentage increase in machine-hours are as follows:

1. Actual prices of individual inputs included in variable overhead costs, such as the price of energy, indirect materials, or indirect labor, are lower than budgeted prices of these inputs. For example, the actual price of electricity may only be \$0.09 per kilowatt-hour, compared with a price of \$0.10 per kilowatt-hour in the flexible budget.

2. Relative to the flexible budget, the percentage increase in the actual usage of individual items in the variable overhead-cost pool is less than the percentage increase in machine-hours. Compared with the flexible-budget amount of 30,000 kilowatt-hours, suppose actual energy used is 32,400 kilowatt-hours, or 8% higher. The fact that this is a smaller percentage increase than the 12.5% increase in machine-hours (4,500 actual machine-hours versus a flexible budget of 4,000 machine hours) will lead to a favorable variable overhead spending variance. The favorable spending variance can be partially or completely traced to the efficient use of energy and other variable overhead items.

As part of the last stage of the five-step decision-making process, Webb's managers will need to examine the signals provided by the variable overhead variances to *evaluate performance and learn*. By understanding the reasons for these variances, Webb can take appropriate actions and make more precise predictions in order to achieve improved results in future periods.

For example, Webb's managers must examine why actual prices of variable overhead cost items are different from budgeted prices. The price effects could be the result of skillful negotiation on the part of the purchasing manager, oversupply in the market, or lower quality of inputs such as indirect materials. Webb's response depends on what is believed to be the cause of the variance. If the concerns are about quality, for instance, Webb may want to put in place new quality management systems.

Similarly, Webb's managers should understand the possible causes for the efficiency with which variable overhead resources are used. These causes include skill levels of workers, maintenance of machines, and the efficiency of the manufacturing process. Webb's managers discovered that Webb used fewer supervision resources per machine-hour because of manufacturing process improvements. As a result, they began organizing crossfunctional teams to see if more process improvements could be achieved.

We emphasize that a favorable variable overhead spending variance is not always desirable. For example, the variable overhead spending variance would be favorable if Webb's managers purchased lower-priced, poor-quality indirect materials, hired less-talented supervisors, or performed less machine maintenance. These decisions, however, are likely to hurt product quality and harm the long-run prospects of the business.

To clarify the concepts of variable overhead efficiency variance and variable overhead spending variance, consider the following example. Suppose that (a) energy is the only item of variable overhead cost and machine-hours is the cost-allocation base; (b) actual machine-hours used equals the number of machine hours under the flexible budget; and (c) the actual price of energy equals the budgeted price. From (a) and (b), it follows that there is no efficiency variance — the company has been efficient with respect to the number of machine-hours (the cost-allocation base) used to produce the actual output. However, and despite (c), there could still be a spending variance. Why? Because even though the company used the correct number of machine hours, the energy consumed *per machine hour* could be higher than budgeted (for example, because the machines have not been maintained correctly). The cost of this higher energy usage would be reflected in an unfavorable spending variance.

Journal Entries for Variable Overhead Costs and Variances

We now prepare journal entries for Variable Overhead Control and the contra account Variable Overhead Allocated.

Entries for variable overhead for April 2011 (data from Exhibit 8-1) are as follows:

1. Variable Overhead Control	130,500	
Accounts Payable and various other accounts		130,500
To record actual variable overhead costs incurred.		
2. Work-in-Process Control	120,000	
Variable Overhead Allocated		120,000
To record variable overhead cost allocated		
(0.40 machine-hour/unit × 10,000 units × \$30/machine-hour). (The costs accumulated in Work-in-Process Control are transferred to Finished Goods Control when production is completed and to Cost of Goods Sold when the products are sold.)		
3. Variable Overhead Allocated	120,000	
Variable Overhead Efficiency Variance	15,000	
Variable Overhead Control		130,500
Variable Overhead Spending Variance		4,500
To record variances for the accounting period.		

These variances are the underallocated or overallocated variable overhead costs. At the end of the fiscal year, the variance accounts are written off to cost of goods sold if immaterial in amount. If the variances are material in amount, they are prorated among Work-in-Process Control, Finished Goods Control, and Cost of Goods Sold on the basis of the variable overhead allocated to these accounts, as described in Chapter 4, pages 117–122. As we discussed in Chapter 7, only unavoidable costs are prorated. Any part of the variances attributable to avoidable inefficiency are written off in the period. Assume that the balances in the variable overhead variance accounts as of April 2011 are also the balances at the end of the 2011 fiscal year and are immaterial in amount. The following journal entry records the write-off of the variance accounts to cost of goods sold:

Cost of Goods Sold	10,500	
Variable Overhead Spending Variance	4,500	
Variable Overhead Efficiency Variance		15,000

We next consider fixed overhead cost variances.

Decision Point ◀

What variances can be calculated for variable overhead costs?

Fixed Overhead Cost Variances

The flexible-budget amount for a fixed-cost item is also the amount included in the static budget prepared at the start of the period. No adjustment is required for differences between actual output and budgeted output for fixed costs, because fixed costs are unaffected by changes in the output level within the relevant range. At the start of 2011, Webb budgeted fixed overhead costs to be $276,000 per month. The actual amount for April 2011 turned out to be $285,000. The **fixed overhead flexible-budget variance** is the difference between actual fixed overhead costs and fixed overhead costs in the flexible budget:

Learning Objective 4

Compute the fixed overhead flexible-budget variance,

. . . difference between actual fixed overhead costs and flexible-budget fixed overhead amounts

the fixed overhead spending variance,

. . . same as the preceding explanation

and the fixed overhead production-volume variance

. . . difference between budgeted fixed overhead and fixed overhead allocated on the basis of actual output produced

$$\frac{\text{Fixed overhead}}{\text{flexible-budget variance}} = \frac{\text{Actual costs}}{\text{incurred}} - \frac{\text{Flexible-budget}}{\text{amount}}$$

$$= \$285,000 - \$276,000$$

$$= \$9,000 \text{ U}$$

The variance is unfavorable because $285,000 actual fixed overhead costs exceed the $276,000 budgeted for April 2011, which decreases that month's operating income by $9,000.

The variable overhead flexible-budget variance described earlier in this chapter was subdivided into a spending variance and an efficiency variance. There is not an efficiency variance for fixed overhead costs. That's because a given lump sum of fixed overhead costs will be unaffected by how efficiently machine-hours are used to produce output in a given budget period. As we will see later on, this does not mean that a company cannot be efficient or inefficient in its use of fixed-overhead-cost resources. As Exhibit 8-2 shows, because there is no efficiency variance, the **fixed overhead spending variance** is the same amount as the fixed overhead flexible-budget variance:

$$\frac{\text{Fixed overhead}}{\text{spending variance}} = \frac{\text{Actual costs}}{\text{incurred}} - \frac{\text{Flexible-budget}}{\text{amount}}$$

$$= \$285,000 - \$276,000$$

$$= \$9,000 \text{ U}$$

Reasons for the unfavorable spending variance could be higher plant-leasing costs, higher depreciation on plant and equipment, or higher administrative costs, such as a higher-than-budgeted salary paid to the plant manager. Webb investigated this variance and found that there was a $9,000 per month unexpected increase in its equipment-leasing costs. However, management concluded that the new lease rates were competitive with lease rates available elsewhere. If this were not the case, management would look to lease equipment from other suppliers.

| Exhibit 8-2 | Columnar Presentation of Fixed Overhead Variance Analysis: Webb Company for April 2011[a] |

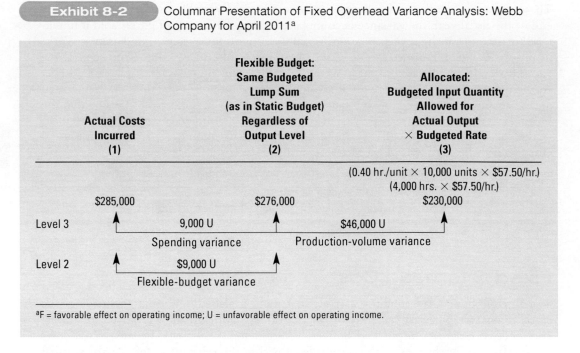

	Actual Costs Incurred (1)	Flexible Budget: Same Budgeted Lump Sum (as in Static Budget) Regardless of Output Level (2)	Allocated: Budgeted Input Quantity Allowed for Actual Output × Budgeted Rate (3)
			(0.40 hr./unit × 10,000 units × $57.50/hr.) (4,000 hrs. × $57.50/hr.)
	$285,000	$276,000	$230,000
Level 3		9,000 U	$46,000 U
		Spending variance	Production-volume variance
Level 2		$9,000 U	
		Flexible-budget variance	

[a]F = favorable effect on operating income; U = unfavorable effect on operating income.

Production-Volume Variance

We now examine a variance—the production-volume variance—that arises only for fixed costs. Recall that at the start of the year, Webb calculated a budgeted fixed overhead rate of $57.50 per machine hour. Under standard costing, Webb's budgeted fixed overhead costs are allocated to actual output produced during the period at the rate of $57.50 per standard machine-hour, equivalent to a rate of $23 per jacket (0.40 machine-hour per jacket × $57.50 per machine-hour). If Webb produces 1,000 jackets, $23,000 ($23 per jacket × 1,000 jackets) out of April's budgeted fixed overhead costs of $276,000 will be allocated to the jackets. If Webb produces 10,000 jackets, $230,000 ($23 per jacket × 10,000 jackets) will be allocated. Only if Webb produces 12,000 jackets (that is, operates at capacity), will all $276,000 ($23 per jacket × 12,000 jackets) of the budgeted fixed overhead cost be allocated to the jacket output. The key point here is that even though Webb budgets fixed overhead costs to be $276,000, it does not necessarily allocate all these costs to output. The reason is that Webb budgets $276,000 of fixed costs to support its planned production of 12,000 jackets. If Webb produces fewer than 12,000 jackets, it only allocates the budgeted cost of capacity actually needed and used to produce the jackets.

The **production-volume variance**, also referred to as the **denominator-level variance**, is the difference between budgeted fixed overhead and fixed overhead allocated on the basis of actual output produced. The allocated fixed overhead can be expressed in terms of allocation-base units (machine-hours for Webb) or in terms of the budgeted fixed cost per unit:

$$\frac{\text{Production}}{\text{volume variance}} = \frac{\text{Budgeted}}{\text{fixed overhead}} - \frac{\text{Fixed overhead allocated}}{\text{for actual output units produced}}$$

$$= \$276,000 - (0.40 \text{ hour per jacket} \times \$57.50 \text{ per hour} \times 10,000 \text{ jackets})$$

$$= \$276,000 - (\$23 \text{ per jacket} \times 10,000 \text{ jackets})$$

$$= \$276,000 - \$230,000$$

$$= \$46,000 \text{ U}$$

As shown in Exhibit 8-2, the budgeted fixed overhead ($276,000) will be the lump sum shown in the static budget and also in any flexible budget within the relevant range. Fixed overhead allocated ($230,000) is the amount of fixed overhead costs allocated; it is calculated by multiplying the number of output units produced during the budget period (10,000 units) by the budgeted cost per output unit ($23). The $46,000 U production-volume variance can also be thought of as $23 per jacket × 2,000 jackets that were *not* produced (12,000 jackets planned – 10,000 jackets produced). We will explore possible causes for the unfavorable production-volume variance and its management implications in the following section.

Exhibit 8-3 is a graphic presentation of the production-volume variance. Exhibit 8-3 shows that for planning and control purposes, fixed (manufacturing) overhead costs do not change in the 0- to 12,000-unit relevant range. Contrast this behavior of fixed costs with how these costs are depicted for the inventory costing purpose in Exhibit 8-3. Under generally accepted accounting principles, fixed (manufacturing) overhead costs are allocated as an inventoriable cost to the output units produced. Every output unit that Webb manufactures will increase the fixed overhead allocated to products by $23. That is, for purposes of allocating fixed overhead costs to jackets, these costs are viewed *as if* they had a variable-cost behavior pattern. As the graph in Exhibit 8-3 shows, the difference between the fixed overhead costs budgeted of $276,000 and the $230,000 of costs allocated is the $46,000 unfavorable production-volume variance.

Managers should always be careful to distinguish the true behavior of fixed costs from the manner in which fixed costs are assigned to products. In particular, while fixed costs are unitized and allocated for inventory costing purposes in a certain way, as described previously, managers should be wary of using the same unitized fixed overhead costs for planning and control purposes. When forecasting fixed costs, managers should concentrate on total lump-sum costs. Similarly, when managers are looking to assign costs for control purposes or identify the best way to use capacity resources that are fixed in the short run, we will see in Chapters 9 and Chapter 11 that the use of unitized fixed costs often leads to incorrect decisions.

Interpreting the Production-Volume Variance

Lump-sum fixed costs represent costs of acquiring capacity that do not decrease automatically if the resources needed turn out to be less than the resources acquired. Sometimes costs are fixed for a specific time period for contractual reasons, such as an annual lease contract for a plant. At other times, costs are fixed because capacity has to be acquired or disposed of in fixed increments, or lumps. For example, suppose that acquiring a sewing machine gives Webb the ability to produce 1,000 jackets. Then, if it is not possible to buy or lease a fraction of a machine, Webb can add capacity only in increments of 1,000 jackets. That is, Webb may choose capacity levels of 10,000; 11,000; or 12,000 jackets, but nothing in between.

Webb's management would want to analyze why this overcapacity occurred. Is demand weak? Should Webb reevaluate its product and marketing strategies? Is there a quality problem? Or did Webb make a strategic mistake by acquiring too much capacity? The causes of the $46,000 unfavorable production-volume variance will drive the actions Webb's managers will take in response to this variance.

In contrast, a favorable production-volume variance indicates an overallocation of fixed overhead costs. That is, the overhead costs allocated to the actual output produced exceed the budgeted fixed overhead costs of $276,000. The favorable production-volume variance comprises the fixed costs recorded in excess of $276,000.

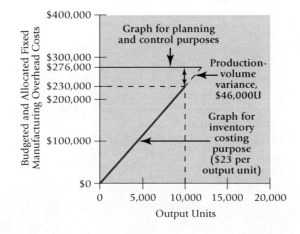

Exhibit 8-3

Behavior of Fixed Manufacturing Overhead Costs: Budgeted for Planning and Control Purposes and Allocated for Inventory Costing Purposes for Webb Company for April 2011

Be careful when drawing conclusions regarding a company's decisions about capacity planning and usage from the type (that is, favorable, F, or unfavorable, U) or the magnitude associated with a production-volume variance. To interpret the $46,000 unfavorable variance, Webb should consider why it sold only 10,000 jackets in April. Suppose a new competitor had gained market share by pricing below Webb's selling price. To sell the budgeted 12,000 jackets, Webb might have had to reduce its own selling price on all 12,000 jackets. Suppose it decided that selling 10,000 jackets at a higher price yielded higher operating income than selling 12,000 jackets at a lower price. The production-volume variance does not take into account such information. The failure of the production-volume variance to consider such information is why Webb should not interpret the $46,000 U amount as the total economic cost of selling 2,000 jackets fewer than the 12,000 jackets budgeted. If, however, Webb's managers anticipate they will not need capacity beyond 10,000 jackets, they may reduce the excess capacity, say, by canceling the lease on some of the machines.

Companies plan their plant capacity strategically on the basis of market information about how much capacity will be needed over some future time horizon. For 2011, Webb's budgeted quantity of output is equal to the maximum capacity of the plant for that budget period. Actual demand (and quantity produced) turned out to be below the budgeted quantity of output, so Webb reports an unfavorable production-volume variance for April 2011. However, it would be incorrect to conclude that Webb's management made a poor planning decision regarding plant capacity. Demand for Webb's jackets might be highly uncertain. Given this uncertainty and the cost of not having sufficient capacity to meet sudden demand surges (including lost contribution margins as well as reduced repeat business), Webb's management may have made a wise choice in planning 2011 plant capacity. Of course, if demand is unlikely to pick up again, Webb's managers may look to cancel the lease on some of the machines or to sublease the machines to other parties with the goal of reducing the unfavorable production-volume variance.

Managers must always explore the why of a variance before concluding that the label unfavorable or favorable necessarily indicates, respectively, poor or good management performance. Understanding the reasons for a variance also helps managers decide on future courses of action. Should Webb's managers try to reduce capacity, increase sales, or do nothing? Based on their analysis of the situation, Webb's managers decided to reduce some capacity but continued to maintain some excess capacity to accommodate unexpected surges in demand. Chapter 9 and Chapter 13 examine these issues in more detail. The Concepts in Action feature on page 280 highlights another example of managers using variances, and the reasons behind them, to help guide their decisions.

Next we describe the journal entries Webb would make to record fixed overhead costs using standard costing.

Journal Entries for Fixed Overhead Costs and Variances

We illustrate journal entries for fixed overhead costs for April 2011 using Fixed Overhead Control and the contra account Fixed Overhead Allocated (data from Exhibit 8-2).

1. Fixed Overhead Control   285,000
          Salaries Payable, Accumulated Depreciation, and various other accounts   285,000
      To record actual fixed overhead costs incurred.
2. Work-in-Process Control   230,000
          Fixed Overhead Allocated   230,000
      To record fixed overhead costs allocated
        (0.40 machine-hour/unit × 10,000 units × $57.50/machine-hour). (The costs accumulated in Work-in-Process Control are transferred to Finished Goods Control when production is completed and to Cost of Goods Sold when the products are sold.)
3. Fixed Overhead Allocated   230,000
      Fixed Overhead Spending Variance   9,000
      Fixed Overhead Production-Volume Variance   46,000
          Fixed Overhead Control   285,000
      To record variances for the accounting period.

Overall, $285,000 of fixed overhead costs were incurred during April, but only $230,000 were allocated to jackets. The difference of $55,000 is precisely the underallocated fixed overhead costs that we introduced when studying normal costing in Chapter 4. The third entry illustrates how the fixed overhead spending variance of $9,000 and the fixed overhead production-volume variance of $46,000 together record this amount in a standard costing system.

At the end of the fiscal year, the fixed overhead spending variance is written off to cost of goods sold if it is immaterial in amount, or prorated among Work-in-Process Control, Finished Goods Control, and Cost of Goods Sold on the basis of the fixed overhead allocated to these accounts as described in Chapter 4, pages 117–122. Some companies combine the write-off and proration methods—that is, they write off the portion of the variance that is due to inefficiency and could have been avoided and prorate the portion of the variance that is unavoidable. Assume that the balance in the Fixed Overhead Spending Variance account as of April 2011 is also the balance at the end of 2011 and is immaterial in amount. The following journal entry records the write-off to Cost of Goods Sold.

| Cost of Goods Sold | 9,000 | |
| Fixed Overhead Spending Variance | | 9,000 |

We now consider the production-volume variance. Assume that the balance in Fixed Overhead Production-Volume Variance as of April 2011 is also the balance at the end of 2011. Also assume that some of the jackets manufactured during 2011 are in work-in-process and finished goods inventory at the end of the year. Many management accountants make a strong argument for writing off to Cost of Goods Sold and not prorating an unfavorable production-volume variance. Proponents of this argument contend that the unfavorable production-volume variance of $46,000 measures the cost of resources expended for 2,000 jackets that were not produced ($23 per jacket × 2,000 jackets = $46,000). Prorating these costs would inappropriately allocate fixed overhead costs incurred for the 2,000 jackets that were not produced to the jackets that were produced. The jackets produced already bear their representative share of fixed overhead costs of $23 per jacket. Therefore, this argument favors charging the unfavorable production-volume variance against the year's revenues so that fixed costs of unused capacity are not carried in work-in-process inventory and finished goods inventory.

There is, however, an alternative view. This view regards the denominator level chosen as a "soft" rather than a "hard" measure of the fixed resources required and needed to produce each jacket. Suppose that either because of the design of the jacket or the functioning of the machines, it took more machine-hours than previously thought to manufacture each jacket. Consequently, Webb could make only 10,000 jackets rather than the planned 12,000 in April. In this case, the $276,000 of budgeted fixed overhead costs support the production of the 10,000 jackets manufactured. Under this reasoning, prorating the fixed overhead production-volume variance would appropriately spread fixed overhead costs among Work-in-Process Control, Finished Goods Control, and Cost of Goods Sold.

What about a favorable production-volume variance? Suppose Webb manufactured 13,800 jackets in April 2011.

$$\text{Production-volume variance} = \begin{matrix} \text{Budgeted} \\ \text{fixed} \\ \text{overhead} \end{matrix} - \begin{matrix} \text{Fixed overhead allocated using} \\ \text{budgeted cost per output unit overhead} \\ \text{allowed for actual output produced} \end{matrix}$$

$$= \$276,000 - (\$23 \text{ per jacket} \times 13,800 \text{ jackets})$$

$$= \$276,000 - \$317,400 = \$41,400 \text{ F}$$

Because actual production exceeded the planned capacity level, clearly the fixed overhead costs of $276,000 supported production of, and so should be allocated to, all 13,800 jackets. Prorating the favorable production-volume variance achieves this outcome and reduces the amounts in Work-in-Process Control, Finished Goods Control, and Cost of Goods Sold. Proration is also the more conservative approach in the sense that it results in a lower operating income than if the entire favorable production-volume variance were credited to Cost of Goods Sold.

One more point is relevant to the discussion of whether to prorate the production-volume variance or to write it off to cost of goods sold. If variances are always written off to cost of goods sold, a company could set its standards to either increase (for financial reporting purposes) or decrease (for tax purposes) operating income. In other words, always writing off variances invites gaming behavior. For example, Webb could generate a favorable (unfavorable) production-volume variance by setting the denominator level used to allocate fixed overhead costs low (high) and thereby increase (decrease) operating income. The proration method has the effect of approximating the allocation of fixed costs based on actual costs and actual output so it is not susceptible to the manipulation of operating income via the choice of the denominator level.

There is no clear-cut or preferred approach for closing out the production-volume variance. The appropriate accounting procedure is a matter of judgment and depends on the circumstances of each case. Variations of the proration method may be desirable. For example, a company may choose to write off a portion of the production-volume variance and prorate the rest. The goal is to write off that part of the production-volume variance that represents the cost of capacity not used to support the production of output during the period. The rest of the production-volume variance is prorated to Work-in-Process Control, Finished Goods Control, and Cost of Goods Sold.

If Webb were to write off the production-volume variance to cost of goods sold, it would make the following journal entry.

Cost of Goods Sold	46,000	
Fixed Overhead Production-Volume Variance		46,000

Decision Point

What variances can be calculated for fixed overhead costs?

Integrated Analysis of Overhead Cost Variances

As our discussion indicates, the variance calculations for variable overhead and fixed overhead differ:

■ Variable overhead has no production-volume variance.

■ Fixed overhead has no efficiency variance.

Exhibit 8-4 presents an integrated summary of the variable overhead variances and the fixed overhead variances computed using standard costs for April 2011. Panel A shows the variances for variable overhead, while Panel B contains the fixed overhead variances. As you study Exhibit 8-4, note how the columns in Panels A and B are aligned to measure the different variances. In both Panels A and B,

■ the difference between columns 1 and 2 measures the spending variance.

■ the difference between columns 2 and 3 measures the efficiency variance (if applicable).

■ the difference between columns 3 and 4 measures the production-volume variance (if applicable).

Panel A contains an efficiency variance; Panel B has no efficiency variance for fixed overhead. As discussed earlier, a lump-sum amount of fixed costs will be unaffected by the degree of operating efficiency in a given budget period.

Panel A does not have a production-volume variance, because the amount of variable overhead allocated is always the same as the flexible-budget amount. Variable costs never have any unused capacity. When production and sales decline from 12,000 jackets to 10,000 jackets, budgeted variable overhead costs proportionately decline. Fixed costs are different. Panel B has a production-volume variance (see Exhibit 8-3) because Webb had to acquire the fixed manufacturing overhead resources it had committed to when it planned production of 12,000 jackets, even though it produced only 10,000 jackets and did not use some of its capacity.

Learning Objective 5

Show how the 4-variance analysis approach reconciles the actual overhead incurred with the overhead amounts allocated during the period

. . . the 4-variance analysis approach identifies spending and efficiency variances for variable overhead costs and spending and production-volume variances for fixed overhead costs

Exhibit 8-4 Columnar Presentation of Integrated Variance Analysis: Webb Company for April 2011[a]

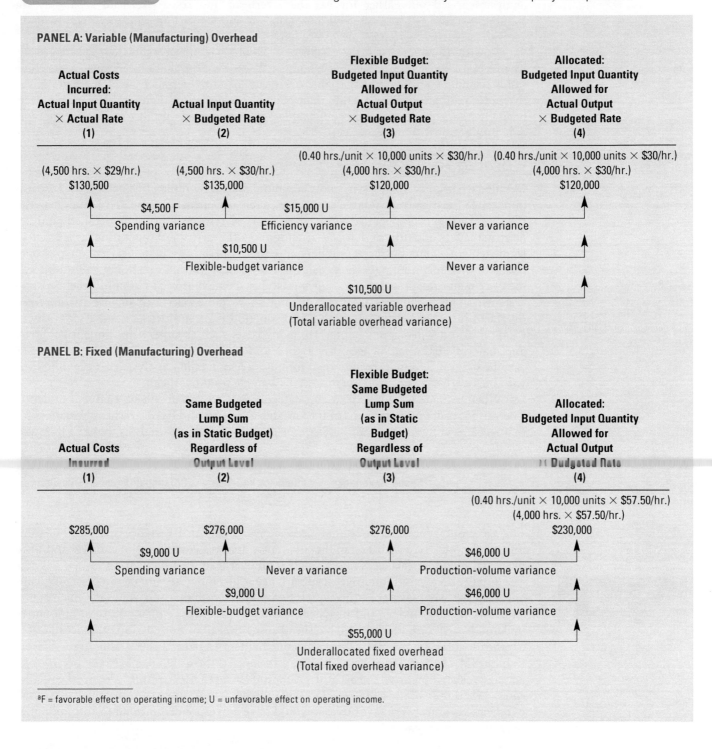

PANEL A: Variable (Manufacturing) Overhead

Actual Costs Incurred: Actual Input Quantity × Actual Rate (1)	Actual Input Quantity × Budgeted Rate (2)	Flexible Budget: Budgeted Input Quantity Allowed for Actual Output × Budgeted Rate (3)	Allocated: Budgeted Input Quantity Allowed for Actual Output × Budgeted Rate (4)
(4,500 hrs. × $29/hr.) $130,500	(4,500 hrs. × $30/hr.) $135,000	(0.40 hrs./unit × 10,000 units × $30/hr.) (4,000 hrs. × $30/hr.) $120,000	(0.40 hrs./unit × 10,000 units × $30/hr.) (4,000 hrs. × $30/hr.) $120,000

$4,500 F — Spending variance
$15,000 U — Efficiency variance
Never a variance

$10,500 U — Flexible-budget variance
Never a variance

$10,500 U — Underallocated variable overhead (Total variable overhead variance)

PANEL B: Fixed (Manufacturing) Overhead

Actual Costs Incurred (1)	Same Budgeted Lump Sum (as in Static Budget) Regardless of Output Level (2)	Flexible Budget: Same Budgeted Lump Sum (as in Static Budget) Regardless of Output Level (3)	Allocated: Budgeted Input Quantity Allowed for Actual Output × Budgeted Rate (4)
$285,000	$276,000	$276,000	(0.40 hrs./unit × 10,000 units × $57.50/hr.) (4,000 hrs. × $57.50/hr.) $230,000

$9,000 U — Spending variance
Never a variance
$46,000 U — Production-volume variance

$9,000 U — Flexible-budget variance
$46,000 U — Production-volume variance

$55,000 U — Underallocated fixed overhead (Total fixed overhead variance)

[a]F = favorable effect on operating income; U = unfavorable effect on operating income.

4-Variance Analysis

When all of the overhead variances are presented together as in Exhibit 8-4, we refer to it as a 4-variance analysis:

	4-Variance Analysis		
	Spending Variance	Efficiency Variance	Production-Volume Variance
Variable overhead	$4,500 F	$15,000 U	Never a variance
Fixed overhead	$9,000 U	Never a variance	$46,000 U

Note that the 4-variance analysis provides the same level of information as the variance analysis carried out earlier for variable overhead and fixed overhead separately (in Exhibits 8-1 and 8-2, respectively), but it does so in a unified presentation that also indicates those variances that are never present.

As with other variances, the variances in Webb's 4-variance analysis are not necessarily independent of each other. For example, Webb may purchase lower-quality machine fluids (leading to a favorable variable overhead spending variance), which results in the machines taking longer to operate than budgeted (causing an unfavorable variable overhead efficiency variance), and producing less than budgeted output (causing an unfavorable production-volume variance).

Combined Variance Analysis

Detailed 4-variance analyses are most common in large, complex businesses, because it is impossible for managers at large companies, such as General Electric and Disney, to keep track of all that is happening within their areas of responsibility. The detailed analyses help managers identify and focus attention on the areas not operating as expected. Managers of small businesses understand their operations better based on personal observations and nonfinancial measures. They find less value in doing the additional measurements required for 4-variance analyses. For example, to simplify their costing systems, small companies may not distinguish variable overhead incurred from fixed overhead incurred because making this distinction is often not clear-cut. As we saw in Chapter 2 and will see in Chapter 10, many costs such as supervision, quality control, and materials handling have both variable- and fixed-cost components that may not be easy to separate. Managers may therefore use a less detailed analysis that *combines* the variable overhead and fixed overhead into a single total overhead.

When a single total overhead cost category is used, it can still be analyzed in depth. The variances are now the sums of the variable overhead and fixed overhead variances for that level, as computed in Exhibit 8-4. The combined variance analysis looks as follows:

	Combined 3-Variance Analysis		
	Spending Variance	Efficiency Variance	Production-Volume Variance
Total overhead	$4,500 U	$15,000 U	$46,000 U

The accounting for 3-variance analysis is simpler than for 4-variance analysis, but some information is lost. In particular, the 3-variance analysis combines the variable and fixed overhead spending variances into a single total overhead spending variance.

Finally, the overall **total-overhead variance** is given by the sum of the preceding variances. In the Webb example, this equals $65,500 U. Note that this amount, which aggregates the flexible-budget and production-volume variances, equals the total amount of underallocated (or underapplied) overhead costs. (Recall our discussion of underallocated overhead costs in normal costing from Chapter 4, page 118.) Using figures from Exhibit 8-4, the $65,500 U total-overhead variance is the difference between (a) the total actual overhead incurred ($130,500 + $285,000 = $415,500) and (b) the overhead allocated ($120,000 + $230,000 = $350,000) to the actual output produced. If the total-overhead variance were favorable, it would have corresponded instead to the amount of overapplied overhead costs.

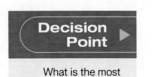

Decision Point ▶

What is the most detailed way for a company to reconcile actual overhead incurred with the amount allocated during a period?

Production-Volume Variance and Sales-Volume Variance

As we complete our study of variance analysis for Webb Company, it is helpful to step back to see the "big picture" and to link the accounting and performance evaluation functions of standard costing. Exhibit 7-2, page 231, subdivided the static-budget variance of $93,100 U into a flexible-budget variance of $29,100 U and a sales-volume variance of $64,000 U. In both Chapter 7 and this chapter, we presented more detailed variances that subdivided, whenever possible, individual flexible-budget variances for selling price, direct materials, direct manufacturing labor, variable overhead, and fixed overhead. Here is a summary:

Selling price	$50,000 F
Direct materials (Price, $44,400 F + Efficiency, $66,000 U)	21,600 U
Direct manufacturing labor (Price, $18,000 U + Efficiency, $20,000 U)	38,000 U
Variable overhead (Spending, $4,500 F + Efficiency, $15,000 U)	10,500 U
Fixed overhead (Spending, $9,000 U)	9,000 U
Total flexible budget variance	$29,100 U

Learning Objective 6

Explain the relationship between the sales-volume variance and the production-volume variance

. . . the production-volume and operating-income volume variances together comprise the sales-volume variance

We also calculated one other variance in this chapter, the production-volume variance, which is not part of the flexible-budget variance. Where does the production-volume variance fit into the "big picture"? As we shall see, the production-volume variance is a component of the sales-volume variance.

Under our assumption of actual production and sales of 10,000 jackets, Webb's costing system debits to Work-in-Process Control the standard costs of the 10,000 jackets produced. These amounts are then transferred to Finished Goods and finally to Cost of Goods Sold:

Direct materials (Chapter 7, p. 240, entry 1b)	
($60 per jacket × 10,000 jackets)	$ 600,000
Direct manufacturing labor (Chapter 7, p. 240, entry 2)	
($16 per jacket × 10,000 jackets)	160,000
Variable overhead (Chapter 8, p. 270, entry 2)	
($12 per jacket × 10,000 jackets)	120,000
Fixed overhead (Chapter 8, p. 274, entry 2)	
($23 per jacket × 10,000 jackets)	230,000
Cost of goods sold at standard cost	
($111 per jacket × 10,000 jackets)	$1,110,000

Webb's costing system also records the revenues from the 10,000 jackets sold at the budgeted selling price of $120 per jacket. The net effect of these entries on Webb's budgeted operating income is as follows:

Revenues at budgeted selling price	
($120 per jacket × 10,000 jackets)	$1,200,000
Cost of goods sold at standard cost	
($111 per jacket × 10,000 jackets)	1,110,000
Operating income based on budgeted profit per jacket	
($9 per jacket × 10,000 jackets)	$ 90,000

A crucial point to keep in mind is that in standard costing, fixed overhead cost is treated as if it is a variable cost. That is, in determining the budgeted operating income of $90,000, only $230,000 ($23 per jacket × 10,000 jackets) of fixed overhead is considered, whereas the budgeted fixed overhead costs are $276,000. Webb's accountants then record the $46,000 unfavorable production-volume variance (the difference between budgeted fixed overhead costs, $276,000, and allocated fixed overhead costs, $230,000, p. 274, entry 2), as well as the various flexible-budget variances (including the fixed overhead spending variance) that total $29,100 unfavorable (see Exhibit 7-2, p. 231). This results in actual operating income of $14,900 as follows:

Operating income based on budgeted profit per jacket	
($9 per jacket × 10,000 jackets)	$ 90,000
Unfavorable production-volume variance	(46,000)
Flexible-budget operating income (Exhibit 7-2)	44,000
Unfavorable flexible-budget variance for operating income (Exhibit 7-2)	(29,100)
Actual operating income (Exhibit 7-2)	$ 14,900

Concepts in Action

Variance Analysis and Standard Costing Help Sandoz Manage Its Overhead Costs

In the United States, the importance of generic pharmaceuticals is growing dramatically. In recent years, Wal-Mart has been selling hundreds of generic drugs for $4 per prescription, a price many competitors have since matched. Moreover, with recent legislation extending health insurance coverage to 32 million previously uninsured Americans, the growing use of generic drugs is certain to accelerate, a trend rooted both in demographics—the aging U.S. population takes more drugs each year—and in the push to cut health care costs.

Sandoz US, a $7.5 billion subsidiary of Swiss-based Novartis AG, is one of the largest developers of generic pharmaceutical substitutes for market-leading therapeutic drugs. Market pricing pressure means that Sandoz, Teva Pharmaceutical, and other generic manufacturers operate on razor-thin margins. As a result, along with an intricate analysis of direct-cost variances, firms like Sandoz must also tackle the challenge of accounting for overhead costs. Sandoz uses standard costing and variance analysis to manage its overhead costs.

Each year, Sandoz prepares an overhead budget based on a detailed production plan, planned overhead spending, and other factors, including inflation, efficiency initiatives, and anticipated capital expenditures and depreciation. Sandoz then uses activity-based costing techniques to assign budgeted overhead costs to different work centers (for example, mixing, blending, tableting, testing, and packaging). Finally, overhead costs are assigned to products based on the activity levels required by each product at each work center. The resulting standard product cost is used in product profitability analysis and as a basis for making pricing decisions. The two main focal points in Sandoz's performance analyses are overhead absorption analysis and manufacturing overhead variance analysis.

Each month, Sandoz uses absorption analysis to compare actual production and actual costs to the standard costs of processed inventory. The monthly analysis evaluates two key trends:

1. Are costs in line with the budget? If not, the reasons are examined and the accountable managers are notified.
2. Are production volume and product mix conforming to plan? If not, Sandoz reviews and adjusts machine capacities and the absorption trend is deemed to be permanent. Plant management uses absorption analysis as a compass to determine if it is on budget and has an appropriate capacity level to efficiently satisfy the needs of its customers.

Manufacturing overhead variances are examined at the work center level. These variances help determine when equipment is not running as expected, which leads to repair or replacement. Variances also help in identifying inefficiencies in processing and setup and cleaning times, which leads to more efficient ways to use equipment. Sometimes, manufacturing overhead variance analysis leads to the review and improvement of the standards themselves—a critical element in planning the level of plant capacity. Management reviews current and future capacity use on a monthly basis, using standard hours entered into the plan's enterprise resource planning system. The standards are a useful tool in identifying capacity constraints and future capital needs.

As the plant controller remarked, "Standard costing at Sandoz produces costs that are not only understood by management accountants and industrial engineers, but by decision makers in marketing and on the production floor. Management accountants at Sandoz achieve this by having a high degree of process understanding and involvement. The result is better pricing and product mix decisions, lower waste, process improvements, and efficient capacity choices—all contributing to overall profitability."

Source: Booming US Generic Drug Market. Delhi, India: RNCOS Ltd, 2010; Conversations with, and documents prepared by, Eric Evans and Erich Erchr (of Sandoz US), 2004; Day, Kathleen. 2006. Wal-Mart sets $4 price for many generic drugs. *Washington Post*, September 22; Halpern, Steven. 2010. Teva: Generic gains from health care reform. *AOL Inc.* "Blogging Stocks" blog, May 13. http://www.bloggingstocks.com/2010/05/13/teva-teva-generic-gains-from-healthcare-reform/

In contrast, the static-budget operating income of $108,000 (p. 229) is not entered in Webb's costing system, because standard costing records budgeted revenues, standard costs, and variances only for the 10,000 jackets actually produced and sold, not for the 12,000 jackets that were *planned* to be produced and sold. As a result, the sales-volume variance of $64,000 U, which is the difference between static-budget operating income,

$108,000, and flexible-budget operating income, $44,000 (Exhibit 7-2, p. 231), is never actually recorded in standard costing. Nevertheless, the sales-volume variance is useful because it helps managers understand the lost contribution margin from selling 2,000 fewer jackets (the sales-volume variance assumes fixed costs remain at the budgeted level of $276,000).

The sales-volume variance has two components. They are as follows:

1. A difference between the static-budget operating income of $108,000 for 12,000 jackets and budgeted operating income of $90,000 for 10,000 jackets. This is the **operating-income volume variance** of $18,000 U ($108,000 − $90,000), and reflects the fact that Webb produced and sold 2,000 fewer units than budgeted.

2. A difference between the budgeted operating income of $90,000 and the flexible budget operating income of $44,000 (Exhibit 7-2, p. 231) for the 10,000 actual units. This difference arises because Webb's costing system treats fixed costs as if they behave in a variable manner and so assumes fixed costs equal the allocated amount of $230,000, rather than the budgeted fixed costs of $276,000. Of course, the difference between the allocated and budgeted fixed costs is precisely the production-volume variance of $46,000 U.

In summary, we have the following:

	Operating-income volume variance	$18,000 U
(+)	Production-volume variance	46,000 U
Equals	Sales-volume variance	$64,000 U

That is, the sales-volume variance is comprised of operating-income volume and production-volume variances.

Decision Point

What is the relationship between the sales-volume variance and the production-volume variance?

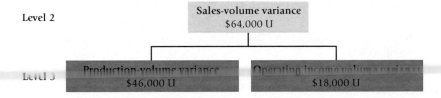

Level 2   Sales-volume variance $64,000 U

Level 3   Production-volume variance $46,000 U   Operating-income volume variance $18,000 U

Variance Analysis and Activity-Based Costing

Activity-based costing (ABC) systems focus on individual activities as the fundamental cost objects. ABC systems classify the costs of various activities into a cost hierarchy—output unit-level costs, batch-level costs, product-sustaining costs, and facility-sustaining costs (see p. 149). In this section, we show how a company that has an ABC system and batch-level costs can benefit from variance analysis. Batch-level costs are the costs of activities related to a group of units of products or services rather than to each individual unit of product or service. We illustrate variance analysis for variable batch-level direct costs and fixed batch-level setup overhead costs.[4]

Consider Lyco Brass Works, which manufactures many different types of faucets and brass fittings. Because of the wide range of products it produces, Lyco uses an activity-based costing system. In contrast, Webb uses a simple costing system because it makes only one type of jacket. One of Lyco's products is Elegance, a decorative brass faucet for home spas. Lyco produces Elegance in batches.

For each product Lyco makes, it uses dedicated materials-handling labor to bring materials to the production floor, transport work in process from one work center to the next, and take the finished goods to the shipping area. Therefore, materials-handling labor costs for Elegance are direct costs of Elegance. Because the materials for a batch are moved together, materials-handling labor costs vary with number of batches rather than with number of units in a batch. Materials-handling labor costs are variable direct batch-level costs.

Learning Objective 7

Calculate variances in activity-based costing

. . . compare budgeted and actual overhead costs of activities

---

[4] The techniques we demonstrate can be applied to analyze variable batch-level overhead costs as well.

To manufacture a batch of Elegance, Lyco must set up the machines and molds. Setting up the machines and molds requires highly trained skills. Hence, a separate setup department is responsible for setting up machines and molds for different batches of products. Setup costs are overhead costs of products. For simplicity, assume that setup costs are fixed with respect to the number of setup-hours. They consist of salaries paid to engineers and supervisors and costs of leasing setup equipment.

Information regarding Elegance for 2012 follows:

	Actual Result	Static-Budget Amount
1. Units of Elegance produced and sold	151,200	180,000
2. Batch size (units per batch)	140	150
3. Number of batches (Line 1 ÷ Line 2)	1,080	1,200
4. Materials-handling labor-hours per batch	5.25	5
5. Total materials-handling labor-hours (Line 3 × Line 4)	5,670	6,000
6. Cost per materials-handling labor-hour	$ 14.50	$ 14
7. Total materials-handling labor costs (Line 5 × Line 6)	$ 82,215	$ 84,000
8. Setup-hours per batch	6.25	6
9. Total setup-hours (Line 3 × Line 8)	6,750	7,200
10. Total fixed setup overhead costs	$220,000	$216,000

Flexible Budget and Variance Analysis for Direct Labor Costs

To prepare the flexible budget for materials-handling labor costs, Lyco starts with the actual units of output produced, 151,200 units, and proceeds with the following steps.

Step 1: Using Budgeted Batch Size, Calculate the Number of Batches that Should Have Been Used to Produce Actual Output. At the budgeted batch size of 150 units per batch, Lyco should have produced the 151,200 units of output in 1,008 batches (151,200 units ÷ 150 units per batch).

Step 2: Using Budgeted Materials-Handling Labor-Hours per Batch, Calculate the Number of Materials-Handling Labor-Hours that Should Have Been Used. At the budgeted quantity of 5 hours per batch, 1,008 batches should have required 5,040 materials-handling labor-hours (1,008 batches × 5 hours per batch).

Step 3: Using Budgeted Cost per Materials-Handling Labor-Hour, Calculate the Flexible-Budget Amount for Materials-Handling Labor-Hours. The flexible-budget amount is 5,040 materials-handling labor-hours × $14 budgeted cost per materials-handling labor-hour = $70,560.

Note how the flexible-budget calculations for materials-handling labor costs focus on batch-level quantities (materials-handling labor-hours per batch rather than per unit). Flexible-budget quantity computations focus at the appropriate level of the cost hierarchy. For example, because materials handling is a batch-level cost, the flexible-budget quantity calculations are made at the batch level—the quantity of materials-handling labor-hours that Lyco should have used based on the number of batches it should have used to produce the actual quantity of 151,200 units. If a cost had been a product-sustaining cost—such as product design cost—the flexible-budget quantity computations would focus at the product-sustaining level, for example, by evaluating the actual complexity of product design relative to the budget.

The flexible-budget variance for materials-handling labor costs can now be calculated as follows:

$$\text{Flexible-budget variance} = \text{Actual costs} - \text{Flexible-budget costs}$$

$$= (5,670 \text{ hours} \times \$14.50 \text{ per hour}) - (5,040 \text{ hours} \times \$14 \text{ per hour})$$

$$= \$82,215 - \$70,560$$

$$= \$11,655 \text{ U}$$

The unfavorable variance indicates that materials-handling labor costs were $11,655 higher than the flexible-budget target. We can get some insight into the possible reasons for this unfavorable outcome by examining the price and efficiency components of the flexible-budget variance. Exhibit 8-5 presents the variances in columnar form.

$$\begin{aligned} \text{Price} \atop \text{variance} &= \left(\begin{matrix} \text{Actual price} \\ \text{of input} \end{matrix} - \begin{matrix} \text{Budgeted price} \\ \text{of input} \end{matrix} \right) \times \begin{matrix} \text{Actual quantity} \\ \text{of input} \end{matrix} \end{aligned}$$

$$= (\$14.50 \text{ per hour} - \$14 \text{ per hour}) \times 5{,}670 \text{ hours}$$

$$= \$0.50 \text{ per hour} \times 5{,}670 \text{ hours}$$

$$= \$2{,}835 \text{ U}$$

The unfavorable price variance for materials-handling labor indicates that the $14.50 actual cost per materials-handling labor-hour exceeds the $14.00 budgeted cost per materials-handling labor-hour. This variance could be the result of Lyco's human resources manager negotiating wage rates less skillfully or of wage rates increasing unexpectedly due to scarcity of labor.

$$\begin{aligned} \text{Efficiency} \atop \text{variance} &= \left(\begin{matrix} \text{Actual} \\ \text{quantity of} \\ \text{input used} \end{matrix} - \begin{matrix} \text{Budgeted quantity} \\ \text{of input allowed} \\ \text{for actual output} \end{matrix} \right) \times \begin{matrix} \text{Budgeted price} \\ \text{of input} \end{matrix} \end{aligned}$$

$$= (5{,}670 \text{ hours} - 5{,}040 \text{ hours}) \times \$14 \text{ per hour}$$

$$= 630 \text{ hours} \times \$14 \text{ per hour}$$

$$= \$8{,}820 \text{ U}$$

The unfavorable efficiency variance indicates that the 5,670 actual materials-handling labor-hours exceeded the 5,040 budgeted materials-handling labor-hours for actual output. Possible reasons for the unfavorable efficiency variance are as follows:

- Smaller actual batch sizes of 140 units, instead of the budgeted batch sizes of 150 units, resulting in Lyco producing the 151,200 units in 1,080 batches instead of 1,008 (151,200 ÷ 150) batches
- Higher actual materials-handling labor-hours per batch of 5.25 hours instead of budgeted materials-handling labor-hours of 5 hours

Reasons for smaller-than-budgeted batch sizes could include quality problems when batch sizes exceed 140 faucets and high costs of carrying inventory.

Exhibit 8-5   Columnar Presentation of Variance Analysis for Direct Materials-Handling Labor Costs: Lyco Brass Works for 2012[a]

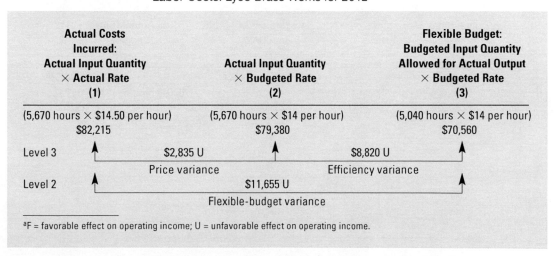

Actual Costs Incurred: Actual Input Quantity × Actual Rate (1)	Actual Input Quantity × Budgeted Rate (2)	Flexible Budget: Budgeted Input Quantity Allowed for Actual Output × Budgeted Rate (3)
(5,670 hours × $14.50 per hour) $82,215	(5,670 hours × $14 per hour) $79,380	(5,040 hours × $14 per hour) $70,560

Level 3   ↑ $2,835 U   ↑ $8,820 U   ↑
       Price variance   Efficiency variance
Level 2   ↑ $11,655 U   ↑
       Flexible-budget variance

[a]F = favorable effect on operating income; U = unfavorable effect on operating income.

Possible reasons for larger actual materials-handling labor-hours per batch are as follows:

■ Inefficient layout of the Elegance production line
■ Materials-handling labor having to wait at work centers before picking up or delivering materials
■ Unmotivated, inexperienced, and underskilled employees
■ Very tight standards for materials-handling time

Identifying the reasons for the efficiency variance helps Lyco's managers develop a plan for improving materials-handling labor efficiency and to take corrective action that will be incorporated into future budgets.

We now consider fixed setup overhead costs.

Flexible Budget and Variance Analysis for Fixed Setup Overhead Costs

Exhibit 8-6 presents the variances for fixed setup overhead costs in columnar form. Lyco's fixed setup overhead flexible-budget variance is calculated as follows:

$$\begin{array}{c}\text{Fixed-setup}\\\text{overhead}\\\text{flexible-budget}\\\text{variance}\end{array} = \begin{array}{c}\text{Actual costs}\\\text{incurred}\end{array} - \begin{array}{c}\text{Flexible-budget}\\\text{costs}\end{array}$$

$$= \$220{,}000 - \$216{,}000$$

$$= \$4{,}000 \text{ U}$$

Note that the flexible-budget amount for fixed setup overhead costs equals the static-budget amount of $216,000. That's because there is no "flexing" of fixed costs. Moreover, because fixed overhead costs have no efficiency variance, the fixed setup overhead spending variance is the same as the fixed overhead flexible-budget variance. The spending variance could be unfavorable because of higher leasing costs of new setup equipment or higher salaries paid to engineers and supervisors. Lyco may have incurred these costs to alleviate some of the difficulties it was having in setting up machines.

Exhibit 8-6   Columnar Presentation of Fixed Setup Overhead Variance Analysis: Lyco Brass Works for 2012[a]

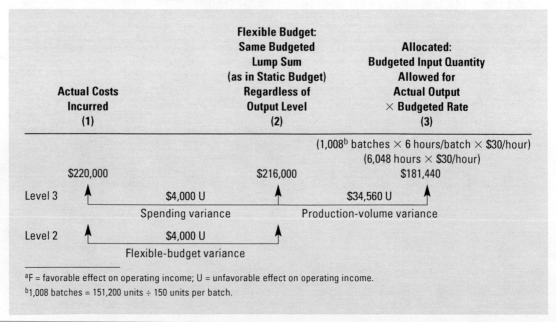

[a]F = favorable effect on operating income; U = unfavorable effect on operating income.
[b]1,008 batches = 151,200 units ÷ 150 units per batch.

To calculate the production-volume variance, Lyco first computes the budgeted cost-allocation rate for fixed setup overhead costs using the same four-step approach described on page 266.

Step 1: Choose the Period to Use for the Budget. Lyco uses a period of 12 months (the year 2012).

Step 2: Select the Cost-Allocation Base to Use in Allocating Fixed Overhead Costs to Output Produced. Lyco uses budgeted setup-hours as the cost-allocation base for fixed setup overhead costs. Budgeted setup-hours in the static budget for 2012 are 7,200 hours.

Step 3: Identify the Fixed Overhead Costs Associated with the Cost-Allocation Base. Lyco's fixed setup overhead cost budget for 2012 is $216,000.

Step 4: Compute the Rate per Unit of the Cost-Allocation Base Used to Allocate Fixed Overhead Costs to Output Produced. Dividing the $216,000 from Step 3 by the 7,200 setup-hours from Step 2, Lyco estimates a fixed setup overhead cost rate of $30 per setup-hour:

$$\frac{\text{Budgeted fixed setup overhead cost per unit of cost-allocation base}}{} = \frac{\text{Budgeted total costs in fixed overhead cost pool}}{\text{Budgeted total quantity of cost-allocation base}} = \frac{\$216,000}{7,200 \text{ setup hours}}$$

$$= \$30 \text{ per setup-hour}$$

$$\frac{\text{Production-volume variance for fixed setup overhead costs}}{} = \frac{\text{Budgeted fixed setup overhead costs}}{} - \frac{\text{Fixed setup overhead allocation using budgeted input allowed for actual output units produced}}{}$$

$$= \$216,000 - (1,008 \text{ batches} \times 6 \text{ hours/batch}) \times \$30/\text{hour}$$

$$= \$216,000 - (6,048 \text{ hours} \times \$30/\text{hour})$$

$$= \$216,000 - \$181,440$$

$$= \$34,560 \text{ U}$$

During 2012, Lyco planned to produce 180,000 units of Elegance but actually produced 151,200 units. The unfavorable production-volume variance measures the amount of extra fixed setup costs that Lyco incurred for setup capacity it had but did not use. One interpretation is that the unfavorable $34,560 production-volume variance represents inefficient use of setup capacity. However, Lyco may have earned higher operating income by selling 151,200 units at a higher price than 180,000 units at a lower price. As a result, Lyco's managers should interpret the production-volume variance cautiously because it does not consider effects on selling prices and operating income.

Overhead Variances in Nonmanufacturing Settings

Our Webb Company example examines variable manufacturing overhead costs and fixed manufacturing overhead costs. Should the overhead costs of the nonmanufacturing areas of the company be examined using the variance analysis framework discussed in this chapter? Companies often use variable-cost information pertaining to nonmanufacturing, as well as manufacturing, costs in pricing and product mix decisions. Managers consider variance analysis of all variable overhead costs when making such decisions and when managing costs. For example, managers in industries in which distribution costs are high, such as automobiles, consumer durables, and cement and steel, may use standard costing to give reliable and timely information on variable distribution overhead spending variances and efficiency variances.

Consider service-sector companies such as airlines, hospitals, hotels, and railroads. The measures of output commonly used in these companies are passenger-miles flown,

Decision Point

How can variance analysis be used in an activity-based costing system?

Learning Objective 8

Examine the use of overhead variances in nonmanufacturing settings

. . . analyze nonmanufacturing variable overhead costs for decision making and cost management; fixed overhead variances are especially important in service settings

patient days provided, room-days occupied, and ton-miles of freight hauled, respectively. Few costs can be traced to these outputs in a cost-effective way. The majority of costs are fixed overhead costs, such as the costs of equipment, buildings, and staff. Using capacity effectively is the key to profitability, and fixed overhead variances can help managers in this task. Retail businesses, such as Kmart, also have high capacity-related fixed costs (lease and occupancy costs). In the case of Kmart, sales declines resulted in unused capacity and unfavorable fixed-cost variances. Kmart reduced fixed costs by closing some of its stores, but it also had to file for Chapter 11 bankruptcy in January 2002.

Consider the following data for the mainline operations of United Airlines for selected years from the past decade. Available seat miles (ASMs) are the actual seats in an airplane multiplied by the distance traveled.

Year	Total ASMs (Millions) (1)	Operating Revenue per ASM (2)	Operating Cost per ASM (3)	Operating Income per ASM (4) = (2) − (3)
2000	175,485	11.0 cents	10.6 cents	0.4 cents
2003	136,630	9.6 cents	10.5 cents	−0.9 cents
2006	143,095	11.5 cents	11.2 cents	0.3 cents
2008	135,861	12.6 cents	15.7 cents	−3.1 cents

After September 11, 2001, as air travel declined, United's revenues decreased but a majority of its costs comprising fixed costs of airport facilities, equipment, and personnel did not. United had a large unfavorable production-volume variance as its capacity was underutilized. As column 1 of the table indicates, United responded by reducing its capacity substantially over the next few years. Available seat miles declined from 175,485 million in 2000 to 136,630 million in 2003. Yet, United was unable to fill even the planes it had retained, so revenue per ASM declined (column 2) and cost per ASM stayed roughly the same (column 3). United filed for Chapter 11 bankruptcy in December 2002 and began seeking government guarantees to obtain the loans it needed. Subsequently, strong demand for airline travel, as well as yield improvements gained by more efficient use of resources and networks, led to increased traffic and higher average ticket prices. By maintaining a disciplined approach to capacity and tight control over growth, United saw close to a 20% increase in its revenue per ASM between 2003 and 2006. The improvement in performance allowed United to come out of bankruptcy on February 1, 2006. In the past year, however, the severe global recession and soaring jet fuel prices have had a significant negative impact on United's performance (and that of its competitor airlines), as reflected in the negative operating income for 2008.

Financial and Nonfinancial Performance Measures

The overhead variances discussed in this chapter are examples of financial performance measures. As the preceding examples illustrate, nonfinancial measures such as those related to capacity utilization and physical measures of input usage also provide useful information. Returning to the Webb example one final time, we can see that nonfinancial measures that managers of Webb would likely find helpful in planning and controlling its overhead costs include the following:

1. Quantity of actual indirect materials used per machine-hour, relative to quantity of budgeted indirect materials used per machine-hour

2. Actual energy used per machine-hour, relative to budgeted energy used per machine-hour

3. Actual machine-hours per jacket, relative to budgeted machine-hours per jacket

These performance measures, like the financial variances discussed in this chapter and Chapter 7, can be described as signals to direct managers' attention to problems. These nonfinancial performance measures probably would be reported daily or hourly on the production floor. The overhead variances we discussed in this chapter capture the financial effects of items such as the three factors listed, which in many cases first appear as nonfinancial performance measures. An especially interesting example along these lines comes from Japan, where some companies have introduced budgeted-to-actual variance analysis and internal trading systems among group units as a means to rein in their CO_2 emissions. The goal is to raise employee awareness of emissions reduction in preparation for the anticipated future costs of greenhouse-gas reduction plans being drawn up by the new Japanese government.

Finally, both financial and nonfinancial performance measures are used to evaluate the performance of managers. Exclusive reliance on either is always too simplistic because each gives a different perspective on performance. Nonfinancial measures (such as those described previously) provide feedback on individual aspects of a manager's performance, whereas financial measures evaluate the overall effect of and the tradeoffs among different nonfinancial performance measures. We provide further discussion of these issues in Chapters 13, 19, and 23.

Decision Point

How are overhead variances useful in nonmanufacturing settings?

Problem for Self-Study

Nina Garcia is the newly appointed president of Laser Products. She is examining the May 2012 results for the Aerospace Products Division. This division manufactures wing parts for satellites. Garcia's current concern is with manufacturing overhead costs at the Aerospace Products Division. Both variable and fixed overhead costs are allocated to the wing parts on the basis of laser-cutting-hours. The following budget information is available:

Budgeted variable overhead rate	$200 per hour
Budgeted fixed overhead rate	$240 per hour
Budgeted laser-cutting time per wing part	1.5 hours
Budgeted production and sales for May 2012	5,000 wing parts
Budgeted fixed overhead costs for May 2012	$1,800,000

Actual results for May 2012 are as follows:

Wing parts produced and sold	4,800 units
Laser-cutting-hours used	8,400 hours
Variable overhead costs	$1,478,400
Fixed overhead costs	$1,832,200

1. Compute the spending variance and the efficiency variance for variable overhead.
2. Compute the spending variance and the production-volume variance for fixed overhead.
3. Give two explanations for each of the variances calculated in requirements 1 and 2.

Required

Solution

1 and 2. See Exhibit 8-7.
3. a. Variable overhead spending variance, $201,600 F. One possible reason for this variance is that the actual prices of individual items included in variable overhead (such as cutting fluids) are lower than budgeted prices. A second possible reason is that the percentage increase in the actual quantity usage of individual items in the variable overhead cost pool is less than the percentage increase in laser-cutting-hours compared to the flexible budget.
   b. Variable overhead efficiency variance, $240,000 U. One possible reason for this variance is inadequate maintenance of laser machines, causing them to take more laser-cutting time per wing part. A second possible reason is use of undermotivated, inexperienced, or underskilled workers with the laser-cutting machines, resulting in more laser-cutting time per wing part.

Exhibit 8-7   Columnar Presentation of Integrated Variance Analysis: Laser Products for May 2012[a]

PANEL A: Variable (Manufacturing) Overhead

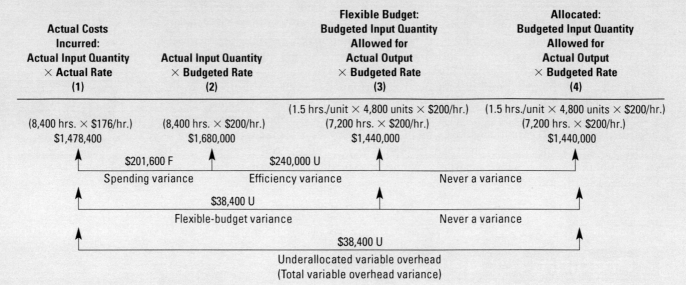

PANEL B: Fixed (Manufacturing) Overhead

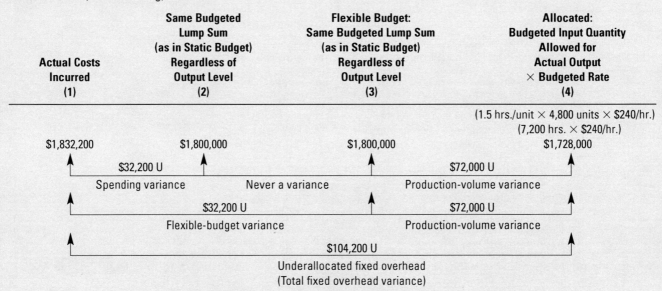

[a]F = favorable effect on operating income; U = unfavorable effect on operating income.

Source: Strategic finance by Paul Sherman. Copyright 2003 by INSTITUTE OF MANAGEMENT ACCOUNTANTS. Reproduced with permission of INSTITUTE OF MANAGEMENT ACCOUNTANTS in the format Other book via Copyright Clearance Center.

c. Fixed overhead spending variance, $32,200 U. One possible reason for this variance is that the actual prices of individual items in the fixed-cost pool unexpectedly increased from the prices budgeted (such as an unexpected increase in machine leasing costs). A second possible reason is misclassification of items as fixed that are in fact variable.

d. Production-volume variance, $72,000 U. Actual production of wing parts is 4,800 units, compared with 5,000 units budgeted. One possible reason for this variance is demand factors, such as a decline in an aerospace program that led to a decline in demand for aircraft parts. A second possible reason is supply factors, such as a production stoppage due to labor problems or machine breakdowns.

Decision Points

The following question-and-answer format summarizes the chapter's learning objectives. Each decision presents a key question related to a learning objective. The guidelines are the answer to that question.

Decision	Guidelines
1. How do managers plan variable overhead costs and fixed overhead costs?	Planning of both variable and fixed overhead costs involves undertaking only activities that add value and then being efficient in that undertaking. The key difference is that for variable-cost planning, ongoing decisions during the budget period play a much larger role; whereas for fixed-cost planning, most key decisions are made before the start of the period.
2. How are budgeted variable overhead and fixed overhead cost rates calculated?	The budgeted variable (fixed) overhead cost rate is calculated by dividing the budgeted variable (fixed) overhead costs by the denominator level of the cost-allocation base.
3. What variances can be calculated for variable overhead costs?	When the flexible budget for variable overhead is developed, an overhead efficiency variance and an overhead spending variance can be computed. The variable overhead efficiency variance focuses on the difference between the actual quantity of the cost-allocation base used relative to the budgeted quantity of the cost-allocation base. The variable overhead spending variance focuses on the difference between the actual variable overhead cost per unit of the cost-allocation base relative to the budgeted variable overhead cost per unit of the cost-allocation base.
4. What variances can be calculated for fixed overhead costs?	For fixed overhead, the static and flexible budgets coincide. The difference between the budgeted and actual amount of fixed overhead is the flexible-budget variance, also referred to as the spending variance. The production-volume variance measures the difference between budgeted fixed overhead and fixed overhead allocated on the basis of actual output produced.
5. What is the most detailed way for a company to reconcile actual overhead incurred with the amount allocated during a period?	A 4-variance analysis presents spending and efficiency variances for variable overhead costs and spending and production-volume variances for fixed overhead costs. By analyzing these four variances together, managers can reconcile the actual overhead costs with the amount of overhead allocated to output produced during a period.
6. What is the relationship between the sales-volume variance and the production-volume variance?	The production-volume variance is a component of the sales-volume variance. The production-volume and operating-income volume variances together comprise the sales-volume variance.
7. How can variance analysis be used in an activity-based costing system?	Flexible budgets in ABC systems give insight into why actual activity costs differ from budgeted activity costs. Using output and input measures for an activity, a 4-variance analysis can be conducted.
8. How are overhead variances useful in nonmanufacturing settings?	Managers consider variance analysis of all variable overhead costs, including those outside the manufacturing function, when making pricing and product mix decisions and when managing costs. Fixed overhead variances are especially important in service settings, where using capacity effectively is the key to profitability. In all cases, the information provided by variances can be supplemented by the use of suitable nonfinancial metrics.

Terms to Learn

The chapter and the Glossary at the end of the book contain definitions of the following important terms:

denominator level (**p. 266**)

denominator-level variance (**p. 272**)

fixed overhead flexible-budget
  variance (**p. 271**)

fixed overhead spending variance
  (**p. 271**)

operating-income volume variance
  (**p. 281**)

production-denominator level (**p. 266**)

production-volume variance (**p. 272**)

standard costing (**p. 264**)

total-overhead variance (**p. 278**)

variable overhead efficiency variance
  (**p. 267**)

variable overhead flexible-budget
  variance (**p. 267**)

variable overhead spending variance
  (**p. 269**)

Assignment Material

MyAccountingLab

Questions

8-1 How do managers plan for variable overhead costs?

8-2 How does the planning of fixed overhead costs differ from the planning of variable overhead costs?

8-3 How does standard costing differ from actual costing?

8-4 What are the steps in developing a budgeted variable overhead cost-allocation rate?

8-5 What are the factors that affect the spending variance for variable manufacturing overhead?

8-6 Assume variable manufacturing overhead is allocated using machine-hours. Give three possible reasons for a favorable variable overhead efficiency variance.

8-7 Describe the difference between a direct materials efficiency variance and a variable manufacturing overhead efficiency variance.

8-8 What are the steps in developing a budgeted fixed overhead rate?

8-9 Why is the flexible-budget variance the same amount as the spending variance for fixed manufacturing overhead?

8-10 Explain how the analysis of fixed manufacturing overhead costs differs for (a) planning and control and (b) inventory costing for financial reporting.

8-11 Provide one caveat that will affect whether a production-volume variance is a good measure of the economic cost of unused capacity.

8-12 "The production-volume variance should always be written off to Cost of Goods Sold." Do you agree? Explain.

8-13 What are the variances in a 4-variance analysis?

8-14 "Overhead variances should be viewed as interdependent rather than independent." Give an example.

8-15 Describe how flexible-budget variance analysis can be used in the control of costs of activity areas.

MyAccountingLab

Exercises

8-16 Variable manufacturing overhead, variance analysis. Esquire Clothing is a manufacturer of designer suits. The cost of each suit is the sum of three variable costs (direct material costs, direct manufacturing labor costs, and manufacturing overhead costs) and one fixed-cost category (manufacturing overhead costs). Variable manufacturing overhead cost is allocated to each suit on the basis of budgeted direct manufacturing labor-hours per suit. For June 2012 each suit is budgeted to take four labor-hours. Budgeted variable manufacturing overhead cost per labor-hour is $12. The budgeted number of suits to be manufactured in June 2012 is 1,040.

Actual variable manufacturing costs in June 2012 were $52,164 for 1,080 suits started and completed. There were no beginning or ending inventories of suits. Actual direct manufacturing labor-hours for June were 4,536.

Required
1. Compute the flexible-budget variance, the spending variance, and the efficiency variance for variable manufacturing overhead.
2. Comment on the results.

8-17 Fixed manufacturing overhead, variance analysis (continuation of 8-16). Esquire Clothing allocates fixed manufacturing overhead to each suit using budgeted direct manufacturing labor-hours per suit. Data pertaining to fixed manufacturing overhead costs for June 2012 are budgeted, $62,400, and actual, $63,916.

Required
1. Compute the spending variance for fixed manufacturing overhead. Comment on the results.
2. Compute the production-volume variance for June 2012. What inferences can Esquire Clothing draw from this variance?

8-18 **Variable manufacturing overhead variance analysis.** The French Bread Company bakes baguettes for distribution to upscale grocery stores. The company has two direct-cost categories: direct materials and direct manufacturing labor. Variable manufacturing overhead is allocated to products on the basis of standard direct manufacturing labor-hours. Following is some budget data for the French Bread Company:

Direct manufacturing labor use	0.02 hours per baguette
Variable manufacturing overhead	$10.00 per direct manufacturing labor-hour

The French Bread Company provides the following additional data for the year ended December 31, 2012:

Planned (budgeted) output	3,200,000 baguettes
Actual production	2,800,000 baguettes
Direct manufacturing labor	50,400 hours
Actual variable manufacturing overhead	$680,400

Required

1. What is the denominator level used for allocating variable manufacturing overhead? (That is, for how many direct manufacturing labor-hours is French Bread budgeting?)
2. Prepare a variance analysis of variable manufacturing overhead. Use Exhibit 8-4 (p. 277) for reference.
3. Discuss the variances you have calculated and give possible explanations for them.

8-19 **Fixed manufacturing overhead variance analysis (continuation of 8-18).** The French Bread Company also allocates fixed manufacturing overhead to products on the basis of standard direct manufacturing labor-hours. For 2012, fixed manufacturing overhead was budgeted at $4.00 per direct manufacturing labor-hour. Actual fixed manufacturing overhead incurred during the year was $272,000.

Required

1. Prepare a variance analysis of fixed manufacturing overhead cost. Use Exhibit 8-4 (p. 277) as a guide.
2. Is fixed overhead underallocated or overallocated? By what amount?
3. Comment on your results. Discuss the variances and explain what may be driving them.

8-20 **Manufacturing overhead, variance analysis.** The Solutions Corporation is a manufacturer of centrifuges. Fixed and variable manufacturing overheads are allocated to each centrifuge using budgeted assembly-hours. Budgeted assembly time is two hours per unit. The following table shows the budgeted amounts and actual results related to overhead for June 2012.

	Home	Insert	Page Layout	Formulas	Data	Review	View	
	A	B	C	D	E	F	G	
1			The Solutions Corporation (June 2012)			Actual Results	Static Budget	
2	Number of centrifuges assembled and sold					216	200	
3	Hours of assembly time					411		
4	Variable manufacturing overhead cost per hour of assembly time						$30.00	
5	Variable manufacturing overhead costs					$12,741		
6	Fixed manufacturing overhead costs					$20,550	$19,200	

Required

1. Prepare an analysis of all variable manufacturing overhead and fixed manufacturing overhead variances using the columnar approach in Exhibit 8-4 (p. 277).
2. Prepare journal entries for Solutions' June 2012 variable and fixed manufacturing overhead costs and variances; write off these variances to cost of goods sold for the quarter ending June 30, 2012.
3. How does the planning and control of variable manufacturing overhead costs differ from the planning and control of fixed manufacturing overhead costs?

8-21 **4-variance analysis, fill in the blanks.** Rozema, Inc., produces chemicals for large biotech companies. It has the following data for manufacturing overhead costs during August 2013:

	Variable	Fixed
Actual costs incurred	$31,000	$18,000
Costs allocated to products	33,000	14,600
Flexible budget	———	13,400
Actual input × budgeted rate	30,800	———

Use F for favorable and U for unfavorable:

	Variable	Fixed
(1) Spending variance	$____	$____
(2) Efficiency variance	____	____
(3) Production-volume variance	____	____
(4) Flexible-budget variance	____	____
(5) Underallocated (overallocated) manufacturing overhead	____	____

8-22 Straightforward 4-variance overhead analysis. The Lopez Company uses standard costing in its manufacturing plant for auto parts. The standard cost of a particular auto part, based on a denominator level of 4,000 output units per year, included 6 machine-hours of variable manufacturing overhead at $8 per hour and 6 machine-hours of fixed manufacturing overhead at $15 per hour. Actual output produced was 4,400 units. Variable manufacturing overhead incurred was $245,000. Fixed manufacturing overhead incurred was $373,000. Actual machine-hours were 28,400.

Required
1. Prepare an analysis of all variable manufacturing overhead and fixed manufacturing overhead variances, using the 4-variance analysis in Exhibit 8-4 (p. 277).
2. Prepare journal entries using the 4-variance analysis.
3. Describe how individual fixed manufacturing overhead items are controlled from day to day.
4. Discuss possible causes of the fixed manufacturing overhead variances.

8-23 Straightforward coverage of manufacturing overhead, standard-costing system. The Singapore division of a Canadian telecommunications company uses standard costing for its machine-paced production of telephone equipment. Data regarding production during June are as follows:

Variable manufacturing overhead costs incurred	$618,840
Variable manufacturing overhead cost rate	$8 per standard machine-hour
Fixed manufacturing overhead costs incurred	$145,790
Fixed manufacturing overhead costs budgeted	$144,000
Denominator level in machine-hours	72,000
Standard machine-hour allowed per unit of output	1.2
Units of output	65,500
Actual machine-hours used	76,400
Ending work-in-process inventory	0

Required
1. Prepare an analysis of all manufacturing overhead variances. Use the 4-variance analysis framework illustrated in Exhibit 8-4 (p. 277).
2. Prepare journal entries for manufacturing overhead costs and their variances.
3. Describe how individual variable manufacturing overhead items are controlled from day to day.
4. Discuss possible causes of the variable manufacturing overhead variances.

8-24 Overhead variances, service sector. Meals on Wheels (MOW) operates a meal home-delivery service. It has agreements with 20 restaurants to pick up and deliver meals to customers who phone or fax orders to MOW. MOW allocates variable and fixed overhead costs on the basis of delivery time. MOW's owner, Josh Carter, obtains the following information for May 2012 overhead costs:

	Actual Results	Static Budget
Meals on Wheels (May 2012)		
Output units (number of deliveries)	8,800	10,000
Hours per delivery		0.70
Hours of delivery time	5,720	
Variable overhead cost per hour of delivery time		$ 1.50
Variable overhead costs	$10,296	
Fixed overhead costs	$38,600	$35,000

1. Compute spending and efficiency variances for MOW's variable overhead in May 2012.
2. Compute the spending variance and production-volume variance for MOW's fixed overhead in May 2012.
3. Comment on MOW's overhead variances and suggest how Josh Carter might manage MOW's variable overhead differently from its fixed overhead costs.

Required

8-25 Total overhead, 3-variance analysis. Furniture, Inc., specializes in the production of futons. It uses standard costing and flexible budgets to account for the production of a new line of futons. For 2011, budgeted variable overhead at a level of 3,600 standard monthly direct labor-hours was $43,200; budgeted total overhead at 4,000 standard monthly direct labor-hours was $103,400. The standard cost allocated to each output included a total overhead rate of 120% of standard direct labor costs. For October, Furniture, Inc., incurred total overhead of $120,700 and direct labor costs of $128,512. The direct labor price variance was $512 unfavorable. The direct labor flexible-budget variance was $3,512 unfavorable. The standard labor price was $25 per hour. The production-volume variance was $34,600 favorable.

1. Compute the direct labor efficiency variance and the spending and efficiency variances for overhead. Also, compute the denominator level.
2. Describe how individual variable overhead items are controlled from day to day. Also, describe how individual fixed overhead items are controlled.

Required

8-26 Overhead variances, missing information. Dvent budgets 18,000 machine-hours for the production of computer chips in August 2011. The budgeted variable overhead rate is $6 per machine-hour. At the end of August, there is a $375 favorable spending variance for variable overhead and a $1,575 unfavorable spending variance for fixed overhead. For the computer chips produced, 14,850 machine-hours are budgeted and 15,000 machine-hours are actually used. Total actual overhead costs are $120,000.

1. Compute efficiency and flexible-budget variances for Dvent's variable overhead in August 2011. Will variable overhead be over- or underallocated? By how much?
2. Compute production-volume and flexible-budget variances for Dvent's fixed overhead in August 2011. Will fixed overhead be over- or underallocated? By how much?

Required

8-27 Identifying favorable and unfavorable variances. Purdue, Inc., manufactures tires for large auto companies. It uses standard costing and allocates variable and fixed manufacturing overhead based on machine-hours. For each independent scenario given, indicate whether each of the manufacturing variances will be favorable or unfavorable or, in case of insufficient information, indicate "CBD" (cannot be determined).

Scenario	Variable Overhead Spending Variance	Variable Overhead Efficiency Variance	Fixed Overhead Spending Variance	Fixed Overhead Production-Volume Variance
Production output is 4% less than budgeted, and actual fixed manufacturing overhead costs are 5% more than budgeted				
Production output is 12% less than budgeted; actual machine-hours are 7% more than budgeted				
Production output is 9% more than budgeted				
Actual machine-hours are 20% less than flexible-budget machine-hours				
Relative to the flexible budget, actual machine-hours are 12% less, and actual variable manufacturing overhead costs are 20% greater				

8-28 Flexible-budget variances, review of Chapters 7 and 8. David James is a cost accountant and business analyst for Doorknob Design Company (DDC), which manufactures expensive brass doorknobs. DDC uses two direct cost categories: direct materials and direct manufacturing labor. James feels that manufacturing overhead is most closely related to material usage. Therefore, DDC allocates manufacturing overhead to production based upon pounds of materials used.

At the beginning of 2012, DDC budgeted annual production of 400,000 doorknobs and adopted the following standards for each doorknob:

	Input	**Cost/Doorknob**
Direct materials (brass)	0.3 lb. @ $10/lb.	$ 3.00
Direct manufacturing labor	1.2 hours @ $20/hour	24.00
Manufacturing overhead:		
Variable	$6/lb. × 0.3 lb.	1.80
Fixed	$15/lb. × 0.3 lb.	4.50
Standard cost per doorknob		$33.30

Actual results for April 2012 were as follows:

Production	35,000 doorknobs
Direct materials purchased	12,000 lb. at $11/lb.
Direct materials used	10,450 lb.
Direct manufacturing labor	38,500 hours for $808,500
Variable manufacturing overhead	$64,150
Fixed manufacturing overhead	$152,000

Required

1. For the month of April, compute the following variances, indicating whether each is favorable (F) or unfavorable (U):
   a. Direct materials price variance (based on purchases)
   b. Direct materials efficiency variance
   c. Direct manufacturing labor price variance
   d. Direct manufacturing labor efficiency variance
   e. Variable manufacturing overhead spending variance
   f. Variable manufacturing overhead efficiency variance
   g. Production-volume variance
   h. Fixed manufacturing overhead spending variance
2. Can James use any of the variances to help explain any of the other variances? Give examples.

MyAccountingLab

Problems

8-29 Comprehensive variance analysis. Kitchen Whiz manufactures premium food processors. The following is some manufacturing overhead data for Kitchen Whiz for the year ended December 31, 2012:

Manufacturing Overhead	Actual Results	Flexible Budget	Allocated Amount
Variable	$ 76,608	$ 76,800	$ 76,800
Fixed	350,208	348,096	376,320

Budgeted number of output units: 888

Planned allocation rate: 2 machine-hours per unit

Actual number of machine-hours used: 1,824

Static-budget variable manufacturing overhead costs: $71,040

Required Compute the following quantities (you should be able to do so in the prescribed order):

1. Budgeted number of machine-hours planned
2. Budgeted fixed manufacturing overhead costs per machine-hour
3. Budgeted variable manufacturing overhead costs per machine-hour
4. Budgeted number of machine-hours allowed for actual output produced
5. Actual number of output units
6. Actual number of machine-hours used per output unit

8-30 Journal entries (continuation of 8-29).

Required

1. Prepare journal entries for variable and fixed manufacturing overhead (you will need to calculate the various variances to accomplish this).
2. Overhead variances are written off to the Cost of Goods Sold (COGS) account at the end of the fiscal year. Show how COGS is adjusted through journal entries.

8-31 Graphs and overhead variances. Best Around, Inc., is a manufacturer of vacuums and uses standard costing. Manufacturing overhead (both variable and fixed) is allocated to products on the basis of budgeted machine-hours. In 2012, budgeted fixed manufacturing overhead cost was $17,000,000. Budgeted variable manufacturing overhead was $10 per machine-hour. The denominator level was 1,000,000 machine-hours.

Required

1. Prepare a graph for fixed manufacturing overhead. The graph should display how Best Around, Inc.'s fixed manufacturing overhead costs will be depicted for the purposes of (a) planning and control and (b) inventory costing.
2. Suppose that 1,125,000 machine-hours were allowed for actual output produced in 2012, but 1,150,000 actual machine-hours were used. Actual manufacturing overhead was $12,075,000, variable, and $17,100,000, fixed. Compute (a) the variable manufacturing overhead spending and efficiency variances and (b) the fixed manufacturing overhead spending and production-volume variances. Use the columnar presentation illustrated in Exhibit 8-4 (p. 277).
3. What is the amount of the under- or overallocated variable manufacturing overhead and the under- or overallocated fixed manufacturing overhead? Why are the flexible-budget variance and the under- or overallocated overhead amount always the same for variable manufacturing overhead but rarely the same for fixed manufacturing overhead?
4. Suppose the denominator level was 1,360,000 rather than 1,000,000 machine-hours. What variances in requirement 2 would be affected? Recompute them.

8-32 4-variance analysis, find the unknowns. Consider the following two situations—cases A and B—independently. Data refer to operations for April 2012. For each situation, assume standard costing. Also assume the use of a flexible budget for control of variable and fixed manufacturing overhead based on machine-hours.

	Cases	
	A	B
(1) Fixed manufacturing overhead incurred	$ 84,920	$22,180
(2) Variable manufacturing overhead incurred	$120,000	—
(3) Denominator level in machine-hours	—	1,000
(4) Standard machine-hours allowed for actual output achieved	6,200	—
(5) Fixed manufacturing overhead (per standard machine-hour)	—	—
Flexible-Budget Data:		
(6) Variable manufacturing overhead (per standard machine-hour)	—	$ 42.00
(7) Budgeted fixed manufacturing overhead	$ 88,200	$20,000
(8) Budgeted variable manufacturing overhead[a]	—	—
(9) Total budgeted manufacturing overhead[a]	—	—
Additional Data:		
(10) Standard variable manufacturing overhead allocated	$124,000	—
(11) Standard fixed manufacturing overhead allocated	$ 86,800	—
(12) Production-volume variance	—	$ 4,000 F
(13) Variable manufacturing overhead spending variance	$ 4,600 F	$ 2,282 F
(14) Variable manufacturing overhead efficiency variance	—	$ 2,478 F
(15) Fixed manufacturing overhead spending variance	—	—
(16) Actual machine-hours used	—	—

[a]For standard machine-hours allowed for actual output produced.

Fill in the blanks under each case. [*Hint:* Prepare a worksheet similar to that in Exhibit 8-4 (p. 277). Fill in the knowns and then solve for the unknowns.]

Required

8-33 Flexible budgets, 4-variance analysis. (CMA, adapted) Nolton Products uses standard costing. It allocates manufacturing overhead (both variable and fixed) to products on the basis of standard direct manufacturing labor-hours (DLH). Nolton develops its manufacturing overhead rate from the current annual budget. The manufacturing overhead budget for 2012 is based on budgeted output of 720,000 units, requiring 3,600,000 DLH. The company is able to schedule production uniformly throughout the year.

A total of 66,000 output units requiring 315,000 DLH was produced during May 2012. Manufacturing overhead (MOH) costs incurred for May amounted to $375,000. The actual costs, compared with the annual budget and 1/12 of the annual budget, are as follows:

	Total Amount	Per Output Unit	Per DLH Input Unit	Monthly MOH Budget May 2012	Actual MOH Costs for May 2012
	Annual Manufacturing Overhead Budget 2012				
Variable MOH					
Indirect manufacturing labor	$ 900,000	$1.25	$0.25	$ 75,000	$ 75,000
Supplies	1,224,000	1.70	0.34	102,000	111,000
Fixed MOH					
Supervision	648,000	0.90	0.18	54,000	51,000
Utilities	540,000	0.75	0.15	45,000	54,000
Depreciation	1,008,000	1.40	0.28	84,000	84,000
Total	$4,320,000	$6.00	$1.20	$360,000	$375,000

Required Calculate the following amounts for Nolton Products for May 2012:

1. Total manufacturing overhead costs allocated
2. Variable manufacturing overhead spending variance
3. Fixed manufacturing overhead spending variance
4. Variable manufacturing overhead efficiency variance
5. Production-volume variance

Be sure to identify each variance as favorable (F) or unfavorable (U).

8-34 Direct Manufacturing Labor and Variable Manufacturing Overhead Variances. Sarah Beth's Art Supply Company produces various types of paints. Actual direct manufacturing labor hours in the factory that produces paint have been higher than budgeted hours for the last few months and the owner, Sarah B. Jones, is concerned about the effect this has had on the company's cost overruns. Because variable manufacturing overhead is allocated to units produced using direct manufacturing labor hours, Sarah feels that the mismanagement of labor will have a twofold effect on company profitability. Following are the relevant budgeted and actual results for the second quarter of 2011.

	Budget Information	Actual Results
Paint set production	25,000	29,000
Direct manuf. labor hours per paint set	2 hours	2.3 hours
Direct manufacturing labor rate	$10/hour	$10.40/hour
Variable manufacturing overhead rate	$20/hour	$18.95/hour

Required

1. Calculate the direct manufacturing labor price and efficiency variances and indicate whether each is favorable (F) or unfavorable (U).
2. Calculate the variable manufacturing overhead spending and efficiency variances and indicate whether each is favorable (F) or unfavorable (U).
3. For both direct manufacturing labor and variable manufacturing overhead, do the price/spending variances help Sarah explain the efficiency variances?
4. Is Sarah correct in her assertion that the mismanagement of labor has a twofold effect on cost overruns? Why might the variable manufacturing overhead efficiency variance not be an accurate representation of the effect of labor overruns on variable manufacturing overhead costs?

8-35 Activity-based costing, batch-level variance analysis. Pointe's Fleet Feet, Inc., produces dance shoes for stores all over the world. While the pairs of shoes are boxed individually, they are crated and shipped in batches. The shipping department records both variable direct batch-level costs and fixed batch-level overhead costs. The following information pertains to shipping department costs for 2011.

	Static-Budget Amounts	Actual Results
Pairs of shoes shipped	250,000	175,000
Average number of pairs of shoes per crate	10	8
Packing hours per crate	1.1 hours	0.9 hour
Variable direct cost per hour	$22	$24
Fixed overhead cost	$55,000	$52,500

Required

1. What is the static budget number of crates for 2011?
2. What is the flexible budget number of crates for 2011?
3. What is the actual number of crates shipped in 2011?
4. Assuming fixed overhead is allocated using crate-packing hours, what is the predetermined fixed overhead allocation rate?
5. For variable direct batch-level costs, compute the price and efficiency variances.
6. For fixed overhead costs, compute the spending and the production-volume variances.

8-36 Activity-based costing, batch-level variance analysis. Jo Nathan Publishing Company specializes in printing specialty textbooks for a small but profitable college market. Due to the high setup costs for each batch printed, Jo Nathan holds the book requests until demand for a book is approximately 500. At that point Jo Nathan will schedule the setup and production of the book. For rush orders, Jo Nathan will produce smaller batches for an additional charge of $400 per setup.

Budgeted and actual costs for the printing process for 2012 were as follows:

	Static-Budget Amounts	Actual Results
Number of books produced	300,000	324,000
Average number of books per setup	500	480
Hours to set up printers	8 hours	8.2 hours
Direct variable cost per setup-hour	$40	$39
Total fixed setup overhead costs	$105,600	$119,000

Required

1. What is the static budget number of setups for 2012?
2. What is the flexible budget number of setups for 2012?
3. What is the actual number of setups in 2012?
4. Assuming fixed setup overhead costs are allocated using setup-hours, what is the predetermined fixed setup overhead allocation rate?
5. Does Jo Nathan's charge of $400 cover the budgeted direct variable cost of an order? The budgeted total cost?
6. For direct variable setup costs, compute the price and efficiency variances.
7. For fixed setup overhead costs, compute the spending and the production-volume variances.
8. What qualitative factors should Jo Nathan consider before accepting or rejecting a special order?

8-37 Production-Volume Variance Analysis and Sales Volume Variance. Dawn Floral Creations, Inc., makes jewelry in the shape of flowers. Each piece is hand-made and takes an average of 1.5 hours to produce because of the intricate design and scrollwork. Dawn uses direct labor hours to allocate the overhead cost to production. Fixed overhead costs, including rent, depreciation, supervisory salaries, and other production expenses, are budgeted at $9,000 per month. These costs are incurred for a facility large enough to produce 1,000 pieces of jewelry a month.

During the month of February, Dawn produced 600 pieces of jewelry and actual fixed costs were $9,200.

Required

1. Calculate the fixed overhead spending variance and indicate whether it is favorable (F) or unfavorable (U).
2. If Dawn uses direct labor hours available at capacity to calculate the budgeted fixed overhead rate, what is the production-volume variance? Indicate whether it is favorable (F) or unfavorable (U).
3. An unfavorable production-volume variance is a measure of the under-allocation of fixed overhead cost caused by production levels at less than capacity. It therefore could be interpreted as the economic cost of unused capacity. Why would Dawn be willing to incur this cost? Your answer should separately consider the following two unrelated factors:
   a. Demand could vary from month to month while available capacity remains constant.
   b. Dawn would not want to produce at capacity unless it could sell all the units produced. What does Dawn need to do to raise demand and what effect would this have on profit?
4. Dawn's budgeted variable cost per unit is $25 and it expects to sell its jewelry for $55 apiece. Compute the sales-volume variance and reconcile it with the production-volume variance calculated in requirement 2. What does each concept measure?

8-38 Comprehensive review of Chapters 7 and 8, working backward from given variances. The Mancusco Company uses a flexible budget and standard costs to aid planning and control of its machining manufacturing operations. Its costing system for manufacturing has two direct-cost categories (direct materials and direct manufacturing labor—both variable) and two overhead-cost categories (variable manufacturing overhead and fixed manufacturing overhead, both allocated using direct manufacturing labor-hours).

At the 40,000 budgeted direct manufacturing labor-hour level for August, budgeted direct manufacturing labor is $800,000, budgeted variable manufacturing overhead is $480,000, and budgeted fixed manufacturing overhead is $640,000.

The following actual results are for August:

Direct materials price variance (based on purchases)	$176,000 F
Direct materials efficiency variance	69,000 U
Direct manufacturing labor costs incurred	522,750
Variable manufacturing overhead flexible-budget variance	10,350 U
Variable manufacturing overhead efficiency variance	18,000 U
Fixed manufacturing overhead incurred	597,460
Fixed manufacturing overhead spending variance	42,540 F

The standard cost per pound of direct materials is $11.50. The standard allowance is three pounds of direct materials for each unit of product. During August, 30,000 units of product were produced. There was no beginning inventory of direct materials. There was no beginning or ending work in process. In August, the direct materials price variance was $1.10 per pound.

In July, labor unrest caused a major slowdown in the pace of production, resulting in an unfavorable direct manufacturing labor efficiency variance of $45,000. There was no direct manufacturing labor price variance. Labor unrest persisted into August. Some workers quit. Their replacements had to be hired at higher wage rates, which had to be extended to all workers. The actual average wage rate in August exceeded the standard average wage rate by $0.50 per hour.

Required

1. Compute the following for August:
   a. Total pounds of direct materials purchased
   b. Total number of pounds of excess direct materials used
   c. Variable manufacturing overhead spending variance
   d. Total number of actual direct manufacturing labor-hours used
   e. Total number of standard direct manufacturing labor-hours allowed for the units produced
   f. Production-volume variance
2. Describe how Mancusco's control of variable manufacturing overhead items differs from its control of fixed manufacturing overhead items.

8-39 Review of Chapters 7 and 8, 3-variance analysis. (CPA, adapted) The Beal Manufacturing Company's costing system has two direct-cost categories: direct materials and direct manufacturing labor. Manufacturing overhead (both variable and fixed) is allocated to products on the basis of standard direct manufacturing labor-hours (DLH). At the beginning of 2012, Beal adopted the following standards for its manufacturing costs:

	Input	Cost per Output Unit
Direct materials	3 lb. at $5 per lb.	$ 15.00
Direct manufacturing labor	5 hrs. at $15 per hr.	75.00
Manufacturing overhead:		
Variable	$6 per DLH	30.00
Fixed	$8 per DLH	40.00
Standard manufacturing cost per output unit		$160.00

The denominator level for total manufacturing overhead per month in 2012 is 40,000 direct manufacturing labor-hours. Beal's flexible budget for January 2012 was based on this denominator level. The records for January indicated the following:

Direct materials purchased	25,000 lb. at $5.20 per lb.
Direct materials used	23,100 lb.
Direct manufacturing labor	40,100 hrs. at $14.60 per hr.
Total actual manufacturing overhead (variable and fixed)	$600,000
Actual production	7,800 output units

Required

1. Prepare a schedule of total standard manufacturing costs for the 7,800 output units in January 2012.
2. For the month of January 2012, compute the following variances, indicating whether each is favorable (F) or unfavorable (U):
   a. Direct materials price variance, based on purchases
   b. Direct materials efficiency variance
   c. Direct manufacturing labor price variance
   d. Direct manufacturing labor efficiency variance
   e. Total manufacturing overhead spending variance
   f. Variable manufacturing overhead efficiency variance
   g. Production-volume variance

8-40 Non-financial variances. Supreme Canine Products produces high quality dog food distributed only through veterinary offices. To ensure that the food is of the highest quality and has taste appeal, Supreme has a rigorous inspection process. For quality control purposes, Supreme has a standard based on the pounds of food inspected per hour and the number of pounds that pass or fail the inspection.

Supreme expects that for every 15,000 pounds of food produced, 1,500 pounds of food will be inspected. Inspection of 1,500 pounds of dog food should take 1 hour. Supreme also expects that 6% of the food inspected will fail the inspection. During the month of May, Supreme produced 3,000,000 pounds of food and inspected 277,500 pounds of food in 215 hours. Of the 277,500 pounds of food inspected, 15,650 pounds of food failed to pass the inspection.

Required

1. Compute two variances that help determine whether the time spent on inspections was more or less than expected. (Follow a format similar to the one used for the variable overhead spending and efficiency variances, but without prices.)
2. Compute two variances that can be used to evaluate the percentage of the food that fails the inspection.

8-41 Overhead variances and sales volume variance. Eco-Green Company manufactures cloth shopping bags that it plans to sell for $5 each. Budgeted production and sales for these bags for 2011 is 800,000 bags, with a standard of 400,000 machine hours for the whole year. Budgeted fixed overhead costs are $470,000, and variable overhead cost is $1.60 per machine hour.

Because of increased demand, actual production and sales of the bags for 2011 are 900,000 bags using 440,000 actual machine hours. Actual variable overhead costs are $699,600 and actual fixed overhead is $501,900. Actual selling price is $6 per bag.

Direct materials and direct labor actual costs were the same as standard costs, which were $1.20 per unit and $1.80 per unit, respectively.

Required

1. Calculate the variable overhead and fixed overhead variances (spending, efficiency, spending and volume).
2. Create a chart like that in Exhibit 7-2 showing Flexible Budget Variances and Sales Volume Variances for revenues, costs, contribution margin, and operating income.
3. Calculate the operating income based on budgeted profit per shopping bag.
4. Reconcile the budgeted operating income from requirement 3 to the actual operating income from your chart in requirement 2.
5. Calculate the operating income volume variance and show how the sales volume variance is comprised of the production volume variance and the operating income volume variance.

Collaborative Learning Problem

8-42 Overhead variances, ethics. Zeller Company uses standard costing. The company has two manufacturing plants, one in Nevada and the other in Ohio. For the Nevada plant, Zeller has budgeted annual output of 4,000,000 units. Standard labor hours per unit are 0.25, and the variable overhead rate for the Nevada plant is $3.25 per direct labor hour. Fixed overhead for the Nevada plant is budgeted at $2,500,000 for the year.

For the Ohio plant, Zeller has budgeted annual output of 4,200,000 units with standard labor hours also 0.25 per unit. However, the variable overhead rate for the Ohio plant is $3 per hour, and the budgeted fixed overhead for the year is only $2,310,000.

Firm management has always used variance analysis as a performance measure for the two plants, and has compared the results of the two plants.

Jack Jones has just been hired as a new controller for Zeller. Jack is good friends with the Ohio plant manager and wants him to get a favorable review. Jack suggests allocating the firm's budgeted common fixed costs of $3,150,000 to the two plants, but on the basis of one-third to the Ohio plant and two-thirds to the Nevada plant. His explanation for this allocation base is that Nevada is a more expensive state than Ohio.

At the end of the year, the Nevada plant reported the following actual results: output of 3,900,000 using 1,014,000 labor hours in total, at a cost of $3,244,800 in variable overhead and $2,520,000 in fixed overhead. Actual results for the Ohio plant are an output of 4,350,000 units using 1,218,000 labor hours with a variable cost of $3,775,800 and fixed overhead cost of $2,400,000. The actual common fixed costs for the year were $3,126,000.

Required

1. Compute the budgeted fixed cost per labor hour for the fixed overhead separately for each plant:
   a. Excluding allocated common fixed costs
   b. Including allocated common fixed costs
2. Compute the variable overhead spending variance and the variable overhead efficiency variance separately for each plant.
3. Compute the fixed overhead spending and volume variances for each plant:
   a. Excluding allocated common fixed costs
   b. Including allocated common fixed costs
4. Did Jack Jones's attempt to make the Ohio plant look better than the Nevada plant by allocating common fixed costs work? Why or why not?
5. Should common fixed costs be allocated in general when variances are used as performance measures? Why or why not?
6. What do you think of Jack Jones's behavior overall?

9

Inventory Costing and Capacity Analysis

9 Inventory Costing and Capacity Analysis

Few numbers capture the attention of managers and shareholders more than operating profits.

In industries that require significant upfront investments in capacity, the decisions made regarding the level of such fixed investments, and the extent to which the capacity is eventually utilized to meet customer demand, have a substantial impact on corporate profits. Unfortunately, the choice of compensation and reward systems, as well as the choice of inventory-costing methods, may induce managerial decisions that benefit short-term earnings at the expense of a firm's long-term health. It may take a substantial external shock, like a sharp economic slowdown, to motivate firms to make the right capacity and inventory choices, as the following article illustrates.

Lean Manufacturing Helps Companies Reduce Inventory and Survive the Recession[1]

Can changing the way a mattress is pieced together save a company during an economic downturn? For Sealy, the world's largest mattress manufacturer, the answer is a resounding "yes!"

Sealy is among thousands of manufacturers that have remained profitable during the recession by using lean manufacturing to become more cost-efficient. Lean manufacturing involves producing output in an uninterrupted flow, rather than as part of unfinished batches, and producing only what customers order. Driving this lean movement is an urgent need to pare inventory, which reduces inventory costs.

Before the adoption of lean practices, the company used to manufacture units at peak capacity. That is, it made as many mattresses as its resources allowed. Sealy employees were also paid based on the number of mattresses produced each day. While factories operated at peak capacity, inventory often piled up, which cost the company millions of dollars each year.

While Sealy launched its lean strategy in 2004, its efforts intensified during the recession. Old processes were reconfigured to be more efficient. As a result, each bed is now completed in 4 hours, down from 21. Median delivery times have been cut to 60 hours from 72, and plants have cut their raw-material inventories by 50%.

Additionally, the company now adheres to a precise production schedule that reflects orders from retailers such as Mattress Discounters

[1] *Source*: Paul Davidson. 2009. Lean manufacturing helps companies survive recession. *USA Today*, November 2; Sealy Corporation. 2009. Annual Report. Trinity, NC: Sealy Corporation, 2010. http://ccbn.10kwizard.com/xml/download.php?repo=tenk&ipage=6709696&format=PDF

and Macy's. While factories no longer run at full capacity, no mattress is made now until a customer orders it.

Sealy's manufacturing and inventory strategy has been key to its survival during the recession. While 2009 sales were 14% less than 2008 sales, earnings rose more than $16 million. Moreover, a large part of the earnings increase was due to reductions in inventory costs, which were lower by 12%, or nearly $8 million, in 2009.

Managers in industries with high fixed costs, like manufacturing, must manage capacity levels and make decisions about the use of available capacity. Managers must also decide on a production and inventory policy (as Sealy did). These decisions and the accounting choices managers make affect the operating incomes of manufacturing companies. This chapter focuses on two types of cost accounting choices:

1. *The inventory-costing choice* determines which manufacturing costs are treated as inventoriable costs. Recall from Chapter 2 (p. 37), *inventoriable costs* are all costs of a product that are regarded as assets when they are incurred and expensed as cost of goods sold when the product is sold. There are three types of inventory costing methods: absorption costing, variable costing, and throughput costing.
2. *The denominator-level capacity choice* focuses on the cost allocation base used to set budgeted fixed manufacturing cost rates. There are four possible choices of capacity levels: theoretical capacity, practical capacity, normal capacity utilization, and master-budget capacity utilization.

Variable and Absorption Costing

Learning Objective 1

Identify what distinguishes variable costing

. . . fixed manufacturing costs excluded from inventoriable costs

from absorption costing

. . . fixed manufacturing costs included in inventoriable costs

The two most common methods of costing inventories in manufacturing companies are *variable costing* and *absorption costing*. We describe each next and then discuss them in detail, using a hypothetical lens-manufacturing company as an example.

Variable Costing

Variable costing is a method of inventory costing in which all variable manufacturing costs (direct and indirect) are included as inventoriable costs. All fixed manufacturing costs are excluded from inventoriable costs and are instead treated as costs of the period in which they are incurred. Note that *variable costing* is a less-than-perfect term to describe this inventory-costing method, because only variable manufacturing costs are inventoried; variable nonmanufacturing costs are still treated as period costs and are expensed. Another common term used to describe this method is **direct costing**. This is also a misnomer because variable costing considers variable manufacturing overhead (an indirect cost) as inventoriable, while excluding direct marketing costs, for example.

Absorption Costing

Absorption costing is a method of inventory costing in which all variable manufacturing costs and all fixed manufacturing costs are included as inventoriable costs. That is, inventory "absorbs" all manufacturing costs. The job costing system you studied in Chapter 4 is an example of absorption costing.

Under both variable costing and absorption costing, all variable manufacturing costs are inventoriable costs and all nonmanufacturing costs in the value chain (such as research and development and marketing), whether variable or fixed, are period costs and are recorded as expenses when incurred.

Comparing Variable and Absoption Costing

The easiest way to understand the difference between variable costing and absorption costing is with an example. We will study Stassen Company, an optical consumer-products manufacturer, in this chapter. We focus in particular on its product line of high-end telescopes for aspiring astronomers.

Stassen uses standard costing:

- Direct costs are traced to products using standard prices and standard inputs allowed for actual outputs produced.

- Indirect (overhead) manufacturing costs are allocated using standard indirect rates times standard inputs allowed for actual outputs produced.

Stassen's management wants to prepare an income statement for 2012 (the fiscal year just ended) to evaluate the performance of the telescope product line. The operating information for the year is as follows:

	A	B
		Units
2	Beginning inventory	0
3	Production	8,000
4	Sales	6,000
5	Ending inventory	2,000

Actual price and cost data for 2012 are as follows:

	A	B
10	Selling price	$ 1,000
11	Variable manufacturing cost per unit	
12	Direct material cost per unit	$ 110
13	Direct manufacturing labor cost per unit	40
14	Manufacturing overhead cost per unit	50
15	Total variable manufacturing cost per unit	$ 200
16	Variable marketing cost per unit sold	$ 185
17	Fixed manufacturing costs (all indirect)	$1,080,000
18	Fixed marketing costs (all indirect)	$1,380,000

For simplicity and to focus on the main ideas, we assume the following about Stassen:

- Stassen incurs manufacturing and marketing costs only. The cost driver for all variable manufacturing costs is units produced; the cost driver for variable marketing costs is units sold. There are no batch-level costs and no product-sustaining costs.

- There are no price variances, efficiency variances, or spending variances. Therefore, the *budgeted* (standard) price and cost data for 2012 are the same as the *actual* price and cost data.

- Work-in-process inventory is zero.

- Stassen budgeted production of 8,000 units for 2012. This was used to calculate the budgeted fixed manufacturing cost per unit of $135 ($1,080,000/8,000 units).

- Stassen budgeted sales of 6,000 units for 2012, which is the same as the actual sales for 2012.

- The actual production for 2012 is 8,000 units. As a result, there is no production-volume variance for manufacturing costs in 2012. Later examples, based on data for 2013 and 2014, do include production-volume variances. However, even in those cases, the income statements contain no variances other than the production-volume variance.

- All variances are written off to cost of goods sold in the period (year) in which they occur.

Based on the preceding information, Stassen's inventoriable costs per unit produced in 2012 under the two inventory costing methods are as follows:

	Variable Costing		Absorption Costing	
Variable manufacturing cost per unit produced:				
Direct materials	$110		$110	
Direct manufacturing labor	40		40	
Manufacturing overhead	50	$200	50	$200
Fixed manufacturing cost per unit produced	—		135	
Total inventoriable cost per unit produced		$200		$335

To summarize, the main difference between variable costing and absorption costing is the accounting for fixed manufacturing costs:

- Under variable costing, fixed manufacturing costs are not inventoried; they are treated as an expense of the period.

- Under absorption costing, fixed manufacturing costs are inventoriable costs. In our example, the standard fixed manufacturing cost is $135 per unit ($1,080,000 ÷ 8,000 units) produced.

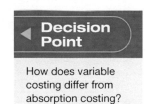

◄ Decision Point

How does variable costing differ from absorption costing?

Variable vs. Absorption Costing: Operating Income and Income Statements

When comparing variable and absorption costing, we must also take into account whether we are looking at short- or long-term numbers. How does the data for a one-year period differ from that of a three-year period under variable and absorption costing?

Comparing Income Statements for One Year

What will Stassen's operating income be if it uses variable costing or absorption costing? The differences between these methods are apparent in Exhibit 9-1. Panel A shows the variable costing income statement and Panel B the absorption-costing income statement for Stassen's telescope product line for 2012. The variable-costing income statement uses the contribution-margin format introduced in Chapter 3. The absorption-costing income statement uses the gross-margin format introduced in Chapter 2. Why these differences in format? The distinction between variable costs and fixed costs is central to variable

| Exhibit 9-1 | Comparison of Variable Costing and Absorption Costing for Stassen Company: Telescope Product-Line Income Statements for 2012 |

	Home	Insert	Page Layout	Formulas	Data	Review	View			
	A		B	C	D		E		F	G
1	Panel A: VARIABLE COSTING					Panel B: ABSORPTION COSTING				
2	Revenues: $1,000 × 6,000 units			$6,000,000		Revenues: $1,000 × 6,000 units				$6,000,000
3	Variable cost of goods sold:					Cost of goods sold:				
4	Beginning inventory		$ 0			Beginning inventory			$ 0	
5	Variable manufacturing costs: $200 × 8,000 units		1,600,000			Variable manufacturing costs: $200 × 8,000 unit			1,600,000	
6						Allocated fixed manufacturing costs: $135 × 8,000 units			1,080,000	
7	Cost of goods available for sale		1,600,000			Cost of goods available for sale			2,680,000	
8	Deduct ending inventory: $200 × 2,000 units		(400,000)			Deduct ending inventory: $335 × 2,000 units			(670,000)	
9	Variable cost of goods sold			1,200,000		Cost of goods sold				2,010,000
10	Variable marketing costs: $185 × 6,000 units sold			1,110,000						
11	Contribution margin			3,690,000		Gross Margin				3,990,000
12	Fixed manufacturing costs			1,080,000		Variable marketing costs: $185 × 6,000 units sold				1,110,000
13	Fixed marketing cost			1,380,000		Fixed marketing costs				1,380,000
14	Operating income			$1,230,000		Operating Income				$1,500,000
15										
16	Manufacturing costs expensed in Panel A:					Manufacturing costs expensed in Panel B:				
17	Variable cost of goods sold			$1,200,000						
18	Fixed manufacturing costs			1,080,000						
19	Total			$2,280,000		Cost of goods sold				$2,010,000

Learning Objective 2

Compute income under absorption costing

. . . using the gross-margin format

and variable costing,

. . . using the contribution-margin format

and explain the difference in income

. . . affected by the unit level of production and sales under absorption costing, but only the unit level of sales under variable costing

costing, and it is highlighted by the contribution-margin format. Similarly, the distinction between manufacturing and nonmanufacturing costs is central to absorption costing, and it is highlighted by the gross-margin format.

Absorption-costing income statements need not differentiate between variable and fixed costs. However, we will make this distinction between variable and fixed costs in the Stassen example to show how individual line items are classified differently under variable costing and absorption costing. In Exhibit 9-1, Panel B, note that inventoriable cost is $335 per unit under absorption costing: allocated fixed manufacturing costs of $135 per unit plus variable manufacturing costs of $200 per unit.

Notice how the fixed manufacturing costs of $1,080,000 are accounted for under variable costing and absorption costing in Exhibit 9-1. The income statement under variable costing deducts the $1,080,000 lump sum as an expense for 2012. In contrast, under absorption costing, the $1,080,000 ($135 per unit × 8,000 units) is initially treated as an inventoriable cost in 2012. Of this $1,080,000, $810,000 ($135 per unit × 6,000 units sold) subsequently becomes a part of cost of goods sold in 2012, and $270,000 ($135 per unit × 2,000 units) remains an asset—part of ending finished goods inventory on December 31, 2012.

Operating income is $270,000 higher under absorption costing compared with variable costing, because only $810,000 of fixed manufacturing costs are expensed under absorption costing, whereas all $1,080,000 of fixed manufacturing costs are expensed under variable costing. Note that the variable manufacturing cost of $200 per unit is accounted for the same way in both income statements in Exhibit 9-1.

These points can be summarized as follows:

	Variable Costing	Absorption Costing
Variable manufacturing costs: $200 per telescope produced	Inventoriable	Inventoriable
Fixed manufacturing costs: $1,080,000 per year	Deducted as an expense of the period	Inventoriable at $135 per telescope produced using budgeted denominator level of 8,000 units produced per year ($1,080,000 ÷ 8,000 units = $135 per unit)

The basis of the difference between variable costing and absorption costing is how fixed manufacturing costs are accounted for. If inventory levels change, operating income will differ between the two methods because of the difference in accounting for fixed manufacturing costs. To see this difference, let's compare telescope sales of 6,000; 7,000; and 8,000 units by Stassen in 2012, when 8,000 units were produced. Of the $1,080,000 total fixed manufacturing costs, the amount expensed in the 2012 income statement under each of these scenarios would be as follows:

		Home	Insert	Page Layout	Formulas	Data	Review	View	
	A	B	C		D	E	G	H	
1			**Variable Costing**				**Absorption Costing**		
2							**Fixed Manufacturing Costs**		
3	**Units**	**Ending**	**Fixed Manufacturing Costs**				**Included in Inventory**	**Amount Expensed**	
4	**Sold**	**Inventory**	**Included in Inventory**	**Amount Expensed**			**=$135 × Ending Inv.**	**=$135 × Units Sold**	
5	6,000	2,000	$0	$1,080,000			$270,000	$ 810,000	
6	7,000	1,000	$0	$1,080,000			$135,000	$ 945,000	
7	8,000	0	$0	$1,080,000			$ 0	$1,080,000	

In the last scenario, where 8,000 units are produced and sold, both variable and absorption costing report the same net income because inventory levels are unchanged. This chapter's appendix describes how the choice of variable costing or absorption costing affects the breakeven quantity of sales when inventory levels are allowed to vary.

Comparing Income Statements for Three Years

To get a more comprehensive view of the effects of variable costing and absorption costing, Stassen's management accountants prepare income statements for three years of operations, starting with 2012. In both 2013 and 2014, Stassen has a production-volume variance, because actual telescope production differs from the budgeted level of production of 8,000 units per year used to calculate budgeted fixed manufacturing cost per unit. The actual quantities sold for 2013 and 2014 are the same as the sales quantities budgeted for these respective years, which are given in units in the following table:

		Home	Insert	Page Layout	Formulas	Data
	E	F	G	H		
1		2012	2013	2014		
2	Budgeted production	8,000	8,000	8,000		
3	Beginning inventory	0	2,000	500		
4	Actual production	8,000	5,000	10,000		
5	Sales	6,000	6,500	7,500		
6	Ending inventory	2,000	500	3,000		

All other 2012 data given earlier for Stassen also apply for 2013 and 2014.

Exhibit 9-2 presents the income statement under variable costing in Panel A and the income statement under absorption costing in Panel B for 2012, 2013, and 2014. As you study Exhibit 9-2, note that the 2012 columns in both Panels A and B show the same figures as Exhibit 9-1. The 2013 and 2014 columns are similar to 2012 *except for the production-volume variance line item under absorption costing in Panel B.* Keep in mind the following points about absorption costing as you study Panel B of Exhibit 9-2:

1. The $135 fixed manufacturing cost rate is based on the budgeted denominator capacity level of 8,000 units in 2012, 2013, and 2014 ($1,080,000 ÷ 8,000 units = $135 per unit). Whenever production (the quantity produced, not the quantity sold) deviates from the denominator level, there will be a production-volume variance. The amount of Stassen's production-volume variance is determined by multiplying $135 per unit by the difference between the actual level of production and the denominator level.

| Exhibit 9-2 | Comparison of Variable Costing and Absorption Costing for Stassen Company: Telescope Product-Line Income Statements for 2012, 2013, and 2014 |

	A	B	C	D	E	F	G
		Home Insert Page Layout Formulas Data Review View					
1	Panel A: VARIABLE COSTING						
2			2012		2013		2014
3	Revenues: $1,000 × 6,000; 6,500; 7,500 units		$6,000,000		$6,500,000		$7,500,000
4	Variable cost of goods sold:						
5	Beginning inventory: $200 × 0; 2,000; 500 units	$ 0		$ 400,000		$ 100,000	
6	Variable manufacturing costs: $200 × 8,000; 5,000; 10,000 units	1,600,000		1,000,000		2,000,000	
7	Cost of goods available for sale	1,600,000		1,400,000		2,100,000	
8	Deduct ending inventory: $200 × 2,000; 500; 3,000 units	(400,000)		(100,000)		(600,000)	
9	Variable cost of goods sold		1,200,000		1,300,000		1,500,000
10	Variable marketing costs: $185 × 6,000; 6,500; 7,500 units		1,110,000		1,202,500		1,387,500
11	Contribution margin		3,690,000		3,997,500		4,612,500
12	Fixed manufacturing costs		1,080,000		1,080,000		1,080,000
13	Fixed marketing costs		1,380,000		1,380,000		1,380,000
14	Operating income		$1,230,000		$1,537,500		$2,152,500
15							
16	Panel B: ABSORPTION COSTING						
17			2012		2013		2014
18	Revenues: $1,000 × 6,000; 6,500; 7,500 units		$6,000,000		$6,500,000		$7,500,000
19	Cost of goods sold:						
20	Beginning inventory: $335 × 0; 2,000; 500 units	$ 0		$ 670,000		$ 167,500	
21	Variable manufacturing costs: $200 × 8,000; 5,000; 10,000 units	1,600,000		1,000,000		2,000,000	
22	Allocated fixed manufacturing costs: $135 × 8,000; 5,000; 10,000 units	1,080,000		675,000		1,350,000	
23	Cost of goods available for sale	2,680,000		2,345,000		3,517,500	
24	Deduct ending inventory: $335 × 2,000; 500; 3,000 units	(670,000)		(167,500)		(1,005,000)	
25	Adjustment for production-volume variance[a]	0		405,000 U		(270,000) F	
26	Cost of goods sold		2,010,000		2,582,500		2,242,500
27	Gross Margin		3,990,000		3,917,500		5,257,500
28	Variable marketing costs: $185 × 6,000; 6,500; 7,500 units		1,110,000		1,202,500		1,387,500
29	Fixed marketing costs		1,380,000		1,380,000		1,380,000
30	Operating Income		$1,500,000		$1,335,000		$2,490,000
31							
32	[a]Production-volume variance = Budgeted fixed manufacturing costs – Fixed manufacturing overhead allocated using budgeted cost per output unit allowed for actual output produced (Panel B, line 22)						
33	2012: $1,080,000 – ($135 × 8,000) = $1,080,000 – $1,080,000 = $0						
34	2013: $1,080,000 – ($135 × 5,000) = $1,080,000 – $675,000 = $405,000 U						
35	2014: $1,080,000 – ($135 × 10,000) = $1,080,000 – $1,350,000 = ($270,000) F						
36							
37	Production volume variance can also be calculated as follows:						
38	Fixed manufacturing cost per unit × (Denominator level – Actual output units produced)						
39	2012: $135 × (8,000 – 8,000) units = $135 × 0 = $0						
40	2013: $135 × (8,000 – 5,000) units = $135 × 3,000 = $405,000 U						
41	2014: $135 × (8,000 – 10,000) units = $135 × (2,000) = ($270,000) F						

In 2013, production was 5,000 units, 3,000 lower than the denominator level of 8,000 units. The result is an unfavorable production-volume variance of $405,000 ($135 per unit × 3,000 units). The year 2014 has a favorable production-volume variance of $270,000 ($135 per unit × 2,000 units), due to production of 10,000 units, which exceeds the denominator level of 8,000 units.

Recall how standard costing works under absorption costing. Each time a unit is manufactured, $135 of fixed manufacturing costs is included in the cost of goods manufactured and available for sale. In 2013, when 5,000 units are manufactured, $675,000 ($135 per unit × 5,000 units) of fixed manufacturing costs is included in the cost of goods available for sale (see Exhibit 9-2, Panel B, line 22). Total fixed manufacturing costs for 2013 are $1,080,000. The production-volume variance of $405,000 U equals the difference between $1,080,000 and $675,000. In Panel B, note how, for each year, the fixed manufacturing costs included in the cost of goods available for sale plus the production-volume variance always equals $1,080,000.

2. The production-volume variance, which relates only to fixed manufacturing overhead, exists under absorption costing but not under variable costing. Under variable costing, fixed manufacturing costs of $1,080,000 are always treated as an expense of the period, regardless of the level of production (and sales).

Here's a summary (using information from Exhibit 9-2) of the operating-income differences for Stassen Company during the 2012 to 2014 period:

	2012	2013	2014
1. Absorption-costing operating income	$1,500,000	$1,335,000	$2,490,000
2. Variable-costing operating income	$1,230,000	$1,537,500	$2,152,500
3. Difference: (1) – (2)	$ 270,000	$ (202,500)	$ 337,500

The sizeable differences in the preceding table illustrate why managers whose performance is measured by reported income are concerned about the choice between variable costing and absorption costing.

Why do variable costing and absorption costing usually report different operating income numbers? In general, if inventory increases during an accounting period, less operating income will be reported under variable costing than absorption costing. Conversely, if inventory decreases, more operating income will be reported under variable costing than absorption costing. The difference in reported operating income is due solely to (a) moving fixed manufacturing costs into inventories as inventories increase and (b) moving fixed manufacturing costs out of inventories as inventories decrease.

The difference between operating income under absorption costing and variable costing can be computed by formula 1, which focuses on fixed manufacturing costs in beginning inventory and ending inventory:

	A	B	C	D	E	F	G	H
1	Formula 1							
2						Fixed manufacturing		Fixed manufacturing
3		Absorption-costing	–	Variable-costing	=	costs in ending inventory	–	costs in beginning inventory
4		operating income		operation income		under absorption costing		under absorption costing
5	2012	$1,500,000	–	$1,230,000	=	($135 × 2,000 units)	–	($135 × 0 units)
6				$ 270,000	=	$270,000		
7								
8	2013	$1,335,000	–	$1,537,500	=	($135 × 500 units)	–	($135 × 2,000 units)
9				($ 202,500)	=	($202,500)		
10								
11	2014	$2,490,000	–	$2,152,500	=	($135 × 3,000 units)	–	($135 × 500 units)
12				$ 337,500	=	$337,500		

Fixed manufacturing costs in ending inventory are deferred to a future period under absorption costing. For example, $270,000 of fixed manufacturing overhead is deferred to 2013 at December 31, 2012. Under variable costing, all $1,080,000 of fixed manufacturing costs are treated as an expense of 2012.

Recall that,

$$\frac{\text{Beginning}}{\text{inventory}} + \frac{\text{Cost of goods}}{\text{manufactured}} = \frac{\text{Cost of goods}}{\text{sold}} + \frac{\text{Ending}}{\text{Inventory}}$$

Therefore, instead of focusing on fixed manufacturing costs in ending and beginning inventory (as in formula 1), we could alternatively look at fixed manufacturing costs in units produced and units sold. The latter approach (see formula 2) highlights how fixed manufacturing costs move between units produced and units sold during the fiscal year.

	Home	Insert		Page Layout		Formulas	Data	Review	View		
	A	B	C	D	E	F		G	H	
16	Formula 2									
17						Fixed manufacturing costs			Fixed manufacturing costs	
18		Absorption-costing	–	Variable-costing	=	inventoried in units produced	–		in cost of goods sold	
19		operating income		operation income		under absorption costing			under absorption costing	
20	2012	$1,500,000	–	$1,230,000	=	($135 × 8,000 units)	–		($135 × 6,000 units)	
21				$ 270,000	=	$270,000				
22										
23	2013	$1,335,000	–	$1,537,500	=	($135 × 5,000 units)	–		($135 × 6,500 units)	
24				($ 202,500)	=	($202,500)				
25										
26	2014	$2,490,000	–	$2,152,500	=	($135 × 10,000 units)	–		($135 × 7,500 units)	
27				$ 337,500	=	$337,500				

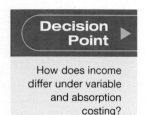

Decision Point ▶

How does income differ under variable and absorption costing?

Managers face increasing pressure to reduce inventory levels. Some companies are achieving steep reductions in inventory levels using policies such as just-in-time production—a production system under which products are manufactured only when needed. Formula 1 illustrates that, as Stassen reduces its inventory levels, operating income differences between absorption costing and variable costing become immaterial. Consider, for example, the formula for 2012. If instead of 2,000 units in ending inventory, Stassen had only 2 units in ending inventory, the difference between absorption-costing operating income and variable-costing operating income would drop from $270,000 to just $270.

Variable Costing and the Effect of Sales and Production on Operating Income

Given a constant contribution margin per unit and constant fixed costs, the period-to-period change in operating income under variable costing is *driven solely by changes in the quantity of units actually sold*. Consider the variable-costing operating income of Stassen in (a) 2013 versus 2012 and (b) 2014 versus 2013. Recall the following:

$$\frac{\text{Contribution}}{\text{margin per unit}} = \text{Selling price} - \frac{\text{Variable manufacturing}}{\text{cost per unit}} - \frac{\text{Variable marketing}}{\text{cost per unit}}$$

$$= \$1,000 \text{ per unit} - \$200 \text{ per unit} - \$185 \text{ per unit}$$

$$= \$615 \text{ per unit}$$

$$\frac{\text{Change in}}{\text{variable-costing}} = \frac{\text{Contribution}}{\text{margin}} \times \frac{\text{Change in quantity}}{\text{of units sold}}$$
$$\text{operating income} \quad \text{per unit}$$

(a) 2013 vs. 2012: $1,537,500 − $1,230,000 = $615 per unit × (6,500 unit − 6,000 units)

$307,500 = $307,500

(b) 2014 vs. 2013: $2,152,500 − $1,537,500 = $615 per unit × (7,500 units − 6,500 units)

$615,000 = $615,000

Under variable costing, Stassen managers cannot increase operating income by "producing for inventory." Why not? Because, as you can see from the preceding computations, when using variable costing, only the quantity of units sold drives operating income. We'll explain later in this chapter that absorption costing enables managers to increase operating income by increasing the unit level of sales, as well as by producing more units. Before you proceed to the next section, make sure that you examine Exhibit 9-3 for a detailed comparison of the differences between variable costing and absorption costing.

| Exhibit 9-3 | Comparative Income Effects of Variable Costing and Absorption Costing |

Question	Variable Costing	Absorption Costing	Comment
Are fixed manufacturing costs inventoried?	No	Yes	Basic theoretical question of when these costs should be expensed
Is there a production-volume variance?	No	Yes	Choice of denominator level affects measurement of operating income under absorption costing only
Are classifications between variable and fixed costs routinely made?	Yes	Infrequently	Absorption costing can be easily modified to obtain subclassifications for variable and fixed costs, if desired (for example, see Exhibit 9-1, Panel B)
How do changes in unit inventory levels affect operating income?[a]			Differences are attributable to the timing of when fixed manufacturing costs are expensed
Production = sales	Equal	Equal	
Production > sales	Lower[b]	Higher[c]	
Production < sales	Higher	Lower	
What are the effects on cost-volume-profit relationship (for a given level of fixed costs and a given contribution margin per unit)?	Driven by unit level of sales	Driven by (a) unit level of sales, (b) unit level of production, and (c) chosen denominator level	Management control benefit: Effects of changes in production level on operating income are easier to understand under variable costing

[a]Assuming that all manufacturing variances are written off as period costs, that no change occurs in work-in-process inventory, and no change occurs in the budgeted fixed manufacturing cost rate between accounting periods.

[b]That is, lower operating income than under absorption costing.

[c]That is, higher operating income than under variable costing.

Absorption Costing and Performance Measurement

Absorption costing is the required inventory method for external reporting in most countries. Many companies use absorption costing for internal accounting as well. Why? Because it is cost-effective and less confusing to managers to use one common method of inventory costing for both external and internal reporting and performance evaluation. A common method of inventory costing can also help prevent managers from taking actions that make their performance measure look good but that hurt the income they report to shareholders. Another advantage of absorption costing is that it measures the cost of all manufacturing resources, whether variable or fixed, necessary to produce inventory. Many companies use inventory costing information for long-run decisions, such as pricing and choosing a product mix. For these long-run decisions, inventory costs should include both variable *and* fixed costs.

One problem with absorption costing is that it enables a manager to increase operating income in a specific period by increasing production—even if there is no customer demand for the additional production! By producing more ending inventory, the firm's margins and income can be made higher. Stassen's managers may be tempted to do this to get higher bonuses based on absorption-costing operating income. Generally, higher operating income also has a positive effect on stock price, which increases managers' stock-based compensation.

To reduce the undesirable incentives to build up inventories that absorption costing can create, a number of companies use variable costing for internal reporting. Variable costing focuses attention on distinguishing variable manufacturing costs from fixed manufacturing costs. This distinction is important for short-run decision making (as in cost-volume-profit analysis in Chapter 3 and in planning and control in Chapters 6, 7, and 8).

Learning Objective 3

Understand how absorption costing can provide undesirable incentives for managers to build up inventory

. . . producing more units for inventory absorbs fixed manufacturing costs and increases operating income

Companies that use both methods for internal reporting—variable costing for short-run decisions and performance evaluation and absorption costing for long-run decisions—benefit from the different advantages of both. In the next section, we explore in more detail the challenges that arise from absorption costing.

Undesirable Buildup of Inventories

Recall that one motivation for an undesirable buildup of inventories could be because a manager's bonus is based on reported absorption-costing operating income. Assume that Stassen's managers have such a bonus plan. Exhibit 9-4 shows how Stassen's absorption costing operating income for 2013 changes as the production level changes. This exhibit assumes that the production-volume variance is written off to cost of goods sold at the end of each year. Beginning inventory of 2,000 units and sales of 6,500 units for 2013 are unchanged from the case shown in Exhibit 9-2. *As you review Exhibit 9-4, keep in mind that the computations are basically the same as those in Exhibit 9-2.*

Exhibit 9-4 shows that production of 4,500 units meets the 2013 sales budget of 6,500 units (2,000 units from beginning inventory + 4,500 units produced). Operating income at this production level is $1,267,500. By producing more than 4,500 units, commonly referred to as *producing for inventory*, Stassen increases absorption-costing operating income. Each additional unit in 2013 ending inventory will increase operating income by $135. For example, if 9,000 units are produced (the last column in Exhibit 9-4), ending inventory will be 4,500 units and operating income increases to $1,875,000. This amount is $607,500 more than the operating income with zero ending inventory ($1,875,000 − $1,267,500, or 4,500 units × $135 per unit = $607,500). Under absorption costing, the company, by producing 4,500 units for inventory, includes $607,500 of fixed manufacturing costs in finished goods inventory, so those costs are not expensed in 2013.

Can top management implement checks and balances that limit managers from producing for inventory under absorption costing? While the answer is yes, as we will see in

---

Exhibit 9-4 Effect on Absorption-Costing Operating Income of Different Production Levels for Stassen Company: Telescope Product-Line Income Statement for 2013 at Sales of 6,500 Units

	A	B	C	D	E	F	G	H	I	J	K
		Home Insert Page Layout Formulas Data Review View									
1	**Unit Data**										
2	Beginning inventory	2,000		2,000		2,000		2,000		2,000	
3	Production	4,500		5,000		6,500		8,000		9,000	
4	Goods available for sale	6,500		7,000		8,500		10,000		11,000	
5	Sales	6,500		6,500		6,500		6,500		6,500	
6	Ending inventory	0		500		2,000		3,500		4,500	
7											
8	**Income Statement**										
9	Revenues	$6,500,000		$6,500,000		$6,500,000		$6,500,000		$6,500,000	
10	Cost of goods sold:										
11	Beginning inventory ($335 × 2,000)	670,000		670,000		670,000		670,000		670,000	
12	Variable manufacturing costs: $200 × production	900,000		1,000,000		1,300,000		1,600,000		1,800,000	
13	Allocated fixed manufacturing costs: $135 × production	607,500		675,000		877,500		1,080,000		1,215,000	
14	Cost of goods available for sale	2,177,500		2,345,000		2,847,500		3,350,000		3,685,000	
15	Deduct ending inventory: $335 × ending inventory	0		(167,500)		(670,000)		(1,172,500)		(1,507,500)	
16	Adjustment for production-volume variance[a]	472,500	U	405,000	U	202,500	U	0		(135,000)	F
17	Cost of goods sold	2,650,000		2,582,500		2,380,000		2,177,500		2,042,500	
18	Gross Margin	3,850,000		3,917,500		4,120,000		4,322,500		4,457,500	
19	Marketing costs: ($1,380,000 + $185 per unit × 6,500 units sold)	2,582,500		2,582,500		2,582,500		2,582,500		2,582,500	
20	Operating Income	$1,267,500		$1,335,000		$1,537,500		$1,740,000		$1,875,000	
21											
22	[a]Production-volume variance = Budgeted fixed manufacturing costs − Allocated fixed manufacturing costs (Income Statement, line 13)										
23	At production of 4,500 units: $1,080,000 − $607,500 = $472,500 U										
24	At production of 5,000 units: $1,080,000 − $675,000 = $405,000 U										
25	At production of 6,500 units: $1,080,000 − $877,500 = $202,500 U										
26	At production of 8,000 units: $1,080,000 − $1,080,000 = $0										
27	At production of 9,000 units: $1,080,000 − $1,215,000 = ($135,000) F										

the next section, producing for inventory cannot completely be prevented. There are many subtle ways a manager can produce for inventory that, if done to a limited extent, may not be easy to detect. For example, consider the following:

- A plant manager may switch to manufacturing products that absorb the highest amount of fixed manufacturing costs, regardless of the customer demand for these products (called "cherry picking" the production line). Production of items that absorb the least or lower fixed manufacturing costs may be delayed, resulting in failure to meet promised customer delivery dates (which, over time, can result in unhappy customers).

- A plant manager may accept a particular order to increase production, even though another plant in the same company is better suited to handle that order.

- To increase production, a manager may defer maintenance beyond the current period. Although operating income in this period may increase as a result, future operating income could decrease by a larger amount if repair costs increase and equipment becomes less efficient.

The example in Exhibit 9-4 focuses on only one year (2013). A Stassen manager who built up ending inventories of telescopes to 4,500 units in 2013 would have to further increase ending inventories in 2014 to increase that year's operating income by producing for inventory. There are limits to how much inventory levels can be increased over time (because of physical constraints on storage space and management supervision and controls). Such limits reduce the likelihood of incurring some of absorption costing's undesirable effects.

Proposals for Revising Performance Evaluation

Top management, with help from the controller and management accountants, can take several steps to reduce the undesirable effects of absorption costing.

- Focus on careful budgeting and inventory planning to reduce management's freedom to build up excess inventory. For example, the budgeted monthly balance sheets have estimates of the dollar amount of inventories. If actual inventories exceed these dollar amounts, top management can investigate the inventory buildups.

- Incorporate a carrying charge for inventory in the internal accounting system. For example, the company could assess an inventory carrying charge of 1% per month on the investment tied up in inventory and for spoilage and obsolescence when it evaluates a manager's performance. An increasing number of companies are beginning to adopt this inventory carrying charge.

- Change the period used to evaluate performance. Critics of absorption costing give examples in which managers take actions that maximize quarterly or annual income at the potential expense of long-run income. When their performance is evaluated over a three- to five-year period, managers will be less tempted to produce for inventory.

- Include nonfinancial as well as financial variables in the measures used to evaluate performance. Examples of nonfinancial measures that can be used to monitor the performance of Stassen's managers in 2014 (see data on p. 305) are as follows:

$$\textbf{(a)} \ \frac{\text{Ending inventory in units in 2014}}{\text{Beginning inventory in units in 2014}} = \frac{3,000}{500} = 6$$

$$\textbf{(b)} \ \frac{\text{Units produced in 2014}}{\text{Units sold in 2014}} = \frac{10,000}{7,500} = 1.33$$

Decision Point

Why might managers build up finished goods inventory if they use absorption costing?

Top management would want to see production equal to sales and relatively stable levels of inventory. Companies that manufacture or sell several products could report these two measures for each of the products they manufacture and sell.

Comparing Inventory Costing Methods

Before we begin our discussion of capacity, we will look at *throughput costing*, a variation of variable costing, and compare the various costing methods.

Throughput Costing

Some managers maintain that even variable costing promotes an excessive amount of costs being inventoried. They argue that only direct materials are "truly variable" in output. **Throughput costing**, which also is called **super-variable costing**, is an extreme form of variable costing in which only direct material costs are included as inventoriable costs. All other costs are costs of the period in which they are incurred. In particular, variable direct manufacturing labor costs and variable manufacturing overhead costs are regarded as period costs and are deducted as expenses of the period.

Exhibit 9-5 is the throughput-costing income statement for Stassen Company for 2012, 2013, and 2014. *Throughput margin* equals revenues minus all direct material cost of the goods sold. Compare the operating income amounts reported in Exhibit 9-5 with those for absorption costing and variable costing:

	2012	2013	2014
Absorption-costing operating income	$1,500,000	$1,335,000	$2,490,000
Variable-costing operating income	$1,230,000	$1,537,500	$2,152,500
Throughput-costing operating income	$1,050,000	$1,672,500	$1,927,500

Only the $110 direct material cost per unit is inventoriable under throughput costing, compared with $335 per unit for absorption costing and $200 per unit for variable costing. When the production quantity exceeds sales as in 2012 and 2014, throughput costing results in the largest amount of expenses in the current period's income statement. Advocates of throughput costing say it provides less incentive to produce for inventory than either variable costing or, especially, absorption costing. Throughput costing is a more recent phenomenon in comparison with variable costing and absorption costing and has avid supporters, but so far it has not been widely adopted.[2]

	Home Insert Page Layout Formulas Data Review View			
	A	B	C	D
1		**2012**	**2013**	**2014**
2	Revenues: $1,000 × 6,000; 6,500; 7,500 units	$6,000,000	$6,500,000	$7,500,000
3	Direct material cost of goods sold			
4	Beginning inventory: $110 × 0; 2,000; 500 units	0	220,000	55,000
5	Direct materials: $110 × 8,000; 5,000; 10,000 units	880,000	550,000	1,100,000
6	Cost of goods available for sale	880,000	770,000	1,155,000
7	Deduct ending inventory: $110 × 2,000; 500; 3,000 units	(220,000)	(55,000)	(330,000)
8	Direct material cost of goods sold	660,000	715,000	825,000
9	Throughput margin[a]	5,340,000	5,785,000	6,675,000
10	Manufacturing costs (other than direct materials)[b]	1,800,000	1,530,000	1,980,000
11	Marketing costs[c]	2,490,000	2,582,500	2,767,500
12	Operating income	$1,050,000	$1,672,500	$1,927,500
13				
14	[a]Throughput margin equals revenues minus all direct material cost of goods sold			
15	[b]Fixed manuf. costs + [(variable manuf. labor cost per unit + variable manuf. overhead cost per unit)			
16	× units produced]; $1,080,000 + [($40 + $50) × 8,000; 5,000; 10,000 units]			
17	[c]Fixed marketing costs + (variable marketing cost per unit × units sold);			
18	$1,380,000 + ($185 × 6,000; 6,500; 7,500 units)			

[2] See E. Goldratt, *The Theory of Constraints* (New York: North River Press, 1990); E. Noreen, D. Smith, and J. Mackey, *The Theory of Constraints and Its Implications for Management Accounting* (New York: North River Press, 1995).

A Comparison of Alternative Inventory-Costing Methods

Variable costing and absorption costing (as well as throughput costing) may be combined with actual, normal, or standard costing. Exhibit 9-6 compares product costing under six alternative inventory-costing systems.

Variable Costing	Absorption Costing
Actual costing	Actual costing
Standard costing	Standard costing
Normal costing	Normal costing

Variable costing has been controversial among accountants, not because of disagreement about the need to delineate between variable and fixed costs for internal planning and control, but as it pertains to *external reporting*. Accountants who favor variable costing for external reporting maintain that the fixed portion of manufacturing costs is more closely related to the capacity to produce than to the actual production of specific units. Hence, fixed costs should be expensed, not inventoried.

Accountants who support absorption costing for *external reporting* maintain that inventories should carry a fixed-manufacturing-cost component. Why? Because both variable manufacturing costs and fixed manufacturing costs are necessary to produce goods. Therefore, both types of costs should be inventoried in order to match all manufacturing costs to revenues, regardless of their different behavior patterns. For external reporting to shareholders, companies around the globe tend to follow the generally accepted accounting principle that all manufacturing costs are inventoriable.

Similarly, for tax reporting in the United States, direct production costs, as well as fixed and variable indirect production costs, must be taken into account in the computation of inventoriable costs in accordance with the "full absorption" method of inventory costing. Indirect production costs include items such as rent, utilities, maintenance, repair expenses, indirect materials, and indirect labor. For other indirect cost categories (including depreciation, insurance, taxes, officers' salaries, factory administrative expenses, and strike-related costs), the portion of the cost that is "incident to and necessary for production or manufacturing operations or processes" is inventoriable for tax

Exhibit 9-6   Comparison of Alternative Inventory-Costing Systems

			Actual Costing	Normal Costing	Standard Costing
Absorption Costing	**Variable Costing**	**Variable Direct Manufacturing Cost**	Actual prices × Actual quantity of inputs used	Actual prices × Actual quantity of inputs used	Standard prices × Standard quantity of inputs allowed for actual output achieved
		Variable Manufacturing Overhead Costs	Actual variable overhead rates × Actual quantity of cost-allocation bases used	Budgeted variable overhead rates × Actual quantity of cost-allocation bases used	Standard variable overhead rates × Standard quantity of cost-allocation bases allowed for actual output achieved
		Fixed Direct Manufacturing Costs	Actual prices × Actual quantity of inputs used	Actual prices × Actual quantity of inputs used	Standard prices × Standard quantity of inputs allowed for actual output achieved
		Fixed Manufacturing Overhead Costs	Actual fixed overhead rates × Actual quantity of cost-allocation bases used	Budgeted fixed overhead rates × Actual quantity of cost-allocation bases used	Standard fixed overhead rates × Standard quantity of cost-allocation bases allowed for actual output achieved

purposes if (and only if) it is treated as inventoriable for the purposes of financial reporting. Accordingly, costs must often be allocated between those portions related to manufacturing activities and those not related to manufacturing.[3]

Denominator-Level Capacity Concepts and Fixed-Cost Capacity Analysis

We have seen that the difference between variable and absorption costing methods arises solely from the treatment of fixed manufacturing costs. Spending on fixed manufacturing costs enables firms to obtain the scale or capacity needed to satisfy the expected demand from customers. Determining the "right" amount of spending, or the appropriate level of capacity, is one of the most strategic and most difficult decisions managers face. Having too much capacity to produce relative to that needed to meet market demand means incurring some costs of unused capacity. Having too little capacity to produce means that demand from some customers may be unfilled. These customers may go to other sources of supply and never return. Therefore, both managers and accountants should have a clear understanding of the issues that arise with capacity costs.

We start by analyzing a key question in absorption costing: Given a level of spending on fixed manufacturing costs, what capacity level should be used to compute the fixed manufacturing cost per unit produced? We then study the broader question of how a firm should decide on its level of capacity investment.

Absorption Costing and Alternative Denominator-Level Capacity Concepts

Earlier chapters, especially Chapters 4, 5, and 8, have highlighted how normal costing and standard costing report costs in an ongoing timely manner throughout a fiscal year. The choice of the capacity level used to allocate budgeted fixed manufacturing costs to products can greatly affect the operating income reported under normal costing or standard costing and the product-cost information available to managers.

Consider the Stassen Company example again. Recall that the annual fixed manufacturing costs of the production facility are $1,080,000. Stassen currently uses absorption costing with standard costs for external reporting purposes, and it calculates its budgeted fixed manufacturing rate on a per unit basis. We will now examine four different capacity levels used as the denominator to compute the budgeted fixed manufacturing cost rate: theoretical capacity, practical capacity, normal capacity utilization, and master-budget capacity utilization.

Theoretical Capacity and Practical Capacity

In business and accounting, capacity ordinarily means a "constraint," an "upper limit." **Theoretical capacity** is the level of capacity based on producing at full efficiency all the time. Stassen can produce 25 units per shift when the production lines are operating at maximum speed. If we assume 360 days per year, the theoretical annual capacity for 2 shifts per day is as follows:

$$25 \text{ units per shift} \times 2 \text{ shifts per day} \times 360 \text{ days} = 18,000 \text{ units}$$

Theoretical capacity is theoretical in the sense that it does not allow for any plant maintenance, shutdown periods, interruptions because of downtime on the assembly lines, or any other factors. Theoretical capacity represents an ideal goal of capacity utilization. Theoretical capacity levels are unattainable in the real world but they provide a target to which a company can aspire.

---

[3] Details regarding tax rules can be found in Section 1.471-11 of the U.S. Internal Revenue Code: Inventories of Manufacturers (see http://ecfr.gpoaccess.gov). Recall from Chapter 2 that costs not related to production, such as marketing, distribution, or research expenses, are treated as period expenses for financial reporting. Under U.S. tax rules, a firm can still consider these costs as inventoriable for tax purposes provided that it does so consistently.

Practical capacity is the level of capacity that reduces theoretical capacity by considering unavoidable operating interruptions, such as scheduled maintenance time, shutdowns for holidays, and so on. Assume that practical capacity is the practical production rate of 20 units per shift (as opposed to 25 units per shift under theoretical capacity) for 2 shifts per day for 300 days a year (as distinguished from 360 days a year under theoretical capacity). The practical annual capacity is as follows:

20 units per shift × 2 shifts per day × 300 days = 12,000 units

Engineering and human resource factors are both important when estimating theoretical or practical capacity. Engineers at the Stassen facility can provide input on the technical capabilities of machines for cutting and polishing lenses. Human-safety factors, such as increased injury risk when the line operates at faster speeds, are also necessary considerations in estimating practical capacity. With difficulty, practical capacity is attainable.

Normal Capacity Utilization and Master-Budget Capacity Utilization

Both theoretical capacity and practical capacity measure capacity levels in terms of what a plant can *supply*—available capacity. In contrast, normal capacity utilization and master-budget capacity utilization measure capacity levels in terms of *demand* for the output of the plant, that is, the amount of available capacity the plant expects to use based on the demand for its products. In many cases, budgeted demand is well below production capacity available.

Normal capacity utilization is the level of capacity utilization that satisfies average customer demand over a period (say, two to three years) that includes seasonal, cyclical, and trend factors. **Master-budget capacity utilization** is the level of capacity utilization that managers expect for the current budget period, which is typically one year. These two capacity-utilization levels can differ—for example, when an industry, such as automobiles or semiconductors, has cyclical periods of high and low demand or when management believes that budgeted production for the coming period is not representative of long-run demand.

Consider Stassen's master budget for 2012, based on production of 8,000 telescopes per year. Despite using this master-budget capacity-utilization level of 8,000 telescopes for 2012, top management believes that over the next three years the normal (average) annual production level will be 10,000 telescopes. It views 2012's budgeted production level of 8,000 telescopes to be "abnormally" low because a major competitor has been sharply reducing its selling price and spending large amounts on advertising. Stassen expects that the competitor's lower price and advertising blitz will not be a long-run phenomenon and that, by 2014 and beyond, Stassen's production and sales will be higher.

Effect on Budgeted Fixed Manufacturing Cost Rate

We now illustrate how each of these four denominator levels affects the budgeted fixed manufacturing cost rate. Stassen has budgeted (standard) fixed manufacturing overhead costs of $1,080,000 for 2012. This lump-sum is incurred to provide the capacity to produce telescopes. The amount includes, among other costs, leasing costs for the facility and the compensation of the facility managers. The budgeted fixed manufacturing cost rates for 2012 for each of the four capacity-level concepts are as follows:

	Home	Insert	Page Layout	Formulas	Data	Review	View		
			A		B	C		D	
1					**Budgeted Fixed**	**Budget**		**Budgeted Fixed**	
2		**Denominator-Level**			**Manufacturing**	**Capacity Level**		**Manufacturing**	
3		**Capacity Concept**			**Costs per Year**	**(in units)**		**Cost per Unit**	
4		**(1)**			**(2)**	**(3)**		**(4) = (2) / (3)**	
5	Theoretical capacity				$1,080,000	18,000		$ 60	
6	Practical capacity				$1,080,000	12,000		$ 90	
7	Normal capacity utilization				$1,080,000	10,000		$108	
8	Master-budget capacity utilization				$1,080,000	8,000		$135	

The significant difference in cost rates (from $60 to $135) arises because of large differences in budgeted capacity levels under the different capacity concepts.

Budgeted (standard) variable manufacturing cost is $200 per unit. The total budgeted (standard) manufacturing cost per unit for alternative capacity-level concepts is as follows:

	A	B	C	D
1		Budgeted Variable	Budgeted Fixed	Budgeted Total
2	**Denominator-Level**	Manufacturing	Manufacturing	Manufacturing
3	**Capacity Concept**	Cost per Unit	Cost per Unit	Cost per Unit
4	(1)	(2)	(3)	(4) = (2) + (3)
5	Theoretical capacity	$200	$ 60	$260
6	Practical capacity	$200	$ 90	$290
7	Normal capacity utilization	$200	$108	$308
8	Master-budget capacity utilization	$200	$135	$335

Because different denominator-level capacity concepts yield different budgeted fixed manufacturing costs per unit, Stassen must decide which capacity level to use. Stassen is not required to use the same capacity-level concept, say, for management planning and control, external reporting to shareholders, and income tax purposes.

Choosing a Capacity Level

As we just saw, at the start of each fiscal year, managers determine different denominator levels for the different capacity concepts and calculate different budgeted fixed manufacturing costs per unit. We now discuss the problems with and effects of different denominator-level choices for different purposes, including (a) product costing and capacity management, (b) pricing, (c) performance evaluation, (d) external reporting, and (e) tax requirements.

Product Costing and Capacity Management

Data from normal costing or standard costing are often used in pricing or product-mix decisions. As the Stassen example illustrates, use of theoretical capacity results in an unrealistically small fixed manufacturing cost per unit because it is based on an idealistic and unattainable level of capacity. Theoretical capacity is rarely used to calculate budgeted fixed manufacturing cost per unit because it departs significantly from the real capacity available to a company.

Many companies favor practical capacity as the denominator to calculate budgeted fixed manufacturing cost per unit. Practical capacity in the Stassen example represents the maximum number of units (12,000) that Stassen can reasonably expect to produce per year for the $1,080,000 it will spend annually on capacity. If Stassen had consistently planned to produce fewer units, say 6,000 telescopes each year, it would have built a smaller plant and incurred lower costs.

Stassen budgets $90 in fixed manufacturing cost per unit based on the $1,080,000 it costs to acquire the capacity to produce 12,000 units. This level of plant capacity is an important strategic decision that managers make well before Stassen uses the capacity and even before Stassen knows how much of the capacity it will actually use. That is, budgeted fixed manufacturing cost of $90 per unit measures the *cost per unit of supplying the capacity*.

Demand for Stassen's telescopes in 2012 is expected to be 8,000 units, which is 4,000 units lower than the practical capacity of 12,000 units. However, it costs Stassen $1,080,000 per year to acquire the capacity to make 12,000 units, so the cost of *supplying* the capacity needed to make 12,000 units is still $90 per unit. The capacity and its cost are fixed *in the short run*; unlike variable costs, the capacity supplied does not automatically reduce to match the capacity needed in 2012. As a result, not all of the capacity supplied at $90 per unit will be needed or used in 2012. Using practical capacity as the denominator level, managers can subdivide the cost of resources supplied into used and unused components. At the supply cost of $90 per unit, the manufacturing resources that Stassen will use equal $720,000 ($90 per unit × 8,000 units). Manufacturing resources that Stassen will not use are $360,000 [$90 per unit × (12,000 – 8,000) units].

Using practical capacity as the denominator level sets the cost of capacity at the cost of supplying the capacity, regardless of the demand for the capacity. Highlighting the cost of capacity acquired but not used directs managers' attention toward managing unused capacity, perhaps by designing new products to fill unused capacity, by leasing unused capacity to others, or by eliminating unused capacity. In contrast, using either of the capacity levels based on the demand for Stassen's telescopes—master-budget capacity utilization or normal capacity utilization—hides the amount of unused capacity. If Stassen had used master-budget capacity utilization as the capacity level, it would have calculated budgeted fixed manufacturing cost per unit as $135 ($1,080,000 ÷ 8,000 units). This calculation does not use data about practical capacity, so it does not separately identify the cost of unused capacity. Note, however, that the cost of $135 per unit includes a charge for unused capacity: It comprises the $90 fixed manufacturing resource that would be used to produce each unit at practical capacity plus the cost of unused capacity allocated to each unit, $45 per unit ($360,000 ÷ 8,000 units).

From the perspective of long-run product costing, which cost of capacity should Stassen use for pricing purposes or for benchmarking its product cost structure against competitors: $90 per unit based on practical capacity or $135 per unit based on master-budget capacity utilization? Probably the $90 per unit based on practical capacity. Why? Because $90 per unit represents the budgeted cost per unit of only the capacity used to produce the product, and it explicitly excludes the cost of any unused capacity. Stassen's customers will be willing to pay a price that covers the cost of the capacity actually used but will not want to pay for unused capacity that provides no other benefits to them. Customers expect Stassen to manage its unused capacity or to bear the cost of unused capacity, not pass it along to them. Moreover, if Stassen's competitors manage unused capacity more effectively, the cost of capacity in the competitors' cost structures (which guides competitors' pricing decisions) is likely to approach $90. In the next section we show how the use of normal capacity utilization or master-budget capacity utilization can result in setting selling prices that are not competitive.

Pricing Decisions and the Downward Demand Spiral

The **downward demand spiral** for a company is the continuing reduction in the demand for its products that occurs when competitor prices are not met; as demand drops further, higher and higher unit costs result in greater reluctance to meet competitors' prices.

The easiest way to understand the downward demand spiral is via an example. Assume Stassen uses master-budget capacity utilization of 8,000 units for product costing in 2012. The resulting manufacturing cost is $335 per unit ($200 variable manufacturing cost per unit + $135 fixed manufacturing cost per unit). Assume that in December 2011, a competitor offers to supply a major customer of Stassen (a customer who was expected to purchase 2,000 units in 2012) telescopes at $300 per unit. The Stassen manager, not wanting to show a loss on the account and wanting to recoup all costs in the long run, declines to match the competitor's price. The account is lost. The loss means budgeted fixed manufacturing costs of $1,080,000 will be spread over the remaining master-budget volume of 6,000 units at a rate of $180 per unit ($1,080,000 ÷ 6,000 units).

Suppose yet another Stassen customer, who also accounts for 2,000 units of budgeted volume, receives a bid from a competitor at a price of $350 per unit. The Stassen manager compares this bid with his revised unit cost of $380 ($200 + $180), declines to match the competition, and the account is lost. Planned output would shrink further to 4,000 units. Budgeted fixed manufacturing cost per unit for the remaining 4,000 telescopes would now be \$270 (\$1,080,000 ÷ 4,000 units). The following table shows the effect of spreading fixed manufacturing costs over a shrinking amount of master-budget capacity utilization:

	Home Insert Page Layout Formulas Data Review View		
	A	B	C	D
1	Master-Budget		Budgeted Fixed	
2	Capacity Utilization	Budgeted Variable	Manufacturing	Budgeted Total
3	Denominator Level	Manufacturing Cost	Cost per Unit	Manufacturing
4	(Units)	per Unit	[$1,080,000 ÷ (1)]	Cost per Unit
5	(1)	(2)	(3)	(4) = (2) + (3)
6	8,000	$200	$135	$335
7	6,000	$200	$180	$380
8	4,000	$200	$270	$470
9	3,000	$200	$360	$560

Practical capacity, by contrast, is a stable measure. The use of practical capacity as the denominator to calculate budgeted fixed manufacturing cost per unit avoids the recalculation of unit costs when expected demand levels change, because the fixed cost rate is calculated based on *capacity available* rather than *capacity used to meet demand*. Managers who use reported unit costs in a mechanical way to set prices are less likely to promote a downward demand spiral when they use practical capacity than when they use normal capacity utilization or master-budget capacity utilization.

Using practical capacity as the denominator level also gives the manager a more accurate idea of the resources needed and used to produce a unit by excluding the cost of unused capacity. As discussed earlier, the cost of manufacturing resources supplied to produce a telescope is \$290 (\$200 variable manufacturing cost per unit plus \$90 fixed manufacturing cost per unit). This cost is lower than the prices offered by Stassen's competitors and would have correctly led the manager to match the prices and retain the accounts (assuming for purposes of this discussion that Stassen has no other costs). If, however, the prices offered by competitors were lower than \$290 per unit, the Stassen manager would not recover the cost of resources used to supply telescopes. This would signal to the manager that Stassen was noncompetitive even if it had no unused capacity. The only way then for Stassen to be profitable and retain customers in the long run would be to reduce its manufacturing cost per unit. The Concepts in Action feature on page 319 highlights the downward spiral currently at work in the traditional landline phone industry.

Performance Evaluation

Consider how the choice among normal capacity utilization, master-budget capacity utilization, and practical capacity affects the evaluation of a marketing manager. Normal capacity utilization is often used as a basis for long-run plans. Normal capacity utilization depends on the time span selected and the forecasts made for each year. *However, normal capacity utilization is an average that provides no meaningful feedback to the marketing manager for a particular year.* Using normal capacity utilization as a reference for judging current performance of a marketing manager is an example of misusing a long-run measure for a short-run purpose. Master-budget capacity utilization, rather than normal capacity utilization or practical capacity, should be used to evaluate a marketing manager's performance in the current year, because the master budget is the principal short-run planning and control tool. Managers feel more obligated to reach the levels specified in the master budget, which should have been carefully set in relation to the maximum opportunities for sales in the current year.

When large differences exist between practical capacity and master-budget capacity utilization, several companies (such as Texas Instruments, Polysar, and Sandoz) classify the difference as *planned unused capacity*. One reason for this approach is performance

| Concepts in Action | The "Death Spiral" and the End of Landline Telephone Service |

Can you imagine a future without traditional landline telephone service? Verizon and AT&T, the two largest telephone service providers in the United States, are already working to make that future a reality. Recently, both companies announced plans to reduce their focus on providing copper-wire telephone service to homes and businesses. According to AT&T, with the rise of mobile phones and Internet communications such as voice over Internet Protocol (VoIP), less than 20% of Americans now rely exclusively on landlines for voice service and another 25% have abandoned them altogether.

But why would telephone companies abandon landlines if 75% of Americans still use them? Continued reduced service demand is leading to higher unit costs, or a downward demand spiral. As AT&T recently told the U.S. Federal Communications Commission, "The business model for legacy phone services is in a death spiral. With an outdated product, falling revenues, and rising costs, the plain-old telephone service business is unsustainable for the long run."

Marketplace statistics support AT&T's claim. From 2000 to 2008, total long-distance access minutes fell by 42%. As a result, revenue from traditional landline phone service decreased by 27% between 2000 and 2007. In 2008 alone, AT&T lost 12% of its landline customers, while Verizon lost 10%. Industry observers estimate that customers are permanently disconnecting 700,000 landline phones every month.

As all these companies lose landline customers and revenue, the costs of maintaining the phone wires strung on poles and dug through trenches is not falling nearly as quickly. It now costs phone companies an average of $52 per year to maintain a copper phone line, up from $43 in 2003, largely because of the declining number of landlines. These costs do not include other expenses required to maintain landline phone service including local support offices, call centers, and garages.

New competitors are taking advantage of this situation. Vonage, the leading Internet phone company, offers its services for as little as $18 per month. Without relying on wires to transmit calls, its direct costs of providing telephone service come to $6.67 a month for each subscriber. And the largest part of that is not true cost, but subsidies to rural phone carriers for connecting long distance calls. As Vonage attracts more customers, its economies of scale will increase while its costs of providing service will decrease for each additional subscriber.

Hamstrung by increasing unit costs, legacy carriers like Verizon and AT&T are unable to compete with Vonage on price. As such, their traditional landline businesses are in permanent decline. So what are these companies doing about it? Verizon is reducing its landline operations by selling large parts of its copper-wire business to smaller companies at a significant discount. AT&T recently petitioned the U.S. government to waive a requirement that it and other carriers maintain their costly landline networks. As the landline phone service "death spiral" continues, the future of telecommunications will include more wireless, fiber optics, and VoIP with less of Alexander Graham Bell's original vision of telephones connected by copper wires.

Source: Comments of AT&T Inc. on the Transition from the Legacy Circuit-switched Network to Broadband. Washington, DC: AT&T Inc., December 21, 2009. http://fjallfoss.fcc.gov/ecfs/document/view?id=7020354032; Hansell, Saul. 2009. Verizon boss hangs up on landline phone business. *New York Times,* September 17; Hansell, Saul. 2009. Will the phone industry need a bailout, too? *New York Times,* May 8.

evaluation. Consider our Stassen telescope example. The managers in charge of capacity planning usually do not make pricing decisions. Top management decided to build a production facility with 12,000 units of practical capacity, focusing on demand over the next five years. But Stassen's marketing managers, who are mid-level managers, make the pricing decisions. These marketing managers believe they should be held accountable only for the manufacturing overhead costs related to their potential customer base in 2012. The master-budget capacity utilization suggests a customer base in 2012 of 8,000 units (2/3 of the 12,000 practical capacity). Using responsibility accounting principles (see Chapter 6, pp. 199–201), only 2/3 of the budgeted total fixed manufacturing costs ($1,080,000 × 2/3 = $720,000) would be attributed to the fixed capacity costs of meeting 2012 demand. The remaining 1/3 of the numerator ($1,080,000 × 1/3 = $360,000) would be separately shown as the capacity cost of meeting increases in long-run demand expected to occur beyond 2012.[4]

External Reporting

The magnitude of the favorable/unfavorable production-volume variance under absorption costing is affected by the choice of the denominator level used to calculate the budgeted fixed manufacturing cost per unit. Assume the following actual operating information for Stassen in 2012:

	A	B	C
1	Beginning inventory	0	
2	Production	8,000	units
3	Sales	6,000	units
4	Ending inventory	2,000	units
5	Selling price	$ 1,000	per unit
6	Variable manufacturing cost	$ 200	per unit
7	Fixed manufacturing costs	$ 1,080,000	
8	Variable marketing cost	$ 185	per unit sold
9	Fixed marketing costs	$ 1,380,000	

Note that this is the same data used to calculate the income under variable and absorption costing for Stassen in Exhibit 9-1. As before, we assume that there are no price, spending, or efficiency variances in manufacturing costs.

Recall from Chapter 8 the equation used to calculate the production-volume variance:

$$\text{Production-volume variance} = \left(\begin{array}{c}\text{Budgeted} \\ \text{fixed} \\ \text{manufacturing} \\ \text{overhead}\end{array}\right) - \left(\begin{array}{c}\text{Fixed manufacturing overhead allocated using} \\ \text{budgeted cost per output unit} \\ \text{allowed for actual output produced}\end{array}\right)$$

The four different capacity-level concepts result in four different budgeted fixed manufacturing overhead cost rates per unit. The different rates will result in different amounts of fixed manufacturing overhead costs allocated to the 8,000 units actually produced and different amounts of production-volume variance. Using the budgeted fixed manufacturing costs of $1,080,000 (equal to actual fixed manufacturing costs) and the rates calculated on page 315 for different denominator levels, the production-volume variance computations are as follows:

$$\text{Production-volume variance (theoretical capacity)} = \$1,080,000 - (8,000 \text{ units} \times \$60 \text{ per unit})$$
$$= \$1,080,000 - 480,000$$
$$= 600,000 \text{ U}$$

$$\text{Production-volume variance (practical capacity)} = \$1,080,000 - (8,000 \text{ units} \times \$90 \text{ per unit})$$
$$= \$1,080,000 - 720,000$$
$$= 360,000 \text{ U}$$

$$\text{Production-volume variance (normal capacity utilization)} = \$1,080,000 - (8,000 \text{ units} \times \$108 \text{ per unit})$$
$$= \$1,080,000 - 864,000$$
$$= 216,000 \text{ U}$$

---

[4] For further discussion, see T. Klammer, *Capacity Measurement and Improvement* (Chicago: Irwin, 1996). This research was facilitated by CAM-I, an organization promoting innovative cost management practices. CAM-I's research on capacity costs explores ways in which companies can identify types of capacity costs that can be reduced (or eliminated) without affecting the required output to meet customer demand. An example is improving processes to successfully eliminate the costs of capacity held in anticipation of handling difficulties due to imperfect coordination with suppliers and customers.

Production-volume variance (master-budget capacity utilization)

$$= \$1,080,000 - (8,000 \text{ units} \times \$135 \text{ per unit})$$

$$= \$1,080,000 - 1,080,000$$

$$= 0$$

How Stassen disposes of its production-volume variance at the end of the fiscal year will determine the effect this variance has on the company's operating income. We now discuss the three alternative approaches Stassen can use to dispose of the production-volume variance. These approaches were first discussed in Chapter 4 (pp. 117–122).

1. **Adjusted allocation-rate approach.** This approach restates all amounts in the general and subsidiary ledgers by using actual rather than budgeted cost rates. Given that actual fixed manufacturing costs are $1,080,000 and actual production is 8,000 units, the recalculated fixed manufacturing cost is $135 per unit ($1,080,000 ÷ 8,000 actual units). Under the adjusted allocation-rate approach, the choice of the capacity level used to calculate the budgeted fixed manufacturing cost per unit has no effect on year-end financial statements. In effect, actual costing is adopted at the end of the fiscal year.

2. **Proration approach.** The underallocated or overallocated overhead is spread among ending balances in Work-in-Process Control, Finished Goods Control, and Cost of Goods Sold. The proration restates the ending balances in these accounts to what they would have been if actual cost rates had been used rather than budgeted cost rates. The proration approach also results in the choice of the capacity level used to calculate the budgeted fixed manufacturing cost per unit having no effect on year-end financial statements.

3. **Write-off variances to cost of goods sold approach.** Exhibit 9-7 shows how use of this approach affects Stassen's operating income for 2012. Recall that Stassen had no beginning inventory, and it had production of 8,000 units and sales of 6,000 units. Therefore, the ending inventory on December 31, 2012, is 2,000 units. Using master-budget capacity utilization as the denominator-level results in assigning the highest amount of fixed manufacturing cost per unit to the 2,000 units in ending inventory (see the line item "deduct ending inventory" in Exhibit 9-7). Accordingly, operating income is highest using master-budget capacity utilization. The differences in operating income for the four denominator-level concepts in Exhibit 9-7 are due to different amounts of fixed manufacturing overhead being inventoried at the end of 2012:

Fixed Manufacturing Overhead
In December 31, 2012, Inventory

Theoretical capacity	2,000 units × $60 per unit = $120,000
Practical capacity	2,000 units × $90 per unit = $180,000
Normal capacity utilization	2,000 units × $108 per unit = $216,000
Master-budget capacity utilization	2,000 units × $135 per unit = $270,000

In Exhibit 9-7, for example, the $54,000 difference ($1,500,000 – $1,446,000) in operating income between master-budget capacity utilization and normal capacity utilization is due to the difference in fixed manufacturing overhead inventoried ($270,000 – $216,000).

What is the common reason and explanation for the increasing operating-income numbers in Exhibit 9-4 (p. 310) and Exhibit 9-7? It is the amount of fixed manufacturing costs incurred that is included in ending inventory at the end of the year. As this amount increases, so does operating income. The amount of fixed manufacturing costs inventoried depends on two factors: the number of units in ending inventory and the rate at which fixed manufacturing costs are allocated to each unit. Exhibit 9-4 shows the effect on operating income of increasing the number of units in ending inventory (by increasing production). Exhibit 9-7 shows the effect on operating income of increasing the fixed manufacturing cost allocated per unit (by decreasing the denominator level used to calculate the rate).

Chapter 8 (pp. 275–276) discusses the various issues managers and management accountants must consider when deciding whether to prorate the production-volume

Exhibit 9-7   Income-Statement Effects of Using Alternative Capacity-Level Concepts: Stassen Company for 2012

	A	B	C	D	E	F	G	H	I
1		Theoretical Capacity		Practical Capacity		Normal Capacity Utilization		Master-Budget Capacity Utilization	
2	Denominator level in cases	18,000		12,000		10,000		8,000	
3	Revenues[a]	$6,000,000		$6,000,000		$6,000,000		$6,000,000	
4	Cost of goods sold								
5	Beginning inventory	0		0		0		0	
6	Variable manufacturing costs[b]	1,600,000		1,600,000		1,600,000		1,600,000	
7	Fixed manufacturing costs[c]	480,000		720,000		864,000		1,080,000	
8	Cost of goods available for sale	2,080,000		2,320,000		2,464,000		2,680,000	
9	Deduct ending inventory[d]	(520,000)		(580,000)		(616,000)		(670,000)	
10	Cost of goods sold (at standard cost)	1,560,000		1,740,000		1,848,000		2,010,000	
11	Adjustment for production-volume variance	600,000	U	360,000	U	216,000	U	0	
12	Cost of goods sold	2,160,000		2,100,000		2,064,000		2,010,000	
13	Gross margin	3,840,000		3,900,000		3,936,000		3,990,000	
14	Marketing costs[e]	2,490,000		2,490,000		2,490,000		2,490,000	
15	Operating income	$1,350,000		$1,410,000		$1,446,000		$1,500,000	
16									
17	[a]$1,000 × 6,000 units = $6,000,000			[d]Ending inventory costs:					
18	[b]$200 × 8,000 units = $1,600,000			($200 + $60) × 2,000 units = $520,000					
19	[c]Fixed manufacturing overhead costs:			($200 + $90) × 2,000 units = $580,000					
20	$60 × 8,000 units = $ 480,000			($200 + $108) × 2,000 units = $616,000					
21	$90 × 8,000 units = $ 720,000			($200 + $135) × 2,000 units = $670,000					
22	$108 × 8,000 units = $ 864,000			[e]Marketing costs:					
23	$135 × 8,000 units = $1,080,000			$1,380,000 + $185 × 6,000 units = $2,490,000					

variance among inventories and cost of goods sold or to simply write off the variance to cost of goods sold. The objective is to write off the portion of the production-volume variance that represents the cost of capacity not used to support the production of output during the period. Determining this amount is almost always a matter of judgment.

Tax Requirements

Decision Point ▶

What are the major factors managers consider in choosing the capacity level to compute the budgeted fixed manufacturing cost rate?

For tax reporting purposes in the United States, the Internal Revenue Service (IRS) requires companies to assign inventoriable indirect production costs by a "method of allocation which fairly apportions such costs among the various items produced." Approaches that involve the use of either overhead rates (which the IRS terms the "manufacturing burden rate method") or standard costs are viewed as acceptable. Under either approach, U.S. tax reporting requires end-of-period reconciliation between actual and applied indirect costs using the adjusted allocation-rate method or the proration method.[5] More interestingly, under either approach, the IRS permits the use of practical capacity to calculate budgeted fixed manufacturing cost per unit. Further, the production-volume variance thus generated can be deducted for tax purposes in the year in which the cost is incurred. The tax benefits from this policy are evident from Exhibit 9-7. Note that the operating income when the

---

[5] For example, Section 1.471-11 of the U.S. Internal Revenue Code states, "The proper use of the standard cost method . . . requires that a taxpayer must reallocate to the goods in ending inventory a pro rata portion of any net negative or net positive overhead variances." Of course, if the variances are not material in amount, they can be expensed (i.e., written off to cost of goods sold), provided the same treatment is carried out in the firm's financial reports.

denominator is set to practical capacity (column D, where the production volume variance of $360,000 is written off to cost of goods sold) is lower than those under normal capacity utilization (column F) or master-budget capacity utilization (column H).

Planning and Control of Capacity Costs

In addition to the issues previously discussed, managers must take a variety of other factors into account when planning capacity levels and in deciding how best to control and assign capacity costs. These include the level of uncertainty regarding both the expected costs and the expected demand for the installed capacity, the presence of capacity-related issues in nonmanufacturing settings, and the potential use of activity-based costing techniques in allocating capacity costs.

Difficulties in Forecasting Chosen Denominator-Level Concept

Practical capacity measures the available supply of capacity. Managers can usually use engineering studies and human-resource considerations (such as worker safety) to obtain a reliable estimate of this denominator level for the budget period. It is more difficult to obtain reliable estimates of demand-side denominator-level concepts, especially longer-term normal capacity utilization figures. For example, many U.S. steel companies in the 1980s believed they were in the downturn of a demand cycle that would have an upturn within two or three years. After all, steel had been a cyclical business in which upturns followed downturns, making the notion of normal capacity utilization appear reasonable. Unfortunately, the steel cycle in the 1980s did not turn up; some companies and numerous plants closed. More recently, the global economic slowdown has made a mockery of demand projections. Consider that in 2006, the forecast for the Indian automotive market was that annual demand for cars and passenger vehicles would hit 1.92 million in the year 2009–2010. In early 2009, the forecast for the same period was revised downward to 1.37 million vehicles. Even ignoring the vagaries of economic cycles, another problem is that marketing managers of firms are often prone to overestimate their ability to regain lost sales and market share. Their estimate of "normal" demand for their product may consequently reflect an overly optimistic outlook. Master-budget capacity utilization focuses only on the expected demand for the next year. Therefore, master-budget capacity utilization can be more reliably estimated than normal capacity utilization. However, it is still just a forecast, and the true demand realization can be either higher or lower than this estimate.

It is important to understand that costing systems, such as normal costing or standard costing, do not recognize uncertainty the way managers recognize it. A single amount, rather than a range of possible amounts, is used as the denominator level when calculating the budgeted fixed manufacturing cost per unit in absorption costing. Consider Stassen's facility, which has an estimated practical capacity of 12,000 units. The estimated master-budget capacity utilization for 2012 is 8,000 units. However, there is still substantial doubt regarding the actual number of units Stassen will have to manufacture in 2012 and in future years. Managers recognize uncertainty in their capacity-planning decisions. Stassen built its current plant with a 12,000 unit practical capacity in part to provide the capability to meet possible demand surges. Even if such surges do not occur in a given period, do not conclude that capacity unused in a given period is wasted resources. The gains from meeting sudden demand surges may well require having unused capacity in some periods.

Difficulties in Forecasting Fixed Manufacturing Costs

The fixed manufacturing cost rate is based on a numerator (budgeted fixed manufacturing costs) and a denominator (some measure of capacity or capacity utilization). Our discussion so far has emphasized issues concerning the choice of the denominator. Challenging issues also arise in measuring the numerator. For example, deregulation of the U.S. electric utility industry has resulted in many electric utilities becoming unprofitable. This situation has led to write-downs in the values of the utilities' plants and equipment. The

Learning Objective 7

Understand other issues that play an important role in capacity planning and control

. . . uncertainty regarding the expected spending on capacity costs and the demand for installed capacity, the role of capacity-related issues in nonmanufacturing areas, and the possible use of activity-based costing techniques in allocating capacity costs

write-downs reduce the numerator because there is less depreciation expense included in the calculation of fixed capacity cost per kilowatt-hour of electricity produced. The difficulty that managers face in this situation is that the amount of write-downs is not clear-cut but, rather, a matter of judgment.

Nonmanufacturing Costs

Capacity costs also arise in nonmanufacturing parts of the value chain. Stassen may acquire a fleet of vehicles capable of distributing the practical capacity of its production facility. When actual production is below practical capacity, there will be unused-capacity cost issues with the distribution function, as well as with the manufacturing function.

As you saw in Chapter 8, capacity cost issues are prominent in many service-sector companies, such as airlines, hospitals, and railroads—even though these companies carry no inventory and so have no inventory costing problems. For example, in calculating the fixed overhead cost per patient-day in its obstetrics and gynecology department, a hospital must decide which denominator level to use: practical capacity, normal capacity utilization, or master-budget capacity utilization. Its decision may have implications for capacity management, as well as pricing and performance evaluation.

Activity-Based Costing

Decision Point

What issues must managers take into account when planning capacity levels and for assigning capacity costs?

To maintain simplicity and the focus on choosing a denominator to calculate a budgeted fixed manufacturing cost rate, our Stassen example assumed that all fixed manufacturing costs had a single cost driver: telescope units produced. As you saw in Chapter 5, activity-based costing systems have multiple overhead cost pools at the output-unit, batch, product-sustaining, and facility-sustaining levels—each with its own cost driver. In calculating activity cost rates (for fixed costs of setups and material handling, say), management must choose a capacity level for the quantity of the cost driver (setup-hours or loads moved). Should management use practical capacity, normal capacity utilization, or master-budget capacity utilization? For all the reasons described in this chapter (such as pricing and capacity management), most proponents of activity-based costing argue that practical capacity should be used as the denominator level to calculate activity cost rates.

Problem for Self-Study

Assume Stassen Company on January 1, 2012, decides to contract with another company to preassemble a large percentage of the components of its telescopes. The revised manufacturing cost structure during the 2012–2014 period is as follows:

Variable manufacturing cost per unit produced	
Direct materials	$ 250
Direct manufacturing labor	20
Manufacturing overhead	5
Total variable manufacturing cost per unit produced	$ 275
Fixed manufacturing costs	$480,000

Under the revised cost structure, a larger percentage of Stassen's manufacturing costs are variable with respect to units produced. The denominator level of production used to calculate budgeted fixed manufacturing cost per unit in 2012, 2013, and 2014 is 8,000 units. Assume no other change from the data underlying Exhibits 9-1 and 9-2. Summary information pertaining to absorption-costing operating income and variable-costing operating income with this revised cost structure is as follows:

	2012	2013	2014
Absorption-costing operating income	$1,500,000	$1,560,000	$2,340,000
Variable-costing operating income	1,380,000	1,650,000	2,190,000
Difference	$ 120,000	$ (90,000)	$ 150,000

1. Compute the budgeted fixed manufacturing cost per unit in 2012, 2013, and 2014.
2. Explain the difference between absorption-costing operating income and variable-costing operating income in 2012, 2013, and 2014, focusing on fixed manufacturing costs in beginning and ending inventory.
3. Why are these differences smaller than the differences in Exhibit 9-2?
4. Assume the same preceding information, except that for 2012, the master-budget capacity utilization is 10,000 units instead of 8,000. How would Stassen's absorption-costing income for 2012 differ from the $1,500,000 shown previously? Show your computations.

Solution

1. $\text{Budgeted fixed manufacturing cost per unit} = \dfrac{\text{Budgeted fixed manufacturing costs}}{\text{Budgeted production units}}$

$$= \frac{\$480,000}{8,000 \text{ units}}$$

$$= \$60 \text{ per unit}$$

2. $\begin{array}{c}\text{Absorption-costing} \\ \text{operating} \\ \text{income}\end{array} - \begin{array}{c}\text{Variable-costing} \\ \text{operating} \\ \text{income}\end{array} = \begin{array}{c}\text{Fixed manufacturing} \\ \text{costs in ending inventory} \\ \text{under absorption costing}\end{array} - \begin{array}{c}\text{Fixed manufacturing costs} \\ \text{in beginning inventory} \\ \text{under absorption costing}\end{array}$

2012: $1,500,000 − $1,380,000 = ($60 per unit × 2,000 units) − ($600 per unit × 0 units)

$120,000 = $120,000

2013: $1,560,000 − $1,650,000 = ($60 per unit × 500 units) − ($60 per unit × 2,000 units)

−$90,000 = −$90,000

2014: $2,340,000 − $2,190,000 = ($60 per unit × 3,000 units) − ($60 per unit × 500 units)

$150,000 = $150,000

3. Subcontracting a large part of manufacturing has greatly reduced the magnitude of fixed manufacturing costs. This reduction, in turn, means differences between absorption costing and variable costing are much smaller than in Exhibit 9-2.
4. Given the higher master-budget capacity utilization level of 10,000 units, the budgeted fixed manufacturing cost rate for 2012 is now as follows:

$$\frac{\$480,000}{10,000 \text{ units}} = \$48 \text{ per unit}$$

The manufacturing cost per unit is $323 ($275 + $48). So, the production-volume variance for 2012 is

$$(10,000 \text{ units} − 8,000 \text{ units}) \times \$48 \text{ per unit} = \$96,000 \text{ U}$$

The absorption-costing income statement for 2012 is as follows:

Revenues: $1,000 per unit × 6,000 units		$6,000,000
Cost of goods sold:		
Beginning inventory	0	
Variable manufacturing costs: $275 per unit × 8,000 units	2,200,000	
Fixed manufacturing costs: $48 per unit × 8,000 units	384,000	
Cost of goods available for sale	2,584,000	
Deduct ending inventory: $323 per unit × 2,000 units	(646,000)	
Cost of goods sold (at standard costs)	1,938,000	
Adjustment for production-volume variance	96,000 U	
Cost of goods sold		2,034,000
Gross margin		3,966,000
Marketing costs: $1,380,000 fixed + ($185 per unit) × (6,000 units sold)		2,490,000
Operating income		$1,476,000

The higher denominator level used to calculate the budgeted fixed manufacturing cost per unit means that fewer fixed manufacturing costs are inventoried ($48 per unit × 2,000 units = $96,000) than when the master-budget capacity utilization was 8,000 units ($60 per unit × 2,000 units = $120,000). This difference of $24,000 ($120,000 – $96,000) results in operating income being lower by $24,000 relative to the prior calculated income level of $1,500,000.

Decision Points

The following question-and-answer format summarizes the chapter's learning objectives. Each decision presents a key question related to a learning objective. The guidelines are the answer to that question.

Decision	Guidelines
1. How does variable costing differ from absorption costing?	Variable costing and absorption costing differ in only one respect: how to account for fixed manufacturing costs. Under variable costing, fixed manufacturing costs are excluded from inventoriable costs and are a cost of the period in which they are incurred. Under absorption costing, fixed manufacturing costs are inventoriable and become a part of cost of goods sold in the period when sales occur.
2. How does income differ under variable and absorption costing?	The variable-costing income statement is based on the contribution-margin format. Under it, operating income is driven by the unit level of sales. Under absorption costing, the income statement follows the gross-margin format. Operating income is driven by the unit level of production, the unit level of sales, and the denominator level used for assigning fixed costs.
3. Why might managers build up finished goods inventory if they use absorption costing?	When absorption costing is used, managers can increase current operating income by producing more units for inventory. Producing for inventory absorbs more fixed manufacturing costs into inventory and reduces costs expensed in the period. Critics of absorption costing label this manipulation of income as the major negative consequence of treating fixed manufacturing costs as inventoriable costs.
4. How does throughput costing differ from variable costing and absorption costing?	Throughput costing treats all costs except direct materials as costs of the period in which they are incurred. Throughput costing results in a lower amount of manufacturing costs being inventoried than either variable or absorption costing.
5. What are the various capacity levels a company can use to compute the budgeted fixed manufacturing cost rate?	Capacity levels can be measured in terms of capacity supplied—theoretical capacity or practical capacity. Capacity can also be measured in terms of output demanded—normal capacity utilization or master-budget capacity utilization.
6. What are the major factors managers consider in choosing the capacity level to compute the budgeted fixed manufacturing cost rate?	The major factors managers consider in choosing the capacity level to compute the budgeted fixed manufacturing cost rate are (a) effect on product costing and capacity management, (b) effect on pricing decisions, (c) effect on performance evaluation, (d) effect on financial statements, and (e) regulatory requirements.
7. What issues must managers take into account when planning capacity levels and for assigning capacity costs?	Critical factors in this regard include the uncertainty about the expected spending on capacity costs and the demand for the installed capacity, the role of capacity-related issues in nonmanufacturing areas, and the possible use of activity-based costing techniques in allocating capacity costs.

Appendix

Breakeven Points in Variable Costing and Absorption Costing

Chapter 3 introduced cost-volume-profit analysis. If variable costing is used, the breakeven point (that's where operating income is $0) is computed in the usual manner. There is only one breakeven point in this case, and it depends on (1) fixed (manufacturing and operating) costs and (2) contribution margin per unit.

The formula for computing the breakeven point under variable costing is a special case of the more general target operating income formula from Chapter 3 (p. 70):

Let Q = Number of units sold to earn the target operating income

$$\text{Then } Q = \frac{\text{Total fixed costs } + \text{ Target operating income}}{\text{Contribution margin per unit}}$$

Breakeven occurs when the target operating income is $0. In our Stassen illustration for 2012 (see Exhibit 9-1, p. 304):

$$Q = \frac{(\$1,080,000 + \$1,380,000) + \$0}{(\$1,000 - (\$200 + \$185))} = \frac{\$2,460,000}{\$615}$$

$$= 4,000 \text{ units}$$

We now verify that Stassen will achieve breakeven under variable costing by selling 4,000 units:

Revenues, $1,000 × 4,000 units	$4,000,000
Variable costs, $385 × 4,000 units	1,540,000
Contribution margin, $615 × 4,000 units	2,460,000
Fixed costs	2,460,000
Operating income	$ 0

If absorption costing is used, the required number of units to be sold to earn a specific target operating income is not unique because of the number of variables involved. The following formula shows the factors that will affect the target operating income under absorption costing:

$$Q = \frac{\begin{array}{c}\text{Total} \\ \text{fixed} \\ \text{costs}\end{array} + \begin{array}{c}\text{Target} \\ \text{operating} \\ \text{income}\end{array} + \left[\begin{array}{c}\text{Fixed} \\ \text{manufacturing} \\ \text{cost rate}\end{array} \times \left(\begin{array}{c}\text{Breakeven} \\ \text{sales} \\ \text{in units}\end{array} - \begin{array}{c}\text{Units} \\ \text{produced}\end{array} \right) \right]}{\text{Contribution margin per unit}}$$

In this formula, the numerator is the sum of three terms (from the perspective of the two "+" signs), compared with two terms in the numerator of the variable-costing formula stated earlier. The additional term in the numerator under absorption costing is as follows:

$$\left[\begin{array}{c}\text{Fixed manufacturing} \\ \text{cost rate}\end{array} \times \left(\begin{array}{c}\text{Breakeven sales} \\ \text{in units}\end{array} - \begin{array}{c}\text{Units} \\ \text{produced}\end{array} \right) \right]$$

This term reduces the fixed costs that need to be recovered when units produced exceed the breakeven sales quantity. When production exceeds the breakeven sales quantity, some of the fixed manufacturing costs that are expensed under variable costing are not expensed under absorption costing; they are instead included in finished goods inventory.[6]

For Stassen Company in 2012, suppose that actual production is 5,280 units. Then, one breakeven point, Q, under absorption costing is as follows:

$$Q = \frac{(\$1,080,000 + \$1,380,000) + \$0 + [\$135 \times (Q - 5,280)]}{(\$1,000 - (\$200 + \$185))}$$

$$= \frac{(\$2,460,000 + \$135Q - \$712,800)}{\$615}$$

$$\$615Q = \$1,747,200 + \$135Q$$

$$\$480Q = \$1,747,200$$

$$Q = 3,640$$

---

[6] The reverse situation, where production is lower than the breakeven sales quantity, is not possible unless the firm has opening inventory. In that case, provided the variable manufacturing cost per unit and the fixed manufacturing cost rate are constant over time, the breakeven formula given is still valid.

We next verify that production of 5,280 units and sales of 3,640 units will lead Stassen to breakeven under absorption costing:

Revenues, $1,000 × 3,640 units		$3,640,000
Cost of goods sold:		
Cost of goods sold at standard cost, $335 × 3,640 units	$1,219,400	
Production-volume variance, $135 × (8,000 – 5,280) units	367,200 U	1,586,600
Gross margin		2,053,400
Marketing costs:		
Variable marketing costs, $185 × 3,640 units	673,400	
Fixed marketing costs	1,380,000	2,053,400
Operating income		$ 0

The breakeven point under absorption costing depends on (1) fixed manufacturing costs, (2) fixed operating (marketing) costs, (3) contribution margin per unit, (4) unit level of production, and (5) the capacity level chosen as the denominator to set the fixed manufacturing cost rate. For Stassen in 2012, a combination of 3,640 units sold, fixed manufacturing costs of $1,080,000, fixed marketing costs of $1,380,000, contribution margin per unit of $615, an 8,000-unit denominator level, and production of 5,280 units would result in an operating income of $0. *Note, however, that there are many combinations of these five factors that would give an operating income of $0.* For example, holding all other factors constant, a combination of 6,240 units produced and 3,370 units sold also results in an operating income of $0 under absorption costing. We provide verification of this alternative breakeven point next:

Revenues, $1,000 × 3,370 units		$3,370,000
Cost of goods sold:		
Cost of goods sold at standard cost, $335 × 3,370 units	$1,128,950	
Production-volume variance, $135 × (8,000 – 6,240) units	237,600 U	1,366,550
Gross margin		2,003,450
Marketing costs:		
Variable marketing costs, $185 × 3,370 units	623,450	
Fixed marketing costs	1,380,000	2,003,450
Operating income		$ 0

Suppose actual production in 2012 was equal to the denominator level, 8,000 units, and there were no units sold and no fixed marketing costs. All the units produced would be placed in inventory, so all the fixed manufacturing costs would be included in inventory. There would be no production-volume variance. Under these conditions, the company could break even under absorption costing with no sales whatsoever! In contrast, under variable costing, the operating loss would be equal to the fixed manufacturing costs of $1,080,000.

Terms to Learn

This chapter and the Glossary at the end of the book contain definitions of the following important terms:

absorption costing (**p. 302**)

direct costing (**p. 302**)

downward demand spiral (**p. 317**)

master-budget capacity utilization (**p. 315**)

normal capacity utilization (**p. 315**)

practical capacity (**p. 315**)

super-variable costing (**p. 312**)

theoretical capacity (**p. 314**)

throughput costing (**p. 312**)

variable costing (**p. 301**)

Assignment Material

Questions

9-1 Differences in operating income between variable costing and absorption costing are due solely to accounting for fixed costs. Do you agree? Explain.

9-2 Why is the term *direct costing* a misnomer?

9-3 Do companies in either the service sector or the merchandising sector make choices about absorption costing versus variable costing?

9-4 Explain the main conceptual issue under variable costing and absorption costing regarding the timing for the release of fixed manufacturing overhead as expense.

9-5 "Companies that make no variable-cost/fixed-cost distinctions must use absorption costing, and those that do make variable-cost/fixed-cost distinctions must use variable costing." Do you agree? Explain.

9-6 The main trouble with variable costing is that it ignores the increasing importance of fixed costs in manufacturing companies. Do you agree? Why?

9-7 Give an example of how, under absorption costing, operating income could fall even though the unit sales level rises.

9-8 What are the factors that affect the breakeven point under (a) variable costing and (b) absorption costing?

9-9 Critics of absorption costing have increasingly emphasized its potential for leading to undesirable incentives for managers. Give an example.

9-10 What are two ways of reducing the negative aspects associated with using absorption costing to evaluate the performance of a plant manager?

9-11 What denominator-level capacity concepts emphasize the output a plant can supply? What denominator-level capacity concepts emphasize the output customers demand for products produced by a plant?

9-12 Describe the downward demand spiral and its implications for pricing decisions.

9-13 Will the financial statements of a company always differ when different choices at the start of the accounting period are made regarding the denominator-level capacity concept?

9-14 What is the IRS's requirement for tax reporting regarding the choice of a denominator-level capacity concept?

9-15 "The difference between practical capacity and master-budget capacity utilization is the best measure of management's ability to balance the costs of having too much capacity and having too little capacity." Do you agree? Explain.

Exercises

MyAccountingLab

9-16 **Variable and absorption costing, explaining operating-income differences.** Nascar Motors assembles and sells motor vehicles and uses standard costing. Actual data relating to April and May 2011 are as follows:

	Home Insert Page Layout Formulas Data Review			
	A	B	C	D
1		April		May
2	Unit data			
3	Beginning inventory	0		150
4	Production	500		400
5	Sales	350		520
6	Variable costs			
7	Manufacturing cost per unit produced	$ 10,000		$ 10,000
8	Operating (marketing) cost per unit sold	3,000		3,000
9	Fixed costs			
10	Manufacturing costs	$2,000,000		$2,000,000
11	Operating (marketing) costs	600,000		600,000

The selling price per vehicle is $24,000. The budgeted level of production used to calculate the budgeted fixed manufacturing cost per unit is 500 units. There are no price, efficiency, or spending variances. Any production-volume variance is written off to cost of goods sold in the month in which it occurs.

Required

1. Prepare April and May 2011 income statements for Nascar Motors under (a) variable costing and (b) absorption costing.

2. Prepare a numerical reconciliation and explanation of the difference between operating income for each month under variable costing and absorption costing.

9-17 **Throughput costing (continuation of 9-16).** The variable manufacturing costs per unit of Nascar Motors are as follows:

	Home Insert Page Layout Formulas Data Review		
	A	B	C
1		April	May
7	Direct material cost per unit	$6,700	$6,700
8	Direct manufacturing labor cost per unit	1,500	1,500
9	Manufacturing overhead cost per unit	1,800	1,800

Required 1. Prepare income statements for Nascar Motors in April and May of 2011 under throughput costing.
2. Contrast the results in requirement 1 with those in requirement 1 of Exercise 9-16.
3. Give one motivation for Nascar Motors to adopt throughput costing.

9-18 Variable and absorption costing, explaining operating-income differences. BigScreen Corporation manufactures and sells 50-inch television sets and uses standard costing. Actual data relating to January, February, and March of 2012 are as follows:

	January	February	March
Unit data			
Beginning inventory	0	300	300
Production	1,000	800	1,250
Sales	700	800	1,500
Variable costs			
Manufacturing cost per unit produced	$ 900	$ 900	$ 900
Operating (marketing) cost per unit sold	$ 600	$ 600	$ 600
Fixed costs			
Manufacturing costs	$400,000	$400,000	$400,000
Operating (marketing) costs	$140,000	$140,000	$140,000

The selling price per unit is $2,500. The budgeted level of production used to calculate the budgeted fixed manufacturing cost per unit is 1,000 units. There are no price, efficiency, or spending variances. Any production-volume variance is written off to cost of goods sold in the month in which it occurs.

Required 1. Prepare income statements for BigScreen in January, February, and March of 2012 under (a) variable costing and (b) absorption costing.
2. Explain the difference in operating income for January, February, and March under variable costing and absorption costing.

9-19 Throughput costing (continuation of 9-18). The variable manufacturing costs per unit of BigScreen Corporation are as follows:

	January	February	March
Direct material cost per unit	$500	$500	$500
Direct manufacturing labor cost per unit	100	100	100
Manufacturing overhead cost per unit	300	300	300
	$900	$900	$900

Required 1. Prepare income statements for BigScreen in January, February, and March of 2012 under throughput costing.
2. Contrast the results in requirement 1 with those in requirement 1 of Exercise 9-18.
3. Give one motivation for BigScreen to adopt throughput costing.

9-20 Variable versus absorption costing. The Zwatch Company manufactures trendy, high-quality moderately priced watches. As Zwatch's senior financial analyst, you are asked to recommend a method of inventory costing. The CFO will use your recommendation to prepare Zwatch's 2012 income statement. The following data are for the year ended December 31, 2012:

Beginning inventory, January 1, 2012	85,000 units
Ending inventory, December 31, 2012	34,500 units
2012 sales	345,400 units
Selling price (to distributor)	$22.00 per unit
Variable manufacturing cost per unit, including direct materials	$5.10 per unit
Variable operating (marketing) cost per unit sold	$1.10 per unit sold
Fixed manufacturing costs	$1,440,000
Denominator-level machine-hours	6,000
Standard production rate	50 units per machine-hour
Fixed operating (marketing) costs	$1,080,000

Assume standard costs per unit are the same for units in beginning inventory and units produced during the year. Also, assume no price, spending, or efficiency variances. Any production-volume variance is written off to cost of goods sold in the month in which it occurs.

1. Prepare income statements under variable and absorption costing for the year ended December 31, 2012. **Required**
2. What is Zwatch's operating income as percentage of revenues under each costing method?
3. Explain the difference in operating income between the two methods.
4. Which costing method would you recommend to the CFO? Why?

9-21 Absorption and variable costing. (CMA) Osawa, Inc., planned and actually manufactured 200,000 units of its single product in 2012, its first year of operation. Variable manufacturing cost was $20 per unit produced. Variable operating (nonmanufacturing) cost was $10 per unit sold. Planned and actual fixed manufacturing costs were $600,000. Planned and actual fixed operating (nonmanufacturing) costs totaled $400,000. Osawa sold 120,000 units of product at $40 per unit.

1. Osawa's 2012 operating income using absorption costing is (a) $440,000, (b) $200,000, (c) $600,000, **Required** (d) $840,000, or (e) none of these. Show supporting calculations.
2. Osawa's 2012 operating income using variable costing is (a) $800,000, (b) $440,000, (c) $200,000, (d) $600,000, or (e) none of these. Show supporting calculations.

9-22 Absorption versus variable costing. Grunewald Company manufacturers a professional grade vacuum cleaner and began operations in 2011. For 2011, Grunewald budgeted to produce and sell 20,000 units. The company had no price, spending, or efficiency variances, and writes off production-volume variance to cost of goods sold. Actual data for 2011 are given as follows:

	A	B
	Home Insert Page Layout Formulas Data	
	A	B
1	Units produced	18,000
2	Units sold	17,500
3	Selling price	$ 425
4	Variable costs:	
5	Manufacturing cost per unit produced	
6	Direct materials	$ 30
7	Direct manufacturing labor	25
8	Manufacturing overhead	00
9	Marketing cost per unit sold	45
10	Fixed costs:	
11	Manufacturing costs	$1,100,000
12	Administrative costs	965,450
13	Marketing	1,366,400

1. Prepare a 2011 income statement for Grunewald Company using variable costing. **Required**
2. Prepare a 2011 income statement for Grunewald Company using absorption costing.
3. Explain the differences in operating incomes obtained in requirement 1 and requirement 2.
4. Grunewald's management is considering implementing a bonus for the supervisors based on gross margin under absorption costing. What incentives will this create for the supervisors? What modifications could Grunewald management make to improve such a plan? Explain briefly.

9-23 Comparison of actual-costing methods. The Rehe Company sells its razors at $3 per unit. The company uses a first-in, first-out actual costing system. A fixed manufacturing cost rate is computed at the end of each year by dividing the actual fixed manufacturing costs by the actual production units. The following data are related to its first two years of operation:

	2011	2012
Sales	1,000 units	1,200 units
Production	1,400 units	1,000 units
Costs:		
Variable manufacturing	$ 700	$ 500
Fixed manufacturing	700	700
Variable operating (marketing)	1,000	1,200
Fixed operating (marketing)	400	400

Required

1. Prepare income statements based on variable costing for each of the two years.
2. Prepare income statements based on absorption costing for each of the two years.
3. Prepare a numerical reconciliation and explanation of the difference between operating income for each year under absorption costing and variable costing.
4. Critics have claimed that a widely used accounting system has led to undesirable buildups of inventory levels. (a) Is variable costing or absorption costing more likely to lead to such buildups? Why? (b) What can be done to counteract undesirable inventory buildups?

9-24 Variable and absorption costing, sales, and operating-income changes. Helmetsmart, a three-year-old company, has been producing and selling a single type of bicycle helmet. Helmetsmart uses standard costing. After reviewing the income statements for the first three years, Stuart Weil, president of Helmetsmart, commented, "I was told by our accountants—and in fact, I have memorized—that our breakeven volume is 49,000 units. I was happy that we reached that sales goal in each of our first two years. But, here's the strange thing: In our first year, we sold 49,000 units and indeed we broke even. Then, in our second year we sold the same volume and had a positive operating income. I didn't complain, of course . . . but here's the bad part. In our third year, we *sold 20% more* helmets, but our *operating income fell by more than 80%* relative to the second year! We didn't change our selling price or cost structure over the past three years and have no price, efficiency, or spending variances . . . so what's going on?!"

	Home	Insert	Page Layout	Formulas	Data	Review	View
	A				B	C	D
1	**Absorption Costing**						
2					**2011**	**2012**	**2013**
3	Sales (units)				49,000	49,000	58,800
4	Revenues				$1,960,000	$1,960,000	$2,352,000
5	Cost of goods sold						
6	Beginning inventory				0	0	352,800
7	Production				1,764,000	2,116,800	1,764,000
8	Available for sale				1,764,000	2,116,800	2,116,800
9	Deduct ending inventory				0	(352,800)	0
10	Adjustment for production-volume variance				0	(215,600)	0
11	Cost of goods sold				1,764,000	1,548,400	2,116,800
12	Gross margin				196,000	411,600	235,200
13	Selling and administrative expenses (all fixed)				196,000	196,000	196,000
14	Operating income				$ 0	$ 215,600	$ 39,200
15							
16	Beginning inventory				0	0	9,800
17	Production (units)				49,000	58,800	49,000
18	Sales (units)				49,000	49,000	58,800
19	Ending inventory				0	9,800	0
20	Variable manufacturing cost per unit				$ 14	$ 14	$ 14
21	Fixed manufacturing overhead costs				$1,078,000	$1,078,000	$1,078,000
22	Fixed manuf. costs allocated per unit produced				$ 22	$ 22	$ 22

Required

1. What denominator level is Helmetsmart using to allocate fixed manufacturing costs to the bicycle helmets? How is Helmetsmart disposing of any favorable or unfavorable production-volume variance at the end of the year? Explain your answer briefly.
2. How did Helmetsmart's accountants arrive at the breakeven volume of 49,000 units?
3. Prepare a variable costing-based income statement for each year. Explain the variation in variable costing operating income for each year based on contribution margin per unit and sales volume.
4. Reconcile the operating incomes under variable costing and absorption costing for each year, and use this information to explain to Stuart Weil the positive operating income in 2012 and the drop in operating income in 2013.

9-25 Capacity management, denominator-level capacity concepts. Match each of the following items with one or more of the denominator-level capacity concepts by putting the appropriate letter(s) by each item:

a. Theoretical capacity
b. Practical capacity
c. Normal capacity utilization
d. Master-budget capacity utilization

1. Measures the denominator level in terms of what a plant can supply
2. Is based on producing at full efficiency all the time
3. Represents the expected level of capacity utilization for the next budget period
4. Measures the denominator level in terms of demand for the output of the plant
5. Takes into account seasonal, cyclical, and trend factors
6. Should be used for performance evaluation in the current year
7. Represents an ideal benchmark
8. Highlights the cost of capacity acquired but not used
9. Should be used for long-term pricing purposes
10. Hides the cost of capacity acquired but not used
11. If used as the denominator-level concept, would avoid the restatement of unit costs when expected demand levels change

9-26 Denominator-level problem. Thunder Bolt, Inc., is a manufacturer of the very popular G36 motorcycles. The management at Thunder Bolt has recently adopted absorption costing and is debating which denominator-level concept to use. The G36 motorcycles sell for an average price of $8,200. Budgeted fixed manufacturing overhead costs for 2012 are estimated at $6,480,000. Thunder Bolt, Inc., uses subassembly operators that provide component parts. The following are the denominator-level options that management has been considering:

a. Theoretical capacity—based on three shifts, completion of five motorcycles per shift, and a 360-day year—3 × 5 × 360 = 5,400.
b. Practical capacity—theoretical capacity adjusted for unavoidable interruptions, breakdowns, and so forth—3 × 4 × 320 = 3,840.
c. Normal capacity utilization—estimated at 3,240 units.
d. Master-budget capacity utilization—the strengthening stock market and the growing popularity of motorcycles have prompted the marketing department to issue an estimate for 2012 of 3,600 units.

1. Calculate the budgeted fixed manufacturing overhead cost rates under the four denominator-level concepts.
2. What are the benefits to Thunder Bolt, Inc., of using either theoretical capacity or practical capacity?
3. Under a cost-based pricing system, what are the negative aspects of a master-budget denominator level? What are the positive aspects?

Required

9-27 Variable and absorption costing and breakeven points. Mega-Air, Inc., manufactures a specialized snowboard made for the advanced snowboarder. Mega-Air began 2011 with an inventory of 240 snowboards. During the year, it produced 900 boards and sold 995 for $750 each. Fixed production costs were $280,000 and variable production costs were $335 per unit. Fixed advertising, marketing, and other general and administrative expenses were $112,000 and variable shipping costs were $15 per board. Assume that the cost of each unit in beginning inventory is equal to 2011 inventory cost.

1. Prepare an income statement assuming Mega-Air uses variable costing.
2. Prepare an income statement assuming Mega-Air uses absorption costing. Mega-Air uses a denominator level of 1,000 units. Production-volume variances are written off to cost of goods sold.
3. Compute the breakeven point in units sold assuming Mega-Air uses the following:
   a. Variable costing
   b. Absorption costing (Production = 900 boards)
4. Provide proof of your preceding breakeven calculations.
5. Assume that $20,000 of fixed administrative costs were reclassified as fixed production costs. Would this change affect breakeven point using variable costing? What if absorption costing were used? Explain.
6. The company that supplies Mega-Air with its specialized impact-resistant material has announced a price increase of $25 for each board. What effect would this have on the breakeven points previously calculated?

Required

MyAccountingLab

Problems

9-28 Variable costing versus absorption costing. The Mavis Company uses an absorption-costing system based on standard costs. Total variable manufacturing cost, including direct material cost, is $3 per unit; the standard production rate is 10 units per machine-hour. Total budgeted and actual fixed manufacturing overhead costs are $420,000. Fixed manufacturing overhead is allocated at $7 per machine-hour ($420,000 ÷ 60,000 machine-hours of denominator level). Selling price is $5 per unit. Variable operating (nonmanufacturing) cost, which is driven by units sold, is $1 per unit. Fixed operating (nonmanufacturing) costs are $120,000. Beginning inventory in 2012 is 30,000 units; ending inventory is 40,000 units. Sales in 2012 are 540,000 units. The same standard unit costs persisted throughout 2011 and 2012. For simplicity, assume that there are no price, spending, or efficiency variances.

Required

1. Prepare an income statement for 2012 assuming that the production-volume variance is written off at year-end as an adjustment to cost of goods sold.
2. The president has heard about variable costing. She asks you to recast the 2012 statement as it would appear under variable costing.
3. Explain the difference in operating income as calculated in requirements 1 and 2.
4. Graph how fixed manufacturing overhead is accounted for under absorption costing. That is, there will be two lines: one for the budgeted fixed manufacturing overhead (which is equal to the actual fixed manufacturing overhead in this case) and one for the fixed manufacturing overhead allocated. Show how the production-volume variance might be indicated in the graph.
5. Critics have claimed that a widely used accounting system has led to undesirable buildups of inventory levels. (a) Is variable costing or absorption costing more likely to lead to such buildups? Why? (b) What can be done to counteract undesirable inventory buildups?

9-29 Variable costing and absorption costing, the All-Fixed Company. (R. Marple, adapted) It is the end of 2011. The All-Fixed Company began operations in January 2010. The company is so named because it has no variable costs. All its costs are fixed; they do not vary with output.

The All-Fixed Company is located on the bank of a river and has its own hydroelectric plant to supply power, light, and heat. The company manufactures a synthetic fertilizer from air and river water and sells its product at a price that is not expected to change. It has a small staff of employees, all paid fixed annual salaries. The output of the plant can be increased or decreased by adjusting a few dials on a control panel.

The following budgeted and actual data are for the operations of the All-Fixed Company. All-Fixed uses budgeted production as the denominator level and writes off any production-volume variance to cost of goods sold.

	2010	2011[a]
Sales	20,000 tons	20,000 tons
Production	40,000 tons	0 tons
Selling price	$ 20 per ton	$ 20 per ton
Costs (all fixed):		
Manufacturing	$320,000	$320,000
Operating (nonmanufacturing)	$ 60,000	$ 60,000

[a] Management adopted the policy, effective January 1, 2011, of producing only as much product as needed to fill sales orders. During 2011, sales were the same as for 2010 and were filled entirely from inventory at the start of 2011.

Required

1. Prepare income statements with one column for 2010, one column for 2011, and one column for the two years together, using (a) variable costing and (b) absorption costing.
2. What is the breakeven point under (a) variable costing and (b) absorption costing?
3. What inventory costs would be carried in the balance sheet on December 31, 2010 and 2011, under each method?
4. Assume that the performance of the top manager of the company is evaluated and rewarded largely on the basis of reported operating income. Which costing method would the manager prefer? Why?

9-30 Comparison of variable costing and absorption costing. Hinkle Company uses standard costing. Tim Bartina, the new president of Hinkle Company, is presented with the following data for 2012:

	A	B	C
		Home Insert Page Layout Formulas Data Review View	
1	Hinkle Company		
2	Income Statements for the Year Ended December 31, 2012		
3		Variable	Absorption
4		Costing	Costing
5	Revenues	$9,000,000	$9,000,000
6	Cost of goods sold (at standard costs)	4,680,000	5,860,000
7	Fixed manufacturing overhead (budgeted)	1,200,000	-
8	Fixed manufacturing overhead variances (all unfavorable):		
9	Spending	100,000	100,000
10	Production volume	-	400,000
11	Total marketing and administrative costs (all fixed)	1,500,000	1,500,000
12	Total costs	7,480,000	7,860,000
13	Operating income	$1,520,000	$1,140,000
14			
15	Inventories (at standard costs)		
16	December 31, 2011	$1,200,000	$1,720,000
17	December 31, 2012	66,000	206,000

Required

1. At what percentage of denominator level was the plant operating during 2012?
2. How much fixed manufacturing overhead was included in the 2011 and the 2012 ending inventory under absorption costing?
3. Reconcile and explain the difference in 2012 operating incomes under variable and absorption costing.
4. Tim Bartina is concerned: He notes that despite an increase in sales over 2011, 2012 operating income has actually declined under absorption costing. Explain how this occurred.

9-31 Effects of differing production levels on absorption costing income: Metrics to minimize inventory buildups. University Press produces textbooks for college courses. The company recently hired a new editor, Leslie White, to handle production and sales of books for an introduction to accounting course. Leslie's compensation depends on the gross margin associated with sales of this book. Leslie needs to decide how many copies of the book to produce. The following information is available for the fall semester 2011:

Estimated sales	20,000 books
Beginning inventory	0 books
Average selling price	$80 per book
Variable production costs	$50 per book
Fixed production costs	$400,000 per semester

The fixed cost allocation rate is based on expected sales and is therefore equal to $400,000/20,000 books = $20 per book

Leslie has decided to produce either 20,000, 24,000, or 30,000 books.

Required

1. Calculate expected gross margin if Leslie produces 20,000, 24,000, or 30,000 books. (Make sure you include the production-volume variance as part of cost of goods sold.)
2. Calculate ending inventory in units and in dollars for each production level.

3. Managers who are paid a bonus that is a function of gross margin may be inspired to produce a product in excess of demand to maximize their own bonus. The chapter suggested metrics to discourage managers from producing products in excess of demand. Do you think the following metrics will accomplish this objective? Show your work.

   a. Incorporate a charge of 10% of the cost of the ending inventory as an expense for evaluating the manager.

   b. Include nonfinancial measures (such as the ones recommended on p. 311) when evaluating management and rewarding performance.

9-32 Alternative denominator-level capacity concepts, effect on operating income. Lucky Lager has just purchased the Austin Brewery. The brewery is two years old and uses absorption costing. It will "sell" its product to Lucky Lager at $45 per barrel. Paul Brandon, Lucky Lager's controller, obtains the following information about Austin Brewery's capacity and budgeted fixed manufacturing costs for 2012:

	Home	Insert	Page Layout	Formulas	Data	Review	View	
	A			B	C	D	E	
1				**Budgeted Fixed**	**Days of**	**Hours of**		
2	**Denominator-Level**			**Manufacturing**	**Production**	**Production**	**Barrels**	
3	**Capacity Concept**			**Overhead per Period**	**per Period**	**per Day**	**per Hour**	
4	Theoretical capacity			$28,000,000	360	24	540	
5	Practical capacity			$28,000,000	350	20	500	
6	Normal capacity utilization			$28,000,000	350	20	400	
7	Master-budget capacity for each half year							
8	(a) January–June 2012			$14,000,000	175	20	320	
9	(b) July–December 2012			$14,000,000	175	20	480	

Required

1. Compute the budgeted fixed manufacturing overhead rate per barrel for each of the denominator-level capacity concepts. Explain why they are different.

2. In 2012, the Austin Brewery reported these production results:

	Home	Insert	Page Layout	Formulas	Data
	A				B
12	Beginning inventory in barrels, 1-1-2012				0
13	Production in barrels				2,600,000
14	Ending inventory in barrels, 12-31-2012				200,000
15	Actual variable manufacturing costs				$78,520,000
16	Actual fixed manufacturing overhead costs				$27,088,000

There are no variable cost variances. Fixed manufacturing overhead cost variances are written off to cost of goods sold in the period in which they occur. Compute the Austin Brewery's operating income when the denominator-level capacity is (a) theoretical capacity, (b) practical capacity, and (c) normal capacity utilization.

9-33 Motivational considerations in denominator-level capacity selection (continuation of 9-32).

Required

1. If the plant manager of the Austin Brewery gets a bonus based on operating income, which denominator-level capacity concept would he prefer to use? Explain.

2. What denominator-level capacity concept would Lucky Lager prefer to use for U.S. income-tax reporting? Explain.

3. How might the IRS limit the flexibility of an absorption-costing company like Lucky Lager attempting to minimize its taxable income?

9-34 Denominator-level choices, changes in inventory levels, effect on operating income. Koshu Corporation is a manufacturer of computer accessories. It uses absorption costing based on standard costs and reports the following data for 2011:

	Home	Insert	Page Layout	Formulas	Data	Review
	A				B	C
1	Theoretical capacity				280,000	units
2	Practical capacity				224,000	units
3	Normal capacity utilization				200,000	units
4	Selling price				$ 40	per unit
5	Beginning inventory				20,000	units
6	Production				220,000	units
7	Sales volume				230,000	units
8	Variable budgeted manufacturing cost				$ 5	per unit
9	Total budgeted fixed manufacturing costs				$2,800,000	
10	Total budgeted operating (nonmanuf.) costs (all fixed)				$ 900,000	

There are no price, spending, or efficiency variances. Actual operating costs equal budgeted operating costs. The production-volume variance is written off to cost of goods sold. For each choice of denominator level, the budgeted production cost per unit is also the cost per unit of beginning inventory.

1. What is the production-volume variance in 2011 when the denominator level is (a) theoretical capacity, (b) practical capacity, and (c) normal capacity utilization?
2. Prepare absorption costing–based income statements for Koshu Corporation using theoretical capacity, practical capacity, and normal capacity utilization as the denominator levels.
3. Why is the operating income under normal capacity utilization lower than the other two scenarios?
4. Reconcile the difference in operating income based on theoretical capacity and practical capacity with the difference in fixed manufacturing overhead included in inventory.

9-35 Effects of denominator-level choice. Carlisle Company is a manufacturer of precision surgical tools. It initiated standard costing and a flexible budget on January 1, 2011. The company president, Monica Carlisle, has been pondering how fixed manufacturing overhead should be allocated to products. Machine-hours have been chosen as the allocation base. Her remaining uncertainty is the denominator level for machine-hours. She decides to wait for the first month's results before making a final choice of what denominator level should be used from that day forward.

During January 2011, the actual units of output had a standard of 37,680 machine-hours allowed. The fixed manufacturing overhead spending variance was $6,000, favorable. If the company used practical capacity as the denominator level, the production-volume variance would be $12,200, unfavorable. If the company used normal capacity utilization as the denominator level, the production-volume variance would be $2,400, unfavorable. Budgeted fixed manufacturing overhead was $96,600 for the month.

1. Compute the denominator level, assuming that the normal-capacity-utilization concept is chosen.
2. Compute the denominator level, assuming that the practical-capacity concept is chosen.
3. Suppose you are the executive vice president. You want to maximize your 2011 bonus, which depends on 2011 operating income. Assume that the production-volume variance is written off to cost of goods sold at year-end, and assume that the company expects inventories to increase during the year. Which denominator level would you favor? Why?

9-36 Downward demand spiral. Spirelli Company is about to enter the highly competitive personal electronics market with a new optical reader. In anticipation of future growth, the company has leased a large manufacturing facility, and has purchased several expensive pieces of equipment. In 2011, the company's first year, Spirelli budgets for production and sales of 25,000 units, compared with its practical capacity of 50,000. The company's cost data follow:

	Home	Insert	Page Layout	Formulas	Data
	A				B
1	Variable manufacturing costs per unit:				
2	Direct materials				$ 24
3	Direct manufacturing labor				36
4	Manufacturing overhead				12
5	Fixed manufacturing overhead				$700,000

Required 1. Assume that Spirelli uses absorption costing, and uses budgeted units produced as the denominator for calculating its fixed manufacturing overhead rate. Selling price is set at 120% of manufacturing cost. Compute Spirelli's selling price.

2. Spirelli enters the market with the selling price computed previously. However, despite growth in the overall market, sales are not as robust as had been expected, and a competitor has priced its product $15 lower than Spirelli's. Enrico Spirelli, the company's president, insists that the competitor must be pricing its product at a loss, and that the competitor will be unable to sustain that. In response, Spirelli makes no price adjustments, but budgets production and sales for 2012 at 22,000 units. Variable and fixed costs are not expected to change. Compute Spirelli's new selling price. Comment on how Spirelli's choice of budgeted production affected its selling price and competitive position.

3. Recompute the selling price using practical capacity as the denominator level of activity. How would this choice have affected Spirelli's position in the marketplace? Generally, how would this choice affect the production-volume variance?

9-37 Absorption costing and production-volume variance—alternative capacity bases. Earth's Best Light (EBL), a producer of energy-efficient light bulbs, expects that demand will increase markedly over the next decade. Due to the high fixed costs involved in the business, EBL has decided to evaluate its financial performance using absorption costing income. The production-volume variance is written off to cost of goods sold. The variable cost of production is $2.70 per bulb. Fixed manufacturing costs are $1,015,000 per year. Variable and fixed selling and administrative expenses are $0.40 per bulb sold and $200,000, respectively. Because its light bulbs are currently popular with environmentally-conscious customers, EBL can sell the bulbs for $9.60 each.

EBL is deciding among various concepts of capacity for calculating the cost of each unit produced. Its choices are as follows:

Theoretical capacity	725,000 bulbs
Practical capacity	406,000 bulbs
Normal capacity	290,000 bulbs (average expected output for the next three years)
Master budget capacity	175,000 bulbs expected production this year

Required 1. Calculate the inventoriable cost per unit using each level of capacity to compute fixed manufacturing cost per unit.

2. Suppose EBL actually produces 250,000 bulbs. Calculate the production-volume variance using each level of capacity to compute the fixed manufacturing overhead allocation rate.

3. Assume EBL has no beginning inventory. If this year's actual sales are 175,000 bulbs, calculate operating income for EBL using each type of capacity to compute fixed manufacturing cost per unit.

9-38 Operating income effects of denominator-level choice and disposal of production-volume variance (continuation of 9-37).

Required 1. If EBL sells all 250,000 bulbs produced, what would be the effect on operating income of using each type of capacity as a basis for calculating manufacturing cost per unit?

2. Compare the results of operating income at different capacity levels when 175,000 bulbs are sold and when 250,000 bulbs are sold. What conclusion can you draw from the comparison?

3. Using the original data (that is, 250,000 units produced and 175,000 units sold) if EBL had used the pro-ration approach to allocate the production-volume variance, what would operating income have been under each level of capacity? (Assume that there is no ending work in process.)

9-39 Cost allocation, downward demand spiral. Cayzer Associates operates a chain of 10 hospitals in the Los Angeles area. Its central food-catering facility, Mealman, prepares and delivers meals to the hospitals. It has the capacity to deliver up to 1,300,000 meals a year. In 2012, based on estimates from each hospital controller, Mealman budgeted for 975,000 meals a year. Budgeted fixed costs in 2012 were $1,521,000. Each hospital was charged $6.46 per meal—$4.90 variable costs plus $1.56 allocated budgeted fixed cost.

Recently, the hospitals have been complaining about the quality of Mealman's meals and their rising costs. In mid-2012, Cayzer's president announces that all Cayzer hospitals and support facilities will be run as profit centers. Hospitals will be free to purchase quality-certified services from outside the system. Ron Smith, Mealman's controller, is preparing the 2013 budget. He hears that three hospitals have decided to use outside suppliers for their meals; this will reduce the 2013 estimated demand to 780,000 meals. No change in variable cost per meal or total fixed costs is expected in 2013.

Required 1. How did Smith calculate the budgeted fixed cost per meal of $1.56 in 2012?

2. Using the same approach to calculating budgeted fixed cost per meal and pricing as in 2012, how much would hospitals be charged for each Mealman meal in 2013? What would their reaction be?

3. Suggest an alternative cost-based price per meal that Smith might propose and that might be more acceptable to the hospitals. What can Mealman and Smith do to make this price profitable in the long run?

9-40 **Cost allocation, responsibility accounting, ethics (continuation of 9-39).** In 2013, only 760,500 Mealman meals were produced and sold to the hospitals. Smith suspects that hospital controllers had systematically inflated their 2013 meal estimates.

1. Recall that Mealman uses the master-budget capacity utilization to allocate fixed costs and to price **Required** meals. What was the effect of production-volume variance on Mealman's operating income in 2013?
2. Why might hospital controllers deliberately overestimate their future meal counts?
3. What other evidence should Cayzer's president seek to investigate Smith's concerns?
4. Suggest two specific steps that Smith might take to reduce hospital controllers' incentives to inflate their estimated meal counts.

Collaborative Learning Problem

9-41 **Absorption, variable, and throughput costing; performance evaluation.** Mile-High Foods, Inc., was formed in March 2011 to provide prepackaged snack boxes for a new low cost regional airline beginning on April 1. The company has just leased warehouse space central to the two airports to store materials.

To move packaged materials from the warehouses to the airports, where final assembly will take place, Mile-High must choose whether to lease a delivery truck and pay a full-time driver at a fixed cost of $5,000 per month, or pay a delivery service a rate equivalent to $0.40 per box. This cost will be included in either fixed manufacturing overhead or variable manufacturing overhead, depending on which option is chosen. The company is hoping for rapid growth, as sales forecasts for the new airline are promising. However, it is essential that Mile-High managers carefully control costs in order to be compliant with their sales contract and remain profitable.

Ron Spencer, the company's president, is trying to determine whether to use absorption, variable, or throughput costing to evaluate the performance of company managers. For absorption costing, he intends to use the practical-capacity level of the facility, which is 20,000 boxes per month. Production-volume variances will be written off to cost of goods sold.

Costs for the three months are expected to remain unchanged. The costs and revenues for April, May, and June are expected to be as follows:

Sales revenue	$6.00 per box
Direct material cost	$1.20 per box
Direct manufacturing labor cost	$0.35 per box
Variable manufacturing overhead cost	$0.15 per box
Variable delivery cost (if this option is chosen)	$0.40 per box
Fixed delivery cost (if this option is chosen)	$5,000 per month
Fixed manufacturing overhead costs	$15,000 per month
Fixed administrative costs	$28,000 per month

Projected production and sales for each month follow. High production in May is the result of an anticipated surge in June employee vacations.

	Sales (in units)	Production
April	12,000	12,200
May	12,500	18,000
June	13,000	9,000
Total	37,500	39,200

1. Compute operating income for April, May, and June under absorption costing, assuming that Mile-High **Required** opts to use
   a. the leased truck and salaried driver.
   b. the variable delivery service.
2. Compute operating income for April, May, and June under variable costing, assuming that Mile-High opts to use
   a. the leased truck and salaried driver.
   b. the variable delivery service.
3. Compute operating income for April, May, and June under throughput costing, assuming that Mile-High opts to use
   a. the leased truck and salaried driver.
   b. the variable delivery service.
4. Should Mile-High choose absorption, variable, or throughput costing for evaluating the performance of managers? Why? What advantages and disadvantages might there be in adopting throughput costing?
5. Should Mile-High opt for the leased truck and salaried driver or the variable delivery service? Explain briefly.

10 Determining How Costs Behave

10 Determining How Costs Behave

What is the value of looking at the past?

Perhaps it is to recall fond memories you've had or help you understand historical events. Maybe your return to the past enables you to better understand and predict the future. When an organization looks at the past, it typically does so to analyze its results, so that the best decisions can be made for the company's future. This activity requires gathering information about costs and how they behave so that managers can predict what they will be "down the road." Gaining a deeper understanding of cost behavior can also spur a firm to reorganize its operations in innovative ways and tackle important challenges, as the following article shows.

Management Accountants at Cisco Embrace Opportunities, Enhance Sustainability[1]

Understanding how costs behave is a valuable technical skill. Managers look to management accountants to help them identify cost drivers, estimate cost relationships, and determine the fixed and variable components of costs. To be effective, management accountants must have a clear understanding of the business's strategy and operations to identify new opportunities to reduce costs and increase profitability. At Cisco Systems, management accountants' in-depth understanding of the company's costs and operations led to reduced costs, while also helping the environment.

Cisco, makers of computer networking equipment including routers and wireless switches, traditionally regarded the used equipment it received back from its business customers as scrap and recycled it at a cost of about $8 million a year. As managers looked at the accumulated costs and realized that they may literally be "throwing away money," they decided to reassess their treatment of scrap material. In 2005, managers at Cisco began trying to find uses for the equipment, mainly because 80% of the returns were in working condition. A value recovery team at Cisco identified groups within the company that could use the returned equipment. These included its customer service group, which supports warranty claims and service

[1] *Source:* Nidumolu, R., C. Prahalad, and M. Rangaswami. 2009. Why sustainability is now the key driver of innovation. *Harvard Business Review,* September 2009; Cisco Systems, Inc. 2009. 2009 corporate social responsibility report. San Jose, CA: Cisco Systems, Inc.

contracts, and the labs that provide technical support, training, and product demonstrations.

Based on the initial success of the value recovery team, in 2005, Cisco designated its recycling group as a company business unit, set clear objectives for it, and assigned the group its own income statement. As a result, the reuse of equipment rose from 5% in 2004 to 45% in 2008, and Cisco's recycling costs fell by 40%. The unit has become a profit center that contributed $153 million to Cisco's bottom line in 2008.

With product returns reducing corporate profitability by an average of about 4% a year, companies like Cisco can leverage management accountants' insight to reduce the cost of these returns while decreasing its environmental footprint. Not only can this turn a cost center into a profitable business, but sustainability efforts like these signals that the company is concerned about preventing environmental damage by reducing waste.

As the Cisco example illustrates, managers must understand how costs behave to make strategic and operating decisions that have a positive environmental impact. Consider several other examples. Managers at FedEx decided to replace old planes with new Boeing 757s that reduced fuel consumption by 36%, while increasing capacity by 20%. At Clorox, managers decided to create a new line of non-synthetic cleaning products that were better for the environment and helped create a new category of 'green' cleaning products worth about $200 million annually.

In each situation, knowledge of cost behavior was needed to answer key questions. This chapter will focus on how managers determine cost-behavior patterns—that is, how costs change in relation to changes in activity levels, in the quantity of products produced, and so on.

Basic Assumptions and Examples of Cost Functions

Learning Objective 1

Describe linear cost functions

. . . graph of cost function is a straight line

and three common ways in which they behave

. . . variable, fixed, and mixed

Managers are able to understand cost behavior through cost functions. A **cost function** is a mathematical description of how a cost changes with changes in the level of an activity relating to that cost. Cost functions can be plotted on a graph by measuring the level of an activity, such as number of batches produced or number of machine-hours used, on the horizontal axis (called the x-axis) and the amount of total costs corresponding to—or, preferably, dependent on—the levels of that activity on the vertical axis (called the y-axis).

Basic Assumptions

Managers often estimate cost functions based on two assumptions:

1. Variations in the level of a single activity (the cost driver) explain the variations in the related total costs.

2. Cost behavior is approximated by a linear cost function within the relevant range. Recall that a relevant range is the range of the activity in which there is a relationship between total cost and the level of activity. For a **linear cost function** represented graphically, total cost versus the level of a single activity related to that cost is a straight line within the relevant range.

We use these two assumptions throughout most, but not all, of this chapter. Not all cost functions are linear and can be explained by a single activity. Later sections will discuss cost functions that do not rely on these assumptions.

Linear Cost Functions

To understand three basic types of linear cost functions and to see the role of cost functions in business decisions, consider the negotiations between Cannon Services and World Wide Communications (WWC) for exclusive use of a videoconferencing line between New York and Paris.

■ **Alternative 1:** $5 per minute used. Total cost to Cannon changes in proportion to the number of minutes used. The number of minutes used is the only factor whose change causes a change in total cost.

Panel A in Exhibit 10-1 presents this *variable cost* for Cannon Services. Under alternative 1, there is no fixed cost. We write the cost function in Panel A of Exhibit 10-1 as

$$y = \$5X$$

where X measures the number of minutes used (on the x-axis), and y measures the total cost of the minutes used (on the y-axis) calculated using the cost function. Panel A illustrates the $5 **slope coefficient**, the amount by which total cost changes when a one-unit change occurs in the level of activity (one minute of usage in the Cannon example). *Throughout the chapter, uppercase letters, such as X, refer to the actual observations, and lowercase letters, such as y, represent estimates or calculations made using a cost function.*

■ **Alternative 2:** Total cost will be fixed at $10,000 per month, regardless of the number of minutes used. (We use the same activity measure, number of minutes used, to compare cost-behavior patterns under the three alternatives.)

Panel B in Exhibit 10-1 presents this *fixed cost* for Cannon Services. We write the cost function in Panel B as

$$y = \$10,000$$

Exhibit 10-1   Examples of Linear Cost Functions

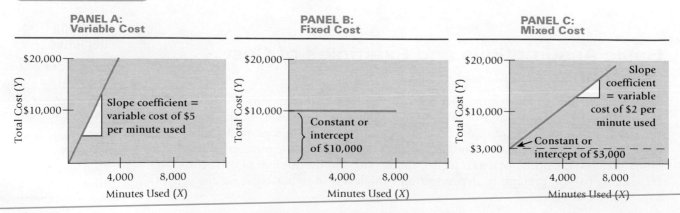

PANEL A:
Variable Cost

Total Cost (Y)

$20,000

$10,000

Slope coefficient = variable cost of $5 per minute used

4,000   8,000
Minutes Used (X)

PANEL B:
Fixed Cost

Total Cost (Y)

$20,000

$10,000

Constant or intercept of $10,000

4,000   8,000
Minutes Used (X)

PANEL C:
Mixed Cost

Total Cost (Y)

$20,000

$10,000

$3,000

Slope coefficient = variable cost of $2 per minute used

Constant or intercept of $3,000

4,000   8,000
Minutes Used (X)

The fixed cost of $10,000 is called a **constant**; it is the component of total cost that does not vary with changes in the level of the activity. Under alternative 2, the constant accounts for all the cost because there is no variable cost. Graphically, the slope coefficient of the cost function is zero; this cost function intersects the y-axis at the constant value, and therefore the *constant* is also called the **intercept**.

■ **Alternative 3:** $3,000 per month plus $2 per minute used. This is an example of a mixed cost. A **mixed cost**—also called a **semivariable cost**—is a cost that has both fixed and variable elements.

Panel C in Exhibit 10-1 presents this *mixed cost* for Cannon Services. We write the cost function in Panel C of Exhibit 10-1 as

$$y = \$3,000 + \$2X$$

Unlike the graphs for alternatives 1 and 2, Panel C has both a constant, or intercept, value of $3,000 and a slope coefficient of $2. In the case of a mixed cost, total cost in the relevant range increases as the number of minutes used increases. Note that total cost does not vary strictly in proportion to the number of minutes used within the relevant range. For example, with 4,000 minutes of usage, the total cost equals $11,000 [$3,000 + ($2 per minute × 4,000 minutes)], but when 8,000 minutes are used, total cost equals $19,000 [$3,000 + ($2 per minute × 8,000 minutes)]. Although the usage in terms of minutes has doubled, total cost has increased by only about 73% [($19,000 – $11,000) ÷ $11,000].

Cannon's managers must understand the cost-behavior patterns in the three alternatives to choose the best deal with WWC. Suppose Cannon expects to do at least 4,000 minutes of videoconferencing per month. Its cost for 4,000 minutes under the three alternatives would be as follows:

■ **Alternative 1:** $20,000 ($5 per minute × 4,000 minutes)

■ **Alternative 2:** $10,000

■ **Alternative 3:** $11,000 [$3,000 + ($2 per minute × 4,000 minutes)]

Alternative 2 is the least costly. Moreover, if Cannon were to use more than 4,000 minutes, as is likely to be the case, alternatives 1 and 3 would be even more costly. Cannon's managers, therefore, should choose alternative 2.

Note that the graphs in Exhibit 10-1 are linear. That is, they appear as straight lines. We simply need to know the constant, or intercept, amount (commonly designated a) and the slope coefficient (commonly designated b). For any linear cost function based on a single activity (recall our two assumptions discussed at the start of the chapter), knowing a and b is sufficient to describe and graphically plot all the values within the relevant range of number of minutes used. We write a general form of this linear cost function as

$$y = a + bX$$

Under alternative 1, a = $0 and b = $5 per minute used; under alternative 2, a = $10,000 and b = $0 per minute used; and under alternative 3, a = $3,000 and b = $2 per minute used. To plot the mixed-cost function in Panel C, we draw a line starting from the point marked $3,000 on the y-axis and increasing at a rate of $2 per minute used, so that at 1,000 minutes, total costs increase by $2,000 ($2 per minute × 1,000 minutes) to $5,000 ($3,000 + $2,000) and at 2,000 minutes, total costs increase by $4,000 ($2 per minute × 2,000 minutes) to $7,000 ($3,000 + $4,000) and so on.

Review of Cost Classification

Before we discuss issues related to the estimation of cost functions, we briefly review the three criteria laid out in Chapter 2 for classifying a cost into its variable and fixed components.

Choice of Cost Object

A particular cost item could be variable with respect to one cost object and fixed with respect to another cost object. Consider Super Shuttle, an airport transportation company. If the fleet of vans it owns is the cost object, then the annual van registration and license costs would be variable costs with respect to the number of vans owned. But if a particular van is the cost object, then the registration and license costs for that van are fixed costs with respect to the miles driven during a year.

Time Horizon

Whether a cost is variable or fixed with respect to a particular activity depends on the time horizon being considered in the decision situation. The longer the time horizon, all other things being equal, the more likely that the cost will be variable. For example, inspection costs at Boeing Company are typically fixed in the short run with respect to inspection-hours used because inspectors earn a fixed salary in a given year regardless of the number of inspection-hours of work done. But, in the long run, Boeing's total inspection costs will vary with the inspection-hours required: More inspectors will be hired if more inspection-hours are needed, and some inspectors will be reassigned to other tasks or laid off if fewer inspection-hours are needed.

Relevant Range

What is a linear cost function and what types of cost behavior can it represent?

Managers should never forget that variable and fixed cost-behavior patterns are valid for linear cost functions only within a given relevant range. Outside the relevant range, variable and fixed cost-behavior patterns change, causing costs to become nonlinear (nonlinear means the plot of the relationship on a graph is not a straight line). For example, Exhibit 10-2 plots the relationship (over several years) between total direct manufacturing labor costs and the number of snowboards produced each year by Ski Authority at its Vermont plant. In this case, the nonlinearities outside the relevant range occur because of labor and other inefficiencies (first because workers are learning to produce snowboards and later because capacity limits are being stretched). Knowing the relevant range is essential to properly classify costs.

Identifying Cost Drivers

Learning Objective 2

Explain the importance of causality in estimating cost functions

. . . only a cause-and-effect relationship establishes an economically plausible relationship between an activity and its costs

The Cannon Services/WWC example illustrates variable-, fixed-, and mixed-cost functions using information about *future* cost structures proposed to Cannon by WWC. Often, however, cost functions are estimated from *past* cost data. Managers use **cost estimation** to measure a relationship based on data from past costs and the related level of an activity. For example, marketing managers at Volkswagen could use cost estimation to understand what causes their marketing costs to change from year to year (for example, the number of new car models introduced or a competitor's sudden recall) and the fixed and variable components of these costs. Managers are interested in estimating past cost-behavior functions primarily because these estimates can help them make more-accurate **cost predictions**, or forecasts, of future costs. Better cost predictions help managers make more-informed planning and control decisions, such as preparing next year's marketing budget. But better management decisions, cost predictions, and estimation of cost functions can be achieved only if managers correctly identify the factors that affect costs.

Exhibit 10-2

Linearity Within Relevant Range for Ski Authority, Inc.

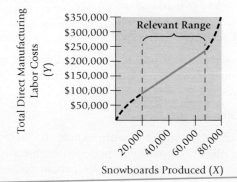

The Cause-and-Effect Criterion

The most important issue in estimating a cost function is determining whether a cause-and-effect relationship exists between the level of an activity and the costs related to that level of activity. Without a cause-and-effect relationship, managers will be less confident about their ability to estimate or predict costs. Recall from Chapter 2 that when a cause-and-effect relationship exists between a change in the level of an activity and a change in the level of total costs, we refer to the activity measure as a *cost driver*. We use the terms *level of activity* and *level of cost driver* interchangeably when estimating cost functions. Understanding the drivers of costs is crucially important for managing costs. The cause-and-effect relationship might arise as a result of the following:

- **A physical relationship between the level of activity and costs.** An example is when units of production are used as the activity that affects direct material costs. Producing more units requires more direct materials, which results in higher total direct material costs.

- **A contractual arrangement.** In alternative 1 of the Cannon Services example described earlier, number of minutes used is specified in the contract as the level of activity that affects the telephone line costs.

- **Knowledge of operations.** An example is when number of parts is used as the activity measure of ordering costs. A product with many parts will incur higher ordering costs than a product with few parts.

Managers must be careful not to interpret a high correlation, or connection, in the relationship between two variables to mean that either variable causes the other. Consider direct material costs and labor costs. For a given product mix, producing more units generally results in higher material costs and higher labor costs. Material costs and labor costs are highly correlated, but neither causes the other. Using labor costs to predict material costs is problematic. Some products require more labor costs relative to material costs, while other products require more material costs relative to labor costs. If the product mix changes toward more labor-intensive products, then labor costs will increase while material costs will decrease. Labor costs are a poor predictor of material costs. By contrast, factors that drive material costs such as product mix, product designs, and manufacturing processes, would have more accurately predicted the changes in material costs.

Only a cause-and-effect relationship—not merely correlation—establishes an economically plausible relationship between the level of an activity and its costs. Economic plausibility is critical because it gives analysts and managers confidence that the estimated relationship will appear again and again in other sets of data from the same situation. Identifying cost drivers also gives managers insights into ways to reduce costs and the confidence that reducing the quantity of the cost drivers will lead to a decrease in costs.

To identify cost drivers on the basis of data gathered over time, always use a long time horizon. Why? Because costs may be fixed in the short run (during which time they have no cost driver), but they are usually variable and have a cost driver in the long run.

Cost Drivers and the Decision-Making Process

Consider Elegant Rugs, which uses state-of-the-art automated weaving machines to produce carpets for homes and offices. Management has made many changes in manufacturing processes and wants to introduce new styles of carpets. It would like to evaluate how these changes have affected costs and what styles of carpets it should introduce. It follows the five-step decision-making process outlined in Chapter 1.

Step 1: Identify the problem and uncertainties. The changes in the manufacturing process were specifically targeted at reducing indirect manufacturing labor costs, and management wants to know whether costs such as supervision, maintenance, and quality control did, in fact, decrease. One option is to simply compare indirect manufacturing labor costs before and after the process change. The problem with this approach is that the volume of activity before and after the process change was very different so costs need to be compared after taking into account the change in activity volume.

Managers were fairly confident about the direct material and direct manufacturing labor costs of the new styles of carpets. They were less certain about the impact that the choice of different styles would have on indirect manufacturing costs.

Step 2: Obtain information. Managers gathered information about potential cost drivers—factors such as machine-hours or direct manufacturing labor-hours that cause indirect manufacturing labor costs to be incurred. They also began considering different techniques (discussed in the next section) such as the industrial engineering method, the conference method, the account analysis method, the high-low method, and the regression method for estimating the magnitude of the effect of the cost driver on indirect manufacturing labor costs. Their goal was to identify the best possible single cost driver.

Step 3: Make predictions about the future. Managers used past data to estimate the relationship between cost drivers and costs and used this relationship to predict future costs.

Step 4: Make decisions by choosing among alternatives. As we will describe later (pp. 353–355), Elegant Rugs chose machine-hours as the cost driver of indirect manufacturing labor costs. Using the regression analysis estimate of indirect manufacturing labor cost per machine-hour, managers estimated the costs of alternative styles of carpets and chose to introduce the most profitable styles.

Step 5: Implement the decision, evaluate performance, and learn. After the managers at Elegant Rugs introduced the new carpet styles, they focused on evaluating the results of their decision. Comparing predicted to actual costs helped managers to learn how accurate the estimates were, to set targets for continuous improvement, and to constantly seek ways to improve efficiency and effectiveness.

Decision Point ▶

What is the most important issue in estimating a cost function?

Cost Estimation Methods

As we mentioned in Step 2, four methods of cost estimation are the industrial engineering method, the conference method, the account analysis method, and the quantitative analysis method (which takes different forms). These methods differ with respect to how expensive they are to implement, the assumptions they make, and the information they provide about the accuracy of the estimated cost function. They are not mutually exclusive, and many organizations use a combination of these methods.

Learning Objective 3

Understand various methods of cost estimation

. . . for example, the regression analysis method determines the line that best fits past data

---

Industrial Engineering Method

The **industrial engineering method**, also called the **work-measurement method**, estimates cost functions by analyzing the relationship between inputs and outputs in physical terms. Consider Elegant Rugs. It uses inputs of cotton, wool, dyes, direct manufacturing labor, machine time, and power. Production output is square yards of carpet. Time-and-motion studies analyze the time required to perform the various operations to produce the carpet. For example, a time-and-motion study may conclude that to produce 10 square yards of carpet requires one hour of direct manufacturing labor. Standards and budgets transform these physical input measures into costs. The result is an estimated cost function relating direct manufacturing labor costs to the cost driver, square yards of carpet produced.

The industrial engineering method is a very thorough and detailed way to estimate a cost function when there is a physical relationship between inputs and outputs, but it can be very time consuming. Some government contracts mandate its use. Many organizations, such as Bose and Nokia, use it to estimate direct manufacturing costs but find it too costly or impractical for analyzing their entire cost structure. For example, physical relationships between inputs and outputs are difficult to specify for some items, such as indirect manufacturing costs, R&D costs, and advertising costs.

Conference Method

The **conference method** estimates cost functions on the basis of analysis and opinions about costs and their drivers gathered from various departments of a company (purchasing, process engineering, manufacturing, employee relations, etc.). The Cooperative Bank in the United Kingdom has a cost-estimating department that develops cost functions for its retail banking products (checking accounts, VISA cards, mortgages, and so on) based on the consensus of estimates from personnel of the particular departments. Elegant Rugs gathers opinions from supervisors and production engineers about how indirect manufacturing labor costs vary with machine-hours and direct manufacturing labor-hours.

The conference method encourages interdepartmental cooperation. The pooling of expert knowledge from different business functions of the value chain gives the conference method credibility. Because the conference method does not require detailed analysis of data, cost functions and cost estimates can be developed quickly. However, the emphasis on opinions rather than systematic estimation means that the accuracy of the cost estimates depends largely on the care and skill of the people providing the inputs.

Account Analysis Method

The **account analysis method** estimates cost functions by classifying various cost accounts as variable, fixed, or mixed with respect to the identified level of activity. Typically, managers use qualitative rather than quantitative analysis when making these cost-classification decisions. The account analysis approach is widely used because it is reasonably accurate, cost-effective, and easy to use.

Consider indirect manufacturing labor costs for a small production area (or cell) at Elegant Rugs. Indirect manufacturing labor costs include wages paid for supervision, maintenance, quality control, and setups. During the most recent 12-week period, Elegant Rugs ran the machines in the cell for a total of 862 hours and incurred total indirect manufacturing labor costs of $12,501. Using qualitative analysis, the manager and the cost analyst determine that over this 12-week period indirect manufacturing labor costs are mixed costs with only one cost driver—machine-hours. As machine-hours vary, one component of the cost (such as supervision cost) is fixed, whereas another component (such as maintenance cost) is variable. The goal is to use account analysis to estimate a linear cost function for indirect manufacturing labor costs with number of machine-hours as the cost driver. The cost analyst uses experience and judgment to separate total indirect manufacturing labor costs ($12,501) into costs that are fixed ($2,157, based on 950 hours of machine capacity for the cell over a 12-week period) and costs that are variable ($10,344) with respect to the number of machine-hours used. Variable cost per machine-hour is $10,344 ÷ 862 machine-hours = $12 per machine-hour. The linear cost equation, $y = a + bX$, in this example is as follows:

$$\text{Indirect manufacturing labor costs} = \$2,157 +$$
$$(\$12 \text{ per machine-hour} \times \text{Number of machine-hours})$$

Management at Elegant Rugs can use the cost function to estimate the indirect manufacturing labor costs of using, say, 950 machine-hours to produce carpet in the next 12-week period. Estimated costs equal $2,157 + (950 machine-hours × $12 per machine-hour) = $13,557.

To obtain reliable estimates of the fixed and variable components of cost, organizations must take care to ensure that individuals thoroughly knowledgeable about the operations make the cost-classification decisions. Supplementing the account analysis method with the conference method improves credibility.

Quantitative Analysis Method

Quantitative analysis uses a formal mathematical method to fit cost functions to past data observations. Excel is a useful tool for performing quantitative analysis. Columns B and C of Exhibit 10-3 show the breakdown of Elegant Rugs' total machine-hours (862) and total indirect manufacturing labor costs ($12,501) into weekly data for the most recent 12-week period. Note that the data are paired; for each week, there is data for the number of machine-hours and corresponding indirect manufacturing labor costs. For example, week 12 shows 48 machine-hours and indirect manufacturing labor costs of $963. The next section uses the data in Exhibit 10-3 to illustrate how to estimate a cost

Decision Point

What are the different methods that can be used to estimate a cost function?

Exhibit 10-3

Weekly Indirect
Manufacturing Labor
Costs and Machine-
Hours for Elegant Rugs

	Home	Insert	Page Layout	Formulas
	A	B	C	
1	Week	Cost Driver: Machine-Hours	Indirect Manufacturing Labor Costs	
2		(X)	(Y)	
3	1	68	$ 1,190	
4	2	88	1,211	
5	3	62	1,004	
6	4	72	917	
7	5	60	770	
8	6	96	1,456	
9	7	78	1,180	
10	8	46	710	
11	9	82	1,316	
12	10	94	1,032	
13	11	68	752	
14	12	48	963	
15	Total	862	$12,501	
16				

function using quantitative analysis. We examine two techniques—the relatively simple high-low method as well as the more common quantitative tool used to examine and understand data, regression analysis.

Steps in Estimating a Cost Function Using Quantitative Analysis

**Learning
Objective** 4

Outline six steps in
estimating a cost
function using
quantitative analysis

. . . the end result
(Step 6) is to evaluate
the cost driver of the
estimated cost function

There are six steps in estimating a cost function using quantitative analysis of a past cost relationship. We illustrate the steps as follows using the Elegant Rugs example.

Step 1: Choose the dependent variable. Choice of the **dependent variable** (the cost to be predicted and managed) will depend on the cost function being estimated. In the Elegant Rugs example, the dependent variable is indirect manufacturing labor costs.

Step 2: Identify the independent variable, or cost driver. The **independent variable** (level of activity or cost driver) is the factor used to predict the dependent variable (costs). When the cost is an indirect cost, as it is with Elegant Rugs, the independent variable is also called a cost-allocation base. Although these terms are sometimes used interchangeably, we use the term *cost driver* to describe the independent variable. Frequently, the cost analyst, working with the management team, will cycle through the six steps several times, trying alternative economically plausible cost drivers to identify a cost driver that best fits the data.

A cost driver should be measurable and have an *economically plausible* relationship with the dependent variable. Economic plausibility means that the relationship (describing how changes in the cost driver lead to changes in the costs being considered) is based on a physical relationship, a contract, or knowledge of operations and makes economic sense to the operating manager and the management accountant. As we saw in Chapter 5, all the individual items of costs included in the dependent variable should have the same cost driver, that is, the cost pool should be homogenous. When all items of costs in the dependent variable do not have the same cost driver, the cost analyst should investigate the possibility of creating homogenous cost pools and estimating more than one cost function, one for each cost item/cost driver pair.

As an example, consider several types of fringe benefits paid to employees and the cost drivers of the benefits:

Fringe Benefit	Cost Driver
Health benefits	Number of employees
Cafeteria meals	Number of employees
Pension benefits	Salaries of employees
Life insurance	Salaries of employees

The costs of health benefits and cafeteria meals can be combined into one homogenous cost pool because they have the same cost driver—the number of employees. Pension benefits and life insurance costs have a different cost driver—the salaries of employees—and, therefore, should not be combined with health benefits and cafeteria meals. Instead, pension benefits and life insurance costs should be combined into a separate homogenous cost pool. The cost pool comprising pension benefits and life insurance costs can be estimated using salaries of employees receiving these benefits as the cost driver.

Step 3:   Collect data on the dependent variable and the cost driver. This is usually the most difficult step in cost analysis. Cost analysts obtain data from company documents, from interviews with managers, and through special studies. These data may be time-series data or cross-sectional data.

Time-series data pertain to the same entity (organization, plant, activity, and so on) over successive past periods. Weekly observations of indirect manufacturing labor costs and number of machine-hours at Elegant Rugs are examples of time-series data. The ideal time-series database would contain numerous observations for a company whose operations have not been affected by economic or technological change. A stable economy and technology ensure that data collected during the estimation period represent the same underlying relationship between the cost driver and the dependent variable. Moreover, the periods used to measure the dependent variable and the cost driver should be consistent throughout the observations.

Cross-sectional data pertain to different entities during the same period. For example, studies of loans processed and the related personnel costs at 50 individual, yet similar, branches of a bank during March 2012 would produce cross-sectional data for that month. The cross-sectional data should be drawn from entities that, within each entity, have a similar relationship between the cost driver and costs. Later in this chapter, we describe the problems that arise in data collection.

Step 4:   Plot the data. The general relationship between the cost driver and costs can be readily observed in a graphical representation of the data, which is commonly called a plot of the data. The plot provides insight into the relevant range of the cost function, and reveals whether the relationship between the driver and costs is approximately linear. Moreover, the plot highlights extreme observations (observations outside the general pattern) that analysts should check. Was there an error in recording the data or an unusual event, such as a work stoppage, that makes these observations unrepresentative of the normal relationship between the cost driver and the costs?

Exhibit 10-4 is a plot of the weekly data from columns B and C of the Excel spreadsheet in Exhibit 10-3. This graph provides strong visual evidence of a positive linear relationship between number of machine-hours and indirect manufacturing labor costs (that is, when machine-hours go up, so do indirect manufacturing labor costs). There do not appear to be any extreme observations in Exhibit 10-4. The relevant range is from 46 to 96 machine-hours per week (weeks 8 and 6, respectively).

Step 5:   Estimate the cost function. We will show two ways to estimate the cost function for our Elegant Rugs data. One uses the high-low method, and the other uses regression analysis, the two most frequently described forms of quantitative analysis. The widespread availability of computer packages such as Excel makes regression analysis much more easy to use. Still, we describe the high-low method to provide some basic intuition for the idea of drawing a line to "fit" a number of data points. We present these methods after Step 6.

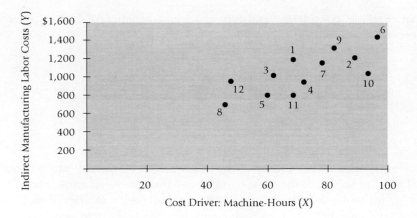

Step 6:   Evaluate the cost driver of the estimated cost function. In this step, we describe criteria for evaluating the cost driver of the estimated cost function. We do this after illustrating the high-low method and regression analysis.

High-Low Method

The simplest form of quantitative analysis to "fit" a line to data points is the **high-low method**. It uses only the highest and lowest observed values of the cost driver within the relevant range and their respective costs to estimate the slope coefficient and the constant of the cost function. It provides a first cut at understanding the relationship between a cost driver and costs. We illustrate the high-low method using data from Exhibit 10-3.

	Cost Driver: Machine-Hours (X)	Indirect Manufacturing Labor Costs (Y)
Highest observation of cost driver (week 6)	96	$1,456
Lowest observation of cost driver (week 8)	46	710
Difference	50	$ 746

The slope coefficient, b, is calculated as follows:

$$\text{Slope coefficient} = \frac{\substack{\text{Difference between costs associated with highest} \\ \text{and lowest observations of the cost driver}}}{\substack{\text{Difference between highest and lowest} \\ \text{observations of the cost driver}}}$$

$$= \$746 \div 50 \text{ machine-hours} = \$14.92 \text{ per machine-hour}$$

To compute the constant, we can use either the highest or the lowest observation of the cost driver. Both calculations yield the same answer because the solution technique solves two linear equations with two unknowns, the slope coefficient and the constant. Because

$$y = a + bX$$
$$a = y - bX$$

At the highest observation of the cost driver, the constant, a, is calculated as follows:

$$\text{Constant} = \$1,456 - (\$14.92 \text{ per machine-hour} \times 96 \text{ machine-hours}) = \$23.68$$

And at the lowest observation of the cost driver,

$$\text{Constant} = \$710 - (\$14.92 \text{ per machine-hour} \times 46 \text{ machine-hours}) = \$23.68$$

Thus, the high-low estimate of the cost function is as follows:

$$y = a + bX$$
$$y = \$23.68 + (\$14.92 \text{ per machine-hour} \times \text{Number of machine-hours})$$

The purple line in Exhibit 10-5 shows the estimated cost function using the high-low method (based on the data in Exhibit 10-3). The estimated cost function is a straight line joining the observations with the highest and lowest values of the cost driver (number of machine-hours). Note how this simple high-low line falls "in-between" the data points with three observations on the line, four above it and five below it. The intercept (a = 23.68), the point where the dashed extension of the purple line meets the y-axis, is the constant component of the equation that provides the best linear approximation of how a cost behaves *within the relevant range* of 46 to 96 machine-hours. The intercept should *not* be interpreted as an estimate of the fixed costs of Elegant Rugs if no machines were run. That's because running no machines and shutting down the plant—that is, using zero machine-hours—is *outside the relevant range.*

Suppose indirect manufacturing labor costs in week 6 were $1,280, instead of $1,456, while 96 machine-hours were used. In this case, the highest observation of the cost driver (96 machine-hours in week 6) will not coincide with the newer highest observation of the costs ($1,316 in week 9). How would this change affect our high-low calculation? Given that the cause-and-effect relationship runs *from* the cost driver *to* the costs in a cost function, we choose the highest and lowest observations of the cost driver (the factor that causes the costs to change). The high-low method would still estimate the new cost function using data from weeks 6 (high) and 8 (low).

There is a danger of relying on only two observations to estimate a cost function. Suppose that because a labor contract guarantees certain minimum payments in week 8, indirect manufacturing labor costs in week 8 were $1,000, instead of $710, when only 46 machine-hours were used. The blue line in Exhibit 10-5 shows the cost function that would be estimated by the high-low method using this revised cost. Other than the two points used to draw the line, all other data lie on or below the line! In this case, choosing the highest and lowest observations for machine-hours would result in an estimated cost function that poorly describes the underlying linear cost relationship between number of machine-hours and indirect manufacturing labor costs. In such situations, the high-low method can be modified so that the two observations chosen to estimate the cost function are a *representative high* and a *representative low.* By using this adjustment, managers can avoid having extreme observations, which arise from abnormal events, influence the estimate of the cost function. The modification allows managers to estimate a cost function that is representative of the relationship between the cost driver and costs and, therefore, is more useful for making decisions (such as pricing and performance evaluation).

The advantage of the high-low method is that it is simple to compute and easy to understand; it gives a quick, initial insight into how the cost driver—number of machine-hours—affects indirect manufacturing labor costs. The disadvantage is that it ignores information from all but two observations when estimating the cost function. We next describe the regression analysis method of quantitative analysis that uses all available data to estimate the cost function.

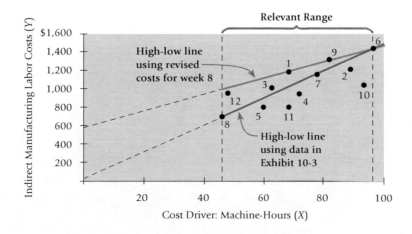

Exhibit 10-5

High-Low Method for Weekly Indirect Manufacturing Labor Costs and Machine-Hours for Elegant Rugs

Regression Analysis Method

Regression analysis is a statistical method that measures the average amount of change in the dependent variable associated with a unit change in one or more independent variables. In the Elegant Rugs example, the dependent variable is total indirect manufacturing labor costs. The independent variable, or cost driver, is number of machine-hours. **Simple regression** analysis estimates the relationship between the dependent variable and *one* independent variable. **Multiple regression** analysis estimates the relationship between the dependent variable and *two or more* independent variables. Multiple regression analysis for Elegant Rugs might use as the independent variables, or cost drivers, number of machine-hours and number of batches. The appendix to this chapter will explore simple regression and multiple regression in more detail.

In later sections, we will illustrate how Excel performs the calculations associated with regression analysis. The following discussion emphasizes how managers interpret and use the output from Excel to make critical strategic decisions. Exhibit 10-6 shows the line developed using regression analysis that best fits the data in columns B and C of Exhibit 10-3. Excel estimates the cost function to be

$$y = \$300.98 + \$10.31X$$

The regression line in Exhibit 10-6 is derived using the least-squares technique. The least-squares technique determines the regression line by minimizing the sum of the squared vertical differences from the data points (the various points in the graph) to the regression line. The vertical difference, called the **residual term**, measures the distance between actual cost and estimated cost for each observation of the cost driver. Exhibit 10-6 shows the residual term for the week 1 data. The line from the observation to the regression line is drawn perpendicular to the horizontal axis, or *x*-axis. The smaller the residual terms, the better the fit between actual cost observations and estimated costs. *Goodness of fit* indicates the strength of the relationship between the cost driver and costs. The regression line in Exhibit 10-6 rises from left to right. The positive slope of this line and small residual terms indicate that, on average, indirect manufacturing labor costs increase as the number of machine-hours increases. The vertical dashed lines in Exhibit 10-6 indicate the relevant range, the range within which the cost function applies.

Instructors and students who want to explore the technical details of estimating the least-squares regression line, can go to the appendix, pages 367–371 and return to this point without any loss of continuity.

The estimate of the slope coefficient, *b*, indicates that indirect manufacturing labor costs vary at the average amount of $10.31 for every machine-hour used within the relevant range. Management can use the regression equation when budgeting for future indirect manufacturing labor costs. For instance, if 90 machine-hours are budgeted for the upcoming week, the predicted indirect manufacturing labor costs would be

$$y = \$300.98 + (\$10.31 \text{ per machine-hour} \times 90 \text{ machine-hours}) = \$1,228.88$$

Exhibit 10-6

Regression Model for Weekly Indirect Manufacturing Labor Costs and Machine-Hours for Elegant Rugs

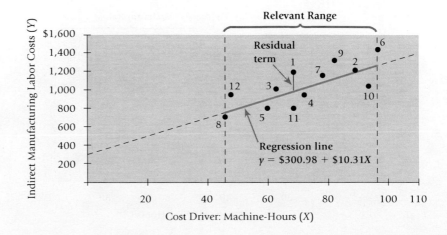

As we have already mentioned, the regression method is more accurate than the high-low method because the regression equation estimates costs using information from all observations, whereas the high-low equation uses information from only two observations. The inaccuracies of the high-low method can mislead managers. Consider the high-low method equation in the preceding section, $y = \$23.68 + \$14.92$ per machine-hour $\times$ Number of machine-hours. For 90 machine-hours, the predicted weekly cost based on the high-low method equation is $\$23.68 + (\$14.92$ per machine-hour $\times$ 90 machine-hours$) = \$1,366.48$. Suppose that for 7 weeks over the next 12-week period, Elegant Rugs runs its machines for 90 hours each week. Assume average indirect manufacturing labor costs for those 7 weeks are $\$1,300$. Based on the high-low method prediction of $\$1,366.48$, Elegant Rugs would conclude it has performed well because actual costs are less than predicted costs. But comparing the $\$1,300$ performance with the more-accurate $\$1,228.88$ prediction of the regression model tells a much different story and would probably prompt Elegant Rugs to search for ways to improve its cost performance.

Accurate cost estimation helps managers predict future costs and evaluate the success of cost-reduction initiatives. Suppose the manager at Elegant Rugs is interested in evaluating whether recent strategic decisions that led to changes in the production process and resulted in the data in Exhibit 10-3 have reduced indirect manufacturing labor costs, such as supervision, maintenance, and quality control. Using data on number of machine-hours used and indirect manufacturing labor costs of the previous process (not shown here), the manager estimates the regression equation,

$$y = \$546.26 + (\$15.86 \text{ per machine-hour} \times \text{Number of machine-hours})$$

The constant ($\$300.98$ versus $\$545.26$) and the slope coefficient ($\$10.31$ versus $\$15.86$) are both smaller for the new process relative to the old process. It appears that the new process has decreased indirect manufacturing labor costs.

◄ Decision Point

What are the steps to estimate a cost function using quantitative analysis?

Evaluating Cost Drivers of the Estimated Cost Function

How does a company determine the best cost driver when estimating a cost function? In many cases, the choice of a cost driver is aided substantially by understanding both operations and cost accounting.

To see why the understanding of operations is needed, consider the costs to maintain and repair metal-cutting machines at Helix Corporation, a manufacturer of treadmills. Helix schedules repairs and maintenance at a time when production is at a low level to avoid having to take machines out of service when they are needed most. An analysis of the monthly data will then show high repair costs in months of low production and low repair costs in months of high production. Someone unfamiliar with operations might conclude that there is an inverse relationship between production and repair costs. The engineering link between units produced and repair costs, however, is usually clear-cut. Over time, there is a cause-and-effect relationship: the higher the level of production, the higher the repair costs. To estimate the relationship correctly, operating managers and analysts will recognize that repair costs will tend to lag behind periods of high production, and hence, they will use production of prior periods as the cost driver.

In other cases, choosing a cost driver is more subtle and difficult. Consider again indirect manufacturing labor costs at Elegant Rugs. Management believes that both the number of machine-hours and the number of direct manufacturing labor-hours are plausible cost drivers of indirect manufacturing labor costs. However, management is not sure which is the better cost driver. Exhibit 10-7 presents weekly data (in Excel) on indirect manufacturing labor costs and number of machine-hours for the most recent 12-week period from Exhibit 10-3, together with data on the number of direct manufacturing labor-hours for the same period.

Learning Objective 5

Describe three criteria used to evaluate and choose cost drivers

. . . economically plausible relationships, goodness of fit, and significant effect of the cost driver on costs

Exhibit 10-7

Weekly Indirect
Manufacturing Labor
Costs, Machine-Hours,
and Direct
Manufacturing Labor-
Hours for Elegant Rugs

	Home	Insert	Page Layout	Formulas	Data	Review
	A	B		C		D
1	Week	Original Cost Driver: Machine-Hours		Alternate Cost Driver: Direct Manufacturing Labor-Hours (X)		Indirect Manufacturing Labor Costs (Y)
2	1	68		30		$ 1,190
3	2	88		35		1,211
4	3	62		36		1,004
5	4	72		20		917
6	5	60		47		770
7	6	96		45		1,456
8	7	78		44		1,180
9	8	46		38		710
10	9	82		70		1,316
11	10	94		30		1,032
12	11	68		29		752
13	12	48		38		963
14	Total	862		462		$12,501
15						

Choosing Among Cost Drivers

What guidance do the different cost-estimation methods provide for choosing among cost drivers? The industrial engineering method relies on analyzing physical relationships between cost drivers and costs, relationships that are difficult to specify in this case. The conference method and the account analysis method use subjective assessments to choose a cost driver and to estimate the fixed and variable components of the cost function. In these cases, managers must rely on their best judgment. Managers cannot use these methods to test and try alternative cost drivers. The major advantages of quantitative methods are that they are objective—a given data set and estimation method result in a unique estimated cost function—and managers can use them to evaluate different cost drivers. We use the regression analysis approach to illustrate how to evaluate different cost drivers.

First, the cost analyst at Elegant Rugs enters data in columns C and D of Exhibit 10-7 in Excel and estimates the following regression equation of indirect manufacturing labor costs based on number of direct manufacturing labor-hours:

$$y = \$744.67 + \$7.72X$$

Exhibit 10-8 shows the plot of the data points for number of direct manufacturing labor-hours and indirect manufacturing labor costs, and the regression line that best fits the data. Recall that Exhibit 10-6 shows the corresponding graph when number of machine-hours is the cost driver. To decide which of the two cost drivers Elegant Rugs should choose, the analyst compares the machine-hour regression equation and the direct manufacturing labor-hour regression equation. There are three criteria used to make this evaluation.

1. **Economic plausibility.** Both cost drivers are economically plausible. However, in the state-of-the-art, highly automated production environment at Elegant Rugs, managers familiar with the operations believe that costs such as machine maintenance are likely to be more closely related to number of machine-hours used than to number of direct manufacturing labor-hours used.

2. **Goodness of fit.** Compare Exhibits 10-6 and 10-8. The vertical differences between actual costs and predicted costs are much smaller for the machine-hours regression than for the direct manufacturing labor-hours regression. Number of machine-hours used, therefore, has a stronger relationship—or goodness of fit—with indirect manufacturing labor costs.

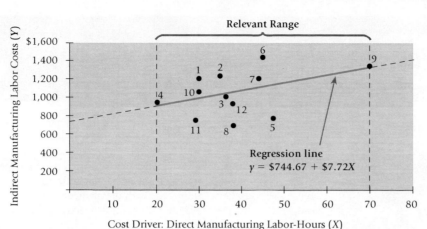

Exhibit 10-8

Regression Model for Weekly Indirect Manufacturing Labor Costs and Direct Manufacturing Labor-Hours for Elegant Rugs

3. **Significance of independent variable.** Again compare Exhibits 10-6 and 10-8 (both of which have been drawn to roughly the same scale). The machine-hours regression line has a steep slope relative to the slope of the direct manufacturing labor-hours regression line. *For the same (or more) scatter of observations about the line (goodness of fit),* a flat, or slightly sloped regression line indicates a weak relationship between the cost driver and costs. In our example, changes in direct manufacturing labor-hours appear to have a small influence or effect on indirect manufacturing labor costs.

Based on this evaluation, managers at Elegant Rugs select number of machine-hours as the cost driver and use the cost function $y = \$300.98 + (\$10.31$ per machine-hour $\times$ Number of machine-hours) to predict future indirect manufacturing labor costs.

Instructors and students who want to explore how regression analysis techniques can be used to choose among different cost drivers can go to the appendix, pages 371–374 and return to this point without any loss of continuity.

Why is choosing the correct cost driver to estimate indirect manufacturing labor costs important? Because identifying the wrong drivers or misestimating cost functions can lead management to incorrect (and costly) decisions along a variety of dimensions. Consider the following strategic decision that management at Elegant Rugs must make. The company is thinking of introducing a new style of carpet that, from a manufacturing standpoint, is similar to the carpets it has manufactured in the past. Prices are set by the market and sales of 650 square yards of this carpet are expected each week. Management estimates 72 machine-hours and 21 direct manufacturing labor-hours would be required per week to produce the 650 square yards of carpet needed. Using the machine-hour regression equation, Elegant Rugs would predict indirect manufacturing labor costs of $y = \$300.98 + (\$10.31$ per machine-hour $\times$ 72 machine-hours) = \$1,043.30. If it used direct manufacturing labor-hours as the cost driver, it would incorrectly predict costs of $\$744.67 + (\$7.72$ per labor-hour $\times$ 21 labor-hours) = \$906.79. If Elegant Rugs chose similarly incorrect cost drivers for other indirect costs as well and systematically underestimated costs, it would conclude that the costs of manufacturing the new style of carpet would be low and basically fixed (fixed because the regression line is nearly flat). But the actual costs driven by number of machine-hours used and other correct cost drivers would be higher. By failing to identify the proper cost drivers, management would be misled into believing the new style of carpet would be more profitable than it actually is. It might decide to introduce the new style of carpet, whereas if Elegant identifies the correct cost driver it might decide not to introduce the new carpet.

Incorrectly estimating the cost function would also have repercussions for cost management and cost control. Suppose number of direct manufacturing labor-hours were used as the cost driver, and actual indirect manufacturing labor costs for the new carpet were \$970. Actual costs would then be higher than the predicted costs of \$906.79. Management would feel compelled to find ways to cut costs. In fact, on the basis of the preferred machine-hour cost driver, the plant would have actual costs lower than the \$1,043.30 predicted costs—a performance that management should seek to replicate, not change!

Concepts in Action

Activity-Based Costing: Identifying Cost and Revenue Drivers

Many cost estimation methods presented in this chapter are essential to service, manufacturing, and retail-sector implementations of activity-based costing across the globe. To determine the cost of an activity in the banking industry, ABC systems often rely on expert analyses and opinions gathered from operating personnel (the conference method). For example, the loan department staff at the Co-operative Bank in the United Kingdom subjectively estimate the costs of the loan processing activity and the quantity of the related cost driver—the number of loans processed, a batch-level cost driver, as distinguished from the amount of the loans, an output unit-level cost driver—to derive the cost of processing a loan.

Elsewhere in the United Kingdom, the City of London police force uses input-output relationships (the industrial engineering method) to identify cost drivers and the cost of an activity. Using a surveying methodology, officials can determine the total costs associated with responding to house robberies, dealing with burglaries, and filling out police reports. In the United States, the Boeing Commercial Airplane Group's Wichita Division used detailed analyses of its commercial airplane-manufacturing methods to support make/buy decisions for complex parts required in airplane assembly. The industrial engineering method is also used by U.S. government agencies such as the U.S. Postal Service to determine the cost of each post office transaction and the U.S. Patent and Trademark Office to identify the costs of each patent examination.

Regression analysis is another helpful tool for determining the cost drivers of activities. Consider how fuel service retailers (that is, gas stations with convenience stores) identify the principal cost driver for labor within their operations. Two possible cost drivers are gasoline sales and convenience store sales. Gasoline sales are batch-level activities because payment transactions occur only once for each gasoline purchase, regardless of the volume of gasoline purchased; whereas convenience store sales are output unit-level activities that vary based on the amount of food, drink, and other products sold. Fuel service retailers generally use convenience store sales as the basis for assigning labor costs because multiple regression analyses confirm that convenience store sales, not gasoline sales, are the major cost driver of labor within their operations.

While popular, these are not the only methods used to evaluate cost drivers. If you recall from chapter five, Charles Schwab is one of the growing number of companies using time-driven activity based costing, which uses time as the cost driver. At Citigroup, the company's internal technology infrastructure group uses time to better manage the labor capacity required to provide reliable, secure, and cost effective technology services to about 60 Citigroup business units around the world.

The trend of using activity-based costing to identify cost and revenue drivers also extends into emerging areas. For example, the U.S. government allocated $19 billion in 2009 to support the adoption of electronic health records. Using the input-output method, many health clinics and doctor's offices are leveraging activity-based costing to identify the cost of adopting this new health information technology tool.

Sources: Barton, T., and J. MacArthur. 2003. Activity-based costing and predatory pricing: The case of the retail industry. *Management Accounting Quarterly* (Spring); Carter, T., A. Sedaghat, and T. Williams. 1998. How ABC changed the post office. *Management Accounting*, (February); The Cooperative Bank. Harvard Business School. Case No. N9-195-196; Federowicz, M., M. Grossman, B. Hayes, and J. Riggs. 2010. A tutorial on activity-based costing of electronic health records. *Quality Management in Health Care* (January–March); Kaplan, Robert, and Steven Anderson. 2008. *Time-driven activity-based costing: A simpler and more powerful path to higher profits*. Boston: Harvard Business School Publishing; Leapman, B. 2006. Police spend £500m filling in forms. *The Daily Telegraph*, January 22; Paduano, Rocco, and Joel Cutcher-Gershenfeld. 2001. Boeing Commercial Airplane Group Wichita Division (Boeing Co.). MIT Labor Aerospace Research Agenda Case Study. Cambridge, MA: MIT; Peckenpaugh, J. 2002. Teaching the ABCs. *Government Executive*, April 1; The United Kingdom Home Office. 2007. *The police service national ABC model: Manual of guidance*. London: Her Majesty's Stationary Office.

Cost Drivers and Activity-Based Costing

Activity-based costing (ABC) systems focus on individual activities—such as product design, machine setup, materials handling, distribution, and customer service—as the fundamental cost objects. To implement ABC systems, managers must identify a cost driver for each activity. For example, using methods described in this chapter, the manager must decide whether the number of loads moved or the weight of loads moved is the cost driver of materials-handling costs.

To choose the cost driver and use it to estimate the cost function in our materials-handling example, the manager collects data on materials-handling costs and the quantities of the two competing cost drivers over a reasonably long period. Why a long period? Because in the short run, materials-handling costs may be fixed and, therefore, will not vary with changes in the level of the cost driver. In the long run, however, there is a clear cause-and-effect relationship between materials-handling costs and the cost driver. Suppose number of loads moved is the cost driver of materials-handling costs. Increases in the number of loads moved will require more materials-handling labor and equipment; decreases will result in equipment being sold and labor being reassigned to other tasks.

ABC systems have a great number and variety of cost drivers and cost pools. That means ABC systems require many cost relationships to be estimated. In estimating the cost function for each cost pool, the manager must pay careful attention to the cost hierarchy. For example, if a cost is a batch-level cost such as setup cost, the manager must only consider batch-level cost drivers like number of setup-hours. In some cases, the costs in a cost pool may have more than one cost driver from different levels of the cost hierarchy. In the Elegant Rugs example, the cost drivers for indirect manufacturing labor costs could be machine-hours and number of production batches of carpet manufactured. Furthermore, it may be difficult to subdivide the indirect manufacturing labor costs into two cost pools and to measure the costs associated with each cost driver. In these cases, companies use multiple regression to estimate costs based on more than one independent variable. The appendix to this chapter discusses multiple regression in more detail.

As the Concepts in Action feature (p. 356) illustrates, managers implementing ABC systems use a variety of methods—industrial engineering, conference, and regression analysis—to estimate slope coefficients. In making these choices, managers trade off level of detail, accuracy, feasibility, and costs of estimating cost functions.

Nonlinear Cost Functions

In practice, cost functions are not always linear. A **nonlinear cost function** is a cost function for which the graph of total costs (based on the level of a single activity) is not a straight line within the relevant range. To see what a nonlinear cost function looks like, return to Exhibit 10-2 (p. 344). The relevant range is currently set at 20,000 to 65,000 snowboards. But if we extend the relevant range to encompass the region from 0 to 80,000 snowboards produced, it is evident that the cost function over this expanded range is graphically represented by a line that is not straight.

Consider another example. Economies of scale in advertising may enable an advertising agency to produce double the number of advertisements for less than double the costs. Even direct material costs are not always linear variable costs because of quantity discounts on direct material purchases. As shown in Exhibit 10-9 (p. 358), Panel A, total direct material costs rise as the units of direct materials purchased increase. But, because of quantity discounts, these costs rise more slowly (as indicated by the slope coefficient) as the units of direct materials purchased increase. This cost function has $b = \$25$ per unit for 1–1,000 units purchased, $b = \$15$ per unit for 1,001 –2,000 units purchased, and $b = \$10$ per unit for 2,001–3,000 units purchased. The direct material cost per unit falls at each price break—that is, the cost per unit decreases with larger purchase orders. If managers are interested in understanding cost behavior over the relevant range from 1 to 3,000 units, the cost function is nonlinear—not a straight line. If, however, managers are only interested in understanding cost behavior over a more narrow relevant range (for example, from 1 to 1,000 units), the cost function is linear.

Step cost functions are also examples of nonlinear cost functions. A **step cost function** is a cost function in which the cost remains the same over various ranges of the level of activity, but the cost increases by discrete amounts—that is, increases in steps—as the level of activity increases from one range to the next. Panel B in Exhibit 10-9 shows a *step variable-cost function*, a step cost function in which cost remains the same over *narrow* ranges of the level of activity in each relevant range. Panel B presents the relationship between units of production and setup costs. The pattern is a step cost function because, as we described in Chapter 5 on activity-based costing, setup costs are

Examples of Nonlinear Cost Functions

PANEL A:
Effects of Quantity
Discounts on Slope
Coefficient of Direct
Material Cost Function

PANEL B:
Step Variable-Cost
Function

PANEL C:
Step Fixed-Cost
Function

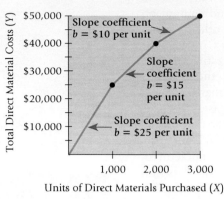

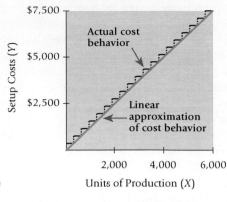

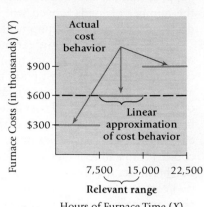

related to each production batch started. If the relevant range is considered to be from 0 to 6,000 production units, the cost function is nonlinear. However, as shown by the blue line in Panel B, managers often approximate step variable costs with a continuously-variable cost function. This type of step cost pattern also occurs when production inputs such as materials-handling labor, supervision, and process engineering labor are acquired in discrete quantities but used in fractional quantities.

Panel C in Exhibit 10-9 shows a *step fixed-cost function* for Crofton Steel, a company that operates large heat-treatment furnaces to harden steel parts. Looking at Panel C and Panel B, you can see that the main difference between a step variable-cost function and a step fixed-cost function is that the cost in a step fixed-cost function remains the same over *wide* ranges of the activity in each relevant range. The ranges indicate the number of furnaces being used (each furnace costs $300,000). The cost increases from one range to the next higher range when the hours of furnace time needed require the use of another furnace. The relevant range of 7,500 to 15,000 hours of furnace time indicates that the company expects to operate with two furnaces at a cost of $600,000. Management considers the cost of operating furnaces as a fixed cost within this relevant range of operation. However, if the relevant range is considered to be from 0 to 22,500 hours, the cost function is nonlinear: The graph in Panel C is not a single straight line; it is three broken lines.

Learning Curves

Nonlinear cost functions also result from learning curves. A **learning curve** is a function that measures how labor-hours per unit decline as units of production increase because workers are learning and becoming better at their jobs. Managers use learning curves to predict how labor-hours, or labor costs, will increase as more units are produced.

The aircraft-assembly industry first documented the effect that learning has on efficiency. In general, as workers become more familiar with their tasks, their efficiency improves. Managers learn how to improve the scheduling of work shifts and how to operate the plant more efficiently. As a result of improved efficiency, unit costs decrease as productivity increases, and the unit-cost function behaves nonlinearly. These nonlinearities must be considered when estimating and predicting unit costs.

Managers have extended the learning-curve notion to other business functions in the value chain, such as marketing, distribution, and customer service, and to costs other than labor costs. The term *experience curve* describes this broader application of the learning curve. An **experience curve** is a function that measures the decline in cost per unit in various business functions of the value chain—marketing, distribution, and so on—as the amount of these activities increases. For companies such as Dell Computer, Wal-Mart, and McDonald's, learning curves and experience curves are key elements of their strategies. These companies use learning curves and experience curves to reduce costs and increase customer satisfaction, market share, and profitability.

We now describe two learning-curve models: the cumulative average-time learning model and the incremental unit-time learning model.

Cumulative Average-Time Learning Model

In the **cumulative average-time learning model**, cumulative average time per unit declines by a constant percentage each time the cumulative quantity of units produced doubles. Consider Rayburn Corporation, a radar systems manufacturer. Rayburn has an 80% learning curve. The 80% means that when the quantity of units produced is doubled from X to $2X$, cumulative average time *per unit* for $2X$ units is 80% of cumulative average time *per unit* for X units. Average time per unit has dropped by 20% (100% − 80%). Exhibit 10-10 is an Excel spreadsheet showing the calculations for the cumulative average-time learning model for Rayburn Corporation. Note that as the number of units produced doubles from 1 to 2 in column A, cumulative average time per unit declines from 100 hours to 80% of 100 hours (0.80 × 100 hours = 80 hours) in column B. As the number of units doubles from 2 to 4, cumulative average time per unit declines to 80% of 80 hours = 64 hours, and so on. To obtain the cumulative total time in column D, multiply cumulative average time per unit by the cumulative number of units produced. For example, to produce 4 cumulative units would require 256 labor-hours (4 units × 64 cumulative average labor-hours per unit).

Exhibit 10-10 Cumulative Average-Time Learning Model for Rayburn Corporation

A	B	C	D	E
Cumulative Number of Units (X)	Cumulative Average Time per Unit (y)*: Labor-Hours		Cumulative Total Time: Labor-Hours (D = Col A × Col B)	Individual Unit Time for Xth Unit: Labor-Hours
1	100.00		100.00	100.00
2	80.00	= (100 × 0.8)	160.00	60.00
3	70.21		210.63	50.63
4	64.00	= (80 × 0.8)	256.00	45.37
5	59.56		297.82	41.82
6	56.17		337.01	39.19
7	53.45		374.14	37.13
8	51.20	= (64 × 0.8)	409.60	35.46
9	49.29		443.65	34.05
10	47.65		476.51	32.86
11	46.21		508.32	31.81
12	44.93		539.22	30.89
13	43.79		569.29	30.07
14	42.76		598.63	29.34
15	41.82		627.30	28.67
16	40.96	= (51.2 × 0.8)	655.36	28.06

E13 = D13 − D12 = 210.63 − 160.00

*The mathematical relationship underlying the cumulative average-time learning model is as follows:

$$y = aX^b$$

where y = Cumulative average time (labor-hours) per unit
  X = Cumulative number of units produced
  a = Time (labor-hours) required to produce the first unit
  b = Factor used to calculate cumulative average time to produce units

The value of b is calculated as

$$\frac{\ln (\text{learning-curve \% in decimal form})}{\ln 2}$$

For an 80% learning curve, $b = \ln 0.8/\ln 2 = -0.2231/0.6931 = -0.3219$
For example, when $X = 3$, $a = 100$, $b = -0.3219$,

$$y = 100 \times 3^{-0.3219} = 70.21 \text{ labor-hours}$$

The cumulative total time when $X = 3$ is 70.21 × 3 = 210.63 labor-hours. Numbers in table may not be exact because of rounding.

Incremental Unit-Time Learning Model

In the **incremental unit-time learning model**, incremental time needed to produce the last unit declines by a constant percentage each time the cumulative quantity of units produced doubles. Again, consider Rayburn Corporation and an 80% learning curve. The 80% here means that when the quantity of units produced is doubled from X to $2X$, the time needed to produce the last unit when $2X$ total units are produced is 80% of the time needed to produce the last unit when X total units are produced. Exhibit 10-11 is an Excel spreadsheet showing the calculations for the incremental unit-time learning model for Rayburn Corporation based on an 80% learning curve. Note how when units produced double from 2 to 4 in column A, the time to produce unit 4 (the last unit when 4 units are produced) is 64 hours in column B, which is 80% of the 80 hours needed to produce unit 2 (the last unit when 2 units are produced). We obtain the cumulative total time in column D by summing individual unit times in column B. For example, to produce 4 cumulative units would require 314.21 labor-hours (100.00 + 80.00 + 70.21 + 64.00).

Exhibit 10-12 presents graphs using Excel for the cumulative average-time learning model (using data from Exhibit 10-10) and the incremental unit-time learning model (using data from Exhibit 10-11). Panel A graphically illustrates cumulative average time per unit as a function of cumulative units produced for each model (column A in Exhibit 10-10 or 10-11). The curve for the cumulative average-time learning model is plotted using the data from Exhibit 10-10, column B, while the curve for the incremental unit-time learning model is plotted using the data from Exhibit 10-11, column E. Panel B graphically illustrates cumulative total labor-hours, again as a function of cumulative units produced for each model. The curve for the cumulative average-time learning model is plotted using the data from Exhibit 10-10, column D, while that for the incremental unit-time learning model is plotted using the data from Exhibit 10-11, column D.

Exhibit 10-11   Incremental Unit-Time Learning Model for Rayburn Corporation

	A	B	C	D	E
1	**Incremental Unit-Time Learning Model for Rayburn Corporation**				
3		**80% Learning Curve**			
5	**Cumulative**	**Individual Unit Time**		**Cumulative**	**Cumulative**
6	**Number**	**for Xth Unit (y)*:**		**Total Time:**	**Average Time**
7	**of Units (X)**	**Labor-Hours**		**Labor-Hours**	**per Unit:**
8					**Labor-Hours**
10					**E = Col D ÷ Col A**
12	1	100.00		100.00	100.00
13	2	80.00	= (100 × 0.8)	180.00	90.00
14	3	70.21		250.21	83.40
15	4	64.00	= (80 × 0.8)	314.21	78.55
16	5	59.56		373.77	74.75
17	6	56.17		429.94	71.66
18	7	53.45		483.39	69.06
19	8	51.20	= (64 × 0.8)	534.59	66.82
20	9	49.29		583.89	64.88
21	10	47.65		631.54	63.15
22	11	46.21		677.75	61.61
23	12	44.93		722.68	60.22
24	13	43.79		766.47	58.96
25	14	42.76		809.23	57.80
26	15	41.82		851.05	56.74
27	16	40.96	= (51.2 × 0.8)	892.01	55.75

Callout: D14 = D13 + B14 = 180.00 + 70.21

*The mathematical relationship underlying the incremental unit-time learning model is as follows:

$$y = aX^b$$

where y = Time (labor-hours) taken to produce the last single unit
X = Cumulative number of units produced
a = Time (labor-hours) required to produce the first unit
b = Factor used to calculate incremental unit time to produce units
$$= \frac{\ln (\text{learning-curve \% in decimal form})}{\ln 2}$$

For an 80% learning curve, $b = \ln 0.8 \div \ln 2 = -0.2231 \div 0.6931 = -0.3219$
For example, when $X = 3$, $a = 100$, $b = -0.3219$,
$y = 100 \times 3^{-0.3219} = 70.21$ labor-hours
The cumulative total time when $X = 3$ is $100 + 80 + 70.21 = 250.21$ labor-hours. Numbers in the table may not be exact because of rounding.

| Exhibit 10-12 | Plots for Cumulative Average-Time Learning Model and Incremental Unit-Time Learning Model for Rayburn Corporation |

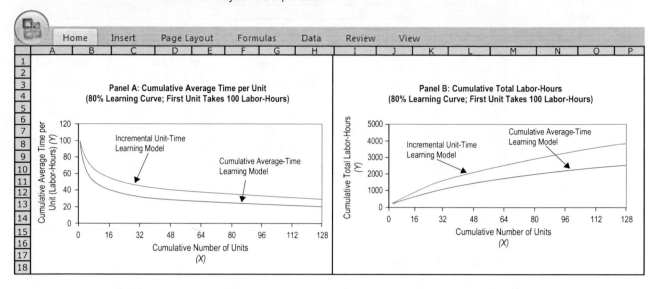

The incremental unit-time learning model predicts a higher cumulative total time to produce 2 or more units than the cumulative average-time learning model, assuming the same learning rate for both models. That is, in Exhibit 10-12, Panel B, the graph for the 80% incremental unit-time learning model lies above the graph for the 80% cumulative average-time learning model. If we compare the results in Exhibit 10-10 (column D) with the results in Exhibit 10-11 (column D), to produce 4 cumulative units, the 80% incremental unit-time learning model predicts 314.21 labor-hours versus 256.00 labor-hours predicted by the 80% cumulative average-time learning model. That's because under the cumulative average-time learning model *average labor-hours needed to produce all 4 units* is 64 hours; the labor-hour amount needed to produce unit 4 is much less than 64 hours—it is 45.37 hours (see Exhibit 10-10). Under the incremental unit-time learning model, the labor-hour amount needed to produce unit 4 is 64 hours, and the labor-hours needed to produce the first 3 units are more than 64 hours, so average time needed to produce all 4 units is more than 64 hours.

How do managers choose which model and what percent learning curve to use? It is important to recognize that managers make their choices on a case-by-case basis. For example, if the behavior of manufacturing labor-hour usage as production levels increase follows a pattern like the one predicted by the 80% learning curve cumulative average-time learning model, then the 80% learning curve cumulative average-time learning model should be used. Engineers, plant managers, and workers are good sources of information on the amount and type of learning actually occurring as production increases. Plotting this information and estimating the model that best fits the data is helpful in selecting the appropriate model.[2]

Incorporating Learning-Curve Effects into Prices and Standards

How do companies use learning curves? Consider the data in Exhibit 10-10 for the cumulative average-time learning model at Rayburn Corporation. Suppose variable costs subject to learning effects consist of direct manufacturing labor, at $20 per hour, and related overhead, at $30 per direct manufacturing labor-hour. Managers should predict the costs shown in Exhibit 10-13.

These data show that the effects of the learning curve could have a major influence on decisions. For example, managers at Rayburn Corporation might set an extremely low selling price on its radar systems to generate high demand. As its production increases to meet this growing demand, cost per unit drops. Rayburn "rides the product down the

---

[2] For details, see C. Bailey, "Learning Curve Estimation of Production Costs and Labor-Hours Using a Free Excel Add-In," *Management Accounting Quarterly*, (Summer 2000: 25–31). Free software for estimating learning curves is available at Dr. Bailey's Web site, www.profbailey.com.

Home	Insert	Page Layout	Formulas	Data	Review	View
	A	B	C	D	E	F
1		Cumulative				
2	Cumulative	Average Time	Cumulative	Cumulative Costs		Additions to
3	Number of	per Unit:	Total Time:	at $50 per		Cumulative
4	Units	Labor-Hours[a]	Labor-Hours[a]	Labor-Hour		Costs
5	1	100.00	100.00	$ 5,000	(100.00 × $50)	$ 5,000
6	2	80.00	160.00	8,000	(160.00 × $50)	3,000
7	4	64.00	256.00	12,800	(256.00 × $50)	4,800
8	8	51.20	409.60	20,480	(409.60 × $50)	7,680
9	16	40.96	655.36	32,768	(655.36 × $50)	12,288
10						
11	[a]Based on the cumulative average-time learning model. See Exhibit 10-10 for the computations					
12	of these amounts.					

learning curve" as it establishes a larger market share. Although it may have earned little operating income on its first unit sold—it may actually have lost money on that unit—Rayburn earns more operating income per unit as output increases.

Alternatively, subject to legal and other considerations, Rayburn's managers might set a low price on just the final 8 units. After all, the total labor and related overhead costs per unit for these final 8 units are predicted to be only $12,288 ($32,768 – $20,480). On these final 8 units, the $1,536 cost per unit ($12,288 ÷ 8 units) is much lower than the $5,000 cost per unit of the first unit produced.

Many companies, such as Pizza Hut and Home Depot, incorporate learning-curve effects when evaluating performance. The Nissan Motor Company expects its workers to learn and improve on the job and evaluates performance accordingly. It sets assembly-labor efficiency standards for new models of cars after taking into account the learning that will occur as more units are produced.

The learning-curve models examined in Exhibits 10-10 to 10-13 assume that learning is driven by a single variable (production output). Other models of learning have been developed (by companies such as Analog Devices and Hewlett-Packard) that focus on how quality—rather than manufacturing labor-hours—will change over time, regardless of whether more units are produced. Studies indicate that factors other than production output, such as job rotation and organizing workers into teams, contribute to learning that improves quality.

**Decision
Point** ▶

What is a nonlinear
cost function and in
what ways do
learning curves give
rise to nonlinearities?

Data Collection and Adjustment Issues

The ideal database for estimating cost functions quantitatively has two characteristics:

**Learning
Objective** **7**

Be aware of data
problems encountered
in estimating cost
functions

. . . for example,
unreliable data and poor
record keeping, extreme
observations, treating
fixed costs as if they are
variable, and a changing
relationship between a
cost driver and cost

1. **The database should contain numerous reliably measured observations of the cost driver (the independent variable) and the related costs (the dependent variable).** Errors in measuring the costs and the cost driver are serious. They result in inaccurate estimates of the effect of the cost driver on costs.

2. **The database should consider many values spanning a wide range for the cost driver.** Using only a few values of the cost driver that are grouped closely considers too small a segment of the relevant range and reduces the confidence in the estimates obtained.

Unfortunately, cost analysts typically do not have the advantage of working with a database having both characteristics. This section outlines some frequently encountered data problems and steps the cost analyst can take to overcome these problems.

1. The time period for measuring the dependent variable (for example, machine-lubricant costs) does not properly match the period for measuring the cost driver. This problem often arises when accounting records are not kept on the accrual basis. Consider a cost function with machine-lubricant costs as the dependent variable and number of machine-hours as the cost driver. Assume that the lubricant is purchased sporadically

and stored for later use. Records maintained on the basis of lubricants purchased will indicate little lubricant costs in many months and large lubricant costs in other months. These records present an obviously inaccurate picture of what is actually taking place. The analyst should use accrual accounting to measure cost of lubricants consumed to better match costs with the machine-hours cost driver in this example.

2. Fixed costs are allocated as if they are variable. For example, costs such as depreciation, insurance, or rent may be allocated to products to calculate cost per unit of output. *The danger is to regard these costs as variable rather than as fixed. They seem to be variable because of the allocation methods used.* To avoid this problem, the analyst should carefully distinguish fixed costs from variable costs and not treat allocated fixed cost per unit as a variable cost.

3. Data are either not available for all observations or are not uniformly reliable. Missing cost observations often arise from a failure to record a cost or from classifying a cost incorrectly. For example, marketing costs may be understated because costs of sales visits to customers may be incorrectly recorded as customer-service costs. Recording data manually rather than electronically tends to result in a higher percentage of missing observations and erroneously entered observations. Errors also arise when data on cost drivers originate outside the internal accounting system. For example, the accounting department may obtain data on testing-hours for medical instruments from the company's manufacturing department and data on number of items shipped to customers from the distribution department. One or both of these departments might not keep accurate records. To minimize these problems, the cost analyst should design data collection reports that regularly and routinely obtain the required data and should follow up immediately whenever data are missing.

4. Extreme values of observations occur from errors in recording costs (for example, a misplaced decimal point), from nonrepresentative periods (for example, from a period in which a major machine breakdown occurred or from a period in which a delay in delivery of materials from an international supplier curtailed production), or from observations outside the relevant range. Analysts should adjust or eliminate unusual observations before estimating a cost relationship.

5. There is no homogeneous relationship between the cost driver and the individual cost items in the dependent variable-cost pool. A homogeneous relationship exists when each activity whose costs are included in the dependent variable has the same cost driver. In this case, a single cost function can be estimated. As discussed in Step 2 for estimating a cost function using quantitative analysis (p. 348), when the cost driver for each activity is different, separate cost functions (each with its own cost driver) should be estimated for each activity. Alternatively, as discussed on pages 372–374, the cost function should be estimated with more than one independent variable using multiple regression.

6. The relationship between the cost driver and the cost is not stationary. That is, the underlying process that generated the observations has not remained stable over time. For example, the relationship between number of machine-hours and manufacturing overhead costs is unlikely to be stationary when the data cover a period in which new technology was introduced. One way to see if the relationship is stationary is to split the sample into two parts and estimate separate cost relationships—one for the period before the technology was introduced and one for the period after the technology was introduced. Then, if the estimated coefficients for the two periods are similar, the analyst can pool the data to estimate a single cost relationship. When feasible, pooling data provides a larger data set for the estimation, which increases confidence in the cost predictions being made.

7. Inflation has affected costs, the cost driver, or both. For example, inflation may cause costs to change even when there is no change in the level of the cost driver. To study the underlying cause-and-effect relationship between the level of the cost driver and costs, the analyst should remove purely inflationary price effects from the data by dividing each cost by the price index on the date the cost was incurred.

In many cases, a cost analyst must expend considerable effort to reduce the effect of these problems before estimating a cost function on the basis of past data.

◀ **Decision Point**

What are the common data problems a company must watch for when estimating costs?

Problem for Self-Study

The Helicopter Division of GLD, Inc., is examining helicopter assembly costs at its Indiana plant. It has received an initial order for eight of its new land-surveying helicopters. GLD can adopt one of two methods of assembling the helicopters:

	A	B	C	D	E
1		Labor-Intensive Assembly Method		Machine-Intensive Assembly Method	
2	Direct material cost per helicopter	$ 40,000		$36,000	
3	Direct-assembly labor time for first helicopter	2,000	labor-hours	800	labor-hours
4	Learning curve for assembly labor time per helicopter	85%	cumulative average time*	90%	incremental unit time**
5	Direct-assembly labor cost	$ 30	per hour	$ 30	per hour
6	Equipment-related indirect manufacturing cost	$ 12	per direct-assembly labor-hour	$ 45	per direct-assembly labor-hour
7	Material-handling-related indirect manufacturing cost	50%	of direct material cost	50%	of direct material cost
8					
9					
10	*Using the formula (p. 359), for an 85% learning curve, $b = \dfrac{\ln 0.85}{\ln 2} = \dfrac{-0.162519}{0.693147} = -0.234465$				
11					
12					
13					
14					
15	**Using the formula (p. 360), for a 90% learning curve, $b = \dfrac{\ln 0.90}{\ln 2} = \dfrac{-0.105361}{0.693147} = -0.152004$				
16					
17					

Required

1. How many direct-assembly labor-hours are required to assemble the first eight helicopters under (a) the labor-intensive method and (b) the machine-intensive method?
2. What is the total cost of assembling the first eight helicopters under (a) the labor-intensive method and (b) the machine-intensive method?

Solution

1. a. The following calculations show the labor-intensive assembly method based on an 85% cumulative average-time learning model (using Excel):

	G	H	I	J	K
1	Cumulative	Cumulative		Cumulative	Individual
2	Number	Average Time		Total Time:	time for
3	of Units	per Unit (y):		Labor-Hours	Xth unit:
4		Labor-Hours			Labor-Hours
5				Col J = Col G × Col H	
6	1	2,000		2,000	2,000
7	2	1,700	(2,000 × 0.85)	3,400	1,400
8	3	1,546		4,637	1,237
9	4	1,445	(1,700 × 0.85)	5,780	1,143
10	5	1,371		6,857	1,077
11	6	1,314		7,884	1,027
12	7	1,267		8,871	987
13	8	1,228.25	(1,445 × 0.85)	9,826	955
14					

Cumulative average-time per unit for the Xth unit in column H is calculated as $y = aX^b$; see Exhibit 10-10 (p. 359). For example, when $X = 3$, $y = 2{,}000 \times 3^{-0.234465} = 1{,}546$ labor-hours.

b. The following calculations show the machine-intensive assembly method based on a 90% incremental unit-time learning model:

	Home	Insert	Page Layout	Formulas	Data	Review	View	
	G	H	I		J		K	
1	Cumulative	Individual			Cumulative		Cumulative	
2	Number	Unit Time			Total Time:		Average Time	
3	of Units	for Xth Unit (y):			Labor-Hours		Per Unit:	
4		Labor-Hours					Labor-Hours	
5							Col K = Col J ÷ Col G	
6	1	800			800		800	
7	2	720	(800 × 0.9)		1,520		760	
8	3	677			2,197		732	
9	4	648	(720 × 0.9)		2,845		711	
10	5	626			3,471		694	
11	6	609			4,081		680	
12	7	595			4,676		668	
13	8	583	(648 × 0.9)		5,258		657	

Individual unit time for the Xth unit in column H is calculated as $y = aX^b$; see Exhibit 10-11 (p. 360). For example, when $X = 3$, $y = 800 \times 3^{-0.152004} = 677$ labor-hours.

2. Total costs of assembling the first eight helicopters are as follows:

	Home	Insert	Page Layout	Formulas	Data	Review	View	
	O					P	Q
1						Labor-Intensive	Machine-Intensive
2						Assembly Method	Assembly Method
3						(using data from part 1a)	(using data from part 1b)
4	Direct materials:						
5	8 helicopters × $40,000; $36,000 per helicopter					$320,000	$288,000
6	Direct-assembly labor:						
7	9,826 hrs.; 5,258 hrs. × $30/hr.					294,780	157,740
8	Indirect manufacturing costs						
9	Equipment related						
10	9,826 hrs. × $12/hr.; 5,258 hrs. × $45/hr.					117,912	236,610
11	Materials-handling related						
12	0.50 × $320,000; $288,000					160,000	144,000
13	Total assembly costs					$892,692	$826,350

The machine-intensive method's assembly costs are $66,342 lower than the labor-intensive method ($892,692 – $826,350).

Decision Points

The following question-and-answer format summarizes the chapter's learning objectives. Each decision presents a key question related to a learning objective. The guidelines are the answer to that question.

Decision	Guidelines
1. What is a linear cost function and what types of cost behavior can it represent?	A linear cost function is a cost function in which, within the relevant range, the graph of total costs based on the level of a single activity is a straight line. Linear cost functions can be described by a constant, *a*, which represents the estimate of the total cost component that, within the relevant range, does not vary with changes in the level of the activity; and a slope coefficient, *b*, which represents the estimate of the amount by which total costs change for each unit change in the level of the activity within the relevant range. Three types of linear cost functions are variable, fixed, and mixed (or semivariable).
2. What is the most important issue in estimating a cost function?	The most important issue in estimating a cost function is determining whether a cause-and-effect relationship exists between the level of an activity and the costs related to that level of activity. Only a cause-and-effect relationship—not merely correlation—establishes an economically plausible relationship between the level of an activity and its costs.
3. What are the different methods that can be used to estimate a cost function?	Four methods for estimating cost functions are the industrial engineering method, the conference method, the account analysis method, and the quantitative analysis method (which includes the high-low method and the regression analysis method). If possible, the cost analyst should apply more than one method. Each method is a check on the others.
4. What are the steps to estimate a cost function using quantitative analysis?	There are six steps to estimate a cost function using quantitative analysis: (a) Choose the dependent variable; (b) identify the cost driver; (c) collect data on the dependent variable and the cost driver; (d) plot the data; (e) estimate the cost function; and (f) evaluate the cost driver of the estimated cost function. In most situations, working closely with operations managers, the cost analyst will cycle through these steps several times before identifying an acceptable cost function.
5. How should a company evaluate and choose cost drivers?	Three criteria for evaluating and choosing cost drivers are (a) economic plausibility, (b) goodness of fit, and (c) significance of independent variable.
6. What is a nonlinear cost function and in what ways do learning curves give rise to nonlinearities?	A nonlinear cost function is one in which the graph of total costs based on the level of a single activity is not a straight line within the relevant range. Nonlinear costs can arise because of quantity discounts, step cost functions, and learning-curve effects. With learning curves, labor-hours per unit decline as units of production increase. In the cumulative average-time learning model, cumulative average-time per unit declines by a constant percentage each time the cumulative quantity of units produced doubles. In the incremental unit-time learning model, the time needed to produce the last unit declines by a constant percentage each time the cumulative quantity of units produced doubles.
7. What are the common data problems a company must watch for when estimating costs?	The most difficult task in cost estimation is collecting high-quality, reliably measured data on the costs and the cost driver. Common problems include missing data, extreme values of observations, changes in technology, and distortions resulting from inflation.

Appendix

Regression Analysis

This appendix describes estimation of the regression equation, several commonly used regression statistics, and how to choose among cost functions that have been estimated by regression analysis. We use the data for Elegant Rugs presented in Exhibit 10-3 (p. 348) and displayed here again for easy reference.

Week	Cost Driver: Machine-Hours (X)	Indirect Manufacturing Labor Costs (Y)
1	68	$ 1,190
2	88	1,211
3	62	1,004
4	72	917
5	60	770
6	96	1,456
7	78	1,180
8	46	710
9	82	1,316
10	94	1,032
11	68	752
12	48	963
Total	862	$12,501

Estimating the Regression Line

The least-squares technique for estimating the regression line minimizes the sum of the squares of the vertical deviations from the data points to the estimated regression line (also called *residual term* in Exhibit 10-6, p. 352). The objective is to find the values of a and b in the linear cost function $y = a + bX$, where y is the *predicted* cost value as distinguished from the *observed* cost value, which we denote by Y. We wish to find the numerical values of a and b that minimize $\Sigma(Y - y)^2$, the sum of the squares of the vertical deviations between Y and y. Generally, these computations are done using software packages such as Excel. For the data in our example,[3] $a = \$300.98$ and $b = \$10.31$, so that the equation of the regression line is $y = \$300.98 + \$10.31X$.

Goodness of Fit

Goodness of fit measures how well the predicted values, y, based on the cost driver, X, match actual cost observations, Y. The regression analysis method computes a measure of goodness of fit, called the **coefficient of determination**. The coefficient of determination (r^2) measures the percentage of variation in Y explained by X (the independent variable).

---

[3] The formulae for a and b are as follows:

$$a = \frac{(\Sigma Y)(\Sigma X^2) - (\Sigma X)(\Sigma XY)}{n(\Sigma X^2) - (\Sigma X)(\Sigma X)} \text{ and } b = \frac{n(\Sigma XY) - (\Sigma X)(\Sigma Y)}{n(\Sigma X^2) - (\Sigma X)(\Sigma X)}$$

where for the Elegant Rugs data in Exhibit 10-3,

n = number of data points = 12

ΣX = sum of the given X values = 68 + 88 + ... + 48 = 862

ΣX^2 = sum of squares of the X values = $(68)^2 + (88)^2 + ... + (48)^2 + 4,624 + 7,744 + ... + 2,304 = 64,900$

ΣY = sum of given Y values = 1,190 + 1,211 + ... + 963 = 12,501

ΣXY = sum of the amounts obtained by multiplying each of the given X values by the associated observed
Y value = (68)(1,190) + (88)(1,211) + ... + (48)(963)
= 80,920 + 106,568 + ... + 46,224 = 928,716

$$a = \frac{(12,501)(64,900) - (862)(928,716)}{12(64,900) - (862)(862)} = \$300.98$$

$$b = \frac{12(928,716) - (862)(12,501)}{12(64,900) - (862)(862)} = \$10.31$$

It is more convenient to express the coefficient of determination as 1 minus the proportion of total variance that is *not* explained by the independent variable—that is, 1 minus the ratio of unexplained variation to total variation. The unexplained variance arises because of differences between the actual values, Y, and the predicted values, y, which in the Elegant Rugs example is given by[4]

$$r^2 = 1 - \frac{\text{Unexplained variation}}{\text{Total variation}} = 1 - \frac{\Sigma(Y - y)^2}{\Sigma(Y - \bar{Y})^2} = 1 - \frac{290,824}{607,699} = 0.52$$

The calculations indicate that r^2 increases as the predicted values, y, more closely approximate the actual observations, Y. The range of r^2 is from 0 (implying no explanatory power) to 1 (implying perfect explanatory power). Generally, an r^2 of 0.30 or higher passes the goodness-of-fit test. However, do not rely exclusively on goodness of fit. It can lead to the indiscriminate inclusion of independent variables that increase r^2 but have no economic plausibility as cost drivers. *Goodness of fit has meaning only if the relationship between the cost drivers and costs is economically plausible.*

An alternative and related way to evaluate goodness of fit is to calculate the *standard error of the regression*. The **standard error of the regression** is the variance of the residuals. It is equal to

$$S = \sqrt{\frac{\Sigma(Y - y)^2}{\text{Degrees of freedom}}} = \sqrt{\frac{\Sigma(Y - y)^2}{n - 2}} = \sqrt{\frac{290,824}{12 - 2}} = \$170.54$$

Degrees of freedom equal the number of observations, 12, *minus* the number of coefficients estimated in the regression (in this case two, a and b). On average, actual Y and the predicted value, y, differ by \$170.54. For comparison, $\bar{Y}$, the average value of Y, is \$1,041.75. The smaller the standard error of the regression, the better the fit and the better the predictions for different values of X.

Significance of Independent Variables

Do changes in the economically plausible independent variable result in significant changes in the dependent variable? Or alternatively stated, is the slope coefficient, b = \$10.31, of the regression line statistically significant (that is, different from \$0)? Recall, for example, that in the regression of number of machine-hours and indirect manufacturing labor costs in the Elegant Rugs illustration, b is estimated from a sample of 12 weekly observations. The estimate, b, is subject to random factors, as are all sample statistics. That is, a different sample of 12 data points would undoubtedly give a different estimate of b. The **standard error of the estimated coefficient** indicates how much the estimated value, b, is likely to be affected by random factors. The t-value of the b coefficient measures how large the value of the estimated coefficient is relative to its standard error.

The cutoff t-value for making inferences about the b coefficient is a function of the number of degrees of freedom, the significance level, and whether it is a one-sided or two-sided test. A 5% level of significance indicates that there is less than a 5% probability that random factors could have affected the coefficient b. A two-sided test assumes that random factors could have caused the coefficient to be either greater than \$10.31 or less than \$10.31 with equal probability. At a 5% level of significance, this means that there is less than a 2.5% (5% ÷ 2) probability that random factors could have caused the coefficient to be greater than \$10.31 and less than 2.5% probability that random factors could have caused the coefficient to be less than \$10.31. Under the expectation that the coefficient of b is positive, a one-sided test at the 5% level of significance assumes that there is less than 5% probability that random factors would have caused the coefficient to be less than \$10.31. The cutoff t-value at the 5% significance level and 10 degrees of freedom for a two-sided test is 2.228. If there were more observations and 60 degrees of freedom, the cutoff t-value would be 2.00 at a 5% significance level for a two-sided test.

The t-value (called t Stat in the Excel output) for the slope coefficient b is the value of the estimated coefficient, \$10.31 ÷ the standard error of the estimated coefficient \$3.12 = 3.30, which exceeds the cutoff t-value of 2.228. In other words, a relationship exists between the independent variable, machine-hours, and the dependent variable that cannot be attributed to random chance alone. Exhibit 10-14 shows a convenient format (in Excel) for summarizing the regression results for number of machine-hours and indirect manufacturing labor costs.

---

[4] From footnote 3, $\Sigma Y = 12,501$ and $\bar{Y} = 12,501 \div 12 = 1,041.75$

$$\Sigma(Y - \bar{Y})^2 = (1,190 - 1,041.75)^2 + (1,211 - 1,041.75)^2 + \ldots + (963 - 1,041.75)^2 = 607,699$$

Each value of X generates a predicted value of y. For example, in week 1, y = \$300.98 + (\$10.31 × 68) = \$1002.06; in week 2, y = \$300.98 + (\$10.31 × 88) = \$1,208.26; and in week 12, y = \$300.98 + (\$10.31 × 48) = \$795.86. Comparing the predicted and actual values,

$$\Sigma(Y - y)^2 = (1,190 - 1,002.06)^2 + (1,211 - 1208.26)^2 + \ldots + (963 - 795.86)^2 = 290,824.$$

Exhibit 10-14	Simple Regression Results with Indirect Manufacturing Labor Costs as Dependent Variable and Machine-Hours as Independent Variable (Cost Driver) for Elegant Rugs

	A	B	C	D	E	F
1		**Coefficients**	**Standard Error**	**t Stat**		= Coefficient/Standard Error
2		(1)	(2)	(3) = (1) ÷ (2)		= B3/C3
3	Intercept	$300.98	$229.75	1.31 ⟶		= 300.98/229.75
4	Independent Variable: Machine-Hours (X)	$ 10.31	$ 3.12	3.30		
5						
6	**Regression Statistics**					
7	R Square	0.52				
8	Durbin-Watson Statistic	2.05				

An alternative way to test that the coefficient b is significantly different from zero is in terms of a *confidence interval*: There is less than a 5% chance that the true value of the machine-hours coefficient lies outside the range $10.31 ± (2.228 × $3.12), or $10.31 ± $6.95, or from $3.36 to $17.26. Because 0 does not appear in the confidence interval, we can conclude that changes in the number of machine-hours do affect indirect manufacturing labor costs. Similarly, using data from Exhibit 10-14, the *t*-value for the constant term *a* is $300.98 ÷ $229.75 = 1.31, which is less than 2.228. This *t*-value indicates that, within the relevant range, the constant term is *not* significantly different from zero. The Durbin-Watson statistic in Exhibit 10-14 will be discussed in the following section.

Specification Analysis of Estimation Assumptions

Specification analysis is the testing of the assumptions of regression analysis. If the assumptions of (1) linearity within the relevant range, (2) constant variance of residuals, (3) independence of residuals, and (4) normality of residuals all hold, then the simple regression procedures give reliable estimates of coefficient values. This section provides a brief overview of specification analysis. When these assumptions are not satisfied, more-complex regression procedures are necessary to obtain the best estimates.[5]

1. **Linearity within the relevant range.** A common assumption—and one that appears to be reasonable in many business applications—is that a linear relationship exists between the independent variable X and the dependent variable Y within the relevant range. If a linear regression model is used to estimate a nonlinear relationship, however, the coefficient estimates obtained will be inaccurate.

   When there is only one independent variable, the easiest way to check for linearity is to study the data plotted in a scatter diagram, a step that often is unwisely skipped. Exhibit 10-6 (p. 352) presents a scatter diagram for the indirect manufacturing labor costs and machine-hours variables of Elegant Rugs shown in Exhibit 10-3 (p. 348). The scatter diagram reveals that linearity appears to be a reasonable assumption for these data.

   The learning-curve models discussed in this chapter (pp. 358–361) are examples of nonlinear cost functions. Costs increase when the level of production increases, but by lesser amounts than would occur with a linear cost function. In this case, the analyst should estimate a nonlinear cost function that incorporates learning effects.

2. **Constant variance of residuals.** The vertical deviation of the observed value Y from the regression line estimate y is called the *residual term, disturbance term,* or *error term, u = Y – y.* The assumption of constant variance implies that the residual terms are unaffected by the level of the cost driver. The assumption also implies that there is a uniform scatter, or dispersion, of the data points about the regression line as in Exhibit 10-15, Panel A. This assumption is likely to be violated, for example, in cross-sectional estimation of costs in operations of different sizes. For example, suppose Elegant Rugs has production areas of varying sizes. The company collects data from these different production areas to estimate the relationship between machine-hours and indirect manufacturing labor costs. It is very possible that the residual terms in this regression will be larger for the larger production

[5] For details see, for example, W. H. Greene, *Econometric Analysis*, 6th ed. (Upper Saddle River, NJ: Prentice Hall, 2007).

Exhibit 10-15   Constant Variance of Residuals Assumption

PANEL A:
Constant Variance
(Uniform Scatter of Data
Points Around Regression Line)

PANEL B:
Nonconstant Variance
(Higher Outputs Have
Larger Residuals)

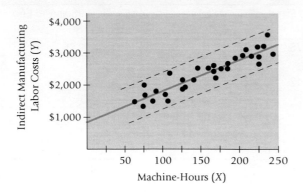

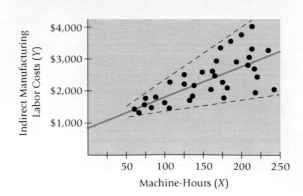

areas that have higher machine-hours and higher indirect manufacturing labor costs. There would not be a uniform scatter of data points about the regression line (see Exhibit 10-15, Panel B). Constant variance is also known as *homoscedasticity*. Violation of this assumption is called *heteroscedasticity*.

Heteroscedasticity does not affect the accuracy of the regression estimates *a* and *b*. It does, however, reduce the reliability of the estimates of the standard errors and thus affects the precision with which inferences about the population parameters can be drawn from the regression estimates.

3. **Independence of residuals.** The assumption of independence of residuals is that the residual term for any one observation is not related to the residual term for any other observation. The problem of *serial correlation* (also called *autocorrelation*) in the residuals arises when there is a systematic pattern in the sequence of residuals such that the residual in observation *n* conveys information about the residuals in observations $n + 1$, $n + 2$, and so on. Consider another production cell at Elegant Rugs that has, over a 20-week period, seen an increase in production and hence machine-hours. Exhibit 10-16 Panel B is a scatter diagram of machine-hours and indirect manufacturing labor costs. Observe the systematic pattern of the residuals in Panel B—positive residuals for extreme (high and low) quantities of machine-hours and negative residuals for moderate quantities of machine-hours. One reason for this observed pattern at low values of the cost driver is the "stickiness" of costs. When machine-hours are below 50 hours, indirect manufacturing labor costs do not decline. When machine-hours increase over time as production is ramped up, indirect manufacturing labor costs increase more as managers at Elegant Rugs struggle

Exhibit 10-16   Independence of Residuals Assumption

PANEL A:
Independence of Residuals
(No Pattern in Residuals)

PANEL B:
Serial Correlation in Residuals
(A Pattern of Positive Residuals for
Extreme Machine-Hours Used;
Negative Residuals for Moderate
Machine-Hours Used)

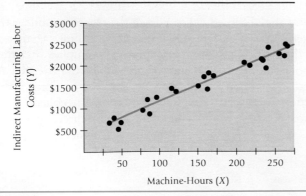

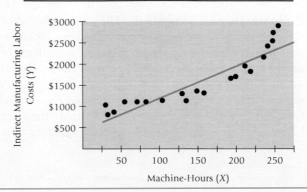

to manage the higher volume. How would the plot of residuals look if there were no auto-correlation? Like the plot in Exhibit 10-16, Panel A that shows no pattern in the residuals.

Like nonconstant variance of residuals, serial correlation does not affect the accuracy of the regression estimates *a* and *b*. It does, however, affect the standard errors of the coefficients, which in turn affect the precision with which inferences about the population parameters can be drawn from the regression estimates.

The Durbin-Watson statistic is one measure of serial correlation in the estimated residuals. For samples of 10 to 20 observations, a Durbin-Watson statistic in the 1.10–2.90 range indicates that the residuals are independent. The Durbin-Watson statistic for the regression results of Elegant Rugs in Exhibit 10-14 is 2.05. Therefore, an assumption of independence in the estimated residuals is reasonable for this regression model.

4. **Normality of residuals.** The normality of residuals assumption means that the residuals are distributed normally around the regression line. The normality of residuals assumption is frequently satisfied when using regression analysis on real cost data. Even when the assumption does not hold, accountants can still generate accurate estimates based on the regression equation, but the resulting confidence interval around these estimates is likely to be inaccurate.

Using Regression Output to Choose Cost Drivers of Cost Functions

Consider the two choices of cost drivers we described earlier in this chapter for indirect manufacturing labor costs (y):

$$y = a + (b \times \text{Number of machine-hours})$$

$$y = a + (b \times \text{Number of direct manufacturing labor-hours})$$

Exhibits 10-6 and 10-8 show plots of the data for the two regressions. Exhibit 10-14 reports regression results for the cost function using number of machine-hours as the independent variable. Exhibit 10-17 presents comparable regression results (in Excel) for the cost function using number of direct manufacturing labor-hours as the independent variable.

On the basis of the material presented in this appendix, which regression is better? Exhibit 10-18 compares these two cost functions in a systematic way. For several criteria, the cost function based on machine-hours is preferable to the cost function based on direct manufacturing labor-hours. The economic plausibility criterion is especially important.

Do not always assume that any one cost function will perfectly satisfy all the criteria in Exhibit 10-18. A cost analyst must often make a choice among "imperfect" cost functions, in the sense that the data of any particular cost function will not perfectly meet one or more of the assumptions underlying regression analysis. For example, both of the cost functions in Exhibit 10-18 are imperfect because, as stated in the section on specification analysis of estimation assumptions, inferences drawn from only 12 observations are not reliable.

Exhibit 10-17 Simple Regression Results with Indirect Manufacturing Labor Costs as Dependent Variable and Direct Manufacturing Labor-Hours as Independent Variable (Cost Driver) for Elegant Rugs

	A	B	C	D	E	F	G	H
		Home Insert Page Layout Formulas Data Review View						
1		**Coefficients**	**Standard Error**	**t Stat**				
2		**(1)**	**(2)**	**(3) = (1) ÷ (2)**				
3	Intercept	$744.67	$217.61	3.42				
4	Independent Variable: Direct Manufacturing Labor-Hours (*X*)	$ 7.72	$ 5.40	1.43		= Coefficient/Standard Error = B4/C4 = 7.72/5.40		
5								
6	**Regression Statistics**							
7	R Square	0.17						
8	Durbin-Watson Statistic	2.26						

Exhibit 10-18	Comparison of Alternative Cost Functions for Indirect Manufacturing Labor Costs Estimated with Simple Regression for Elegant Rugs

Criterion	Cost Function 1: Machine-Hours as Independent Variable	Cost Function 2: Direct Manufacturing Labor-Hours as Independent Variable
Economic plausibility	A positive relationship between indirect manufacturing labor costs (technical support labor) and machine-hours is economically plausible in Elegant Rugs' highly automated plant	A positive relationship between indirect manufacturing labor costs and direct manufacturing labor-hours is economically plausible, but less so than machine-hours in Elegant Rugs' highly automated plant on a week-to-week basis.
Goodness of fit[a]	$r^2 = 0.52$; standard error of regression = \$170.50. Excellent goodness of fit.	$r^2 = 0.17$; standard error of regression = \$224.60. Poor goodness of fit.
Significance of independent variable(s)	The t-value of 3.30 is significant at the 0.05 level.	The t-value of 1.43 is not significant at the 0.05 level.
Specification analysis of estimation assumptions	Plot of the data indicates that assumptions of linearity, constant variance, independence of residuals (Durbin-Watson statistic = 2.05), and normality of residuals hold, but inferences drawn from only 12 observations are not reliable.	Plot of the data indicates that assumptions of linearity, constant variance, independence of residuals (Durbin-Watson statistic = 2.26), and normality of residuals hold, but inferences drawn from only 12 observations are not reliable.

[a]If the number of observations available to estimate the machine-hours regression differs from the number of observations available to estimate the direct manufacturing labor-hours regression, an *adjusted* r^2 can be calculated to take this difference (in degrees of freedom) into account. Programs such as Excel calculate and present *adjusted* r^2.

Multiple Regression and Cost Hierarchies

In some cases, a satisfactory estimation of a cost function may be based on only one independent variable, such as number of machine-hours. In many cases, however, basing the estimation on more than one independent variable (that is, *multiple regression*) is more economically plausible and improves accuracy. The most widely used equations to express relationships between two or more independent variables and a dependent variable are linear in the form

$$y = a + b_1X_1 + b_2X_2 + ... + u$$

where,

y = Cost to be predicted

$X_1, X_2, ...$ = Independent variables on which the prediction is to be based

$a, b_1, b_2, ...$ = Estimated coefficients of the regression model

u = Residual term that includes the net effect of other factors not in the model as well as measurement errors in the dependent and independent variables

Example: Consider the Elegant Rugs data in Exhibit 10-19. The company's ABC analysis indicates that indirect manufacturing labor costs include large amounts incurred for setup and changeover costs when a new batch of carpets is started. Management believes that in addition to number of machine-hours (an output unit-level cost driver), indirect manufacturing labor costs are also affected by the number of batches of carpet produced during each week (a batch-level driver). Elegant Rugs estimates the relationship between two independent variables, number of machine-hours and number of production batches of carpet manufactured during the week, and indirect manufacturing labor costs.

Exhibit 10-19

Weekly Indirect
Manufacturing Labor
Costs, Machine-Hours,
Direct Manufacturing
Labor-Hours, and
Number of Production
Batches for
Elegant Rugs

	A	B	C	D	E
	Week	Machine-Hours (X_1)	Number of Production Batches (X_2)	Direct Manufacturing Labor-Hours	Indirect Manufacturing Labor Costs (Y)
1					
2	1	68	12	30	$ 1,190
3	2	88	15	35	1,211
4	3	62	13	36	1,004
5	4	72	11	20	917
6	5	60	10	47	770
7	6	96	12	45	1,456
8	7	78	17	44	1,180
9	8	46	7	38	710
10	9	82	14	70	1,316
11	10	94	12	30	1,032
12	11	68	7	29	752
13	12	48	14	38	963
14	Total	862	144	462	$12,501
15					

Exhibit 10-20 presents results (in Excel) for the following multiple regression model, using data in columns B, C, and E of Exhibit 10-19:

$$y = \$42.58 + \$7.60X_1 + \$37.77X_2$$

where X_1 is the number of machine-hours and X_2 is the number of production batches. It is economically plausible that both number of machine-hours and number of production batches would help explain variations in indirect manufacturing labor costs at Elegant Rugs. The r^2 of 0.52 for the simple regression using number of machine-hours (Exhibit 10-14) increases to 0.72 with the multiple regression in Exhibit 10-20. The t-values suggest that the independent variable coefficients of both number of machine-hours ($\$7.60$) and number of production batches ($\$37.77$) are significantly different from zero ($t = 2.74$ is the t-value for number of machine-hours, and $t = 2.48$ is the t-value for number of production batches compared to the cut-off t-value of 2.26). The multiple regression model in Exhibit 10-20 satisfies both economic plausibility and statistical criteria, and it explains much greater variation (that

Exhibit 10-20 Multiple Regression Results with Indirect Manufacturing Labor Costs and Two Independent Variables of Cost Drivers (Machine-Hours and Production Batches) for Elegant Rugs

	A	B	C	D	E	F
1		Coefficients	Standard Error	t Stat		
2		(1)	(2)	(3) = (1) ÷ (2)		
3	Intercept	$42.58	$213.91	0.20		
4	Independent Variable 1: Machine-Hours ($X1$)	$ 7.60	$ 2.77	2.74		= Coefficient/Standard Error = B4/C4 = 7.60/2.77
5	Independent Variable 2: Number of Production Batches ($X2$)	$37.77	$ 15.25	2.48		
6						
7	**Regression Statistics**					
8	R Square	0.72				
9	Durbin-Watson Statistic	2.49				

is, r^2 of 0.72 versus r^2 of 0.52) in indirect manufacturing labor costs than the simple regression model using only number of machine-hours as the independent variable.[6] The standard error of the regression equation that includes number of batches as an independent variable is

$$\sqrt{\frac{\Sigma(Y - y)^2}{n - 3}} = \sqrt{\frac{170,156}{9}} = \$137.50$$

which is lower than the standard error of the regression with only machine-hours as the independent variable, $170.50. That is, even though adding a variable reduces the degrees of freedom in the denominator, it substantially improves fit so that the numerator, $\Sigma(Y - y)^2$, decreases even more. Number of machine-hours and number of production batches are both important cost drivers of indirect manufacturing labor costs at Elegant Rugs.

In Exhibit 10-20, the slope coefficients—$7.60 for number of machine-hours and $37.77 for number of production batches—measure the change in indirect manufacturing labor costs associated with a unit change in an independent variable (assuming that the other independent variable is held constant). For example, indirect manufacturing labor costs increase by $37.77 when one more production batch is added, assuming that the number of machine-hours is held constant.

An alternative approach would create two separate cost pools for indirect manufacturing labor costs: one for costs related to number of machine-hours and another for costs related to number of production batches. Elegant Rugs would then estimate the relationship between the cost driver and the costs in each cost pool. The difficult task under this approach is to properly subdivide the indirect manufacturing labor costs into the two cost pools.

Multicollinearity

A major concern that arises with multiple regression is multicollinearity. **Multicollinearity** exists when two or more independent variables are highly correlated with each other. Generally, users of regression analysis believe that a *coefficient of correlation* between independent variables greater than 0.70 indicates multicollinearity. Multicollinearity increases the standard errors of the coefficients of the individual variables. That is, variables that are economically and statistically significant will appear not to be significantly different from zero.

The matrix of correlation coefficients of the different variables described in Exhibit 10-19 are as follows:

	Indirect Manufacturing Labor Costs	Machine-Hours	Number of Production Batches	Direct Manufacturing Labor-Hours
Indirect manufacturing labor costs	1			
Machine-hours	0.72	1		
Number of production batches	0.69	0.4	1	
Direct manufacturing labor-hours	0.41	0.12	0.31	1

These results indicate that multiple regressions using any pair of the independent variables in Exhibit 10-19 are not likely to encounter multicollinearity problems.

When multicollinearity exists, try to obtain new data that do not suffer from multicollinearity problems. Do not drop an independent variable (cost driver) that should be included in a model because it is correlated with another independent variable. Omitting such a variable will cause the estimated coefficient of the independent variable included in the model to be biased away from its true value.

---

[6] Adding another variable always increases r^2. The question is whether adding another variable increases r^2 sufficiently. One way to get insight into this question is to calculate an adjusted r^2 as follows:

Adjusted $r^2 = 1 - (1 - r^2)\dfrac{n - 1}{n - p - 1}$, where n is the number of observations and p is the number of coefficients estimated. In the model with only machine-hours as the independent variable, adjusted $r^2 = 1 - (1 - 0.52)\dfrac{12 - 1}{12 - 2 - 1} = 0.41$. In the model with both machine-hours and number of batches as independent variables, adjusted $r^2 = 1 - (1 - 0.72)\dfrac{12 - 1}{12 - 3 - 1} = 0.62$. Adjusted r^2 does not have the same interpretation as r^2 but the increase in adjusted r^2 when number of batches is added as an independent variable suggests that adding this variable significantly improves the fit of the model in a way that more than compensates for the degree of freedom lost by estimating another coefficient.

Terms to Learn

This chapter and the Glossary at the end of this book contain definitions of the following important terms:

account analysis method (**p. 347**)
coefficient of determination (r^2) (**p. 367**)
conference method (**p. 346**)
constant (**p. 343**)
cost estimation (**p. 344**)
cost function (**p. 341**)
cost predictions (**p. 344**)
cumulative average-time learning
  model (**p. 359**)
dependent variable (**p. 348**)
experience curve (**p. 358**)
high-low method (**p. 350**)

incremental unit-time learning model
  (**p. 360**)
independent variable (**p. 348**)
industrial engineering method (**p. 346**)
intercept (**p. 343**)
learning curve (**p. 358**)
linear cost function (**p. 342**)
mixed cost (**p. 343**)
multicollinearity (**p. 374**)
multiple regression (**p. 352**)
nonlinear cost function (**p. 357**)
regression analysis (**p. 352**)

residual term (**p. 352**)
semivariable cost (**p. 343**)
simple regression (**p. 352**)
slope coefficient (**p. 342**)
specification analysis (**p. 369**)
standard error of the estimated
  coefficient (**p. 368**)
standard error of the regression
  (**p. 368**)
step cost function (**p. 357**)
work-measurement method (**p. 346**)

Assignment Material

Questions

10-1 What two assumptions are frequently made when estimating a cost function?

10-2 Describe three alternative linear cost functions.

10-3 What is the difference between a linear and a nonlinear cost function? Give an example of each type of cost function.

10-4 "High correlation between two variables means that one is the cause and the other is the effect." Do you agree? Explain.

10-5 Name four approaches to estimating a cost function.

10-6 Describe the conference method for estimating a cost function. What are two advantages of this method?

10-7 Describe the account analysis method for estimating a cost function.

10-8 List the six steps in estimating a cost function on the basis of an analysis of a past cost relationship. Which step is typically the most difficult for the cost analyst?

10-9 When using the high-low method, should you base the high and low observations on the dependent variable or on the cost driver?

10-10 Describe three criteria for evaluating cost functions and choosing cost drivers.

10-11 Define learning curve. Outline two models that can be used when incorporating learning into the estimation of cost functions.

10-12 Discuss four frequently encountered problems when collecting cost data on variables included in a cost function.

10-13 What are the four key assumptions examined in specification analysis in the case of simple regression?

10-14 "All the independent variables in a cost function estimated with regression analysis are cost drivers." Do you agree? Explain.

10-15 "Multicollinearity exists when the dependent variable and the independent variable are highly correlated." Do you agree? Explain.

Exercises

10-16 **Estimating a cost function.** The controller of the Ijiri Company wants you to estimate a cost function from the following two observations in a general ledger account called Maintenance:

Month	Machine-Hours	Maintenance Costs Incurred
January	6,000	$4,000
February	10,000	5,400

Required

1. Estimate the cost function for maintenance.
2. Can the constant in the cost function be used as an estimate of fixed maintenance cost per month? Explain.

10-17 Identifying variable-, fixed-, and mixed-cost functions. The Pacific Corporation operates car rental agencies at more than 20 airports. Customers can choose from one of three contracts for car rentals of one day or less:

- Contract 1: $50 for the day
- Contract 2: $30 for the day plus $0.20 per mile traveled
- Contract 3: $1 per mile traveled

Required

1. Plot separate graphs for each of the three contracts, with costs on the vertical axis and miles traveled on the horizontal axis.
2. Express each contract as a linear cost function of the form $y = a + bX$.
3. Identify each contract as a variable-, fixed-, or mixed-cost function.

10-18 Various cost-behavior patterns. (CPA, adapted) Select the graph that matches the numbered manufacturing cost data (requirements 1–9). Indicate by letter which graph best fits the situation or item described.

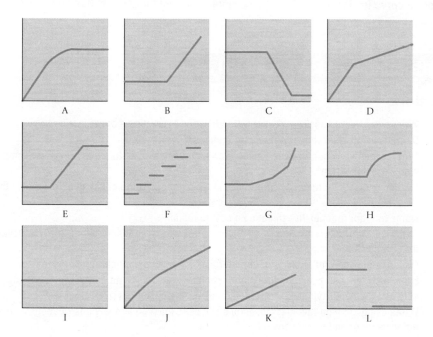

The vertical axes of the graphs represent total cost, and the horizontal axes represent units produced during a calendar year. In each case, the zero point of dollars and production is at the intersection of the two axes. The graphs may be used more than once.

Required

1. Annual depreciation of equipment, where the amount of depreciation charged is computed by the machine-hours method.
2. Electricity bill—a flat fixed charge, plus a variable cost after a certain number of kilowatt-hours are used, in which the quantity of kilowatt-hours used varies proportionately with quantity of units produced.
3. City water bill, which is computed as follows:

First 1,000,000 gallons or less	$1,000 flat fee
Next 10,000 gallons	$0.003 per gallon used
Next 10,000 gallons	$0.006 per gallon used
Next 10,000 gallons	$0.009 per gallon used
and so on	and so on

The gallons of water used vary proportionately with the quantity of production output.
4. Cost of direct materials, where direct material cost per unit produced decreases with each pound of material used (for example, if 1 pound is used, the cost is $10; if 2 pounds are used, the cost is $19.98; if 3 pounds are used, the cost is $29.94), with a minimum cost per unit of $9.20.

5. Annual depreciation of equipment, where the amount is computed by the straight-line method. When the depreciation schedule was prepared, it was anticipated that the obsolescence factor would be greater than the wear-and-tear factor.

6. Rent on a manufacturing plant donated by the city, where the agreement calls for a fixed-fee payment unless 200,000 labor-hours are worked, in which case no rent is paid.

7. Salaries of repair personnel, where one person is needed for every 1,000 machine-hours or less (that is, 0 to 1,000 hours requires one person, 1,001 to 2,000 hours requires two people, and so on).

8. Cost of direct materials used (assume no quantity discounts).

9. Rent on a manufacturing plant donated by the county, where the agreement calls for rent of $100,000 to be reduced by $1 for each direct manufacturing labor-hour worked in excess of 200,000 hours, but a minimum rental fee of $20,000 must be paid.

10-19 Matching graphs with descriptions of cost and revenue behavior. (D. Green, adapted) Given here are a number of graphs.

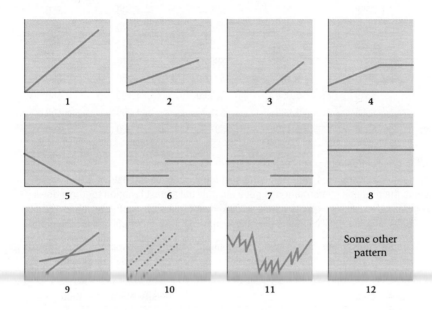

The horizontal axis represents the units produced over the year and the vertical axis represents total cost or revenues. Indicate by number which graph best fits the situation or item described (a–h). Some graphs may be used more than once; some may not apply to any of the situations.

a. Direct material costs

b. Supervisors' salaries for one shift and two shifts

c. A cost-volume-profit graph

d. Mixed costs—for example, car rental fixed charge plus a rate per mile driven

e. Depreciation of plant, computed on a straight-line basis

f. Data supporting the use of a variable-cost rate, such as manufacturing labor cost of $14 per unit produced

g. Incentive bonus plan that pays managers $0.10 for every unit produced above some level of production

h. Interest expense on $2 million borrowed at a fixed rate of interest

10-20 Account analysis method. Lorenzo operates a car wash. Incoming cars are put on an automatic conveyor belt. Cars are washed as the conveyor belt carries them from the start station to the finish station. After a car moves off the conveyor belt, it is dried manually. Workers then clean and vacuum the inside of the car. Lorenzo serviced 80,000 cars in 2012. Lorenzo reports the following costs for 2012:

Account Description	Costs
Car wash labor	$260,000
Soap, cloth, and supplies	42,000
Water	38,000
Electric power to move conveyor belt	72,000
Depreciation	64,000
Salaries	46,000

Required

1. Classify each account as variable or fixed with respect to the number of cars washed. Explain.
2. Suppose Lorenzo washed 90,000 cars in 2012. Use the cost classification you developed in requirement 1 to estimate Lorenzo's total costs in 2012. Depreciation is computed on a straight-line basis.

10-21 Account analysis, high-low. Java Joe Coffees wants to find an equation to estimate monthly utility costs. Java Joe's has been in business for one year and has collected the following cost data for utilities:

Month	Electricity Bill	Kilowatt Hours Used	Telephone Bill	Telephone Minutes Used	Water Bill	Gallons of Water Used
January	$360	1,200	$92.00	1,100	$60	30,560
February	$420	1,400	$91.20	1,060	$60	26,800
March	$549	1,830	$94.80	1,240	$60	31,450
April	$405	1,350	$89.60	980	$60	29,965
May	$588	1,960	$98.00	1,400	$60	30,568
June	$624	2,080	$98.80	1,440	$60	25,540
July	$522	1,740	$93.40	1,170	$60	32,690
August	$597	1,990	$96.20	1,310	$60	31,222
September	$630	2,100	$95.60	1,280	$60	33,540
October	$615	2,050	$93.80	1,190	$60	31,970
November	$594	1,980	$91.00	1,050	$60	28,600
December	$633	2,110	$97.00	1,350	$60	34,100

Required

1. Which of the preceding costs is variable? Fixed? Mixed? Explain.
2. Using the high-low method, determine the cost function for each cost.
3. Combine the preceding information to get a monthly utility cost function for Java Joe's.
4. Next month, Java Joe's expects to use 2,200 kilowatt hours of electricity, make 1,500 minutes of telephone calls, and use 32,000 gallons of water. Estimate total cost of utilities for the month.

10-22 Account analysis method. Gower, Inc., a manufacturer of plastic products, reports the following manufacturing costs and account analysis classification for the year ended December 31, 2012.

Account	Classification	Amount
Direct materials	All variable	$300,000
Direct manufacturing labor	All variable	225,000
Power	All variable	37,500
Supervision labor	20% variable	56,250
Materials-handling labor	50% variable	60,000
Maintenance labor	40% variable	75,000
Depreciation	0% variable	95,000
Rent, property taxes, and administration	0% variable	100,000

Gower, Inc., produced 75,000 units of product in 2012. Gower's management is estimating costs for 2013 on the basis of 2012 numbers. The following additional information is available for 2013.

a. Direct materials prices in 2013 are expected to increase by 5% compared with 2012.
b. Under the terms of the labor contract, direct manufacturing labor wage rates are expected to increase by 10% in 2013 compared with 2012.
c. Power rates and wage rates for supervision, materials handling, and maintenance are not expected to change from 2012 to 2013.
d. Depreciation costs are expected to increase by 5%, and rent, property taxes, and administration costs are expected to increase by 7%.
e. Gower expects to manufacture and sell 80,000 units in 2013.

Required

1. Prepare a schedule of variable, fixed, and total manufacturing costs for each account category in 2013. Estimate total manufacturing costs for 2013.
2. Calculate Gower's total manufacturing cost per unit in 2012, and estimate total manufacturing cost per unit in 2013.
3. How can you obtain better estimates of fixed and variable costs? Why would these better estimates be useful to Gower?

10-23 **Estimating a cost function, high-low method.** Reisen Travel offers helicopter service from suburban towns to John F. Kennedy International Airport in New York City. Each of its 10 helicopters makes between 1,000 and 2,000 round-trips per year. The records indicate that a helicopter that has made 1,000 round-trips in the year incurs an average operating cost of $350 per round-trip, and one that has made 2,000 round-trips in the year incurs an average operating cost of $300 per round-trip.

1. Using the high-low method, estimate the linear relationship $y = a + bX$, where y is the total annual operating cost of a helicopter and X is the number of round-trips it makes to JFK airport during the year.
2. Give examples of costs that would be included in a and in b.
3. If Reisen Travel expects each helicopter to make, on average, 1,200 round-trips in the coming year, what should its estimated operating budget for the helicopter fleet be?

Required

10-24 **Estimating a cost function, high-low method.** Laurie Daley is examining customer-service costs in the southern region of Capitol Products. Capitol Products has more than 200 separate electrical products that are sold with a six-month guarantee of full repair or replacement with a new product. When a product is returned by a customer, a service report is prepared. This service report includes details of the problem and the time and cost of resolving the problem. Weekly data for the most recent 8-week period are as follows:

Week	Customer-Service Department Costs	Number of Service Reports
1	$13,700	190
2	20,900	275
3	13,000	115
4	18,800	395
5	14,000	265
6	21,500	455
7	16,900	340
8	21,000	305

1. Plot the relationship between customer-service costs and number of service reports. Is the relationship economically plausible?
2. Use the high-low method to compute the cost function, relating customer-service costs to the number of service reports.
3. What variables, in addition to number of service reports, might be cost drivers of weekly customer-service costs of Capitol Products?

Required

10-25 **Linear cost approximation.** Terry Lawler, managing director of the Chicago Reviewers Group, is examining how overhead costs behave with changes in monthly professional labor-hours billed to clients. Assume the following historical data:

Total Overhead Costs	Professional Labor-Hours Billed to Clients
$335,000	2,000
400,000	3,000
430,000	4,000
472,000	5,000
533,000	6,500
582,000	7,500

1. Compute the linear cost function, relating total overhead costs to professional labor-hours, using the representative observations of 3,000 and 6,500 hours. Plot the linear cost function. Does the constant component of the cost function represent the fixed overhead costs of the Chicago Reviewers Group? Why?
2. What would be the predicted total overhead costs for (a) 4,000 hours and (b) 7,500 hours using the cost function estimated in requirement 1? Plot the predicted costs and actual costs for 4,000 and 7,500 hours.
3. Lawler had a chance to accept a special job that would have boosted professional labor-hours from 3,000 to 4,000 hours. Suppose Lawler, guided by the linear cost function, rejected this job because it would have brought a total increase in contribution margin of $35,000, before deducting the predicted increase in total overhead cost, $38,000. What is the total contribution margin actually forgone?

Required

10-26 Cost-volume-profit and regression analysis. Goldstein Corporation manufactures a children's bicycle, model CT8. Goldstein currently manufactures the bicycle frame. During 2012, Goldstein made 32,000 frames at a total cost of $1,056,000. Ryan Corporation has offered to supply as many frames as Goldstein wants at a cost of $32.50 per frame. Goldstein anticipates needing 35,000 frames each year for the next few years.

Required

1. **a.** What is the average cost of manufacturing a bicycle frame in 2012? How does it compare to Ryan's offer?
   b. Can Goldstein use the answer in requirement 1a to determine the cost of manufacturing 35,000 bicycle frames? Explain.
2. Goldstein's cost analyst uses annual data from past years to estimate the following regression equation with total manufacturing costs of the bicycle frame as the dependent variable and bicycle frames produced as the independent variable:

$$y = \$435,000 + \$19X$$

During the years used to estimate the regression equation, the production of bicycle frames varied from 31,000 to 35,000. Using this equation, estimate how much it would cost Goldstein to manufacture 35,000 bicycle frames. How much more or less costly is it to manufacture the frames rather than to acquire them from Ryan?

3. What other information would you need to be confident that the equation in requirement 2 accurately predicts the cost of manufacturing bicycle frames?

10-27 Regression analysis, service company. (CMA, adapted) Bob Jones owns a catering company that prepares food and beverages for banquets and parties. For a standard party the cost on a per-person basis is as follows:

Food and beverages	$15
Labor (0.5 hour × $10 per hour)	5
Overhead (0.5 hour × $14 per hour)	7
Total cost per person	$27

Jones is quite certain about his estimates of the food, beverages, and labor costs but is not as comfortable with the overhead estimate. The overhead estimate was based on the actual data for the past 12 months, which are presented here. These data indicate that overhead costs vary with the direct labor-hours used. The $14 estimate was determined by dividing total overhead costs for the 12 months by total labor-hours.

Month	Labor-Hours	Overhead Costs
January	2,500	$ 55,000
February	2,700	59,000
March	3,000	60,000
April	4,200	64,000
May	7,500	77,000
June	5,500	71,000
July	6,500	74,000
August	4,500	67,000
September	7,000	75,000
October	4,500	68,000
November	3,100	62,000
December	6,500	73,000
Total	57,500	$805,000

Jones has recently become aware of regression analysis. He estimated the following regression equation with overhead costs as the dependent variable and labor-hours as the independent variable:

$$y = \$48,271 + \$3.93X$$

Required

1. Plot the relationship between overhead costs and labor-hours. Draw the regression line and evaluate it using the criteria of economic plausibility, goodness of fit, and slope of the regression line.
2. Using data from the regression analysis, what is the variable cost per person for a standard party?
3. Bob Jones has been asked to prepare a bid for a 200-person standard party to be given next month. Determine the minimum bid price that Jones would be willing to submit to recoup variable costs.

10-28 High-low, regression. Melissa Crupp is the new manager of the materials storeroom for Canton Manufacturing. Melissa has been asked to estimate future monthly purchase costs for part #4599, used in two of Canton's products. Melissa has purchase cost and quantity data for the past nine months as follows:

Month	Cost of Purchase	Quantity Purchased
January	$10,390	2,250 parts
February	10,550	2,350
March	14,400	3,390
April	13,180	3,120
May	10,970	2,490
June	11,580	2,680
July	12,690	3,030
August	8,560	1,930
September	12,450	2,960

Estimated monthly purchases for this part based on expected demand of the two products for the rest of the year are as follows:

Month	Purchase Quantity Expected
October	2,800 parts
November	3,100
December	2,500

Required

1. The computer in Melissa's office is down and Melissa has been asked to immediately provide an equation to estimate the future purchase cost for part # 4599. Melissa grabs a calculator and uses the high-low method to estimate a cost equation. What equation does she get?
2. Using the equation from requirement 1, calculate the future expected purchase costs for each of the last three months of the year.
3. After a few hours Melissa's computer is fixed. Melissa uses the first nine months of data and regression analysis to estimate the relationship between the quantity purchased and purchase costs of part #4599. The regression line Melissa obtains is as follows:

$$y = \$1,779.6 + 3.67X$$

Evaluate the regression line using the criteria of economic plausibility, goodness of fit, and significance of the independent variable. Compare the regression equation to the equation based on the high-low method. Which is a better fit? Why?
4. Use the regression results to calculate the expected purchase costs for October, November, and December. Compare the expected purchase costs to the expected purchase costs calculated using the high-low method in requirement 2. Comment on your results.

10-29 Learning curve, cumulative average-time learning model. Global Defense manufactures radar systems. It has just completed the manufacture of its first newly designed system, RS-32. Manufacturing data for the RS-32 follow:

	Home	Insert	Page Layout	Formulas	Data	Review	View		
	A						B	C	
1	Direct material cost						$160,000	per unit of RS-32	
2	Direct manufacturing labor time for first unit						6,000	direct manufacturing labor-hours	
3	Learning curve for manufacturing labor time per radar system						85%	cumulative average time[a]	
4	Direct manufacturing labor cost						$ 30	per direct manufacturing labor-hour	
5	Variable manufacturing overhead cost						$ 20	per direct manufacturing labor-hour	
6									
7	[a]Using the formula (p. 359), for a 85% learning curve, $b = \dfrac{\ln 0.85}{\ln 2} = \dfrac{-0.162519}{0.693147} = -0.234465$								
8									

Required Calculate the total variable costs of producing 2, 4, and 8 units.

10-30 Learning curve, incremental unit-time learning model. Assume the same information for Global Defense as in Exercise 10-29, except that Global Defense uses an 85% incremental unit-time learning model as a basis for predicting direct manufacturing labor-hours. (An 85% learning curve means $b = -0.234465$.)

Required
1. Calculate the total variable costs of producing 2, 3, and 4 units.
2. If you solved Exercise 10-29, compare your cost predictions in the two exercises for 2 and 4 units. Why are the predictions different? How should Global Defense decide which model it should use?

MyAccountingLab

Problems

10-31 High-low method. Ken Howard, financial analyst at KMW Corporation, is examining the behavior of quarterly maintenance costs for budgeting purposes. Howard collects the following data on machine-hours worked and maintenance costs for the past 12 quarters:

Quarter	Machine-Hours	Maintenance Costs
1	100,000	$205,000
2	120,000	240,000
3	110,000	220,000
4	130,000	260,000
5	95,000	190,000
6	115,000	235,000
7	105,000	215,000
8	125,000	255,000
9	105,000	210,000
10	125,000	245,000
11	115,000	200,000
12	140,000	280,000

Required
1. Estimate the cost function for the quarterly data using the high-low method.
2. Plot and comment on the estimated cost function.
3. Howard anticipates that KMW will operate machines for 100,000 hours in quarter 13. Calculate the predicted maintenance costs in quarter 13 using the cost function estimated in requirement 1.

10-32 High-low method and regression analysis. Local Harvest, a cooperative of organic family-owned farms outside of Columbus, Ohio, has recently started a fresh produce club to provide support to the group's member farms, and to promote the benefits of eating organic, locally-produced food to the nearby suburban community. Families pay a seasonal membership fee of $50, and place their orders a week in advance for a price of $40 per week. In turn, Local Harvest delivers fresh-picked seasonal local produce to several neighborhood distribution points. Eight hundred families joined the club for the first season, but the number of orders varied from week to week.

Harvey Hendricks has run the produce club for the first 10-week season. Before becoming a farmer, Harvey had been a business major in college, and he remembers a few things about cost analysis. In planning for next year, he wants to know how many orders will be needed each week for the club to break even, but first he must estimate the club's fixed and variable costs. He has collected the following data over the club's first 10 weeks of operation:

Week	Number of Orders per Week	Weekly Total Costs
1	351	$18,795
2	385	21,597
3	410	22,800
4	453	22,600
5	425	21,900
6	486	24,600
7	455	23,900
8	467	22,900
9	525	25,305
10	510	24,500

1. Plot the relationship between number of orders per week and weekly total costs.
2. Estimate the cost equation using the high-low method, and draw this line on your graph.
3. Harvey uses his computer to calculate the following regression formula:

Total weekly costs = $8,631 + ($31.92 × Number of weekly orders)

Draw the regression line on your graph. Use your graph to evaluate the regression line using the criteria of economic plausibility, goodness of fit, and significance of the independent variable. Is the cost function estimated using the high-low method a close approximation of the cost function estimated using the regression method? Explain briefly.
4. Did Fresh Harvest break even this season? Remember that each of the families paid a seasonal membership fee of $50.
5. Assume that 900 families join the club next year, and that prices and costs do not change. How many orders, on average, must Fresh Harvest receive each week to break even?

10-33 High-low method; regression analysis. (CIMA, adapted) Anna Martinez, the financial manager at the Casa Real restaurant, is checking to see if there is any relationship between newspaper advertising and sales revenues at the restaurant. She obtains the following data for the past 10 months:

Month	Revenues	Advertising Costs
March	$50,000	$2,000
April	70,000	3,000
May	55,000	1,500
June	65,000	3,500
July	55,000	1,000
August	65,000	2,000
September	45,000	1,500
October	80,000	4,000
November	55,000	2,500
December	60,000	2,500

She estimates the following regression equation:

Monthly revenues = $39,502 + ($8.723 × Advertising costs)

1. Plot the relationship between advertising costs and revenues.
2. Draw the regression line and evaluate it using the criteria of economic plausibility, goodness of fit, and slope of the regression line.
3. Use the high-low method to compute the function, relating advertising costs and revenues.
4. Using (a) the regression equation and (b) the high-low equation, what is the increase in revenues for each $1,000 spent on advertising within the relevant range? Which method should Martinez use to predict the effect of advertising costs on revenues? Explain briefly.

10-34 Regression, activity-based costing, choosing cost drivers. Fitzgerald Manufacturing has been using activity-based costing to determine the cost of product X-678. One of the activities, "Inspection," occurs just before the product is finished. Fitzgerald inspects every 10th unit, and has been using "number of units inspected" as the cost driver for inspection costs. A significant component of inspection costs is the cost of the test-kit used in each inspection.

Neela McFeen, the line manager, is wondering if inspection labor-hours might be a better cost driver for inspection costs. Neela gathers information for weekly inspection costs, units inspected, and inspection labor-hours as follows:

Week	Units Inspected	Inspection Labor-Hours	Inspection Costs
1	1,400	190	$3,700
2	400	70	1,800
3	1,700	230	4,500
4	2,400	240	5,900
5	2,100	210	5,300
6	700	90	2,400
7	900	110	2,900

Neela runs regressions on each of the possible cost drivers and estimates these cost functions:

$$\text{Inspection Costs} = \$977 + (\$2.05 \times \text{Number of units inspected})$$
$$\text{Inspection Costs} = \$478 + (\$20.31 \times \text{Inspection labor-hours})$$

Required

1. Explain why number of units inspected and inspection labor-hours are plausible cost drivers of inspection costs.
2. Plot the data and regression line for units inspected and inspection costs. Plot the data and regression line for inspection labor-hours and inspection costs. Which cost driver of inspection costs would you choose? Explain.
3. Neela expects inspectors to work 140 hours next period and to inspect 1,100 units. Using the cost driver you chose in requirement 2, what amount of inspection costs should Neela budget? Explain any implications of Neela choosing the cost driver you did not choose in requirement 2 to budget inspection costs.

10-35 Interpreting regression results, matching time periods. Brickman Apparel produces equipment for the extreme-sports market. It has four peak periods, each lasting two months, for manufacturing the merchandise suited for spring, summer, fall, and winter. In the off-peak periods, Brickman schedules equipment maintenance. Brickman's controller, Sascha Green, wants to understand the drivers of equipment maintenance costs. The data collected is shown in the table as follows:

Month	Machine-Hours	Maintenance Costs
January	5,000	$ 1,300
February	5,600	2,200
March	1,500	12,850
April	6,500	1,665
May	5,820	2,770
June	1,730	15,250
July	7,230	1,880
August	5,990	2,740
September	2,040	15,350
October	6,170	1,620
November	5,900	2,770
December	1,500	14,700

A regression analysis of one year of monthly data yields the following relationships:

$$\text{Maintenance costs} = \$18,552 - (\$2.683 \times \text{Number of machine-hours})$$

Upon examining the results, Green comments, "So, all I have to do to reduce maintenance costs is run my machines longer?! This is hard to believe, but numbers don't lie! I would have guessed just the opposite."

Required

1. Explain why Green made this comment. What is wrong with her analysis?
2. Upon further reflection, Sascha Green reanalyzes the data, this time comparing quarterly machine-hours with quarterly maintenance expenditures. This time, the results are very different. The regression yields the following formula:

$$\text{Maintenance costs} = \$2,622.80 + (\$1.175 \times \text{Number of machine-hours})$$

What caused the formula to change, in light of the fact that the data was the same?

10-36 Cost estimation, cumulative average-time learning curve. The Nautilus Company, which is under contract to the U.S. Navy, assembles troop deployment boats. As part of its research program, it completes the assembly of the first of a new model (PT109) of deployment boats. The Navy is impressed with the PT109. It requests that Nautilus submit a proposal on the cost of producing another six PT109s.

Nautilus reports the following cost information for the first PT109 assembled and uses a 90% cumulative average-time learning model as a basis for forecasting direct manufacturing labor-hours for the next six PT109s. (A 90% learning curve means $b = -0.152004$.)

	Home	Insert	Page Layout	Formulas	Data	Review	View	
	A					B		C
1	Direct material					$200,000		
2	Direct manufacturing labor time for first boat					15,000	labor-hours	
3	Direct manufacturing labor rate					$ 40	per direct manufacturing labor-hour	
4	Variable manufacturing overhead cost					$ 25	per direct manufacturing labor-hour	
5	Other manufacturing overhead					20%	of direct manufacturing labor costs	
6	Tooling costs[a]					$280,000		
7	Learning curve for manufacturing labor time per boat					90%	cumulative average time[b]	
8								
9	[a]Tooling can be reused at no extra cost because all of its cost has been assigned to the first deployment boat.							
10								
11	[b]Using the formula (p. 359), for a 90% learning curve, $b = \dfrac{\ln 0.9}{\ln 2} = \dfrac{-0.105361}{0.693147} = -0.152004$							
12								

1. Calculate predicted total costs of producing the six PT109s for the Navy. (Nautilus will keep the first deployment boat assembled, costed at $1,575,000, as a demonstration model for potential customers.) **Required**
2. What is the dollar amount of the difference between (a) the predicted total costs for producing the six PT109s in requirement 1, and (b) the predicted total costs for producing the six PT109s, assuming that there is no learning curve for direct manufacturing labor? That is, for (b) assume a linear function for units produced and direct manufacturing labor-hours.

10-37 Cost estimation, incremental unit-time learning model. Assume the same information for the Nautilus Company as in Problem 10-36 with one exception. This exception is that Nautilus uses a 90% incremental unit-time learning model as a basis for predicting direct manufacturing labor-hours in its assembling operations. (A 90% learning curve means $b = -0.152004$.)

1. Prepare a prediction of the total costs for producing the six PT109s for the Navy. **Required**
2. If you solved requirement 1 of Problem 10-36, compare your cost prediction there with the one you made here. Why are the predictions different? How should Nautilus decide which model it should use?

10-38 Regression; choosing among models. Tilbert Toys (TT) makes the popular Floppin' Freddy Frog and Jumpin' Jill Junebug dolls in batches. TT has recently adopted activity-based costing. TT incurs setup costs for each batch of dolls that it produces. TT uses "number of setups" as the cost driver for setup costs.

TT has just hired Bebe Williams, an accountant. Bebe thinks that "number of setup-hours" might be a better cost driver because the setup time for each product is different. Bebe collects the following data.

	Home	Insert	Page Layout	Formulas	Data	Review	View
	A	B		C		D	
1	Month	Number of Setups		Number of Setup Hours		Setup Costs	
2	1	300		1,840		$104,600	
3	2	410		2,680		126,700	
4	3	150		1,160		57,480	
5	4	480		3,800		236,840	
6	5	310		3,680		178,880	
7	6	460		3,900		213,760	
8	7	420		2,980		209,620	
9	8	300		1,200		90,080	
10	9	270		3,280		221,040	

Required

1. Estimate the regression equation for (a) setup costs and number of setups and (b) setup costs and number of setup-hours. You should obtain the following results:

Regression 1: Setup costs = $a + (b \times$ Number of setups)

Variable	Coefficient	Standard Error	t-Value
Constant	$12,890	$61,365	0.21
Independent variable 1: No. of setups	$ 426.77	$ 171	2.49

$r^2 = 0.47$; Durbin-Watson statistic = 1.65

Regression 2: Setup costs = $a + (b \times$ Number of setup-hours)

Variable	Coefficient	Standard Error	t-Value
Constant	$6,573	$25,908	0.25
Independent variable 1: No. of setup-hours	$ 56.27	$ 8.90	6.32

$r^2 = 0.85$; Durbin-Watson statistic = 1.50

2. On two different graphs plot the data and the regression lines for each of the following cost functions:
   a. Setup costs = $a + (b \times$ Number of setups)
   b. Setup costs = $a + (b \times$ Number of setup-hours)
3. Evaluate the regression models for "Number of setups" and "Number of setup-hours" as the cost driver according to the format of Exhibit 10-18 (p. 372).
4. Based on your analysis, which cost driver should Tilbert Toys use for setup costs, and why?

10-39 Multiple regression (continuation of 10-38). Bebe Williams wonders if she should run a multiple regression with both number of setups and number of setup-hours, as cost drivers.

Required

1. Run a multiple regression to estimate the regression equation for setup costs using both number of setups and number of setup-hours as independent variables. You should obtain the following result:

Regression 3: Setup costs = $a (b_1 \times$ No. of setups) + ($b_2 \times$ No. of setup-hours)

Variable	Coefficient	Standard Error	t-Value
Constant	−$2,807	$34,850	−0.08
Independent variable 1: No. of setups	$ 58.62	$ 133.42	0.44
Independent variable 2: No. of setup-hours	$ 52.31	$ 13.08	4.00

$r^2 = 0.86$; Durbin-Watson statistic = 1.38

2. Evaluate the multiple regression output using the criteria of economic plausibility goodness of fit, significance of independent variables, and specification of estimation assumptions. (Assume linearity, constant variance, and normality of residuals.)
3. What difficulties do not arise in simple regression analysis that may arise in multiple regression analysis? Is there evidence of such difficulties in the multiple regression presented in this problem? Explain.
4. Which of the regression models from Problems 10-38 and 10-39 would you recommend Bebe Williams use? Explain.

10-40 Purchasing department cost drivers, activity-based costing, simple regression analysis. Fashion Bling operates a chain of 10 retail department stores. Each department store makes its own purchasing decisions. Barry Lee, assistant to the president of Fashion Bling, is interested in better understanding the drivers of purchasing department costs. For many years, Fashion Bling has allocated purchasing department costs to products on the basis of the dollar value of merchandise purchased. A $100 item is allocated 10 times as many overhead costs associated with the purchasing department as a $10 item.

Lee recently attended a seminar titled "Cost Drivers in the Retail Industry." In a presentation at the seminar, Couture Fabrics, a leading competitor that has implemented activity-based costing, reported number of purchase orders and number of suppliers to be the two most important cost drivers of purchasing department costs. The dollar value of merchandise purchased in each purchase order was not found to be a significant cost driver. Lee interviewed several members of the purchasing department at the Fashion Bling store in Miami. They believed that Couture Fabrics' conclusions also applied to their purchasing department.

Lee collects the following data for the most recent year for Fashion Bling's 10 retail department stores:

	Home	Insert	Page Layout	Formulas	Data	Review	View
	A		B	C	D	E	
1	Department Store		Purchasing Department Costs (PDC)	Dollar Value of Merchandise Purchased (MP$)	Number of Purchase Orders (No. of POs)	Number of Suppliers (No. of Ss)	
2	Baltimore		$1,522,000	$ 68,307,000	4,345	125	
3	Chicago		1,095,000	33,463,000	2,548	230	
4	Los Angeles		542,000	121,800,000	1,420	8	
5	Miami		2,053,000	119,450,000	5,935	188	
6	New York		1,068,000	33,575,000	2,786	21	
7	Phoenix		517,000	29,836,000	1,334	29	
8	Seattle		1,544,000	102,840,000	7,581	101	
9	St. Louis		1,761,000	38,725,000	3,623	127	
10	Toronto		1,605,000	139,300,000	1,712	202	
11	Vancouver		1,263,000	130,110,000	4,736	196	

Lee decides to use simple regression analysis to examine whether one or more of three variables (the last three columns in the table) are cost drivers of purchasing department costs. Summary results for these regressions are as follows:

Regression 1: PDC = a + (b × MP$)

Variable	Coefficient	Standard Error	t-Value
Constant	$1,041,421	$040,709	3.00
Independent variable 1: MP$	0.0031	0.0038	0.83

$r^2 = 0.08$; Durbin-Watson statistic = 2.41

Regression 2: PDC = a (b × No. of POs)

Variable	Coefficient	Standard Error	t-Value
Constant	$722,538	$265,835	2.72
Independent variable 1: No. of POs	$ 159.48	$ 64.84	2.46

$r^2 = 0.43$; Durbin-Watson statistic = 1.97

Regression 3: PDC = a + (b × No. of Ss)

Variable	Coefficient	Standard Error	t-Value
Constant	$828,814	$246,570	3.36
Independent variable 1: No. of Ss	$ 3,816	$ 1,698	2.25

$r^2 = 0.39$; Durbin-Watson statistic = 2.01

Required

1. Compare and evaluate the three simple regression models estimated by Lee. Graph each one. Also, use the format employed in Exhibit 10-18 (p. 372) to evaluate the information.
2. Do the regression results support the Couture Fabrics' presentation about the purchasing department's cost drivers? Which of these cost drivers would you recommend in designing an ABC system?
3. How might Lee gain additional evidence on drivers of purchasing department costs at each of Fashion Bling's stores?

10-41 **Purchasing department cost drivers, multiple regression analysis (continuation of 10-40).** Barry Lee decides that the simple regression analysis used in Problem 10-40 could be extended to a multiple regression analysis. He finds the following results for two multiple regression analyses:

Regression 4: PDC = $a + (b_1 \times$ No. of POs$) + (b_2 \times$ No. of Ss$)$

Variable	Coefficient	Standard Error	t-Value
Constant	$484,522	$256,684	1.89
Independent variable 1: No. of POs	$ 126.66	$ 57.80	2.19
Independent variable 2: No. of Ss	$ 2,903	$ 1,459	1.99

$r^2 = 0.64$; Durbin-Watson statistic = 1.91

Regression 5: PDC = $a + (b_1 \times$ No. of POs$) + (b_2 \times$ No. of Ss$) + (b_3 \times$ MP$)$

Variable	Coefficient	Standard Error	t-Value
Constant	$483,560	$312,554	1.55
Independent variable 1: No. of POs	$ 126.58	$ 63.75	1.99
Independent variable 2: No. of Ss	$ 2,901	$ 1,622	1.79
Independent variable 3: MP$	0.00002	0.0029	0.01

$r^2 = 0.64$; Durbin-Watson statistic = 1.91

The coefficients of correlation between combinations of pairs of the variables are as follows:

	PDC	MP$	No. of POs
MP$	0.28		
No. of POs	0.66	0.27	
No. of Ss	0.62	0.30	0.29

Required

1. Evaluate regression 4 using the criteria of economic plausibility, goodness of fit, significance of independent variables and specification analysis. Compare regression 4 with regressions 2 and 3 in Problem 10-40. Which one of these models would you recommend that Lee use? Why?
2. Compare regression 5 with regression 4. Which one of these models would you recommend that Lee use? Why?
3. Lee estimates the following data for the Baltimore store for next year: dollar value of merchandise purchased, $78,000,000; number of purchase orders, 4,000; number of suppliers, 95. How much should Lee budget for purchasing department costs for the Baltimore store for next year?
4. What difficulties do not arise in simple regression analysis that may arise in multiple regression analysis? Is there evidence of such difficulties in either of the multiple regressions presented in this problem? Explain.
5. Give two examples of decisions in which the regression results reported here (and in Problem 10-40) could be informative.

Collaborative Learning Problem

10-42 **Interpreting regression results, matching time periods, ethics.** Jayne Barbour is working as a summer intern at Mode, a trendy store specializing in clothing for twenty-somethings. Jayne has been working closely with her cousin, Gail Hubbard, who plans promotions for Mode. The store has only been in business for 10 months, and Valerie Parker, the store's owner, has been unsure of the effectiveness of the store's advertising. Wanting to impress Valerie with the regression analysis skills she acquired in a cost accounting course the previous semester, Jayne decides to prepare an analysis of the effect of advertising on revenues. She collects the following data:

	Home	Insert	Page Layout	Formulas
	A	B		C
1	Month	Advertising Expense		Revenue
2	October	4,560		$35,400
3	November	3,285		44,255
4	December	1,200		56,300
5	January	4,099		28,764
6	February	3,452		49,532
7	March	1,075		43,200
8	April	4,768		30,600
9	May	4,775		52,137
10	June	1,845		49,640
11	July	1,430		29,542

Jayne performs a regression analysis, comparing each month's advertising expense with that month's revenue, and obtains the following formula:

$$\text{Revenue} = \$47{,}801 - (1.92 \times \text{Advertising expense})$$

Variable	Coefficient	Standard Error	t-Value
Constant	$47,801.72	7,628.39	6.27
Independent variable: Advertising expense	−1.92	2.26	−0.85

$r^2 = 0.43$; Standard error = 10,340.18

1. Plot the preceding data on a graph and draw the regression line. What does the cost formula indicate about the relationship between monthly advertising expense and monthly revenues? Is the relationship economically plausible? **Required**

2. Jayne worries that if she makes her presentation to the owner as planned, it will reflect poorly on her cousin Gail's performance. Is she ethically obligated to make the presentation?

3. Jayne thinks further about her analysis, and discovers a significant flaw in her approach. She realizes that advertising done in a given month should be expected to influence the following month's sales, not necessarily the current month's. She modifies her analysis by comparing, for example, October advertising expense with November sales revenue. The modified regression yields the following:

$$\text{Revenue} = \$23{,}538 + (5.92 \times \text{Advertising expense})$$

Variable	Coefficient	Standard Error	t-Value
Constant	$23,538.45	4,996.60	4.71
Independent variable: Previous month's advertising expense	5.92	1.42	4.18

$r^2 = 0.71$; Standard error = 6,015.67

What does the revised cost formula indicate? Plot the revised data on a graph. (You will need to discard October revenue and July advertising expense from the data set.) Is this relationship economically plausible?

4. Can Jayne conclude that there is a cause and effect relationship between advertising expense and sales revenue? Why or why not?

11

Decision Making and Relevant Information

11

Decision Making and Relevant Information

How many decisions have you made today?

Maybe you made a big one, such as accepting a job offer. Or maybe your decision was as simple as settling on your plans for the weekend or choosing a restaurant for dinner. Regardless of whether decisions are significant or routine, most people follow a simple, logical process when making them. This process involves gathering information, making predictions, making a choice, acting on the choice, and evaluating results. It also includes deciding what costs and benefits each choice affords. Some costs are irrelevant. For example, once a coffee maker is purchased, its cost is irrelevant when deciding how much money a person saves each time he or she brews coffee at home versus buying it at Starbucks. The cost of the coffee maker was incurred in the past, and the money is spent and can't be recouped. This chapter will explain which costs and benefits are relevant and which are not—and how you should think of them when choosing among alternatives.

Relevant Costs, JetBlue, and Twitter[1]

What does it cost JetBlue to fly a customer on a round-trip flight from New York City to Nantucket? The incremental cost is very small, around $5 for beverages, because the other costs (the plane, pilots, ticket agents, fuel, airport landing fees, and baggage handlers) are fixed. Because most costs are fixed, would it be worthwhile for JetBlue to fill a seat provided it earns at least $5 for that seat? The answer depends on whether the flight is full.

Suppose JetBlue normally charges $330 for this round-trip ticket. If the flight is full, JetBlue would not sell the ticket for anything less than $330, because there are still customers willing to pay this fare for the flight. What if there are empty seats? Selling a ticket for something more than $5 is better than leaving the seat empty and earning nothing.

If a customer uses the Internet to purchase the ticket a month in advance, JetBlue will likely quote $330 because it expects the flight to be full. If, on the Monday before the scheduled Friday departure, JetBlue finds that the plane will not be full, the airline may be willing to lower its prices dramatically in hopes of attracting more customers and earning a profit on the unfilled seats.

---

[1] *Source*: Jones, Charisse. 2009. JetBlue and United give twitter a try to sell airline seats fast. *USA Today*, August 2. www.usatoday.com/travel/flights/2009-08-02-jetblue-united-twitter-airfares_N.htm

Enter Twitter. Like the e-mails that Jet Blue has sent out to customers for years, the widespread messaging service allows JetBlue to quickly connect with customers and fill seats on flights that might otherwise take off less than full. When JetBlue began promoting last-minute fare sales on Twitter in 2009 and Twitter-recipients learned that $330 round-trip tickets from New York City to Nantucket were available for just $18, the flights filled up quickly. JetBlue's Twitter fare

sales usually last only eight hours, or until all available seats are sold. To use such a pricing strategy requires a deep understanding of costs in different decision situations.

Just like JetBlue, managers in corporations around the world use a decision process to help them make decisions. Managers at JPMorgan Chase gather information about financial markets, consumer preferences, and economic trends before determining whether to offer new services to customers. Macy's managers examine all the relevant information related to domestic and international clothing manufacturing before selecting vendors. Managers at Porsche gather cost information to decide whether to manufacture a component part or purchase it from a supplier. The decision process may not always be easy, but as Napoleon Bonaparte said, "Nothing is more difficult, and therefore more precious, than to be able to decide."

Information and the Decision Process

Managers usually follow a *decision model* for choosing among different courses of action. A **decision model** is a formal method of making a choice that often involves both quantitative and qualitative analyses. Management accountants analyze and present relevant data to guide managers' decisions.

Consider a strategic decision facing management at Precision Sporting Goods, a manufacturer of golf clubs: Should it reorganize its manufacturing operations to reduce manufacturing labor costs? Precision Sporting Goods has only two alternatives: Do not reorganize or reorganize.

Reorganization will eliminate all manual handling of materials. Current manufacturing labor consists of 20 workers—15 workers operate machines, and 5 workers handle materials. The 5 materials-handling workers have been hired on contracts that

Learning Objective 1

Use the five-step decision-making process to make decisions

. . . the five steps are identify the problem and uncertainties; obtain information; make predictions about the future; make decisions by choosing among alternatives; and implement the decision, evaluate performance, and learn

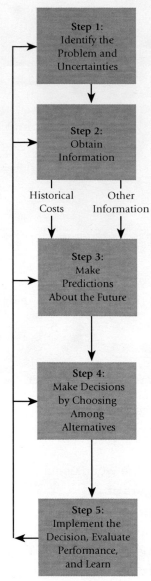

Exhibit 11-1

Five-Step Decision-
Making Process
for Precision
Sporting Goods

Step 1:
Identify the
Problem and
Uncertainties

Should Precision Sporting Goods reorganize its
manufacturing operations to reduce manufacturing
labor costs? An important uncertainty is how the
reorganization will affect employee morale.

Step 2:
Obtain
Information

Historical hourly wage rates are $14 per hour. However, a
recently negotiated increase in employee benefits of $2 per
hour will increase wages to $16 per hour. The reorganization
of manufacturing operations is expected to reduce the number
of workers from 20 to 15 by eliminating all 5 workers who
handle materials. The reorganization is likely to have negative
effects on employee morale.

Historical   Other
Costs   Information

Step 3:
Make
Predictions
About the Future

Managers use information from Step 2 as a basis for predicting
future manufacturing labor costs. Under the existing do-not-
reorganize alternative, costs are predicted to be $640,000
(20 workers × 2,000 hours per worker per year × $16 per
hour), and under the reorganize alternative, costs are predicted
to be $480,000 (15 workers × 2,000 hours per worker per
year ×$16 per hour). Recall, the reorganization is predicted
to cost $90,000 per year.

Step 4:
Make Decisions
by Choosing
Among
Alternatives

Managers compare the predicted benefits calculated in Step 3
($640,000 − $480,000 = $160,000—that is, savings from
eliminating materials-handling labor costs, 5 workers × 2,000
hours per worker per year × $16 per hour = $160,000) against
the cost of the reorganization ($90,000) along with other
considerations (such as likely negative effects on employee
morale). Management chooses the reorganize alternative
because the financial benefits are significant and the effects on
employee morale are expected to be temporary and relatively small.

Step 5:
Implement the
Decision, Evaluate
Performance,
and Learn

Evaluating performance after the decision is implemented
provides critical feedback for managers, and the five-step
sequence is then repeated in whole or in part. Managers
learn from actual results that the new manufacturing labor
costs are $540,000, rather than the predicted $480,000,
because of lower-than-expected manufacturing labor
productivity. This (now) historical information can
help managers make better subsequent predictions that
allow for more learning time. Alternatively, managers may
improve implementation via employee training and better
supervision.

permit layoffs without additional payments. Each worker works 2,000 hours annually.
Reorganization is predicted to cost $90,000 each year (mostly for new equipment
leases). Production output of 25,000 units as well as the selling price of $250, the direct
material cost per unit of $50, manufacturing overhead of $750,000, and marketing
costs of $2,000,000 will be unaffected by the reorganization.

Managers use the five-step decision-making process presented in Exhibit 11-1 and
first introduced in Chapter 1 to make this decision. Study the sequence of steps in this
exhibit and note how Step 5 evaluates performance to provide feedback about actions
taken in the previous steps. This feedback might affect future predictions, the prediction
methods used, the way choices are made, or the implementation of the decision.

**Decision
Point** ▶

What is the five-step
process that
managers can use to
make decisions?

The Concept of Relevance

Much of this chapter focuses on Step 4 in Exhibit 11-1 and on the concepts of relevant
costs and relevant revenues when choosing among alternatives.

Relevant Costs and Relevant Revenues

Relevant costs are *expected future costs,* and **relevant revenues** are *expected future revenues* that differ among the alternative courses of action being considered. Revenues and costs that are *not relevant* are said to be *irrelevant.* It is important to recognize that to be relevant costs and relevant revenues they *must:*

- **Occur in the future**—every decision deals with selecting a course of action based on its expected future results.

- **Differ among the alternative courses of action**—costs and revenues that do not differ will not matter and, hence, will have no bearing on the decision being made.

Learning Objective 2

Distinguish relevant from irrelevant information in decision situations

. . . only costs and revenues that are expected to occur in the future and differ among alternative courses of action are relevant

The question is always, "What difference will an action make?"

Exhibit 11-2 presents the financial data underlying the choice between the do-not-reorganize and reorganize alternatives for Precision Sporting Goods. There are two ways to analyze the data. The first considers "All revenues and costs," while the second considers only "Relevant revenues and costs."

The first two columns describe the first way and present *all data.* The last two columns describe the second way and present *only relevant costs*—the $640,000 and $480,000 expected future manufacturing labor costs and the $90,000 expected future reorganization costs that differ between the two alternatives. The revenues, direct materials, manufacturing overhead, and marketing items can be ignored because they will remain the same whether or not Precision Sporting Goods reorganizes. They do not differ between the alternatives and, therefore, are irrelevant.

Note, the past (historical) manufacturing hourly wage rate of $14 and total past (historical) manufacturing labor costs of $560,000 (20 workers × 2,000 hours per worker per year × $14 per hour) do not appear in Exhibit 11-2. *Although they may be a useful basis for making informed predictions of the expected future manufacturing labor costs of $640,000 and $480,000, historical costs themselves are past costs that, therefore, are irrelevant to decision making.* Past costs are also called **sunk costs** because they are unavoidable and cannot be changed no matter what action is taken.

The analysis in Exhibit 11-2 indicates that reorganizing the manufacturing operations will increase predicted operating income by $70,000 each year. Note that the managers at Precision Sporting Goods reach the same conclusion whether they use all data or include only relevant data in the analysis. By confining the analysis to only the relevant data, managers

---

Exhibit 11-2   Determining Relevant Revenues and Relevant Costs for Precision Sporting Goods

	All Revenues and Costs		Relevant Revenues and Costs	
	Alternative 1: Do Not Reorganize	**Alternative 2: Reorganize**	**Alternative 1: Do Not Reorganize**	**Alternative 2: Reorganize**
Revenues[a]	$6,250,000	$6,250,000	—	—
Costs:				
Direct materials[b]	1,250,000	1,250,000	—	—
Manufacturing labor	640,000[c]	480,000[d]	$ 640,000[c]	$ 480,000[d]
Manufacturing overhead	750,000	750,000	—	—
Marketing	2,000,000	2,000,000	—	—
Reorganization costs	—	90,000	—	90,000
Total costs	4,640,000	4,570,000	640,000	570,000
Operating income	$1,610,000	$1,680,000	$(640,000)	$(570,000)
		$70,000 Difference		$70,000 Difference

[a]25,000 units ×$250 per unit = $6,250,000
[b]25,000 units × $50 per unit = $1,250,000
[c]20 workers × 2,000 hours per worker × $16 per hour = $640,000
[d]15 workers × 2,000 hours per worker × $16 per hour = $480,000

| Exhibit 11-3 | Key Features of Relevant Information |

- Past (historical) costs may be helpful as a basis for making *predictions.* However, past costs themselves are always irrelevant when making *decisions.*
- Different alternatives can be compared by examining differences in expected total future revenues and expected total future costs.
- Not all expected future revenues and expected future costs are relevant. Expected future revenues and expected future costs that do not differ among alternatives are irrelevant and, hence, can be eliminated from the analysis. The key question is always, "What difference will an action make?"
- Appropriate weight must be given to qualitative factors and quantitative nonfinancial factors.

can clear away the clutter of potentially confusing irrelevant data. Focusing on the relevant data is especially helpful when all the information needed to prepare a detailed income statement is unavailable. Understanding which costs are relevant and which are irrelevant helps the decision maker concentrate on obtaining only the pertinent data and is more efficient.

Qualitative and Quantitative Relevant Information

Managers divide the outcomes of decisions into two broad categories: *quantitative* and *qualitative.* **Quantitative factors** are outcomes that are measured in numerical terms. Some quantitative factors are financial; they can be expressed in monetary terms. Examples include the cost of direct materials, direct manufacturing labor, and marketing. Other quantitative factors are nonfinancial; they can be measured numerically, but they are not expressed in monetary terms. Reduction in new product-development time and the percentage of on-time flight arrivals are examples of quantitative nonfinancial factors. **Qualitative factors** are outcomes that are difficult to measure accurately in numerical terms. Employee morale is an example.

Relevant-cost analysis generally emphasizes quantitative factors that can be expressed in financial terms. *But just because qualitative factors and quantitative nonfinancial factors cannot be measured easily in financial terms does not make them unimportant.* In fact, managers must wisely weigh these factors. In the Precision Sporting Goods example, managers carefully considered the negative effect on employee morale of laying-off materials-handling workers, a qualitative factor, before choosing the reorganize alternative. Comparing and trading off nonfinancial and financial considerations is seldom easy.

Exhibit 11-3 summarizes the key features of relevant information.

An Illustration of Relevance: Choosing Output Levels

The concept of relevance applies to all decision situations. In this and the following several sections of this chapter, we present some of these decision situations. Later chapters describe other decision situations that require application of the relevance concept, such as Chapter 12 on pricing, Chapter 16 on joint costs, Chapter 19 on quality and timeliness, Chapter 20 on inventory management and supplier evaluation, Chapter 21 on capital investment, and Chapter 22 on transfer pricing. We start by considering decisions that affect output levels such as whether to introduce a new product or to try to sell more units of an existing product.

One-Time-Only Special Orders

One type of decision that affects output levels is accepting or rejecting special orders when there is idle production capacity and the special orders have no long-run implications. We use the term **one-time-only special order** to describe these conditions.

Example 1: Surf Gear manufactures quality beach towels at its highly auto-mated Burlington, North Carolina, plant. The plant has a production capacity of 48,000 towels each month. Current monthly production is 30,000 towels. Retail department stores account for all existing sales. Expected results for the coming month (August) are shown in Exhibit 11-4. (These amounts are predictions based on past costs.) We assume all costs can be classified as either fixed or variable with respect to a single cost driver (units of output).

As a result of a strike at its existing towel supplier, Azelia, a luxury hotel chain, has offered to buy 5,000 towels from Surf Gear in August at $11 per towel. No subsequent sales to Azelia are anticipated. Fixed manufacturing costs are based on the 48,000-towel production capacity. That is, fixed manufacturing costs relate to the production capacity available and not the actual capacity used. If Surf Gear accepts the special order, it will use existing idle capacity to produce the 5,000 towels, and fixed manufacturing costs will not change. No marketing costs will be necessary for the 5,000-unit one-time-only special order. Accepting this special order is not expected to affect the selling price or the quantity of towels sold to regular customers. Should Surf Gear accept Azelia's offer?

Exhibit 11-4 presents data for this example on an absorption-costing basis (that is, both variable and fixed manufacturing costs are included in inventoriable costs and cost of goods sold). In this exhibit, the manufacturing cost of $12 per unit and the marketing cost of $7 per unit include both variable and fixed costs. The sum of all costs (variable and fixed) in a particular business function of the value chain, such as manufacturing costs or marketing costs, are called **business function costs. Full costs of the product,** in this case $19 per unit, are the sum of all variable and fixed costs in all business functions of the value chain (R&D, design, production, marketing, distribution, and customer service). For Surf Gear, full costs of the product consist of costs in manufacturing and marketing because these are the only business functions. No marketing costs are necessary for the special order, so the manager of Surf Gear will focus

	A	B	C	D
		Total	Per Unit	
1		**Total**	**Per Unit**	
2	Units sold	30,000		
3				
4	Revenues	$600,000	$20.00	
5	Cost of goods sold (manufacturing costs)			
6	Variable manufacturing costs	225,000	7.50[b]	
7	Fixed manufacturing costs	135,000	4.50[c]	
8	Total cost of goods sold	360,000	12.00	
9	Marketing costs			
10	Variable marketing costs	150,000	5.00	
11	Fixed marketing costs	60,000	2.00	
12	Total marketing costs	210,000	7.00	
13	Full costs of the product	570,000	19.00	
14	Operating income	$ 30,000	$ 1.00	
15				
16	[a]Surf Gear incurs no R&D, product-design, distribution, or customer-service costs			
17	[b]Variable manufacturing = Direct material + Variable direct manufacturing + Variable manufacturing			
18	cost per unit cost per unit labor cost per unit overhead cost per unit			
19	= $6.00 + $0.50 + $1.00 = $7.50			
20	[c]Fixed manufacturing = Fixed direct manufacturing + Fixed manufacturing			
21	cost per unit labor cost per unit overhead cost per unit			
22	= $1.50 + $3.00 = $4.50			

only on manufacturing costs. Based on the manufacturing cost per unit of $12—which is greater than the $11-per-unit price offered by Azelia—the manager might decide to reject the offer.

Exhibit 11-5 separates manufacturing and marketing costs into their variable- and fixed-cost components and presents data in the format of a contribution income statement. The relevant revenues and costs are the expected future revenues and costs that differ as a result of accepting the special offer—revenues of $55,000 ($11 per unit × 5,000 units) and variable manufacturing costs of $37,500 ($7.50 per unit × 5,000 units). The fixed manufacturing costs and all marketing costs (*including variable marketing costs*) are irrelevant in this case because these costs will not change in total whether the special order is accepted or rejected. Surf Gear would gain an additional $17,500 (relevant revenues, $55,000 – relevant costs, $37,500) in operating income by accepting the special order. In this example, comparing total amounts for 30,000 units versus 35,000 units or focusing only on the relevant amounts in the difference column in Exhibit 11-5 avoids a misleading implication—the implication that would result from comparing the $11-per-unit selling price against the manufacturing cost per unit of $12 (Exhibit 11-4), which includes both variable and fixed manufacturing costs.

The assumption of no long-run or strategic implications is crucial to management's analysis of the one-time-only special-order decision. Suppose Surf Gear concludes that the retail department stores (its regular customers) will demand a lower price if it sells towels at $11 apiece to Azelia. In this case, revenues from regular customers will be relevant. Why? Because the future revenues from regular customers will differ depending on whether the special order is accepted or rejected. The relevant-revenue and relevant-cost analysis of the Azelia order would have to be modified to consider both the short-run benefits from accepting the order and the long-run consequences on profitability if prices were lowered to all regular customers.

Exhibit 11-5

One-Time-Only Special-Order Decision for Surf Gear: Comparative Contribution Income Statements

	A	B	C	D	E	F	G	H
		Home Insert Page Layout Formulas Data Review View						
1		Without the Special Order				With the Special Order		Difference: Relevant Amounts
2		30,000				35,000		for the
3		Units to be Sold				Units to be Sold		5,000
4		Per Unit		Total		Total		Units Special Order
5		(1)		(2) = (1) × 30,000		(3)		(4) = (3) – (2)
6	Revenues	$20.00		$600,000		$655,000		$55,000[a]
7	Variable costs:							
8	Manufacturing	7.50		225,000		262,500		37,500[b]
9	Marketing	5.00		150,000		150,000		0[c]
10	Total variable costs	12.50		375,000		412,500		37,500
11	Contribution margin	7.50		225,000		242,500		17,500
12	Fixed costs:							
13	Manufacturing	4.50		135,000		135,000		0[d]
14	Marketing	2.00		60,000		60,000		0[d]
15	Total fixed costs	6.50		195,000		195,000		0
16	Operating income	$ 1.00		$ 30,000		$ 47,500		$17,500
17								
18	[a]5,000 units × $11.00 per unit = $55,000.							
19	[b]5,000 units × $7.50 per unit = $37,500.							
20	[c]No variable marketing costs would be incurred for the 5,000-unit one-time-only special order.							
21	[d]Fixed manufacturing costs and fixed marketing costs would be unaffected by the special order.							

Potential Problems in Relevant-Cost Analysis

Managers should avoid two potential problems in relevant-cost analysis. First, they must watch for incorrect general assumptions, such as all variable costs are relevant and all fixed costs are irrelevant. In the Surf Gear example, the variable marketing cost of $5 per unit is irrelevant because Surf Gear will incur no extra marketing costs by accepting the special order. But fixed manufacturing costs could be relevant. The extra production of 5,000 towels per month does not affect fixed manufacturing costs because we assumed that the relevant range is from 30,000 to 48,000 towels per month. In some cases, however, producing the extra 5,000 towels might increase fixed manufacturing costs. Suppose Surf Gear would need to run three shifts of 16,000 towels per shift to achieve full capacity of 48,000 towels per month. Increasing the monthly production from 30,000 to 35,000 would require a partial third shift because two shifts could produce only 32,000 towels. The extra shift would increase fixed manufacturing costs, thereby making these additional fixed manufacturing costs relevant for this decision.

Second, unit-cost data can potentially mislead decision makers in two ways:

1. **When irrelevant costs are included.** Consider the $4.50 of fixed manufacturing cost per unit (direct manufacturing labor, $1.50 per unit, plus manufacturing overhead, $3.00 per unit) included in the $12-per-unit manufacturing cost in the one-time-only special-order decision (see Exhibits 11-4 and 11-5). This $4.50-per-unit cost is irrelevant, given the assumptions in our example, so it should be excluded.

2. **When the same unit costs are used at different output levels.** Generally, managers use total costs rather than unit costs because total costs are easier to work with and reduce the chance for erroneous conclusions. Then, if desired, the total costs can be unitized. In the Surf Gear example, total fixed manufacturing costs remain at $135,000 even if Surf Gear accepts the special order and produces 35,000 towels. Including the fixed manufacturing cost per unit of $4.50 as a cost of the special order would lead to the erroneous conclusion that total fixed manufacturing costs would increase to $157,500 ($4.50 per towel × 35,000 towels).

The best way for managers to avoid these two potential problems is to keep focusing on (1) total revenues and total costs (rather than unit revenue and unit cost) and (2) the relevance concept. Managers should always require all items included in an analysis to be expected total future revenues and expected total future costs that differ among the alternatives.

Insourcing-versus-Outsourcing and Make-versus-Buy Decisions

We now apply the concept of relevance to another strategic decision: whether a company should make a component part or buy it from a supplier. We again assume idle capacity.

Outsourcing and Idle Facilities

Outsourcing is purchasing goods and services from outside vendors rather than producing the same goods or providing the same services within the organization, which is **insourcing**. For example, Kodak prefers to manufacture its own film (insourcing) but has IBM do its data processing (outsourcing). Honda relies on outside vendors to supply some component parts but chooses to manufacture other parts internally.

Decisions about whether a producer of goods or services will insource or outsource are also called **make-or-buy decisions**. Surveys of companies indicate that managers consider quality, dependability of suppliers, and costs as the most important factors in the make-or-buy decision. Sometimes, however, qualitative factors dominate management's make-or-buy decision. For example, Dell Computer buys the Pentium chip for its personal computers from Intel because Dell does not have the know-how and technology to make

◄ Decision Point

When is a revenue or cost item relevant for a particular decision and what potential problems should be avoided in relevant cost analysis?

Learning Objective 3

Explain the opportunity-cost concept and why it is used in decision making

. . . in all decisions, it is important to consider the contribution to income forgone by choosing a particular alternative and rejecting others

the chip itself. In contrast, to maintain the secrecy of its formula, Coca-Cola does not out-source the manufacture of its concentrate.

Example 2: The Soho Company manufactures a two-in-one video system con-sisting of a DVD player and a digital media receiver (that downloads movies and video from internet sites such as NetFlix). Columns 1 and 2 of the follow-ing table show the expected total and per-unit costs for manufacturing the DVD-player of the video system. Soho plans to manufacture the 250,000 units in 2,000 batches of 125 units each. Variable batch-level costs of $625 per batch vary with the number of batches, not the total number of units produced.

	Expected Total Costs of Producing 250,000 Units in 2,000 Batches Next Year (1)	Expected Cost per Unit (2) = (1) ÷ 250,000
Direct materials ($36 per unit × 250,000 units)	$ 9,000,000	$36.00
Direct manufacturing labor ($10 per unit × 250,000 units)	2,500,000	10.00
Variable manufacturing overhead costs of power and utilities ($6 per unit × 250,000 units)	1,500,000	6.00
Mixed (variable and fixed) batch-level manufacturing overhead costs of materials handling and setup [$750,000 + ($625 per batch × 2,000 batches)]	2,000,000	8.00
Fixed manufacturing overhead costs of plant lease, insurance, and administration	3,000,000	12.00
Total manufacturing cost	$18,000,000	$72.00

Broadfield, Inc., a manufacturer of DVD players, offers to sell Soho 250,000 DVD players next year for $64 per unit on Soho's preferred delivery schedule. Assume that financial factors will be the basis of this make-or-buy decision. Should Soho make or buy the DVD player?

Columns 1 and 2 of the preceding table indicate the expected total costs and expected cost per unit of producing 250,000 DVD players next year. The expected manufacturing cost per unit for next year is $72. At first glance, it appears that the company should buy DVD players because the expected $72-per-unit cost of making the DVD player is more than the $64 per unit to buy it. But a make-or-buy decision is rarely obvious. To make a deci-sion, management needs to answer the question, "What is the difference in relevant costs between the alternatives?"

For the moment, suppose (a) the capacity now used to make the DVD players will become idle next year if the DVD players are purchased and (b) the $3,000,000 of fixed manufacturing overhead will continue to be incurred next year regardless of the decision made. Assume the $750,000 in fixed salaries to support materials handling and setup will not be incurred if the manufacture of DVD players is completely shut down.

Exhibit 11-6 presents the relevant-cost computations. Note that Soho will *save* $1,000,000 by making DVD players rather than buying them from Broadfield. Making DVD players is the preferred alternative.

Note how the key concepts of relevance presented in Exhibit 11-3 apply here:

▪ Exhibit 11-6 compares differences in expected total future revenues and expected total future costs. Past costs are always irrelevant when making decisions.

▪ Exhibit 11-6 shows $2,000,000 of future materials-handling and setup costs under the make alternative but not under the buy alternative. Why? Because buying DVD players and not manufacturing them will save $2,000,000 in future variable costs per batch and avoidable fixed costs. The $2,000,000 represents future costs that differ between the alternatives and so is relevant to the make-or-buy decision.

Relevant Items	Total Relevant Costs		Relevant Cost Per Unit	
	Make	**Buy**	**Make**	**Buy**
Outside purchase of parts ($64 × 250,000 units)		$16,000,000		$64
Direct materials	$ 9,000,000		$36	
Direct manufacturing labor	2,500,000		10	
Variable manufacturing overhead	1,500,000		6	
Mixed (variable and fixed) materials-handling and setup overhead	2,000,000		8	
Total relevant costs[a]	$15,000,000	$16,000,000	$58	$64
Difference in favor of making DVD players	$1,000,000		$4	

[a]The $3,000,000 of plant-lease, plant-insurance, and plant-administration costs could be included under both alternatives. Conceptually, they do not belong in a listing of relevant costs because these costs are irrelevant to the decision. Practically, some managers may want to include them in order to list all costs that will be incurred under each alternative.

■ Exhibit 11-6 excludes the $3,000,000 of plant-lease, insurance, and administration costs under both alternatives. Why? Because these future costs will not differ between the alternatives, so they are irrelevant.

A common term in decision making is *incremental cost*. An **incremental cost** is the additional total cost incurred for an activity. In Exhibit 11-6, the incremental cost of making DVD players is the additional total cost of $15,000,000 that Soho will incur if it decides to make DVD players. The $3,000,000 of fixed manufacturing overhead is not an incremental cost because Soho will incur these costs whether or not it makes DVD players. Similarly, the incremental cost of buying DVD players from Broadfield is the additional total cost of $16,000,000 that Soho will incur if it decides to buy DVD players. A **differential cost** is the difference in total cost between two alternatives. In Exhibit 11-6, the differential cost between the make-DVD-players and buy-DVD-players alternatives is $1,000,000 ($16,000,000 − $15,000,000). Note that *incremental cost* and *differential cost* are sometimes used interchangeably in practice. When faced with these terms, always be sure to clarify what they mean.

We define *incremental revenue* and *differential revenue* similarly to incremental cost and differential cost. **Incremental revenue** is the additional total revenue from an activity. **Differential revenue** is the difference in total revenue between two alternatives.

Strategic and Qualitative Factors

Strategic and qualitative factors affect outsourcing decisions. For example, Soho may prefer to manufacture DVD players in-house to retain control over the design, quality, reliability, and delivery schedules of the DVD players it uses in its video-systems. Conversely, despite the cost advantages documented in Exhibit 11-6, Soho may prefer to outsource, become a leaner organization, and focus on areas of its core competencies—the manufacture and sale of video systems. As an example of focus, advertising companies, such as J. Walter Thompson, only do the creative and planning aspects of advertising (their core competencies), and outsource production activities, such as film, photographs, and illustrations.

Outsourcing is not without risks. As a company's dependence on its suppliers increases, suppliers could increase prices and let quality and delivery performance slip. To minimize these risks, companies generally enter into long-run contracts specifying costs, quality, and delivery schedules with their suppliers. Intelligent managers build close partnerships or alliances with a few key suppliers. Toyota goes so far as to send its own engineers to improve suppliers' processes. Suppliers of companies such as Ford, Hyundai, Panasonic, and Sony have researched and developed innovative products, met demands for increased quantities, maintained quality and on-time delivery, and lowered costs—actions that the companies themselves would not have had the competencies to achieve.

Concepts in Action

Pringles Prints and the Offshoring of Innovation

According to a recent survey, 67% of U.S. companies are engaged in the rapidly-evolving process of "offshoring," which is the outsourcing of business processes and jobs to other countries. Offshoring was initially popular with companies because it yielded immediate labor-cost savings for activities such as software development, call centers, and technical support.

While the practice remains popular today, offshoring has transformed from lowering costs on back-office processes to accessing global talent for innovation. With global markets expanding and domestic talent scarce, companies are now hiring qualified engineers, scientists, inventors, and analysts all over the world for research and development (R&D), new product development (NPD), engineering, and knowledge services.

Innovation Offshoring Services

R&D	NPD	Engineering	Knowledge Services
■ Programming	■ Prototype design	■ Testing	■ Market analysis
■ Code development	■ Product development	■ Reengineering	■ Credit analysis
■ New technologies	■ Systems design	■ Drafting/modeling	■ Data mining
■ New materials/ process research	■ Support services	■ Embedded systems development	■ Forecasting
			■ Risk management

By utilizing offshoring innovation, companies not only continue to reduce labor costs, but cut back-office costs as well. Companies also obtain local market knowledge and access to global best practices in many important areas.

Some companies are leveraging offshore resources by creating global innovation networks. Procter & Gamble (P&G), for instance, established "Connect and Develop," a multi-national effort to create and leverage innovative ideas for product development. When the company wanted to create a new line of Pringles potato chips with pictures and words—trivia questions, animal facts, and jokes—printed on each chip, the company turned to offshore innovation.

Rather than trying to invent the technology required to print images on potato chips in-house, Procter & Gamble created a technology brief that defined the problems it needed to solve, and circulated it throughout the company's global innovation network for possible solutions. As a result, P&G discovered a small bakery in Bologna, Italy, run by a university professor who also manufactured baking equipment. He had invented an ink-jet method for printing edible images on cakes and cookies, which the company quickly adapted for potato chips.

As a result, Pringles Prints were developed in less than a year—as opposed to a more traditional two year process—and immediately led to double-digit product growth.

Sources: Cuoto, Vinay, Mahadeva Mani, Vikas Sehgal, Arie Lewin, Stephan Manning, and Jeff Russell. 2007. *Offshoring 2.0: Contracting knowledge and innovation to expand global capabilities.* Duke University Offshoring Research Network: Durham, NC. Heijmen, Ton, Arie Lewin, Stephan Manning, Nidthida Prem-Ajchariyawong, and Jeff Russell. 2008. *Offshoring reaches the c-suite.* Duke University Offshoring Research Network: Durham, NC. Huston, Larry and Nabil Sakkab. 2006. Connect and develop: Inside Procter & Gamble's new model for innovation. *Harvard Business Review,* March.

Outsourcing decisions invariably have a long-run horizon in which the financial costs and benefits of outsourcing become more uncertain. Almost always, strategic and qualitative factors such as the ones described here become important determinants of the outsourcing decision. Weighing all these factors requires the exercise of considerable management judgment and care.

International Outsourcing

What additional factors would Soho have to consider if the supplier of DVD players was based in Mexico? The most important would be exchange-rate risk. Suppose the Mexican supplier offers to sell Soho 250,000 DVD players for 192,000,000 Pesos. Should Soho make or buy? The answer depends on the exchange rate that Soho expects next year. If Soho forecasts an exchange rate of 12 Pesos per $1, Soho's expected purchase cost equals

$16,000,000 (192,000,000 Pesos/12 Pesos per $) greater than the $15,000,000 relevant costs for making the DVD players in Exhibit 11-6, so Soho would prefer to make DVD players rather than buy them. If, however, Soho anticipates an exchange rate of 13.50 Pesos per $1, Soho's expected purchase cost equals $14,222,222 (192,000,000 Pesos/13.50 Pesos per $), which is less than the $15,000,000 relevant costs for making the DVD players, so Soho would prefer to buy rather than make the DVD players.

Another option is for Soho to enter into a forward contract to purchase 192,000,000 Pesos. A forward contract allows Soho to contract today to purchase pesos next year at a predetermined, fixed cost, thereby protecting itself against exchange rate risk. If Soho decides to go this route, it would make (buy) DVD players if the cost of the contract is greater (less) than $15,000,000. International outsourcing requires companies to evaluate exchange rate risks and to implement strategies and costs for managing them. The Concepts in Action feature (p. 400) describes *offshoring*—the practice of outsourcing services to lower-cost countries.

Opportunity Costs and Outsourcing

In the simple make-or-buy decision in Exhibit 11-6, we assumed that the capacity currently used to make DVD players will remain idle if Soho purchases the parts from Broadfield. Often, however, the released capacity can be used for other, profitable purposes. In this case, the choice Soho's managers are faced with is not whether to make or buy; the choice now centers on how best to use available production capacity.

Example 3: Suppose that if Soho decides to buy DVD players for its video systems from Broadfield, then Soho's best use of the capacity that becomes available is to produce 100,000 Digiteks, a portable, stand-alone DVD player. From a manufacturing standpoint, Digiteks are similar to DVD players made for the video system. With help from operating managers, Soho's management accountant estimates the following future revenues and costs if Soho decides to manufacture and sell Digiteks:

Incremental future revenues		$8,000,000
Incremental future costs		
Direct materials	$3,400,000	
Direct manufacturing labor	1,000,000	
Variable overhead (such as power, utilities)	600,000	
Materials-handling and setup overheads	500,000	
Total incremental future costs		5,500,000
Incremental future operating income		$2,500,000

Because of capacity constraints, Soho can make either DVD players for its video-system unit or Digiteks, but not both. Which of the following two alternatives should Soho choose?

1. Make video-system DVD players and do not make Digiteks
2. Buy video-system DVD players and make Digiteks

Exhibit 11-7, Panel A, summarizes the "total-alternatives" approach—the future costs and revenues for *all* products. Alternative 2, buying video-system DVD players and using the available capacity to make and sell Digiteks, is the preferred alternative. The future incremental costs of buying video-system DVD players from an outside supplier ($16,000,000) exceed the future incremental costs of making video-system DVD players in-house ($15,000,000). Soho can use the capacity freed up by buying video-system DVD players to gain $2,500,000 in operating income (incremental future revenues of $8,000,000 minus total incremental future costs of $5,500,000) by making and selling Digiteks. The *net relevant* costs of buying video-system DVD players and making and selling Digiteks are $16,000,000 – $2,500,000 = $13,500,000.

Exhibit 11-7	Total-Alternatives Approach and Opportunity-Cost Approach to Make-or-Buy Decisions for Soho Company

	Alternatives for Soho	
Relevant Items	**1. Make Video-System DVD Players and Do Not Make Digitek**	**2. Buy Video-System DVD Players and Make Digitek**
PANEL A Total-Alternatives Approach to Make-or-Buy Decisions		
Total incremental future costs of making/buying video-system DVD players (from Exhibit 11-6)	$15,000,000	$16,000,000
Deduct excess of future revenues over future costs from Digitek	0	(2,500,000)
Total relevant costs under total-alternatives approach	$15,000,000	$13,500,000
	1. Make Video-System DVD Players	**2. Buy Video-System DVD Players**
PANEL B Opportunity-Cost Approach to Make-or-Buy Decisions		
Total incremental future costs of making/buying video-system DVD players (from Exhibit 11-6)	$15,000,000	$16,000,000
Opportunity cost: Profit contribution forgone because capacity will not be used to make Digitek, the next-best alternative	2,500,000	0
Total relevant costs under opportunity-cost approach	$17,500,000	$16,000,000

Note that the differences in costs across the columns in Panels A and B are the same: The cost of alternative 3 is $1,500,000 less than the cost of alternative 1, and $2,500,000 less than the cost of alternative 2.

The Opportunity-Cost Approach

Deciding to use a resource in a particular way causes a manager to forgo the opportunity to use the resource in alternative ways. This lost opportunity is a cost that the manager must consider when making a decision. **Opportunity cost** is the contribution to operating income that is forgone by not using a limited resource in its next-best alternative use. For example, the (relevant) cost of going to school for an MBA degree is not only the cost of tuition, books, lodging, and food, but also the income sacrificed (opportunity cost) by not working. Presumably, the estimated future benefits of obtaining an MBA (for example, a higher-paying career) will exceed these costs.

Exhibit 11-7, Panel B, displays the opportunity-cost approach for analyzing the alternatives faced by Soho. *Note that the alternatives are defined differently in the total alternatives approach (1. Make Video-System DVD Players and Do Not Make Digiteks and 2. Buy Video-System DVD Players and Make Digiteks) and the opportunity cost approach (1. Make Video-System DVD Players and 2. Buy Video-System DVD Players), which does not reference Digiteks. Under the opportunity-cost approach, the cost of each alternative includes (1) the incremental costs and (2) the opportunity cost, the profit forgone from not making Digiteks. This opportunity cost arises because Digitek is excluded from formal consideration in the alternatives.*

Consider alternative 1, making video-system DVD players. What are all the costs of making video-system DVD players? Certainly Soho will incur $15,000,000 of incremental costs to make video-system DVD players, but is this the entire cost? No, because by deciding to use limited manufacturing resources to make video-system DVD players, Soho will give up the opportunity to earn $2,500,000 by not using these resources to make Digiteks. Therefore, the relevant costs of making video-system DVD players are the incremental costs of $15,000,000 plus the opportunity cost of $2,500,000.

Next, consider alternative 2, buy video-system DVD players. The incremental cost of buying video-system DVD players will be $16,000,000. The opportunity cost is zero.

Why? Because by choosing this alternative, Soho will not forgo the profit it can earn from making and selling Digiteks.

Panel B leads management to the same conclusion as Panel A: buying video-system DVD players and making Digiteks is the preferred alternative.

Panels A and B of Exhibit 11-7 describe two consistent approaches to decision making with capacity constraints. The total-alternatives approach in Panel A includes all future incremental costs and revenues. For example, under alternative 2, the additional future operating income from *using capacity to make and sell Digiteks* ($2,500,000) is subtracted from the future incremental cost of buying video-system DVD players ($16,000,000). The opportunity-cost analysis in Panel B takes the opposite approach. It focuses only on video-system DVD players. *Whenever capacity is not going to be used to make and sell Digiteks* the future forgone operating income is added as an opportunity cost of making video-system DVD players, as in alternative 1. (Note that when Digiteks are made, as in alternative 2, there is no "opportunity cost of not making Digiteks.") Therefore, whereas Panel A *subtracts* $2,500,000 under alternative 2, Panel B *adds* $2,500,000 under alternative 1. *Panel B highlights the idea that when capacity is constrained, the relevant revenues and costs of any alternative equal (1) the incremental future revenues and costs plus (2) the opportunity cost.* However, when more than two alternatives are being considered simultaneously, it is generally easier to use the total-alternatives approach.

Opportunity costs are not recorded in financial accounting systems. Why? Because historical record keeping is limited to transactions involving alternatives that were *actually selected*, rather than alternatives that were rejected. Rejected alternatives do not produce transactions and so they are not recorded. If Soho makes video-system DVD players, it will not make Digiteks, and it will not record any accounting entries for Digiteks. Yet the opportunity cost of making video-system DVD players, which equals the operating income that Soho forgoes by not making Digiteks, is a crucial input into the make-or-buy decision. Consider again Exhibit 11-7, Panel B. On the basis of only the incremental costs that are systematically recorded in accounting systems, it is less costly for Soho to make rather than buy video-system DVD players. Recognizing the opportunity cost of $2,500,000 leads to a different conclusion: Buying video-system DVD players is preferable.

Suppose Soho has sufficient capacity to make Digiteks even if it makes video-system DVD players. In this case, the opportunity cost of making video-system DVD players is $0 because Soho does not give up the $2,500,000 operating income from making Digiteks even if it chooses to make video-system DVD players. The relevant costs are $15,000,000 (incremental costs of $15,000,000 plus opportunity cost of $0). Under these conditions, Soho would prefer to make video-system DVD players, rather than buy them, and also make Digiteks.

Besides quantitative considerations, the make-or-buy decision should also consider strategic and qualitative factors. If Soho decides to buy video-system DVD players from an outside supplier, it should consider factors such as the supplier's reputation for quality and timely delivery. Soho would also want to consider the strategic consequences of selling Digiteks. For example, will selling Digiteks take Soho's focus away from its video-system business?

Carrying Costs of Inventory

To see another example of an opportunity cost, consider the following data for Soho:

Annual estimated video-system DVD player requirements for next year	250,000 units
Cost per unit when each purchase is equal to 2,500 units	$64.00
Cost per unit when each purchase is equal to or greater than 125,000 units; $64 minus 1% discount	$63.36
Cost of a purchase order	$500
Alternatives under consideration:	

    A. Make 100 purchases of 2,500 units each during next year
    B. Make 2 purchases of 125,000 units during the year

Average investment in inventory:

A. (2,500 units × $64.00 per unit) ÷ 2[a]	$80,000
B. (125,000 units × $63.36 per unit) ÷ 2[a]	$3,960,000
Annual rate of return if cash is invested elsewhere (for example, bonds or stocks) at the same level of risk as investment in inventory)	9%

[a] The example assumes that video-system-DVD-player purchases will be used uniformly throughout the year. The average investment in inventory during the year is the cost of the inventory when a purchase is received plus the cost of inventory just before the next purchase is delivered (in our example, zero) divided by 2.

Soho will pay cash for the video-system DVD players it buys. Which purchasing alternative is more economical for Soho?

The following table presents the analysis using the total alternatives approach recognizing that Soho has, on average, $3,960,000 of cash available to invest. If Soho invests only $80,000 in inventory as in alternative A, it will have $3,880,000 ($3,960,000 − $80,000) of cash available to invest elsewhere, which at a 9% rate of return will yield a total return of $349,200. This income is subtracted from the ordering and purchasing costs incurred under alternative A. If Soho invests all $3,960,000 in inventory as in alternative B, it will have $0 ($3,960,000 − $3,960,000) available to invest elsewhere and will earn no return on the cash.

	Alternative A: Make 100 Purchases of 2,500 Units Each During the Year and Invest Any Excess Cash (1)	Alternative B: Make 2 Purchases of 125,000 Units Each During the Year and Invest Any Excess Cash (2)	Difference (3) = (1) − (2)
Annual purchase-order costs (100 purch. orders × $500/purch. order; 2 purch. orders × $500/purch. order)	$ 50,000	$ 1,000	$ 49,000
Annual purchase costs (250,000 units × $64.00/unit; 250,000 units × $63.36/unit)	16,000,000	15,840,000	160,000
Deduct annual rate of return earned by investing cash not tied up in inventory elsewhere at the same level of risk [0.09 × ($3,960,000 − $80,000); 0.09 × ($3,960,000 − $3,960,000)	(349,200)	0	(349,200)
Relevant costs	$15,700,800	$15,841,000	$(140,200)

Consistent with the trends toward holding smaller inventories, purchasing smaller quantities of 2,500 units 100 times a year is preferred to purchasing 125,000 units twice a year by $140,200.

The following table presents the two alternatives using the opportunity cost approach. Each alternative is defined only in terms of the two purchasing choices with no explicit reference to investing the excess cash.

	Alternative A: Make 100 Purchases of 2,500 Units Each During the Year (1)	Alternative B: Make 2 Purchases of 125,000 Units Each During the Year (2)	Difference (3) = (1) − (2)
Annual purchase-order costs (100 purch. orders × $500/purch. order; 2 purch. orders × $500/purch. order)	$ 50,000	$ 1,000	$ 49,000
Annual purchase costs (250,000 units × $64.00/unit; 250,000 units × $63.36/unit)	16,000,000	15,840,000	160,000
Opportunity cost: Annual rate of return that could be earned if investment in inventory were invested elsewhere at the same level of risk (0.09 × $80,000; 0.09 × $3,960,000)	7,200	356,400	(349,200)
Relevant costs	$16,057,200	$16,197,400	$(140,200)

Recall that under the opportunity cost approach, the relevant cost of any alternative is (1) the incremental cost of the alternative plus (2) the opportunity cost of the profit forgone from choosing that alternative. The opportunity cost of holding inventory is the income forgone by tying up money in inventory and not investing it elsewhere. The opportunity cost would not be recorded in the accounting system because, once the money is invested in inventory, there is no money available to invest elsewhere, and hence no return related to this investment to record. On the basis of the costs recorded in the accounting system (purchase-order costs and purchase costs), Soho would erroneously conclude that making two purchases of 125,000 units each is the less costly alternative. Column 3, however, indicates that, as in the total alternatives approach, purchasing smaller quantities of 2,500 units 100 times a year is preferred to purchasing 125,000 units twice during the year by $140,200. Why? Because the lower opportunity cost of holding smaller inventory exceeds the higher purchase and ordering costs. If the opportunity cost of money tied up in inventory were greater than 9% per year, or if other incremental benefits of holding lower inventory were considered— such as lower insurance, materials-handling, storage, obsolescence, and breakage costs—making 100 purchases would be even more economical.

Decision Point

What is an opportunity cost and why should it be included when making decisions?

Product-Mix Decisions with Capacity Constraints

We now examine how the concept of relevance applies to **product-mix decisions**—the decisions made by a company about which products to sell and in what quantities. These decisions usually have only a short-run focus, because they typically arise in the context of capacity constraints that can be relaxed in the long run. In the short run, for example, BMW, the German car manufacturer, continually adapts the mix of its different models of cars (for example, 325i, 525i, and 740i) to fluctuations in selling prices and demand.

To determine product mix, a company maximizes operating income, subject to constraints such as capacity and demand. Throughout this section, we assume that as short-run changes in product mix occur, the only costs that change are costs that are variable with respect to the number of units produced (and sold). Under this assumption, the analysis of individual product contribution margins provides insight into the product mix that maximizes operating income.

Learning Objective 4

Know how to choose which products to produce when there are capacity constraints

. . . select the product with the highest contribution margin per unit of the limiting resource

Example 4: Power Recreation assembles two engines, a snowmobile engine and a boat engine, at its Lexington, Kentucky, plant.

	Snowmobile Engine	Boat Engine
Selling price	$800	$1,000
Variable cost per unit	560	625
Contribution margin per unit	$240	$ 375
Contribution margin percentage ($240 ÷ $800; $375 ÷ $1,000)	30%	37.5%

Assume that only 600 machine-hours are available daily for assembling engines. Additional capacity cannot be obtained in the short run. Power Recreation can sell as many engines as it produces. The constraining resource, then, is machine-hours. It takes two machine-hours to produce one snowmobile engine and five machine-hours to produce one boat engine. What product mix should Power Recreation's managers choose to maximize its operating income?

In terms of contribution margin per unit and contribution margin percentage, boat engines are more profitable than snowmobile engines. The product that Power Recreation should produce and sell, however, is not necessarily the product with the higher individual contribution margin per unit or contribution margin percentage. Managers should choose the product with *the highest contribution margin per unit of the constraining resource (factor)*. That's the resource that restricts or limits the production or sale of products.

	Snowmobile Engine	Boat Engine
Contribution margin per unit	$240	$375
Machine-hours required to produce one unit	2 machine-hours	5 machine-hours
Contribution margin per machine-hour		
$240 per unit ÷ 2 machine-hours/unit	$120/machine-hour	
$375 per unit ÷ 5 machine-hours/unit		$75/machine-hour
Total contribution margin for 600 machine-hours		
$120/machine-hour × 600 machine-hours	$72,000	
$75/machine-hour × 600 machine-hours		$45,000

The number of machine-hours is the constraining resource in this example and snow-mobile engines earn more contribution margin per machine-hour ($120/machine-hour) compared to boat engines ($75/machine-hour). Therefore, choosing to produce and sell snowmobile engines maximizes *total* contribution margin ($72,000 versus $45,000 from producing and selling boat engines) and operating income. Other constraints in manufacturing settings can be the availability of direct materials, components, or skilled labor, as well as financial and sales factors. In a retail department store, the constraining resource may be linear feet of display space. Regardless of the specific constraining resource, managers should always focus on maximizing *total* contribution margin by choosing products that give the highest contribution margin per unit of the constraining resource.

In many cases, a manufacturer or retailer has the challenge of trying to maximize total operating income for a variety of products, each with more than one constraining resource. Some constraints may require a manufacturer or retailer to stock minimum quantities of products even if these products are not very profitable. For example, supermarkets must stock less-profitable products because customers will be willing to shop at a supermarket only if it carries a wide range of products that customers desire. To determine the most profitable production schedule and the most profitable product mix, the manufacturer or retailer needs to determine the maximum total contribution margin in the face of many constraints. Optimization techniques, such as linear programming discussed in the appendix to this chapter, help solve these more-complex problems.

Finally, there is the question of managing the bottleneck constraint to increase output and, therefore, contribution margin. Can the available machine-hours for assembling engines be increased beyond 600, for example, by reducing idle time? Can the time needed to assemble each snowmobile engine (two machine-hours) and each boat engine (five machine-hours) be reduced, for example, by reducing setup time and processing time of assembly? Can quality be improved so that constrained capacity is used to produce only good units rather than some good and some defective units? Can some of the assembly operations be outsourced to allow more engines to be built? Implementing any of these options will likely require Power Recreation to incur incremental costs. Power Recreation will implement only those options where the increase in contribution margins exceeds the increase in costs. *Instructors and students who, at this point, want to explore these issues in more detail can go to the section in Chapter 19, pages 686–688, titled "Theory of Constraints and Throughput Contribution Analysis" and then return to this chapter without any loss of continuity.*

Decision Point ▶

When resources are constrained, how should managers choose which of multiple products to produce and sell?

Learning Objective 5

Discuss factors managers must consider when adding or dropping customers or segments

. . . managers should focus on how total costs differ among alternatives and ignore allocated overhead costs

Customer Profitability, Activity-Based Costing, and Relevant Costs

Not only must companies make choices regarding which products and how much of each product to produce, they must often make decisions about adding or dropping a product line or a business segment. Similarly, if the cost object is a customer, companies must make decisions about adding or dropping customers (analogous to a product line) or a branch office (analogous to a business segment). We illustrate relevant-revenue and relevant-cost analysis for these kinds of decisions using customers rather than products as the cost object.

Example 5: Allied West, the West Coast sales office of Allied Furniture, a wholesaler of specialized furniture, supplies furniture to three local retailers: Vogel, Brenner, and Wisk. Exhibit 11-8 presents expected revenues and costs of Allied West by customer for the upcoming year using its activity-based costing system. Allied West assigns costs to customers based on the activities needed to support each customer. Information on Allied West's costs for different activities at various levels of the cost hierarchy follows:

■ Furniture-handling labor costs vary with the number of units of furniture shipped to customers.

■ Allied West reserves different areas of the warehouse to stock furniture for different customers. For simplicity, assume that furniture-handling equipment in an area and depreciation costs on the equipment that Allied West has already acquired are identified with individual customers (customer-level costs). Any unused equipment remains idle. The equipment has a one-year useful life and zero disposal value.

■ Allied West allocates rent to each customer on the basis of the amount of warehouse space reserved for that customer.

■ Marketing costs vary with the number of sales visits made to customers.

■ Sales-order costs are batch-level costs that vary with the number of sales orders received from customers; delivery-processing costs are batch-level costs that vary with the number of shipments made.

■ Allied West allocates fixed general-administration costs (facility-level costs) to customers on the basis of customer revenues.

■ Allied Furniture allocates its fixed corporate-office costs to sales offices on the basis of the square feet area of each sales office. Allied West then allocates these costs to customers on the basis of customer revenues.

In the following sections, we consider several decisions that Allied West's managers face: Should Allied West drop the Wisk account? Should it add a fourth customer, Loral? Should Allied Furniture close down Allied West? Should it open another sales office, Allied South, whose revenues and costs are identical to those of Allied West?

Exhibit 11-8

Customer Profitability Analysis for Allied West

	Customer			
	Vogel	**Brenner**	**Wisk**	**Total**
Revenues	$500,000	$300,000	$400,000	$1,200,000
Cost of goods sold	370,000	220,000	330,000	920,000
Furniture-handling labor	41,000	18,000	33,000	92,000
Furniture-handling equipment cost written off as depreciation	12,000	4,000	9,000	25,000
Rent	14,000	8,000	14,000	36,000
Marketing support	11,000	9,000	10,000	30,000
Sales-order and delivery processing	13,000	7,000	12,000	32,000
General administration	20,000	12,000	16,000	48,000
Allocated corporate-office costs	10,000	6,000	8,000	24,000
Total costs	491,000	284,000	432,000	1,207,000
Operating income	$ 9,000	$ 16,000	$ (32,000)	$ (7,000)

Relevant-Revenue and Relevant-Cost Analysis of Dropping a Customer

Exhibit 11-8 indicates a loss of $32,000 on the Wisk account. Allied West's managers believe the reason for the loss is that Wisk places low-margin orders with Allied, and has relatively high sales-order, delivery-processing, furniture-handling, and marketing costs. Allied West is considering several possible actions with respect to the Wisk account: reducing its own costs of supporting Wisk by becoming more efficient, cutting back on some of the services it offers Wisk; asking Wisk to place larger, less frequent orders; charging Wisk higher prices; or dropping the Wisk account. The following analysis focuses on the operating-income effect of dropping the Wisk account for the year.

To determine what to do, Allied West's managers must answer the question, what are the relevant revenues and relevant costs? Information about the effect of dropping the Wisk account follows:

■ Dropping the Wisk account will save cost of goods sold, furniture-handling labor, marketing support, sales-order, and delivery-processing costs incurred on the account.

■ Dropping the Wisk account will leave idle the warehouse space and furniture-handling equipment currently used to supply products to Wisk.

■ Dropping the Wisk account will have no effect on fixed general-administration costs or corporate-office costs.

Exhibit 11-9, column 1, presents the relevant-revenue and relevant-cost analysis using data from the Wisk column in Exhibit 11-8. Allied West's operating income will be $15,000 lower if it drops the Wisk account—the cost savings from dropping the Wisk account, $385,000, will not be enough to offset the loss of $400,000 in revenues—so Allied West's managers decide to keep the account. Note that there is no opportunity cost of using warehouse space for Wisk because without Wisk, the space and equipment will remain idle.

Depreciation on equipment that Allied West has already acquired is a past cost and therefore irrelevant; rent, general-administration, and corporate-office costs are future costs that will not change if Allied West drops the Wisk account, and hence irrelevant. Overhead costs allocated to the sales office and individual customers are always irrelevant. The only question is, will expected total corporate-office costs decrease as a result of dropping the Wisk account? In our example, they will not, so these costs are irrelevant. *If expected total corporate-office costs* were to decrease by dropping the Wisk account, those savings would be relevant even if *the amount allocated to Allied West did not change.*

	(Incremental Loss in Revenues) and Incremental Savings in Costs from Dropping Wisk Account (1)	Incremental Revenues and (Incremental Costs) from Adding Loral Account (2)
Revenues	$(400,000)	$400,000
Cost of goods sold	330,000	(330,000)
Furniture-handling labor	33,000	(33,000)
Furniture-handling equipment cost written off as depreciation	0	(9,000)
Rent	0	0
Marketing support	10,000	(10,000)
Sales-order and delivery processing	12,000	(12,000)
General administration	0	0
Corporate-office costs	0	0
Total costs	385,000	(394,000)
Effect on operating income (loss)	$ (15,000)	$ 6,000

Exhibit 11-9

Relevant-Revenue and Relevant-Cost Analysis for Dropping the Wisk Account and Adding the Loral Account

Now suppose that if Allied West drops the Wisk account, it could lease the extra warehouse space to Sanchez Corporation for $20,000 per year. Then $20,000 would be Allied's opportunity cost of continuing to use the warehouse to service Wisk. Allied West would gain $5,000 by dropping the Wisk account ($20,000 from lease revenue minus lost operating income of $15,000). Before reaching a decision, Allied West's managers must examine whether Wisk can be made more profitable so that supplying products to Wisk earns more than the $20,000 from leasing to Sanchez. The managers must also consider strategic factors such as the effect of the decision on Allied West's reputation for developing stable, long-run business relationships with its customers.

Relevant-Revenue and Relevant-Cost Analysis of Adding a Customer

Suppose that in addition to Vogel, Brenner, and Wisk, Allied West's managers are evaluating the profitability of adding a customer, Loral. There is no other alternative use of the Allied West facility. Loral has a customer profile much like Wisk's. Suppose Allied West's managers predict revenues and costs of doing business with Loral to be the same as the revenues and costs described under the Wisk column of Exhibit 11-8. In particular, Allied West would have to acquire furniture-handling equipment for the Loral account costing $9,000, with a one-year useful life and zero disposal value. If Loral is added as a customer, warehouse rent costs ($36,000), general-administration costs ($48,000), and *actual total* corporate-office costs will not change. Should Allied West add Loral as a customer?

Exhibit 11-9, column 2, shows incremental revenues exceed incremental costs by $6,000. The opportunity cost of adding Loral is $0 because there is no alternative use of the Allied West facility. On the basis of this analysis, Allied West's managers would recommend adding Loral as a customer. Rent, general-administration, and corporate-office costs are irrelevant because these costs will not change if Loral is added as a customer. However, the cost of new equipment to support the Loral order (written off as depreciation of $9,000 in Exhibit 11-9, column 2), is relevant. That's because this cost can be avoided if Allied West decides not to add Loral as a customer. Note the critical distinction here: *Depreciation cost is irrelevant in deciding whether to drop Wisk as a customer because depreciation on equipment that has already been purchased is a past cost, but the cost of purchasing new equipment in the future, that will then be written off as depreciation, is relevant in deciding whether to add Loral as a customer.*

Relevant-Revenue and Relevant-Cost Analysis of Closing or Adding Branch Offices or Segments

Companies periodically confront decisions about closing or adding branch offices or business segments. For example, given Allied West's expected loss of $7,000 (see Exhibit 11-8), should it be closed for the year? Assume that closing Allied West will have no effect on total corporate-office costs and that there is no alternative use for the Allied West space.

Exhibit 11-10, column 1, presents the relevant-revenue and relevant-cost analysis using data from the "Total" column in Exhibit 11-8. The revenue losses of $1,200,000 will exceed the cost savings of $1,158,000, leading to a decrease in operating income of $42,000. Allied West should not be closed. The key reasons are that closing Allied West will not save depreciation cost or actual total corporate-office costs. Depreciation cost is past or sunk because it represents the cost of equipment that Allied West has already purchased. Corporate-office costs allocated to various sales offices will change *but the total amount of these costs will not decline.* The $24,000 no longer allocated to Allied West will be allocated to other sales offices. Therefore, the $24,000 of allocated corporate-office costs is irrelevant, because it does not represent expected cost savings from closing Allied West.

Now suppose Allied Furniture has the opportunity to open another sales office, Allied South, whose revenues and costs would be identical to Allied West's costs, including a cost of $25,000 to acquire furniture-handling equipment with a one-year useful life and zero disposal value. Opening this office will have no effect on total corporate-office costs.

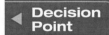

◄ **Decision Point**

In deciding to add or drop customers or to add or discontinue branch offices or segments, what should managers focus on and how should they take into account allocated overhead costs?

| **Exhibit 11-10** | Relevant-Revenue and Relevant-Cost Analysis for Closing Allied West and Opening Allied South |

	(Incremental Loss in Revenues) and Incremental Savings in Costs from Closing Allied West (1)	Incremental Revenues and (Incremental Costs) from Opening Allied South (2)
Revenues	$(1,200,000)	$1,200,000
Cost of goods sold	920,000	(920,000)
Furniture-handling labor	92,000	(92,000)
Furniture-handling equipment cost written off as depreciation	0	(25,000)
Rent	36,000	(36,000)
Marketing support	30,000	(30,000)
Sales-order and delivery processing	32,000	(32,000)
General administration	48,000	(48,000)
Corporate-office costs	0	0
Total costs	1,158,000	(1,183,000)
Effect on operating income (loss)	$ (42,000)	$ 17,000

Should Allied Furniture open Allied South? Exhibit 11-10, column 2, indicates that it should do so because opening Allied South will increase operating income by $17,000. As before, the cost of new equipment to be purchased in the future (and written off as depreciation) is relevant and *allocated* corporate-office costs should be ignored. Total corporate-office costs will not change if Allied South is opened, therefore these costs are irrelevant.

Irrelevance of Past Costs and Equipment-Replacement Decisions

Learning Objective **6**

Explain why book value of equipment is irrelevant in equipment-replacement decisions

. . . it is a past cost

At several points in this chapter, when discussing the concept of relevance, we reasoned that past (historical or sunk) costs are irrelevant to decision making. That's because a decision cannot change something that has already happened. We now apply this concept to decisions about replacing equipment. We stress the idea that **book value**—original cost minus accumulated depreciation—of existing equipment is a past cost that is irrelevant.

Example 6: Toledo Company, a manufacturer of aircraft components, is considering replacing a metal-cutting machine with a newer model. The new machine is more efficient than the old machine, but it has a shorter life. Revenues from aircraft parts ($1.1 million per year) will be unaffected by the replacement decision. Here are the data the management accountant prepares for the existing (old) machine and the replacement (new) machine:

	Old Machine	New Machine
Original cost	$1,000,000	$600,000
Useful life	5 years	2 years
Current age	3 years	0 years
Remaining useful life	2 years	2 years
Accumulated depreciation	$600,000	Not acquired yet
Book value	$400,000	Not acquired yet
Current disposal value (in cash)	$40,000	Not acquired yet
Terminal disposal value (in cash 2 years from now)	$0	$0
Annual operating costs (maintenance, energy, repairs, coolants, and so on)	$800,000	$460,000

Toledo Corporation uses straight-line depreciation. To focus on relevance, we ignore the time value of money and income taxes.[2] Should Toledo replace its old machine?

Exhibit 11-11 presents a cost comparison of the two machines. Consider why each of the four items in Toledo's equipment-replacement decision is relevant or irrelevant:

1. **Book value of old machine, $400,000.** Irrelevant, because it is a past or sunk cost. All past costs are "down the drain." Nothing can change what has already been spent or what has already happened.

2. **Current disposal value of old machine, $40,000.** Relevant, because it is an expected future benefit that will only occur if the machine is replaced.

3. **Loss on disposal, $360,000.** This is the difference between amounts in items 1 and 2. It is a meaningless combination blurring the distinction between the irrelevant book value and the relevant disposal value. Each should be considered separately, as was done in items 1 and 2.

4. **Cost of new machine, $600,000.** Relevant, because it is an expected future cost that will only occur if the machine is purchased.

Exhibit 11-11 should clarify these four assertions. Column 3 in Exhibit 11-11 shows that the book value of the old machine does not differ between the alternatives and could be ignored for decision-making purposes. No matter what the timing of the write-off— whether a lump-sum charge in the current year or depreciation charges over the next two years—the total amount is still $400,000 because it is a past (historical) cost. In contrast, the $600,000 cost of the new machine and the current disposal value of $40,000 for the old machine are relevant because they would not arise if Toledo's managers decided not to replace the machine. Note that the operating income from replacing is $120,000 higher for the two years together.

To provide focus, Exhibit 11-12 concentrates only on relevant items. Note that the same answer—higher operating income as a result of lower costs of $120,000 by replacing the machine—is obtained even though the book value is omitted from the calculations. The only relevant items are the cash operating costs, the disposal value of the old machine, and the cost of the new machine that is represented as depreciation in Exhibit 11-12.

Decision Point

Is book value of existing equipment relevant in equipment replacement decisions?

Exhibit 11-11

Operating Income Comparison: Replacement of Machine, Relevant, and Irrelevant Items for Toledo Company

	Two Years Together		
	Keep (1)	**Replace (2)**	**Difference (3) = (1) – (2)**
Revenues	$2,200,000	$2,200,000	—
Operating costs			
Cash operating costs			
($800,000/yr. × 2 years;			
$460,000/yr. × 2 years)	1,600,000	920,000	$ 680,000
Book value of old machine			
Periodic write-off as depreciation or	400,000	—	—
Lump-sum write-off	—	400,000[a]	
Current disposal value of old machine	—	(40,000)[a]	40,000
New machine cost, written off periodically			
as depreciation	—	600,000	(600,000)
Total operating costs	2,000,000	1,880,000	120,000
Operating income	$ 200,000	$ 320,000	$(120,000)

[a]In a formal income statement, these two items would be combined as "loss on disposal of machine" of $360,000.

---

[2] See Chapter 21 for a discussion of time-value-of-money and income-tax considerations in capital investment decisions.

Exhibit 11-12

Cost Comparison:
Replacement of
Machine, Relevant
Items Only, for Toledo
Company

	Two Years Together		
	Keep (1)	Replace (2)	Difference (3) = (1) – (2)
Cash operating costs	$1,600,000	$ 920,000	$680,000
Current disposal value of old machine	—	(40,000)	40,000
New machine, written off periodically as depreciation	—	600,000	(600,000)
Total relevant costs	$1,600,000	$1,480,000	$120,000

Decisions and Performance Evaluation

Consider our equipment-replacement example in light of the five-step sequence in Exhibit 11-1 (p. 392):

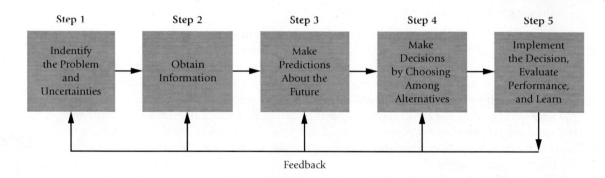

Feedback

The decision model analysis (Step 4), which is presented in Exhibits 11-11 and 11-12, dictates replacing the machine rather than keeping it. In the real world, however, would the manager replace it? An important factor in replacement decisions is the manager's perception of whether the decision model is consistent with how the manager's performance will be judged after the decision is implemented (the performance-evaluation model in Step 5).

From the perspective of their own careers, it is no surprise that managers tend to favor the alternative that makes their performance look better. If the performance-evaluation model conflicts with the decision model, the performance-evaluation model often prevails in influencing managers' decisions. For example, if the promotion or bonus of the manager at Toledo hinges on his or her first year's operating income performance under accrual accounting, the manager's temptation *not* to replace will be overwhelming. Why? Because the accrual accounting model for measuring performance will show a higher first-year operating income if the old machine is kept rather than replaced (as the following table shows):

First-Year Results: Accrual Accounting		Keep		Replace
Revenues		$1,100,000		$1,100,000
Operating costs				
Cash-operating costs	$800,000		$460,000	
Depreciation	200,000		300,000	
Loss on disposal	—		360,000	
Total operating costs		1,000,000		1,120,000
Operating income (loss)		$ 100,000		$ (20,000)

Even though top management's goals encompass the two-year period (consistent with the decision model), the manager will focus on first-year results if his or her evaluation is based on short-run measures such as the first-year's operating income.

Resolving the conflict between the decision model and the performance-evaluation model is frequently a baffling problem in practice. In theory, resolving the difficulty seems obvious: Design models that are consistent. Consider our replacement example. Year-by-year effects on operating income of replacement can be budgeted for the two-year planning horizon. The manager then would be evaluated on the expectation that the first year would be poor and the next year would be much better. Doing this for every decision, however, makes the performance evaluation model very cumbersome. As a result of these practical difficulties, accounting systems rarely track each decision separately. Performance evaluation focuses on responsibility centers for a specific period, not on projects or individual items of equipment over their useful lives. Thus, the impacts of many different decisions are combined in a single performance report and evaluation measure, say operating income. Lower-level managers make decisions to maximize operating income, and top management—through the reporting system—is rarely aware of particular desirable alternatives that were *not* chosen by lower-level managers because of conflicts between the decision and performance-evaluation models.

Consider another conflict between the decision model and the performance-evaluation model. Suppose a manager buys a particular machine only to discover shortly thereafter that a better machine could have been purchased instead. The decision model may suggest replacing the machine that was just bought with the better machine, but will the manager do so? Probably not. Why? Because replacing the machine so soon after its purchase will reflect badly on the manager's capabilities and performance. If the manager's bosses have no knowledge of the better machine, the manager may prefer to keep the recently purchased machine rather than alert them to the better machine.

Chapter 23 discusses performance evaluation models in more detail and ways to reduce conflict between the decision model and the performance evaluation model.

Decision Point

How can conflicts arise between the decision model used by a manager and the performance-evaluation model used to evaluate that manager?

Problem for Self-Study

Wally Lewis is manager of the engineering development division of Goldcoast Products. Lewis has just received a proposal signed by all 15 of his engineers to replace the workstations with networked personal computers (networked PCs). Lewis is not enthusiastic about the proposal.

Data on workstations and networked PCs are as follows:

	Workstations	Networked PCs
Original cost	$300,000	$135,000
Useful life	5 years	3 years
Current age	2 years	0 years
Remaining useful life	3 years	3 years
Accumulated depreciation	$120,000	Not acquired yet
Current book value	$180,000	Not acquired yet
Current disposal value (in cash)	$95,000	Not acquired yet
Terminal disposal value (in cash 3 years from now)	$0	$0
Annual computer-related cash operating costs	$40,000	$10,000
Annual revenues	$1,000,000	$1,000,000
Annual noncomputer-related operating costs	$880,000	$880,000

Lewis's annual bonus includes a component based on division operating income. He has a promotion possibility next year that would make him a group vice president of Goldcoast Products.

Required

1. Compare the costs of workstations and networked PCs. Consider the cumulative results for the three years together, ignoring the time value of money and income taxes.
2. Why might Lewis be reluctant to purchase the networked PCs?

Solution

1. The following table considers all cost items when comparing future costs of work-stations and networked PCs:

All Items	Three Years Together		
	Workstations (1)	Networked PCs (2)	Difference (3) = (1) − (2)
Revenues	$3,000,000	$3,000,000	—
Operating costs			
Noncomputer-related operating costs	2,640,000	2,640,000	—
Computer-related cash operating costs	120,000	30,000	$ 90,000
Workstations' book value			
Periodic write-off as depreciation or	180,000	—	—
Lump-sum write-off	—	180,000 }	
Current disposal value of workstations	—	(95,000)	95,000
Networked PCs, written off periodically			
as depreciation	—	135,000	(135,000)
Total operating costs	2,940,000	2,890,000	50,000
Operating income	$ 60,000	$ 110,000	$ (50,000)

Alternatively, the analysis could focus on only those items in the preceding table that differ between the alternatives.

Relevant Items	Three Years Together		
	Workstations	Networked PCs	Difference
Computer-related cash operating costs	$120,000	$ 30,000	$90,000
Current disposal value of workstations	—	(95,000)	95,000
Networked PCs, written off periodically			
as depreciation	—	135,000	(135,000)
Total relevant costs	$120,000	$ 70,000	$ 50,000

The analysis suggests that it is cost-effective to replace the workstations with the networked PCs.

2. The accrual-accounting operating incomes *for the first year* under the keep work-stations versus the buy networked PCs alternatives are as follows:

	Keep Workstations	Buy Networked PCs
Revenues	$1,000,000	$1,000,000
Operating costs		
Noncomputer-related operating costs	$880,000	$880,000
Computer-related cash operating costs	40,000	10,000
Depreciation	60,000	45,000
Loss on disposal of workstations	—	85,000[a]
Total operating costs	980,000	1,020,000
Operating income (loss)	$ 20,000	$ (20,000)

[a] $85,000 = Book value of workstations, $180,000 − Current disposal value, $95,000.

Lewis would be less happy with the expected operating loss of $20,000 if the networked PCs are purchased than he would be with the expected operating income of $20,000 if the workstations are kept. Buying the networked PCs would eliminate the component of his bonus based on operating income. He might also perceive the $20,000 operating loss as reducing his chances of being promoted to a group vice president.

Decision Points

The following question-and-answer format summarizes the chapter's learning objectives. Each decision presents a key question related to a learning objective. The guidelines are the answer to that question.

Decision	Guidelines
1. What is the five-step process that managers can use to make decisions?	The five-step decision-making process is (a) identify the problem and uncertainties, (b) obtain information, (c) make predictions about the future, (d) make decisions by choosing among alternatives, and (e) implement the decision, evaluate performance, and learn.
2. When is a revenue or cost item relevant for a particular decision and what potential problems should be avoided in relevant-cost analysis?	To be relevant for a particular decision, a revenue or cost item must meet two criteria: (a) It must be an expected future revenue or expected future cost, and (b) it must differ among alternative courses of action. The outcomes of alternative actions can be quantitative and qualitative. Quantitative outcomes are measured in numerical terms. Some quantitative outcomes can be expressed in financial terms, others cannot. Qualitative factors, such as employee morale, are difficult to measure accurately in numerical terms. Consideration must be given to relevant quantitative and qualitative factors in making decisions.

Two potential problems to avoid in relevant-cost analysis are (a) making incorrect general assumptions—such as all variable costs are relevant and all fixed costs are irrelevant—and (b) losing sight of total amounts, focusing instead on unit amounts. |
3. What is an opportunity cost and why should it be included when making decisions?	Opportunity cost is the contribution to income that is forgone by not using a limited resource in its next-best alternative use. Opportunity cost is included in decision making because the relevant cost of any decision is (1) the incremental cost of the decision plus (2) the opportunity cost of the profit forgone from making that decision.
4. When resources are constrained, how should managers choose which of multiple products to produce and sell?	When resources are constrained, managers should select the product that yields the highest contribution margin per unit of the constraining or limiting resource (factor). In this way, total contribution margin will be maximized.
5. In deciding to add or drop customers or to add or discontinue branch offices or segments, what should managers focus on and how should they take into account allocated overhead costs?	When making decisions about adding or dropping customers or adding or discontinuing branch offices and segments, managers should focus on only those costs that will change and any opportunity costs. Managers should ignore allocated overhead costs.
6. Is book value of existing equipment relevant in equipment-replacement decisions?	Book value of existing equipment is a past (historical or sunk) cost and, therefore, is irrelevant in equipment-replacement decisions.
7. How can conflicts arise between the decision model used by a manager and the performance-evaluation model used to evaluate that manager?	Top management faces a persistent challenge: making sure that the performance-evaluation model of lower-level managers is consistent with the decision model. A common inconsistency is to tell these managers to take a multiple-year view in their decision making but then to judge their performance only on the basis of the current year's operating income.

Appendix

Linear Programming

In this chapter's Power Recreation example (pp. 405–406), suppose both the snowmobile and boat engines must be tested on a very expensive machine before they are shipped to customers. The available machine-hours for testing are limited. Production data are as follows:

| Department | Available Daily Capacity in Hours | Use of Capacity in Hours per Unit of Product | | Daily Maximum Production in Units | |
		Snowmobile Engine	Boat Engine	Snowmobile Engine	Boat Engine
Assembly	600 machine-hours	2.0 machine-hours	5.0 machine-hours	300[a] snow engines	120 boat engines
Testing	120 testing-hours	1.0 machine-hour	0.5 machine-hour	120 snow engines	240 boat engines

[a] For example, 600 machine-hours ÷ 2.0 machine-hours per snowmobile engine = 300, the maximum number of snowmobile engines that the assembly department can make if it works exclusively on snowmobile engines.

Exhibit 11-13 summarizes these and other relevant data. In addition, as a result of material shortages for boat engines, Power Recreation cannot produce more than 110 boat engines per day. How many engines of each type should Power Recreation produce and sell daily to maximize operating income?

Because there are multiple constraints, a technique called *linear programming* or *LP* can be used to determine the number of each type of engine Power Recreation should produce. LP models typically assume that all costs are either variable or fixed with respect to a single cost driver (units of output). As we shall see, LP models also require certain other linear assumptions to hold. When these assumptions fail, other decision models should be considered.[3]

Steps in Solving an LP Problem

We use the data in Exhibit 11-13 to illustrate the three steps in solving an LP problem. Throughout this discussion, S equals the number of units of snowmobile engines produced and sold, and B equals the number of units of boat engines produced and sold.

Step 1: Determine the objective function. The **objective function** of a linear program expresses the objective or goal to be maximized (say, operating income) or minimized (say, operating costs). In our example, the objective is to find the combination of snowmobile engines and boat engines that maximizes total contribution margin. Fixed costs remain the same regardless of the product-mix decision and are irrelevant. The linear function expressing the objective for the total contribution margin (TCM) is as follows:

$$TCM = \$240S + \$375B$$

Step 2: Specify the constraints. A **constraint** is a mathematical inequality or equality that must be satisfied by the variables in a mathematical model. The following linear inequalities express the relationships in our example:

Assembly department constraint	$2S + 5B \leq 600$
Testing department constraint	$1S + 0.5B \leq 120$
Materials-shortage constraint for boat engines	$B \leq 110$
Negative production is impossible	$S \geq 0$ and $B \geq 0$

| Exhibit 11-13 | Operating Data for Power Recreation |

| | Department Capacity (per Day) In Product Units | | Selling Price | Variable Cost per Unit | Contribution Margin per Unit |
	Assembly	Testing			
Only snowmobile engines	300	120	$ 800	$560	$240
Only boat engines	120	240	$1,000	$625	$375

[3] Other decision models are described in J. Moore and L. Weatherford, *Decision Modeling with Microsoft Excel*, 6th ed. (Upper Saddle River, NJ: Prentice Hall, 2001); and S. Nahmias, *Production and Operations Analysis*, 6th ed. (New York: McGraw-Hill/Irwin, 2008).

The three solid lines on the graph in Exhibit 11-14 show the existing constraints for assembly and testing and the materials-shortage constraint.[4] The feasible or technically possible alternatives are those combinations of quantities of snowmobile engines and boat engines that satisfy all the constraining resources or factors. The shaded "area of feasible solutions" in Exhibit 11-14 shows the boundaries of those product combinations that are feasible.

Step 3: Compute the optimal solution. Linear programming (LP) is an optimization technique used to maximize the *objective function* when there are multiple *constraints*. We present two approaches for finding the optimal solution using LP: trial-and-error approach and graphic approach. These approaches are easy to use in our example because there are only two variables in the objective function and a small number of constraints. Understanding these approaches provides insight into LP. In most real-world LP applications, managers use computer software packages to calculate the optimal solution.[5]

Trial-and-Error Approach

The optimal solution can be found by trial and error, by working with coordinates of the corners of the area of feasible solutions.

First, select any set of corner points and compute the total contribution margin. Five corner points appear in Exhibit 11-14. It is helpful to use simultaneous equations to obtain the exact coordinates in the graph. To illustrate, the corner point ($S = 75$, $B = 90$) can be derived by solving the two pertinent constraint inequalities as simultaneous equations:

$$2S + 5B = 600 \quad (1)$$

$$1S + 0.5B = 120 \quad (2)$$

Multiplying (2) by 2: $\quad 2S + B = 240 \quad (3)$

Subtracting (3) from (1): $\quad 4B = 360$

Therefore, $\quad B = 360 \div 4 = 90$

Substituting for B in (2): $1S + 0.5(90) = 120$

$$S = 120 - 45 = 75$$

Given $S = 75$ snowmobile engines and $B = 90$ boat engines, TCM = ($210 per snowmobile engine × 75 snowmobile engines) + ($375 per boat engine × 90 boat engines) = $51,750.

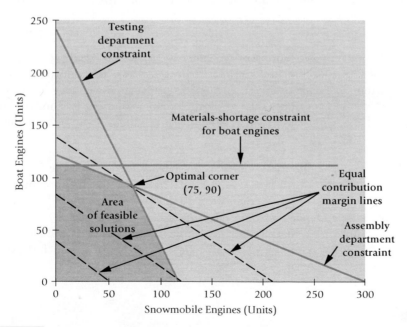

Exhibit 11-14

Linear Programming: Graphic Solution for Power Recreation

---

[4] As an example of how the lines are plotted in Exhibit 11-14, use equal signs instead of inequality signs and assume for the assembly department that $B = 0$; then $S = 300$ (600 machine-hours ÷ 2 machine-hours per snowmobile engine). Assume that $S = 0$; then $B = 120$ (600 machine-hours ÷ 5 machine-hours per boat engine). Connect those two points with a straight line.

[5] Standard computer software packages rely on the simplex method. The *simplex method* is an iterative step-by-step procedure for determining the optimal solution to an LP problem. It starts with a specific feasible solution and then tests it by substitution to see whether the result can be improved. These substitutions continue until no further improvement is possible and the optimal solution is obtained.

Second, move from corner point to corner point and compute the total contribution margin at each corner point.

Trial	Corner Point (S, B)	Snowmobile Engines (S)	Boat Engines (B)	Total Contribution Margin
1	(0, 0)	0	0	$240(0) + $375(0) = $0
2	(0, 110)	0	110	$240(0) + $375(110) = $41,250
3	(25,110)	25	110	$240(25) + $375(110) = $47,250
4	(75, 90)	75	90	$240(75) + $375(90) = $51,750[a]
5	(120, 0)	120	0	$240(120) + $375(0) = $28,800

[a] The optimal solution.

The optimal product mix is the mix that yields the highest total contribution: 75 snowmobile engines and 90 boat engines. To understand the solution, consider what happens when moving from the point (25,110) to (75,90). Power Recreation gives up $7,500 [$375 × (110 − 90)] in contribution margin from boat engines while gaining $12,000 [$240 × (75 − 25)] in contribution margin from snowmobile engines. This results in a net increase in contribution margin of $4,500 ($12,000 − $7,500), from $47,250 to $51,750.

Graphic Approach

Consider all possible combinations that will produce the same total contribution margin of, say, $12,000. That is,

$$\$240S + \$375B = \$12,000$$

This set of $12,000 contribution margins is a straight dashed line through [S = 50 ($12,000 ÷ $240); B = 0)] and [S = 0, B = 32 ($12,000 ÷ $375)] in Exhibit 11-14. Other equal total contribution margins can be represented by lines parallel to this one. In Exhibit 11-14, we show three dashed lines. Lines drawn farther from the origin represent more sales of both products and higher amounts of equal contribution margins.

The optimal line is the one farthest from the origin but still passing through a point in the area of feasible solutions. This line represents the highest total contribution margin. The optimal solution—the number of snowmobile engines and boat engines that will maximize the objective function, total contribution margin—is the corner point (S = 75, B = 90). This solution will become apparent if you put a straight-edge ruler on the graph and move it outward from the origin and parallel with the $12,000 contribution margin line. Move the ruler as far away from the origin as possible—that is, increase the total contribution margin—without leaving the area of feasible solutions. In general, the optimal solution in a maximization problem lies at the corner where the dashed line intersects an extreme point of the area of feasible solutions. Moving the ruler out any farther puts it outside the area of feasible solutions.

Sensitivity Analysis

What are the implications of uncertainty about the accounting or technical coefficients used in the objective function (such as the contribution margin per unit of snowmobile engines or boat engines) or the constraints (such as the number of machine-hours it takes to make a snowmobile engine or a boat engine)? Consider how a change in the contribution margin of snowmobile engines from $240 to $300 per unit would affect the optimal solution. Assume the contribution margin for boat engines remains unchanged at $375 per unit. The revised objective function will be as follows:

$$TCM = \$300S + \$375B$$

Using the trial-and-error approach to calculate the total contribution margin for each of the five corner points described in the previous table, the optimal solution is still (S = 75, B = 90). What if the contribution margin of snowmobile engines falls to $160 per unit? The optimal solution remains the same (S = 75, B = 90). Thus, big changes in the contribution margin per unit of snowmobile engines have no effect on the optimal solution in this case. That's because, although the slopes of the equal contribution margin lines in Exhibit 11-14 change as the contribution margin of snowmobile engines changes from $240 to $300 to $160 per unit, the farthest point at which the equal contribution margin lines intersect the area of feasible solutions is still (S = 75, B = 90).

Terms to Learn

This chapter and the Glossary at the end of the book contain definitions of the following important terms:

insourcing (**p. 397**)

linear programming (LP) (**p. 417**)

make-or-buy decisions (**p. 397**)

objective function (**p. 416**)

one-time-only special order (**p. 394**)

opportunity cost (**p. 402**)

outsourcing (**p. 397**)

product-mix decisions (**p. 405**)

qualitative factors (**p. 394**)

quantitative factors (**p. 394**)

relevant costs (**p. 393**)

relevant revenues (**p. 393**)

sunk costs (**p. 393**)

Assignment Material

Questions

11-1 Outline the five-step sequence in a decision process.

11-2 Define relevant costs. Why are historical costs irrelevant?

11-3 "All future costs are relevant." Do you agree? Why?

11-4 Distinguish between quantitative and qualitative factors in decision making.

11-5 Describe two potential problems that should be avoided in relevant-cost analysis.

11-6 "Variable costs are always relevant, and fixed costs are always irrelevant." Do you agree? Why?

11-7 "A component part should be purchased whenever the purchase price is less than its total manufacturing cost per unit." Do you agree? Why?

11-8 Define opportunity cost.

11-9 "Managers should always buy inventory in quantities that result in the lowest purchase cost per unit." Do you agree? Why?

11-10 "Management should always maximize sales of the product with the highest contribution margin per unit." Do you agree? Why?

11-11 "A branch office or business segment that shows negative operating income should be shut down." Do you agree? Explain briefly.

11-12 "Cost written off as depreciation on equipment already purchased is always irrelevant." Do you agree? Why?

11-13 "Managers will always choose the alternative that maximizes operating income or minimizes costs in the decision model." Do you agree? Why?

11-14 Describe the three steps in solving a linear programming problem.

11-15 How might the optimal solution of a linear programming problem be determined?

Exercises

11-16 **Disposal of assets.** Answer the following questions.

1. A company has an inventory of 1,100 assorted parts for a line of missiles that has been discontinued. The inventory cost is $78,000. The parts can be either (a) remachined at total additional costs of $24,500 and then sold for $33,000 or (b) sold as scrap for $6,500. Which action is more profitable? Show your calculations.

2. A truck, costing $101,000 and uninsured, is wrecked its first day in use. It can be either (a) disposed of for $17,500 cash and replaced with a similar truck costing $103,500 or (b) rebuilt for $89,500, and thus be brand-new as far as operating characteristics and looks are concerned. Which action is less costly? Show your calculations.

11-17 **Relevant and irrelevant costs.** Answer the following questions.

1. DeCesare Computers makes 5,200 units of a circuit board, CB76 at a cost of $280 each. Variable cost per unit is $190 and fixed cost per unit is $90. Peach Electronics offers to supply 5,200 units of CB76 for $260. If DeCesare buys from Peach it will be able to save $10 per unit in fixed costs but continue to incur the remaining $80 per unit. Should DeCesare accept Peach's offer? Explain.

2. LN Manufacturing is deciding whether to keep or replace an old machine. It obtains the following information:

	Old Machine	New Machine
Original cost	$10,700	$9,000
Useful life	10 years	3 years
Current age	7 years	0 years
Remaining useful life	3 years	3 years
Accumulated depreciation	$7,490	Not acquired yet
Book value	$3,210	Not acquired yet
Current disposal value (in cash)	$2,200	Not acquired yet
Terminal disposal value (3 years from now)	$0	$0
Annual cash operating costs	$17,500	$15,500

LN Manufacturing uses straight-line depreciation. Ignore the time value of money and income taxes. Should LN Manufacturing replace the old machine? Explain.

11-18 Multiple choice. (CPA) Choose the best answer.

1. The Woody Company manufactures slippers and sells them at $10 a pair. Variable manufacturing cost is $4.50 a pair, and allocated fixed manufacturing cost is $1.50 a pair. It has enough idle capacity available to accept a one-time-only special order of 20,000 pairs of slippers at $6 a pair. Woody will not incur any marketing costs as a result of the special order. What would the effect on operating income be if the special order could be accepted without affecting normal sales: (a) $0, (b) $30,000 increase, (c) $90,000 increase, or (d) $120,000 increase? Show your calculations.

2. The Reno Company manufactures Part No. 498 for use in its production line. The manufacturing cost per unit for 20,000 units of Part No. 498 is as follows:

Direct materials	$ 6
Direct manufacturing labor	30
Variable manufacturing overhead	12
Fixed manufacturing overhead allocated	16
Total manufacturing cost per unit	$64

The Tray Company has offered to sell 20,000 units of Part No. 498 to Reno for $60 per unit. Reno will make the decision to buy the part from Tray if there is an overall savings of at least $25,000 for Reno. If Reno accepts Tray's offer, $9 per unit of the fixed overhead allocated would be eliminated. Furthermore, Reno has determined that the released facilities could be used to save relevant costs in the manufacture of Part No. 575. For Reno to achieve an overall savings of $25,000, the amount of relevant costs that would have to be saved by using the released facilities in the manufacture of Part No. 575 would be which of the following: (a) $80,000, (b) $85,000, (c) $125,000, or (d) $140,000? Show your calculations.

11-19 Special order, activity-based costing. (CMA, adapted) The Award Plus Company manufactures medals for winners of athletic events and other contests. Its manufacturing plant has the capacity to produce 10,000 medals each month. Current production and sales are 7,500 medals per month. The company normally charges $150 per medal. Cost information for the current activity level is as follows:

Variable costs that vary with number of units produced	
Direct materials	$ 262,500
Direct manufacturing labor	300,000
Variable costs (for setups, materials handling, quality control, and so on) that vary with number of batches, 150 batches × $500 per batch	75,000
Fixed manufacturing costs	275,000
Fixed marketing costs	175,000
Total costs	$1,087,500

Award Plus has just received a special one-time-only order for 2,500 medals at $100 per medal. Accepting the special order would not affect the company's regular business. Award Plus makes medals for its existing customers in batch sizes of 50 medals (150 batches × 50 medals per batch = 7,500 medals). The special order requires Award Plus to make the medals in 25 batches of 100 each.

Required

1. Should Award Plus accept this special order? Show your calculations.
2. Suppose plant capacity were only 9,000 medals instead of 10,000 medals each month. The special order must either be taken in full or be rejected completely. Should Award Plus accept the special order? Show your calculations.
3. As in requirement 1, assume that monthly capacity is 10,000 medals. Award Plus is concerned that if it accepts the special order, its existing customers will immediately demand a price discount of $10 in the month in which the special order is being filled. They would argue that Award Plus's capacity costs are now being spread over more units and that existing customers should get the benefit of these lower costs. Should Award Plus accept the special order under these conditions? Show your calculations.

11-20 Make versus buy, activity-based costing. The Svenson Corporation manufactures cellular modems. It manufactures its own cellular modem circuit boards (CMCB), an important part of the cellular modem. It reports the following cost information about the costs of making CMCBs in 2011 and the expected costs in 2012:

	Current Costs in 2011	Expected Costs in 2012
Variable manufacturing costs		
Direct material cost per CMCB	$ 180	$ 170
Direct manufacturing labor cost per CMCB	50	45
Variable manufacturing cost per batch for setups, materials handling, and quality control	1,600	1,500
Fixed manufacturing cost		
Fixed manufacturing overhead costs that can be avoided if CMCBs are not made	320,000	320,000
Fixed manufacturing overhead costs of plant depreciation, insurance, and administration that cannot be avoided even if CMCBs are not made	800,000	800,000

Svenson manufactured 8,000 CMCBs in 2011 in 40 batches of 200 each. In 2012, Svenson anticipates needing 10,000 CMCBs. The CMCBs would be produced in 80 batches of 125 each.

The Minton Corporation has approached Svenson about supplying CMCBs to Svenson in 2012 at $300 per CMCB on whatever delivery schedule Svenson wants.

1. Calculate the total expected manufacturing cost per unit of making CMCBs in 2012.
2. Suppose the capacity currently used to make CMCBs will become idle if Svenson purchases CMCBs from Minton. On the basis of financial considerations alone, should Svenson make CMCBs or buy them from Minton? Show your calculations.
3. Now suppose that if Svenson purchases CMCBs from Minton, its best alternative use of the capacity currently used for CMCBs is to make and sell special circuit boards (CB3s) to the Essex Corporation. Svenson estimates the following incremental revenues and costs from CB3s:

Total expected incremental future revenues	$2,000,000
Total expected incremental future costs	$2,150,000

On the basis of financial considerations alone, should Svenson make CMCBs or buy them from Minton? Show your calculations.

Required

11-21 Inventory decision, opportunity costs. Lawn World, a manufacturer of lawn mowers, predicts that it will purchase 264,000 spark plugs next year. Lawn World estimates that 22,000 spark plugs will be required each month. A supplier quotes a price of $7 per spark plug. The supplier also offers a special discount option: If all 264,000 spark plugs are purchased at the start of the year, a discount of 2% off the $7 price will be given. Lawn World can invest its cash at 10% per year. It costs Lawn World $260 to place each purchase order.

Required

1. What is the opportunity cost of interest forgone from purchasing all 264,000 units at the start of the year instead of in 12 monthly purchases of 22,000 units per order?
2. Would this opportunity cost be recorded in the accounting system? Why?
3. Should Lawn World purchase 264,000 units at the start of the year or 22,000 units each month? Show your calculations.

11-22 Relevant costs, contribution margin, product emphasis. The Seashore Stand is a take-out food store at a popular beach resort. Susan Sexton, owner of the Seashore Stand, is deciding how much refrigerator space to devote to four different drinks. Pertinent data on these four drinks are as follows:

	Cola	Lemonade	Punch	Natural Orange Juice
Selling price per case	$18.75	$20.50	$27.75	$39.30
Variable cost per case	$13.75	$15.60	$20.70	$30.40
Cases sold per foot of shelf space per day	22	12	6	13

Sexton has a maximum front shelf space of 12 feet to devote to the four drinks. She wants a minimum of 1 foot and a maximum of 6 feet of front shelf space for each drink.

Required

1. Calculate the contribution margin per case of each type of drink.
2. A coworker of Sexton's recommends that she maximize the shelf space devoted to those drinks with the highest contribution margin per case. Evaluate this recommendation.
3. What shelf-space allocation for the four drinks would you recommend for the Seashore Stand? Show your calculations.

11-23 Selection of most profitable product. Body-Builders, Inc., produces two basic types of weight-lifting equipment, Model 9 and Model 14. Pertinent data are as follows:

		A	B	C
1			Per Unit	
2			Model 9	Model 14
3	Selling price		$100.00	$70.00
4	Costs			
5		Direct material	28.00	13.00
6		Direct manufacturing labor	15.00	25.00
7		Variable manufacturing overhead*	25.00	12.50
8		Fixed manufacturing overhead*	10.00	5.00
9		Marketing (all variable)	14.00	10.00
10		Total cost	92.00	65.50
11	Operating income		$ 8.00	$ 4.50
12				
13	*Allocated on the basis of machine-hours			

The weight-lifting craze is such that enough of either Model 9 or Model 14 can be sold to keep the plant operating at full capacity. Both products are processed through the same production departments.

Required Which products should be produced? Briefly explain your answer.

11-24 Which center to close, relevant-cost analysis, opportunity costs. Fair Lakes Hospital Corporation has been operating ambulatory surgery centers in Groveton and Stockdale, two small communities each about an hour away from its main hospital. As a cost control measure the hospital has decided that it needs only one of those two centers permanently, so one must be shut down. The decision regarding which center to close will be made on financial considerations alone. The following information is available:

a. The Groveton center was built 15 years ago at a cost of $5 million on land leased from the City of Groveton at a cost of $40,000 per year. The land and buildings will immediately revert back to the city if the center is closed. The center has annual operating costs of $2.5 million, all of which will be saved if the center is closed. In addition, Fair Lakes allocates $800,000 of common administrative costs to the Groveton center. If the center is closed, these costs would be reallocated to other ambulatory centers. If the center is kept open, Fair Lakes plans to invest $1 million in a fixed income note, which will earn the $40,000 that Fair Lakes needs for the lease payments.

b. The Stockdale center was built 20 years ago at a cost of $4.8 million, of which Fair Lakes and the City of Stockdale each paid half, on land donated by a hospital benefactor. Two years ago, Fair Lakes spent $2 million to renovate the facility. If the center is closed, the property will be sold to developers for $7 million. The operating costs of the center are $3 million per year, all of which will be saved if the center is closed. Fair Lakes allocates $1 million of common administrative costs to the Stockdale center. If the center is closed, these costs would be reallocated to other ambulatory centers.

c. Fair Lakes estimates that the operating costs of whichever center remains open will be $3.5 million per year.

Required The City Council of Stockdale has petitioned Fair Lakes to close the Groveton facility, thus sparing the Stockdale center. The Council argues that otherwise the $2 million spent on recent renovations would be wasted. Do you agree with the Stockdale City Council's arguments and conclusions? In your answer, identify and explain all costs that you consider relevant and all costs that you consider irrelevant for the center-closing decision.

11-25 Closing and opening stores. Sanchez Corporation runs two convenience stores, one in Connecticut and one in Rhode Island. Operating income for each store in 2012 is as follows:

	Connecticut Store	Rhode Island Store
Revenues	$1,070,000	$860,000
Operating costs		
Cost of goods sold	750,000	660,000
Lease rent (renewable each year)	90,000	75,000
Labor costs (paid on an hourly basis)	42,000	42,000
Depreciation of equipment	25,000	22,000
Utilities (electricity, heating)	43,000	46,000
Allocated corporate overhead	50,000	40,000
Total operating costs	1,000,000	885,000
Operating income (loss)	$ 70,000	$ (25,000)

The equipment has a zero disposal value. In a senior management meeting, Maria Lopez, the management accountant at Sanchez Corporation, makes the following comment, "Sanchez can increase its profitability by closing down the Rhode Island store or by adding another store like it."

Required

1. By closing down the Rhode Island store, Sanchez can reduce overall corporate overhead costs by $44,000. Calculate Sanchez's operating income if it closes the Rhode Island store. Is Maria Lopez's statement about the effect of closing the Rhode Island store correct? Explain.

2. Calculate Sanchez's operating income if it keeps the Rhode Island store open and opens another store with revenues and costs identical to the Rhode Island store (including a cost of $22,000 to acquire equipment with a one-year useful life and zero disposal value). Opening this store will increase corporate overhead costs by $4,000. Is Maria Lopez's statement about the effect of adding another store like the Rhode Island store correct? Explain.

11-26 Choosing customers. Broadway Printers operates a printing press with a monthly capacity of 2,000 machine-hours. Broadway has two main customers: Taylor Corporation and Kelly Corporation. Data on each customer for January follows:

	Taylor Corporation	Kelly Corporation	Total
Revenues	$120,000	$80,000	$200,000
Variable costs	42,000	48,000	90,000
Contribution margin	78,000	32,000	110,000
Fixed costs (allocated)	60,000	40,000	100,000
Operating income	$ 18,000	$ (8,000)	$ 10,000
Machine-hours required	1,500 hours	500 hours	2,000 hours

Kelly Corporation indicates that it wants Broadway to do an *additional* $80,000 worth of printing jobs during February. These jobs are identical to the existing business Broadway did for Kelly in January in terms of variable costs and machine-hours required. Broadway anticipates that the business from Taylor Corporation in February will be the same as that in January. Broadway can choose to accept as much of the Taylor and Kelly business for February as its capacity allows. Assume that total machine-hours and fixed costs for February will be the same as in January.

Required

What action should Broadway take to maximize its operating income? Show your calculations.

11-27 Relevance of equipment costs. The Auto Wash Company has just today paid for and installed a special machine for polishing cars at one of its several outlets. It is the first day of the company's fiscal year. The machine costs $20,000. Its annual cash operating costs total $15,000. The machine will have a four-year useful life and a zero terminal disposal value.

After the machine has been used for only one day, a salesperson offers a different machine that promises to do the same job at annual cash operating costs of $9,000. The new machine will cost $24,000 cash, installed. The "old" machine is unique and can be sold outright for only $10,000, minus $2,000 removal cost. The new machine, like the old one, will have a four-year useful life and zero terminal disposal value.

Revenues, all in cash, will be $150,000 annually, and other cash costs will be $110,000 annually, regardless of this decision.

For simplicity, ignore income taxes and the time value of money.

Required

1. a. Prepare a statement of cash receipts and disbursements for each of the four years under each alternative. What is the cumulative difference in cash flow for the four years taken together?

b. Prepare income statements for each of the four years under each alternative. Assume straight-line depreciation. What is the cumulative difference in operating income for the four years taken together?

c. What are the irrelevant items in your presentations in requirements a and b? Why are they irrelevant?

2. Suppose the cost of the "old" machine was $1 million rather than $20,000. Nevertheless, the old machine can be sold outright for only $10,000, minus $2,000 removal cost. Would the net differences in requirements 1a and 1b change? Explain.

3. Is there any conflict between the decision model and the incentives of the manager who has just purchased the "old" machine and is considering replacing it a day later?

11-28 Equipment upgrade versus replacement. (A. Spero, adapted) The TechGuide Company produces and sells 7,500 modular computer desks per year at a selling price of $750 each. Its current production equipment, purchased for $1,800,000 and with a five-year useful life, is only two years old. It has a terminal disposal value of $0 and is depreciated on a straight-line basis. The equipment has a current disposal price of $450,000. However, the emergence of a new molding technology has led TechGuide to consider either upgrading or replacing the production equipment. The following table presents data for the two alternatives:

	Home	Insert	Page Layout	Formulas	Data	Review
	A				B	C
1					**Upgrade**	**Replace**
2	One-time equipment costs				$3,000,000	$4,800,000
3	Variable manufacturing cost per desk				$ 150	$ 75
4	Remaining useful life of equipment (years)				3	3
5	Terminal disposal value of equipment				$ 0	$ 0

All equipment costs will continue to be depreciated on a straight-line basis. For simplicity, ignore income taxes and the time value of money.

Required

1. Should TechGuide upgrade its production line or replace it? Show your calculations.

2. Now suppose the one-time equipment cost to replace the production equipment is somewhat negotiable. All other data are as given previously. What is the maximum one-time equipment cost that TechGuide would be willing to pay to replace the old equipment rather than upgrade it?

3. Assume that the capital expenditures to replace and upgrade the production equipment are as given in the original exercise, but that the production and sales quantity is not known. For what production and sales quantity would TechGuide (i) upgrade the equipment or (ii) replace the equipment?

4. Assume that all data are as given in the original exercise. Dan Doria is TechGuide's manager, and his bonus is based on operating income. Because he is likely to relocate after about a year, his current bonus is his primary concern. Which alternative would Doria choose? Explain.

MyAccountingLab

Problems

11-29 Special Order. Louisville Corporation produces baseball bats for kids that it sells for $32 each. At capacity, the company can produce 50,000 bats a year. The costs of producing and selling 50,000 bats are as follows:

	Cost per Bat	Total Costs
Direct materials	$12	$ 600,000
Direct manufacturing labor	3	150,000
Variable manufacturing overhead	1	50,000
Fixed manufacturing overhead	5	250,000
Variable selling expenses	2	100,000
Fixed selling expenses	4	200,000
Total costs	$27	$1,350,000

Required

1. Suppose Louisville is currently producing and selling 40,000 bats. At this level of production and sales, its fixed costs are the same as given in the preceding table. Ripkin Corporation wants to place a one-time special order for 10,000 bats at $25 each. Louisville will incur no variable selling costs for this special order. Should Louisville accept this one-time special order? Show your calculations.

2. Now suppose Louisville is currently producing and selling 50,000 bats. If Louisville accepts Ripkin's offer it will have to sell 10,000 fewer bats to its regular customers. (a) On financial considerations alone, should Louisville accept this one-time special order? Show your calculations. (b) On financial considerations alone, at what price would Louisville be indifferent between accepting the special order and continuing to sell to its regular customers at $32 per bat. (c) What other factors should Louisville consider in deciding whether to accept the one-time special order?

11-30 International outsourcing. Bernie's Bears, Inc., manufactures plush toys in a facility in Cleveland, Ohio. Recently, the company designed a group of collectible resin figurines to go with the plush toy line. Management is trying to decide whether to manufacture the figurines themselves in existing space in the Cleveland facility or to accept an offer from a manufacturing company in Indonesia. Data concerning the decision follows:

Expected annual sales of figurines (in units)	400,000
Average selling price of a figurine	$5
Price quoted by Indonesian company, in Indonesian Rupiah (IDR), for each figurine	27,300 IDR
Current exchange rate	9,100 IDR = $1
Variable manufacturing costs	$2.85 per unit
Incremental annual fixed manufacturing costs associated with the new product line	$200,000
Variable selling and distribution costs[a]	$0.50 per unit
Annual fixed selling and distribution costs[a]	$285,000

[a] Selling and distribution costs are the same regardless of whether the figurines are manufactured in Cleveland or imported.

Required

1. Should Bernie's Bears manufacture the 400,000 figurines in the Cleveland facility or purchase them from the Indonesian supplier? Explain.
2. Bernie's Bears believes that the US dollar may weaken in the coming months against the Indonesian Rupiah and does not want to face any currency risk. Assume that Bernie's Bears can enter into a forward contract today to purchase 27,300 IDRs for $3.40. Should Bernie's Bears manufacture the 400,000 figurines in the Cleveland facility or purchase them from the Indonesian supplier? Explain.
3. What are some of the qualitative factors that Bernie's Bears should consider when deciding whether to outsource the figurine manufacturing to Indonesia?

11-31 Relevant costs, opportunity costs. Larry Miller, the general manager of Basil Software, must decide when to release the new version of Basil's spreadsheet package, Easyspread 2.0. Development of Easyspread 2.0 is complete; however, the diskettes, compact discs, and user manuals have not yet been produced. The product can be shipped starting July 1, 2011.

The major problem is that Basil has overstocked the previous version of its spreadsheet package, Easyspread 1.0. Miller knows that once Easyspread 2.0 is introduced, Basil will not be able to sell any more units of Easyspread 1.0. Rather than just throwing away the inventory of Easyspread 1.0, Miller is wondering if it might be better to continue to sell Easyspread 1.0 for the next three months and introduce Easyspread 2.0 on October 1, 2011, when the inventory of Easyspread 1.0 will be sold out.

The following information is available:

	Easyspread 1.0	Easyspread 2.0
Selling price	$160	$195
Variable cost per unit of diskettes, compact discs, user manuals	25	30
Development cost per unit	70	100
Marketing and administrative cost per unit	35	40
Total cost per unit	130	170
Operating income per unit	$ 30	$ 25

Development cost per unit for each product equals the total costs of developing the software product divided by the anticipated unit sales over the life of the product. Marketing and administrative costs are fixed costs in 2011, incurred to support all marketing and administrative activities of Basil Software. Marketing and administrative costs are allocated to products on the basis of the budgeted revenues of each product. The preceding unit costs assume Easyspread 2.0 will be introduced on October 1, 2011.

Required

1. On the basis of financial considerations alone, should Miller introduce Easyspread 2.0 on July 1, 2011, or wait until October 1, 2011? Show your calculations, clearly identifying relevant and irrelevant revenues and costs.
2. What other factors might Larry Miller consider in making a decision?

11-32 Opportunity costs. (H. Schaefer) The Wild Boar Corporation is working at full production capacity producing 13,000 units of a unique product, Rosebo. Manufacturing cost per unit for Rosebo is as follows:

Direct materials	$ 5
Direct manufacturing labor	1
Manufacturing overhead	7
Total manufacturing cost	$13

Manufacturing overhead cost per unit is based on variable cost per unit of $4 and fixed costs of $39,000 (at full capacity of 13,000 units). Marketing cost per unit, all variable, is $2, and the selling price is $26.

A customer, the Miami Company, has asked Wild Boar to produce 3,500 units of Orangebo, a modification of Rosebo. Orangebo would require the same manufacturing processes as Rosebo. Miami has offered to pay Wild Boar $20 for a unit of Orangebo and share half of the marketing cost per unit.

Required

1. What is the opportunity cost to Wild Boar of producing the 3,500 units of Orangebo? (Assume that no overtime is worked.)
2. The Buckeye Corporation has offered to produce 3,500 units of Rosebo for Wild Boar so that Wild Boar may accept the Miami offer. That is, if Wild Boar accepts the Buckeye offer, Wild Boar would manufacture 9,500 units of Rosebo and 3,500 units of Orangebo and purchase 3,500 units of Rosebo from Buckeye. Buckeye would charge Wild Boar $18 per unit to manufacture Rosebo. On the basis of financial considerations alone, should Wild Boar accept the Buckeye offer? Show your calculations.
3. Suppose Wild Boar had been working at less than full capacity, producing 9,500 units of Rosebo at the time the Miami offer was made. Calculate the minimum price Wild Boar should accept for Orangebo under these conditions. (Ignore the previous $20 selling price.)

11-33 Product mix, special order. (N. Melumad, adapted) Pendleton Engineering makes cutting tools for metalworking operations. It makes two types of tools: R3, a regular cutting tool, and HP6, a high-precision cutting tool. R3 is manufactured on a regular machine, but HP6 must be manufactured on both the regular machine and a high-precision machine. The following information is available.

	R3	HP6
Selling price	$ 100	$ 150
Variable manufacturing cost per unit	$ 60	$ 100
Variable marketing cost per unit	$ 15	$ 35
Budgeted total fixed overhead costs	$350,000	$550,000
Hours required to produce one unit on the regular machine	1.0	0.5

Additional information includes the following:

a. Pendleton faces a capacity constraint on the regular machine of 50,000 hours per year.
b. The capacity of the high-precision machine is not a constraint.
c. Of the $550,000 budgeted fixed overhead costs of HP6, $300,000 are lease payments for the high-precision machine. This cost is charged entirely to HP6 because Pendleton uses the machine exclusively to produce HP6. The lease agreement for the high-precision machine can be canceled at any time without penalties.
d. All other overhead costs are fixed and cannot be changed.

Required

1. What product mix—that is, how many units of R3 and HP6—will maximize Pendleton's operating income? Show your calculations.
2. Suppose Pendleton can increase the annual capacity of its regular machines by 15,000 machine-hours at a cost of $150,000. Should Pendleton increase the capacity of the regular machines by 15,000 machine-hours? By how much will Pendleton's operating income increase? Show your calculations.
3. Suppose that the capacity of the regular machines has been increased to 65,000 hours. Pendleton has been approached by Carter Corporation to supply 20,000 units of another cutting tool, S3, for $120 per unit. Pendleton must either accept the order for all 20,000 units or reject it totally. S3 is exactly like R3 except that its variable manufacturing cost is $70 per unit. (It takes one hour to produce one unit of S3 on the regular machine, and variable marketing cost equals $15 per unit.) What product mix should Pendleton choose to maximize operating income? Show your calculations.

11-34 Dropping a product line, selling more units. The Northern Division of Grossman Corporation makes and sells tables and beds. The following estimated revenue and cost information from the division's activity-based costing system is available for 2011.

	4,000 Tables	5,000 Beds	Total
Revenues ($125 × 4,000; $200 × 5,000)	$500,000	$1,000,000	$1,500,000
Variable direct materials and direct manufacturing labor costs ($75 × 4,000; $105 × 5,000)	300,000	525,000	825,000
Depreciation on equipment used exclusively by each product line	42,000	58,000	100,000
Marketing and distribution costs $40,000 (fixed) + ($750 per shipment × 40 shipments)	70,000		
$60,000 (fixed) + ($750 per shipment × 100 shipments)		135,000 }	205,000
Fixed general-administration costs of the division allocated to product lines on the basis of revenue	110,000	220,000	330,000
Corporate-office costs allocated to product lines on the basis of revenues	50,000	100,000	150,000
Total costs	572,000	1,038,000	1,610,000
Operating income (loss)	$(72,000)	$ (38,000)	$ (110,000)

Additional information includes the following:

   a. On January 1, 2011, the equipment has a book value of $100,000, a one-year useful life, and zero disposal value. Any equipment not used will remain idle.
   b. Fixed marketing and distribution costs of a product line can be avoided if the line is discontinued.
   c. Fixed general-administration costs of the division and corporate-office costs will not change if sales of individual product lines are increased or decreased or if product lines are added or dropped.

Required

   1. On the basis of financial considerations alone, should the Northern Division discontinue the tables product line for the year, assuming the released facilities remain idle? Show your calculations.
   2. What would be the effect on the Northern Division's operating income if it were to sell 4,000 more tables? Assume that to do so the division would have to acquire additional equipment costing $42,000 with a one-year useful life and zero terminal disposal value. Assume further that the fixed marketing and distribution costs would not change but that the number of shipments would double. Show your calculations.
   3. Given the Northern Division's expected operating loss of $110,000, should Grossman Corporation shut it down for the year? Assume that shutting down the Northern Division will have no effect on corporate-office costs but will lead to savings of all general-administration costs of the division. Show your calculations.
   4. Suppose Grossman Corporation has the opportunity to open another division, the Southern Division, whose revenues and costs are expected to be identical to the Northern Division's revenues and costs (including a cost of $100,000 to acquire equipment with a one-year useful life and zero terminal disposal value). Opening the new division will have no effect on corporate-office costs. Should Grossman open the Southern Division? Show your calculations.

11-35 Make or buy, unknown level of volume. (A. Atkinson) Oxford Engineering manufactures small engines. The engines are sold to manufacturers who install them in such products as lawn mowers. The company currently manufactures all the parts used in these engines but is considering a proposal from an external supplier who wishes to supply the starter assemblies used in these engines.

The starter assemblies are currently manufactured in Division 3 of Oxford Engineering. The costs relating to the starter assemblies for the past 12 months were as follows:

Direct materials	$200,000
Direct manufacturing labor	150,000
Manufacturing overhead	400,000
Total	$750,000

Over the past year, Division 3 manufactured 150,000 starter assemblies. The average cost for each starter assembly is $5 ($750,000 ÷ 150,000).

Further analysis of manufacturing overhead revealed the following information. Of the total manufacturing overhead, only 25% is considered variable. Of the fixed portion, $150,000 is an allocation of general overhead that will remain unchanged for the company as a whole if production of the starter assemblies is discontinued. A further $100,000 of the fixed overhead is avoidable if production of the starter assemblies is discontinued. The balance of the current fixed overhead, $50,000, is the division manager's salary. If production of the starter assemblies is discontinued, the manager of Division 3 will be transferred to Division 2 at the same salary. This move will allow the company to save the $40,000 salary that would otherwise be paid to attract an outsider to this position.

Required

1. Tidnish Electronics, a reliable supplier, has offered to supply starter-assembly units at $4 per unit. Because this price is less than the current average cost of $5 per unit, the vice president of manufacturing is eager to accept this offer. On the basis of financial considerations alone, should the outside offer be accepted? Show your calculations. (*Hint:* Production output in the coming year may be different from production output in the past year.)

2. How, if at all, would your response to requirement 1 change if the company could use the vacated plant space for storage and, in so doing, avoid $50,000 of outside storage charges currently incurred? Why is this information relevant or irrelevant?

11-36 **Make versus buy, activity-based costing, opportunity costs.** The Weaver Company produces gas grills. This year's expected production is 20,000 units. Currently, Weaver makes the side burners for its grills. Each grill includes two side burners. Weaver's management accountant reports the following costs for making the 40,000 burners:

	Cost per Unit	Costs for 40,000 Units
Direct materials	$5.00	$200,000
Direct manufacturing labor	2.50	100,000
Variable manufacturing overhead	1.25	50,000
Inspection, setup, materials handling		4,000
Machine rent		8,000
Allocated fixed costs of plant administration, taxes, and insurance		50,000
Total costs		$412,000

Weaver has received an offer from an outside vendor to supply any number of burners Weaver requires at $9.25 per burner. The following additional information is available:

a. Inspection, setup, and materials-handling costs vary with the number of batches in which the burners are produced. Weaver produces burners in batch sizes of 1,000 units. Weaver will produce the 40,000 units in 40 batches.

b. Weaver rents the machine used to make the burners. If Weaver buys all of its burners from the outside vendor, it does not need to pay rent on this machine.

Required

1. Assume that if Weaver purchases the burners from the outside vendor, the facility where the burners are currently made will remain idle. On the basis of financial considerations alone, should Weaver accept the outside vendor's offer at the anticipated volume of 40,000 burners? Show your calculations.

2. For this question, assume that if the burners are purchased outside, the facilities where the burners are currently made will be used to upgrade the grills by adding a rotisserie attachment. (Note: Each grill contains two burners and one rotisserie attachment.) As a consequence, the selling price of grills will be raised by $30. The variable cost per unit of the upgrade would be $24, and additional tooling costs of $100,000 per year would be incurred. On the basis of financial considerations alone, should Weaver make or buy the burners, assuming that 20,000 grills are produced (and sold)? Show your calculations.

3. The sales manager at Weaver is concerned that the estimate of 20,000 grills may be high and believes that only 16,000 grills will be sold. Production will be cut back, freeing up work space. This space can be used to add the rotisserie attachments whether Weaver buys the burners or makes them in-house. At this lower output, Weaver will produce the burners in 32 batches of 1,000 units each. On the basis of financial considerations alone, should Weaver purchase the burners from the outside vendor? Show your calculations.

11-37 **Multiple choice, comprehensive problem on relevant costs.** The following are the Class Company's unit costs of manufacturing and marketing a high-style pen at an output level of 20,000 units per month:

Manufacturing cost	
Direct materials	$1.00
Direct manufacturing labor	1.20
Variable manufacturing overhead cost	0.80
Fixed manufacturing overhead cost	0.50
Marketing cost	
Variable	1.50
Fixed	0.90

Required

The following situations refer only to the preceding data; there is *no connection* between the situations. Unless stated otherwise, assume a regular selling price of $6 per unit. Choose the best answer to each question. Show your calculations.

1. For an inventory of 10,000 units of the high-style pen presented in the balance sheet, the appropriate unit cost to use is (a) $3.00, (b) $3.50, (c) $5.00, (d) $2.20, or (e) $5.90.

2. The pen is usually produced and sold at the rate of 240,000 units per year (an average of 20,000 per month). The selling price is $6 per unit, which yields total annual revenues of $1,440,000. Total costs are $1,416,000, and operating income is $24,000, or $0.10 per unit. Market research estimates that unit sales could be increased by 10% if prices were cut to $5.80. Assuming the implied cost-behavior patterns continue, this action, if taken, would

   a. decrease operating income by $7,200.

   b. decrease operating income by $0.20 per unit ($48,000) but increase operating income by 10% of revenues ($144,000), for a net increase of $96,000.

   c. decrease fixed cost per unit by 10%, or $0.14, per unit, and thus decrease operating income by $0.06 ($0.20 − $0.14) per unit.

   d. increase unit sales to 264,000 units, which at the $5.80 price would give total revenues of $1,531,200 and lead to costs of $5.90 per unit for 264,000 units, which would equal $1,557,600, and result in an operating loss of $26,400.

   e. None of these

3. A contract with the government for 5,000 units of the pens calls for the reimbursement of all manufacturing costs plus a fixed fee of $1,000. No variable marketing costs are incurred on the government contract. You are asked to compare the following two alternatives:

Sales Each Month to	Alternative A	Alternative B
Regular customers	15,000 units	15,000 units
Government	0 units	5,000 units

   Operating income under alternative B is greater than that under alternative A by (a) $1,000, (b) $2,500, (c) $3,500, (d) $300, or (e) none of these.

4. Assume the same data with respect to the government contract as in requirement 3 except that the two alternatives to be compared are as follows:

Sales Each Month to	Alternative A	Alternative B
Regular customers	20,000 units	15,000 units
Government	0 units	5,000 units

   Operating income under alternative B relative to that under alternative A is (a) $4,000 less, (b) $3,000 greater, (c) $6,500 less, (d) $500 greater, or (e) none of these.

5. The company wants to enter a foreign market in which price competition is keen. The company seeks a one-time-only special order for 10,000 units on a minimum-unit-price basis. It expects that shipping costs for this order will amount to only $0.75 per unit, but the fixed costs of obtaining the contract will be $4,000. The company incurs no variable marketing costs other than shipping costs. Domestic business will be unaffected. The selling price to break even is (a) $3.50, (b) $4.15, (c) $4.25, (d) $3.00, or (e) $5.00.

6. The company has an inventory of 1,000 units of pens that must be sold immediately at reduced prices. Otherwise, the inventory will become worthless. The unit cost that is relevant for establishing the minimum selling price is (a) $4.50, (b) $4.00, (c) $3.00, (d) $5.90, or (e) $1.50.

7. A proposal is received from an outside supplier who will make and ship the high-style pens directly to the Class Company's customers as sales orders are forwarded from Class's sales staff. Class's fixed marketing costs will be unaffected, but its variable marketing costs will be slashed by 20%. Class's plant will be idle, but its fixed manufacturing overhead will continue at 50% of present levels. How much per unit would the company be able to pay the supplier without decreasing operating income? (a) $4.75, (b) $3.95, (c) $2.95, (d) $5.35, or (e) none of these.

11-38 Closing down divisions. Belmont Corporation has four operating divisions. The budgeted revenues and expenses for each division for 2011 follows:

	Division			
	A	**B**	**C**	**D**
Sales	$630,000	$ 632,000	$960,000	$1,240,000
Cost of goods sold	550,000	620,000	765,000	925,000
Selling, general, and administrative expenses	120,000	135,000	144,000	210,000
Operating income/loss	$ (40,000)	$(123,000)	$ 51,000	$ 105,000

Further analysis of costs reveals the following percentages of variable costs in each division:

Cost of goods sold	90%	80%	90%	85%
Selling, general, and administrative expenses	50%	50%	60%	60%

Closing down any division would result in savings of 40% of the fixed costs of that division.

Top management is very concerned about the unprofitable divisions (A and B) and is considering closing them for the year.

Required

1. Calculate the increase or decrease in operating income if Belmont closes division A.
2. Calculate the increase or decrease in operating income if Belmont closes division B.
3. What other factors should the top management of Belmont consider before making a decision?

11-39 Product mix, constrained resource. Westford Company produces three products, A110, B382, and C657. Unit data for the three products follows:

	Product		
	A110	**B382**	**C657**
Selling price	$84	$56	70
Variable costs			
Direct materials	24	15	9
Labor and other costs	28	27	40
Quantity of Bistide per unit	8 lb.	5 lb.	3 lb.

All three products use the same direct material, Bistide. The demand for the products far exceeds the direct materials available to produce the products. Bistide costs $3 per pound and a maximum of 5,000 pounds is available each month. Westford must produce a minimum of 200 units of each product.

Required

1. How many units of product A110, B382, and C657 should Westford produce?
2. What is the maximum amount Westford would be willing to pay for another 1,000 pounds of Bistide?

11-40 Optimal product mix. (CMA adapted) Della Simpson, Inc., sells two popular brands of cookies: Della's Delight and Bonny's Bourbon. Della's Delight goes through the Mixing and Baking departments, and Bonny's Bourbon, a filled cookie, goes through the Mixing, Filling, and Baking departments.

Michael Shirra, vice president for sales, believes that at the current price, Della Simpson can sell all of its daily production of Della's Delight and Bonny's Bourbon. Both cookies are made in batches of 3,000. In each department, the time required per batch and the total time available each day are as follows:

	A	B	C	D
		Home Insert Page Layout Formulas Data Review		
1		**Department Minutes**		
2		**Mixing**	**Filling**	**Baking**
3	Della's Delight	30	0	10
4	Bonny's Bourbon	15	15	15
5	Total available per day	660	270	300

Revenue and cost data for each type of cookie are as follows:

	A	B	C
		Home Insert Page Layout Formulas Data	
7		**Della's**	**Bonny's**
8		**Delight**	**Bourbon**
9	Revenue per batch	$ 475	$ 375
10	Variable cost per batch	175	125
11	Contribution margin per batch	$ 300	$ 250
12	Monthly fixed costs		
13	(allocated to each product)	$18,650	$22,350

Required

1. Using D to represent the batches of Della's Delight and B to represent the batches of Bonny's Bourbon made and sold each day, formulate Shirra's decision as an LP model.
2. Compute the optimal number of batches of each type of cookie that Della Simpson, Inc., should make and sell each day to maximize operating income.

11-41 Dropping a customer, activity-based costing, ethics. Jack Arnoldson is the management accountant for Valley Restaurant Supply (VRS). Bob Gardner, the VRS sales manager, and Jack are meeting to discuss the profitability of one of the customers, Franco's Pizza. Jack hands Bob the following analysis of Franco's activity during the last quarter, taken from Valley's activity-based costing system:

Sales	$15,600
Cost of goods sold (all variable)	9,350
Order processing (25 orders processed at $200 per order)	5,000
Delivery (2,500 miles driven at $0.50 per mile)	1,250
Rush orders (3 rush orders at $110 per rush order)	330
Sales calls (3 sales calls at $100 per call)	300
Profits	($ 630)

Bob looks at the report and remarks, "I'm glad to see all my hard work is paying off with Franco's. Sales have gone up 10% over the previous quarter!"

Jack replies, "Increased sales are great, but I'm worried about Franco's margin, Bob. We were showing a profit with Franco's at the lower sales level, but now we're showing a loss. Gross margin percentage this quarter was 40%, down five percentage points from the prior quarter. I'm afraid that corporate will push hard to drop them as a customer if things don't turn around."

"That's crazy," Bob responds. "A lot of that overhead for things like order processing, deliveries, and sales calls would just be allocated to other customers if we dropped Franco's. This report makes it look like we're losing money on Franco's when we're not. In any case, I am sure you can do something to make its profitability look closer to what we think it is. No one doubts that Franco is a very good customer."

Required

1. Assume that Bob is partly correct in his assessment of the report. Upon further investigation, it is determined that 10% of the order processing costs and 20% of the delivery costs would not be avoidable if VRS were to drop Franco's. Would VRS benefit from dropping Franco's? Show your calculations.
2. Bob's bonus is based on meeting sales targets. Based on the preceding information regarding gross margin percentage, what might Bob have done last quarter to meet his target and receive his bonus? How might VRS revise its bonus system to address this?
3. Should Jack rework the numbers? How should he respond to Bob's comments about making Franco look more profitable?

Collaborative Learning Problem

11-42 Equipment replacement decisions and performance evaluation. Bob Moody manages the Knoxville plant of George Manufacturing. He has been approached by a representative of Darda Engineering regarding the possible replacement of a large piece of manufacturing equipment that George uses in its process with a more efficient model. While the representative made some compelling arguments in favor of replacing the 3-year old equipment, Moody is hesitant. Moody is hoping to be promoted next year to manager of the larger Chicago plant, and he knows that the accrual-basis net operating income of the Knoxville plant will be evaluated closely as part of the promotion decision. The following information is available concerning the equipment replacement decision:

■ The historic cost of the old machine is $300,000. It has a current book value of $120,000, two remaining years of useful life, and a market value of $72,000. Annual depreciation expense is $60,000. It is expected to have a salvage value of $0 at the end of its useful life.

■ The new equipment will cost $180,000. It will have a two-year useful life and a $0 salvage value. George uses straight-line depreciation on all equipment.

■ The new equipment will reduce electricity costs by $35,000 per year, and will reduce direct manufacturing labor costs by $30,000 per year.

For simplicity, ignore income taxes and the time value of money.

Required

1. Assume that Moody's priority is to receive the promotion, and he makes the equipment replacement decision based on next year's accrual-based net operating income. Which alternative would he choose? Show your calculations.
2. What are the relevant factors in the decision? Which alternative is in the best interest of the company over the next two years? Show your calculations.
3. At what cost of the new equipment would Moody be willing to purchase it? Explain.

17 Process Costing

17 Process Costing

Learning Objectives

1. Identify the situations in which process-costing systems are appropriate

2. Understand the basic concepts of process-costing and compute average unit costs

3. Describe the five steps in process costing and calculate equivalent units

4. Use the weighted-average method and first-in, first-out (FIFO) method of process costing

5. Apply process-costing methods to situations with transferred-in costs

6. Understand the need for hybrid-costing systems such as operation-costing

Companies that produce identical or similar units of a product or service (for example, an oil-refining company) often use process costing.

A key part of process costing is valuing inventory, which entails determining how many units of the product the firm has on hand at the end of an accounting reporting period, evaluating the units' stages of completion, and assigning costs to the units. There are different methods for doing this, each of which can result in different profits. At times, variations in international rules and customs make it difficult to compare inventory costs across competitors. In the case of ExxonMobil, differences in accounting rules between the United States and Europe also reduce the company's profits and tax liability.

ExxonMobil and Accounting Differences in the Oil Patch[1]

In 2010, ExxonMobil was number two on the *Fortune* 500 annual ranking of the largest U.S. companies. In 2009, the company had $284 billion dollars in revenue with more than $19 billion in profits. Believe it or not, however, by one measure ExxonMobil's profits are *understated*.

ExxonMobil, like most U.S. energy companies, uses last-in, first-out (LIFO) accounting. Under this treatment, ExxonMobil records its cost of inventory at the latest price paid for crude oil in the open market, even though it is often selling oil produced at a much lower cost. This increases the company's cost of goods sold, which in turn reduces profit. The benefit of using LIFO accounting for financial reporting is that ExxonMobil is then permitted to use LIFO for tax purposes as well, thereby lowering its payments to the tax authorities.

In contrast, International Financial Reporting Standards (IFRS) do not permit the use of LIFO accounting. European oil companies such as Royal Dutch Shell and British Petroleum use the first-in, first-out (FIFO) methodology instead when accounting for inventory. Under FIFO, oil companies use the cost of the oldest crude in their inventory to calculate the cost of barrels of oil sold. This reduces costs on the income statement, therefore increasing gross margins.

Assigning costs to inventory is a critical part of process costing, and a company's choice of method can result in substantially different

---

[1] *Source:* Exxon Mobil Corporation. 2010. 2009 Annual Report. Irving, TX: Exxon Mobil Corporation; Kaminska, Izabella. 2010. Shell, BP, and the increasing cost of inventory. *Financial Times.* "FT Alphaville" blog, April 29; Reilly, David. 2006. Big oil's accounting methods fuel criticism. *Wall Street Journal,* August 8.

profits. For instance, ExxonMobil's 2009 net income would have been $7.1 billion higher under FIFO. Moreover, at the end of fiscal 2009, the cumulative difference—or "LIFO Reserve"—between the value of inventory ExxonMobil was carrying on its balance sheet based on the initial cost versus the current replacement cost of that inventory was $17.1 billion. This number takes on special relevance in the context of current efforts to achieve convergence between U.S. GAAP and IFRS. Should that happen, and if U.S. firms are forced to adopt FIFO for financial and tax reporting, they would have to pay additional taxes on the cumulative savings to date from showing a higher cost of goods sold in LIFO. As an approximation, applying a marginal tax rate of 35% to ExxonMobil's LIFO Reserve of $17.1 billion suggests an incremental tax burden of almost $6 billion.

Companies such as ExxonMobil, Coca-Cola, and Novartis produce many identical or similar units of a product using mass-production techniques. The focus of these companies on individual production processes gives rise to process costing. This chapter describes how companies use process costing methods to determine the costs of products or services and to value inventory and cost of goods sold (using methods like FIFO).

Illustrating Process Costing

Before we examine process costing in more detail, let's briefly compare job costing and process costing. Job-costing and process-costing systems are best viewed as ends of a continuum:

Job-costing system	Process-costing system
Distinct, identifiable units of a product or service (for example, custom-made machines and houses)	Masses of identical or similar units of a product or service (for example, food or chemical processing)

In a *process-costing system*, the unit cost of a product or service is obtained by assigning total costs to many identical or similar units of output. In other words, unit costs are calculated by dividing total costs incurred by the number of units of output from the production process. In a manufacturing process-costing setting, each unit receives the same or similar amounts of direct material costs, direct manufacturing labor costs, and indirect manufacturing costs (manufacturing overhead).

The main difference between process costing and job costing is the *extent of averaging* used to compute unit costs of products or services. In a job-costing system, individual jobs use different quantities of production resources, so it would be incorrect to cost each job at the same average production cost. In contrast, when identical or similar units of products or services are mass-produced, not processed as individual jobs, process costing is used to calculate an average production cost for all units produced. Some processes such as clothes manufacturing have aspects of both process costing (cost per unit of each operation, such as cutting or sewing, is identical) and job costing (different materials are used in different batches of clothing, say, wool versus cotton). The final section in this chapter describes "hybrid" costing systems that combine elements of both job and process costing.

Consider the following illustration of process costing: Suppose that Pacific Electronics manufactures a variety of cell phone models. These models are assembled in the assembly department. Upon completion, units are transferred to the testing department. We focus on the assembly department process for one model, SG-40. All units of SG-40 are identical and must meet a set of demanding performance specifications. The process-costing system for SG-40 in the assembly department has a single direct-cost category—direct materials— and a single indirect-cost category—conversion costs. Conversion costs are all manufacturing costs other than direct material costs, including manufacturing labor, energy, plant depreciation, and so on. Direct materials are added at the beginning of the assembly process. Conversion costs are added evenly during assembly.

The following graphic represents these facts:

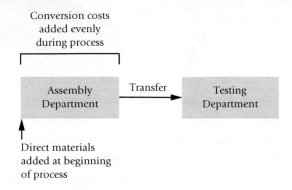

Process-costing systems separate costs into cost categories according to *when costs are introduced into the process*. Often, as in our Pacific Electronics example, only two cost classifications—direct materials and conversion costs—are necessary to assign costs to products. Why only two? Because *all* direct materials are added to the process at one time and all conversion costs generally are added to the process evenly through time. If, however, two different direct materials were added to the process at different times, two different direct-materials categories would be needed to assign these costs to products. Similarly, if manufacturing labor costs were added to the process at a different time from when the other conversion costs were added, an additional cost category—direct manufacturing labor costs—would be needed to separately assign these costs to products.

We will use the production of the SG-40 component in the assembly department to illustrate process costing in three cases, starting with the simplest case and introducing additional complexities in subsequent cases:

- Case 1—Process costing with zero beginning and zero ending work-in-process inventory of SG-40. (That is, all units are started and fully completed within the accounting period.) *This case presents the most basic concepts of process costing and illustrates the feature of averaging of costs.*

- Case 2—Process costing with zero beginning work-in-process inventory and some ending work-in-process inventory of SG-40. (That is, some units of SG-40 started during the accounting period are incomplete at the end of the period.) *This case introduces the five steps of process costing and the concept of equivalent units.*

- Case 3—Process costing with both some beginning and some ending work-in-process inventory of SG-40. *This case adds more complexity and illustrates the effect of weighted-average and first-in, first-out (FIFO) cost flow assumptions on cost of units completed and cost of work-in-process inventory.*

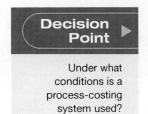

Under what conditions is a process-costing system used?

Case 1: Process Costing with No Beginning or Ending Work-in-Process Inventory

On January 1, 2012, there was no beginning inventory of SG-40 units in the assembly department. During the month of January, Pacific Electronics started, completely assembled, and transferred out to the testing department 400 units.

Data for the assembly department for January 2012 are as follows:

Physical Units for January 2012

Work in process, beginning inventory (January 1)	0 units
Started during January	400 units
Completed and transferred out during January	400 units
Work in process, ending inventory (January 31)	0 units

Learning Objective 2

Understand the basic concepts of process-costing and compute average unit costs

... divide total costs by total units in a given accounting period

Physical units refer to the number of output units, whether complete or incomplete. In January 2012, all 400 physical units started were completed.

Total Costs for January 2012

Direct material costs added during January	$32,000
Conversion costs added during January	24,000
Total assembly department costs added during January	$56,000

Pacific Electronics records direct material costs and conversion costs in the assembly department as these costs are incurred. By averaging, assembly cost of SG-40 is $56,000 ÷ 400 units = $140 per unit, itemized as follows:

Direct material cost per unit ($32,000 ÷ 400 units)	$ 80
Conversion cost per unit ($24,000 ÷ 400 units)	60
Assembly department cost per unit	$140

Case 1 shows that in a process-costing system, average unit costs are calculated by dividing total costs in a given accounting period by total units produced in that period. Because each unit is identical, we assume all units receive the same amount of direct material costs and conversion costs. Case 1 applies whenever a company produces a homogeneous product or service but has no incomplete units when each accounting period ends, which is a common situation in service-sector organizations. For example, a bank can adopt this process-costing approach to compute the unit cost of processing 100,000 customer deposits, each similar to the other, made in a month.

◄ **Decision Point**

How are average unit costs computed when no inventories are present?

Case 2: Process Costing with Zero Beginning and Some Ending Work-in-Process Inventory

In February 2012, Pacific Electronics places another 400 units of SG-40 into production. Because all units placed into production in January were completely assembled, there is no beginning inventory of partially completed units in the assembly department on February 1. Some customers order late, so not all units started in February are completed by the end of the month. Only 175 units are completed and transferred to the testing department.

Data for the assembly department for February 2012 are as follows:

	Home	Insert	Page Layout	Formulas	Data	Review	View			
			A				B	C	D	E
1							Physical Units (SG-40s) (1)	Direct Materials (2)	Conversion Costs (3)	Total Costs (4) = (2) + (3)
2	Work in process, beginning inventory (February 1)						0			
3	Started during February						400			
4	Completed and transferred out during February						175			
5	Work in process, ending inventory (February 29)						225			
6	Degree of completion of ending work in process							100%	60%	
7	Total costs added during February							$32,000	$18,600	$50,600

The 225 partially assembled units as of February 29, 2012, are fully processed with respect to direct materials, because all direct materials in the assembly department are added at the beginning of the assembly process. Conversion costs, however, are added evenly during assembly. Based on the work completed relative to the total work required

**Learning
Objective 3**

Describe the five steps
in process costing

. . . to assign total
costs to units completed
and to units in work
in process

and calculate
equivalent units

. . . output units adjusted
for incomplete units

to complete the SG-40 units still in process at the end of February, an assembly department supervisor estimates that the partially assembled units are, on average, 60% complete with respect to conversion costs.

The accuracy of the completion estimate of conversion costs depends on the care, skill, and experience of the estimator and the nature of the conversion process. Estimating the degree of completion is usually easier for direct material costs than for conversion costs, because the quantity of direct materials needed for a completed unit and the quantity of direct materials in a partially completed unit can be measured more accurately. In contrast, the conversion sequence usually consists of a number of operations, each for a specified period of time, at various steps in the production process.[2] The degree of completion for conversion costs depends on the proportion of the total conversion costs needed to complete one unit (or a batch of production) that has already been incurred on the units still in process. It is a challenge for management accountants to make this estimate accurately.

Because of these uncertainties, department supervisors and line managers—individuals most familiar with the process—often make conversion cost estimates. Still, in some industries, such as semiconductor manufacturing, no exact estimate is possible; in other settings, such as the textile industry, vast quantities in process make the task of estimation too costly. In these cases, it is necessary to assume that all work in process in a department is complete to some preset degree with respect to conversion costs (for example, one-third, one-half, or two-thirds complete).

The point to understand here is that a partially assembled unit is not the same as a fully assembled unit. Faced with some fully assembled units and some partially assembled units, we require a common metric that will enable us to compare the work done in each category and, more important, obtain a total measure of work done. The concept we will use in this regard is that of *equivalent units*. We will explain this notion in greater detail next as part of the set of five steps required to calculate (1) the cost of fully assembled units in February 2012 and (2) the cost of partially assembled units still in process at the end of that month, for Pacific Electronics. The five steps of process costing are as follows:

Step 1: Summarize the flow of physical units of output.

Step 2: Compute output in terms of equivalent units.

Step 3: Summarize total costs to account for.

Step 4: Compute cost per equivalent unit.

Step 5: Assign total costs to units completed and to units in ending work in process.

Physical Units and Equivalent Units (Steps 1 and 2)

Step 1 tracks physical units of output. Recall that physical units are the number of output units, whether complete or incomplete. Where did physical units come from? Where did they go? The physical-units column of Exhibit 17-1 tracks where the physical units came from (400 units started) and where they went (175 units completed and transferred out, and 225 units in ending inventory). Remember, when there is no opening inventory, units started must equal the sum of units transferred out and ending inventory.

Because not all 400 physical units are fully completed, output in **Step 2** is computed in *equivalent units*, not in *physical units*. To see what we mean by equivalent units, let's say that during a month, 50 physical units were started but not completed by the end of the month. These 50 units in ending inventory are estimated to be 70% complete with respect to conversion costs. Let's examine those units from the perspective of the conversion costs already incurred to get the units to be 70% complete. Suppose we put all the conversion costs represented in the 70% into making fully completed units. How many units could have been 100% complete by the end of the month? The answer is 35 units. Why? Because 70% of conversion costs incurred on 50 incomplete units could have been incurred to make 35 (0.70×50) complete units by the end of the month. That is, if all the conversion-cost input in the 50 units in inventory had been used to make completed output units, the company would have produced 35 completed units (also called *equivalent units*) of output.

---

[2] For example, consider the conventional tanning process for converting hide to leather. Obtaining 250–300 kg of leather requires putting one metric ton of raw hide through as many as 15 steps: from soaking, liming, and pickling to tanning, dyeing, and fatliquoring, the step in which oils are introduced into the skin before the leather is dried.

Exhibit 17-1

Steps 1 and 2:
Summarize Output in
Physical Units and
Compute Output in
Equivalent Units for
Assembly Department
of Pacific Electronics
for February 2012

	Home	Insert	Page Layout	Formulas	Data	Review	View		
	A				B	C	D		
1					(Step 1)	(Step 2)			
2						Equivalent Units			
3	Flow of Production				Physical Units	Direct Materials	Conversion Costs		
4	Work in process, beginning				0				
5	Started during current period				400				
6	To account for				400				
7	Completed and transferred out during current period				175	175	175		
8	Work in process, ending[a]				225				
9	(225 × 100%; 225 × 60%)					225	135		
10	Accounted for				400				
11	Equivalent units of work done in current period					400	310		
12									
13	[a]Degree of completion in this department; direct materials, 100%; conversion costs, 60%.								

Equivalent units is a derived amount of output units that (1) takes the quantity of each input (factor of production) in units completed and in incomplete units of work in process and (2) converts the quantity of input into the amount of completed output units that could be produced with that quantity of input. Note that equivalent units are calculated separately for each input (such as direct materials and conversion costs). Moreover, every completed unit, by definition, is composed of one equivalent unit of each input required to make it. This chapter focuses on equivalent-unit calculations in manufacturing settings. Equivalent-unit concepts are also found in nonmanufacturing settings. For example, universities convert their part-time student enrollments into "full-time student equivalents."

When calculating equivalent units in Step 2, focus on quantities. Disregard dollar amounts until after equivalent units are computed. In the Pacific Electronics example, all 400 physical units—the 175 fully assembled units and the 225 partially assembled units— are 100% complete with respect to direct materials because all direct materials are added in the assembly department at the start of the process. Therefore, Exhibit 17-1 shows output as 400 *equivalent units* for direct materials: 175 equivalent units for the 175 physical units assembled and transferred out, and 225 equivalent units for the 225 physical units in ending work-in-process inventory.

The 175 fully assembled units are also completely processed with respect to conversion costs. The partially assembled units in ending work in process are 60% complete (on average). Therefore, conversion costs in the 225 partially assembled units are *equivalent* to conversion costs in 135 (60% of 225) fully assembled units. Hence, Exhibit 17-1 shows output as 310 *equivalent units* with respect to conversion costs: 175 equivalent units for the 175 physical units assembled and transferred out and 135 equivalent units for the 225 physical units in ending work-in-process inventory.

Calculation of Product Costs (Steps 3, 4, and 5)

Exhibit 17-2 shows Steps 3, 4, and 5. Together, they are called the *production cost worksheet*.

Step 3 summarizes total costs to account for. Because the beginning balance of work-in-process inventory is zero on February 1, total costs to account for (that is, the total charges or debits to the Work in Process—Assembly account) consist only of costs added during February: direct materials of $32,000 and conversion costs of $18,600, for a total of $50,600.

Step 4 in Exhibit 17-2 calculates cost per equivalent unit separately for direct materials and for conversion costs by dividing direct material costs and conversion costs added during February by the related quantity of equivalent units of work done in February (as calculated in Exhibit 17-1).

To see the importance of using equivalent units in unit-cost calculations, compare conversion costs for January and February 2012. Total conversion costs of $18,600 for the 400 units worked on during February are lower than the conversion costs of

Exhibit 17-2 Steps 3, 4, and 5: Summarize Total Costs to Account For, Compute Cost per Equivalent Unit, and Assign Total Costs to Units Completed and to Units in Ending Work in Process for Assembly Department of Pacific Electronics for February 2012

	Home	Insert	Page Layout	Formulas	Data	Review	View		
	A	B				C	D	E	

	A	B	Total Production Costs (C)	Direct Materials (D)	Conversion Costs (E)
1					
2	(Step 3)	Costs added during February	$50,600	$32,000	$18,600
3		Total costs to account for	$50,600	$32,000	$18,600
4					
5	(Step 4)	Costs added in current period	$50,600	$32,000	$18,600
6		Divide by equivalent units of work done in current period (Exhibit 17-1)		÷ 400	÷ 310
7		Cost per equivalent unit		$ 80	$ 60
8					
9	(Step 5)	Assignment of costs:			
10		Completed and transferred out (175 units)	$24,500	$(175^a \times \$80)$ + $(175^a \times \$60)$	
11		Work in process, ending (225 units):	26,100	$(225^b \times \$80)$ + $(135^b \times \$60)$	
12		Total costs accounted for	$50,600	$32,000 + $18,600	
13					
14		[a]Equivalent units completed and transferred out from Exhibit 17-1, step 2.			
15		[b]Equivalent units in ending work in process from Exhibit 17-1, step 2.			

$24,000 for the 400 units worked on in January. However, in this example, the conversion costs to fully assemble a unit are $60 in both January and February. Total conversion costs are lower in February because fewer equivalent units of conversion-costs work were completed in February (310) than in January (400). Using physical units instead of equivalent units in the per-unit calculation would have led to the erroneous conclusion that conversion costs per unit declined from $60 in January to $46.50 ($18,600 ÷ 400 units) in February. This incorrect costing might have prompted Pacific Electronics to presume that greater efficiencies in processing had been achieved and to lower the price of SG-40, for example, when in fact costs had not declined.

Step 5 in Exhibit 17-2 assigns these costs to units completed and transferred out and to units still in process at the end of February 2012. The idea is to attach dollar amounts to the equivalent output units for direct materials and conversion costs of (a) units completed and (b) ending work in process, as calculated in Exhibit 17-1, Step 2. *Equivalent output units for each input are multiplied by cost per equivalent unit, as calculated in Step 4 of Exhibit 17-2.* For example, costs assigned to the 225 physical units in ending work-in-process inventory are as follows:

Direct material costs of 225 equivalent units (Exhibit 17-1, Step 2) × $80 cost per equivalent unit of direct materials calculated in Step 4	$18,000
Conversion costs of 135 equivalent units (Exhibit 17-1, Step 2) × $60 cost per equivalent unit of conversion costs calculated in Step 4	8,100
Total cost of ending work-in-process inventory	$26,100

Note that total costs to account for in Step 3 ($50,600) equal total costs accounted for in Step 5.

Journal Entries

Journal entries in process-costing systems are similar to the entries made in job-costing systems with respect to direct materials and conversion costs. The main difference is that, in process costing, there is one Work in Process account for each process. In our example, there are accounts for Work in Process—Assembly and Work in Process—Testing. Pacific Electronics purchases direct materials as needed. These materials are delivered directly to the assembly department. Using amounts from Exhibit 17-2, summary journal entries for February are as follows:

1. Work in Process—Assembly   32,000
    Accounts Payable Control   32,000
    To record direct materials purchased and used in production during February.

2. Work in Process—Assembly   18,600
    Various accounts such as Wages Payable Control and   18,600
    Accumulated Depreciation
    To record conversion costs for February; examples include energy, manufacturing supplies, all manufacturing labor, and plant depreciation.

3. Work in Process—Testing   24,500
    Work in Process—Assembly   24,500
    To record cost of goods completed and transferred from assembly to testing during February.

Exhibit 17-3 shows a general framework for the flow of costs through T-accounts. Notice how entry 3 for $24,500 follows the physical transfer of goods from the assembly to the testing department. The T-account Work in Process—Assembly shows February 2012's ending balance of $26,100, which is the beginning balance of Work in Process—Assembly in March 2012. It is important to ensure that all costs have been accounted for and that the ending inventory of the current month is the beginning inventory of the following month.

> ◄ **Decision Point**
>
> What are the five steps in a process-costing system and how are equivalent units calculated?

Case 3: Process Costing with Some Beginning and Some Ending Work-in-Process Inventory

At the beginning of March 2012, Pacific Electronics had 225 partially assembled SG-40 units in the assembly department. It started production of another 275 units in March. Data for the assembly department for March are as follows:

	Home Insert Page Layout Formulas Data Review View				
	A	B	C	D	E
1		**Physical Units (SG-40s)** (1)	**Direct Materials** (2)	**Conversion Costs** (3)	**Total Costs** (4) = (2) + (3)
2	Work in process, beginning inventory (March 1)	225	$18,000[a]	$8,100[a]	$26,100
3	Degree of completion of beginning work in process		100%	60%	
4	Started during March	275			
5	Completed and transferred out during March	400			
6	Work in process, ending inventory (March 31)	100			
7	Degree of completion of ending work in process		100%	50%	
8	Total costs added during March		$19,800	$16,380	$36,180
9					
10					
11	[a]Work in process, beginning inventory (equals work in process, ending inventory for February)				
12	Direct materials: 225 physical units × 100% completed × $80 per unit = $18,000				
13	Conversion costs: 225 physical units × 60% completed × $60 per unit = $8,100				

Pacific Electronics now has incomplete units in both beginning work-in-process inventory and ending work-in-process inventory for March 2012. We can still use the five steps described earlier to calculate (1) cost of units completed and transferred out and (2) cost of ending work in process. To assign costs to each of these categories, however, we first need to choose an inventory-valuation method. We next describe the five-step approach for two important methods—the *weighted-average method* and the *first-in, first-out method*. These different valuation methods produce different amounts for cost of units completed and for ending work in process when the unit cost of inputs changes from one period to the next.

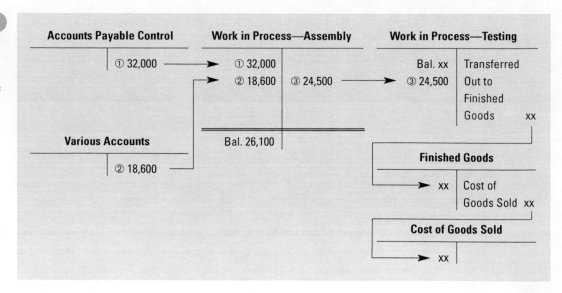

Weighted-Average Method

The **weighted-average process-costing method** calculates cost per equivalent unit of all *work done to date* (regardless of the accounting period in which it was done) and assigns this cost to equivalent units completed and transferred out of the process and to equivalent units in ending work-in-process inventory. The weighted-average cost is the total of all costs entering the Work in Process account (whether the costs are from beginning work in process or from work started during the current period) divided by total equivalent units of work done to date. We now describe the weighted-average method using the five-step procedure introduced on page 610.

Step 1: Summarize the Flow of Physical Units of Output. The physical-units column of Exhibit 17-4 shows where the units came from—225 units from beginning inventory and 275 units started during the current period—and where they went—400 units completed and transferred out and 100 units in ending inventory.

Step 2: Compute Output in Terms of Equivalent Units. The weighted-average cost of inventory is calculated by merging together the costs of beginning inventory and the manufacturing costs of a period and dividing by the total number of units in beginning inventory and units produced during the accounting period. We apply the same concept here

	Home Insert Page Layout Formulas Data Review View			
	A	B	C	D
1		(Step 1)	(Step 2)	
2			Equivalent Units	
3	**Flow of Production**	Physical Units	Direct Materials	Conversion Costs
4	Work in process, beginning (given, p. 613)	225		
5	Started during current period (given, p. 613)	275		
6	To account for	500		
7	Completed and transferred out during current period	400	400	400
8	Work in process, ending[a] (given, p. 613)	100		
9	(100 × 100%; 100 × 50%)		100	50
10	Accounted for	500		
11	Equivalent units of work done to date		500	450
12				
13	[a]Degree of completion in this department; direct materials, 100%; conversion costs, 50%.			

except that calculating the units—in this case equivalent units—is done differently. We use the relationship shown in the following equation:

$$\begin{array}{c} \text{Equivalent units} \\ \text{in beginning work} \\ \text{in process} \end{array} + \begin{array}{c} \text{Equivalent units} \\ \text{of work done in} \\ \text{current period} \end{array} = \begin{array}{c} \text{Equivalent units} \\ \text{completed and transferred} \\ \text{out in current period} \end{array} + \begin{array}{c} \text{Equivalent units} \\ \text{in ending work} \\ \text{in process} \end{array}$$

Although we are interested in calculating the left-hand side of the preceding equation, it is easier to calculate this sum using the equation's right-hand side: (1) equivalent units completed and transferred out in the current period plus (2) equivalent units in ending work in process. *Note that the stage of completion of the current-period beginning work in process is not used in this computation.*

The equivalent-units columns in Exhibit 17-4 show equivalent units of work done to date: 500 equivalent units of direct materials and 450 equivalent units of conversion costs. All completed and transferred-out units are 100% complete as to both direct materials and conversion costs. Partially completed units in ending work in process are 100% complete as to direct materials because direct materials are introduced at the beginning of the process, and 50% complete as to conversion costs, based on estimates made by the assembly department manager.

Step 3: Summarize Total Costs to Account For. Exhibit 17-5 presents Step 3. Total costs to account for in March 2012 are described in the example data on page 615: beginning work in process, $26,100 (direct materials, $18,000, plus conversion costs, $8,100), plus costs added during March, $36,180 (direct materials, $19,800, plus conversion costs, $16,380). The total of these costs is $62,280.

Step 4: Compute Cost per Equivalent Unit. Exhibit 17-5, Step 4, shows the computation of weighted-average cost per equivalent unit for direct materials and conversion costs. Weighted-average cost per equivalent unit is obtained by dividing the sum of costs for beginning work in process plus costs for work done in the current period by total

---

Exhibit 17-5   Steps 3, 4, and 5: Summarize Total Costs to Account For, Compute Cost per Equivalent Unit, and Assign Total Costs to Units Completed and to Units in Ending Work in Process Using Weighted-Average Method of Process Costing for Assembly Department of Pacific Electronics for March 2012

	A	B	C	D	E
			Total Production Costs	Direct Materials	Conversion Costs
1					
2	(Step 3)	Work in process, beginning (given, p. 613)	$26,100	$18,000	$ 8,100
3		Costs added in current period (given, p. 613)	36,180	19,800	16,380
4		Total costs to account for	$62,280	$37,800	$24,480
5					
6	(Step 4)	Costs incurred to date		$37,800	$24,480
7		Divide by equivalent units of work done to date (Exhibit 17-4)		÷ 500	÷ 450
8		Cost per equivalent unit of work done to date		$ 75.60	$ 54.40
9					
10	(Step 5)	Assignment of costs:			
11		Completed and transferred out (400 units)	$52,000	(400[a] × $75.60)	+(400[a] × $54.40)
12		Work in process, ending (100 units):	10,280	(100[b] × $75.60)	+ (50[b] × $54.40)
13		Total costs accounted for	$62,280	$37,800	+ $24,480
14					
15	[a]Equivalent units completed and transferred out from Exhibit 17-4, Step 2.				
16	[b]Equivalent units in ending work in process from Exhibit 17-4, Step 2.				

equivalent units of work done to date. When calculating weighted-average conversion cost per equivalent unit in Exhibit 17-5, for example, we divide total conversion costs, $24,480 (beginning work in process, $8,100, plus work done in current period, $16,380), by total equivalent units of work done to date, 450 (equivalent units of conversion costs in beginning work in process and in work done in current period), to obtain weighted-average cost per equivalent unit of $54.40.

Step 5: Assign Total Costs to Units Completed and to Units in Ending Work in Process. Step 5 in Exhibit 17-5 takes the equivalent units completed and transferred out and equivalent units in ending work in process calculated in Exhibit 17-4, Step 2, and assigns dollar amounts to them using the weighted-average cost per equivalent unit for direct materials and conversion costs calculated in Step 4. For example, total costs of the 100 physical units in ending work in process are as follows:

Direct materials:		
100 equivalent units × weighted-average cost per equivalent unit of $75.60		$ 7,560
Conversion costs:		
50 equivalent units × weighted-average cost per equivalent unit of $54.40		2,720
Total costs of ending work in process		$10,280

The following table summarizes total costs to account for ($62,280) and how they are accounted for in Exhibit 17-5. The arrows indicate that the costs of units completed and transferred out and units in ending work in process are calculated using weighted-average total costs obtained after merging costs of beginning work in process and costs added in the current period.

Costs to Account For		Costs Accounted for Calculated on a Weighted-Average Basis	
Beginning work in process	$26,100	Completed and transferred out	$52,000
Costs added in current period	36,180	Ending work in process	10,280
Total costs to account for	$62,280	Total costs accounted for	$62,280

Before proceeding, review Exhibits 17-4 and 17-5 to check your understanding of the weighted-average method. Note: Exhibit 17-4 deals with only physical and equivalent units, not costs. Exhibit 17-5 shows the cost amounts.

Using amounts from Exhibit 17-5, the summary journal entries under the weighted-average method for March 2012 at Pacific Electronics are as follows:

1. Work in Process—Assembly 19,800
    Accounts Payable Control 19,800
  To record direct materials purchased and used in production during March.

2. Work in Process—Assembly 16,380
    Various accounts such as Wages Payable Control and Accumulated
    Depreciation 16,380
  To record conversion costs for March; examples include energy,
  manufacturing supplies, all manufacturing labor, and plant depreciation.

3. Work in Process—Testing 52,000
    Work in Process—Assembly 52,000
  To record cost of goods completed and transferred from assembly to
  testing during March.

The T-account Work in Process—Assembly, under the weighted-average method, is as follows:

Work in Process—Assembly

Beginning inventory, March 1	26,100	③ Completed and transferred	52,000
① Direct materials	19,800	out to Work in Process—	
② Conversion costs	16,380	Testing	
Ending inventory, March 31	10,280		

First-In, First-Out Method

The **first-in, first-out (FIFO) process-costing method** (1) assigns the cost of the previous accounting period's equivalent units in beginning work-in-process inventory to the first units completed and transferred out of the process, and (2) assigns the cost of equivalent units worked on during the *current* period first to complete beginning inventory, next to start and complete new units, and finally to units in ending work-in-process inventory. The FIFO method assumes that the earliest equivalent units in work in process are completed first.

A distinctive feature of the FIFO process-costing method is that work done on beginning inventory before the current period is kept separate from work done in the current period. Costs incurred and units produced in the current period are used to calculate cost per equivalent unit of work done in the current period. In contrast, equivalent-unit and cost-per-equivalent-unit calculations under the weighted-average method *merge* units and costs in beginning inventory with units and costs of work done in the current period.

We now describe the FIFO method using the five-step procedure introduced on page 610.

Step 1:   Summarize the Flow of Physical Units of Output. Exhibit 17-6, Step 1, traces the flow of physical units of production. The following observations help explain the calculation of physical units under the FIFO method for Pacific Electronics.

- The first physical units assumed to be completed and transferred out during the period are 225 units from beginning work-in-process inventory.

- The March data on page 613 indicate that 400 physical units were completed during March. The FIFO method assumes that of these 400 units, 175 units (400 units − 225 units from beginning work-in-process inventory) must have been started and completed during March.

- Ending work-in-process inventory consists of 100 physical units—the 275 physical units started minus the 175 units that were started and completed.

- The physical units "to account for" equal the physical units "accounted for" (500 units).

Step 2:   Compute Output in Terms of Equivalent Units. Exhibit 17-6 also presents the computations for Step 2 under the FIFO method. *The equivalent-unit calculations for each cost category focus on equivalent units of work done in the current period (March) only.*

Under the FIFO method, equivalent units of work done in March on the beginning work-in-process inventory equal 225 physical units times *the percentage of work remaining to be done in March to complete these units*: 0% for direct materials, because beginning work in process is 100% complete with respect to direct materials, and 40% for conversion costs, because beginning work in process is 60% complete with respect to conversion costs. The results are 0 (0% × 225) equivalent units of work for direct materials and 90 (40% × 225) equivalent units of work for conversion costs.

The equivalent units of work done on the 175 physical units started and completed equals 175 units times 100% for both direct materials and conversion costs, because all work on these units is done in the current period.

The equivalent units of work done on the 100 units of ending work in process equal 100 physical units times 100% for direct materials (because all direct materials for these units are added in the current period) and 50% for conversion costs (because 50% of the conversion-costs work on these units is done in the current period).

Step 3:   Summarize Total Costs to Account For. Exhibit 17-7 presents Step 3 and summarizes total costs to account for in March 2012 (beginning work in process and costs added in the current period) of $62,280, as described in the example data (p. 613).

Step 4:   Compute Cost per Equivalent Unit. Exhibit 17-7 shows the Step 4 computation of cost per equivalent unit for *work done in the current period only* for direct materials and conversion costs. For example, conversion cost per equivalent unit of $52 is obtained by dividing current-period conversion costs of $16,380 by current-period conversion-costs equivalent units of 315.

Step 5:   Assign Total Costs to Units Completed and to Units in Ending Work in Process. Exhibit 17-7 shows the assignment of costs under the FIFO method. Costs of work done in the current period are assigned (1) first to the additional work done to complete the beginning

Exhibit 17-6

Steps 1 and 2:
Summarize Output in
Physical Units and
Compute Output in
Equivalent Units Using
FIFO Method of
Process Costing for
Assembly Department
of Pacific Electronics
for March 2012

	A	B	C	D
		(Step 1)	(Step 2)	
1		**(Step 1)**	**(Step 2)**	
2			**Equivalent Units**	
3	**Flow of Production**	**Physical Units**	**Direct Materials**	**Conversion Costs**
4	Work in process, beginning (given, p. 613)	225	(work done before current period)	
5	Started during current period (given, p. 613)	275		
6	To account for	500		
7	Completed and transferred out during current period:			
8	From beginning work in process[a]	225		
9	[225 × (100% – 100%); 225 × (100% – 60%)]		0	90
10	Started and completed	175[b]		
11	(175 × 100%; 175 × 100%)		175	175
12	Work in process, ending[c] (given, p. 613)	100		
13	(100 × 100%; 100 × 50%)		100	50
14	Accounted for	500		
15	Equivalent units of work done in current period		275	315
16				
17	[a]Degree of completion in this department; direct materials, 100%; conversion costs, 60%.			
18	[b]400 physical units completed and transferred out minus 225 physical units completed and			
19	transferred out from beginning work-in-process inventory.			
20	[c]Degree of completion in this department: direct materials, 100%; conversion costs, 50%.			

work in process, then (2) to work done on units started and completed during the current period, and finally (3) to ending work in process. *Step 5 takes each quantity of equivalent units calculated in Exhibit 17-6, Step 2, and assigns dollar amounts to them (using the cost-per-equivalent-unit calculations in Step 4).* The goal is to use the cost of work done in the current period to determine total costs of all units completed from beginning inventory and from work started and completed in the current period, and costs of ending work in process.

Of the 400 completed units, 225 units are from beginning inventory and 175 units are started and completed during March. The FIFO method starts by assigning the costs of beginning work-in-process inventory of $26,100 to the first units completed and transferred out. As we saw in Step 2, an additional 90 equivalent units of conversion costs are needed to complete these units in the current period. Current-period conversion cost per equivalent unit is $52, so $4,680 (90 equivalent units × $52 per equivalent unit) of additional costs are incurred to complete beginning inventory. Total production costs for units in beginning inventory are $26,100 + $4,680 = $30,780. The 175 units started and completed in the current period consist of 175 equivalent units of direct materials and 175 equivalent units of conversion costs. These units are costed at the cost per equivalent unit in the current period (direct materials, $72, and conversion costs, $52) for a total production cost of $21,700 [175 × ($72 + $52)].

Under FIFO, ending work-in-process inventory comes from units that were started but not fully completed during the current period. Total costs of the 100 partially assembled physical units in ending work in process are as follows:

Direct materials:
    100 equivalent units × $72 cost per equivalent unit in March $7,200
Conversion costs:
    50 equivalent units × $52 cost per equivalent unit in March   2,600
Total cost of work in process on March 31 $9,800

The following table summarizes total costs to account for and costs accounted for of $62,280 in Exhibit 17-7. Notice how under the FIFO method, the layers of beginning work in process and costs added in the current period are kept separate. The arrows

Exhibit 17-7	Steps 3, 4, and 5: Summarize Total Costs to Account For, Compute Cost per Equivalent Unit, and Assign Total Costs to Units Completed and to Units in Ending Work in Process Using FIFO Method of Process Costing for Assembly Department of Pacific Electronics for March 2012

	Home	Insert	Page Layout	Formulas	Data	Review	View			
	A		B					C	D	E
1								Total Production Costs	Direct Material	Conversion Costs
2	(Step 3)	Work in process, beginning (given, p. 613)						$26,100	$18,000	$ 8,100
3		Costs added in current period (given, p. 613)						36,180	19,800	16,380
4		Total costs to account for						$62,280	$37,800	$24,480
5										
6	(Step 4)	Costs added in current period							$19,800	$16,380
7		Divide by equivalent units of work done in current period (Exhibit 17-6)							÷ 275	÷ 315
8		Cost per equivalent unit of work done in current period							$ 72	$ 52
9										
10	(Step 5)	Assignment of costs:								
11		Completed and transferred out (400 units):								
12		Work in process, beginning (225 units)						$26,100	$18,000 + $8,100	
13		Costs added to beginning work in process in current period						4,680	$(0^a \times \$72)$ + $(90^a \times \$52)$	
14		Total from beginning inventory						30,780		
15		Started and completed (175 units)						21,700	$(175^b \times \$72)$ + $(175^b \times \$52)$	
16		Total costs of units completed and transferred out						52,480		
17		Work in process, ending (100 units):						9,800	$(100^c \times \$72)$ + $(50^c \times \$52)$	
18		Total costs accounted for						$62,280	$37,800 + $24,480	
19										
20	[a]Equivalent units used to complete beginning work in process from Exhibit 17-6, Step 2.									
21	[b]Equivalent units started and completed from Exhibit 17-6, Step 2.									
22	[c]Equivalent units in ending work in process from Exhibit 17-6, Step 2.									

indicate where the costs in each layer go—that is, to units completed and transferred out or to ending work in process. Be sure to include costs of beginning work in process ($26,100) when calculating costs of units completed from beginning inventory.

Costs to Account for			Costs Accounted for Calculated on a FIFO Basis	
			Completed and transferred out	
Beginning work in process	$26,100	→	Beginning work in process	$26,100
Costs added in current period	36,180		Used to complete beginning work in process	4,680
			Started and completed	21,700
			Completed and transferred out	52,480
			Ending work in process	9,800
Total costs to account for	$62,280		Total costs accounted for	$62,280

Before proceeding, review Exhibits 17-6 and 17-7 to check your understanding of the FIFO method. Note: Exhibit 17-6 deals with only physical and equivalent units, not costs. Exhibit 17-7 shows the cost amounts.

The journal entries under the FIFO method are identical to the journal entries under the weighted-average method except for one difference. The entry to record the cost of goods completed and transferred out would be $52,480 under the FIFO method instead of $52,000 under the weighted-average method.

Keep in mind that FIFO is applied within each department to compile the cost of units *transferred out*. As a practical matter, however, units *transferred in* during a given period usually are carried at a single average unit cost. For example, the assembly department uses FIFO in the preceding example to distinguish between monthly batches of production. The resulting average cost of units transferred out of the assembly department is $52,480 ÷ 400 units = $131.20 per SG-40 unit. The succeeding department, testing, however, costs these units (which consist of costs incurred in both February and March) at one average unit cost ($131.20 in this illustration). If this averaging were not done, the attempt to track costs on a pure FIFO basis throughout a series of processes would be cumbersome. As a result, the FIFO method should really be called a *modified* or *department* FIFO method.

Comparison of Weighted-Average and FIFO Methods

Consider the summary of the costs assigned to units completed and to units still in process under the weighted-average and FIFO process-costing methods in our example for March 2012:

	Weighted Average (from Exhibit 17-5)	FIFO (from Exhibit 17-7)	Difference
Cost of units completed and transferred out	$52,000	$52,480	+ $480
Work in process, ending	10,280	9,800	− $480
Total costs accounted for	$62,280	$62,280	

The weighted-average ending inventory is higher than the FIFO ending inventory by $480, or 4.9% ($480 ÷ $9,800 = 0.049, or 4.9%). This would be a significant difference when aggregated over the many thousands of products that Pacific Electronics makes. When completed units are sold, the weighted-average method in our example leads to a lower cost of goods sold and, therefore, higher operating income and higher income taxes than the FIFO method. To see why the weighted-average method yields a lower cost of units completed, recall the data on page 613. Direct material cost per equivalent unit in beginning work-in-process inventory is $80, and conversion cost per equivalent unit in beginning work-in-process inventory is $60. These costs are greater, respectively, than the $72 direct materials cost and the $52 conversion cost per equivalent unit of work done during the current period. The current-period costs could be lower due to a decline in the prices of direct materials and conversion-cost inputs, or as a result of Pacific Electronics becoming more efficient in its processes by using smaller quantities of inputs per unit of output, or both.

For the assembly department, FIFO assumes that (1) all the higher-cost units from the previous period in beginning work in process are the first to be completed and transferred out of the process and (2) ending work in process consists of only the lower-cost current-period units. The weighted-average method, however, smooths out cost per equivalent unit by assuming that (1) more of the lower-cost units are completed and transferred out and (2) some of the higher-cost units are placed in ending work in process. The decline in the current-period cost per equivalent unit results in a lower cost of units completed and transferred out and a higher ending work-in-process inventory under the weighted-average method compared with FIFO.

Cost of units completed and, hence, operating income can differ materially between the weighted-average and FIFO methods when (1) direct material or conversion cost per equivalent unit varies significantly from period to period and (2) physical-inventory levels of work in process are large in relation to the total number of units transferred out of the process. As companies move toward long-term procurement contracts that reduce differences in unit costs from period to period and reduce inventory levels, the difference in cost of units completed under the weighted-average and FIFO methods will decrease.[3]

---

[3] For example, suppose beginning work-in-process inventory for March were 125 physical units (instead of 225), and suppose costs per equivalent unit of work done in the current period (March) were direct materials, $75, and conversion costs, $55. Assume that all other data for March are the same as in our example. In this case, the cost of units completed and transferred out would be $52,833 under the weighted-average method and $53,000 under the FIFO method. The work-in-process ending inventory would be $10,417 under the weighted-average method and $10,250 under the FIFO method (calculations not shown). These differences are much smaller than in the chapter example. The weighted-average ending inventory is higher than the FIFO ending inventory by only $167 ($10,417 − $10,250), or 1.6% ($167 ÷ $10,250 = 0.016, or 1.6%), compared with 4.9% higher in the chapter example.

Managers use information from process-costing systems to aid them in pricing and product-mix decisions and to provide them with feedback about their performance. FIFO provides managers with information about changes in costs per unit from one period to the next. Managers can use this information to adjust selling prices based on current conditions (for example, based on the $72 direct material cost and $52 conversion cost in March). They can also more easily evaluate performance in the current period compared with a budget or relative to performance in the previous period (for example, recognizing the decline in both unit direct material and conversion costs relative to the prior period). By focusing on work done and costs of work done during the current period, the FIFO method provides useful information for these planning and control purposes.

The weighted-average method merges unit costs from different accounting periods, obscuring period-to-period comparisons. For example, the weighted-average method would lead managers at Pacific Electronics to make decisions based on the $75.60 direct materials and $54.40 conversion costs, rather than the costs of $72 and $52 prevailing in the current period. Advantages of the weighted-average method, however, are its relative computational simplicity and its reporting of a more-representative average unit cost when input prices fluctuate markedly from month to month.

Activity-based costing plays a significant role in our study of job costing, but how is activity-based costing related to process costing? Each process—assembly, testing, and so on—can be considered a different (production) activity. However, no additional activities need to be identified within each process. That's because products are homogeneous and use resources of each process in a uniform way. The bottom line is that activity-based costing has less applicability in process-costing environments. *The appendix illustrates the use of the standard costing method for the assembly department.*

Transferred-In Costs in Process Costing

Many process-costing systems have two or more departments or processes in the production cycle. As units move from department to department, the related costs are also transferred by monthly journal entries. **Transferred-in costs** (also called **previous-department costs**) are costs incurred in previous departments that are carried forward as the product's cost when it moves to a subsequent process in the production cycle.

We now extend our Pacific Electronics example to the testing department. As the assembly process is completed, the assembly department of Pacific Electronics immediately transfers SG-40 units to the testing department. Conversion costs are added evenly during the testing department's process. At the *end of the process* in testing, units receive additional direct materials, including crating and other packing materials to prepare units for shipment. As units are completed in testing, they are immediately transferred to Finished Goods. Computation of testing department costs consists of transferred-in costs, as well as direct materials and conversion costs that are added in testing.

The following diagram represents these facts:

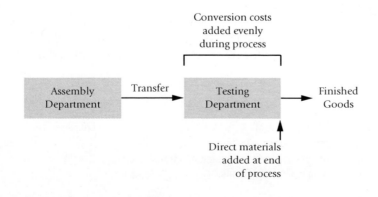

Data for the testing department for March 2012 are as follows:

	A	B	C	D	E
		Physical Units (SG-40s)	Transferred-In Costs	Direct Materials	Conversion Costs
1					
2	Work in process, beginning inventory (March 1)	240	$33,600	$ 0	$18,000
3	Degree of completion of beginning work in process		100%	0%	62.5%
4	Transferred in during March	400			
5	Completed and transferred out during March	440			
6	Work in process, ending inventory (March 31)	200			
7	Degree of completion of ending work in process		100%	0%	80%
8	Total costs added during March				
9	Direct materials and conversion costs			$13,200	$48,600
10	Transferred in (Weighted-average from Exhibit 17-5)[a]		$52,000		
11	Transferred in (FIFO from Exhibit 17-7)[a]		$52,480		
12					
13	[a]The transferred-in costs during March are different under the weighted-average method (Exhibit 17-5) and the FIFO method (Exhibit 17-7). In our example, beginning work-in-process inventory, $51,600 ($33,600 + $0 + $18,000) is the same under both the weighted-average and FIFO inventory methods because we assume costs per equivalent unit to be the same in both January and February. If costs per equivalent unit had been different in the two months, work-in-process inventory at the end of February (beginning of March) would be costed differently under the weighted-average and FIFO methods. The basic approach to process costing with transferred-in costs, however, would still be the same as what we describe in this section.				

Transferred-in costs are treated as if they are a separate type of direct material added at the beginning of the process. That is, transferred-in costs are always 100% complete as of the beginning of the process in the new department. When successive departments are involved, transferred units from one department become all or a part of the direct materials of the next department; however, they are called transferred-in costs, not direct material costs.

Transferred-In Costs and the Weighted-Average Method

To examine the weighted-average process-costing method with transferred-in costs, we use the five-step procedure described earlier (p. 610) to assign costs of the testing department to units completed and transferred out and to units in ending work in process.

Exhibit 17-8 shows Steps 1 and 2. The computations are similar to the calculations of equivalent units under the weighted-average method for the assembly department in Exhibit 17-4. The one difference here is that we have transferred-in costs as an additional input. All units, whether completed and transferred out during the period or in ending work in process, are always fully complete with respect to transferred-in costs. The reason is that the transferred-in costs refer to costs incurred in the assembly department, and any units received in the testing department must have first been completed in the assembly department. However, direct material costs have a zero degree of completion in both beginning and ending work-in-process inventories because, in testing, direct materials are introduced at the *end* of the process.

Exhibit 17-9 describes Steps 3, 4, and 5 for the weighted-average method. Beginning work in process and work done in the current period are combined for purposes of computing cost per equivalent unit for transferred-in costs, direct material costs, and conversion costs.

The journal entry for the transfer from testing to Finished Goods (see Exhibit 17-9) is as follows:

Finished Goods Control	120,890	
Work in Process—Testing		120,890
To record cost of goods completed and transferred from testing to Finished Goods.		

Entries in the Work in Process—Testing account (see Exhibit 17-9) are as follows:

Work in Process—Testing

Beginning inventory, March 1	51,600	Transferred out	120,890
Transferred-in costs	52,000		
Direct materials	13,200		
Conversion costs	48,600		
Ending inventory, March 31	44,510		

Exhibit 17-8 Steps 1 and 2: Summarize Output in Physical Units and Compute Output in Equivalent Units Using Weighted-Average Method of Process Costing for Testing Department of Pacific Electronics for March 2012

	Home	Insert	Page Layout	Formulas	Data	Review	View		
	A				B	C	D	E	
1					(Step 1)		(Step 2)		
2							Equivalent Units		
3	Flow of Production				Physical Units	Transferred-In Costs	Direct Materials	Conversion Costs	
4	Work in process, beginning (given, p. 622)				240				
5	Transferred in during current period (given, p. 622)				400				
6	To account for				640				
7	Completed and transferred out during current period				440	440	440	440	
8	Work in process, ending[a] (given, p. 622)				200				
9	(200 × 100%; 200 × 0%; 200 × 80%)					200	0	160	
10	Accounted for				640				
11	Equivalent units of work done to date					640	440	600	
12									
13	[a]Degree of completion in this department: transferred-in costs, 100%; direct materials, 0%; conversion costs, 80%.								

Exhibit 17-9 Steps 3, 4, and 5: Summarize Total Costs to Account For, Compute Cost per Equivalent Unit, and Assign Total Costs to Units Completed and to Units in Ending Work in Process Using Weighted-Average Method of Process Costing for Testing Department of Pacific Electronics for March 2012

	Home	Insert	Page Layout	Formulas	Data	Review	View		
	A	B			C	D	E	F	
1					Total Production Costs	Transferred-In Costs	Direct Materials	Conversion Costs	
2	(Step 3)	Work in process, beginning (given, p. 622)			$ 51,600	$33,600	$ 0	$18,000	
3		Costs added in current period (given, p. 622)			113,800	52,000	13,200	48,600	
4		Total costs to account for			$165,400	$85,600	$13,200	$66,600	
5									
6	(Step 4)	Costs incurred to date				$85,600	$13,200	$66,600	
7		Divide by equivalent units of work done to date (Exhibit 17-8)				÷ 640	÷ 440	÷ 600	
8		Cost per equivalent unit of work done to date				$133.75	$ 30.00	$111.00	
9									
10	(Step 5)	Assignment of costs:							
11		Completed and transferred out (440 units)			$120,890	(440[a] × $133.75) +	(440[a] × $30) +	(440[a] × $111)	
12		Work in process, ending (200 units):			44,510	(200[b] × $133.75) +	(0[b] × $30) +	(160[b] × $111)	
13		Total costs accounted for			$165,400	$85,600 +	$13,200 +	$66,600	
14									
15	[a]Equivalent units completed and transferred out from Exhibit 17-8, Step 2.								
16	[b]Equivalent units in ending work in process from Exhibit 17-8, Step 2.								

Transferred-In Costs and the FIFO Method

To examine the FIFO process-costing method with transferred-in costs, we again use the five-step procedure. Exhibit 17-10 shows Steps 1 and 2. Other than considering transferred-in costs, computations of equivalent units are the same as under the FIFO method for the assembly department shown in Exhibit 17-6.

Exhibit 17-11 describes Steps 3, 4, and 5. In Step 3, total costs to account for of $165,880 under the FIFO method differs from the corresponding amount under the weighted-average method of $165,400. The reason is the difference in cost of completed units transferred in from the assembly department under the two methods—$52,480 under FIFO and $52,000 under weighted average. Cost per equivalent unit for the current period in Step 4 is calculated on the basis of costs transferred in and work done in the current period only. Step 5 then accounts for the total costs of $165,880 by assigning them to the units transferred out and those in ending work in process. Again, other than considering transferred-in costs, the calculations mirror those under the FIFO method for the assembly department shown in Exhibit 17-7.

Remember that in a series of interdepartmental transfers, each department is regarded as separate and distinct for accounting purposes. The journal entry for the transfer from testing to Finished Goods (see Exhibit 17-11) is as follows:

Finished Goods Control	122,360	
Work in Process—Testing		122,360
To record cost of goods completed and		
transferred from testing to Finished Goods.		

Exhibit 17-10 Steps 1 and 2: Summarize Output in Physical Units and Compute Output in Equivalent Units Using FIFO Method of Process Costing for Testing Department of Pacific Electronics for March 2012

	Home Insert Page Layout Formulas Data Review View				
	A	B	C	D	E
1		**(Step 1)**		**(Step 2)**	
2				**Equivalent Units**	
3	**Flow of Production**	**Physical Units**	**Transferred-In Costs**	**Direct Materials**	**Conversion Costs**
4	Work in process, beginning (given, p. 622)	240	(work done before current period)		
5	Transferred in during current period (given, p. 622)	400			
6	To account for	640			
7	Completed and transferred out during current period:				
8	From beginning work in process[a]	240			
9	[240 × (100% − 100%); 240 × (100% − 0%); 240 × (100% − 62.5%)]		0	240	90
10	Started and completed	200[b]			
11	(200 × 100%; 200 × 100%; 200 × 100%)		200	200	200
12	Work in process, ending[c] (given, p. 000)	200			
13	(200 × 100%; 200 × 0%; 200 × 80%)		200	0	160
14	Accounted for	640			
15	Equivalent units of work done in current period		400	440	450
16					
17	[a]Degree of completion in this department: transferred-in costs, 100%; direct materials, 0%; conversion costs, 62.5%.				
18	[b]440 physical units completed and transferred out minus 240 physical units completed and transferred out from beginning				
19	work-in-process inventory.				
20	[c]Degree of completion in this department: transferred-in costs, 100%; direct materials, 0%; conversion costs, 80%.				

| Exhibit 17-11 | Steps 3, 4, and 5: Summarize Total Costs to Account For, Compute Cost per Equivalent Unit, and Assign Total Costs to Units Completed and to Units in Ending Work in Process Using FIFO Method of Process Costing for Testing Department of Pacific Electronics for March 2012 |

| | Home | Insert | Page Layout | Formulas | Data | Review | View | | | |

	A	B	C	D	E	F
1			Total Production Costs	Transferred-In Cost	Direct Material	Conversion Costs
2	(Step 3)	Work in process, beginning (given, p. 622)	$ 51,600	$33,600	$ 0	$18,000
3		Costs added in current period (given, p. 622)	114,280	52,480	13,200	48,600
4		Total costs to account for	$165,880	$86,080	$13,200	$66,600
5						
6	(Step 4)	Costs added in current period		$52,480	$13,200	$48,600
7		Divide by equivalent units of work done in current period (Exhibit 17-10)		÷ 400	÷ 440	÷ 450
8		Cost per equivalent unit of work done in current period		$131.20	$ 30	$ 108
9						
10	(Step 5)	Assignment of costs:				
11		Completed and transferred out (440 units)				
12		Work in process, beginning (240 units)	$ 51,600	$33,600 +	$0 +	$18,000
13		Costs added to beginning work in process in current period	16,920	$(0^a \times \$131.20)$ +	$(240^a \times \$30)$ +	$(90^a \times \$108)$
14		Total from beginning inventory	68,520			
15		Started and completed (200 units)	53,840	$(200^b \times \$131.20)$ +	$(200^b \times \$30)$ +	$(200^b \times \$108)$
16		Total costs of units completed and transferred out	122,360			
17		Work in process, ending (200 units):	43,520	$(200^c \times \$131.20)$ +	$(0^c \times \$30)$ +	$(160^c \times \$108)$
18		Total costs accounted for	$165,880	$86,080 +	$13,200 +	$66,600
19						
20		^{a}Equivalent units used to complete beginning work in process from Exhibit 17-10, Step 2.				
21		^{b}Equivalent units started and completed from Exhibit 17-10, Step 2.				
22		^{c}Equivalent units in ending work in process from Exhibit 17-10, Step 2.				

Entries in the Work in Process—Testing account (see Exhibit 17-11) are as follows:

Work in Process—Testing

Beginning inventory, March 1	51,600	Transferred out	122,360
Transferred-in costs	52,480		
Direct materials	13,200		
Conversion costs	48,600		
Ending inventory, March 31	43,520		

Points to Remember About Transferred-In Costs

Some points to remember when accounting for transferred-in costs are as follows:

1. Be sure to include transferred-in costs from previous departments in your calculations.

2. In calculating costs to be transferred on a FIFO basis, do not overlook costs assigned in the previous period to units that were in process at the beginning of the current period but are now included in the units transferred. For example, do not overlook the $51,600 in Exhibit 17-11.

3. Unit costs may fluctuate between periods. Therefore, transferred units may contain batches accumulated at different unit costs. For example, the 400 units transferred in

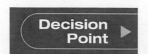

Decision Point ▶

How are the weighted-average and FIFO process-costing methods applied to transferred-in costs?

at $52,480 in Exhibit 17-11 using the FIFO method consist of units that have different unit costs of direct materials and conversion costs when these units were worked on in the assembly department (see Exhibit 17-7). Remember, however, that when these units are transferred to the testing department, they are costed at *one average unit cost* of $131.20 ($52,480 ÷ 400 units), as in Exhibit 17-11.

4. Units may be measured in different denominations in different departments. Consider each department separately. For example, unit costs could be based on kilograms in the first department and liters in the second department. Accordingly, as units are received in the second department, their measurements must be converted to liters.

Hybrid Costing Systems

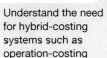

Learning Objective 6

Understand the need for hybrid-costing systems such as operation-costing

. . . when product-costing does not fall into job-costing or process-costing categories

Product-costing systems do not always fall neatly into either job-costing or process-costing categories. Consider Ford Motor Company. Automobiles may be manufactured in a continuous flow (suited to process costing), but individual units may be customized with a special combination of engine size, transmission, music system, and so on (which requires job costing). A **hybrid-costing system** blends characteristics from both job-costing and process-costing systems. Product-costing systems often must be designed to fit the particular characteristics of different production systems. Many production systems are a hybrid: They have some features of custom-order manufacturing and other features of mass-production manufacturing. Manufacturers of a relatively wide variety of closely related standardized products (for example, televisions, dishwashers, and washing machines) tend to use hybrid-costing systems. The Concepts in Action feature (p. 627) describes a hybrid-costing system at Adidas. The next section explains *operation costing*, a common type of hybrid-costing system.

Overview of Operation-Costing Systems

An **operation** is a standardized method or technique that is performed repetitively, often on different materials, resulting in different finished goods. Multiple operations are usually conducted within a department. For instance, a suit maker may have a cutting operation and a hemming operation within a single department. The term *operation*, however, is often used loosely. It may be a synonym for a department or process. For example, some companies may call their finishing department a finishing process or a finishing operation.

An **operation-costing system** is a hybrid-costing system applied to batches of similar, but not identical, products. Each batch of products is often a variation of a single design, and it proceeds through a sequence of operations. Within each operation, all product units are treated exactly alike, using identical amounts of the operation's resources. A key point in the operation system is that each batch does not necessarily move through the same operations as other batches. Batches are also called production runs.

In a company that makes suits, management may select a single basic design for every suit to be made, but depending on specifications, each batch of suits varies somewhat from other batches. Batches may vary with respect to the material used or the type of stitching. Semiconductors, textiles, and shoes are also manufactured in batches and may have similar variations from batch to batch.

An operation-costing system uses work orders that specify the needed direct materials and step-by-step operations. Product costs are compiled for each work order. Direct materials that are unique to different work orders are specifically identified with the appropriate work order, as in job costing. However, each unit is assumed to use an identical amount of conversion costs for a given operation, as in process costing. A single average conversion cost per unit is calculated for each operation, by dividing total conversion costs for that operation by the number of units that pass through it. This average cost is then assigned to each unit passing through the operation. Units that do not pass through an operation are not allocated any costs of that

Concepts in Action | Hybrid Costing for Customized Shoes at Adidas

Adidas has been designing and manufacturing athletic footwear for nearly 90 years. Although shoemakers have long individually crafted shoes for professional athletes like Reggie Bush of the New Orleans Saints, Adidas took this concept a step further when it initiated the *mi adidas* program. *Mi adidas* gives customers the opportunity to create shoes to their exact personal specifications for function, fit, and aesthetics. *Mi adidas* is available in retail stores around the world, and in special *mi adidas* "Performance Stores" in cities such as New York, Chicago, and San Francisco.

The process works as follows: The customer goes to a *mi adidas* station, where a salesperson develops an in-depth customer profile, a 3-D computer scanner develops a scan of the customer's feet, and the customer selects from among 90 to 100 different styles and colors for his or her modularly designed shoe. During the three-step, 30-minute high-tech process, *mi adidas* experts take customers through the "mi fit," "mi performance," and "mi design" phases, resulting in a customized shoe to fit their needs. The resulting data are transferred to an Adidas plant, where small, multiskilled teams produce the customized shoe. The measuring and fitting process is free, but purchasing your own specially made shoes costs between $40 and $65 on top of the normal retail price, depending on the style.

Historically, costs associated with individually customized products have fallen into the domain of job costing. Adidas, however, uses a hybrid-costing system—job costing for the material and customizable components that customers choose and process costing to account for the conversion costs of production. The cost of making each pair of shoes is calculated by accumulating all production costs and dividing by the number of shoes made. In other words, even though each pair of shoes is different, the conversion cost of each pair is assumed to be the same.

The combination of customization with certain features of mass production is called mass customization. It is the consequence of being able to digitize information that individual customers indicate is important to them. Various products that companies are now able to customize within a mass-production setting (for example, personal computers, blue jeans, bicycles) still require job costing of materials and considerable human intervention. However, as manufacturing systems become flexible, companies are also using process costing to account for the standardized conversion costs.

Sources: Adidas. 2010. New Orleans Saints running back Reggie Bush designs custom Adidas shoes to aid in Haiti relief efforts. AG press release. Portland, OR: February 5; Kamenev, Marina. 2006. Adidas' high tech footwear. *BusinessWeek.com*, November 3; Seifert, Ralf. 2003. The "mi adidas" mass customization initiative. IMD No. 159. Lausanne, Switzerland: International Institute for Management Development.

operation. Our examples assume only two cost categories—direct materials and conversion costs—but operation costing can have more than two cost categories. Costs in each category are identified with specific work orders using job-costing or process-costing methods as appropriate.

Managers find operation costing useful in cost management because operation costing focuses on control of physical processes, or operations, of a given production system. For example, in clothing manufacturing, managers are concerned with fabric waste, how many fabric layers that can be cut at one time, and so on. Operation costing measures, in financial terms, how well managers have controlled physical processes.

Illustration of an Operation-Costing System

The Baltimore Clothing Company, a clothing manufacturer, produces two lines of blazers for department stores: those made of wool and those made of polyester. Wool blazers use better-quality materials and undergo more operations than polyester blazers do.

Operations information on work order 423 for 50 wool blazers and work order 424 for 100 polyester blazers is as follows:

	Work Order 423	Work Order 424
Direct materials	Wool	Polyester
	Satin full lining	Rayon partial lining
	Bone buttons	Plastic buttons
Operations		
1. Cutting cloth	Use	Use
2. Checking edges	Use	Do not use
3. Sewing body	Use	Use
4. Checking seams	Use	Do not use
5. Machine sewing of collars and lapels	Do not use	Use
6. Hand sewing of collars and lapels	Use	Do not use

Cost data for these work orders, started and completed in March 2012, are as follows:

	Work Order 423	Work Order 424
Number of blazers	50	100
Direct material costs	$ 6,000	$3,000
Conversion costs allocated:		
Operation 1	580	1,160
Operation 2	400	—
Operation 3	1,900	3,800
Operation 4	500	—
Operation 5	—	875
Operation 6	700	—
Total manufacturing costs	$10,080	$8,835

As in process costing, all product units in any work order are assumed to consume identical amounts of conversion costs of a particular operation. Baltimore's operation-costing system uses a budgeted rate to calculate the conversion costs of each operation. The budgeted rate for Operation 1 (amounts assumed) is as follows:

$$\text{Operation 1 budgeted conversion-cost rate for 2012} = \frac{\text{Operation 1 budgeted conversion costs for 2012}}{\text{Operation 1 budgeted product units for 2012}}$$

$$= \frac{\$232,000}{20,000 \text{ units}}$$

$$= \$11.60 \text{ per unit}$$

Budgeted conversion costs of Operation 1 include labor, power, repairs, supplies, depreciation, and other overhead of this operation. If some units have not been completed (so all units in Operation 1 have not received the same amounts of conversion costs), the conversion-cost rate is computed by dividing budgeted conversion costs by *equivalent units* of conversion costs, as in process costing.

As goods are manufactured, conversion costs are allocated to the work orders processed in Operation 1 by multiplying the $11.60 conversion cost per unit by the number of units processed. Conversion costs of Operation 1 for 50 wool blazers (work order 423) are $11.60 per blazer × 50 blazers = $580, and for 100 polyester blazers (work order 424) are $11.60 per blazer × 100 blazers = $1,160. When equivalent units are used to calculate the conversion-cost rate, costs are allocated to work orders by multiplying conversion cost per equivalent unit by number of equivalent units in the work order. Direct material costs of $6,000 for the 50 wool blazers (work order 423) and $3,000 for the 100 polyester blazers (work order 424) are specifically identified with each order, as in job costing. Remember the basic point in operation costing: Operation unit costs are assumed to be the same regardless of the work order, but direct material costs vary across orders when the materials for each work order vary.

Journal Entries

Actual conversion costs for Operation 1 in March 2012—assumed to be $24,400, including actual costs incurred for work order 423 and work order 424—are entered into a Conversion Costs Control account:

1. Conversion Costs Control	24,400	
Various accounts (such as Wages Payable		
Control and Accumulated Depreciation)		24,400

Summary journal entries for assigning costs to polyester blazers (work order 424) follow. Entries for wool blazers would be similar. Of the $3,000 of direct materials for work order 424, $2,975 are used in Operation 1, and the remaining $25 of materials are used in another operation. The journal entry to record direct materials used for the 100 polyester blazers in March 2012 is as follows:

2. Work in Process, Operation 1	2,975	
Materials Inventory Control		2,975

The journal entry to record the allocation of conversion costs to products uses the budgeted rate of $11.60 per blazer times the 100 polyester blazers processed, or $1,160:

3. Work in Process, Operation 1	1,160	
Conversion Costs Allocated		1,160

The journal entry to record the transfer of the 100 polyester blazers (at a cost of $2,975 + $1,160) from Operation 1 to Operation 3 (polyester blazers do not go through Operation 2) is as follows:

4. Work in Process, Operation 3	4,135	
Work in Process, Operation 1		4,135

After posting these entries, the Work in Process, Operation 1, account appears as follows:

Work in Process, Operation 1

② Direct materials	2,975	④ Transferred to Operation 3	4,135
③ Conversion costs allocated	1,160		
Ending inventory, March 31	0		

Costs of the blazers are transferred through the operations in which blazers are worked on and then to finished goods in the usual manner. Costs are added throughout the fiscal year in the Conversion Costs Control account and the Conversion Costs Allocated account. Any overallocation or underallocation of conversion costs is disposed of in the same way as overallocated or underallocated manufacturing overhead in a job-costing system (see pp. 117–122).

Decision Point

What is an operation-costing system and when is it a better approach to product-costing?

Problem for Self-Study

Allied Chemicals operates a thermo-assembly process as the second of three processes at its plastics plant. Direct materials in thermo-assembly are added at the end of the process. Conversion costs are added evenly during the process. The following data pertain to the thermo-assembly department for June 2012:

	Home	Insert	Page Layout	Formulas	Data	Review	View			
	A					B	C	D	E	
1						Physical Units	Transferred-In Costs	Direct Materials	Conversion Costs	
2	Work in process, beginning inventory					50,000				
3	Degree of completion of beginning work in process						100%	0%	80%	
4	Transferred in during current period					200,000				
5	Completed and transferred out during current period					210,000				
6	Work in process, ending inventory					?				
7	Degree of completion of ending work in process						100%	0%	40%	

Required Compute equivalent units under (1) the weighted-average method and (2) the FIFO method.

Solution

1. The weighted-average method uses equivalent units of work done to date to compute cost per equivalent unit. The calculations of equivalent units follow:

	Home	Insert	Page Layout	Formulas	Data	Review	View		
	A			B	C	D	E		
1				(Step 1)		(Step 2)			
2						Equivalent Units			
3	Flow of Production			Physical Units	Transferred-In Costs	Direct Materials	Conversion Costs		
4	Work in process, beginning (given)			50,000					
5	Transferred in during current period (given)			200,000					
6	To account for			250,000					
7	Completed and transferred out during current period			210,000	210,000	210,000	210,000		
8	Work in process, ending[a]			40,000[b]					
9	(40,000 × 100%; 40,000 × 0%; 40,000 × 40%)				40,000	0	16,000		
10	Accounted for			250,000					
11	Equivalent units of work done to date				250,000	210,000	226,000		
12									
13	[a]Degree of completion in this department: transferred-in costs, 100%; direct materials, 0%; conversion costs, 40%.								
14	[b]250,000 physical units to account for minus 210,000 physical units completed and transferred out.								

2. The FIFO method uses equivalent units of work done in the current period only to compute cost per equivalent unit. The calculations of equivalent units follow:

	Home Insert Page Layout Formulas Data Review View				
	A	B	C	D	E
1		(Step 1)		(Step 2)	
2				Equivalent Units	
3	Flow of Production	Physical Units	Transferred-In Costs	Direct Materials	Conversion Costs
4	Work in process, beginning (given)	50,000			
5	Transferred in during current period (given)	200,000			
6	To account for	250,000			
7	Completed and transferred out during current period:				
8	From beginning work in process[a]	50,000			
9	[50,000 × (100% – 100%); 50,000 × (100% – 0%); 50,000 × (100% – 80%)]		0	50,000	10,000
10	Started and completed	160,000[b]			
11	(160,000 × 100%; 160,000 × 100%; 160,000 × 100%)		160,000	160,000	160,000
12	Work in process, ending[c]	40,000[d]			
13	(40,000 × 100%; 40,000 × 0%; 40,000 × 40%)		40,000	0	16,000
14	Accounted for	250,000			
15	Equivalent units of work done in current period		200,000	210,000	186,000
16					
17	[a]Degree of completion in this department: transferred-in costs, 100%; direct materials, 0%; conversion costs, 80%.				
18	[b]210,000 physical units completed and transferred out minus 50,000 physical units completed and transferred out from beginning work-in-process inventory.				
19	[c]Degree of completion in this department: transferred-in costs, 100%; direct materials, 0%; conversion costs, 40%.				
20	[d]250,000 physical units to account for minus 210,000 physical units completed and transferred out.				

Decision Points

The following question-and-answer format summarizes the chapter's learning objectives. Each decision presents a key question related to a learning objective. The guidelines are the answer to that question.

Decision	Guidelines
1. Under what conditions is a process-costing system used?	A process-costing system is used to determine cost of a product or service when masses of identical or similar units are produced. Industries using process-costing systems include food, textiles, and oil refining.
2. How are average unit costs computed when no inventories are present?	Average unit costs are computed by dividing total costs in a given accounting period by total units produced in that period.
3. What are the five steps in a process-costing system and how are equivalent units calculated?	The five steps in a process-costing system are (1) summarize the flow of physical units of output, (2) compute output in terms of equivalent units, (3) summarize total costs to account for, (4) compute cost per equivalent unit, and (5) assign total costs to units completed and to units in ending work in process.
	Equivalent units is a derived amount of output units that (a) takes the quantity of each input (factor of production) in units completed or in incomplete units in work in process and (b) converts the quantity of input into the amount of completed output units that could be made with that quantity of input.

4. What are the weighted-average and first-in, first-out methods of process costing? Under what conditions will they yield different levels of operating income?

The weighted-average method computes unit costs by dividing total costs in the Work in Process account by total equivalent units completed to date, and assigns this average cost to units completed and to units in ending work-in-process inventory.

The first-in, first-out (FIFO) method computes unit costs based on costs incurred during the current period and equivalent units of work done in the current period.

Operating income can differ materially between the two methods when (1) direct material or conversion cost per equivalent unit varies significantly from period to period and (2) physical-inventory levels of work in process are large in relation to the total number of units transferred out of the process.

5. How are the weighted-average and FIFO process-costing methods applied to transferred-in costs?

The weighted-average method computes transferred-in costs per unit by dividing total transferred-in costs to date by total equivalent transferred-in units completed to date, and assigns this average cost to units completed and to units in ending work-in-process inventory. The FIFO method computes transferred-in costs per unit based on costs transferred in during the current period and equivalent units of transferred-in costs of work done in the current period. The FIFO method assigns transferred-in costs in beginning work in process to units completed and costs transferred in during the current period first to complete beginning inventory, next to start and complete new units, and finally to units in ending work-in-process inventory.

6. What is an operation-costing system and when is it a better approach to product-costing?

Operation-costing is a hybrid-costing system that blends characteristics from both job-costing and process-costing systems. It is a better approach to product-costing when production systems share some features of custom-order manufacturing and other features of mass-production manufacturing.

Appendix

Standard-Costing Method of Process Costing

Chapter 7 described accounting in a standard-costing system. Recall that this involves making entries using standard costs and then isolating variances from these standards in order to support management control. This appendix describes how the principles of standard costing can be employed in process-costing systems.

Benefits of Standard Costing

Companies that use process-costing systems produce masses of identical or similar units of output. In such companies, it is fairly easy to set standards for quantities of inputs needed to produce output. Standard cost per input unit can then be multiplied by input quantity standards to develop standard cost per output unit.

The weighted-average and FIFO methods become very complicated when used in process industries that produce a wide variety of similar products. For example, a steel-rolling mill uses various steel alloys and produces sheets of various sizes and finishes. The different types of direct materials used and the operations performed are few, but used in various combinations, they yield a wide variety of products. Similarly, complex conditions are frequently found, for example, in plants that manufacture rubber products, textiles, ceramics, paints, and packaged food products. In each of these cases, if the broad averaging procedure of *actual* process costing were used, the result would be inaccurate costs for each product. Therefore, the standard-costing method of process costing is widely used in these industries.

Under the standard-costing method, teams of design and process engineers, operations personnel, and management accountants work together to determine *separate* standard costs per equivalent unit on the basis of different technical processing specifications for each product. Identifying standard costs for each product overcomes the disadvantage of costing all products at a single average amount, as under actual costing.

Computations Under Standard Costing

We return to the assembly department of Pacific Electronics, but this time we use standard costs. Assume the same standard costs apply in February and March of 2012. Data for the assembly department are as follows:

	Home Insert Page Layout Formulas Data Review View				
	A	Physical Units (SG-40s) (1)	Direct Materials (2)	Conversion Costs (3)	Total Costs (4) = (2) + (3)
2	Standard cost per unit		$ 74	$ 54	
3	Work in process, beginning inventory (March 1)	225			
4	Degree of completion of beginning work in process		100%	60%	
5	Beginning work in process inventory at standard costs		$16,650[a]	$ 7,290[a]	$23,940
6	Started during March	275			
7	Completed and transferred out during March	400			
8	Work in process, ending inventory (March 31)	100			
9	Degree of completion of ending work in process		100%	50%	
10	Actual total costs added during March		$19,800	$16,380	$36,180
11					
12	[a]Work in process, beginning inventory at standard costs				
13	Direct materials: 225 physical units × 100% completed × $74 per unit = $16,650				
14	Conversion costs: 225 physical units × 60% completed × $54 per unit = $7,290				

We illustrate the standard-costing method of process costing using the five-step procedure introduced earlier (p. 610).

Exhibit 17-12 presents Steps 1 and 2. These steps are identical to the steps described for the FIFO method in Exhibit 17-6 because, as in FIFO, the standard-costing method also assumes that the earliest equivalent units in beginning work in process are completed first. Work done in the current period for direct materials is 275 equivalent units. Work done in the current period for conversion costs is 315 equivalent units.

Exhibit 17-13 describes Steps 3, 4, and 5. In Step 3, total costs to account for (that is, the total debits to Work in Process—Assembly) differ from total debits to Work in Process—Assembly under the actual-cost-based weighted-average

Exhibit 17-12

Steps 1 and 2: Summarize Output in Physical Units and Compute Output in Equivalent Units Using Standard-Costing Method of Process Costing for Assembly Department of Pacific Electronics for March 2012

	Home Insert Page Layout Formulas Data Review View			
	A	B	C	D
1		(Step 1)	(Step 2)	
2			Equivalent Units	
3	Flow of Production	Physical Units	Direct Materials	Conversion Costs
4	Work in process, beginning (given, p. 633)	225		
5	Started during current period (given, p. 633)	275		
6	To account for	500		
7	Completed and transferred out during current period:			
8	From beginning work in process[a]	225		
9	[225 × (100% – 100%); 225 × (100% – 60%)]		0	90
10	Started and completed	175[b]		
11	(175 × 100%; 175 × 100%)		175	175
12	Work in process, ending[c] (given, p. 633)	100		
13	(100 × 100%; 100 × 50%)		100	50
14	Accounted for	500		
15	Equivalent units of work done in current period		275	315
16				
17	[a]Degree of completion in this department: direct materials, 100%; conversion costs, 60%.			
18	[b]400 physical units completed and transferred out minus 225 physical units completed and transferred out from beginning work-in-process inventory.			
19	[c]Degree of completion in this department: direct materials, 100%; conversion costs, 50%.			

Exhibit 17-13 Steps 3, 4, and 5: Summarize Total Costs to Account For, Compute Cost per Equivalent Unit, and Assign Total Costs to Units Completed and to Units in Ending Work in Process Using Standard-Costing Method of Process Costing for Assembly Department of Pacific Electronics for March 2012

	Home	Insert	Page Layout	Formulas	Data	Review	View		

	A	B	C	D	E	F	G
1			Total Production Costs	Direct Materials		Conversion Costs	
2	**(Step 3)**	Work in process, beginning (given, p. 633)					
3		Direct materials, 225 × $74; Conversion costs, 135 × $54	$23,940	$16,650		$ 7,290	
4		Costs added in current period at standard costs					
5		Direct materials, 275 × $74; Conversion costs, 315 × $54	37,360	20,350		17,010	
6		Total costs to account for	$61,300	$37,000		$24,300	
7							
8	**(Step 4)**	Standard cost per equivalent unit (given, p. 633)		$ 74		$ 54	
9							
10	**(Step 5)**	Assignment of costs at standard costs:					
11		Completed and transferred out (400 units):					
12		Work in process, beginning (225 units)	$23,940	$16,650	+	$ 7,290	
13		Costs added to beginning work in process in current period	4,860	($0[a] × $74)	+	(90[a] × $54)	
14		Total from beginning inventory	28,800				
15		Started and completed (175 units)	22,400	(175[b] × $74)	+	(175[b] × $54)	
16		Total costs of units completed and transferred out	51,200				
17		Work in process, ending (100 units):	10,100	(100[c] × $74)	+	(50[c] × $54)	
18		Total costs accounted for	$61,300	$37,000	+	$24,300	
19							
20		Summary of variances for current performance:					
21		Costs added in current period at standard costs (see step 3)		$20,350		$17,010	
22		Actual costs incurred (given, p. 633)		$19,800		$16,380	
23		Variance		$ 550	F	$ 630	F
24							
25		[a]Equivalent units used to complete beginning work in process from Exhibit 17-12, Step 2.					
26		[b]Equivalent units started and completed from Exhibit 17-12, Step 2.					
27		[c]Equivalent units in ending work in process from Exhibit 17-12, Step 2.					

and FIFO methods. That's because, as in all standard-costing systems, the debits to the Work in Process account are at standard costs, rather than actual costs. These standard costs total $61,300 in Exhibit 17-13. In Step 4, costs per equivalent unit are standard costs: direct materials, $74, and conversion costs, $54. *Therefore, costs per equivalent unit do not have to be computed as they were for the weighted-average and FIFO methods.*

Exhibit 17-13, Step 5, assigns total costs to units completed and transferred out and to units in ending work-in-process inventory, as in the FIFO method. Step 5 assigns amounts of standard costs to equivalent units calculated in Exhibit 17-12. These costs are assigned (1) first to complete beginning work-in-process inventory, (2) next to start and complete new units, and (3) finally to start new units that are in ending work-in-process inventory. Note how the $61,300 total costs accounted for in Step 5 of Exhibit 17-13 equal total costs to account for.

Accounting for Variances

Process-costing systems using standard costs record actual direct material costs in Direct Materials Control and actual conversion costs in Conversion Costs Control (similar to Variable and Fixed Overhead Control in Chapter 8). In the journal entries that follow, the first two record these *actual costs.* In entries 3 and 4a, the Work-in-Process—Assembly account accumulates direct material costs and conversion costs at *standard costs.* Entries 3 and 4b isolate total variances. The final entry transfers out completed goods at standard costs.

1. Assembly Department Direct Materials Control (at actual costs)   19,800
          Accounts Payable Control   19,800
      To record direct materials purchased and used in production during March. This cost control account is debited with actual costs.

2. Assembly Department Conversion Costs Control (at actual costs)   16,380

    Various accounts such as Wages Payable Control and Accumulated Depreciation   16,380

  To record assembly department conversion costs for March. This cost control account is debited with actual costs.

Entries 3, 4, and 5 use standard cost amounts from Exhibit 17-13.

3. Work in Process—Assembly (at standard costs)   20,350

    Direct Materials Variances   550

    Assembly Department Direct Materials Control   19,800

  To record standard costs of direct materials assigned to units worked on and total direct materials variances.

4a. Work in Process—Assembly (at standard costs)   17,010

    Assembly Department Conversion Costs Allocated   17,010

  To record conversion costs allocated at standard rates to the units worked on during March.

4b. Assembly Department Conversion Costs Allocated   17,010

    Conversion Costs Variances   630

    Assembly Department Conversion Costs Control   16,380

  To record total conversion costs variances.

5. Work in Process—Testing (at standard costs)   51,200

    Work in Process—Assembly (at standard costs)   51,200

  To record standard costs of units completed and transferred out from assembly to testing.

Variances arise under standard costing, as in entries 3 and 4b. That's because the standard costs assigned to products on the basis of work done in the current period do not equal actual costs incurred in the current period. Recall that variances that result in higher income than expected are termed favorable, while those that reduce income are unfavorable. From an accounting standpoint, favorable cost variances are credit entries, while unfavorable ones are debits. In the preceding example, both direct materials and conversion cost variances are favorable. This is also reflected in the "F" designations for both variances in Exhibit 17-13.

Variances can be analyzed in little or great detail for planning and control purposes, as described in Chapters 7 and 8. Sometimes direct materials price variances are isolated at the time direct materials are purchased and only efficiency variances are computed in entry 3. Exhibit 17-14 shows how the costs flow through the general-ledger accounts under standard costing.

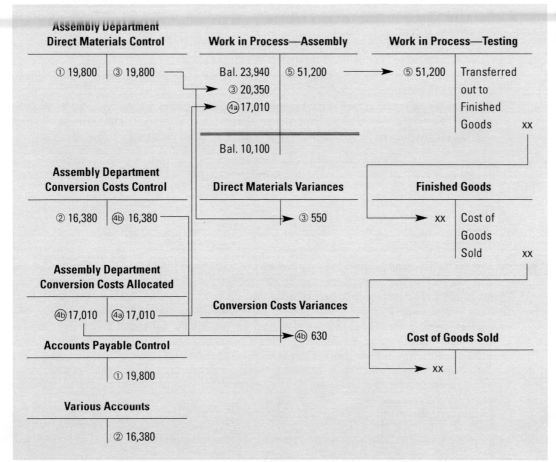

Exhibit 17-14

Flow of Standard Costs in a Process-Costing System for Assembly Department of Pacific Electronics for March 2012

Terms to Learn

This chapter and the Glossary at the end of the book contain definitions of the following important terms:

equivalent units (**p. 611**)

first-in, first-out (FIFO) process-costing
  method (**p. 617**)

hybrid-costing system (**p. 626**)

operation (**p. 626**)

operation-costing system (**p. 626**)

previous-department costs (**p. 621**)

transferred-in costs (**p. 621**)

weighted-average process-costing
  method (**p. 614**)

Assignment Material

Questions

17-1 Give three examples of industries that use process-costing systems.

17-2 In process costing, why are costs often divided into two main classifications?

17-3 Explain equivalent units. Why are equivalent-unit calculations necessary in process costing?

17-4 What problems might arise in estimating the degree of completion of semiconductor chips in a semiconductor plant?

17-5 Name the five steps in process costing when equivalent units are computed.

17-6 Name the three inventory methods commonly associated with process costing.

17-7 Describe the distinctive characteristic of weighted-average computations in assigning costs to units completed and to units in ending work in process.

17-8 Describe the distinctive characteristic of FIFO computations in assigning costs to units completed and to units in ending work in process.

17-9 Why should the FIFO method be called a modified or department FIFO method?

17-10 Identify a major advantage of the FIFO method for purposes of planning and control.

17-11 Identify the main difference between journal entries in process costing and job costing.

17-12 "The standard-costing method is particularly applicable to process-costing situations." Do you agree? Why?

17-13 Why should the accountant distinguish between transferred-in costs and additional direct material costs for each subsequent department in a process-costing system?

17-14 "Transferred-in costs are those costs incurred in the preceding accounting period." Do you agree? Explain.

17-15 "There's no reason for me to get excited about the choice between the weighted-average and FIFO methods in my process-costing system. I have long-term contracts with my materials suppliers at fixed prices." Do you agree with this statement made by a plant controller? Explain.

Exercises

17-16 Equivalent units, zero beginning inventory. Nihon, Inc., is a manufacturer of digital cameras. It has two departments: assembly and testing. In January 2012, the company incurred $750,000 on direct materials and $798,000 on conversion costs, for a total manufacturing cost of $1,548,000.

Required

1. Assume there was no beginning inventory of any kind on January 1, 2012. During January, 10,000 cameras were placed into production and all 10,000 were fully completed at the end of the month. What is the unit cost of an assembled camera in January?

2. Assume that during February 10,000 cameras are placed into production. Further assume the same total assembly costs for January are also incurred in February, but only 9,000 cameras are fully completed at the end of the month. All direct materials have been added to the remaining 1,000 cameras. However, on average, these remaining 1,000 cameras are only 50% complete as to conversion costs. (a) What are the equivalent units for direct materials and conversion costs and their respective costs per equivalent unit for February? (b) What is the unit cost of an assembled camera in February 2012?

3. Explain the difference in your answers to requirements 1 and 2.

17-17 Journal entries (continuation of 17-16). Refer to requirement 2 of Exercise 17-16.

Prepare summary journal entries for the use of direct materials and incurrence of conversion costs. Also prepare a journal entry to transfer out the cost of goods completed. Show the postings to the Work in Process account.

Required

17-18 Zero beginning inventory, materials introduced in middle of process. Roary Chemicals has a mixing department and a refining department. Its process-costing system in the mixing department has two direct materials cost categories (chemical P and chemical Q) and one conversion costs pool. The following data pertain to the mixing department for July 2012:

Units	
Work in process, July 1	0
Units started	50,000
Completed and transferred to refining department	35,000
Costs	
Chemical P	$250,000
Chemical Q	70,000
Conversion costs	135,000

Chemical P is introduced at the start of operations in the mixing department, and chemical Q is added when the product is three-fourths completed in the mixing department. Conversion costs are added evenly during the process. The ending work in process in the mixing department is two-thirds complete.

1. Compute the equivalent units in the mixing department for July 2012 for each cost category.
2. Compute (a) the cost of goods completed and transferred to the refining department during July and (b) the cost of work in process as of July 31, 2012.

Required

17-19 Weighted-average method, equivalent units. Consider the following data for the assembly division of Fenton Watches, Inc.:

The assembly division uses the weighted-average method of process costing.

	Physical Units (Watches)	Direct Materials	Conversion Costs
Beginning work in process (May 1)[a]	80	$ 493,360	$ 91,040
Started in May 2012	500		
Completed during May 2012	460		
Ending work in process (May 31)[b]	120		
Total costs added during May 2012		$3,220,000	$1,392,000

[a]Degree of completion: direct materials, 90%; conversion costs, 40%.
[b]Degree of completion: direct materials, 60%; conversion costs, 30%.

Compute equivalent units for direct materials and conversion costs. Show physical units in the first column of your schedule.

Required

17-20 Weighted-average method, assigning costs (continuation of 17-19).

For the data in Exercise 17-19, summarize total costs to account for, calculate cost per equivalent unit for direct materials and conversion costs, and assign total costs to units completed (and transferred out) and to units in ending work in process.

Required

17-21 FIFO method, equivalent units. Refer to the information in Exercise 17-19. Suppose the assembly division at Fenton Watches, Inc., uses the FIFO method of process costing instead of the weighted-average method.

Compute equivalent units for direct materials and conversion costs. Show physical units in the first column of your schedule.

Required

17-22 FIFO method, assigning costs (continuation of 17-21).

For the data in Exercise 17-19, use the FIFO method to summarize total costs to account for, calculate cost per equivalent unit for direct materials and conversion costs, and assign total costs to units completed (and transferred out) and to units in ending work in process.

Required

17-23 Operation Costing. Whole Goodness Bakery needs to determine the cost of two work orders for the month of June. Work order 215 is for 1,200 packages of dinner rolls and work order 216 is for 1,400 loaves of multigrain bread. Dinner rolls are mixed and cut into individual rolls before being baked and then packaged. Multigrain loaves are mixed and shaped before being baked, sliced, and packaged. The following information applies to work order 215 and work order 216:

	Work Order 215	Work Order 216
Quantity (packages)	1,200	1,400
Operations		
1. Mix	Use	Use
2. Shape loaves	Do not use	Use
3. Cut rolls	Use	Do not use
4. Bake	Use	Use
5. Slice loaves	Do not use	Use
6. Package	Use	Use

Selected budget information for June follows:

	Dinner Rolls	Multigrain Loaves	Total
Packages	4,800	6,500	11,300
Direct material costs	$2,640	$5,850	$ 8,490

Budgeted conversion costs for each operation for June follow:

Mixing	$9,040
Shaping	1,625
Cutting	720
Baking	7,345
Slicing	650
Packaging	8,475

Required

1. Using budgeted number of packages as the denominator, calculate the budgeted conversion-cost rates for each operation.
2. Using the information in requirement 1, calculate the budgeted cost of goods manufactured for the two June work orders.
3. Calculate the cost per package of dinner rolls and multigrain loaves for work order 215 and 216.

17-24 Weighted-average method, assigning costs. Bio Doc Corporation is a biotech company based in Milpitas. It makes a cancer-treatment drug in a single processing department. Direct materials are added at the start of the process. Conversion costs are added evenly during the process. Bio Doc uses the weighted-average method of process costing. The following information for July 2011 is available.

		Equivalent Units	
	Physical Units	Direct Materials	Conversion Costs
Work in process, July 1	8,500[a]	8,500	1,700
Started during July	35,000		
Completed and transferred out during July	33,000	33,000	33,000
Work in process, July 31	10,500[b]	10,500	6,300

[a]Degree of completion: direct materials, 100%; conversion costs, 20%.
[b]Degree of completion: direct materials, 100%; conversion costs, 60%.

Total Costs for July 2008

Work in process, beginning		
Direct materials	$63,100	
Conversion costs	45,510	$108,610
Direct materials added during July		284,900
Conversion costs added during July		485,040
Total costs to account for		$878,550

Required

1. Calculate cost per equivalent unit for direct materials and conversion costs.
2. Summarize total costs to account for, and assign total costs to units completed (and transferred out) and to units in ending work in process.

17-25 FIFO method, assigning costs.

Do Exercise 17-24 using the FIFO method. Note that you first need to calculate the equivalent units of work **Required** done in the current period (for direct materials and conversion costs) to complete beginning work in process, to start and complete new units, and to produce ending work in process.

17-26 Standard-costing method, assigning costs. Refer to the information in Exercise 17-24. Suppose Bio Doc determines standard costs of $8.25 per equivalent unit for direct materials and $12.70 per equivalent unit for conversion costs for both beginning work in process and work done in the current period.

1. Do Exercise 17-24 using the standard-costing method. Note that you first need to calculate the equiv- **Required** alent units of work done in the current period (for direct materials and conversion costs) to complete beginning work in process, to start and complete new units, and to produce ending work in process.
2. Compute the total direct materials and conversion costs variances for July 2011.

17-27 Transferred-in costs, weighted-average method. Asaya Clothing, Inc., is a manufacturer of winter clothes. It has a knitting department and a finishing department. This exercise focuses on the finishing department. Direct materials are added at the end of the process. Conversion costs are added evenly during the process. Asaya uses the weighted-average method of process costing. The following information for June 2012 is available.

	A	Physical Units (tons)	Transferred-In Costs	Direct Materials	Conversion Costs
1		**Physical Units (tons)**	**Transferred-In Costs**	**Direct Materials**	**Conversion Costs**
2	Work in process, beginning inventory (June 1)	75	$ 75,000	$ 0	$30,000
3	Degree of completion, beginning work in process		100%	0%	60%
4	Transferred in during June	135			
5	Completed and transferred out during June	150			
6	Work in process, ending inventory (June 30)	60			
7	Degree of completion, ending work in process		100%	0%	75%
8	Total costs added during June		$142,500	$37,500	$70,000

1. Calculate equivalent units of transferred-in costs, direct materials, and conversion costs. **Required**
2. Summarize total costs to account for, and calculate the cost per equivalent unit for transferred-in costs, direct materials, and conversion costs.
3. Assign total costs to units completed (and transferred out) and to units in ending work in process.

17-28 Transferred-in costs, FIFO method. Refer to the information in Exercise 17-27. Suppose that Asaya uses the FIFO method instead of the weighted-average method in all of its departments. The only changes to Exercise 17-27 under the FIFO method are that total transferred-in costs of beginning work in process on June 1 are $60,000 (instead of $75,000) and total transferred-in costs added during June are $130,800 (instead of $142,500).

Do Exercise 17-27 using the FIFO method. Note that you first need to calculate equivalent units of work done **Required** in the current period (for transferred-in costs, direct materials, and conversion costs) to complete beginning work in process, to start and complete new units, and to produce ending work in process.

17-29 Operation Costing. UB Healthy Company manufactures three different types of vitamins: vitamin A, vitamin B, and a multivitamin. The company uses four operations to manufacture the vitamins: mixing, tableting, encapsulating, and bottling. Vitamins A and B are produced in tablet form (in the tableting department) and the multivitamin is produced in capsule form (in the encapsulating department). Each bottle contains 200 vitamins, regardless of the product.

Conversion costs are applied based on the number of bottles in the tableting and encapsulating departments. Conversion costs are applied based on labor hours in the mixing department. It takes 1.5 minutes to mix the ingredients for a 200-unit bottle for each product. Conversion costs are applied based on machine hours in the bottling department. It takes 1 minute of machine time to fill a 200-unit bottle, regardless of the product.

UB Healthy is planning to complete one batch of each type of vitamin in July. The budgeted number of bottles and expected direct material cost for each type of vitamin is as follows:

	Vitamin A	Vitamin B	Multivitamin
Number of 200 unit bottles	12,000	9,000	18,000
Direct material cost	$23,040	$21,600	$47,520

The budgeted conversion costs for each department for July are as follows:

Department	Budgeted Conversion Cost
Mixing	$ 8,190
Tableting	24,150
Encapsulating	25,200
Bottling	3,510

Required

1. Calculate the conversion cost rates for each department.
2. Calculate the budgeted cost of goods manufactured for vitamin A, vitamin B, and the multivitamin for the month of July.
3. Calculate the cost per 200-unit bottle for each type of vitamin for the month of July.

MyAccountingLab

Problems

17-30 Weighted-average method. Larsen Company manufactures car seats in its San Antonio plant. Each car seat passes through the assembly department and the testing department. This problem focuses on the assembly department. The process-costing system at Larsen Company has a single direct-cost category (direct materials) and a single indirect-cost category (conversion costs). Direct materials are added at the beginning of the process. Conversion costs are added evenly during the process. When the assembly department finishes work on each car seat, it is immediately transferred to testing.

Larsen Company uses the weighted-average method of process costing. Data for the assembly department for October 2012 are as follows:

	Physical Units (Car Seats)	Direct Materials	Conversion Costs
Work in process, October 1[a]	5,000	$1,250,000	$ 402,750
Started during October 2012	20,000		
Completed during October 2012	22,500		
Work in process, October 31[b]	2,500		
Total costs added during October 2012		$4,500,000	$2,337,500

[a]Degree of completion: direct materials, ?%; conversion costs, 60%.
[b]Degree of completion: direct materials, ?%; conversion costs, 70%.

Required

1. For each cost category, compute equivalent units in the assembly department. Show physical units in the first column of your schedule.
2. For each cost category, summarize total assembly department costs for October 2012 and calculate the cost per equivalent unit.
3. Assign total costs to units completed and transferred out and to units in ending work in process.

17-31 Journal entries (continuation of 17-30).

Required

Prepare a set of summarized journal entries for all October 2012 transactions affecting Work in Process—Assembly. Set up a T-account for Work in Process—Assembly and post your entries to it.

17-32 FIFO method (continuation of 17-30).

Required

Do Problem 17-30 using the FIFO method of process costing. Explain any difference between the cost per equivalent unit in the assembly department under the weighted-average method and the FIFO method.

17-33 Transferred-in costs, weighted-average method (related to 17-30 to 17-32). Larsen Company, as you know, is a manufacturer of car seats. Each car seat passes through the assembly department and testing department. This problem focuses on the testing department. Direct materials are added when the testing department process is 90% complete. Conversion costs are added evenly during the testing department's process. As work in assembly is completed, each unit is immediately transferred to testing. As each unit is completed in testing, it is immediately transferred to Finished Goods.

Larsen Company uses the weighted-average method of process costing. Data for the testing department for October 2012 are as follows:

	Physical Units (Car Seats)	Transferred-In Costs	Direct Materials	Conversion Costs
Work in process, October 1[a]	7,500	$2,932,500	$ 0	$ 835,460
Transferred in during October 2012	?			
Completed during October 2012	26,300			
Work in process, October 31[b]	3,700			
Total costs added during October 2012		$7,717,500	$9,704,700	$3,955,900

[a]Degree of completion: transferred-in costs, ?%; direct materials, ?%; conversion costs, 70%.
[b]Degree of completion: transferred-in costs, ?%; direct materials, ?%; conversion costs, 60%.

1. What is the percentage of completion for (a) transferred-in costs and direct materials in beginning work-in-process inventory, and (b) transferred-in costs and direct materials in ending work-in-process inventory? **Required**
2. For each cost category, compute equivalent units in the testing department. Show physical units in the first column of your schedule.
3. For each cost category, summarize total testing department costs for October 2012, calculate the cost per equivalent unit, and assign total costs to units completed (and transferred out) and to units in ending work in process.
4. Prepare journal entries for October transfers from the assembly department to the testing department and from the testing department to Finished Goods.

17-34 Transferred-in costs, FIFO method (continuation of 17-33). Refer to the information in Problem 17-33. Suppose that Larsen Company uses the FIFO method instead of the weighted-average method in all of its departments. The only changes to Problem 17-33 under the FIFO method are that total transferred-in costs of beginning work in process on October 1 are $2,881,875 (instead of $2,932,500) and that total transferred-in costs added during October are $7,735,250 (instead of $7,717,500).

Using the FIFO process-costing method, complete Problem 17-33. **Required**

17-35 Weighted-average method. Ashworth Handcraft is a manufacturer of picture frames for large retailers. Every picture frame passes through two departments: the assembly department and the finishing department. This problem focuses on the assembly department. The process-costing system at Ashworth has a single direct-cost category (direct materials) and a single indirect-cost category (conversion costs). Direct materials are added when the assembly department process is 10% complete. Conversion costs are added evenly during the assembly department's process.

Ashworth uses the weighted-average method of process costing. Consider the following data for the assembly department in April 2012:

	Physical Unit (Frames)	Direct Materials	Conversion Costs
Work in process, April 1[a]	95	$ 1,665	$ 988
Started during April 2012	490		
Completed during April 2012	455		
Work in process, April 30[b]	130		
Total costs added during April 2012		$17,640	$11,856

[a]Degree of completion: direct materials, 100%; conversion costs, 40%.
[b]Degree of completion: direct materials, 100%; conversion costs, 30%.

Summarize total assembly department costs for April 2012, and assign total costs to units completed (and transferred out) and to units in ending work in process. **Required**

17-36 Journal entries (continuation of 17-35).

Prepare a set of summarized journal entries for all April transactions affecting Work in Process—Assembly. **Required**
Set up a T-account for Work in Process—Assembly and post your entries to it.

17-37 FIFO method (continuation of 17-35).

Do Problem 17-35 using the FIFO method of process costing. If you did Problem 17-35, explain any difference **Required**
between the cost of work completed and transferred out and the cost of ending work in process in the assembly department under the weighted-average method and the FIFO method.

17-38 Transferred-in costs, weighted-average method. Bookworm, Inc., has two departments: printing and binding. Each department has one direct-cost category (direct materials) and one indirect-cost category (conversion costs). This problem focuses on the binding department. Books that have undergone the printing process are immediately transferred to the binding department. Direct material is added when the binding process is 80% complete. Conversion costs are added evenly during binding operations. When those operations are done, the books are immediately transferred to Finished Goods. Bookworm, Inc., uses the weighted-average method of process costing. The following is a summary of the April 2012 operations of the binding department.

	A	B	C	D	E
		Physical Units (books)	Transferred-In Costs	Direct Materials	Conversion Costs
2	Beginning work in process	1,050	$ 32,550	$ 0	$13,650
3	Degree of completion, beginning work in process		100%	0%	50%
4	Transferred in during April 2012	2,400			
5	Completed and transferred out during April	2,700			
6	Ending work in process (April 30)	750			
7	Degree of completion, ending work in process		100%	0%	70%
8	Total costs added during April		$129,600	$23,490	$70,200

Required

1. Summarize total binding department costs for April 2012, and assign these costs to units completed (and transferred out) and to units in ending work in process.
2. Prepare journal entries for April transfers from the printing department to the binding department and from the binding department to Finished Goods.

17-39 Transferred-in costs, FIFO method. Refer to the information in Problem 17-38. Suppose that Bookworm, Inc., uses the FIFO method instead of the weighted-average method in all of its departments. The only changes to Problem 17-38 under the FIFO method are that total transferred-in costs of beginning work in process on April 1 are $36,750 (instead of $32,550) and that total transferred-in costs added during April are $124,800 (instead of $129,600).

Required

1. Using the FIFO process-costing method, complete Problem 17-38.
2. If you did Problem 17-38, explain any difference between the cost of work completed and transferred out and the cost of ending work in process in the binding department under the weighted-average method and the FIFO method.

17-40 Transferred-in costs, weighted-average and FIFO methods. Frito-Lay, Inc., manufactures convenience foods, including potato chips and corn chips. Production of corn chips occurs in four departments: cleaning, mixing, cooking, and drying and packaging. Consider the drying and packaging department, where direct materials (packaging) are added at the end of the process. Conversion costs are added evenly during the process. The accounting records of a Frito-Lay plant provide the following information for corn chips in its drying and packaging department during a weekly period (week 37):

	Physical Units (Cases)	Transferred-In Costs	Direct Materials	Conversion Costs
Beginning work in process[a]	1,200	$26,750	$ 0	$ 4,020
Transferred in during week 37 from cooking department	4,200			
Completed during week 37	4,000			
Ending work in process, week 37[b]	1,400			
Total costs added during week 37		$91,510	$23,000	$27,940

[a]Degree of completion: transferred-in costs, 100%; direct materials, ?%; conversion costs, 25%.
[b]Degree of completion: transferred-in costs, 100%; direct materials, ?%; conversion costs, 50%.

Required

1. Using the weighted-average method, summarize the total drying and packaging department costs for week 37, and assign total costs to units completed (and transferred out) and to units in ending work in process.
2. Assume that the FIFO method is used for the drying and packaging department. Under FIFO, the transferred-in costs for work-in-process beginning inventory in week 37 are $28,920 (instead of $26,750 under the weighted-average method), and the transferred-in costs during week 37 from the cooking department are $93,660 (instead of $91,510 under the weighted-average method). All other data are unchanged. Summarize the total drying and packaging department costs for week 37, and assign total costs to units completed and transferred out and to units in ending work in process using the FIFO method.

17-41 **Standard-costing with beginning and ending work in process.** Penelope's Pearls Company (PPC) is a manufacturer of knock off jewelry. Penelope attends Fashion Week in New York City every September and February to gauge the latest fashion trends in jewelry. She then makes trendy jewelry at a fraction of the cost of those designers who participate in Fashion Week. This Fall's biggest item is triple-stranded pearl necklaces. Because of her large volume, Penelope uses process costing to account for her production. In October, she had started some of the triple strands. She continued to work on those in November. Costs and output figures are as follows:

Penelope's Pearls Company
Process Costing
For the Month Ended November 30, 2012

	Units	Direct Materials	Conversion Costs
Standard cost per unit		$3.00	$10.50
Work in process, beginning inventory (Nov. 1)	24,000	$72,000	$176,400
Degree of completion of beginning work in process		100%	70%
Started during November	124,400		
Completed and transferred out	123,000		
Work in process, ending inventory (Nov. 30)	25,400		
Degree of completion of ending work in process		100%	50%
Total costs added during November		$329,000	$1,217,000

1. Compute equivalent units for direct materials and conversion costs. Show physical units in the first column of your schedule. **Required**
2. Compute the total standard costs of pearls transferred out in November and the total standard costs of the November 30 inventory of work in process.
3. Compute the total November variances for direct materials and conversion costs.

Collaborative Learning Problem

17-42 **Standard-costing method.** Ozumo's Gardening makes several different kinds of mulch. Its busy period is in the summer months. In August, the controller suddenly quit due to a stress-related disorder. He took with him the standard costing results for RoseBark, Ozumo's highest quality mulch. The controller had already completed the assignment of costs to finished goods and work in process, but Ozumo does not know standard costs or the completion levels of inventory. The following information is available:

Physical and Equivalent Units for RoseBark
For the Month Ended August 31, 2012

	Physical Units (Yards of Mulch)	Equivalent Units (yards) Direct Materials	Equivalent Units (yards) Conversion Costs
Completion of beginning work in process	965,000	—	434,250
Started and completed	845,000	845,000	845,000
Work on ending work in process	1,817,000	1,817,000	1,090,200
		2,662,000	2,369,450
Units to account for	3,627,000		

	Costs
Cost of units completed from beginning work in process	$ 7,671,750
Cost of new units started and completed	6,717,750
Cost of units completed in August	14,389,500
Cost of ending work in process	12,192,070
Total costs accounted for	$26,581,570

1. Calculate the completion percentages of beginning work in process with respect to the two inputs. **Required**
2. Calculate the completion percentages of ending work in process with respect to the two inputs.
3. What are the standard costs per unit for the two inputs?
4. What is the total cost of work-in-process inventory as of August 1, 2012?

22 Management Control Systems, Transfer Pricing, and Multinational Considerations

Management Control Systems, Transfer Pricing, and Multinational Considerations

Transfer pricing is the price one subunit of a company charges for the services it provides another subunit of the same company.

Top management uses transfer prices (1) to focus managers' attention on the performance of their own subunits and (2) to plan and coordinate the actions of different subunits to maximize the company's income as a whole. While transfer pricing is productive, it can also be contentious, because managers of different subunits often have very different preferences about how transfer prices should be set. For example, some managers prefer the prices be based on market prices. Others prefer the prices be based on costs alone. Controversy also arises when multinational corporations seek to reduce their overall income tax burden by charging high transfer prices to units located in countries with high tax rates. Many countries, including the United States, attempt to restrict this practice, as the following article shows.

Symantec Wins $545 million Opinion in Transfer Pricing Dispute with the IRS[1]

Symantec Corp., a large U.S. software company, won a significant court decision in December 2009, potentially saving it $545 million in contested back taxes. The Internal Revenue Service (IRS) had been seeking back taxes it alleged were owed by Veritas Software Corp., a company acquired by Symantec in 2005. The dispute was over the company's formula for "transfer pricing," a complex set of rules determining how companies set prices, fees, and cost-allocation arrangements between their operations in different tax jurisdictions.

At issue were the fees and cost-allocation arrangements between Veritas and its Irish subsidiary. Ireland has emerged as a popular tax haven for U.S. technology companies. Veritas granted rights to Veritas Ireland to conduct research and development on various intangibles (such as computer programs and manufacturing process technologies) related to data storage software and related devices. Under the agreement in effect, Veritas Ireland paid $160 million for this grant of rights from 1999 to 2001. Based on a discounted cash flow analysis, the IRS contended that the true value of the transferred rights was closer to $1.675 billion. As a consequence, it claimed that the transaction artificially increased the income of Veritas Ireland at the

[1] *Source:* Chinnis, Cabell et al. 2009. Tax court upends IRS's billion dollar buy-in valuation adjustment in "Veritas." Mondaq Business Briefing, December 17; Letzing, John. 2009. Symantec wins $545M opinion in tax case. *Dow Jones News Service,* December 11.

expense of income in the U.S. parent corporation, consequently lowering the U.S. tax bills during this period.

Veritas, however, maintained that it acted appropriately. The company testified that the $160 million figure was based on royalty rates it had received from seven original equipment manufacturers (OEMs) for rights to incorporate Veritas United States' software and technologies into an operating system, with adjustments made for purposes of comparability. At trial, the United States Tax Court supported this position, and called the IRS's valuation of the intangibles "arbitrary, capricious, and unreasonable." Among other things, the court took issue with the discount and growth rates used in the IRS expert's analysis, and disagreed with his assumption that the transferred intangibles had a perpetual useful life.

Though not all companies face multinational tax concerns, transfer-pricing issues are common to many companies. In these companies, transfer pricing is part of the larger management control system. This chapter develops the links among strategy, organization structure, management control systems, and accounting information. We'll examine the benefits and costs of centralized and decentralized organization structures, and we'll look at the pricing of products or services transferred between subunits of the same company. We emphasize how accounting information, such as costs, budgets, and prices, helps in planning and coordinating actions of subunits.

Management Control Systems

A **management control system** is a means of gathering and using information to aid and coordinate the planning and control decisions throughout an organization and to guide the behavior of its managers and other employees. Some companies design their management control system around the concept of the balanced scorecard. For example, ExxonMobil's management control system contains financial and nonfinancial information in each of the four perspectives of the balanced scorecard (see Chapter 13 for details). Well-designed management control systems use information both from within the company, such as net income and employee satisfaction, and from outside the company, such as stock price and customer satisfaction.

Formal and Informal Systems

Management control systems consist of formal and informal control systems. The formal management control system of a company includes explicit rules, procedures, performance measures, and incentive plans that guide the behavior of its managers and other employees. The formal control system is comprised of several systems, such as the

Learning Objective 1

Describe a management control system

. . . gathers information for planning and control decisions

and its three key properties

. . . aligns with strategy, supports organizational responsibility of managers, and motivates employees

management accounting system, which provides information regarding costs, revenues, and income; the human resources systems, which provide information on recruiting, training, absenteeism, and accidents; and the quality systems, which provide information on yield, defective products, and late deliveries to customers.

The informal management control system includes shared values, loyalties, and mutual commitments among members of the organization, company culture, and the unwritten norms about acceptable behavior for managers and other employees. Examples of company slogans that reinforce values and loyalties are "At Ford, Quality Is Job 1," and "At Home Depot, Low Prices Are Just the Beginning."

Effective Management Control

To be effective, management control systems should be closely aligned with the organization's strategies and goals. Two examples of strategies at ExxonMobil are (1) providing innovative products and services to increase market share in key customer segments (by targeting customers who are willing to pay more for faster service, better facilities, and well-stocked convenience stores) and (2) reducing costs and targeting price-sensitive customers. Suppose ExxonMobil decides to pursue the former strategy. The management control system must then reinforce this goal, and ExxonMobil should tie managers' rewards to achieving the targeted measures.

Management control systems should also be designed to support the organizational responsibilities of individual managers. Different levels of management at ExxonMobil need different kinds of information to perform their tasks. For example, top management needs stock-price information to evaluate how much shareholder value the company has created. Stock price, however, is less important for line managers supervising individual refineries. They are more concerned with obtaining information about on-time delivery of gasoline, equipment downtime, product quality, number of days lost to accidents and environmental problems, cost per gallon of gasoline, and employee satisfaction. Similarly, marketing managers are more concerned with information about service at gas stations, customer satisfaction, and market share.

Effective management control systems should also motivate managers and other employees. **Motivation** is the desire to attain a selected goal (the *goal-congruence* aspect) combined with the resulting pursuit of that goal (the *effort* aspect).

Goal congruence exists when individuals and groups work toward achieving the organization's goals—that is, managers working in their own best interest take actions that align with the overall goals of top management. Suppose the goal of ExxonMobil's top management is to maximize operating income. If the management control system evaluates the refinery manager *only* on the basis of costs, the manager may be tempted to make decisions that minimize cost but overlook product quality or timely delivery to retail stations. This oversight is unlikely to maximize operating income of the company as a whole. In this case, the management control system will not achieve goal congruence.

Effort is the extent to which managers strive or endeavor in order to achieve a goal. Effort goes beyond physical exertion, such as a worker producing at a faster rate, to include mental actions as well. For example, effort includes the diligence or acumen with which a manager gathers and analyzes data before authorizing a new investment. It is impossible to directly observe or reward effort. As a result, management control systems motivate employees to exert effort by rewarding them for the achievement of observable goals, such as profit targets or stock returns. This induces managers to exert effort because higher levels of effort increase the likelihood that the goals are achieved. The rewards can be monetary (such as cash, shares of company stock, use of a company car, or membership in a club) or nonmonetary (such as a better title, greater responsibility, or authority over a larger number of employees).

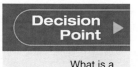

Decision Point ▶

What is a management control system and how should it be designed?

Decentralization

Management control systems must fit an organization's structure. An organization whose structure is decentralized has additional issues to consider for its management control system to be effective.

Decentralization is the freedom for managers at lower levels of the organization to make decisions. **Autonomy** is the degree of freedom to make decisions. The greater the freedom, the greater the autonomy. As we discuss the issues of decentralization and autonomy, we use the term "subunit" to refer to any part of an organization. A subunit may be a large division, such as the refining division of ExxonMobil, or a small group, such as a two-person advertising department of a local clothing chain.

Until the mid-twentieth century, many firms were organized in a centralized, hierarchical fashion. Power was concentrated at the top and there was relatively little freedom for managers at the lower levels to make decisions. Perhaps the most famous example of a highly centralized structure is the Soviet Union, prior to its collapse in the late 1980s. Today, organizations are far more decentralized and many companies have pushed decision-making authority down to subunit managers. Examples of firms with decentralized structures include Nucor, the U.S. steel giant, which allows substantial operational autonomy to the general managers of its plants, and Tesco, Britain's largest retailer, which offers great latitude to its store managers. Of course, no firm is completely decentralized. At Nucor headquarters management still retains responsibility for overall strategic planning, company financing, setting base salary levels and bonus targets, purchase of steel scrap, etc. How much decentralization is optimal? Companies try to choose the degree of decentralization that maximizes benefits over costs. From a practical standpoint, top management can seldom quantify either the benefits or the costs of decentralization. Still, the cost-benefit approach helps management focus on the key issues.

Learning Objective 2

Describe the benefits of decentralization

. . . responsiveness to customers, faster decision making, management development

and the costs of decentralization

. . . loss of control, duplication of activities

Benefits of Decentralization

Supporters of decentralizing decision making and granting responsibilities to managers of subunits advocate the following benefits:

1. **Creates greater responsiveness to needs of a subunit's customers, suppliers, and employees.** Good decisions cannot be made without good information. Compared with top managers, subunit managers are better informed about their customers, competitors, suppliers, and employees, as well as about local factors that affect performance, such as ways to decrease costs, improve quality, and be responsive to customers. Eastman Kodak reports that two advantages of decentralization are an "increase in the company's knowledge of the marketplace and improved service to customers."

2. **Leads to gains from faster decision making by subunit managers.** Decentralization speeds decision making, creating a competitive advantage over centralized organizations. Centralization slows decision making as responsibility for decisions creeps upward through layer after layer of management. Interlake, a manufacturer of materials handling equipment, cites this benefit of decentralization: "We have distributed decision-making powers more broadly to the cutting edge of product and market opportunity." Interlake's materials-handling equipment must often be customized to fit customers' needs. Delegating decision making to the sales force allows Interlake to respond faster to changing customer requirements.

3. **Increases motivation of subunit managers.** Subunit managers are more motivated and committed when they can exercise initiative. Hawei & Hawei, a highly decentralized company, maintains that "Decentralization = Creativity = Productivity."

4. **Assists management development and learning.** Giving managers more responsibility helps develop an experienced pool of management talent to fill higher-level management positions. The company also learns which people are unlikely to be successful top managers. According to Tektronix, an electronics instruments company, "Decentralized units provide a training ground for general managers and a visible field of combat where product champions can fight for their ideas."

5. **Sharpens the focus of subunit managers, broadens the reach of top management.** In a decentralized setting, the manager of a subunit has a concentrated focus. The head of Yahoo Japan, for example, can develop country-specific knowledge and expertise (local advertising trends, cultural norms, payment forms, etc.) and focus attention on maximizing Yahoo's profits in Japan. At the same time, this relieves Yahoo's top

management in Sunnyvale, CA from the burden of controlling day-to-day operating decisions in Japan. The American managers can now spend more time and effort on strategic planning for the entire organization.

Costs of Decentralization

Advocates of more-centralized decision making point to the following costs of decentralizing decision making:

1. **Leads to suboptimal decision making.** This cost arises because top management has given up control over decision making. If the subunit managers do not have the necessary expertise or talent to handle this responsibility, the company, as a whole, is worse off.

   Even if subunit managers are sufficiently skilled, **suboptimal decision making—** also called **incongruent decision making** or **dysfunctional decision making**—occurs when a decision's benefit to one subunit is more than offset by the costs to the organization as a whole. This is most prevalent when the subunits in the company are highly interdependent, such as when the end product of one subunit is used or sold by another subunit. For example, suppose that Nintendo's marketing group receives an order for additional Wii consoles in Australia following the release of some unexpectedly popular new games. A manufacturing manager in Japan who is evaluated on the basis of costs may be unwilling to arrange this rush order since altering production schedules invariably increases manufacturing costs. From Nintendo's viewpoint, however, supplying the consoles may be optimal, both because the Australian customers are willing to pay a premium price and because the current shipment is expected to stimulate orders for other Nintendo games and consoles in the future.

2. **Focuses manager's attention on the subunit rather than the company as a whole.** Individual subunit managers may regard themselves as competing with managers of other subunits in the same company as if they were external rivals. This pushes them to view the relative performance of the subunit as more important than the goals of the company. Consequently, managers may be unwilling to assist when another subunit faces an emergency (as in the Nintendo example) or share important information. In the recent Congressional hearings on the recall of Toyota vehicles, it was revealed that it was common for Toyota's Japan unit to not share information about engineering problems or reported defects between its United States, Asian, and European operations. Toyota has since asserted that this dysfunctional behavior will no longer be tolerated.

3. **Results in duplication of output.** If subunits provide similar products or services, their internal competition could lead to failure in the external markets. The reason is that divisions may find it easier to steal market share from one another, by mimicking each other's successful products, rather than from outside firms. Eventually, this leads to confusion in the minds of customers, and the loss of each division's distinctive strengths. The classic example is General Motors, which has had to wind down its Oldsmobile, Pontiac, and Saturn divisions and is now in bankruptcy reorganization. Similarly, Condé Nast Publishing's initially distinct (and separately run) food magazines, *Bon Appétit* and *Gourmet*, eventually ended up chasing the same readers and advertisers, to the detriment of both. *Gourmet* magazine stopped publication in November 2009.[2]

4. **Results in duplication of activities.** Even if the subunits operate in distinct markets, several individual subunits of the company may undertake the same activity separately. In a highly decentralized company, each subunit may have personnel to carry out staff functions such as human resources or information technology. Centralizing these functions helps to streamline and use fewer resources for these activities, and eliminates wasteful duplication. For example, ABB (Switzerland), a global leader in power and automation technology, is decentralized but has generated significant cost savings of late by centralizing its sourcing decisions across business units for parts, such as pipe pumps and fittings, as well as engineering and erection services. The

---

[2] For an intriguing comparison of the failure of decentralization in these disparate settings, see Jack Shafer's article, "How Condé Nast is Like General Motors: The Magazine Empire as Car Wreck," Slate, October 5, 2009, www.slate.com/id/2231177/.

growing popularity of the "shared service center" model, especially for financial transactions and human resources, is predicated on the 30%–40% savings enabled by the consolidation of such functions, rather than allowing them to be controlled by the subunits.[3]

Comparison of Benefits and Costs

To choose an organization structure that will implement a company's strategy, top managers must compare the benefits and costs of decentralization, often on a function-by-function basis. Surveys of U.S. and European companies report that the decisions made most frequently at the decentralized level are related to product mix and product advertising. In these areas, subunit managers develop their own operating plans and performance reports and make faster decisions based on local information. Decisions related to the type and source of long-term financing and income taxes are made least frequently at the decentralized level. Corporate managers have better information about financing terms in different markets and can obtain the best terms. Centralizing income tax strategies allows the organization to trade off and manage income in a subunit with losses in others. The benefits of decentralization are generally greater when companies face uncertainties in their environments, require detailed local knowledge for performing various jobs, and have few interdependencies among divisions.

Decentralization in Multinational Companies

Multinational companies—companies that operate in multiple countries—are often decentralized because centralized control of a company with subunits around the world is often physically and practically impossible. Also, language, customs, cultures, business practices, rules, laws, and regulations vary significantly across countries. Decentralization enables managers in different countries to make decisions that exploit their knowledge of local business and political conditions and enables them to deal with uncertainties in their individual environments. For example, Philips, a global electronics company headquartered in the Netherlands, delegates marketing and pricing decisions for its television business in the Indian and Singaporean markets to the managers in those countries. Multinational corporations often rotate managers between foreign locations and corporate headquarters. Job rotation combined with decentralization helps develop managers' abilities to operate in the global environment.

There are drawbacks to decentralizing multinational companies. One of the most important is the lack of control and the resulting risks. Barings PLC, a British investment banking firm, went bankrupt and had to be sold when one of its traders in Singapore caused the firm to lose more than £1 billion on unauthorized trades that were not detected until after the trades were made. Similarly, a trader at Sumitomo Corporation racked up $2.6 billion in copper-trading losses because poor controls failed to detect the magnitude of the trader's activities. Multinational corporations that implement decentralized decision making usually design their management control systems to measure and monitor division performance. Information and communications technology helps the flow of information for reporting and control.

Choices About Responsibility Centers

Recall from Chapter 6 that a responsibility center is a segment or subunit of the organization whose manager is accountable for a specified set of activities. To measure the performance of subunits in centralized or decentralized companies, the management control system uses one or a mix of the four types of responsibility centers:

1. *Cost center*—the manager is accountable for costs only.
2. *Revenue center*—the manager is accountable for revenues only.
3. *Profit center*—the manager is accountable for revenues and costs.
4. *Investment center*—the manager is accountable for investments, revenues, and costs.

Centralization or decentralization is not mentioned in the descriptions of these centers because each type of responsibility center can be found in either centralized or decentralized companies.

---

[3] For more on this topic, see http://www.sap.com/solutions/business-suite/erp/pdf/BWP_WP_Shared_Services.pdf.

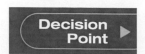

Decision Point ▶

What are the benefits and costs of decentralization?

A common misconception is that *profit center*—and, in some cases, *investment center*—is a synonym for a decentralized subunit, and *cost center* is a synonym for a centralized subunit. *Profit centers can be coupled with a highly centralized organization, and cost centers can be coupled with a highly decentralized organization.* For example, managers in a division organized as a profit center may have little freedom in making decisions. They may need to obtain approval from corporate headquarters for introducing new products and services, or to make expenditures over some preset limit. When Michael Eisner ran Walt Disney Co., the giant media and entertainment conglomerate, the strategic-planning division applied so much scrutiny to business proposals that managers were reluctant to even pitch new ideas.[4] In other companies, divisions such as Information Technology may be organized as cost centers, but their managers may have great latitude with regard to capital expenditures and the purchase of materials and services. In short, the labels "profit center" and "cost center" are independent of the degree of centralization or decentralization in a company.

Transfer Pricing

In decentralized organizations, much of the decision-making power resides in its individual subunits. In these cases, the management control system often uses *transfer prices* to coordinate the actions of the subunits and to evaluate their performance.

As you may recall from the opener, a **transfer price** is the price one subunit (department or division) charges for a product or service supplied to another subunit of the same organization. If, for example, a car manufacturer has a separate division that manufactures engines, the transfer price is the price the engine division charges when it transfers engines to the car assembly division. The transfer price creates revenues for the selling subunit (the engine division in our example) and purchase costs for the buying subunit (the assembly division in our example), affecting each subunit's operating income. These operating incomes can be used to evaluate subunits' performances and to motivate their managers. The product or service transferred between subunits of an organization is called an **intermediate product**. This product may either be further worked on by the receiving subunit (as in the engine example) or, if transferred from production to marketing, sold to an external customer.

In one sense, transfer pricing is a curious phenomenon. Activities within an organization are clearly nonmarket in nature; products and services are not bought and sold as they are in open-market transactions. Yet, establishing prices for transfers among subunits of a company has a distinctly market flavor. The rationale for transfer prices is that subunit managers (such as the manager of the engine division), when making decisions, need only focus on how their decisions will affect their subunit's performance without evaluating their impact on company-wide performance. In this sense, transfer prices ease the subunit managers' information-processing and decision-making tasks. In a well-designed transfer-pricing system, a manager focuses on optimizing subunit performance (the performance of the engine division) and in so doing optimizes the performance of the company as a whole.

Criteria for Evaluating Transfer Prices

As in all management control systems, transfer prices should help achieve a company's strategies and goals and fit its organization structure. We describe four criteria to evaluate transfer pricing: (1) Transfer prices should promote goal congruence. (2) They should induce managers to exert a high level of effort. Subunits selling a product or service should be motivated to hold down their costs; subunits buying the product or service should be motivated to acquire and use inputs efficiently. (3) The transfer price should help top management evaluate the performance of individual subunits. (4) If top management favors a high degree of decentralization, transfer prices should preserve a high degree of subunit autonomy in decision making. That is, a subunit manager seeking to maximize the operating income of the subunit should have the freedom to transact with other subunits of the company (on the basis of transfer prices) or to transact with external parties.

Learning Objective 3

Explain transfer prices

. . . price one subunit charges another for product

and four criteria used to evaluate alternative transfer-pricing methods

. . . goal congruence, management effort, subunit performance evaluation, and subunit autonomy

---

[4] When Robert Iger replaced Eisner as CEO in 2005, one of his first acts was to disassemble the strategic-planning division, thereby giving more authority to Disney's business units (parks and resorts, consumer products, and media networks).

Calculating Transfer Prices

There are three broad categories of methods for determining transfer prices. They are as follows:

1. **Market-based transfer prices.** Top management may choose to use the price of a similar product or service publicly listed in, say, a trade association Web site. Also, top management may select, for the internal price, the external price that a subunit charges to outside customers.

2. **Cost-based transfer prices.** Top management may choose a transfer price based on the cost of producing the product in question. Examples include variable production cost, variable and fixed production costs, and full cost of the product. Full cost of the product includes all production costs plus costs from other business functions (R&D, design, marketing, distribution, and customer service). The cost used in cost-based transfer prices can be actual cost or budgeted cost. Sometimes, the cost-based transfer price includes a markup or profit margin that represents a return on subunit investment.

3. **Hybrid transfer prices.** Hybrid transfer prices take into account both cost and market information. Top management may administer such prices, for example by specifying a transfer price that is an average of the cost of producing and transporting the product internally and the market price for comparable products. At other times, a hybrid transfer price may take the form where the revenue recognized by the selling unit is different from the cost recognized by the buying unit. The most common form of hybrid prices arise via negotiation—the subunits of a company are asked to negotiate the transfer price between them and to decide whether to buy and sell internally or deal with external parties. The eventual transfer price is then the outcome of a bargaining process between selling and buying subunits. Even though there is no requirement that the chosen transfer price bear any specific relationship to cost or market-price data, information regarding costs and prices plays a critical role in the negotiation process. Negotiated transfer prices are often employed when market prices are volatile and change constantly.

To see how each of the three transfer-pricing methods works and to see the differences among them, we examine transfer pricing at Horizon Petroleum against the four criteria of promoting goal congruence, motivating management effort, evaluating subunit performance, and preserving subunit autonomy (if desired).

An Illustration of Transfer Pricing

Horizon Petroleum has two divisions, each operating as a profit center. The transportation division purchases crude oil in Matamoros, Mexico, and transports it from Matamoros to Houston, Texas. The refining division processes crude oil into gasoline. For simplicity, we assume gasoline is the only salable product the Houston refinery makes and that it takes two barrels of crude oil to yield one barrel of gasoline.

Variable costs in each division are variable with respect to a single cost driver: barrels of crude oil transported by the transportation division, and barrels of gasoline produced by the refining division. The fixed cost per unit is based on the budgeted annual fixed costs and practical capacity of crude oil that can be transported by the transportation division, and the budgeted fixed costs and practical capacity of gasoline that can be produced by the refining division. Horizon Petroleum reports all costs and revenues of its non-U.S. operations in U.S. dollars using the prevailing exchange rate.

■ The transportation division has obtained rights to certain oil fields in the Matamoros area. It has a long-term contract to purchase crude oil produced from these fields at $72 per barrel. The division transports the oil to Houston and then "sells" it to the refining division. The pipeline from Matamoros to Houston has the capacity to carry 40,000 barrels of crude oil per day.

■ The refining division has been operating at capacity (30,000 barrels of crude oil a day), using oil supplied by Horizon's transportation division (an average of 10,000 barrels per day) and oil bought from another producer and delivered to the Houston refinery (an average of 20,000 barrels per day at $85 per barrel).

■ The refining division sells the gasoline it produces to outside parties at $190 per barrel.

Exhibit 22-1 summarizes Horizon Petroleum's variable and fixed costs per barrel of crude oil in the transportation division and variable and fixed costs per barrel of gasoline in the refining division, the external market prices of buying crude oil, and the external market price of selling gasoline. What's missing in the exhibit is the actual transfer price from the transportation division to the refining division. This transfer price will vary depending on the transfer-pricing method used. Transfer prices from the transportation division to the refining division under each of the three methods are as follows:

1. Market-based transfer price of $85 per barrel of crude oil based on the competitive market price in Houston.

2. Cost-based transfer prices at, say, 105% of full cost, where full cost is the cost of the crude oil purchased in Matamoros plus the transportation division's own variable and fixed costs (from Exhibit 22-1): 1.05 × ($72 + $1 + $3) = $79.80.

3. Hybrid transfer price of, say, $82 per barrel of crude oil, which is between the market-based and cost-based transfer prices. We describe later in this section the various ways in which hybrid prices can be determined.

Exhibit 22-2 presents division operating incomes per 100 barrels of crude oil purchased under each transfer-pricing method. Transfer prices create income for the selling division and corresponding costs for the buying division that cancel out when division results are consolidated for the company as a whole. The exhibit assumes all three transfer-pricing methods yield transfer prices that are in a range that does not cause division managers to change the business relationships shown in Exhibit 22-1. That is, Horizon Petroleum's total operating income from purchasing, transporting, and refining the 100 barrels of crude oil and selling the 50 barrels of gasoline is the same, $1,200, *regardless of the internal transfer prices used*.

$$\begin{array}{c}\text{Operating} \\ \text{income}\end{array} = \text{Revenues} - \begin{array}{c}\text{Cost of crude} \\ \text{oil purchases} \\ \text{in Matamoros}\end{array} - \begin{array}{c}\text{Transportation} \\ \text{Division} \\ \text{costs}\end{array} - \begin{array}{c}\text{Refining} \\ \text{Division} \\ \text{costs}\end{array}$$

$$= (\$190 \times 50 \text{ barrels of gasoline}) - (\$72 \times 100 \text{ barrels of crude oil})$$

$$- (\$4 \times 100 \text{ barrels of crude oil}) - (\$14 \times 50 \text{ barrels of gasoline})$$

$$= \$9,500 - \$7,200 - \$400 - \$700 = \$1,200$$

Note further that under all three methods, summing the two division operating incomes equals Horizon Petroleum's total operating income of $1,200. By keeping total operating

Exhibit 22-1   Operating Data for Horizon Petroleum

	A	B	C	D	E	F	G	H
1								
2				**Transportation Division**				
3	Contract price per barrel of crude oil supplied in Matamoros			Variable cost per barrel of crude oil	$1			
4		= $72		Fixed cost per barrel of crude oil	3			
5				Full cost per barrel of crude oil	$4			
6								
7								
8				Barrels of crude oil transferred				
9								
10								
11				**Refining Division**				
12	Market price per barrel of crude oil supplied to Houston refinery			Variable cost per barrel of gasoline	$ 8		Market price per barrel of gasoline sold to external parties	
13		= $85		Fixed cost per barrel of gasoline	6			= $190
14				Full cost per barrel of gasoline	$14			
15								

Exhibit 22-2   Division Operating Income of Horizon Petroleum for 100 Barrels of Crude Oil Under Alternative Transfer-Pricing Methods

	A	B	C	D	E	F	G	H
1	**Production and Sales Data**							
2	Barrels of crude oil transferred =	100						
3	Barrels of gasoline sold =	50						
4								
5		**Internal Transfers at**			**Internal Transfers at**			
6		**Market Price =**			**105% of Full Cost =**		**Hybrid Price =**	
7		**$85 per Barrel**			**$79.80 per Barrel**		**$82 per Barrel**	
8	**Transportation Division**							
9	Revenues, $85, $79.80, $82 × 100 barrels of crude oil	$8,500			$7,980		$8,200	
10	Costs							
11	Crude oil purchase costs, $72 × 100 barrels of crude oil	7,200			7,200		7,200	
12	Division variable costs, $1 × 100 barrels of crude oil	100			100		100	
13	Division fixed costs, $3 × 100 barrels of crude oil	300			300		300	
14	Total division costs	7,600			7,600		7,600	
15	Division operating income	$ 900			$ 380		$ 600	
16								
17	**Refining Division**							
18	Revenues, $190 × 50 barrels of gasoline	$9,500			$9,500		$9,500	
19	Costs							
20	Transferred-in costs, $85, $79.80, $82							
21	× 100 barrels of crude oil	8,500			7,980		8,200	
22	Division variable costs, $8 × 50 barrels of gasoline	400			400		400	
23	Division fixed costs, $6 × 50 barrels of gasoline	300			300		300	
24	Total division costs	9,200			8,680		8,900	
25	Division operating income	$ 300			$ 820		$ 600	
26	Operating income of both divisions together	$1,200			$1,200		$1,200	

income the same, we focus attention on the effects of different transfer-pricing methods on the operating income of each division. Subsequent sections of this chapter show that different transfer-pricing methods can cause managers to take different actions leading to different total operating incomes.

Consider the two methods in the first two columns of Exhibit 22-2. The operating income of the transportation division is $520 more ($900 − $380) if transfer prices are based on market prices rather than on 105% of full cost. The operating income of the refining division is $520 more ($820 − $300) if transfer prices are based on 105% of full cost rather than market prices. If the transportation division's sole criterion were to maximize its own division operating income, it would favor transfer prices at market prices. In contrast, the refining division would prefer transfer prices at 105% of full cost to maximize its own division operating income. The hybrid transfer price of $82 is between the 105% of full cost and market-based transfer prices. It splits the $1,200 of operating income equally between the divisions, and could arise as a result of negotiations between the transportation and refining division managers.

It's not surprising that subunit managers, especially those whose compensation or promotion directly depends on subunit operating income, take considerable interest in setting transfer prices. To reduce the excessive focus of subunit managers on their own subunits, many companies compensate subunit managers on the basis of both subunit and company-wide operating incomes.

We next examine market-based, cost-based, and hybrid transfer prices in more detail. We show how the choice of transfer-pricing method combined with managers' sourcing decisions can determine the size of the company-wide operating-income pie itself.

◄ **Decision Point**

What are alternative ways of calculating transfer prices, and what criteria should be used to evaluate them?

Market-Based Transfer Prices

Learning Objective 4

Illustrate how market-based transfer prices promote goal congruence in perfectly competitive markets

. . . division managers transacting internally are motivated to take the same actions as if they were transacting externally

Transferring products or services at market prices generally leads to optimal decisions when three conditions are satisfied: (1) The market for the intermediate product is perfectly competitive, (2) interdependencies of subunits are minimal, and (3) there are no additional costs or benefits to the company as a whole from buying or selling in the external market instead of transacting internally.

Perfectly-Competitive-Market Case

A **perfectly competitive market** exists when there is a homogeneous product with buying prices equal to selling prices and no individual buyers or sellers can affect those prices by their own actions. By using market-based transfer prices in perfectly competitive markets, a company can (1) promote goal congruence, (2) motivate management effort, (3) evaluate subunit performance, and (4) preserve subunit autonomy.

Consider Horizon Petroleum again. Assume there is a perfectly competitive market for crude oil in the Houston area. As a result, the transportation division can sell and the refining division can buy as much crude oil as each wants at $85 per barrel. Horizon would prefer its managers to buy or sell crude oil internally. Think about the decisions that Horizon's division managers would make if each had the autonomy to sell or buy crude oil externally. If the transfer price between Horizon's transportation and refining divisions is set below $85, the manager of the transportation division will be motivated to sell all crude oil to external buyers in the Houston area at $85 per barrel. If the transfer price is set above $85, the manager of the refining division will be motivated to purchase all crude oil requirements from external suppliers. Only an $85 transfer price will motivate the transportation division and the refining division to buy and sell internally. That's because neither division profits by buying or selling in the external market.

Suppose Horizon evaluates division managers on the basis of their individual division's operating income. The transportation division will sell, either internally or externally, as much crude oil as it can profitably transport, and the refining division will buy, either internally or externally, as much crude oil as it can profitably refine. An $85-per-barrel transfer price achieves goal congruence—the actions that maximize each division's operating income are also the actions that maximize operating income of Horizon Petroleum as a whole. Furthermore, because the transfer price is not based on costs, it motivates each division manager to exert management effort to maximize his or her own division's operating income. Market prices also serve to evaluate the economic viability and profitability of each division individually. For example, Koch Industries, the second-largest private company in the United States, uses market-based pricing for all internal transfers. As their CFO, Steve Feilmeier, notes, "We believe that the alternative for any given asset should always be considered in order to best optimize the profitability of the asset. If you simply transfer price between two different divisions at cost, then you may be subsidizing your whole operation and not know it." Returning to our Horizon example, suppose that under market-based transfer prices, the refining division consistently shows small or negative profits. Then, Horizon may consider shutting down the refining division and simply transport and sell the oil to other refineries in the Houston area.

Distress Prices

When supply outstrips demand, market prices may drop well below their historical averages. If the drop in prices is expected to be temporary, these low market prices are sometimes called "distress prices." Deciding whether a current market price is a distress price is often difficult. Prior to the worldwide spike in commodity prices in the 2006–2008 period, the market prices of several mineral and agricultural commodities, including nickel, uranium, and wheat, stayed for many years at what people initially believed were temporary distress levels!

Which transfer price should be used for judging performance if distress prices prevail? Some companies use the distress prices themselves, but others use long-run average prices, or "normal" market prices. In the short run, the manager of the selling subunit should supply the product or service at the distress price as long as it exceeds the *incremental costs of supplying the product or service.* If the distress price is used as the transfer price, the selling division will show a loss because the distress price will not exceed the *full cost* of the division. If the long-run average market price is used, forcing the manager to buy internally at a price above the current market price will hurt the buying division's short-run operating income. But the long-run average market price will provide a better measure of the long-run profitability and viability of the supplier division. Of course, if the price remains low in the long run, the company should use the low market price as the transfer price. If this price is lower than the variable and fixed costs that can be saved if manufacturing facilities are shut down, the production facilities of the selling subunit should be sold, and the buying subunit should purchase the product from an external supplier.

Imperfect Competition

If markets are not perfectly competitive, selling prices affect the quantity of product sold. If the selling division sells its product in the external market, the selling division manager would choose a price and quantity combination that would maximize the division's operating income. If the transfer price is set at this selling price, the buying division may find that acquiring the product is too costly and results in a loss. It may decide not to purchase the product. Yet, from the point of view of the company as a whole, it may well be that profits are maximized if the selling division transfers the product to the buying division for further processing and sale. For this reason, when the market for the intermediate good is imperfectly competitive, the transfer price must generally be set below the external market price (but above the selling division's variable cost) in order to induce efficient transfers.[5]

◀ Decision Point

Under what market conditions do market-based transfer prices promote goal congruence?

Cost-Based Transfer Prices

Cost-based transfer prices are helpful when market prices are unavailable, inappropriate, or too costly to obtain, such as when markets are not perfectly competitive, when the product is specialized, or when the internal product is different from the products available externally in terms of quality and customer service.

Learning Objective 5

Understand how to avoid making suboptimal decisions when transfer prices are based on full cost plus a markup

. . . in situations when buying divisions regard the fixed costs and the markup as variable costs

Full-Cost Bases

In practice, many companies use transfer prices based on full cost. To approximate market prices, cost-based transfer prices are sometimes set at full cost plus a margin. These transfer prices, however, can lead to suboptimal decisions. Suppose Horizon Petroleum makes internal transfers at 105% of full cost. Recall that the refining division purchases, on average, 20,000 barrels of crude oil per day from a local Houston supplier, who delivers the crude oil to the refinery at a price of $85 per barrel. To reduce crude oil costs, the refining division has located an independent producer in Matamoros—Gulfmex Corporation—that is willing to sell 20,000 barrels of crude oil per day at $79 per barrel, delivered to Horizon's pipeline in Matamoros. Given Horizon's organization structure, the transportation division would purchase the 20,000 barrels of crude oil in Matamoros from Gulfmex, transport it to Houston, and then sell it to the refining division. The pipeline has unused capacity and can ship the 20,000 barrels per day at its variable cost of $1 per barrel without affecting the shipment of the 10,000 barrels of crude oil per day acquired under its existing long-term contract arrangement. Will Horizon Petroleum incur lower costs by

---

[5] Consider a firm where division S produces the intermediate product. S has a capacity of 15 units and a variable cost per unit of $2. The imperfect competition is reflected in a downward-sloping demand curve for the intermediate product—if S wants to sell Q units, it has to lower the market price to P = 20 − Q. The division's profit function is therefore given by Q × (20 − Q) − 2Q = 18Q − Q². Simple calculus reveals that it is optimal for S to sell 9 units of the intermediate product at a price of $11, thereby making a profit of $81. Now, suppose that division B in the same firm can take the intermediate product, incur an additional variable cost of $4 and sell it in the external market for $12. Since S has surplus capacity (it only uses 9 of its 15 units of capacity), it is clearly in the firm's interest to have S make additional units and transfer them to B. The firm makes an incremental profit of $12 − $2 − $4 = $6 for each transferred unit. However, if the transfer price for the intermediate product were set equal to the market price of $11, B would reject the transaction since it would lose money on it ($12 − $11 − $4 = −$3 per unit).

   To resolve this conflict, the transfer price should be set at a suitable *discount* to the external price in order to induce the buying division to seek internal transfers. In our example, the selling price must be greater than S's variable cost of $2, but less than B's contribution margin of $8. That is, the transfer price has to be discounted relative to the market price ($11) by a minimum of $3. We explore the issue of feasible transfer pricing ranges further in the section on hybrid transfer prices.

purchasing crude oil from Gulfmex in Matamoros or by purchasing crude oil from the Houston supplier? Will the refining division show lower crude oil purchasing costs by acquiring oil from Gulfmex or by acquiring oil from its current Houston supplier?

The following analysis shows that Horizon Petroleum's operating income would be maximized by purchasing oil from Gulfmex. The analysis compares the incremental costs in both divisions under the two alternatives. The analysis assumes the fixed costs of the transportation division will be the same regardless of the alternative chosen. That is, the transportation division cannot save any of its fixed costs if it does not transport Gulfmex's 20,000 barrels of crude oil per day.

- ■ **Alternative 1:** Buy 20,000 barrels from the Houston supplier at $85 per barrel. Total costs to Horizon Petroleum are 20,000 barrels × $85 per barrel = $1,700,000.

- ■ **Alternative 2:** Buy 20,000 barrels in Matamoros at $79 per barrel and transport them to Houston at a variable cost of $1 per barrel. Total costs to Horizon Petroleum are 20,000 barrels × ($79 + $1) per barrel = $1,600,000.

There is a reduction in total costs to Horizon Petroleum of $100,000 ($1,700,000 − $1,600,000) by acquiring oil from Gulfmex.

Suppose the transportation division's transfer price to the refining division is 105% of full cost. The refining division will see its reported division costs increase if the crude oil is purchased from Gulfmex:

$$\text{Transfer price} = 1.05 \times \left(\begin{array}{c} \text{Purchase price} \\ \text{from} \\ \text{Gulfmex} \end{array} + \begin{array}{c} \text{Variable cost per unit} \\ \text{of Transportation} \\ \text{Division} \end{array} + \begin{array}{c} \text{Fixed cost per unit} \\ \text{of Transportation} \\ \text{Division} \end{array} \right)$$

$$= 1.05 \times (\$79 + \$1 + \$3) = 1.05 \times \$83 = \$87.15 \text{ per barrel}$$

- ■ **Alternative 1:** Buy 20,000 barrels from Houston supplier at $85 per barrel. Total costs to refining division are 20,000 barrels × $85 per barrel = $1,700,000.

- ■ **Alternative 2:** Buy 20,000 barrels from the transportation division of Horizon Petroleum that were purchased from Gulfmex. Total costs to refining division are 20,000 barrels × $87.15 per barrel = $1,743,000.

As a profit center, the refining division can maximize its short-run division operating income by purchasing from the Houston supplier at $1,700,000.

The refining division looks at each barrel that it obtains from the transportation division as a variable cost of $87.15 per barrel; if 10 barrels are transferred, it costs the refining division $871.50; if 100 barrels are transferred, it costs $8,715. In fact, the variable cost per barrel is $80 ($79 to purchase the oil from Gulfmex plus $1 to transport it to Houston). The remaining $7.15 ($87.15 − $80) per barrel is the transportation division's fixed cost and markup. *The full cost plus a markup transfer-pricing method causes the refining division to regard the fixed cost (and the 5% markup) of the transportation division as a variable cost and leads to goal incongruence.*

Should Horizon's top management interfere and force the refining division to buy from the transportation division? Top management interference would undercut the philosophy of decentralization, so Horizon's top management would probably view the decision by the refining division to purchase crude oil from external suppliers as an inevitable cost of decentralization and not interfere. Of course, some interference may occasionally be necessary to prevent costly blunders. But recurring interference and constraints would simply transform Horizon from a decentralized company into a centralized company.

What transfer price will promote goal congruence for both the transportation and refining divisions? The minimum transfer price is $80 per barrel. A transfer price below $80 does not provide the transportation division with an incentive to purchase crude oil from Gulfmex in Matamoros because it is below the transportation division's incremental costs. The maximum transfer price is $85 per barrel. A transfer price above $85 will cause the refining division to purchase crude oil from the external market rather than from the transportation division. A transfer price between the minimum and maximum transfer prices of $80 and $85 will promote goal congruence: Each division will increase its own reported operating income while increasing Horizon Petroleum's operating income if the refining division purchases crude oil from Gulfmex in Matamoros.

In the absence of a market-based transfer price, senior management at Horizon Petroleum cannot easily determine the profitability of the investment made in the transportation division and hence whether Horizon should keep or sell the pipeline. Furthermore, if the transfer price had been based on the actual costs of the transportation division, it would provide the division with no incentive to control costs. That's because all cost inefficiencies of the transportation division would get passed along as part of the actual full-cost transfer price. In fact, every additional dollar of cost arising from wastefulness in the transportation division would generate an additional five cents in profit for the division under the "105% of full cost" rule!

Surveys indicate that, despite the limitations, managers generally prefer to use full-cost-based transfer prices. That's because these transfer prices represent relevant costs for long-run decisions, they facilitate external pricing based on variable and fixed costs, and they are the least costly to administer. However, full-cost transfer pricing does raise many issues. How are each subunit's indirect costs allocated to products? Have the correct activities, cost pools, and cost-allocation bases been identified? Should the chosen fixed-cost rates be actual or budgeted? The issues here are similar to the issues that arise in allocating fixed costs, which were introduced in Chapter 14. Many companies determine the transfer price based on budgeted rates and practical capacity because it overcomes the problem of inefficiencies in actual costs and costs of unused capacity getting passed along to the buying division.

Variable-Cost Bases

Transferring 20,000 barrels of crude oil from the transportation division to the refining division at the variable cost of $80 per barrel achieves goal congruence, as shown in the preceding section. The refining division would buy from the transportation division because the transportation division's variable cost is less than the $85 price charged by external suppliers. Setting the transfer price equal to the variable cost has other benefits. Knowledge of the variable cost per barrel of crude oil is very helpful to the refining division for many decisions such as the short-run pricing decisions discussed in Chapters 11 and 12. However, at the $80-per-barrel transfer price, the transportation division would record an operating loss, and the refining division would show large profits because it would be charged only for the variable costs of the transportation division. One approach to addressing this problem is to have the refining division make a lump-sum transfer payment to cover fixed costs and generate some operating income for the transportation division while the transportation division continues to make transfers at variable cost. The fixed payment is the price the refining division pays for using the capacity of the transportation division. The income earned by each division can then be used to evaluate the performance of each division and its manager.

◄ Decision Point

What problems can arise when full cost plus a markup is used as the transfer price?

Hybrid Transfer Prices

Consider again Horizon Petroleum. As we saw earlier, the transportation division has unused capacity it can use to transport oil from Matamoros to Houston at an incremental cost of $80 per barrel of crude oil. Horizon Petroleum, as a whole, maximizes operating income if the refining division purchases crude oil from the transportation division rather than from the Houston market (incremental cost per barrel of $80 versus price per barrel of $85). Both divisions would be interested in transacting with each other (and the firm achieves goal congruence) if the transfer price is between $80 and $85.

For any internal transaction, there is generally a minimum transfer price the selling division will not go below, based on its cost structure. In the Horizon Petroleum example, the minimum price acceptable to the transportation division is $80. There is also a maximum price the buying division will not wish to exceed, given by the lower of two quantities—the eventual contribution it generates from an internal transaction and the price of purchasing a comparable intermediate product from an outside party. For the

Learning Objective 6

Describe the range of feasible transfer prices when there is unused capacity

. . . from variable cost to market price of the product transferred

refining division, each barrel of gasoline sold to external parties generates $182 in contribution (the $190 price less the $8 variable cost of refining). Since it takes two barrels of crude oil to generate a barrel of gasoline, this is equivalent to a contribution of $91 per barrel of crude. For any price higher than $91, the refining division would lose money for each barrel of crude it takes from the transportation division. On the other hand, the refining division can purchase crude oil on the open market for $85 rather than having it transported internally. The maximum feasible transfer price is thus the lower of $91 and $85, or $85 in this instance. We saw previously that a transfer price between the minimum price ($80) and the maximum ($85) would promote goal congruence. We now describe three different ways in which firms attempt to determine the specific transfer price within these bounds.

Prorating the Difference Between Maximum and Minimum Transfer Prices

One approach that Horizon Petroleum could pursue is to choose a transfer price that splits, on some fair basis, the $5 difference between the $85-per-barrel market-based maximum price the refining division is willing to pay and the $80-per-barrel variable cost-based minimum price the transportation division wants to receive. An easy solution is to split the difference equally, resulting in a transfer price of $82.50. However, this solution ignores the relative costs incurred by the two divisions and might lead to disparate profit margins on the work contributed by each division to the final product. As an alternative approach, Horizon Petroleum could allocate the $5 difference on the basis of the variable costs of the two divisions. Using the data in Exhibit 22-1 (p. 782), variable costs are as follows:

Transportation division's variable costs to transport 100 barrels of crude oil ($1 × 100)	$100
Refining division's variable costs to refine 100 barrels of crude oil and produce 50 barrels of gasoline ($8 × 50)	400
Total variable costs	$500

Of the $5 difference, the transportation division gets to keep ($100 ÷ $500) × $5.00 = $1.00, and the refining division gets to keep ($400 ÷ $500) × $5.00 = $4.00. That is, the transfer price is $81 per barrel of crude oil ($79 purchase cost + $1 variable cost + $1 that the transportation division gets to keep). In effect, this approach results in a budgeted variable-cost-plus transfer price. The "plus" indicates the setting of a transfer price above variable cost.

To decide on the $1 and $4 allocations of the $5 incremental benefit to total company operating income per barrel, the divisions must share information about their variable costs. In effect, each division does not operate (at least for this transaction) in a totally decentralized manner. Furthermore, each division has an incentive to overstate its variable costs to receive a more-favorable transfer price. In the preceding example, suppose the transportation division claims a cost of $2 per barrel to ship crude oil from Gulfmex to Houston. This increased cost raises the variable cost-based minimum price to $79 + $2 = $81 per barrel; the maximum price remains $85. Of the $4 difference between the minimum and maximum, the transportation division now gets to keep ($200 ÷ ($200 + $400)) × $4.00 = $1.33, resulting in a higher transfer price of $82.33. The refining division similarly benefits from asserting that its variable cost to refine 100 barrels of crude oil is greater than $400. As a consequence, proration methods either require a high degree of trust and information exchange among divisions or include provisions for objective audits of cost information in order to be successful.

Negotiated Pricing

This is the most common hybrid method. Under this approach, top management does not administer a specific split of the eventual profits across the transacting divisions. Rather, the eventual transfer price results from a bargaining process between the selling and buying subunits. In the Horizon Petroleum case, for example, the transportation division and the refining division would be free to negotiate a price that is mutually acceptable to both.

As described earlier, the minimum and maximum feasible transfer prices are $80 and $85, respectively, per barrel of crude oil. Where between $80 and $85 will the transfer price per barrel be set? Under a negotiated transfer price, the answer depends on several things: the bargaining strengths of the two divisions; information the transportation division has about the price minus incremental marketing costs of supplying crude oil to outside refineries; and the information the refining division has about its other available sources of crude oil. Negotiations become particularly sensitive because Horizon Petroleum can now evaluate each division's performance on the basis of division operating income. The price negotiated by the two divisions will, in general, have no specific relationship to either costs or market price. But cost and price information is often the starting point in the negotiation process.

Consider the following situation: Suppose the refining division receives an order to supply specially processed gasoline. The incremental cost to purchase and supply crude oil is still $80 per barrel. However, suppose the refining division will profit from this order only if the transportation division can supply crude oil at a price not exceeding $82 per barrel.[6] In this case, the transfer price that would benefit both divisions must be greater than $80 but less than $82. Negotiations would allow the two divisions to achieve an acceptable transfer price. By contrast, a rule-based transfer price, such as a market-based price of $85 or a 105% of full-cost-based price of $87.15, would result in Horizon passing up a profitable opportunity.

A negotiated transfer price strongly preserves division autonomy. It also has the advantage that each division manager is motivated to put forth effort to increase division operating income. Surveys have found that approximately 15%–20% of firms set transfer prices based on negotiation among divisions. The key reason cited by firms that do not use negotiated prices is the cost of the bargaining process, that is, the time and energy spent by managers haggling over transfer prices.

Dual Pricing

There is seldom a single transfer price that simultaneously meets the criteria of promoting goal congruence, motivating management effort, evaluating subunit performance, and preserving subunit autonomy. As a result, some companies choose **dual pricing**, using two separate transfer-pricing methods to price each transfer from one subunit to another. An example of dual pricing arises when the selling division receives a full-cost-based price and the buying division pays the market price for the internally transferred products. Assume Horizon Petroleum purchases crude oil from Gulfmex in Matamoros at $79 per barrel. One way of recording the journal entry for the transfer between the transportation division and the refining division is as follows:

1. Debit the refining division (the buying division) with the market-based transfer price of $85 per barrel of crude oil.

2. Credit the transportation division (the selling division) with the 105%-of-full-cost transfer price of $87.15 per barrel of crude oil.

3. Debit a corporate cost account for the $2.15 ($87.15 − $85) per barrel difference between the two transfer prices.

The dual-pricing system promotes goal congruence because it makes the refining division no worse off if it purchases the crude oil from the transportation division rather than from the external supplier at $85 per barrel. The transportation division receives a corporate subsidy. In dual pricing, the operating income for Horizon Petroleum as a whole is less than the sum of the operating incomes of the divisions.

Dual pricing is not widely used in practice even though it reduces the goal incongruence associated with a pure cost-based transfer-pricing method. One concern with dual pricing is that it leads to problems in computing the taxable income of subunits located in different tax jurisdictions, such as in our example, where the transportation division is taxed in Mexico while the refining division is taxed in the United States. A second concern is that dual pricing insulates managers from the frictions of the marketplace because costs, not market prices, affect the revenues of the supplying division.

◀ **Decision Point**

Within a range of feasible transfer prices, what are alternative ways for firms to arrive at the eventual price?

---

[6] For example, suppose a barrel of specially processed gasoline could be sold for $200 but also required a higher variable cost of refining of $36 per barrel. In this setting, the incremental contribution to the refining division is $164 per barrel of gasoline, which implies that it will pay at most $82 for a barrel of crude oil (since two barrels of crude are required for one barrel of gasoline).

A General Guideline for Transfer-Pricing Situations

Exhibit 22-3 summarizes the properties of market-based, cost-based, and negotiated transfer-pricing methods using the criteria described in this chapter. As the exhibit indicates, it is difficult for a transfer-pricing method to meet all criteria. Market conditions, the goal of the transfer-pricing system, and the criteria of promoting goal congruence, motivating management effort, evaluating subunit performance, and preserving subunit autonomy (if desired) must all be considered simultaneously. The transfer price a company will eventually choose depends on the economic circumstances and the decision at hand. Surveys of company practice indicate that the full-cost-based transfer price is generally the most frequently used transfer-pricing method around the world, followed by market-based transfer price and negotiated transfer price.

Our discussion thus far highlight that, barring settings in which a perfectly competitive market exists for the intermediate product, there is generally a range of possible transfer prices that would induce goal congruence. We now provide a general guideline for determining the minimum price in that range. The following formula is a helpful first step in setting the minimum transfer price in many situations:

$$
\text{Minimum transfer price} = \begin{array}{c} \text{Incremental cost} \\ \text{per unit} \\ \text{incurred up} \\ \text{to the point of transfer} \end{array} + \begin{array}{c} \text{Opportunity cost} \\ \text{per unit} \\ \text{to the selling subunit} \end{array}
$$

Incremental cost in this context means the additional cost of producing and transferring the product or service. Opportunity cost here is the maximum contribution margin forgone by the selling subunit if the product or service is transferred internally. For example, if the selling subunit is operating at capacity, the opportunity cost of transferring a unit internally rather than selling it externally is equal to the market price minus variable cost. That's because by transferring a unit internally, the subunit forgoes the contribution margin it could have obtained by selling the unit in the external market. We distinguish incremental cost from opportunity cost because financial accounting systems record incremental cost but do not record opportunity cost. The guideline measures a *minimum* transfer price because it represents the selling unit's cost of transferring the product. We illustrate the general guideline in some specific situations using data from Horizon Petroleum.

1. **A perfectly competitive market for the intermediate product exists, and the selling division has no unused capacity.** If the market for crude oil in Houston is perfectly

Criteria	Market-Based	Cost-Based	Negotiated
Achieves goal congruence	Yes, when markets are competitive	Often, but not always	Yes
Motivates management effort	Yes	Yes, when based on budgeted costs; less incentive to control costs if transfers are based on actual costs	Yes
Useful for evaluating subunit performance	Yes, when markets are competitive	Difficult unless transfer price exceeds full cost and even then is somewhat arbitrary	Yes, but transfer prices are affected by bargaining strengths of the buying and selling divisions
Preserves subunit autonomy	Yes, when markets are competitive	No, because it is rule-based	Yes, because it is based on negotiations between subunits
Other factors	Market may not exist, or markets may be imperfect or in distress	Useful for determining full cost of products and services; easy to implement	Bargaining and negotiations take time and may need to be reviewed repeatedly as conditions change

competitive, the transportation division can sell all the crude oil it transports to the external market at $85 per barrel, and it will have no unused capacity. The transportation division's incremental cost (as shown in Exhibit 22-1, p. 782) is $73 per barrel (purchase cost of $72 per barrel plus variable transportation cost of $1 per barrel) for oil purchased under the long-term contract or $80 per barrel (purchase cost of $79 plus variable transportation cost of $1) for oil purchased at current market prices from Gulfmex. The transportation division's opportunity cost per barrel of transferring the oil internally is the contribution margin per barrel forgone by not selling the crude oil in the external market: $12 for oil purchased under the long-term contract (market price, $85, minus variable cost, $73) and $5 for oil purchased from Gulfmex (market price, $85, minus variable cost, $80). In either case,

$$\begin{array}{c} \text{Minimum transfer price} \\ \text{per barrel} \end{array} = \begin{array}{c} \text{Incremental cost} \\ \text{per barrel} \end{array} + \begin{array}{c} \text{Opportunity cost} \\ \text{per barrel} \end{array}$$

$$= \$73 + \$12 = \$85$$

$$\text{or}$$

$$= \$80 + \$5 = \$85$$

2. **An intermediate market exists that is not perfectly competitive, and the selling division has unused capacity.** In markets that are not perfectly competitive, capacity utilization can only be increased by decreasing prices. Unused capacity exists because decreasing prices is often not worthwhile—it decreases operating income.

   If the transportation division has unused capacity, its opportunity cost of transferring the oil internally is zero because the division does not forgo any external sales or contribution margin from internal transfers. In this case,

$$\begin{array}{c} \text{Minimum transfer price} \\ \text{per barrel} \end{array} = \begin{array}{c} \text{Incremental cost} \\ \text{per barrel} \end{array} = \begin{array}{l} \$73 \text{ per barrel for oil purchased under the} \\ \text{long-term contract or } \$80 \text{ per barrel for} \\ \text{oil purchased from Gulfmex in Matamoros} \end{array}$$

In general, when markets are not perfectly competitive, the potential to influence demand and operating income through prices complicates the measurement of opportunity costs. The transfer price depends on constantly changing levels of supply and demand. There is not just one transfer price. Rather, the transfer prices for various quantities supplied and demanded depend on the incremental costs and opportunity costs of the units transferred.

3. **No market exists for the intermediate product.** This situation would occur for the Horizon Petroleum case if the crude oil transported by the transportation division could be used only by the Houston refinery (due to, say, its high tar content) and would not be wanted by external parties. Here, the opportunity cost of supplying crude oil internally is zero because the inability to sell crude oil externally means no contribution margin is forgone. For the transportation division of Horizon Petroleum, the minimum transfer price under the general guideline is the incremental cost per barrel (either $73 or $80). As in the previous case, any transfer price between the incremental cost and $85 will achieve goal congruence.

Multinational Transfer Pricing and Tax Considerations

Transfer pricing is an important accounting priority for managers around the world. A 2007 Ernst & Young survey of multinational enterprises in 24 countries found that 74% of parent firms and 81% of subsidiary respondents believed that transfer pricing was "absolutely critical" or "very important" to their organizations. The reason is that parent companies identify transfer pricing as the single most important tax issue they face. The sums of money involved are often staggering. Google, for example, has a 90% market share of UK internet searches and earned £1.6 billion in advertising revenues last year in Britain; yet, Google UK reported a pretax loss of £26 million. The reason is that revenues from customers in Britain are transferred to Google's European headquarters in Dublin. By paying the low Irish corporate tax rate of 12.5%, Google saved £450 million in UK taxes in 2009 alone. Transfer prices affect not just income taxes, but

◀ **Decision Point**

What is the general guideline for determining a minimum transfer price?

Learning Objective 8

Incorporate income tax considerations in multinational transfer pricing

. . . set transfer prices to minimize tax payments to the extent permitted by tax authorities

also payroll taxes, customs duties, tariffs, sales taxes, value-added taxes, environment-related taxes, and other government levies. Our aim here is to highlight tax factors, and in particular income taxes, as important considerations in determining transfer prices.

Transfer Pricing for Tax Minimization

Consider the Horizon Petroleum data in Exhibit 22-2 (p. 783). Assume that the transportation division based in Mexico pays Mexican income taxes at 30% of operating income and that the refining division based in the United States pays income taxes at 20% of operating income. Horizon Petroleum would minimize its total income tax payments with the 105%-of-full-cost transfer-pricing method, as shown in the following table, because this method minimizes income reported in Mexico, where income is taxed at a higher rate than in the United States.

	Operating Income for 100 Barrels of Crude Oil			Income Tax on 100 Barrels of Crude Oil		
Transfer-Pricing Method	**Transportation Division (Mexico) (1)**	**Refining Division (United States) (2)**	**Total (3) = (1) + (2)**	**Transportation Division (Mexico) (4) = 0.30 × (1)**	**Refining Division (United States) (5) = 0.20 × (2)**	**Total (6) = (4) + (5)**
Market price	$900	$300	$1,200	$270	$ 60	$330
105% of full costs	380	820	1,200	114	164	278
Hybrid price	600	600	1,200	180	120	300

Income tax considerations raise additional issues. Tax issues may conflict with other objectives of transfer pricing. Suppose the market for crude oil in Houston is perfectly competitive. In this case, the market-based transfer price achieves goal congruence, provides incentives for management effort, and helps Horizon to evaluate the economic profitability of the transportation division. But it is costly from the perspective of income taxes. To minimize income taxes, Horizon would favor using 105% of full cost for tax reporting. Tax laws in the United States and Mexico, however, constrain this option. In particular, the Mexican tax authorities, aware of Horizon's incentives to minimize income taxes by reducing the income reported in Mexico, would challenge any attempts to shift income to the refining division through an unreasonably low transfer price (see also Concepts in Action, p. 793).

Section 482 of the U.S. Internal Revenue Code governs taxation of multinational transfer pricing. Section 482 requires that transfer prices between a company and its foreign division or subsidiary, for both tangible and intangible property, equal the price that would be charged by an unrelated third party in a comparable transaction. Regulations related to Section 482 recognize that transfer prices can be market-based or cost-plus-based, where the plus represents margins on comparable transactions.[7]

If the market for crude oil in Houston is perfectly competitive, Horizon would be required to calculate taxes using the market price of $85 for transfers from the transportation division to the refining division. Horizon might successfully argue that the transfer price should be set below the market price because the transportation division incurs no marketing and distribution costs when selling crude oil to the refining division. For example, if marketing and distribution costs equal $2 per barrel, Horizon could set the transfer price at $83 ($85 − $2) per barrel, the selling price net of marketing and distribution costs. Under the U.S. Internal Revenue Code, Horizon could obtain advanced approval of the transfer-pricing arrangements from the tax authorities, called an *advanced pricing agreement* (*APA*). The APA is a binding agreement for a specified number of years. The goal of the APA program is to avoid costly transfer-pricing disputes between taxpayers and tax authorities. In 2007, there were 81 APAs executed, of which 54 were bilateral agreements with other tax treaty countries. Included in this was the completion of the first bilateral APA between the United States and China, involving Wal-Mart Stores.

The current global recession has pushed governments around the world to impose tighter trading rules and more aggressively pursue tax revenues. The number of countries

---

[7] J. Styron, "Transfer Pricing and Tax Planning: Opportunities for US Corporations Operating Abroad," *CPA Journal Online* (November 2007); R. Feinschreiber (Ed.), *Transfer Pricing Handbook*, 3rd ed. (New York: John Wiley & Sons, 2002).

Concepts in Action | Transfer Pricing Dispute Temporarily Stops the Flow of Fiji Water

Tax authorities and government officials across the globe pay close attention to taxes paid by multinational companies operating within their boundaries. At the heart of the issue are the transfer prices that companies use to transfer products from one country to another. Since 2008, Fiji Water, LLC, a U.S.-based company that markets its famous brand of bottled water in more than a dozen counties, has been engaged in a fierce transfer-pricing dispute with the government of the Fiji Islands, where its water bottling plant is located.

While Fiji Water is produced in the Fiji Islands, all other activities in the company's value chain—importing, distributing, and retailing—occur in the countries where Fiji Water is sold. Over time, the Fiji Islands government became concerned that Fiji Water was engaging in transfer price manipulations, selling the water shipments produced in the Fiji Islands at a very low price to the company headquarters in Los Angeles. It was feared that very little of the wealth generated by Fiji Water, the country's second largest exporter, was coming into the Fiji Islands as foreign reserves from export earnings, which Fiji badly needed to fund its imports. To the Fiji Islands government, Fiji Water was funneling most of its cash to the United States.

As a result of these concerns, the Fiji Islands Revenue and Customs Authority (FIRCA) decided to take action against Fiji Water. FIRCA halted exports in January 2008 at ports in the Fiji Islands by putting 200 containers loaded with Fiji Water bottled under armed guard, and issuing a statement accusing Fiji Water of transfer price manipulations. FIRCA's chief executive, Jitoko Tikolevu, said, "The wholly U.S.-owned Fijian subsidiary sold its water exclusively to its U.S. parent at the declared rate, in Fiji, of $4 a carton. In the U.S., though, the same company then sold it for up to $50 a carton."

Fiji Water immediately filed a lawsuit against FIRCA with the High Court of Fiji. The court issued an interim order, allowing the company to resume shipment of the embargoed containers upon payment of a bond to the court. In the media and subsequent court filings, the company stated that on a global basis it sold each carton of water for $20–28, and it did not make a profit due to "heavy investments in assets, employees, and marketing necessary to aggressively grow a successful branded product."

The dispute between FIRCA and Fiji Water remains unresolved in the Fiji Islands court system. In the interim, Fiji Water has maintained its previous transfer price of $4 for water produced at its bottling plant in the Fiji Islands. To pressure the company to change its transfer pricing practices, the Fiji Islands government considered adding a 20-cents-per-litre excise tax on water produced in the country, but the tax was ultimately rejected as too draconian. As this high-profile case demonstrates, transfer pricing formulas and taxation details remain a contentious issue for governments and countries around the globe.

Source: Matau, Robert. 2008. Fiji water explains saga. *Fiji Times*, February 9; McMaster, James and Jan Novak. 2009. Fiji water and corporate social responsibility—Green makeover or 'green-washing'? The University of Western Ontario Richard Ivey School of Business No. 909A08, London, Ontario: Ivey Publishing.

that have imposed transfer pricing regulations has approximately quadrupled from 1995 to 2007, according to a 2008 KPMG report. Officials in China, where foreign businesses enjoyed favorable treatment until last year, recently issued new rules requiring multinationals to submit extensive transfer-pricing documentation. Countries such as India, Canada, Turkey, and Greece have brought greater scrutiny to bear on transfer pricing, focusing in particular on intellectual-property values, costs of back-office functions and losses of any type. In the United States, the Obama administration plans to shrink a "tax gap" the IRS estimates may be as high as $345 billion by restricting or closing several widely used tax loopholes. While the plan does not directly address transfer pricing practice, the IRS has become even more aggressive with enforcement. The agency added 1,200 people to its international staff in 2009, and the 2010 budget called for hiring another 800.

Transfer Prices Designed for Multiple Objectives

To meet multiple transfer-pricing objectives, such as minimizing income taxes, achieving goal congruence, and motivating management effort, a company may choose to keep one set of accounting records for tax reporting and a second set for internal management reporting.

Of course, it is costly to maintain two sets of books and companies such as Case New Holland, a world leader in the agricultural and construction equipment business, also oppose it for conceptual reasons. However, a survey by the AnswerThink Consulting Group of large companies (more than $2 billion in revenues) found that 77% used separate reporting systems to track internal pricing information, compared with about 25% of large companies outside that "best practices" group. Microsoft, for example, believes in "delinking" transfer pricing and employs an internal measurement system (Microsoft Accounting Principles, or MAPs) that uses a separate set of company-designed rules and accounts.[8] A key aspect of management control at Microsoft is the desire to hold local managers accountable for product profitability and to establish appropriate sales and marketing spending levels for every product line. To establish these sales and spending levels, the firm creates a profitability statement for every product in every region, and allocates G&A and R&D costs across sales divisions in ways that aren't necessarily the most tax efficient.

Even if a company does not have such formal separated reporting systems, it can still informally adjust transfer prices to satisfy the tradeoff between tax minimization and incentive provision. Consider a multinational firm that makes semiconductor products that it sells through its sales organization in a higher-tax country. To minimize taxes, the parent sets a high transfer price, thereby lowering the operating income of the foreign sales organization. It would be inappropriate to penalize the country sales manager for this low income since the sales organization has no say in determining the transfer price. As an alternative, the company can evaluate the sales manager on the direct contribution (revenues minus marketing costs) incurred in the country. That is, the transfer price incurred to acquire the semiconductor products is omitted for performance-evaluation purposes. Of course, this is not a perfect solution. By ignoring the cost of acquiring the products, the sales manager is given incentives to overspend on local marketing relative to what would be optimal from the firm's overall perspective. If the dysfunctional effects of this are suitably large, corporate managers must then step in and dictate specific operational decisions and goals for the manager based on the information available to them. More generally, adoption of a tax-compliant transfer pricing policy creates a need for nonfinancial performance indicators at lower management levels in order to better evaluate and reward performance.[9]

Additional Issues in Transfer Pricing

Additional factors that arise in multinational transfer pricing include tariffs and customs duties levied on imports of products into a country. The issues here are similar to income tax considerations; companies will have incentives to lower transfer prices for products imported into a country to reduce tariffs and customs duties charged on those products.

In addition to the motivations for choosing transfer prices already described, multinational transfer prices are sometimes influenced by restrictions that some countries place on dividend- or income-related payments to parties outside their national borders. By increasing the prices of goods or services transferred into divisions in these countries, companies can seek to increase the cash paid out of these countries without violating dividend- or income-related restrictions.

Decision Point ▶

How do income tax considerations affect transfer pricing in multinationals?

Problem for Self-Study

The Pillercat Corporation is a highly decentralized company. Each division manager has full authority for sourcing decisions and selling decisions. The machining division of Pillercat has been the major supplier of the 2,000 crankshafts that the tractor division needs each year.

The tractor division, however, has just announced that it plans to purchase all its crankshafts in the forthcoming year from two external suppliers at $200 per crankshaft.

---

[8] For further details, see I. Springsteel, "Separate but Unequal," *CFO Magazine*, August 1999.

[9] Cools et al. "Management control in the transfer pricing tax compliant multinational enterprise," *Accounting, Organizations and Society*, August 2008 provides an illustrative case study of this issue in the context of a semiconductor product division of a multinational firm.

The machining division of Pillercat recently increased its selling price for the forthcoming year to $220 per unit (from $200 per unit in the current year).

Juan Gomez, manager of the machining division, feels that the 10% price increase is justified. It results from a higher depreciation charge on some new specialized equipment used to manufacture crankshafts and an increase in labor costs. Gomez wants the president of Pillercat Corporation to force the tractor division to buy all its crankshafts from the machining division at the price of $220. The following table summarizes the key data.

	A	B
	Home Insert Page Layout Formulas Data Review	
	A	B
1	Number of crankshafts purchased by tractor division	2,000
2	External supplier's market price per crankshaft	$ 200
3	Variable cost per crankshaft in machining division	$ 190
4	Fixed cost per crankshaft in machining division	$ 20

1. Compute the advantage or disadvantage in terms of annual operating income to the Pillercat Corporation as a whole if the tractor division buys crankshafts internally from the machining division under each of the following cases:
   a. The machining division has no alternative use for the facilities used to manufacture crankshafts.
   b. The machining division can use the facilities for other production operations, which will result in annual cash operating savings of $29,000.
   c. The machining division has no alternative use for its facilities, and the external supplier drops the price to $185 per crankshaft.
2. As the president of Pillercat, how would you respond to Juan Gomez's request that you force the tractor division to purchase all of its crankshafts from the machining division? Would your response differ according to the three cases described in requirement 1? Explain.

Required

Solution

1. Computations for the tractor division buying crankshafts internally for one year under cases **a, b,** and **c** are as follows:

	A	B	C	D
	Home Insert Page Layout Formulas Data Review View			
	A	B	C	D
1			Case	
2		a	b	c
3	Number of crankshafts purchased by tractor division	2,000	2,000	2,000
4	External supplier's market price per crankshaft	$ 200	$ 200	$ 185
5	Variable cost per crankshaft in machining division	$ 190	$ 190	$ 190
6	Opportunity costs of the machining division supplying crankshafts to the tractor division	-	$ 29,000	-
7				
8	Total purchase costs if buying from an external supplier			
9	(2,000 shafts × $200, $200, $185 per shaft)	$400,000	$400,000	$370,000
10	Incremental cost of buying from the machining division			
11	(2,000 shafts × $190 per shaft)	380,000	380,000	380,000
12	Total opportunity costs of the machining division	-	29,000	-
13	Total relevant costs	380,000	409,000	380,000
14	Annual operating income advantage (disadvantage) to			
15	Pillercat of buying from the machining division	$ 20,000	$ (9,000)	$ (10,000)

The general guideline that was introduced in the chapter (p. 790) as a first step in setting a transfer price can be used to highlight the alternatives:

	Home	Insert		Page Layout		Formulas	Data	Review	View	
	A	B	C	D	E	F	G			
1	Case	Incremental Cost per Unit Incurred to Point of Transfer	+	Opportunity Cost per Unit to the Supplying Division	=	Transfer Price	External Market Price			
2	a	$190	+	$0	=	$190.00	$200			
3	b	$190	+	$14.50[a]	=	$204.50	$200			
4	c	$190	+	$0	=	$190.00	$185			
5										
6	[a]Opportunity cost per unit	=	Total opportunity costs	÷	Number of crankshafts	= $29,000 ÷ 2,000 = $14.50				
7										

Comparing transfer price to external-market price, the tractor division will maximize annual operating income of Pillercat Corporation as a whole by purchasing from the machining division in case **a** and by purchasing from the external supplier in cases **b** and **c**.

2. Pillercat Corporation is a highly decentralized company. If no forced transfer were made, the tractor division would use an external supplier, a decision that would be in the best interest of the company as a whole in cases **b** and **c** of requirement 1 but not in case **a**.

   Suppose in case **a**, the machining division refuses to meet the price of $200. This decision means that the company will be $20,000 worse off in the short run. Should top management interfere and force a transfer at $200? This interference would undercut the philosophy of decentralization. Many top managers would not interfere because they would view the $20,000 as an inevitable cost of a suboptimal decision that can occur under decentralization. But how high must this cost be before the temptation to interfere would be irresistible? $30,000? $40,000?

   Any top management interference with lower-level decision making weakens decentralization. Of course, Pillercat's management may occasionally interfere to prevent costly mistakes. But recurring interference and constraints would hurt Pillercat's attempts to operate as a decentralized company.

Decision Points

The following question-and-answer format summarizes the chapter's learning objectives. Each decision presents a key question related to a learning objective. The guidelines are the answer to that question.

Decision

1. What is a management control system and how should it be designed?

Guidelines

A management control system is a means of gathering and using information to aid and coordinate the planning and control decisions throughout the organization and to guide the behavior of managers and other employees. Effective management control systems (a) are closely aligned to the organization's strategy, (b) support the organizational responsibilities of individual managers, and (c) motivate managers and other employees to give effort to achieve the organization's goals.

2. What are the benefits and costs of decentralization?

The benefits of decentralization include (a) greater responsiveness to local needs, (b) gains from faster decision making, (c) increased motivation of subunit managers, (d) greater management development and learning, and (e) sharpened focus of subunit managers. The costs of decentralization include (a) suboptimal decision making, (b) excessive focus on the subunit rather than the company as a whole, (c) increased costs of information gathering, and (d) duplication of activities.

3. What are alternative ways of calculating transfer prices, and what criteria should be used to evaluate them?

A transfer price is the price one subunit charges for a product or service supplied to another subunit of the same organization. Transfer prices can be (a) market-based, (b) cost-based, or (c) hybrid. Different transfer-pricing methods produce different revenues and costs for individual subunits, and hence, different operating incomes for the subunits. Transfer prices seek to (a) promote goal congruence, (b) motivate management effort, (c) help evaluate subunit performance, and (d) preserve subunit autonomy (if desired).

4. Under what market conditions do market-based transfer prices promote goal congruence?

In perfectly competitive markets, there is no unused capacity, and division managers can buy and sell as much of a product or service as they want at the market price. In such settings, using the market price as the transfer price motivates division managers to transact internally and to take exactly the same actions as they would if they were transacting in the external market.

5. What problems can arise when full cost plus a markup is used as the transfer price?

A transfer price based on full cost plus a markup may lead to suboptimal decisions because it leads the buying division to regard the fixed costs and the markup of the selling division as a variable cost. The buying division may then purchase products from an external supplier expecting savings in costs that, in fact, will not occur.

6. Within a range of feasible transfer prices, what are alternative ways for firms to arrive at the eventual price?

When there is unused capacity, the transfer-price range lies between the minimum price at which the selling division is willing to sell (its variable cost per unit) and the maximum price the buying division is willing to pay (the lower of its contribution or price at which the product is available from external suppliers). Methods for arriving at a price in this range include proration (such as splitting the difference equally or on the basis of relative variable costs), negotiation between divisions, and dual pricing.

7. What is the general guideline for determining a minimum transfer price?

The general guideline states that the minimum transfer price equals the incremental cost per unit incurred up to the point of transfer plus the opportunity cost per unit to the selling division resulting from transferring products or services internally.

8. How do income tax considerations affect transfer pricing in multinationals?

Transfer prices can reduce income tax payments by reporting more income in low-tax-rate countries and less income in high-tax-rate countries. However, tax regulations of different countries restrict the transfer prices that companies can use.

Terms to Learn

This chapter and the Glossary at the end of the book contain definitions of the following important terms:

autonomy (**p. 777**)

decentralization (**p. 777**)

dual pricing (**p. 789**)

dysfunctional decision making (**p. 778**)

effort (**p. 776**)

goal congruence (**p. 776**)

incongruent decision making (**p. 778**)

intermediate product (**p. 780**)

management control system (**p. 775**)

motivation (**p. 776**)

perfectly competitive market (**p. 784**)

suboptimal decision making (**p. 778**)

transfer price (**p. 780**)

Assignment Material

Questions

MyAccountingLab

22-1 What is a management control system?

22-2 Describe three criteria you would use to evaluate whether a management control system is effective.

22-3 What is the relationship among motivation, goal congruence, and effort?

22-4 Name three benefits and two costs of decentralization.

22-5 "Organizations typically adopt a consistent decentralization or centralization philosophy across all their business functions." Do you agree? Explain.

22-6 "Transfer pricing is confined to profit centers." Do you agree? Explain.

22-7 What are the three methods for determining transfer prices?

22-8 What properties should transfer-pricing systems have?

22-9 "All transfer-pricing methods give the same division operating income." Do you agree? Explain.

22-10 Under what conditions is a market-based transfer price optimal?

22-11 What is one potential limitation of full-cost-based transfer prices?

22-12 Give two reasons why the dual-pricing system of transfer pricing is not widely used.

22-13 "Cost and price information play no role in negotiated transfer prices." Do you agree? Explain.

22-14 "Under the general guideline for transfer pricing, the minimum transfer price will vary depending on whether the supplying division has unused capacity or not." Do you agree? Explain.

22-15 How should managers consider income tax issues when choosing a transfer-pricing method?

MyAccountingLab

Exercises

22-16 Evaluating management control systems, balanced scorecard. Adventure Parks Inc. (API) operates ten theme parks throughout the United States. The company's slogan is "Name Your Adventure," and its mission is to offer an exciting theme park experience to visitors of all ages. API's corporate strategy supports this mission by stressing the importance of sparkling clean surroundings, efficient crowd management and, above all, cheerful employees. Of course, improved shareholder value drives this strategy.

Required

1. Assuming that API uses a balanced scorecard approach (see Chapter 13) to formulating its management control system. List three measures that API might use to evaluate each of the four balanced scorecard perspectives: financial perspective, customer perspective, internal-business-process perspective, and learning-and-growth perspective.

2. How would the management controls related to financial and customer perspectives at API differ between the following three managers: a souvenir shop manager, a park general manager, and the corporation's CEO?

22-17 Cost centers, profit centers, decentralization, transfer prices. Fenster Corporation manufactures windows with wood and metal frames. Fenster has three departments: glass, wood, and metal. The glass department makes the window glass and sends it to either the wood or metal department where the glass is framed. The window is then sold. Upper management sets the production schedules for the three departments and evaluates them on output quantity, cost variances, and product quality.

Required

1. Are the three departments cost centers, revenue centers, or profit centers?
2. Are the three departments centralized or decentralized?
3. Can a centralized department be a profit center? Why or why not?
4. Suppose the upper management of Fenster Corporation decides to let the three departments set their own production schedules, buy and sell products in the external market, and have the wood and metal departments negotiate with the glass department for the glass panes using a transfer price.
   a. Will this change your answers to requirements 1 and 2?
   b. How would you recommend upper management evaluate the three departments if this change is made?

22-18 Benefits and costs of decentralization. Jackson Markets, a chain of traditional supermarkets, is interested in gaining access to the organic and health food retail market by acquiring a regional company in that sector. Jackson intends to operate the newly-acquired stores independently from its supermarkets.

One of the prospects is Health Source, a chain of twenty stores in the mid-Atlantic. Buying for all twenty stores is done by the company's central office. Store managers must follow strict guidelines for all aspects of store management in an attempt to maintain consistency among stores. Store managers are evaluated on the basis of achieving profit goals developed by the central office.

The other prospect is Harvest Moon, a chain of thirty stores in the Northeast. Harvest Moon managers are given significant flexibility in product offerings, allowing them to negotiate purchases with local organic farmers. Store managers are rewarded for exceeding self-developed return on investment goals with company stock options. Some managers have become significant shareholders in the company, and have even decided on their own to open additional store locations to improve market penetration. However, the increased autonomy has led to competition and price cutting among Harvest Moon stores within the same geographic market, resulting in lower margins.

Required

1. Would you describe Health Source as having a centralized or a decentralized structure? Explain.
2. Would you describe Harvest Moon as having a centralized or a decentralized structure? Discuss some of the benefits and costs of that type of structure.

3. Would stores in each chain be considered cost centers, revenue centers, profit centers, or investment centers? How does that tie into the evaluation of store managers?

4. Assume that Jackson chooses to acquire Harvest Moon. What steps can Jackson take to improve goal congruence between store managers and the larger company?

22-19 Multinational transfer pricing, effect of alternative transfer-pricing methods, global income tax minimization. Tech Friendly Computer, Inc., with headquarters in San Francisco, manufactures and sells a desktop computer. Tech Friendly has three divisions, each of which is located in a different country:

a. China division—manufactures memory devices and keyboards

b. South Korea division—assembles desktop computers using locally manufactured parts, along with memory devices and keyboards from the China division

c. U.S. division—packages and distributes desktop computers

Each division is run as a profit center. The costs for the work done in each division for a single desktop computer are as follows:

China division: Variable cost = 900 yuan

Fixed cost = 1,980 yuan

South Korea division: Variable cost = 350,000 won

Fixed cost = 470,000 won

U.S. division: Variable cost = $125

Fixed cost = $325

■ Chinese income tax rate on the China division's operating income: 40%
■ South Korean income tax rate on the South Korea division's operating income: 20%
■ U.S. income tax rate on the U.S. division's operating income: 30%

Each desktop computer is sold to retail outlets in the United States for $3,800. Assume that the current foreign exchange rates are as follows:

9 yuan = $1 U.S.

1,000 won = $1 U.S.

Both the China and the South Korea divisions sell part of their production under a private label. The China division sells the comparable memory/keyboard package used in each Tech Friendly desktop computer to a Chinese manufacturer for 4,500 yuan. The South Korea division sells the comparable desktop computer to a South Korean distributor for 1,340,000 won.

1. Calculate the after-tax operating income per unit earned by each division under the following transfer-pricing methods: (a) market price, (b) 200% of full cost, and (c) 350% of variable cost. (Income taxes are not included in the computation of the cost-based transfer prices.)   **Required**

2. Which transfer-pricing method(s) will maximize the after-tax operating income per unit of Tech Friendly Computer?

22-20 Transfer-pricing methods, goal congruence. British Columbia Lumber has a raw lumber division and a finished lumber division. The variable costs are as follows:

■ Raw lumber division: $100 per 100 board-feet of raw lumber
■ Finished lumber division: $125 per 100 board-feet of finished lumber

Assume that there is no board-feet loss in processing raw lumber into finished lumber. Raw lumber can be sold at $200 per 100 board-feet. Finished lumber can be sold at $275 per 100 board-feet.

1. Should British Columbia Lumber process raw lumber into its finished form? Show your calculations.   **Required**

2. Assume that internal transfers are made at 110% of variable cost. Will each division maximize its division operating-income contribution by adopting the action that is in the best interest of British Columbia Lumber as a whole? Explain.

3. Assume that internal transfers are made at market prices. Will each division maximize its division operating-income contribution by adopting the action that is in the best interest of British Columbia Lumber as a whole? Explain.

22-21 Effect of alternative transfer-pricing methods on division operating income. (CMA, adapted) Ajax Corporation has two divisions. The mining division makes toldine, which is then transferred to the metals division. The toldine is further processed by the metals division and is sold to customers at a price of $150 per unit. The mining division is currently required by Ajax to transfer its total yearly output of

200,000 units of toldine to the metals division at 110% of full manufacturing cost. Unlimited quantities of toldine can be purchased and sold on the outside market at $90 per unit.

The following table gives the manufacturing cost per unit in the mining and metals divisions for 2012:

	Mining Division	Metals Division
Direct material cost	$12	$ 6
Direct manufacturing labor cost	16	20
Manufacturing overhead cost	32[a]	25[b]
Total manufacturing cost per unit	$60	$51

[a]Manufacturing overhead costs in the mining division are 25% fixed and 75% variable.
[b]Manufacturing overhead costs in the metals division are 60% fixed and 40% variable.

Required

1. Calculate the operating incomes for the mining and metals divisions for the 200,000 units of toldine transferred under the following transfer-pricing methods: (a) market price and (b) 110% of full manufacturing cost.
2. Suppose Ajax rewards each division manager with a bonus, calculated as 1% of division operating income (if positive). What is the amount of bonus that will be paid to each division manager under the transfer-pricing methods in requirement 1? Which transfer-pricing method will each division manager prefer to use?
3. What arguments would Brian Jones, manager of the mining division, make to support the transfer-pricing method that he prefers?

22-22 Transfer pricing, general guideline, goal congruence. (CMA, adapted). Quest Motors, Inc., operates as a decentralized multidivision company. The Vivo division of Quest Motors purchases most of its airbags from the airbag division. The airbag division's incremental cost for manufacturing the airbags is $90 per unit. The airbag division is currently working at 80% of capacity. The current market price of the airbags is $125 per unit.

Required

1. Using the general guideline presented in the chapter, what is the minimum price at which the airbag division would sell airbags to the Vivo division?
2. Suppose that Quest Motors requires that whenever divisions with unused capacity sell products internally, they must do so at the incremental cost. Evaluate this transfer-pricing policy using the criteria of goal congruence, evaluating division performance, motivating management effort, and preserving division autonomy.
3. If the two divisions were to negotiate a transfer price, what is the range of possible transfer prices? Evaluate this negotiated transfer-pricing policy using the criteria of goal congruence, evaluating division performance, motivating management effort, and preserving division autonomy.
4. Instead of allowing negotiation, suppose that Quest specifies a hybrid transfer price that "splits the difference" between the minimum and maximum prices from the divisions' standpoint. What would be the resulting transfer price for airbags?

22-23 Multinational transfer pricing, global tax minimization. The Mornay Company manufactures telecommunications equipment at its plant in Toledo, Ohio. The company has marketing divisions throughout the world. A Mornay marketing division in Vienna, Austria, imports 10,000 units of Product 4A36 from the United States. The following information is available:

U.S. income tax rate on the U.S. division's operating income	35%
Austrian income tax rate on the Austrian division's operating income	40%
Austrian import duty	15%
Variable manufacturing cost per unit of Product 4A36	$ 550
Full manufacturing cost per unit of Product 4A36	$ 800
Selling price (net of marketing and distribution costs) in Austria	$1,150

Suppose the United States and Austrian tax authorities only allow transfer prices that are between the full manufacturing cost per unit of $800 and a market price of $950, based on comparable imports into Austria. The Austrian import duty is charged on the price at which the product is transferred into Austria. Any import duty paid to the Austrian authorities is a deductible expense for calculating Austrian income taxes due.

Required

1. Calculate the after-tax operating income earned by the United States and Austrian divisions from transferring 10,000 units of Product 4A36 (a) at full manufacturing cost per unit and (b) at market price of comparable imports. (Income taxes are not included in the computation of the cost-based transfer prices.)
2. Which transfer price should the Mornay Company select to minimize the total of company import duties and income taxes? Remember that the transfer price must be between the full manufacturing cost per unit of $800 and the market price of $950 of comparable imports into Austria. Explain your reasoning.

22-24 Multinational transfer pricing, goal congruence (continuation of 22-23). Suppose that the U.S. division could sell as many units of Product 4A36 as it makes at $900 per unit in the U.S. market, net of all marketing and distribution costs.

Required

1. From the viewpoint of the Mornay Company as a whole, would after-tax operating income be maximized if it sold the 10,000 units of Product 4A36 in the United States or in Austria? Show your computations.
2. Suppose division managers act autonomously to maximize their division's after-tax operating income. Will the transfer price calculated in requirement 2 of Exercise 22-23 result in the U.S. division manager taking the actions determined to be optimal in requirement 1 of this exercise? Explain.
3. What is the minimum transfer price that the U.S. division manager would agree to? Does this transfer price result in the Mornay Company as a whole paying more import duty and taxes than the answer to requirement 2 of Exercise 22-23? If so, by how much?

22-25 Transfer-pricing dispute. The Allison-Chambers Corporation, manufacturer of tractors and other heavy farm equipment, is organized along decentralized product lines, with each manufacturing division operating as a separate profit center. Each division manager has been delegated full authority on all decisions involving the sale of that division's output both to outsiders and to other divisions of Allison-Chambers. Division C has in the past always purchased its requirement of a particular tractor-engine component from division A. However, when informed that division A is increasing its selling price to $150, division C's manager decides to purchase the engine component from external suppliers.

Division C can purchase the component for $135 per unit in the open market. Division A insists that, because of the recent installation of some highly specialized equipment and the resulting high depreciation charges, it will not be able to earn an adequate return on its investment unless it raises its price. Division A's manager appeals to top management of Allison-Chambers for support in the dispute with division C and supplies the following operating data:

C's annual purchases of the tractor-engine component	1,000 units
A's variable cost per unit of the tractor-engine component	$120
A's fixed cost per unit of the tractor-engine component	$ 20

Required

1. Assume that there are no alternative uses for internal facilities of division A. Determine whether the company as a whole will benefit if division C purchases the component from external suppliers for $135 per unit. What should the transfer price for the component be set at so that division managers acting in their own divisions' best interests take actions that are also in the best interest of the company as a whole?
2. Assume that internal facilities of division A would not otherwise be idle. By not producing the 1,000 units for division C, division A's equipment and other facilities would be used for other production operations that would result in annual cash-operating savings of $18,000. Should division C purchase from external suppliers? Show your computations.
3. Assume that there are no alternative uses for division A's internal facilities and that the price from outsiders drops $20. Should division C purchase from external suppliers? What should the transfer price for the component be set at so that division managers acting in their own divisions' best interests take actions that are also in the best interest of the company as a whole?

22-26 Transfer-pricing problem (continuation of 22-25). Refer to Exercise 22-25. Assume that division A can sell the 1,000 units to other customers at $155 per unit, with variable marketing cost of $5 per unit.

Required

Determine whether Allison-Chambers will benefit if division C purchases the 1,000 units from external suppliers at $135 per unit. Show your computations.

Problems

22-27 General guideline, transfer pricing. The Slate Company manufactures and sells television sets. Its assembly division (AD) buys television screens from the screen division (SD) and assembles the TV sets. The SD, which is operating at capacity, incurs an incremental manufacturing cost of $65 per screen. The SD can sell all its output to the outside market at a price of $100 per screen, after incurring a variable marketing and distribution cost of $8 per screen. If the AD purchases screens from outside suppliers at a price of $100 per screen, it will incur a variable purchasing cost of $7 per screen. Slate's division managers can act autonomously to maximize their own division's operating income.

Required

1. What is the minimum transfer price at which the SD manager would be willing to sell screens to the AD?
2. What is the maximum transfer price at which the AD manager would be willing to purchase screens from the SD?
3. Now suppose that the SD can sell only 70% of its output capacity of 20,000 screens per month on the open market. Capacity cannot be reduced in the short run. The AD can assemble and sell more than 20,000 TV sets per month.
   a. What is the minimum transfer price at which the SD manager would be willing to sell screens to the AD?

b. From the point of view of Slate's management, how much of the SD output should be transferred to the AD?

c. If Slate mandates the SD and AD managers to "split the difference" on the minimum and maximum transfer prices they would be willing to negotiate over, what would be the resulting transfer price? Does this price achieve the outcome desired in requirement 3b?

22-28 Pertinent transfer price. Europa, Inc., has two divisions, A and B, that manufacture expensive bicycles. Division A produces the bicycle frame, and division B assembles the rest of the bicycle onto the frame. There is a market for both the subassembly and the final product. Each division has been designated as a profit center. The transfer price for the subassembly has been set at the long-run average market price. The following data are available for each division:

Selling price for final product	$300
Long-run average selling price for intermediate product	200
Incremental cost per unit for completion in division B	150
Incremental cost per unit in division A	120

The manager of division B has made the following calculation:

Selling price for final product		$300
Transferred-in cost per unit (market)	$200	
Incremental cost per unit for completion	150	350
Contribution (loss) on product		$(50)

Required

1. Should transfers be made to division B if there is no unused capacity in division A? Is the market price the correct transfer price? Show your computations.
2. Assume that division A's maximum capacity for this product is 1,000 units per month and sales to the intermediate market are now 800 units. Should 200 units be transferred to division B? At what transfer price? Assume that for a variety of reasons, division A will maintain the $200 selling price indefinitely. That is, division A is not considering lowering the price to outsiders even if idle capacity exists.
3. Suppose division A quoted a transfer price of $150 for up to 200 units. What would be the contribution to the company as a whole if a transfer were made? As manager of division B, would you be inclined to buy at $150? Explain.

22-29 Pricing in imperfect markets (continuation of 22-28). Refer to Problem 22-28.

Required

1. Suppose the manager of division A has the option of (a) cutting the external price to $195, with the certainty that sales will rise to 1,000 units or (b) maintaining the external price of $200 for the 800 units and transferring the 200 units to division B at a price that would produce the same operating income for division A. What transfer price would produce the same operating income for division A? Is that price consistent with that recommended by the general guideline in the chapter so that the resulting decision would be desirable for the company as a whole?
2. Suppose that if the selling price for the intermediate product were dropped to $195, sales to external parties could be increased to 900 units. Division B wants to acquire as many as 200 units if the transfer price is acceptable. For simplicity, assume that there is no external market for the final 100 units of division A's capacity.
   a. Using the general guideline, what is (are) the minimum transfer price(s) that should lead to the correct economic decision? Ignore performance-evaluation considerations.
   b. Compare the total contributions under the alternatives to show why the transfer price(s) recommended lead(s) to the optimal economic decision.

22-30 Effect of alternative transfer-pricing methods on division operating income. Crango Products is a cranberry cooperative that operates two divisions, a harvesting division and a processing division. Currently, all of harvesting's output is converted into cranberry juice by the processing division, and the juice is sold to large beverage companies that produce cranberry juice blends. The processing division has a yield of 500 gallons of juice per 1,000 pounds of cranberries. Cost and market price data for the two divisions are as follows:

	Home	Insert	Page Layout	Formulas	Data	Review	View		
	A				B	C	D		E
1	**Harvesting Division**						**Processing Division**		
2	Variable cost per pound of cranberries				$0.10		Variable processing cost per gallon of juice produced		$0.20
3	Fixed cost per pound of cranberries				$0.25		Fixed cost per gallon of juice produced		$0.40
4	Selling price per pound of cranberries in outside market				$0.60		Selling price per gallon of juice		$2.10

1. Compute Crango's operating income from harvesting 400,000 pounds of cranberries during June 2012 **Required**
and processing them into juice.
2. Crango rewards its division managers with a bonus equal to 5% of operating income. Compute the
bonus earned by each division manager in June 2012 for each of the following transfer pricing methods:
   a. 200% of full cost
   b. Market price
3. Which transfer-pricing method will each division manager prefer? How might Crango resolve any conflicts that may arise on the issue of transfer pricing?

**22-31 Goal-congruence problems with cost-plus transfer-pricing methods, dual-pricing system
(continuation of 22-30).** Assume that Pat Borges, CEO of Crango, had mandated a transfer price equal to
200% of full cost. Now he decides to decentralize some management decisions and sends around a memo
that states the following: "Effective immediately, each division of Crango is free to make its own decisions
regarding the purchase of direct materials and the sale of finished products."

1. Give an example of a goal-congruence problem that will arise if Crango continues to use a transfer **Required**
price of 200% of full cost and Borges's decentralization policy is adopted.
2. Borges feels that a dual transfer-pricing policy will improve goal congruence. He suggests that transfers
out of the harvesting division be made at 200% of full cost and transfers into the processing division be
made at market price. Compute the operating income of each division under this dual transfer pricing
method when 400,000 pounds of cranberries are harvested during June 2012 and processed into juice.
3. Why is the sum of the division operating incomes computed in requirement 2 different from Crango's
operating income from harvesting and processing 400,000 pounds of cranberries?
4. Suggest two problems that may arise if Crango implements the dual transfer prices described in
requirement 2.

22-32 Multinational transfer pricing, global tax minimization. Industrial Diamonds, Inc., based in
Los Angeles, has two divisions:

- ■ South African mining division, which mines a rich diamond vein in South Africa
- ■ U.S. processing division, which polishes raw diamonds for use in industrial cutting tools

The processing division's yield is 50%: It takes 2 pounds of raw diamonds to produce 1 pound of top-quality pol-
ished industrial diamonds. Although all of the mining division's output of 8,000 pounds of raw diamonds is sent for
processing in the United States, there is also an active market for raw diamonds in South Africa. The foreign
exchange rate is 6 ZAR (South African Rand) = $1 U.S. The following information is known about the two divisions:

	A	B	C	D	F	G
1	**South African Mining Division**					
2	Variable cost per pound of raw diamonds				600	ZAR
3	Fixed cost per pound of raw diamonds				1,200	ZAR
4	Market price per pound of raw diamonds				3,600	ZAR
5	Tax rate				25%	
6						
7	**U.S. Processing Division**					
8	Variable cost per pound of polished diamonds				220	U.S. dollars
9	Fixed cost per pound of polished diamonds				850	U.S. dollars
10	Market price per pound of polished diamonds				3,500	U.S. dollars
11	Tax rate				40%	

1. Compute the annual pretax operating income, in U.S. dollars, of each division under the following **Required**
transfer-pricing methods: (a) 250% of full cost and (b) market price.
2. Compute the after-tax operating income, in U.S. dollars, for each division under the transfer-pricing
methods in requirement 1. (Income taxes are not included in the computation of cost-based transfer
price, and Industrial Diamonds does not pay U.S. income tax on income already taxed in South Africa.)
3. If the two division managers are compensated based on after-tax division operating income, which
transfer-pricing method will each prefer? Which transfer-pricing method will maximize the total after-
tax operating income of Industrial Diamonds?
4. In addition to tax minimization, what other factors might Industrial Diamonds consider in choosing a
transfer-pricing method?

22-33 International transfer pricing, taxes, goal congruence. Argone division of Gemini Corporation is located in the United States. Its effective income tax rate is 30%. Another division of Gemini, Calcia, is located in Canada, where the income tax rate is 42%. Calcia manufactures, among other things, an intermediate product for Argone called IP-2007. Calcia operates at capacity and makes 15,000 units of IP-2007 for Argone each period, at a variable cost of $60 per unit. Assume that there are no outside customers for IP-2007. Because the IP-2007 must be shipped from Canada to the United States, it costs Calcia an additional $4 per unit to ship the IP-2007 to Argone. There are no direct fixed costs for IP-2007. Calcia also manufactures other products.

A product similar to IP-2007 that Argone could use as a substitute is available in the United States for $75 per unit.

Required

1. What is the minimum and maximum transfer price that would be acceptable to Argone and Calcia for IP-2007, and why?

2. What transfer price would minimize income taxes for Gemini Corporation as a whole? Would Calcia and Argone want to be evaluated on operating income using this transfer price?

3. Suppose Gemini uses the transfer price from requirement 2, and each division is evaluated on its own after-tax division operating income. Now suppose Calcia has an opportunity to sell 8,000 units of IP-2007 to an outside customer for $68 each. Calcia will not incur shipping costs because the customer is nearby and offers to pay for shipping. Assume that if Calcia accepts the special order, Argone will have to buy 8,000 units of the substitute product in the United States at $75 per unit.
   a. Will accepting the special order maximize after-tax operating income for Gemini Corporation as a whole?
   b. Will Argone want Calcia to accept this special order? Why or why not?
   c. Will Calcia want to accept this special order? Explain.
   d. Suppose Gemini Corporation wants to operate in a decentralized manner. What transfer price should Gemini set for IP-2007 so that each division acting in its own best interest takes actions with respect to the special order that are in the best interests of Gemini Corporation as a whole?

22-34 Transfer pricing, goal congruence. The Bosh Corporation makes and sells 20,000 multisystem music players each year. Its assembly division purchases components from other divisions of Bosh or from external suppliers and assembles the multisystem music players. In particular, the assembly division can purchase the CD player from the compact disc division of Bosh or from Hawei Corporation. Hawei agrees to meet all of Bosh's quality requirements and is currently negotiating with the assembly division to supply 20,000 CD players at a price between $44 and $52 per CD player.

A critical component of the CD player is the head mechanism that reads the disc. To ensure the quality of its multisystem music players, Bosh requires that if Hawei wins the contract to supply CD players, it must purchase the head mechanism from Bosh's compact disc division for $24 each.

The compact disc division can manufacture at most 22,000 CD players annually. It also manufactures as many additional head mechanisms as can be sold. The incremental cost of manufacturing the head mechanism is $18 per unit. The incremental cost of manufacturing a CD player (including the cost of the head mechanism) is $30 per unit, and any number of CD players can be sold for $45 each in the external market.

Required

1. What are the incremental costs minus revenues from sale to external buyers for the company as a whole if the compact disc division transfers 20,000 CD players to the assembly division and sells the remaining 2,000 CD players on the external market?

2. What are the incremental costs minus revenues from sales to external buyers for the company as a whole if the compact disc division sells 22,000 CD players on the external market and the assembly division accepts Hawei's offer at (a) $44 per CD player or (b) $52 per CD player?

3. What is the minimum transfer price per CD player at which the compact disc division would be willing to transfer 20,000 CD players to the assembly division?

4. Suppose that the transfer price is set to the minimum computed in requirement 3 plus $2, and the division managers at Bosh are free to make their own profit-maximizing sourcing and selling decisions. Now, Hawei offers 20,000 CD players for $52 each.
   a. What decisions will the managers of the compact disc division and assembly division make?
   b. Are these decisions optimal for Bosh as a whole?
   c. Based on this exercise, at what price would you recommend the transfer price be set?

22-35 Transfer pricing, goal congruence, ethics. Jeremiah Industries manufactures high-grade aluminum luggage made from recycled metal. The company operates two divisions: metal recycling and luggage fabrication. Each division operates as a decentralized entity. The metal recycling division is free to sell sheet aluminum to outside buyers, and the luggage fabrication division is free to purchase recycled sheet aluminum from other sources. Currently, however, the recycling division sells all of its output to the fabrication division, and the fabrication division does not purchase materials from any outside suppliers.

Aluminum is transferred from the recycling division to the fabrication division at 110% of full cost. The recycling division purchases recyclable aluminum for $0.50 per pound. The division's other variable costs equal $2.80 per pound, and fixed costs at a monthly production level of 50,000 pounds are $1.50 per pound.

During the most recent month, 50,000 pounds of aluminum were transferred between the two divisions. The recycling division's capacity is 70,000 pounds.

Due to increased demand, the fabrication division expects to use 60,000 pounds of aluminum next month. Metalife Corporation has offered to sell 10,000 pounds of recycled aluminum next month to the fabrication division for $5.00 per pound.

Required

1. Calculate the transfer price per pound of recycled aluminum. Assuming that each division is considered a profit center, would the fabrication manager choose to purchase 10,000 pounds next month from Metalife?

2. Is the purchase in the best interest of Jeremiah Industries? Show your calculations. What is the cause of this goal incongruence?

3. The fabrication division manager suggests that $5.00 is now the market price for recycled sheet aluminum, and that this should be the new transfer price. Jeremiah's corporate management tends to agree. The metal recycling manager is suspicious. Metalife's prices have always been considerably higher than $5.00 per pound. Why the sudden price cut? After further investigation by the recycling division manager, it is revealed that the $5.00 per pound price was a one-time-only offer made to the fabrication division due to excess inventory at Metalife. Future orders would be priced at $5.50 per pound. Comment on the validity of the $5.00 per pound market price and the ethics of the fabrication manager. Would changing the transfer price to $5.00 matter to Jeremiah Industries?

Collaborative Learning Problem

22-36 Transfer pricing, utilization of capacity. (J. Patell, adapted) The California Instrument Company (CIC) consists of the semiconductor division and the process-control division, each of which operates as an independent profit center. The semiconductor division employs craftsmen who produce two different electronic components: the new high-performance Super-chip and an older product called Okay-chip. These two products have the following cost characteristics:

	Super-chip	Okay-chip
Direct materials	$ 5	$ 2
Direct manufacturing labor, 3 hours × $20; 1 hour × $20	60	20

Due to the high skill level necessary for the craftsmen, the semiconductor division's capacity is set at 45,000 hours per year.

Maximum demand for the Super-chip is 15,000 units annually, at a price of $80 per chip. There is unlimited demand for the Okay-chip at $26 per chip.

The process-control division produces only one product, a process-control unit, with the following cost structure:

- Direct materials (circuit board): $70
- Direct manufacturing labor (3 hours × $15): $45

The current market price for the control unit is $132 per unit.

A joint research project has just revealed that a single Super-chip could be substituted for the circuit board currently used to make the process-control unit. Direct labor cost of the process-control unit would be unchanged. The improved process-control unit could be sold for $145.

Required

1. Calculate the contribution margin per direct-labor hour of selling Super-chip and Okay-chip. If no transfers of Super-chip are made to the process-control division, how many Super-chips and Okay-chips should the semiconductor division manufacture and sell? What would be the division's annual contribution margin? Show your computations.

2. The process-control division expects to sell 5,000 process-control units this year. From the viewpoint of California Instruments as a whole, should 5,000 Super-chips be transferred to the process-control division to replace circuit boards? Show your computations.

3. What transfer price, or range of prices, would ensure goal congruence among the division managers? Show your calculations.

4. If labor capacity in the semiconductor division were 60,000 hours instead of 45,000, would your answer to requirement 3 differ? Show your calculations.

Appendix A

Notes on Compound Interest and Interest Tables

Interest is the cost of using money. It is the rental charge for funds, just as renting a building and equipment entails a rental charge. When the funds are used for a period of time, it is necessary to recognize interest as a cost of using the borrowed ("rented") funds. This requirement applies even if the funds represent ownership capital and if interest does not entail an outlay of cash. Why must interest be considered? Because the selection of one alternative automatically commits a given amount of funds that could otherwise be invested in some other alternative.

Interest is generally important, even when short-term projects are under consideration. Interest looms correspondingly larger when long-run plans are studied. The rate of interest has significant enough impact to influence decisions regarding borrowing and investing funds. For example, $100,000 invested now and compounded annually for 10 years at 8% will accumulate to $215,900; at 20%, the $100,000 will accumulate to $619,200.

Interest Tables

Many computer programs and pocket calculators are available that handle computations involving the time value of money. You may also turn to the following four basic tables to compute interest.

Table 1—Future Amount of $1

Table 1 shows how much $1 invested now will accumulate in a given number of periods at a given compounded interest rate per period. Consider investing $1,000 now for three years at 8% compound interest. A tabular presentation of how this $1,000 would accumulate to $1,259.70 follows:

Year	Interest per Year	Cumulative Interest Called Compound Interest	Total at End of Year
0	$ —	$ —	$1,000.00
1	80.00 (0.08 × $1,000)	80.00	1,080.00
2	86.40 (0.08 × $1,080)	166.40	1,166.40
3	93.30 (0.08 × $1,166.40)	259.70	1,259.70

This tabular presentation is a series of computations that could appear as follows, where S is the future amount and the subscripts 1, 2, and 3 indicate the number of time periods.

$$S_1 = \$1,000(1.08)^1 = \$1,080$$

$$S_2 = \$1,080(1.08) = \$1,000(1.08)^2 = \$1,166.40$$

$$S_3 = \$1,166.40 \times (1.08) = \$1,000(1.08)^3 = \$1,259.70$$

The formula for the "amount of P", often called the "future value of P" or "future amount of P", can be written as follows:

$$S = P(1 + r)^n$$

S is the future value amount; P is the present value, r is the rate of interest; and n is the number of time periods.

When $P = \$1,000$, $n = 3$, $r = 0.08$, $S = \$1,000(1 + .08)^3 = \$1,259.70$

Fortunately, tables make key computations readily available. A facility in selecting the *proper* table will minimize computations. Check the accuracy of the preceding answer using Table 1, page 842.

Table 2—Present Value of $1

In the previous example, if $1,000 compounded at 8% per year will accumulate to $1,259.70 in three years, then $1,000 must be the present value of $1,259.70 due at the end of three years. The formula for the present value can be derived by reversing the process of *accumulation* (finding the future amount) that we just finished.
If

$$S = P(1 + r)^n$$

then

$$P = \frac{S}{(1 + r)^n}$$

In our example, $S = \$1,259.70$, $n = 3$, $r = 0.08$, so

$$P = \frac{\$1,259.70}{(1.08)^3} = \$1,000$$

Use Table 2, page 843, to check this calculation.

When accumulating, we advance or roll forward in time. The difference between our original amount and our accumulated amount is called *compound interest*. When discounting, we retreat or roll back in time. The difference between the future amount and the present value is called *compound discount*. Note the following formulas:

$$\text{Compound interest} = P[(1 + r)^n - 1]$$

In our example, $P = \$1,000$, $n = 3$, $r = 0.08$, so

$$\text{Compound interest} = \$1,000[(1.08)^3 - 1] = \$259.70$$

$$\text{Compound discount} = S\left[1 - \frac{1}{(1 + r)^n}\right]$$

In our example, $S = \$1,259.70$, $n = 3$, $r = 0.08$, so

$$\text{Compound discount} = \$1,259.70\left[1 - \frac{1}{(1.08)^3}\right] = \$259.70$$

Table 3—Amount of Annuity of $1

An (ordinary) *annuity* is a series of equal payments (receipts) to be paid (or received) at the end of successive periods of equal length. Assume that $1,000 is invested at the end of each of three years at 8%:

End of Year			Amount
1st payment	$1,000.00 ⟶	$1,080.00 ⟶	$1,166.40, which is $1,000(1.08)²
2nd payment		$1,000.00 ⟶	1,080.00, which is $1,000(1.08)¹
3rd payment			1,000.00
Accumulation (future amount)			$3,246.40

The preceding arithmetic may be expressed algebraically as the amount of an ordinary annuity of $1,000 for 3 years = $1,000(1 + r)^2 + $1,000(1 + r)^1 + $1,000.

We can develop the general formula for S_n, the amount of an ordinary annuity of $1, by using the preceding example as a basis where $n = 3$ and $r = 0.08$:

1. $$S_3 = 1 + (1 + r)^1 + (1 + r)^2$$

2. Substitute: $\qquad$ $S_3 = 1 + (1.08)^1 + (1.08)^2$

3. Multiply (2) by $(1 + r)$: $\qquad$ $(1.08)S_3 = (1.08)^1 + (1.08)^2 + (1.08)^3$

4. Subtract (2) from (3): Note that all terms on the right-hand side are removed except $(1.08)^3$ in equation (3) and 1 in equation (2). $\qquad$ $1.08S_3 - S_3 = (1.08)^3 - 1$

5. Factor (4): $\qquad$ $S_3(1.08 - 1) = (1.08)^3 - 1$

6. Divide (5) by $(1.08 - 1)$:

$$S_3 = \frac{(1.08)^3 - 1}{1.08 - 1} = \frac{(1.08)^3 - 1}{.08} = \frac{0.2597}{0.08} = 3.246$$

7. The general formula for the amount of an ordinary annuity of \$1 becomes:

$$S_n = \frac{(1 + r)^n - 1}{r} \text{ or } \frac{\text{Compound interest}}{\text{Rate}}$$

This formula is the basis for Table 3, page 844. Check the answer in the table.

Table 4—Present Value of an Ordinary Annuity of \$1

Using the same example as for Table 3, we can show how the formula of P_n, *the present value of an ordinary annuity*, is developed.

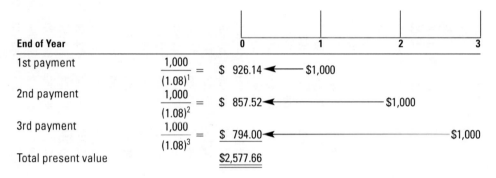

End of Year		0	1	2	3
1st payment	$\dfrac{1,000}{(1.08)^1} = $ \$ 926.14	◄── \$1,000			
2nd payment	$\dfrac{1,000}{(1.08)^2} = $ \$ 857.52	◄──────── \$1,000			
3rd payment	$\dfrac{1,000}{(1.08)^3} = $ \$ 794.00	◄──────────────── \$1,000			
Total present value	\$2,577.66				

We can develop the general formula for P_n by using the preceding example as a basis where $n = 3$ and $r = 0.08$:

1. $\qquad$ $P_3 = \dfrac{1}{1 + r} + \dfrac{1}{(1 + r)^2} + \dfrac{1}{(1 + r)^3}$

2. Substitute: $\qquad$ $P_3 = \dfrac{1}{1.08} + \dfrac{1}{(1.08)^2} + \dfrac{1}{(1.08)^3}$

3. Multiply by $\dfrac{1}{1.08}$: $\qquad$ $P_3\dfrac{1}{1.08} = \dfrac{1}{(1.08)^2} + \dfrac{1}{(1.08)^3} + \dfrac{1}{(1.08)^4}$

4. Subtract (3) from (2): $\qquad$ $P_3 - P_3\dfrac{1}{1.08} = \dfrac{1}{1.08} - \dfrac{1}{(1.08)^4}$

5. Factor (4): $\qquad$ $P_3\left(1 - \dfrac{1}{(1.08)}\right) = \dfrac{1}{1.08}\left[1 - \dfrac{1}{(1.08)^3}\right]$

6. or $\qquad$ $P_3\left(\dfrac{.08}{1.08}\right) = \dfrac{1}{1.08}\left[1 - \dfrac{1}{(1.08)^3}\right]$

7. Multiply by $\dfrac{1.08}{.08}$: $\qquad$ $P_3 = \dfrac{1}{.08}\left[1 - \dfrac{1}{(1.08)^3}\right] = \dfrac{.2062}{.08} = 2.577$

The general formula for the present value of an annuity of \$1.00 is as follows:

$$P_n = \frac{1}{r}\left[1 - \frac{1}{(1 + r)^n}\right] = \frac{\text{Compound discount}}{\text{Rate}}$$

The formula is the basis for Table 4, page 845. Check the answer in the table. The present value tables, Tables 2 and 4, are used most frequently in capital budgeting.

The tables for annuities are not essential. With Tables 1 and 2, compound interest and compound discount can readily be computed. It is simply a matter of dividing either of these by the rate to get values equivalent to those shown in Tables 3 and 4.

Table 1

Compound Amount of $1.00 (The Future Value of $1.00)

$S = P(1 + i)^n$. In this table $P = \$1.00$

Periods	2%	4%	6%	8%	10%	12%	14%	16%	18%	20%	22%	24%	26%	28%	30%	32%	40%	Periods
1	1.020	1.040	1.060	1.080	1.100	1.120	1.140	1.160	1.180	1.200	1.220	1.240	1.260	1.280	1.300	1.320	1.400	1
2	1.040	1.082	1.124	1.166	1.210	1.254	1.300	1.346	1.392	1.440	1.488	1.538	1.588	1.638	1.690	1.742	1.960	2
3	1.061	1.125	1.191	1.260	1.331	1.405	1.482	1.561	1.643	1.728	1.816	1.907	2.000	2.097	2.197	2.300	2.744	3
4	1.082	1.170	1.262	1.360	1.464	1.574	1.689	1.811	1.939	2.074	2.215	2.364	2.520	2.684	2.856	3.036	3.842	4
5	1.104	1.217	1.338	1.469	1.611	1.762	1.925	2.100	2.288	2.488	2.703	2.932	3.176	3.436	3.713	4.007	5.378	5
6	1.126	1.265	1.419	1.587	1.772	1.974	2.195	2.436	2.700	2.986	3.297	3.635	4.002	4.398	4.827	5.290	7.530	6
7	1.149	1.316	1.504	1.714	1.949	2.211	2.502	2.826	3.185	3.583	4.023	4.508	5.042	5.629	6.275	6.983	10.541	7
8	1.172	1.369	1.594	1.851	2.144	2.476	2.853	3.278	3.759	4.300	4.908	5.590	6.353	7.206	8.157	9.217	14.758	8
9	1.195	1.423	1.689	1.999	2.358	2.773	3.252	3.803	4.435	5.160	5.987	6.931	8.005	9.223	10.604	12.166	20.661	9
10	1.219	1.480	1.791	2.159	2.594	3.106	3.707	4.411	5.234	6.192	7.305	8.594	10.086	11.806	13.786	16.060	28.925	10
11	1.243	1.539	1.898	2.332	2.853	3.479	4.226	5.117	6.176	7.430	8.912	10.657	12.708	15.112	17.922	21.199	40.496	11
12	1.268	1.601	2.012	2.518	3.138	3.896	4.818	5.936	7.288	8.916	10.872	13.215	16.012	19.343	23.298	27.983	56.694	12
13	1.294	1.665	2.133	2.720	3.452	4.363	5.492	6.886	8.599	10.699	13.264	16.386	20.175	24.759	30.288	36.937	79.371	13
14	1.319	1.732	2.261	2.937	3.797	4.887	6.261	7.988	10.147	12.839	16.182	20.319	25.421	31.691	39.374	48.757	111.120	14
15	1.346	1.801	2.397	3.172	4.177	5.474	7.138	9.266	11.974	15.407	19.742	25.196	32.030	40.565	51.186	64.359	155.568	15
16	1.373	1.873	2.540	3.426	4.595	6.130	8.137	10.748	14.129	18.488	24.086	31.243	40.358	51.923	66.542	84.954	217.795	16
17	1.400	1.948	2.693	3.700	5.054	6.866	9.276	12.468	16.672	22.186	29.384	38.741	50.851	66.461	86.504	112.139	304.913	17
18	1.428	2.026	2.854	3.996	5.560	7.690	10.575	14.463	19.673	26.623	35.849	48.039	64.072	85.071	112.455	148.024	426.879	18
19	1.457	2.107	3.026	4.316	6.116	8.613	12.056	16.777	23.214	31.948	43.736	59.568	80.731	108.890	146.192	195.391	597.630	19
20	1.486	2.191	3.207	4.661	6.727	9.646	13.743	19.461	27.393	38.338	53.358	73.864	101.721	139.380	190.050	257.916	836.683	20
21	1.516	2.279	3.400	5.034	7.400	10.804	15.668	22.574	32.324	46.005	65.096	91.592	128.169	178.406	247.065	340.449	1171.356	21
22	1.546	2.370	3.604	5.437	8.140	12.100	17.861	26.186	38.142	55.206	79.418	113.574	161.492	228.360	321.184	449.393	1639.898	22
23	1.577	2.465	3.820	5.871	8.954	13.552	20.362	30.376	45.008	66.247	96.889	140.831	203.480	292.300	417.539	593.199	2295.857	23
24	1.608	2.563	4.049	6.341	9.850	15.179	23.212	35.236	53.109	79.497	118.205	174.631	256.385	374.144	542.801	783.023	3214.200	24
25	1.641	2.666	4.292	6.848	10.835	17.000	26.462	40.874	62.669	95.396	144.210	216.542	323.045	478.905	705.641	1033.590	4499.880	25
26	1.673	2.772	4.549	7.396	11.918	19.040	30.167	47.414	73.949	114.475	175.936	268.512	407.037	612.998	917.333	1364.339	6299.831	26
27	1.707	2.883	4.822	7.988	13.110	21.325	34.390	55.000	87.260	137.371	214.642	332.955	512.867	784.638	1192.533	1800.927	8819.764	27
28	1.741	2.999	5.112	8.627	14.421	23.884	39.204	63.800	102.967	164.845	261.864	412.864	646.212	1004.336	1550.293	2377.224	12347.670	28
29	1.776	3.119	5.418	9.317	15.863	26.750	44.693	74.009	121.501	197.814	319.474	511.952	814.228	1285.550	2015.381	3137.935	17286.737	29
30	1.811	3.243	5.743	10.063	17.449	29.960	50.950	85.850	143.371	237.376	389.758	634.820	1025.927	1645.505	2619.996	4142.075	24201.432	30
35	2.000	3.946	7.686	14.785	28.102	52.800	98.100	180.314	327.997	590.668	1053.402	1861.054	3258.135	5653.911	9727.860	16599.217	130161.112	35
40	2.208	4.801	10.286	21.725	45.259	93.051	188.884	378.721	750.378	1469.772	2847.038	5455.913	10347.175	19426.689	36118.865	66520.767	700037.697	40

Table 2 (Place a clip on this page for easy reference.)

Present Value of $1.00

$P = \dfrac{S}{(1 + r)^n}$. In this table S = $1.00.

Periods	2%	4%	6%	8%	10%	12%	14%	16%	18%	20%	22%	24%	26%	28%	30%	32%	40%	Periods
1	0.980	0.962	0.943	0.926	0.909	0.893	0.877	0.862	0.847	0.833	0.820	0.806	0.794	0.781	0.769	0.758	0.714	1
2	0.961	0.925	0.890	0.857	0.826	0.797	0.769	0.743	0.718	0.694	0.672	0.650	0.630	0.610	0.592	0.574	0.510	2
3	0.942	0.889	0.840	0.794	0.751	0.712	0.675	0.641	0.609	0.579	0.551	0.524	0.500	0.477	0.455	0.435	0.364	3
4	0.924	0.855	0.792	0.735	0.683	0.636	0.592	0.552	0.516	0.482	0.451	0.423	0.397	0.373	0.350	0.329	0.260	4
5	0.906	0.822	0.747	0.681	0.621	0.567	0.519	0.476	0.437	0.402	0.370	0.341	0.315	0.291	0.269	0.250	0.186	5
6	0.888	0.790	0.705	0.630	0.564	0.507	0.456	0.410	0.370	0.335	0.303	0.275	0.250	0.227	0.207	0.189	0.133	6
7	0.871	0.760	0.665	0.583	0.513	0.452	0.400	0.354	0.314	0.279	0.249	0.222	0.198	0.178	0.159	0.143	0.095	7
8	0.853	0.731	0.627	0.540	0.467	0.404	0.351	0.305	0.266	0.233	0.204	0.179	0.157	0.139	0.123	0.108	0.068	8
9	0.837	0.703	0.592	0.500	0.424	0.361	0.308	0.263	0.225	0.194	0.167	0.144	0.125	0.108	0.094	0.082	0.048	9
10	0.820	0.676	0.558	0.463	0.386	0.322	0.270	0.227	0.191	0.162	0.137	0.116	0.099	0.085	0.073	0.062	0.035	10
11	0.804	0.650	0.527	0.429	0.350	0.287	0.237	0.195	0.162	0.135	0.112	0.094	0.079	0.066	0.056	0.047	0.025	11
12	0.788	0.625	0.497	0.397	0.319	0.257	0.208	0.168	0.137	0.112	0.092	0.076	0.062	0.052	0.043	0.036	0.018	12
13	0.773	0.601	0.469	0.368	0.290	0.229	0.182	0.145	0.116	0.093	0.075	0.061	0.050	0.040	0.033	0.027	0.013	13
14	0.758	0.577	0.442	0.340	0.263	0.205	0.160	0.125	0.099	0.078	0.062	0.049	0.039	0.032	0.025	0.021	0.009	14
15	0.743	0.555	0.417	0.315	0.239	0.183	0.140	0.108	0.084	0.065	0.051	0.040	0.031	0.025	0.020	0.016	0.006	15
16	0.728	0.534	0.394	0.292	0.218	0.163	0.123	0.093	0.071	0.054	0.042	0.032	0.025	0.019	0.015	0.012	0.005	16
17	0.714	0.513	0.371	0.270	0.198	0.146	0.108	0.080	0.060	0.045	0.034	0.026	0.020	0.015	0.012	0.009	0.003	17
18	0.700	0.494	0.350	0.250	0.180	0.130	0.095	0.069	0.051	0.038	0.028	0.021	0.016	0.012	0.009	0.007	0.002	18
19	0.686	0.475	0.331	0.232	0.164	0.116	0.083	0.060	0.043	0.031	0.023	0.017	0.012	0.009	0.007	0.005	0.002	19
20	0.673	0.456	0.312	0.215	0.149	0.104	0.073	0.051	0.037	0.026	0.019	0.014	0.010	0.007	0.005	0.004	0.001	20
21	0.660	0.439	0.294	0.199	0.135	0.093	0.064	0.044	0.031	0.022	0.015	0.011	0.008	0.006	0.004	0.003	0.001	21
22	0.647	0.422	0.278	0.184	0.123	0.083	0.056	0.038	0.026	0.018	0.013	0.009	0.006	0.004	0.003	0.002	0.001	22
23	0.634	0.406	0.262	0.170	0.112	0.074	0.049	0.033	0.022	0.015	0.010	0.007	0.005	0.003	0.002	0.002	0.000	23
24	0.622	0.390	0.247	0.158	0.102	0.066	0.043	0.028	0.019	0.013	0.008	0.006	0.004	0.003	0.002	0.001	0.000	24
25	0.610	0.375	0.233	0.146	0.092	0.059	0.038	0.024	0.016	0.010	0.007	0.005	0.003	0.002	0.001	0.001	0.000	25
26	0.598	0.361	0.220	0.135	0.084	0.053	0.033	0.021	0.014	0.009	0.006	0.004	0.002	0.002	0.001	0.001	0.000	26
27	0.586	0.347	0.207	0.125	0.076	0.047	0.029	0.018	0.011	0.007	0.005	0.003	0.002	0.001	0.001	0.001	0.000	27
28	0.574	0.333	0.196	0.116	0.069	0.042	0.026	0.016	0.010	0.006	0.004	0.002	0.002	0.001	0.001	0.000	0.000	28
29	0.563	0.321	0.185	0.107	0.063	0.037	0.022	0.014	0.008	0.005	0.003	0.002	0.001	0.001	0.000	0.000	0.000	29
30	0.552	0.308	0.174	0.099	0.057	0.033	0.020	0.012	0.007	0.004	0.003	0.002	0.001	0.001	0.000	0.000	0.000	30
35	0.500	0.253	0.130	0.068	0.036	0.019	0.010	0.006	0.003	0.002	0.001	0.001	0.000	0.000	0.000	0.000	0.000	35
40	0.453	0.208	0.097	0.046	0.022	0.011	0.005	0.003	0.001	0.001	0.000	0.000	0.000	0.000	0.000	0.000	0.000	40

Table 3

Compound Amount of Annuity of $1.00 in Arrears* (Future Value of Annuity)

$$S_n = \frac{(1+r)^n - 1}{r}$$

Periods	2%	4%	6%	8%	10%	12%	14%	16%	18%	20%	22%	24%	26%	28%	30%	32%	40%	Periods
1	1.000	1.000	1.000	1.000	1.000	1.000	1.000	1.000	1.000	1.000	1.000	1.000	1.000	1.000	1.000	1.000	1.000	1
2	2.020	2.040	2.060	2.080	2.100	2.120	2.140	2.160	2.180	2.200	2.220	2.240	2.260	2.280	2.300	2.320	2.400	2
3	3.060	3.122	3.184	3.246	3.310	3.374	3.440	3.506	3.572	3.640	3.708	3.778	3.848	3.918	3.990	4.062	4.360	3
4	4.122	4.246	4.375	4.506	4.641	4.779	4.921	5.066	5.215	5.368	5.524	5.684	5.848	6.016	6.187	6.362	7.104	4
5	5.204	5.416	5.637	5.867	6.105	6.353	6.610	6.877	7.154	7.442	7.740	8.048	8.368	8.700	9.043	9.398	10.946	5
6	6.308	6.633	6.975	7.336	7.716	8.115	8.536	8.977	9.442	9.930	10.442	10.980	11.544	12.136	12.756	13.406	16.324	6
7	7.434	7.898	8.394	8.923	9.487	10.089	10.730	11.414	12.142	12.916	13.740	14.615	15.546	16.534	17.583	18.696	23.853	7
8	8.583	9.214	9.897	10.637	11.436	12.300	13.233	14.240	15.327	16.499	17.762	19.123	20.588	22.163	23.858	25.678	34.395	8
9	9.755	10.583	11.491	12.488	13.579	14.776	16.085	17.519	19.086	20.799	22.670	24.712	26.940	29.369	32.015	34.895	49.153	9
10	10.950	12.006	13.181	14.487	15.937	17.549	19.337	21.321	23.521	25.959	28.657	31.643	34.945	38.593	42.619	47.062	69.814	10
11	12.169	13.486	14.972	16.645	18.531	20.655	23.045	25.733	28.755	32.150	35.962	40.238	45.031	50.398	56.405	63.122	98.739	11
12	13.412	15.026	16.870	18.977	21.384	24.133	27.271	30.850	34.931	39.581	44.874	50.895	57.739	65.510	74.327	84.320	139.235	12
13	14.680	16.627	18.882	21.495	24.523	28.029	32.089	36.786	42.219	48.497	55.746	64.110	73.751	84.853	97.625	112.303	195.929	13
14	15.974	18.292	21.015	24.215	27.975	32.393	37.581	43.672	50.818	59.196	69.010	80.496	93.926	109.612	127.913	149.240	275.300	14
15	17.293	20.024	23.276	27.152	31.772	37.280	43.842	51.660	60.965	72.035	85.192	100.815	119.347	141.303	167.286	197.997	386.420	15
16	18.639	21.825	25.673	30.324	35.950	42.753	50.980	60.925	72.939	87.442	104.935	126.011	151.377	181.868	218.472	262.356	541.988	16
17	20.012	23.698	28.213	33.750	40.545	48.884	59.118	71.673	87.068	105.931	129.020	157.253	191.735	233.791	285.014	347.309	759.784	17
18	21.412	25.645	30.906	37.450	45.599	55.750	68.394	84.141	103.740	128.117	158.405	195.994	242.585	300.252	371.518	459.449	1064.697	18
19	22.841	27.671	33.760	41.446	51.159	63.440	78.969	98.603	123.414	154.740	194.254	244.033	306.658	385.323	483.973	607.472	1491.576	19
20	24.297	29.778	36.786	45.762	57.275	72.052	91.025	115.380	146.628	186.688	237.989	303.601	387.389	494.213	630.165	802.863	2089.206	20
21	25.783	31.969	39.993	50.423	64.002	81.699	104.768	134.841	174.021	225.026	291.347	377.465	489.110	633.593	820.215	1060.779	2925.889	21
22	27.299	34.248	43.392	55.457	71.403	92.503	120.436	157.415	206.345	271.031	356.443	469.056	617.278	811.999	1067.280	1401.229	4097.245	22
23	28.845	36.618	46.996	60.893	79.543	104.603	138.297	183.601	244.487	326.237	435.861	582.630	778.771	1040.358	1388.464	1850.622	5737.142	23
24	30.422	39.083	50.816	66.765	88.497	118.155	158.659	213.978	289.494	392.484	532.750	723.461	982.251	1332.659	1806.003	2443.821	8032.999	24
25	32.030	41.646	54.865	73.106	98.347	133.334	181.871	249.214	342.603	471.981	650.955	898.092	1238.636	1706.803	2348.803	3226.844	11247.199	25
26	33.671	44.312	59.156	79.954	109.182	150.334	208.333	290.088	405.272	567.377	795.165	1114.634	1561.682	2185.708	3054.444	4260.434	15747.079	26
27	35.344	47.084	63.706	87.351	121.100	169.374	238.499	337.502	479.221	681.853	971.102	1383.146	1968.719	2798.706	3971.778	5624.772	22046.910	27
28	37.051	49.968	68.528	95.339	134.210	190.699	272.889	392.503	566.481	819.223	1185.744	1716.101	2481.586	3583.344	5164.311	7425.699	30866.674	28
29	38.792	52.966	73.640	103.966	148.631	214.583	312.094	456.303	669.447	984.068	1447.608	2128.965	3127.798	4587.680	6714.604	9802.923	43214.343	29
30	40.568	56.085	79.058	113.263	164.494	241.333	356.787	530.312	790.948	1181.882	1767.081	2640.916	3942.026	5873.231	8729.985	12940.859	60501.081	30
35	49.994	73.652	111.435	172.317	271.024	431.663	693.573	1120.713	1816.652	2948.341	4783.645	7750.225	12527.442	20188.966	32422.868	51869.427	325400.279	35
40	60.402	95.026	154.762	259.057	442.593	767.091	1342.025	2360.757	4163.213	7343.858	12936.535	22728.803	39792.982	69377.460	120392.883	207874.272	1750091.741	40

*Payments (or receipts) at the end of each period.

Table 4 (Place a clip on this page for easy reference.)

Present Value of Annuity $1.00 in Arrears*

$$P_n = \frac{1}{r}\left[1 - \frac{1}{(1+r)^n}\right]$$

Periods	2%	4%	6%	8%	10%	12%	14%	16%	18%	20%	22%	24%	26%	28%	30%	32%	40%	Periods
1	0.980	0.962	0.943	0.926	0.909	0.893	0.877	0.862	0.847	0.833	0.820	0.806	0.794	0.781	0.769	0.758	0.714	1
2	1.942	1.886	1.833	1.783	1.736	1.690	1.647	1.605	1.566	1.528	1.492	1.457	1.424	1.392	1.361	1.331	1.224	2
3	2.884	2.775	2.673	2.577	2.487	2.402	2.322	2.246	2.174	2.106	2.042	1.981	1.923	1.868	1.816	1.766	1.589	3
4	3.808	3.630	3.465	3.312	3.170	3.037	2.914	2.798	2.690	2.589	2.494	2.404	2.320	2.241	2.166	2.096	1.849	4
5	4.713	4.452	4.212	3.993	3.791	3.605	3.433	3.274	3.127	2.991	2.864	2.745	2.635	2.532	2.436	2.345	2.035	5
6	5.601	5.242	4.917	4.623	4.355	4.111	3.889	3.685	3.498	3.326	3.167	3.020	2.885	2.759	2.643	2.534	2.168	6
7	6.472	6.002	5.582	5.206	4.868	4.564	4.288	4.039	3.812	3.605	3.416	3.242	3.083	2.937	2.802	2.677	2.263	7
8	7.325	6.733	6.210	5.747	5.335	4.968	4.639	4.344	4.078	3.837	3.619	3.421	3.241	3.076	2.925	2.786	2.331	8
9	8.162	7.435	6.802	6.247	5.759	5.328	4.946	4.607	4.303	4.031	3.786	3.566	3.366	3.184	3.019	2.868	2.379	9
10	8.983	8.111	7.360	6.710	6.145	5.650	5.216	4.833	4.494	4.192	3.923	3.682	3.465	3.269	3.092	2.930	2.414	10
11	9.787	8.760	7.887	7.139	6.495	5.938	5.453	5.029	4.656	4.327	4.035	3.776	3.543	3.335	3.147	2.978	2.438	11
12	10.575	9.385	8.384	7.536	6.814	6.194	5.660	5.197	4.793	4.439	4.127	3.851	3.606	3.387	3.190	3.013	2.456	12
13	11.348	9.986	8.853	7.904	7.103	6.424	5.842	5.342	4.910	4.533	4.203	3.912	3.656	3.427	3.223	3.040	2.469	13
14	12.106	10.563	9.295	8.244	7.367	6.628	6.002	5.468	5.008	4.611	4.265	3.962	3.695	3.459	3.249	3.061	2.478	14
15	12.849	11.118	9.712	8.559	7.606	6.811	6.142	5.575	5.092	4.675	4.315	4.001	3.726	3.483	3.268	3.076	2.484	15
16	13.578	11.652	10.106	8.851	7.824	6.974	6.265	5.668	5.162	4.730	4.357	4.033	3.751	3.503	3.283	3.088	2.489	16
17	14.292	12.166	10.477	9.122	8.022	7.120	6.373	5.749	5.222	4.775	4.391	4.059	3.771	3.518	3.295	3.097	2.492	17
18	14.992	12.659	10.828	9.372	8.201	7.250	6.467	5.818	5.273	4.812	4.419	4.080	3.786	3.529	3.304	3.104	2.494	18
19	15.678	13.134	11.158	9.604	8.365	7.366	6.550	5.877	5.316	4.843	4.442	4.097	3.799	3.539	3.311	3.109	2.496	19
20	16.351	13.590	11.470	9.818	8.514	7.469	6.623	5.929	5.353	4.870	4.460	4.110	3.808	3.546	3.316	3.113	2.497	20
21	17.011	14.029	11.764	10.017	8.649	7.562	6.687	5.973	5.384	4.891	4.476	4.121	3.816	3.551	3.320	3.116	2.498	21
22	17.658	14.451	12.042	10.201	8.772	7.645	6.743	6.011	5.410	4.909	4.488	4.130	3.822	3.556	3.323	3.118	2.498	22
23	18.292	14.857	12.303	10.371	8.883	7.718	6.792	6.044	5.432	4.925	4.499	4.137	3.827	3.559	3.325	3.120	2.499	23
24	18.914	15.247	12.550	10.529	8.985	7.784	6.835	6.073	5.451	4.937	4.507	4.143	3.831	3.562	3.327	3.121	2.499	24
25	19.523	15.622	12.783	10.675	9.077	7.843	6.873	6.097	5.467	4.948	4.514	4.147	3.834	3.564	3.329	3.122	2.499	25
26	20.121	15.983	13.003	10.810	9.161	7.896	6.906	6.118	5.480	4.956	4.520	4.151	3.837	3.566	3.330	3.123	2.500	26
27	20.707	16.330	13.211	10.935	9.237	7.943	6.935	6.136	5.492	4.964	4.524	4.154	3.839	3.567	3.331	3.123	2.500	27
28	21.281	16.663	13.406	11.051	9.307	7.984	6.961	6.152	5.502	4.970	4.528	4.157	3.840	3.568	3.331	3.124	2.500	28
29	21.844	16.984	13.591	11.158	9.370	8.022	6.983	6.166	5.510	4.975	4.531	4.159	3.841	3.569	3.332	3.124	2.500	29
30	22.396	17.292	13.765	11.258	9.427	8.055	7.003	6.177	5.517	4.979	4.534	4.160	3.842	3.569	3.332	3.125	2.500	30
35	24.999	18.665	14.498	11.655	9.644	8.176	7.070	6.215	5.539	4.992	4.541	4.164	3.845	3.571	3.333	3.125	2.500	35
40	27.355	19.793	15.046	11.925	9.779	8.244	7.105	6.233	5.548	4.997	4.544	4.166	3.846	3.571	3.333	3.125	2.500	40

*Payments (or receipts) at the end of each period.

845

Glossary

Glossary

Abnormal spoilage. Spoilage that would not arise under efficient operating conditions; it is not inherent in a particular production process. (646)

Absorption costing. Method of inventory costing in which all variable manufacturing costs and all fixed manufacturing costs are included as inventoriable costs. (302)

Account analysis method. Approach to cost function estimation that classifies various cost accounts as variable, fixed, or mixed with respect to the identified level of activity. Typically, qualitative rather than quantitative analysis is used when making these cost-classification decisions. (347)

Accrual accounting rate of return (AARR) method. Capital budgeting method that divides an accrual accounting measure of average annual income of a project by an accrual accounting measure of its investment. See also *return on investment (ROI)*. (749)

Activity. An event, task, or unit of work with a specified purpose. (146)

Activity-based budgeting (ABB). Budgeting approach that focuses on the budgeted cost of the activities necessary to produce and sell products and services. (193)

Activity-based costing (ABC). Approach to costing that focuses on individual activities as the fundamental cost objects. It uses the costs of these activities as the basis for assigning costs to other cost objects such as products or services. (146)

Activity-based management (ABM). Method of management decision-making that uses activity-based costing information to improve customer satisfaction and profitability. (156)

Actual cost. Cost incurred (a historical or past cost), as distinguished from a budgeted or forecasted cost. (27)

Actual costing. A costing system that traces direct costs to a cost object by using the actual direct-cost rates times the actual quantities of the direct-cost inputs and allocates indirect costs based on the actual indirect-cost rates times the actual quantities of the cost allocation bases. (102)

Actual indirect-cost rate. Actual total indirect costs in a cost pool divided by the actual total quantity of the cost-allocation base for that cost pool. (110)

Adjusted allocation-rate approach. Restates all overhead entries in the general ledger and subsidiary ledgers using actual cost rates rather than budgeted cost rates. (118)

Allowable cost. Cost that the contract parties agree to include in the costs to be reimbursed. (559)

Appraisal costs. Costs incurred to detect which of the individual units of products do not conform to specifications. (673)

Artificial costs. See *complete reciprocated costs*. (554)

Autonomy. The degree of freedom to make decisions. (777)

Average cost. See *unit cost*. (35)

Average waiting time. The average amount of time that an order will wait in line before the machine is set up and the order is processed. (683)

Backflush costing. Costing system that omits recording some of the journal entries relating to the stages from purchase of direct material to the sale of finished goods. (719)

Balanced scorecard. A framework for implementing strategy that translates an organization's mission and strategy into a set of performance measures. (470)

Batch-level costs. The costs of activities related to a group of units of products or services rather than to each individual unit of product or service. (149)

Belief systems. Lever of control that articulates the mission, purpose, norms of behaviors, and core values of a company intended to inspire managers and other employees to do their best. (827)

Benchmarking. The continuous process of comparing the levels of performance in producing products and services and executing activities against the best levels of performance in competing companies or in companies having similar processes. (244)

Book value. The original cost minus accumulated depreciation of an asset. (410)

Bottleneck. An operation where the work to be performed approaches or exceeds the capacity available to do it. (682)

Boundary systems. Lever of control that describes standards of behavior and codes of conduct expected of all employees, especially actions that are off-limits. (826)

Breakeven point (BEP). Quantity of output sold at which total revenues equal total costs, that is where the operating income is zero. (68)

Budget. Quantitative expression of a proposed plan of action by management for a specified period and an aid to coordinating what needs to be done to implement that plan. (10)

Budgetary slack. The practice of underestimating budgeted revenues, or overestimating budgeted costs, to make budgeted targets more easily achievable. (201)

Budgeted cost. Predicted or forecasted cost (future cost) as distinguished from an actual or historical cost. (27)

Budgeted indirect-cost rate. Budgeted annual indirect costs in a cost pool divided by the budgeted annual quantity of the cost allocation base. (104)

Budgeted performance. Expected performance or a point of reference to compare actual results. (227)

Bundled product. A package of two or more products (or services) that is sold for a single price, but whose individual components may be sold as separate items at their own "stand-alone" prices. (561)

Business function costs. The sum of all costs (variable and fixed) in a particular business function of the value chain. (395)

Byproducts. Products from a joint production process that have low total sales values compared with the total sales value of the main product or of joint products. (578)

Capital budgeting. The making of long-run planning decisions for investments in projects. (739)

Carrying costs. Costs that arise while holding inventory of goods for sale. (704)

Cash budget. Schedule of expected cash receipts and disbursements. (207)

Cause-and-effect diagram. Diagram that identifies potential causes of defects. Four categories of potential causes of failure are human factors, methods and design factors, machine-related factors, and materials and components factors. Also called a *fishbone diagram*. (676)

Chief financial officer (CFO). Executive responsible for overseeing the financial operations of an organization. Also called *finance director*. (13)

Choice criterion. Objective that can be quantified in a decision model. (84)

Coefficient of determination (r^2). Measures the percentage of variation in a dependent variable explained by one or more independent variables. (367)

Collusive pricing. Companies in an industry conspire in their pricing and production decisions to achieve a price above the competitive price and so restrain trade. (452)

Common cost. Cost of operating a facility, activity, or like cost object that is shared by two or more users. (557)

Complete reciprocated costs. The support department's own costs plus any interdepartmental cost allocations. Also called the *artificial costs* of the support department. (554)

Composite unit. Hypothetical unit with weights based on the mix of individual units. (521)

Conference method. Approach to cost function estimation on the basis of analysis and opinions about costs and their drivers gathered from various departments of a company (purchasing, process engineering, manufacturing, employee relations, and so on). (346)

Conformance quality. Refers to the performance of a product or service relative to its design and product specifications. (672)

Constant. The component of total cost that, within the relevant range, does not vary with changes in the level of the activity. Also called *intercept*. (343)

Constant gross-margin percentage NRV method. Method that allocates joint costs to joint products in such a way that the overall gross-margin percentage is identical for the individual products. (584)

Constraint. A mathematical inequality or equality that must be satisfied by the variables in a mathematical model. (416)

Continuous budget. See *rolling budget*. (188)

Contribution income statement. Income statement that groups costs into variable costs and fixed costs to highlight the contribution margin. (65)

Contribution margin. Total revenues minus total variable costs. (64)

Contribution margin per unit. Selling price minus the variable cost per unit. (65)

Contribution margin percentage. Contribution margin per unit divided by selling price. Also called *contribution margin ratio*. (65)

Contribution margin ratio. See *contribution margin percentage*. (65)

Control. Taking actions that implement the planning decisions, deciding how to evaluate performance, and providing feedback and learning that will help future decision making. (10)

Control chart. Graph of a series of successive observations of a particular step, procedure, or operation taken at regular intervals of time. Each observation is plotted relative to specified ranges that represent the limits within which observations are expected to fall. (675)

Controllability. Degree of influence that a specific manager has over costs, revenues, or related items for which he or she is responsible. (200)

Controllable cost. Any cost that is primarily subject to the influence of a given responsibility center manager for a given period. (200)

Controller. The financial executive primarily responsible for management accounting and financial accounting. Also called *chief accounting officer*. (13)

Conversion costs. All manufacturing costs other than direct material costs. (43)

Cost. Resource sacrificed or forgone to achieve a specific objective. (27)

Cost accounting. Measures, analyzes, and reports financial and nonfinancial information relating to the costs of acquiring or using resources in an organization. It provides information for both management accounting and financial accounting. (4)

Cost Accounting Standards Board (CASB). Government agency that has the exclusive authority to make, put into effect, amend, and rescind cost accounting standards and interpretations thereof designed to achieve uniformity and consistency in regard to measurement, assignment, and allocation of costs to government contracts within the United States. (559)

Cost accumulation. Collection of cost data in some organized way by means of an accounting system. (28)

Cost allocation. Assignment of indirect costs to a particular cost object. (29)

Cost-allocation base. A factor that links in a systematic way an indirect cost or group of indirect costs to a cost object. (100)

Cost-application base. Cost-allocation base when the cost object is a job, product, or customer. (100)

Cost assignment. General term that encompasses both (1) tracing accumulated costs that have a direct relationship to a cost object and (2) allocating accumulated costs that have an indirect relationship to a cost object. (29)

Cost-benefit approach. Approach to decision-making and resource allocation based on a comparison of the expected benefits from attaining company goals and the expected costs. (12)

Cost center. Responsibility center where the manager is accountable for costs only. (199)

Cost driver. A variable, such as the level of activity or volume, that causally affects costs over a given time span. (32)

Cost estimation. The attempt to measure a past relationship based on data from past costs and the related level of an activity. (344)

Cost function. Mathematical description of how a cost changes with changes in the level of an activity relating to that cost. (341)

Cost hierarchy. Categorization of indirect costs into different cost pools on the basis of the different types of cost drivers, or cost-allocation bases, or different degrees of difficulty in determining cause-and-effect (or benefits received) relationships. (149)

Cost incurrence. Describes when a resource is consumed (or benefit forgone) to meet a specific objective. (442)

Cost leadership. Organization's ability to achieve lower costs relative to competitors through productivity and efficiency improvements, elimination of waste, and tight cost control. (468)

Cost management. The approaches and activities of managers to use resources to increase value to customers and to achieve organizational goals. (4)

Cost object. Anything for which a measurement of costs is desired. (27)

Cost of capital. See *required rate of return (RRR)*. (742)

Cost of goods manufactured. Cost of goods brought to completion, whether they were started before or during the current accounting period. (41)

Cost pool. A grouping of individual cost items. (100)

Cost predictions. Forecasts about future costs. (344)

Cost tracing. Describes the assignment of direct costs to a particular cost object. (28)

Costs of quality (COQ). Costs incurred to prevent, or the costs arising as a result of, the production of a low-quality product. (672)

Cost-volume-profit (CVP) analysis. Examines the behavior of total revenues, total costs, and operating income as changes occur in the units sold, the selling price, the variable cost per unit, or the fixed costs of a product. (63)

Cumulative average-time learning model. Learning curve model in which the cumulative average time per unit declines by a constant percentage each time the cumulative quantity of units produced doubles. (359)

Current cost. Asset measure based on the cost of purchasing an asset today identical to the one currently held, or the cost of purchasing an asset that provides services like the one currently held if an identical asset cannot be purchased. (815)

Customer-cost hierarchy. Hierarchy that categorizes costs related to customers into different cost pools on the basis of different types of cost drivers, or cost-allocation bases, or different degrees of difficulty in determining cause-and-effect or benefits-received relationships. (511)

Customer life-cycle costs. Focuses on the total costs incurred by a customer to acquire, use, maintain, and dispose of a product or service. (449)

Customer-profitability analysis. The reporting and analysis of revenues earned from customers and the costs incurred to earn those revenues. (510)

Customer-response time. Duration from the time a customer places an order for a product or service to the time the product or service is delivered to the customer. (681)

Customer service. Providing after-sale support to customers. (6)

Decentralization. The freedom for managers at lower levels of the organization to make decisions. (777)

Decision model. Formal method for making a choice, often involving both quantitative and qualitative analyses. (391)

Decision table. Summary of the alternative actions, events, outcomes, and probabilities of events in a decision model. (85)

Degree of operating leverage. Contribution margin divided by operating income at any given level of sales. (76)

Denominator level. The denominator in the budgeted fixed overhead rate computation. (266)

Denominator-level variance. See *production-volume variance*. (272)

Dependent variable. The cost to be predicted. (348)

Design of products and processes. The detailed planning and engineering of products and processes. (6)

Design quality. Refers to how closely the characteristics of a product or service meet the needs and wants of customers. (672)

Designed-in costs. See *locked-in costs*. (442)

Diagnostic control systems. Lever of control that monitors critical performance variables that help managers track progress toward achieving a company's strategic goals. Managers are held accountable for meeting these goals. (826)

Differential cost. Difference in total cost between two alternatives. (399)

Differential revenue. Difference in total revenue between two alternatives. (399)

Direct costing. See *variable costing*. (302)

Direct costs of a cost object. Costs related to the particular cost object that can be traced to that object in an economically feasible (cost-effective) way. (28)

Direct manufacturing labor costs. Include the compensation of all manufacturing labor that can be traced to the cost object (work in process and then finished goods) in an economically feasible way. (37)

Direct material costs. Acquisition costs of all materials that eventually become part of the cost object (work in process and then finished goods), and that can be traced to the cost object in an economically feasible way. (37)

Direct materials inventory. Direct materials in stock and awaiting use in the manufacturing process. (37)

Direct materials mix variance. The difference between (1) budgeted cost for actual mix of the actual total quantity of direct materials used and (2) budgeted cost of budgeted mix of the actual total quantity of direct materials used. (527)

Direct materials yield variance. The difference between (1) budgeted cost of direct materials based on the actual total quantity of direct materials used and (2) flexible-budget cost of direct materials based on the budgeted total quantity of direct materials allowed for the actual output produced. (527)

Direct method. Cost allocation method that allocates each support department's costs to operating departments only. (550)

Discount rate. See *required rate of return (RRR)*. (742)

Discounted cash flow (DCF) methods. Capital budgeting methods that measure all expected future cash inflows and outflows of a project as if they occurred at the present point in time. (741)

Discounted payback method. Capital budgeting method that calculates the amount of time required for the discounted expected future cash flows to recoup the net initial investment in a project. (748)

Discretionary costs. Arise from periodic (usually annual) decisions regarding the maximum amount to be incurred and have no measurable cause-and-effect relationship between output and resources used. (486)

Distribution. Delivering products or services to customers. (6)

Downsizing. An integrated approach of configuring processes, products, and people to match costs to the activities that need to be performed to operate effectively and efficiently in the present and future. Also called *rightsizing*. (487)

Downward demand spiral. Pricing context where prices are raised to spread capacity costs over a smaller number of output units. Continuing reduction in the demand for products that occurs when the prices of competitors' products are not met and, as demand drops further, higher and higher unit costs result in more and more reluctance to meet competitors' prices. (317)

Dual pricing. Approach to transfer pricing using two separate transfer-pricing methods to price each transfer from one subunit to another. (789)

Dual-rate method. Allocation method that classifies costs in each cost pool into two pools (a variable-cost pool and a fixed-cost pool) with each pool using a different cost-allocation base. (544)

Dumping. Under U.S. laws, it occurs when a non-U.S. company sells a product in the United States at a price below the market value in the country where it is produced, and this lower price materially injures or threatens to materially injure an industry in the United States. (452)

Dysfunctional decision making. See *suboptimal decision making*. (778)

Economic order quantity (EOQ). Decision model that calculates the optimal quantity of inventory to order under a set of assumptions. (704)

Economic value added (EVA®). After-tax operating income minus the (after-tax) weighted-average cost of capital multiplied by total assets minus current liabilities. (812)

Effectiveness. The degree to which a predetermined objective or target is met. (243)

Efficiency. The relative amount of inputs used to achieve a given output level. (243)

Efficiency variance. The difference between actual input quantity used and budgeted input quantity allowed for actual output, multiplied by budgeted price. Also called *usage variance*. (236)

Effort. Exertion toward achieving a goal. (776)

Engineered costs. Costs that result from a cause-and-effect relationship between the cost driver, output, and the (direct or indirect) resources used to produce that output. (486)

Equivalent units. Derived amount of output units that (a) takes the quantity of each input (factor of production) in

units completed and in incomplete units of work in process and (b) converts the quantity of input into the amount of completed output units that could be produced with that quantity of input. (611)

Event. A possible relevant occurrence in a decision model. (84)

Expected monetary value. See *expected value*. (85)

Expected value. Weighted average of the outcomes of a decision with the probability of each outcome serving as the weight. Also called *expected monetary value*. (85)

Experience curve. Function that measures the decline in cost per unit in various business functions of the value chain, such as manufacturing, marketing, distribution, and so on, as the amount of these activities increases. (358)

External failure costs. Costs incurred on defective products after they are shipped to customers. (673)

Facility-sustaining costs. The costs of activities that cannot be traced to individual products or services but support the organization as a whole. (149)

Factory overhead costs. See *indirect manufacturing costs*. (37)

Favorable variance. Variance that has the effect of increasing operating income relative to the budgeted amount. Denoted F. (229)

Finance director. See *chief financial officer (CFO)*. (13)

Financial accounting. Measures and records business transactions and provides financial statements that are based on generally accepted accounting principles. It focuses on reporting to external parties such as investors and banks. (3)

Financial budget. Part of the master budget that focuses on how operations and planned capital outlays affect cash. It is made up of the capital expenditures budget, the cash budget, the budgeted balance sheet, and the budgeted statement of cash flows. (189)

Financial planning models. Mathematical representations of the relationships among operating activities, financial activities, and other factors that affect the master budget. (197)

Finished goods inventory. Goods completed but not yet sold. (37)

First-in, first-out (FIFO) process-costing method. Method of process costing that assigns the cost of the previous accounting period's equivalent units in beginning work-in-process inventory to the first units completed and transferred out of the process, and assigns the cost of equivalent units worked on during the current period first to complete beginning inventory, next to start and complete new units, and finally to units in ending work-in-process inventory. (617)

Fixed cost. Cost that remains unchanged in total for a given time period, despite wide changes in the related level of total activity or volume. (30)

Fixed overhead flexible-budget variance. The difference between actual fixed overhead costs and fixed overhead costs in the flexible budget. (271)

Fixed overhead spending variance. Same as the fixed overhead flexible-budget variance. The difference between actual fixed overhead costs and fixed overhead costs in the flexible budget. (271)

Flexible budget. Budget developed using budgeted revenues and budgeted costs based on the actual output in the budget period. (230)

Flexible-budget variance. The difference between an actual result and the corresponding flexible-budget amount based on the actual output level in the budget period. (231)

Full costs of the product. The sum of all variable and fixed costs in all business functions of the value chain (R&D, design, production, marketing, distribution, and customer service). (395)

Goal congruence. Exists when individuals and groups work toward achieving the organization's goals. Managers working in their own best interest take actions that align with the overall goals of top management. (776)

Gross margin percentage. Gross margin divided by revenues. (82)

Growth component. Change in operating income attributable solely to the change in the quantity of output sold between one period and the next. (479)

High-low method. Method used to estimate a cost function that uses only the highest and lowest observed values of the cost driver within the relevant range and their respective costs. (350)

Homogeneous cost pool. Cost pool in which all the costs have the same or a similar cause-and-effect or benefits-received relationship with the cost-allocation base. (509)

Hurdle rate. See *required rate of return (RRR)*. (742)

Hybrid-costing system. Costing system that blends characteristics from both job-costing systems and process-costing systems. (626)

Idle time. Wages paid for unproductive time caused by lack of orders, machine breakdowns, material shortages, poor scheduling, and the like. (45)

Imputed costs. Costs recognized in particular situations but not incorporated in financial accounting records. (810)

Incongruent decision making. See *suboptimal decision making*. (778)

Incremental cost. Additional total cost incurred for an activity. (399)

Incremental cost-allocation method. Method that ranks the individual users of a cost object in the order of users most responsible for the common cost and then uses this ranking to allocate cost among those users. (557)

Incremental revenue. Additional total revenue from an activity. (399)

Incremental revenue-allocation method. Method that ranks individual products in a bundle according to criteria determined by management (for example, sales), and then uses this ranking to allocate bundled revenues to the individual products. (562)

Incremental unit-time learning model. Learning curve model in which the incremental time needed to produce the last unit declines by a constant percentage each time the cumulative quantity of units produced doubles. (360)

Independent variable. Level of activity or cost driver used to predict the dependent variable (costs) in a cost estimation or prediction model. (348)

Indirect costs of a cost object. Costs related to the particular cost object that cannot be traced to that object in an economically feasible (cost-effective) way. (28)

Indirect manufacturing costs. All manufacturing costs that are related to the cost object (work in process and then finished goods) but that cannot be traced to that cost object in an economically feasible way. Also called *manufacturing overhead costs* and *factory overhead costs*. (37)

Industrial engineering method. Approach to cost function estimation that analyzes the relationship between inputs and outputs in physical terms. Also called *work measurement method*. (346)

Inflation. The decline in the general purchasing power of the monetary unit, such as dollars. (762)

Input-price variance. See *price variance*. (236)

Insourcing. Process of producing goods or providing services within the organization rather than purchasing those same goods or services from outside vendors. (397)

Inspection point. Stage of the production process at which products are examined to determine whether they are acceptable or unacceptable units. (647)

Interactive control systems. Formal information systems that managers use to focus organization attention and learning on key strategic issues. (827)

Intercept. See *constant*. (343)

Intermediate product. Product transferred from one subunit to another subunit of an organization. This product may either be further worked on by the receiving subunit or sold to an external customer. (780)

Internal failure costs. Costs incurred on defective products before they are shipped to customers. (673)

Internal rate-of-return (IRR) method. Capital budgeting discounted cash flow (DCF) method that calculates the discount rate at which the present value of expected cash inflows from a project equals the present value of its expected cash outflows. (743)

Inventoriable costs. All costs of a product that are considered as assets in the balance sheet when they are incurred and that become cost of goods sold only when the product is sold. (37)

Inventory management. Planning, coordinating, and controlling activities related to the flow of inventory into, through, and out of an organization. (703)

Investment. Resources or assets used to generate income. (808)

Investment center. Responsibility center where the manager is accountable for investments, revenues, and costs. (199)

Job. A unit or multiple units of a distinct product or service. (100)

Job-cost record. Source document that records and accumulates all the costs assigned to a specific job, starting when work begins. Also called *job-cost sheet*. (104)

Job-cost sheet. See *job-cost record*. (104)

Job-costing system. Costing system in which the cost object is a unit or multiple units of a distinct product or service called a job. (100)

Joint costs. Costs of a production process that yields multiple products simultaneously. (577)

Joint products. Two or more products that have high total sales values compared with the total sales values of other products yielded by a joint production process. (578)

Just-in-time (JIT) production. Demand-pull manufacturing system in which each component in a production line is produced as soon as, and only when, needed by the next step in the production line. Also called *lean production*. (715)

Just-in-time (JIT) purchasing. The purchase of materials (or goods) so that they are delivered just as needed for production (or sales). (711)

Kaizen budgeting. Budgetary approach that explicitly incorporates continuous improvement anticipated during the budget period into the budget numbers. (203)

Labor-time sheet. Source document that contains information about the amount of labor time used for a specific job in a specific department. (106)

Lean accounting. Costing method that supports creating value for the customer by costing the entire value stream, not individual products or departments, thereby eliminating waste in the accounting process. (727)

Lean production. See *just-in-time (JIT) production*. (715)

Learning. Involves managers examining past performance and systematically exploring alternative ways to make better-informed decisions and plans in the future. (10)

Learning curve. Function that measures how labor-hours per unit decline as units of production increase because workers are learning and becoming better at their jobs. (358)

Life-cycle budgeting. Budget that estimates the revenues and business function costs of the value chain attributable to each product from initial R&D to final customer service and support. (448)

Life-cycle costing. System that tracks and accumulates business function costs of the value chain attributable to each product from initial R&D to final customer service and support. (448)

Line management. Managers (for example, in production, marketing, or distribution) who are directly responsible for attaining the goals of the organization. (13)

Linear cost function. Cost function in which the graph of total costs versus the level of a single activity related to that cost is a straight line within the relevant range. (342)

Linear programming (LP). Optimization technique used to maximize an objective function (for example, contribution margin of a mix of products), when there are multiple constraints. (417)

Locked-in costs. Costs that have not yet been incurred but, based on decisions that have already been made, will be incurred in the future. Also called *designed-in costs*. (442)

Main product. Product from a joint production process that has a high total sales value compared with the total sales values of all other products of the joint production process. (578)

Make-or-buy decisions. Decisions about whether a producer of goods or services will insource (produce goods or services within the firm) or outsource (purchase them from outside vendors). (397)

Management accounting. Measures, analyzes, and reports financial and nonfinancial information that helps managers make decisions to fulfill the goals of an organization. It focuses on internal reporting. (4)

Management by exception. Practice of focusing management attention on areas not operating as expected and giving less attention to areas operating as expected. (227)

Management control system. Means of gathering and using information to aid and coordinate the planning and control decisions throughout an organization and to guide the behavior of its managers and employees. (775)

Manufacturing cells. Grouping of all the different types of equipment used to make a given product. (715)

Manufacturing cycle efficiency (MCE). Value-added manufacturing time divided by manufacturing cycle time. (681)

Manufacturing cycle time. See *manufacturing lead time*. (681)

Manufacturing lead time. Duration between the time an order is received by manufacturing to the time a finished good is produced. Also called *manufacturing cycle time*. (681)

Manufacturing overhead allocated. Amount of manufacturing overhead costs allocated to individual jobs, products, or services based on the budgeted rate multiplied by the actual quantity used of the cost-allocation base. Also called *manufacturing overhead applied*. (113)

Manufacturing overhead applied. See *manufacturing overhead allocated*. (113)

Manufacturing overhead costs. See *indirect manufacturing costs*. (37)

Manufacturing-sector companies. Companies that purchase materials and components and convert them into various finished goods. (36)

Margin of safety. Amount by which budgeted (or actual) revenues exceed breakeven revenues. (74)

Marketing. Promoting and selling products or services to customers or prospective customers. (6)

Market-share variance. The difference in budgeted contribution margin for actual market size in units caused solely by actual market share being different from budgeted market share. (249)

Market-size variance. The difference in budgeted contribution margin at the budgeted market share caused solely by actual market size in units being different from budgeted market size in units. (249)

Master budget. Expression of management's operating and financial plans for a specified period (usually a fiscal year) including a set of budgeted financial statements. Also called *pro forma statements*. (185)

Master-budget capacity utilization. The expected level of capacity utilization for the current budget period (typically one year). (315)

Materials requirements planning (MRP). Push-through system that manufactures finished goods for inventory on the basis of demand forecasts. (714)

Materials-requisition record. Source document that contains information about the cost of direct materials used on a specific job and in a specific department. (105)

Matrix method. See *reciprocal method*. (554)

Merchandising-sector companies. Companies that purchase and then sell tangible products without changing their basic form. (36)

Mixed cost. A cost that has both fixed and variable elements. Also called a *semivariable cost*. (343)

Moral hazard. Describes situations in which an employee prefers to exert less effort (or to report distorted information) compared with the effort (or accurate information) desired by the owner because the employee's effort (or validity of the reported information) cannot be accurately monitored and enforced. (822)

Motivation. The desire to attain a selected goal (the goal-congruence aspect) combined with the resulting pursuit of that goal (the effort aspect). (776)

Multicollinearity. Exists when two or more independent variables in a multiple regression model are highly correlated with each other. (374)

Multiple regression. Regression model that estimates the relationship between the dependent variable and two or more independent variables. (352)

Net income. Operating income plus nonoperating revenues (such as interest revenue) minus nonoperating costs (such as interest cost) minus income taxes. (70)

Net present value (NPV) method. Capital budgeting discounted cash flow (DCF) method that calculates the expected monetary gain or loss from a project by discounting all expected future cash inflows and outflows to the present point in time, using the required rate of return. (742)

Net realizable value (NRV) method. Method that allocates joint costs to joint products on the basis of final sales value minus separable costs of total production of the joint products during the accounting period. (583)

Nominal rate of return. Made up of three elements: (a) a risk-free element when there is no expected inflation, (b) a business-risk element, and (c) an inflation element. (762)

Nonlinear cost function. Cost function in which the graph of total costs based on the level of a single activity is not a straight line within the relevant range. (357)

Nonvalue-added cost. A cost that, if eliminated, would not reduce the actual or perceived value or utility (usefulness) customers obtain from using the product or service. (442)

Normal capacity utilization. The level of capacity utilization that satisfies average customer demand over a period (say, two to three years) that includes seasonal, cyclical, and trend factors. (315)

Normal costing. A costing system that traces direct costs to a cost object by using the actual direct-cost rates times the actual quantities of the direct-cost inputs and that allocates indirect costs based on the budgeted indirect-cost rates times the actual quantities of the cost-allocation bases. (104)

Normal spoilage. Spoilage inherent in a particular production process that arises even under efficient operating conditions. (646)

Objective function. Expresses the objective to be maximized (for example, operating income) or minimized (for example, operating costs) in a decision model (for example, a linear programming model). (416)

On-time performance. Delivering a product or service by the time it is scheduled to be delivered. (682)

One-time-only special order. Orders that have no long-run implications. (394)

Operating budget. Budgeted income statement and its supporting budget schedules. (189)

Operating department. Department that directly adds value to a product or service. Also called a *production department* in manufacturing companies. (543)

Operating income. Total revenues from operations minus cost of goods sold and operating costs (excluding interest expense and income taxes). (42)

Operating-income volume variance. The difference between static-budget operating income and the operating income based on budgeted profit per unit and actual units of output. (281)

Operating leverage. Effects that fixed costs have on changes in operating income as changes occur in units sold and hence in contribution margin. (76)

Operation. A standardized method or technique that is performed repetitively, often on different materials, resulting in different finished goods. (626)

Operation-costing system. Hybrid-costing system applied to batches of similar, but not identical, products. Each batch of products is often a variation of a single design, and it proceeds through a sequence of operations, but each batch does not necessarily move through the same operations as other batches. Within each operation, all product units use identical amounts of the operation's resources. (626)

Opportunity cost. The contribution to operating income that is forgone or rejected by not using a limited resource in its next-best alternative use. (402)

Opportunity cost of capital. See *required rate of return (RRR)*. (742)

Ordering costs. Costs of preparing, issuing, and paying purchase orders, plus receiving and inspecting the items included in the orders. (704)

Organization structure. Arrangement of lines of responsibility within the organization. (199)

Outcomes. Predicted economic results of the various possible combinations of actions and events in a decision model. (85)

Output unit-level costs. The costs of activities performed on each individual unit of a product or service. (149)

Outsourcing. Process of purchasing goods and services from outside vendors rather than producing the same goods or providing the same services within the organization. (397)

Overabsorbed indirect costs. See *overallocated indirect costs*. (118)

Overallocated indirect costs. Allocated amount of indirect costs in an accounting period is greater than the actual (incurred) amount in that period. Also called *overapplied indirect costs* and *overabsorbed indirect costs*. (118)

Overapplied indirect costs. See *overallocated indirect costs*. (118)

Overtime premium. Wage rate paid to workers (for both direct labor and indirect labor) in excess of their straight-time wage rates. (44)

Pareto diagram. Chart that indicates how frequently each type of defect occurs, ordered from the most frequent to the least frequent. (676)

Partial productivity. Measures the quantity of output produced divided by the quantity of an individual input used. (493)

Payback method. Capital budgeting method that measures the time it will take to recoup, in the form of expected future cash flows, the net initial investment in a project. (746)

Peak-load pricing. Practice of charging a higher price for the same product or service when the demand for it approaches the physical limit of the capacity to produce that product or service. (450)

Perfectly competitive market. Exists when there is a homogeneous product with buying prices equal to selling prices and no individual buyers or sellers can affect those prices by their own actions. (784)

Period costs. All costs in the income statement other than cost of goods sold. (38)

Physical-measure method. Method that allocates joint costs to joint products on the basis of the relative weight, volume, or other physical measure at the splitoff point of total production of these products during the accounting period. (582)

Planning. Selecting organization goals, predicting results under various alternative ways of achieving those goals, deciding how to attain the desired goals, and communicating the goals and how to attain them to the entire organization. (10)

Practical capacity. The level of capacity that reduces theoretical capacity by unavoidable operating interruptions such as scheduled maintenance time, shutdowns for holidays, and so on. (315)

Predatory pricing. Company deliberately prices below its costs in an effort to drive out competitors and restrict supply and then raises prices rather than enlarge demand. (451)

Prevention costs. Costs incurred to preclude the production of products that do not conform to specifications. (673)

Previous-department costs. See *transferred-in costs*. (621)

Price discount. Reduction in selling price below list selling price to encourage increases in customer purchases. (511)

Price discrimination. Practice of charging different customers different prices for the same product or service. (450)

Price-recovery component. Change in operating income attributable solely to changes in prices of inputs and outputs between one period and the next. (479)

Price variance. The difference between actual price and budgeted price multiplied by actual quantity of input. Also called *input-price variance* or *rate variance*. (236)

Prime costs. All direct manufacturing costs. (43)

Pro forma statements. Budgeted financial statements. (185)

Probability. Likelihood or chance that an event will occur. (84)

Probability distribution. Describes the likelihood (or the probability) that each of the mutually exclusive and collectively exhaustive set of events will occur. (84)

Process-costing system. Costing system in which the cost object is masses of identical or similar units of a product or service. (101)

Product. Any output that has a positive total sales value (or an output that enables an organization to avoid incurring costs). (578)

Product cost. Sum of the costs assigned to a product for a specific purpose. (45)

Product-cost cross-subsidization. Costing outcome where one undercosted (overcosted) product results in at least one other product being overcosted (undercosted). (140)

Product differentiation. Organization's ability to offer products or services perceived by its customers to be superior and unique relative to the products or services of its competitors. (468)

Product life cycle. Spans the time from initial R&D on a product to when customer service and support is no longer offered for that product. (447)

Product-mix decisions. Decisions about which products to sell and in what quantities. (405)

Product overcosting. A product consumes a low level of resources but is reported to have a high cost per unit. (140)

Product-sustaining costs. The costs of activities undertaken to support individual products regardless of the number of units or batches in which the units are produced. (149)

Product undercosting. A product consumes a high level of resources but is reported to have a low cost per unit. (140)

Production. Acquiring, coordinating, and assembling resources to produce a product or deliver a service. (6)

Production-denominator level. The denominator in the budgeted manufacturing fixed overhead rate computation. (266)

Production department. See *operating department*. (543)

Production-volume variance. The difference between budgeted fixed overhead and fixed overhead allocated on the basis of actual output produced. Also called *denominator-level variance*. (272)

Productivity. Measures the relationship between actual inputs used (both quantities and costs) and actual outputs produced; the lower the inputs for a given quantity of outputs or the higher the outputs for a given quantity of inputs, the higher the productivity. (492)

Productivity component. Change in costs attributable to a change in the quantity of inputs used in the current period relative to the quantity of inputs that would have been used in the prior period to produce the quantity of current period output. (479)

Profit center. Responsibility center where the manager is accountable for revenues and costs. (199)

Proration. The spreading of underallocated manufacturing overhead or overallocated manufacturing overhead among ending work in process, finished goods, and cost of goods sold. (119)

Purchase-order lead time. The time between placing an order and its delivery. (704)

Purchasing costs. Cost of goods acquired from suppliers including incoming freight or transportation costs. (703)

PV graph. Shows how changes in the quantity of units sold affect operating income. (70)

Qualitative factors. Outcomes that are difficult to measure accurately in numerical terms. (394)

Quality. The total features and characteristics of a product made or a service performed according to specifications to satisfy customers at the time of purchase and during use. (671)

Quantitative factors. Outcomes that are measured in numerical terms. (394)

Rate variance. See *price variance*. (236)

Real rate of return. The rate of return demanded to cover investment risk (with no inflation). It has a risk-free element and a business-risk element. (762)

Reciprocal method. Cost allocation method that fully recognizes the mutual services provided among all support departments. Also called *matrix method*. (553)

Reengineering. The fundamental rethinking and redesign of business processes to achieve improvements in critical measures of performance, such as cost, quality, service, speed, and customer satisfaction. (469)

Refined costing system. Costing system that reduces the use of broad averages for assigning the cost of resources to cost objects (jobs, products, services) and provides better measurement of the costs of indirect resources used by different cost objects—no matter how differently various cost objects use indirect resources. (145)

Regression analysis. Statistical method that measures the average amount of change in the dependent variable associated with a unit change in one or more independent variables. (352)

Relevant costs. Expected future costs that differ among alternative courses of action being considered. (393)

Relevant range. Band of normal activity level or volume in which there is a specific relationship between the level of activity or volume and the cost in question. (33)

Relevant revenues. Expected future revenues that differ among alternative courses of action being considered. (393)

Reorder point. The quantity level of inventory on hand that triggers a new purchase order. (707)

Required rate of return (RRR). The minimum acceptable annual rate of return on an investment. Also called the *discount rate*, *hurdle rate*, *cost of capital*, or *opportunity cost of capital*. (742)

Research and development. Generating and experimenting with ideas related to new products, services, or processes. (6)

Residual income (RI). Accounting measure of income minus a dollar amount for required return on an accounting measure of investment. (810)

Residual term. The vertical difference or distance between actual cost and estimated cost for each observation in a regression model. (352)

Responsibility accounting. System that measures the plans, budgets, actions, and actual results of each responsibility center. (199)

Responsibility center. Part, segment, or subunit of an organization whose manager is accountable for a specified set of activities. (199)

Return on investment (ROI). An accounting measure of income divided by an accounting measure of investment. See also *accrual accounting rate of return method*. (809)

Revenue allocation. The allocation of revenues that are related to a particular revenue object but cannot be traced to it in an economically feasible (cost-effective) way. (561)

Revenue center. Responsibility center where the manager is accountable for revenues only. (199)

Revenue driver. A variable, such as volume, that causally affects revenues. (68)

Revenue object. Anything for which a separate measurement of revenue is desired. (561)

Revenues. Inflows of assets (usually cash or accounts receivable) received for products or services provided to customers. (38)

Rework. Units of production that do not meet the specifications required by customers for finished units that are subsequently repaired and sold as good finished units. (645)

Rightsizing. See *downsizing*. (487)

Rolling budget. Budget or plan that is always available for a specified future period by adding a period (month, quarter, or year) to the period that just ended. Also called *continuous budget*. (188)

Safety stock. Inventory held at all times regardless of the quantity of inventory ordered using the EOQ model. (707)

Sales mix. Quantities of various products or services that constitute total unit sales. (77)

Sales-mix variance. The difference between (1) budgeted contribution margin for the actual sales mix, and (2) budgeted contribution margin for the budgeted sales mix. (521)

Sales-quantity variance. The difference between (1) budgeted contribution margin based on actual units sold of all products at the budgeted mix and (2) contribution margin in the static budget (which is based on the budgeted units of all products to be sold at the budgeted mix). (521)

Sales value at splitoff method. Method that allocates joint costs to joint products on the basis of the relative total sales value at the splitoff point of the total production of these products during the accounting period. (580)

Sales-volume variance. The difference between a flexible-budget amount and the corresponding static-budget amount. (231)

Scrap. Residual material left over when making a product. (645)

Selling-price variance. The difference between the actual selling price and the budgeted selling price multiplied by the actual units sold. (233)

Semivariable cost. See *mixed cost*. (343)

Sensitivity analysis. A what-if technique that managers use to calculate how an outcome will change if the original predicted data are not achieved or if an underlying assumption changes. (73)

Separable costs. All costs (manufacturing, marketing, distribution, and so on) incurred beyond the splitoff point that are assignable to each of the specific products identified at the splitoff point. (577)

Sequential allocation method. See *step-down method*. (552)

Sequential tracking. Approach in a product-costing system in which recording of the journal entries occurs in the same order as actual purchases and progress in production. (718)

Service department. See *support department*. (543)

Service-sector companies. Companies that provide services or intangible products to their customers. (36)

Service-sustaining costs. The costs of activities undertaken to support individual services. (149)

Shrinkage costs. Costs that result from theft by outsiders, embezzlement by employees, misclassifications, and clerical errors. (704)

Simple regression. Regression model that estimates the relationship between the dependent variable and one independent variable. (352)

Single-rate method. Allocation method that allocates costs in each cost pool to cost objects using the same rate per unit of a single allocation base. (544)

Slope coefficient. Coefficient term in a cost estimation model that indicates the amount by which total cost changes when a one-unit change occurs in the level of activity within the relevant range. (342)

Source document. An original record that supports journal entries in an accounting system. (104)

Specification analysis. Testing of the assumptions of regression analysis. (369)

Splitoff point. The juncture in a joint-production process when two or more products become separately identifiable. (577)

Spoilage. Units of production that do not meet the specifications required by customers for good units and that are discarded or sold at reduced prices. (645)

Staff management. Staff (such as management accountants and human resources managers) who provide advice and assistance to line management. (13)

Stand-alone cost-allocation method. Method that uses information pertaining to each user of a cost object as a separate entity to determine the cost-allocation weights. (557)

Stand-alone revenue-allocation method. Method that uses product-specific information on the products in the bundle as weights for allocating the bundled revenues to the individual products. (561)

Standard. A carefully determined price, cost, or quantity that is used as a benchmark for judging performance. It is usually expressed on a per unit basis. (234)

Standard cost. A carefully determined cost of a unit of output. (235)

Standard costing. Costing system that traces direct costs to output produced by multiplying the standard prices or rates by the standard quantities of inputs allowed for actual outputs produced and allocates overhead costs on the basis of the standard overhead-cost rates times the standard quantities of the allocation bases allowed for the actual outputs produced. (264)

Standard error of the estimated coefficient. Regression statistic that indicates how much the estimated value of the coefficient is likely to be affected by random factors. (368)

Standard error of the regression. Statistic that measures the variance of residuals in a regression analysis. (368)

Standard input. A carefully determined quantity of input required for one unit of output. (235)

Standard price. A carefully determined price that a company expects to pay for a unit of input. (235)

Static budget. Budget based on the level of output planned at the start of the budget period. (229)

Static-budget variance. Difference between an actual result and the corresponding budgeted amount in the static budget. (229)

Step cost function. A cost function in which the cost remains the same over various ranges of the level of activity, but the cost increases by discrete amounts (that is, increases in steps) as the level of activity changes from one range to the next. (357)

Step-down method. Cost allocation method that partially recognizes the mutual services provided among all support departments. Also called *sequential allocation method*. (552)

Stockout costs. Costs that result when a company runs out of a particular item for which there is customer demand. The company must act to meet that demand or suffer the costs of not meeting it. (704)

Strategic cost management. Describes cost management that specifically focuses on strategic issues. (5)

Strategy. Specifies how an organization matches its own capabilities with the opportunities in the marketplace to accomplish its objectives. (5)

Strategy map. A diagram that describes how an organization creates value by connecting strategic objectives in explicit cause-and-effect relationships with each other in the financial, customer, internal business process, and learning and growth perspectives. (471)

Suboptimal decision making. Decisions in which the benefit to one subunit is more than offset by the costs or loss of benefits to the organization as a whole. Also called *incongruent decision making* or *dysfunctional decision making*. (778)

Sunk costs. Past costs that are unavoidable because they cannot be changed no matter what action is taken. (393)

Super-variable costing. See *throughput costing*. (312)

Supply chain. Describes the flow of goods, services, and information from the initial sources of materials and services to the delivery of products to consumers, regardless of whether those activities occur in the same organization or in other organizations. (7)

Support department. Department that provides the services that assist other internal departments (operating departments and other support departments) in the company. Also called a *service department*. (543)

Target cost per unit. Estimated long-run cost per unit of a product or service that enables the company to achieve its target operating income per unit when selling at the target price. Target cost per unit is derived by subtracting the target operating income per unit from the target price. (440)

Target operating income per unit. Operating income that a company aims to earn per unit of a product or service sold. (440)

Target price. Estimated price for a product or service that potential customers will pay. (439)

Target rate of return on investment. The target annual operating income that an organization aims to achieve divided by invested capital. (446)

Theoretical capacity. The level of capacity based on producing at full efficiency all the time. (314)

Theory of constraints (TOC). Describes methods to maximize operating income when faced with some bottleneck and some nonbottleneck operations. (686)

Throughput costing. Method of inventory costing in which only variable direct material costs are included as inventoriable costs. Also called *super-variable costing*. (312)

Throughput margin. Revenues minus the direct material costs of the goods sold. (686)

Time driver. Any factor in which a change in the factor causes a change in the speed of an activity. (682)

Time value of money. Takes into account that a dollar (or any other monetary unit) received today is worth more than a dollar received at any future time. (741)

Total factor productivity (TFP). The ratio of the quantity of output produced to the costs of all inputs used, based on current period prices. (494)

Total-overhead variance. The sum of the flexible-budget variance and the production-volume variance. (278)

Transfer price. Price one subunit (department or division) charges for a product or service supplied to another subunit of the same organization. (780)

Transferred-in costs. Costs incurred in previous departments that are carried forward as the product's costs when it moves to a subsequent process in the production cycle. Also called *previous department costs*. (621)

Trigger point. Refers to a stage in the cycle from purchase of direct materials to sale of finished goods at which journal entries are made in the accounting system. (719)

Uncertainty. The possibility that an actual amount will deviate from an expected amount. (75)

Underabsorbed indirect costs. See *underallocated indirect costs*. (118)

Underallocated indirect costs. Allocated amount of indirect costs in an accounting period is less than the actual (incurred) amount in that period. Also called *underapplied indirect costs* or *underabsorbed indirect costs*. (118)

Underapplied indirect costs. See *underallocated indirect costs*. (118)

Unfavorable variance. Variance that has the effect of decreasing operating income relative to the budgeted amount. Denoted U. (230)

Unit cost. Cost computed by dividing total cost by the number of units. Also called *average cost*. (35)

Unused capacity. The amount of productive capacity available over and above the productive capacity employed to meet consumer demand in the current period. (486)

Usage variance. See *efficiency variance*. (236)

Value-added cost. A cost that, if eliminated, would reduce the actual or perceived value or utility (usefulness) customers obtain from using the product or service. (442)

Value chain. The sequence of business functions in which customer usefulness is added to products or services of a company. (6)

Value engineering. Systematic evaluation of all aspects of the value chain, with the objective of reducing costs and achieving a quality level that satisfies customers. (441)

Value streams. All valued-added activities needed to design, manufacture, and deliver a given product or product line to customers. (726)

Variable cost. Cost that changes in total in proportion to changes in the related level of total activity or volume. (30)

Variable costing. Method of inventory costing in which only all variable manufacturing costs are included as inventoriable costs. Also called *direct costing*. (301)

Variable overhead efficiency variance. The difference between the actual quantity of variable overhead cost-allocation base used and budgeted quantity of variable overhead cost-allocation base that should have been used to produce actual output, multiplied by budgeted variable overhead cost per unit of cost-allocation base. (267)

Variable overhead flexible-budget variance. The difference between actual variable overhead costs incurred and flexible-budget variable overhead amounts. (267)

Variable overhead spending variance. The difference between actual variable overhead cost per unit and budgeted variable overhead cost per unit of the cost-allocation base, multiplied by actual quantity of variable overhead cost-allocation base used for actual output. (269)

Variance. The difference between actual result and expected performance. (227)

Weighted-average process-costing method. Method of process costing that assigns the equivalent-unit cost of the work done to date (regardless of the accounting period in which it was done) to equivalent units completed and transferred out of the process and to equivalent units in ending work-in-process inventory. (614)

Whale curve. A typically backward-bending curve that represents the results from customer profitability analysis by first ranking customers from best to worst and then plotting their cumulative profitability level. (516)

Work-in-process inventory. Goods partially worked on but not yet completed. Also called *work in progress*. (37)

Work in progress. See *work-in-process inventory*. (37)

Work-measurement method. See *industrial engineering method*. (346)

Index

Author

A
Adamy, J., 237
Anderson, S., 146n, 356
Anderson, S. R., 160
Andrews, E., 452
Ansari, S., 440n
Areeda, P., 451n
Arrington, M., 484
Atkinson, A., 688n
Atkinson, A. A., 202n, 557n
Atkinson, C., 716n

B
Baggaley, B., 727n
Bailey, C., 361n
Banker, R., 478n
Baraldi, E., 441
Barkman, A., 451n
Barton, T., 356
Bell, J., 440n
Berk, J., 812n
Biderman, D., 226n
Birger, J., 78
Blair, N., 806n
Borjesson, S., 194n
Boyle, M., 262
Brunton, N., 558n
Brown, S., 680n
Brownlee, R., 590
Bruno, A., 2n
Bunkley, N., 26n
Bustillo, M., 502n
Buskirk, E., 717

C
Cagilo, A., 716n
Carbone, J., 138n
Carter, T., 356
Champy, J., 469n
Chartrand, S., 717
Chinnis, C., 774n
Clark, P., 676n
Clifford, S., 78
Clinton, B., 547n
Cokins, G., 146n, 511n
Cooper, R., 146n, 511n
Corkery, M., 825
Cox, J., 686n
Cuoto, V., 400
Cutcher-Gershenfeld, J., 356

D
Dash, E., 15
Datar, S., 478n
Davenport, T. H., 716n
Davidson, P., 300n
Day, K., 280
Delmar, E., 183n
DeMarzo, P., 812n

Demski, J., 558n
Dillon, D., 108
Ding, D., 738n
Dombrowski, R.F., 590n

E
Edwards, C., 684
Eikenes, B., 587n
Eisenhardt, K., 680n
Eldon, E., 484
Elliot, D., 825
Erchr, E., 280
Evans, E., 280

F
Fazard, R., 518
Federowicz, M., 356
Fox, J., 824n
Fraser, R., 186n, 478n

G
Gage, J., 198
Gandel, S., 825
Garling, W., 15
Garrity, J., 15
Garthwaite, J., 542n
Gatti, J. F., 586n
Giridharadas, A., 432n
Goff, J., 198
Goldratt, E., 312n, 686n
Goldstein, J. L., 451n
Gollakota, K., 15n
Graham, J., 745n
Green, M., 15
Gregory, A., 226n
Grinnell, D. J., 586n
Grossman, M., 356
Gunderson, E., 62n
Gumbus, A., 15
Gupta, V., 15

H
Hacking, A., 576n
Halpern, S., 280
Hammer, M., 469n
Hansell, S., 319
Harrington, J., 451n
Harris, C., 237
Harris, J. K., 519n
Harvey, C., 745n
Hayzen, A., 478n
Hayes, B., 356
Heijmen, T., 400
Holm, E., 806n
Hope, J., 186n, 478n
Horvath, P., 187n
Huddart, S., 821n
Humphries, S., 717
Huston, L., 400

I
Iqbal, M. X., 819n

J
Jaffe, M., 542n
Jargon, J., 237
Jolley, J., 451n
Jones, C., 390n
Jurkus, A., 680n

K
Kageyama, Y., 670n
Kamenev, M., 627
Kaminska, I., 606n
Kaplan, R., 356
Kaplan, R. S., 146n, 160, 202n, 466n, 470n, 478n, 511n, 516n, 557n
Kaplow, L., 505n
Kapner, S., 262
Kaufman, W., 670n
Keegan, P., 33
Kesmodel, D., 237
Klammer, T., 320n
Knudson, B., 108
Kripalani, M., 432n
Kruz, L., 558n

L
Lacayo, R., 108
Laimon, S., 646n
Lampe, S., 198
Latham, G., 187n
Leapman, B., 356
Leber, J., 576n
Lewin, A., 400
Linebaugh, K., 670n
Loomis, C., 26n
Lublin, J., 825
Lunsford, L., 644n
Lyons, B., 15

M
Macario, A., 264
MacArthur, J., 356
Mackey, J., 312n, 686n
Mackie, B., 547n
Mani, M., 400
Manning, S., 400
Maragonelli, L., 441
Marshall, P. D., 590n
Martinez-Jerez, F. A., 160, 466n
Matau, R., 793
Matlack, C., 644n
Maynard, M., 670n
McGregor, J., 702n
McWilliams, G., 502n
McMaster, J., 793
Melumad, N., 821n
Miller, K., 466n
Misawa, M., 758
Moore, J., 86n, 416n
Moriarity, S., 558n
Morris, J., 684

Company